Patterns for Computer-Mediated Interaction

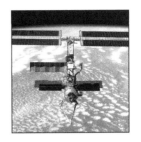

Patterns for Computer-Mediated Interaction

Till Schümmer
Stephan Lukosch

John Wiley & Sons, Ltd

Copyright © 2007   John Wiley & Sons Ltd, The Atrium, Southern Gate, Chichester,
West Sussex PO19 8SQ, England

Telephone (+44) 1243 779777

Email (for orders and customer service enquiries): cs-books@wiley.co.uk
Visit our Home Page on www.wileyeurope.com or www.wiley.com

All Rights Reserved. No part of this publication may be reproduced, stored in a retrieval system or transmitted in any form or by any means, electronic, mechanical, photocopying, recording, scanning or otherwise, except under the terms of the Copyright, Designs and Patents Act 1988 or under the terms of a licence issued by the Copyright Licensing Agency Ltd, 90 Tottenham Court Road, London W1T 4LP, UK, without the permission in writing of the Publisher. Requests to the Publisher should be addressed to the Permissions Department, John Wiley & Sons Ltd, The Atrium, Southern Gate, Chichester, West Sussex PO19 8SQ, England, or emailed to permreq@wiley.co.uk, or faxed to (+44) 1243 770620.

Designations used by companies to distinguish their products are often claimed as trademarks. All brand names and product names used in this book are trade names, service marks, trademarks or registered trademarks of their respective owners. The Publisher is not associated with any product or vendor mentioned in this book.

This publication is designed to provide accurate and authoritative information in regard to the subject matter covered. It is sold on the understanding that the Publisher is not engaged in rendering professional services. If professional advice or other expert assistance is required, the services of a competent professional should be sought.

Other Wiley Editorial Offices

John Wiley & Sons Inc., 111 River Street, Hoboken, NJ 07030, USA

Jossey-Bass, 989 Market Street, San Francisco, CA 94103-1741, USA

Wiley-VCH Verlag GmbH, Boschstr. 12, D-69469 Weinheim, Germany

John Wiley & Sons Australia Ltd, 42 McDougall Street, Milton, Queensland 4064, Australia

John Wiley & Sons (Asia) Pte Ltd, 2 Clementi Loop #02-01, Jin Xing Distripark, Singapore 129809

John Wiley & Sons Canada Ltd, 6045 Freemont Blvd, Mississauga, Ontario, L5R 4J3, Canada

Wiley also publishes its books in a variety of electronic formats. Some content that appears in print may not be available in electronic books.

Library of Congress Cataloging-in-Publication Data:

Schümmer, Till.
  Patterns for computer-mediated interaction / Till Schümmer, Stephan Lukosch.
     p. cm.
  Includes bibliographical references and index.
  ISBN 978-0-470-02561-1 (cloth : alk. paper)
1. Groupware (Computer software) 2. Telematics. 3. Virtual work teams. I. Lukosch, Stephan. II. Title.
  HD66.2.S34 2007
  303.48'34—dc22

2007009229

British Library Cataloguing in Publication Data

A catalogue record for this book is available from the British Library

ISBN-13: 978-0-470-02561-1

Typeset in 10/12 Sabon by Laserwords Private Limited, Chennai, India
Printed and bound in Great Britain by Antony Rowe Ltd, Chippenham, Wiltshire
This book is printed on acid-free paper responsibly manufactured from sustainable forestry
in which at least two trees are planted for each one used for paper production.

To Jutta, Noah, and Liam.

Till Schümmer

For Heide and Greta.

Stephan Lukosch

Contents

Chapter 1	**Introduction**	**1**
	1.1 Groupware: Systems that Support Computer-Mediated Interaction	4
	1.2 A Day with Paul Smith	10
	1.3 Outline	16
	1.4 Acknowledgments	18
Chapter 2	**From Patterns to a Pattern-Oriented Development Process**	**21**
	2.1 Patterns and Pattern Languages	23
	2.1.1 Towards a Holistic Understanding of Socio-Technical Forces	23
	2.1.2 Representations of Patterns	25
	2.1.3 A Pattern Style for Computer-Mediated Interaction	30
	2.1.4 How Patterns should be Applied	34
	2.1.5 Relationships among Patterns in a Pattern Language	39
	2.2 An Overview of our Pattern Language for Computer-Mediated Interaction	43
	2.2.1 The Three Layers of our Pattern Language	43
	2.2.2 Topic Clusters in the Different Layers	44
	2.2.3 Related Pattern Languages	49
	2.3 The Oregon Software Development Process (OSDP)	54
	2.3.1 Conceptual Iteration	55
	2.3.2 Development Iteration	58
	2.3.3 Tailoring Iteration	61
	2.3.4 Applicability of OSDP	61
Chapter 3	**Community Support**	**65**
	3.1 Welcome me... or how to arrive in the community	69
	3.1.1 QUICK REGISTRATION **	72
	3.1.2 LOGIN **	80

		3.1.3 WELCOME AREA *	86
		3.1.4 MENTOR	92
		3.1.5 VIRTUAL ME **	97
		3.1.6 USER GALLERY *	104
		3.1.7 BUDDY LIST **	109
		3.1.8 Welcome me... applied	115
	3.2	Guide me... or how to deal with quality	118
		3.2.1 QUALITY INSPECTION *	120
		3.2.2 LETTER OF RECOMMENDATION *	126
		3.2.3 BIRDS OF A FEATHER	134
		3.2.4 EXPERT FINDER	138
		3.2.5 HALL OF FAME *	143
		3.2.6 REWARD	148
		3.2.7 Guide me... applied	154
	3.3	Save me... or how to protect users	157
		3.3.1 RECIPROCITY *	160
		3.3.2 MASQUERADE *	165
		3.3.3 AVAILABILITY STATUS **	170
		3.3.4 ATTENTION SCREEN *	175
		3.3.5 QUICK GOODBYE *	180
		3.3.6 Save me... applied	185

Chapter 4 Group Support 187

	4.1	Touch me... or how to modify shared material together	191
		4.1.1 GROUP *	194
		4.1.2 SHARED FILE REPOSITORY **	198
		4.1.3 SHARED BROWSING *	202
		4.1.4 VOTE *	208
		4.1.5 APPLICATION SHARING **	215
		4.1.6 SHARED EDITING **	219
		4.1.7 FLOOR CONTROL **	226
		4.1.8 Touch me... applied	230
	4.2	Meet me... or how to create places for collaboration	233
		4.2.1 ROOM **	236
		4.2.2 ACTIVE MAP *	242
		4.2.3 INTERACTION DIRECTORY **	248
		4.2.4 BELL **	252
		4.2.5 INVITATION **	255
		4.2.6 BLIND DATE	260
		4.2.7 Meet me... applied	265

4.3 Read me... or how to support textual communication — 268
    4.3.1 EMBEDDED CHAT ** — 271
    4.3.2 FORUM ** — 277
    4.3.3 THREADED DISCUSSIONS * — 281
    4.3.4 FLAG — 287
    4.3.5 SHARED ANNOTATION — 291
    4.3.6 FEEDBACK LOOP * — 298
    4.3.7 DIGITAL EMOTIONS ** — 302
    4.3.8 FAQ — 307
    4.3.9 Read me... applied — 312

4.4 Feel me... or how to provide synchronous group awareness — 315
    4.4.1 USER LIST ** — 319
    4.4.2 SPONTANEOUS COLLABORATION * — 327
    4.4.3 ACTIVE NEIGHBORS — 332
    4.4.4 INTERACTIVE USER INFO * — 337
    4.4.5 REMOTE FIELD OF VISION * — 342
    4.4.6 REMOTE SELECTION * — 348
    4.4.7 REMOTE CURSOR ** — 353
    4.4.8 TELEPOINTER * — 359
    4.4.9 ACTIVITY INDICATOR * — 363
    4.4.10 Feel me... applied — 367

4.5 Remember me... or how to maintain asynchronous group awareness — 369
    4.5.1 ACTIVITY LOG ** — 371
    4.5.2 TIMELINE — 377
    4.5.3 PERIODIC REPORT ** — 383
    4.5.4 CHANGE INDICATOR ** — 387
    4.5.5 ALIVENESS INDICATOR — 393
    4.5.6 AWAY MESSAGE * — 399
    4.5.7 Remember me... applied — 405

Chapter 5 Base Technology — 407
5.1 Connect me... or how to handle sessions — 409
    5.1.1 COLLABORATIVE SESSION ** — 411
    5.1.2 PERSISTENT SESSION * — 416
    5.1.3 STATE TRANSFER ** — 420
    5.1.4 REPLAY — 425
    5.1.5 Connect Me... applied — 430

	5.2	Share me… or how systems manage common data	431
		5.2.1 CENTRALIZED OBJECTS **	433
		5.2.2 REMOTE SUBSCRIPTION **	437
		5.2.3 REPLICATED OBJECTS **	441
		5.2.4 NOMADIC OBJECTS	446
		5.2.5 MEDIATED UPDATES **	450
		5.2.6 DECENTRALIZED UPDATES *	455
		5.2.7 DISTRIBUTED COMMAND *	460
		5.2.8 Share me… applied	465
	5.3	Control me… or how systems ensure data consistency	467
		5.3.1 PESSIMISTIC LOCKING *	470
		5.3.2 OPTIMISTIC CONCURRENCY CONTROL **	475
		5.3.3 CONFLICT DETECTION **	480
		5.3.4 OPERATIONAL TRANSFORMATION *	484
		5.3.5 LOVELY BAGS	490
		5.3.6 IMMUTABLE VERSIONS *	495
		5.3.7 Control me… applied	500
Chapter 6	**Examples of Applying the Pattern Language**		**501**
	6.1	BSCW	504
		6.1.1 Community Support	505
		6.1.2 Group Support	511
		6.1.3 Base Technology	523
	6.2	CoWord	526
		6.2.1 Group Support	528
		6.2.2 Base Technology	534
Chapter 7	**Epilogue**		**537**
Bibliography			**543**
Index			**569**

Foreword

The Internet has changed the way we interact and communicate. Two to three decades ago the only way to stay in touch with people was to see them in person, write letters, or use a fixed network phone. At work, we had video conferencing and fax, but that was basically it. The Internet was available, but only few of us actually had an e-mail account—and if we had, we often had to share it with others. Those were the days...

Today everything is different. Most of us have a mobile phone, a PDA, and a computer connected to the Internet. Flat rates and high-speed Internet connections make communication and access to information easy and cheap. We don't need actually to meet our friends anymore, but can communicate with them remotely and in realtime, via (IP) telephony, e-mail, instant messaging, chat forums, and Internet communities. In addition to voice and text, we can also exchange photos or even live video streams easily. At work, the picture is similar. Many projects require colloboratation both in and with distributed teams—often across countries, continents, cultures, and time-zones. *Communication enabled business processes*, as described and advocated by Gartner, are a growing trend in the support of business value chains in enterprises and firms. Consequently there is a huge need for communication and collaboration tools that allow distributed groups of people to coordinate their activities and share and work on a common set of artifacts effectively and in real-time.

There is a flip-side to this scenario. Group communication and collaboration via electronic devices and the Internet require appropriate ways of interaction with the systems. In computer-mediated interaction there is no sense of real human personality in the communication. Simply put, you can't use your human senses, but are limited to the senses offered by the collaboration and communication tools you are using. As a result you may feel unsafe, uncertain, or even lost. Many of you probably know such a situation from communicating or working with a person you haven't yet met in person—just via e-mail, phone, and other means of electronic communication and collaboration. In such a scenario you often feel uncertain or unsafe about how to interpret an e-mail, letter, or memo, simply because you have no real clue about the personality of the person who wrote it. What a difference there is in the communication, however, if you know the person with whom you interact: her face, voice, habits, personality. The same e-mail that sounded strange to you before you met makes perfect sense now. From the tone of the exchanged information you know how she is feeling or what is annoying her or making her happy. You feel safer and more comfortable—and the interaction with the remote person becomes more effective.

The lesson we can learn from the above story is clear: tools and applications for computer-mediated communication and interaction must address the needs of both of the humans using them and the needs of the type of communication and interaction they provide or support. In particular, users must be invited to use the applications and need guidance to feel safe, rather than lost, in them. Users also need a sense of the personalities of their communication partners, but, at the same time, their privacy must be protected. In the same way, the communication and interaction between people that is supported by the tools must be both efficient and effective. For example, data exchanged or shared between people must be consistent for all parties, especially when it can be modified during the collaboration. Voice and video must be transmitted in real-time so that everybody sees and hears the same thing, and any interaction between people causes no unnecessary delays. Collaborative sessions often also need explicit guidance and moderation to be effective.

In a nutshell, there is a whole range of really challenging topics that developers of computer-mediated collaboration tools and applications must address, or that users of such tools and applications need to be aware of. But what are the approaches to addressing these challenges? And what are the specific solutions for mastering them? This is what this book is all about. Till and Stephan, two experts in the field of human-computer-human interaction, collected the best practices in computer-mediated interaction and captured them in a pattern language. By means of this language, Till's and Stephan's knowledge becomes readily available and accessible for you. The patterns in the language present the specific practices in computer-mediated interaction, distilled into bite-sized chunks expressed in an appealing writing style, which allows you to easily grasp and understand them and to apply them in your own applications. The language itself shows how all these practices relate to, and depend on, one another. All topics of importance are addressed: welcoming users to a community, guiding them through the topics and interactions in a group, protecting their privacy, modifying shared artifacts, supporting communication within a group, keeping a group alive and vital, guiding collaboration sessions, and managing data and ensuring its consistency.

In other words, the pattern language in this book guides you through key areas of relevance in computer-mediated interaction and the timeless, best practices within these areas. Thus it can help you build group communication and collaboration applications more effectively and successfully, if you are a developer, and to understand how they (should) work if you are using such applications. There is no other book on the topic of computer-mediated interaction that provides the same practical and useful advice as the one you are holding.

I hope you enjoy reading this book as much as I did—and, after reading it, look upon computer-mediated interaction with different eyes than before.

Frank Buschmann

Principal Engineer
Siemens Corporate Technology

Figure/Photo credits

Reproduced by permission of M A Gerosa
Figure 1.2, p8

Reproduced from paypal.com
Figure 3.5, p75

Reproduced from google.com
Figures 3.6, p76; 4.7, p201; 4.32, p259; 4.51, p297

Reproduced by permission of spinchat.com
Figures 3.7, p77; 3.8, p78; 3.9, p79

Reproduced by permission of ©istockphoto.com
Photos p80; p120; p126; p143; p148; p175; p180; p194; p198; p208; p215; p219; p226; p242; p248; p260; p271; p298; p319; p327; p332; p337; p342; p353; p363; p371; p377; p387; p393; p437; p441; p484; p495;

Reproduced from ebay.com
Figures 3.10, p83; 3.33, p129

Reproduced by permission of Atomic Blue (www.planeshift.it)
Figure 3.11, p84

Reproduced from visualbuilder.com
Figure 3.12, p89

Reproduced from communities.com
Figure 3.13, p89

Reproduced from xing.com
Figures 3.14, p90; 3.19, p102; 3.24, p113; 3.50, p168; 4.102, p398

xvi Figure/Photo credits

Reproduced by permission of Kresta King Cutcher
Photo p92; p109

Microsoft product screen shot(s) reprinted with permission from Microsoft Corporation
Figures 3.15, p95; 3.51, p173; 4.13, p218; 4.16, p223; 4.52, p304; 4.53, p305; 4.63, p322; 4.72, p339; 4.86, p361; 4.88, p365;

Reproduced from ACM Press
Figures 3.16, p95; 3.37, p141; 4.27, p247; 4.46, p286; 4.48, p294;

Reproduced by permission of Oliver Müller
Photo p97

Reproduced from Mozilla Thunderbird
Figures 3.17, p100; 3.25, p113; 3.53, p178;

Reproduced by permission of Girgensohn and Lee
Figures 3.18, p101; 3.20, p106

Reproduced by permission of Michael Koch
Figure 3.21, p107; 4.68, p325

Reproduced from icq.com
Figure 3.22, p111

Reproduced from World of Warcraft, Blizzard Entertainment
Figure 3.23, p112; 4.33, p262

Reproduced with permission of Yahoo! Inc. © 2007 by Yahoo! Inc. YAHOO! and the YAHOO! logo are trademarks of Yahoo! Inc.
Figure 3.32, p123; 3.54, p183; 4.30, p251; 4.43, p280;

Reproduced from Seti@home.com
Figure 3.34, p130

Reproduced from ratemyprofessors.com
Figure 3.35, p131

Reproduced from Amazon.com
Figures 3.36, p131; 3.39, p147

Reproduced by permission of Bruce Wood
Photo p134

Reproduced by permission of Caroline Hernandez
Photo p138

Reproduced from freshmeat.co.uk
Figure 3.38, p146

Figure/Photo credits

Reproduced from sourceforge.net
Figure 3.42, p154

Reproduced by permission of Carina Silfverduk
Photo p160

Reproduced by permission of Steve Evans
Photo p165

Reproduced by permission of Ira Struebel
Photo p170

Reproduced from StarWars Galaxies, Lucas Film Ltd
Figures 3.52, p173; 4.42, p275; 4.74, p340

Reproduced from Skype.com
Figure 4.6, p196

Reproduced by permission of D Stotts
Figure 4.8, p205

Reproduced from starcraft.org
Figure 4.10, p211

Reproduced by permission of Axel Guicking
Figure 4.12, p213

Reproduced from flashmeeting.com
Figure 4.18, p229

Reproduced by permission of The Chronicle of Higher Education
Figure 4.25, p240

Reproduced by permission of eclipse.org
Figures 4.41, p274; 4.47, p290

Reproduced by permission of IEEE
Figure 4.49, p296; 4.89, p366

Reproduced by permission of T. Herrmann, University of Bochum, Germany
Figure 4.50, p296

Reproduced from activeworlds.com
Figure 4.52, p304

Reproduced by permission of W S Sarle
Figure 4.56, p310

Reproduced from phpWebThings.com
Figure 4.64, p323

Reproduced by permission of mvnForum.com
Figure 4.65, p323

Reproduced by permission of Jay Budzik
Figure 4.71, p335

Reproduced from vBulletin.com
Figure 4.73, p340

Reproduced by permission of Carl Gutwin
Figure 4.78, p346; 4.79, p350; 4.84, p357; 4.85, p358

Reproduced by permission of J M Caroll
Figure 4.94, p379

Reproduced by permission of T Erickson
Figure 4.95, p380

Reproduced by permission of WinEdt.com
Figure 4.99, p391

Lotus Notes Screen Capture Copyright 2007 IBM Corporation. Used with permission of IBM Corporation. Lotus and Notes are trademarks of IBM Corporation, in the United States, other countries, or both.
Figure 5.8, p448

Reproduced by permission of NASA
Photo, p460

Reproduced by permission of Fraunhofer FIT
Figures 6.2, p506; 6.3, p507; 6.4, p508; 6.5, p509; 6.6, p511; 6.7, p512; 6.8, p513; 6.9, p514; 6.10, p516; 6.11, p516; 6.12, p517; 6.13, p518; 6.14, p518; 6.15, p519; 6.16, p520; 6.17, p521; 6.18, p521; 6.19, p522; 6.20, p523; 6.21, p524; 6.22, p525

Reproduced by permission of Professor Chengzheng Sun
Figures 6.23, p526; 6.24, p527; 6.25, p528; 6.26, p528; 6.27, p529; 6.28, p530; 6.29, p530; 6.30, p531; 6.31, p532; 6.32, p533; 6.33, p533; 6.34, p534; 6.35, p534; 6.36, p535; 6.37, p536

We additionally thank all our colleagues and friends who volunteered to appear on pictures not mentioned in the above list.

CHAPTER 1

Introduction

New technologies have changed the ways in which people interact and collaborate over a distance. Users can stay connected over a network and practice new ways of collaborative working. Instead of working face-to-face most of the time, today many people collaborate with remote peers via the Internet. In professional work life, employees in distributed companies collaborate via distributed work groups, workers in distant parts of a virtual organization can form dynamic ad-hoc teams for a step in a production process, and people participate in virtual communities to increase their professional capabilities. This process is also visible in private life, where computer users increasingly participate in communities to make their lives easier or more interesting.

As a result, more and more applications are designed for use by more than one user. Domains in which this has become obvious are multi-player games, websites that foster interaction among visitors, applications for interaction between mobile users, systems that foster collaborative learning, interactive workspaces and smart environments, or peer-to-peer applications, to name only a few. In such areas we can see a shift in interest from human computer interaction to computer-mediated human interaction.

This book discusses how applications for supporting computer-mediated interaction or *groupware* applications can be built. A groupware application is a combination of software, hardware and social processes that supports groups in their interaction. The groupware thus is what mediates interaction in computer-mediated interaction.

We will use a *pattern language* to build such groupware systems. Pattern languages combine *patterns* from a specific application domain, and consist of patterns and the relations between these patterns. Patterns capture design knowledge and rationale so that a novice can make design decisions in the same way that experts would. By means of design patterns one can describe expert knowledge in the form of rules of thumb that helps to solve a problem in the application domain of the pattern language.

Depending on your role in the development process of a groupware system, you would make use of a pattern language in different ways:

— As a *software developer*, you would find guidance on how to implement groupware applications. The patterns would outline different functional components that need to be developed when approaching groupware-typical problems.

— As a *user*, the patterns would provide you with an idea on how the groupware applications might look and how social processes might change when groupware comes into play. Your role would probably require you to identify functional aspects of your envisioned groupware application and communicate them to the software developers. This can raise your level of participation and help to ensure that the solution fits into your context. In the case of high-level patterns, you might also be able to implement the pattern on your own by tailoring an existing groupware environment.

— Finally, as a *student* or *researcher* in the field of computer-supported collaborative work, you might use patterns to frame your research: a pattern language documents best practices that have evolved during recent years, and in the case of most patterns, provides you with links to research literature in which such practices have been discussed.

To complement the patterns, we will provide a common scenario that serves as an example of how to apply the pattern approach in a concrete case of groupware development. We have chosen the case of a distributed software development team that wants to make use of groupware technology to support the distributed development of a collaborative game engine better. We will tell the story of Paul Smith, who is the project leader of the collaborative game engine project. The story will tell you about how social interaction is intertwined with professional activities, and how Paul interacts with a global network of people to achieve his project's goals.

The fact that we have selected collaborative software development does not, however, mean that the application of this book is restricted to that domain. As you will see in the scenarios, many of the issues that arise in the collaboration of distributed software developers are to the same degree relevant in other application domains such as distributed management, distributed product development, or distributed learning. You can consider this in the same way as an architect would understand the creation of houses: in our example we will build a metaphorical *office building* for software developers. But the skills required to create such a building can also be used to build a school or a building for car design engineers. It is you as end user who will introduce the domain-specific context of your group, while this book concentrates on groupware infrastructure.

1.1 Groupware: Systems that Support Computer-Mediated Interaction

A famous definition of the term groupware defines groupware systems as "intentional group processes plus software to support them" (Johnson-Lenz and Johnson-Lenz, 1981). This definition includes various aspects that we have to consider when designing groupware solutions:

— The core of the definition is the *group*. A group of users wants to interact using groupware. Naturally, the members of the group should play an important role in the design of groupware. The groupware design has the purpose of creating a solution that satisfies the user's needs. *End-user requirements* therefore have to be the central issue during groupware design.

— The group interacts in an *intentional group process*. The *interaction between people* thus needs to play an important role in the design of any groupware solution. It has to become clear who interacts with whom. How strict the intentional group process is must be considered, ranging from unplanned interaction in virtual communities up to formally structured workflows in a distributed workgroup.

— The process is supported by *software*. The fact that software is mentioned third here emphasizes that the software itself should be a supportive facility to ease the interaction between people. The software should be adapted to the users' needs to best fulfill its supportive role. At this point the *software developer* comes into play. As software supports the group process, the software developer should support the users in adapting or creating software that fits the process.

Compared to a focus on design, which has the goal of supporting the group in the manipulation of content, support for social group interaction needs a broader focus, that of the relationships between users. Tools for manipulation are in most cases used by one user (even in collaborative systems), so they affect the relationship between the user and shared artifacts. Social interaction, on the other hand, affects the relationships between users and needs to address issues like trust and privacy. In contrast to the design of tools for the manipulation of artifacts, which mainly affects human-computer interaction, the focus should thus be on human-computer-human interaction (HCHI). The design of tools therefore focuses on the interaction of the user with the artifact, and considers the human-human interaction as a marginal aspect.

To provide customized designs of groupware mechanisms, we have to make use of a design process that is flexible enough to adapt to the group's needs. Experiences with the design of single user applications have already shown that many software development projects fail because of requirements inadequacies (Dorfman, 1997).

In such cases, the customer is typically involved in the early stages of the project as a source of design requirements. This set of requirements is then implemented by the software developers and subsequently the customer assesses the result. However, if the requirements were not specified correctly, customers receive a product that does not match their needs. This means that requirements in the context of computer-mediated interaction must always address social aspects as well as technical aspects, which is why they are called *socio-technical requirements*.

Unfortunately, these socio-technical requirements are often less clear to the stakeholders involved in the development of groupware applications. Two factors make this part of groupware development difficult:

— While in single user tasks, such as word processing or image editing, only one actor interacts with an artifact, groupware needs to support the interaction of many users with each other. An interaction partner is thus not a technical, deterministic, artifact, but a non-deterministic human.

— Users are not as familiar with using these new opportunities for interaction compared with single-user applications.

The theory of socio-technical design views a community from two perspectives: the social system, including group processes, roles, and flow of information, and the technical system, which includes tools used within the community, such as IT infrastructure or buildings. From a socio-technical perspective these two systems are highly interrelated. A socio-technical perspective on groupware design has to be aware of three key aspects (Bikson and Eveland, 1996):

— It is difficult to predict the reciprocal effect of changes to either the social or the technical system.

— The process used to create the socio-technical system will affect the acceptance of the system.

— Both social and technical systems change over time.

The tools in the technical system, i.e. the software that supports intentional group processes (Johnson-Lenz and Johnson-Lenz, 1981), can be classified in many different ways. One popular way to classify groupware is to distinguish how it support groups. Teufel et al. (1995) introduced such a model and distinguish between three different main support functionalities:

1. *Communication* focuses on the information exchange between cooperating group members.
2. *Coordination* concentrates on coordinating group tasks.
3. *Cooperation* adds the ability to accomplish group goals to the above support functionalities.

As all main support functionalities start with the letter C, Borghoff and Schlichter (2000) later on called this approach *3C-classification*. In their initial proposal

Teufel et al. (1995) positioned the three main functionalities in a triangle to cluster groupware applications in *system classes* of common functionality, i.e. *communication systems*, *workflow management systems*, *shared information spaces*, and *workgroup computing systems*.

In contrast to the initial approach of Teufel et al. (1995), we propose a different approach. Figure 1.1 places well-known groupware applications in two-dimensional

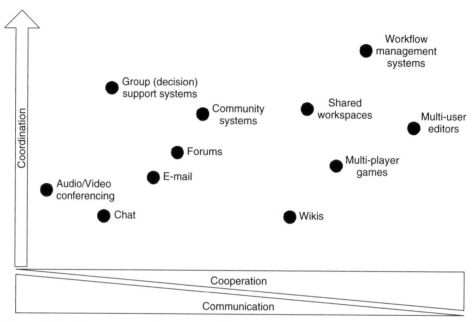

Figure 1.1 Groupware applications in relation to their support of communication, coordination, and cooperation

space. The vertical axis denotes the application's support for coordination, while the horizontal axis is used to denote the degree of communication and cooperation that an application supports. This is possible because a higher degree of communication implies a lower degree of cooperation. By placing an application in this two-dimensional space, the individual degree of communication, coordination, and cooperation can be visualized much better for each of the application types.

In particular, we distinguish the following groupware applications in Figure 1.1:

— *Audio/video conferencing* tools allow users to communicate by various means, so they have a high degree of communication and a low degree of cooperation. Compared to workflow management systems, for example, they do not explicitly offer functionality for scheduling or organizing tasks. We thus see them at a medium degree of coordination.

— *Chat* tools have a lower degree of communication than audio/video conferencing tools, as non-verbal information is omitted when communicating via a chat application. For the same reason, the degree of coordination is reduced.

— *Group Decision Support Systems (GDSS)* are explicitly designed to support groups in decision-making. For that purpose, they offer synchronous as well as asynchronous communication tools, group votes, etc. They therefore have a high degree of communication and coordination.

— *E-mail* is the most popular groupware application. E-mail can be used for many purposes, but its main purpose is to support communication. As the communication is asynchronous and text-based, the degree of communication is reduced compared to chat tools. However, as users can structure their information when using e-mails, the degree of coordination is increased.

— *Forums* allow users to discuss a topic in which they are interested. The communicating group is therefore defined by the topic. Compared to e-mail, communication is more public. However, if used in a company, forums allow coordination of a group that is cooperating on a common task.

— *Community Systems* integrate a variety of tools and allow a large group of users, i.e. a community, to communicate, to share information, or to coordinate common activities. Often, these tools are web-based. Compared to the tools listed above, community systems have better support for accomplishing and coordinating group goals. However, the degree of communication possible is lower, as there is no possibility of communicating directly with individual community members.

— *Wikis* are web-based systems that allow users to change the content of the web pages. Wikis have their origin in the design patterns community. The first Wiki was the *Portland Pattern Repository*, which was created in 1995 by Ward Cunningham. As Wikis allow users to create and share content, they have a high degree of cooperation, but as they do not explicitly support communication or coordination, they are low in these respects.

— *Shared workspaces* such as BCSW (see Section 1.1) allow users to share content. In the most cases, they also allow structuring of the shared content to coordinate common tasks. For that reason, shared workspaces have a higher degree of cooperation and coordination than Wikis.

— *Multi-player games* are becoming more and more popular. They allow users to solve tasks or quests jointly, and support a number of coordination functionalities for that purpose. Communication is mainly short and used only for coordination, which explains the degree of communication, coordination, and cooperation they exhibit.

— *Workflow Management Systems (WfMS)* are tools that allow modeling, coordination, supervision, and evaluation of a workflow by a cooperating team. For that reason they exhibit the highest degree of coordination of all tools. As their main purpose is to coordinate users in accomplishing a group goal, they have also a high degree of cooperation. WfMS only use communication for coordination purposes, for example to pass on a task or to notify about a completed task, so they show a quite low degree of communication.

— *Multiuser editors* such as CoWord (see Section 1.2) allow cooperating users to create a shared artifact synchronously, for example a text document, drawing, or a spreadsheet, and thus accomplish group goals. This explains the high degree of cooperation of such tools. Multiuser editors use a lot of coordination functionalities as well, for example to avoid conflicting changes. Communication is not explicitly supported, thus the degree of communication is low.

Apart from the various main functionalities that are supported by a groupware application, *awareness* plays an important role. Of the tools listed above, multiuser editors, for example, make use of awareness widgets that show the working area of other users, with the goal to avoid conflicting changes in a shared artifact. Awareness can be seen as a mediator between these three main functionalities.

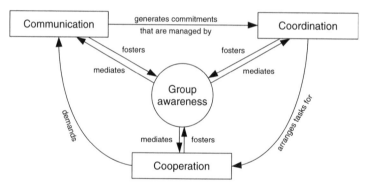

Figure 1.2 Relationship between communication, coordination, cooperation, and mediating group awareness

Gerosa et al. (2004) describe this as shown in Figure 1.2. In this figure, cooperating users must be able to communicate and to coordinate themselves. When communicating, users might generate commitments and define tasks that must be completed to accomplish the common group goal. These tasks must be coordinated so that they are accomplished in the correct order and at the correct time with respect to possible external restrictions. To accomplish these tasks the users have to cooperate in a shared environment. However, while cooperating, unexpected situations might emerge that demand new communication. In such communication new commitments and tasks might be defined, which again must be coordinated to be accomplished in cooperation. Apart from this cyclic aspect of cooperation, Gerosa et al. place awareness in a central position in Figure 1.2. Every user action that is performed during communication, coordination, or cooperation generates information. Some of this information involves two or even more users, and should be made available to all cooperating users so that they can become aware of each other. This helps to mediate further communication, coordination, and cooperation. Based on this information, users are able to build up a shared understanding of their common group goals and to synchronize their cooperation.

Now that we have clarified our understanding of groupware, the following section presents a scenario in the not too far distant future. This will serve as a running scenario throughout the book. It will relate the patterns in the book to a practical example and show how they can be applied in the scenario.

1.2 A Day with Paul Smith

Join us on a ride with a time machine. Our destination is a typical working day in the life of Paul Smith. Paul is a software engineer and works in the software development department of a leading entertainment device company in London. Currently, Paul is the project leader in the COGE project in which a *Cooperative Game Engine* is being developed.

Paul's company has subsidiaries all over the world. The members of Paul's team are distributed as shown in Figure 1.3. One team of developers is located in Rio de Janeiro, one in London, and a third in Hong Kong. The main customer is a large game manufacturer located in Germany, which has the goal of building an educational game that helps better understanding of water supply in African countries. The game manufacturer has a group of African pilot users located in Ethiopia and Malawi.

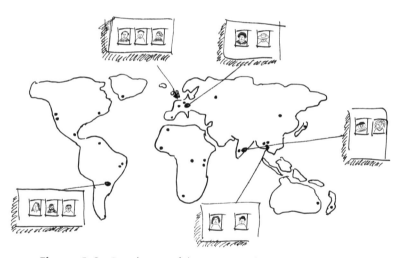

Figure 1.3 Distribution of the team members in Paul's project

Most of the projects in Paul's department are performed in teams to benefit from the synergy of people with varied expertise. Currently, the following interaction constellations are present in the COGE project: the developers from London continue to work on the results that were created only hours before in Hong Kong. Both software teams communicate to plan the internal architecture of the game engine. In other meetings, the London team collaborates with the German customer, which integrates the game engine in its project. The German customer also communicates with some of the developers in Hong Kong or Rio if time shifts allow interaction.

Finally, the German customer interacts with their pilot users and collects suggestions from them on how the game could be improved.

For their common tasks, team members interact daily using their computing devices. Let's now take a look how Paul's typical working day starts.

6:30 AM. The alarm-clock rings and Paul gets out of bed. After a shower and a shave Paul prepares his breakfast. While eating his cereal and enjoying his freshly brewed coffee, Paul has a look at his electronic newspaper (see Figure 1.4). The electronic newspaper is connected to the Internet. According to the preferences Paul has configured, the electronic newspaper shows Paul the latest news in specific categories in which he is interested. Paul is an enthusiastic member of the pattern community and participates in a online community that writes, discusses, and shepherds patterns. He has therefore configured a special section in his electronic newspaper that shows him the latest pattern community news and information about his buddies. The daily report tells Paul what has happened in his online community and allows him to keep track of interesting discussions. A sidebar in the newspaper shows Paul's buddy list. As some of Paul's buddies are already awake, Paul has a short chat with them and agrees to arrange a meeting in the evening.

Figure 1.4 Paul has his breakfast

To plan his working day, Paul checks his main tasks for the day and the achievements of his colleagues during the night. In Hong Kong they have solved one of the major problems with the network protocol for the new cooperative game engine. However, the solution has raised some new problems in a module that is developed by the team in Rio. Paul therefore decides to announce a meeting with the colleagues in Rio for the afternoon. He enters the collaboration space and sends invitations to those involved.

8:30 AM. Paul leaves his house in a small neighborhood in the London suburbs, gets into his car, and sets off for his office in the city. In the car Paul recalls the destination from his favorite destinations folder. The navigation system of the car not only connects to GPS satellites, but also to the Internet to plan the best route into the city. It uses GPS to detect Paul's position and the Internet to avoid traffic jams. Additionally, Paul sends his route to his office in an online travel portal that mediates travel mates. Travel mates are selected not only according the destination but also according to Paul's topics of interest. The latter is quite important for Paul, as he does not want to share a ride with someone with whom he has nothing to talk about. In most cases, this allows Paul to pick up a travel mate on his way into the city.

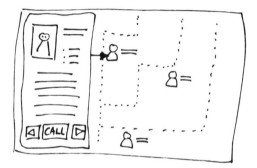

Figure 1.5 Paul looks for a new travel mate

This morning the travel portal suggests a new travel mate (see Figure 1.5). Paul does not know this person, but the portal uses a recommendation system, and the travel mate is ranked as a trustworthy and interesting person. Paul has an additional look at the user gallery and reads the introduction of the proposed travel mate. Paul is satisfied with the suggestion and decides to stop on his way into the city and to pick up the suggested travel mate. The car navigation system calculates the estimated pick-up time and notifies the travel mate. It also keeps the travel mate aware of probable changes so that she does not have to wait too long.

9:30 AM. After picking up the travel mate and dropping her at her destination, Paul arrives in his office. A biometric security check at the entrance proves Paul's identity, and Paul moves to the project's group room where he meets his colleagues. Video screens show the offices of colleagues in Frankfurt, Hong Kong, and Rio de Janeiro in a permanent video stream. One of the colleagues in London starts a discussion about the project's current problems. Paul suggests postponing the discussion until the afternoon when colleagues from Brazil will also be available. Currently, nobody is in the office in Rio, as it is not yet morning there.

As plenty of time is left before the general meeting, Paul joins a group that discusses the software architecture of the current project (see Figure 1.6). This group meets in

Figure 1.6 Paul participates in a virtual reality conference about the software architecture of the current project

a special room that allows 3D projections. Currently, the group is discussing parts of the architecture for the user interface. Luckily, this group is not affected by the problem that was raised by the solution from China, and makes good progress.

When the meeting about the software architecture is over, Paul goes to his office to start up his desktop computer. He enters the group's collaboration space and is pleased to see that everyone has accepted his invitation to discuss the new problems with the network protocol. The collaboration space also notifies Paul about newly received mails, who else is on line in the collaboration space, and open tasks. As the group has decided to use an open awareness concept, Paul can also see what everyone is currently doing by moving his mouse cursor over the images in his buddy list. This information is often used to start a spontaneous collaboration and discussion about ongoing problems. However, teammates who do not want to be disturbed indicate this in the buddy list so that the collaboration space does not allow direct communication.

1:00 PM. After a few more hours of work and a good lunch in the company's canteen, it is time for the group meeting to discuss the new problems with the network protocol. The video screens show that the necessary people are available at all locations. Paul contacts them and announces the start of the meeting, and all his colleagues move to the group meeting room. This room is equipped with the 3D projector Paul used in the morning. This projector displays video streams for each participant from the various locations (see Figure 1.7), the virtual room for the meeting in the team's collaboration space, and the current shared documents containing the description of the network protocol. This allows everyone to see each other and the material for discussion.

14   Chapter 1   Introduction

Figure 1.7 Paul participates in a conference to discuss problems with his colleagues overseas

Paul opens the meeting by passing the floor to his colleague Gwan in Hong Kong. Gwan explains how they have solved one of the major problems with the network protocol. To do this, Gwan uses a virtual pointer that allows him to point to the corresponding lines in the source code. Other colleagues can discuss Gwan's presentation using synchronous textual chat so that Gwan is not disturbed. They can also annotate the source code and post questions to a blackboard that will be discussed after Gwan's explanation.

Everyone is impressed with Gwan's presentation, although they know that his solution raises a new problem. After the open questions have been answered, Paul hands the moderation over to Rio de Janeiro and Ana explains the new problem. Ana's presentation raises a lot of open questions on the shared blackboard. The group clusters the open questions and splits into subgroups to address these question clusters. The subgroups create new virtual rooms in the team's collaboration space to discuss the open questions. Before the groups retreat to their new virtual rooms, Paul schedules a new meeting for tomorrow for the groups to present their results.

4:00 PM. Paul has his last meeting for the day. David, a colleague from Detroit, visits the lab. After giving David a short guided tour of the office, Paul tells him about the new problems with the network protocol. David starts smiling, as he knows how to solve part of the problem. Paul and David therefore enter the collaboration space and knock at the virtual door of the subgroup that formed this afternoon and whose questions David can answer. David offers himself as a mentor and to explain the technology that can solve part of the problem. Soon, David and the other colleagues are in deep discussion and Paul leaves to do other work in his office. Two hours later, David leaves the lab to catch his flight back to Detroit. The subgroup tells Paul that they have nominated David as an expert for specific topics in the collaboration space. This might help David with his next evaluation and wage bargaining.

8:00 PM. Paul has finally finished his most important tasks for the day. He uses his MDA[1] to connect to his online community. As soon as he is on line his friends contact him. They had thought that Paul had forgotten about their appointment. Paul had, and excuses himself for being late. Paul's friends suggest watching a movie in one of the new cinemas downtown. A quick vote shows that all agree. They run a recommender system for movies, and after a short discussion agree on what to see (see Figure 1.8). Adriana offers to buy the tickets and reserve the seats in the cinema's online booking system.

So a long working day finally ends, and Paul leaves his office to watch a movie with his friends. We can step back into our time machine and go on a short ride back to the present.

Figure 1.8 Paul uses the recommender system

---

[1] MDA is an abbreviation for *mobile digital assistant* which is a combination of a mobile phone and a personal digital assistant (PDA).

1.3 Outline

The scenario of Paul Smith shows one vision of the future. Our main prediction is that in future people will interact more and more using computing devices. In combination with software these computing devices will mediate interaction among people.

As the overview of groupware approaches shows, the scenario is not too far in the future, as most of the computer-mediated interaction it describes already happens in our lives, although not as an integral part of daily life. To mention a few, Paul's day starts with a look at the Periodic Report of his favorite online community, then at his Buddy List to see who else is already on line. The team is using a collaboration space that is based on virtual Rooms, Paul's colleague David acts as a Mentor, and finally Paul and his friends use a recommender system with Letters of Recommendation to select a movie for the evening.

The terms set in Small Caps are patterns that are part of our pattern language for computer-mediated interaction. These and other patterns can be found in different chapters of this book, which is structured as follows:

— Chapter 2 *From Patterns to a Pattern-oriented Development Process* introduces the reader to the theory of patterns. It looks at the original and more recent publications by Christopher Alexander. Using an end-user centered view, we transfer ideas to the domain of computer-mediated interaction. This results in a pattern form that is different than the pattern forms used in more technical pattern languages. While technical pattern languages use design diagrams or code fragments to illustrate solutions, we prefer a narrative way of presenting the patterns. This ensures that both end users *and* developers will be able to read the solution.

In the remaining part of this chapter, we will introduce OSDP, a pattern-oriented process for groupware development, which is based on piecemeal growth via short design and development iterations, as well as frequent diagnosis and reflection on working practices and how the application supports them.

— Chapter 3 *Community Support* describes patterns at a high level of abstraction. The patterns in this chapter describe group processes and the use of computer technology to support such processes. Its main focus lies on the early phases of the group process. It answers questions such as:

- How to arrive in the community
- How to find out what is interesting in the community
- How to protect users

— Chapter 4 *Group Support* provides patterns at the user interface level of a collaborative application. The patterns are both technical (describing how to design group interfaces) and social (elaborating on successful application of groupware technology). Problems solved are:

- How to modify shared material together
- How to shape places for collaboration
- How to organize textual communication
- How to become aware of other user's actions
- How to notice absent participants

— Chapter 5 *Base Technology* discusses the technical layer of groupware applications. The patterns are mainly technical and answer the questions:

- How systems bootstrap for collaboration
- How systems manage shared data
- How systems ensure data consistency

— Chapter 6 *Examples of Applying the Pattern Language* presents two case studies, one on BCSW and another on CoWord. These case studies show how group interaction can be supported by HCHI technology. The goal of this chapter is to put the patterns together and to illustrate how they are used by two well-known groupware applications.

1.4 Acknowledgments

The patterns in this book have evolved over the last five years with the help of many brilliant practitioners in the areas of groupware development, human computer interaction, software development, and social practice design. We would like to express our deepest thanks to all of them and hope that we have not forgotten too many of the colleagues who crossed our paths in the last years.

When we made our first steps towards a groupware pattern language, we had discussions with Alejandro Fernandez, Torsten Holmer (who also contributed the pictures of Paul in the introduction), Jessica Rubart, and Robert Slagter. These discussions were the seed for the idea of a comprehensive groupware pattern language, although we did not anticipate that we would finally manage to write all the patterns in these days.

Our first attempt to write patterns was made in the publication of three initial awareness patterns that were discussed at EuroPLoP 2002. When we look back at the results of this attempt, those patterns look rather naïve now. However, getting in touch with the pattern culture of the EuroPLoP community was probably the most important step towards this book. In endless discussions with shepherds and other authors in writer's workshops we learned to express our patterns in a hopefully clear way that is useful to the book's audience. We are indebted to the EuroPLoP community for being both open to novice pattern authors and at the same time showing a high level of professionalism in the craft of pattern writing.

The following people invested many hours of their time by acting as shepherds for patterns in this book and providing numerous suggestions for improvement: Antonio Rito Silva (EuroPLoP 2002), Kristian Elof Soerensen (EuroPLoP 2003), Joseph Bergin (EuroPLoP 2004), Andreas Rüping (EuroPLoP 2004), Uwe Zdun (CHI2004), Alan O'Callaghan (EuroPLoP 2005), Lise B. Hvatum (EuroPLoP 2005), Ofra Homsky (EuroPLoP 2006), and Munawar Hafiz (PLoP 2006). Uwe Zdun in addition helped us as a shepherd for the whole book. His critical comments forced us to concentrate on the core patterns of the language and bring them to the shape you see today.

Almost seventy pattern authors commented our patterns in writer's workshops at EuroPLoP and PLoP, as well as in pattern workshops at the CSCW conference, the European CSCW conference (ECSCW), and the CHI conference. They are, in alphabetic order: Juan I. Asensio, Paris Avgeriou, Pippin Barr, Joseph Bergin, Bettina Biel, Diethelm Bienhaus, Jan Borchers, Andrea Botero Cabrera, Lynwood Brown, Mishka Bugajska, Frank Buschmann, Jens Coldeway, Andy Crabtree, Catalina Danis, Jutta Eckstein, Amr Elssamadisy, Tom Erickson, Karl Flieder, Richard Gabriel, Ian Graham, Sharon Greene, Tom Gross, Liz Guy, Darren Hayes, Fabian Hermann, Thomas Herrmann, Rod Holland, Torsten Holmer, Stefan Holtel, Ofra Homsky, Lise Hvatum, Mads Ingstrup, Jim Kile, Daniel Kluender, Kari-Hans Kommonen, Gabriele Kunau, Greg Laudemen, Jouni Linkola, Donald Little, Rui Lopes, Michael

Lyons, Mary Lynn Manns, Mika Myller, Mark Prince, Amir Raveh, Simos Retalis, Rebecca Rikner, Judy Roell, Andreas Rüping, Andy Schneider, Dirk Schnelle, Wolfram Schobert, Didi Schütz, Helen Sharp, Marianna Sipos, Guy Steele, Winfried Tautges, Lucia Terrenghi, John C. Thomas, Markus Völter, Aake Walldius, Charles Weir, Michael Weiss, Leon Welicki, Dave West, Elizabeth Whitworth, Michael Wissen, Mary Zajicek, Uwe Zdun, and Jürgen Ziegler.

Several colleagues in the research field of Computer-Supported Collaborative Work (CSCW) provided us with interesting insights into research prototypes, participated in discussions on the nature of collaborative applications, or helped us to find known uses for the patterns in this book. To name only the most important contributors, we would like to thank Christian Schuckmann, Jan Schümmer, Holger Kleinsorgen, Hans Scholz, Andrea Kienle, Peter Tandler, Michael Koch, and Carl Gutwin. Special thanks are due to Elke Hinrichs (Fraunhofer FIT), Wolfgang Graether (Fraunhofer FIT), and Thomas Koch (OrbiTeam) for giving us a guided tour through the visual and invisible parts of BSCW. Their input greatly helped to document the BSCW case study. Similarly, special thanks are due to Chengzheng Sun and Steven Xia, of the School of Computer Engineering, Nanyang Technological University, Singapore, for their help and input for the CoWord case study.

Jörg and Anja Haake encouraged us to use the book in our classes on designing collaborative systems. We hope that many classes of future students will benefit from this decision. In this context, we would also like to thank our students, who started using the pattern language from the winter term 2004. Observing their use of the pattern language to design collaborative applications helped us to see the language from a student's point of view.

We thank all the people who have actively participated in the production of the book. These are the series editor Frank Buschmann, Gaynor Redvers-Mutton, Sally Tickner, Rosie Kemp, Andrew Kennerley, Hannah Clement, and everyone else at John Wiley & Sons. Special thanks are due to our copy-editor Steve Rickaby, who showed patience even on a very tight schedule. It was a pleasure to discuss the nuances of the English language with Steve.

Above all, we would like to express our gratitude to our families. Without their support, a book like this would not have been possible.

And finally, we thank you for your interest in this book. We hope that our pattern language will prove useful to you and become a tool in your daily work when shaping better computer-mediated interaction.

CHAPTER 2

From Patterns to a Pattern-Oriented Development Process

The use and development of groupware applications challenges users and developers in new ways. Users are faced with new technologies they have often not experienced before.

In the case of our scenario, this means that members of the game development project have to learn how they can establish a community and structure their interaction in a globally distributed team. They have to find ways of coordinating their modifications in the source code and staying aware of other developers' actions and expertise. They have to design their communication in a way that allows new members to catch up easily with previous discussions and to ensure that developers do not leave the community because of a lack of motivation.

These are traditionally not the skills of average software developers, who may have experience of interacting in locally operating teams, but who have also often performed their tasks in isolation. Developers building groupware applications are challenged with technical problems that are outside the focus of average software developers. They have to consider applications that have more than one control flow: different users use the application in parallel, which makes it a more subtle problem to ensure that changes in the application state are propagated correctly and that users stay aware of concurrent actions.

In this book we present a set of patterns that explain how developers and users can solve the problems of designing computer-mediated interaction. The patterns themselves are presented in Chapters 3 to 5, while this chapter provides the theoretical foundations for a pattern-based approach to groupware development. We provide a brief overview of the theory of patterns and discuss how patterns can be part of a participatory design process for collaborative applications. If you are familiar with the pattern concept and with pattern-based development processes, you should concentrate on Section 2.1.3, where we discuss the pattern format used in this book, and on Section 2.2, which contains an outline of the whole pattern language. If, alternatively, you are deeply interested in the theoretical foundations of pattern languages and how they alter the way in which users and developers design applications, you might not find this chapter comprehensive enough. In this case, we suggest that you look at *A Pattern Approach to End-User Centered Groupware Development* (Schümmer, 2005), a book that discusses the ideas presented in this chapter in more depth.

2.1 Patterns and Pattern Languages

2.1.1 Towards a Holistic Understanding of Socio-Technical Forces

Users are subject to different forces: wishes and responsibilities. The forces of different users interact in a socio-technical context in which the technology itself adds additional forces.

As an example, consider a group consisting of Fred and George, two distributed software developers. One of Fred's personal goals could be that he wants to finish a specific software component. The forces related to this goal are that Fred needs to be able to modify the source code and that he has understood the changes that need to be applied to the source code. The latter is a potential cause of a conflicting force, since the code was initially written by George in a way that nobody other than George is able to understand. A social solution that resolves Fred's conflicting forces would be to pair Fred and George so that George can explain the source code to Fred. However, Fred and George don't work in the same place, which raises a technical force: Fred and George would like to modify the same source code, but they are not collocated and therefore cannot access the same computer. Communication is also complicated by the distributed setting.

This example shows how social and technical forces coexist and how they relate to each other. In reality, the context and connections between forces in a real collaboration setting are much more complex than this. We therefore need solutions that take this complex context into account.

Traditional approaches to requirements engineering have tried to focus on subproblems, so that the big problem can be understood while taking as little context into account as possible. By isolating the requirements, they become disconnected from the context, and the developer should be able to create a solution that perfectly satisfies the isolated requirements. The vision is that the solution can be described as an encapsulated component that can be reused whenever the problem recurs.

If this view of reality were true, it would radically ease the process of designing components. Unfortunately, most requirements cannot easily be disconnected from their context. Instead of isolating a solution from the design context, we have to consider the context, so that the solution is situated in the user's environment. As Stahl (1993) pointed out, the understanding of requirements requires a "situatedness" of the actors. In such a situation, the user has full access to *all* dependencies that currently constitute the context. To make a design decision, designers need to be collocated either physically or in thought, and the situation needs to be as close as possible to the situation of the anticipated users.

But what is the main benefit of looking at a field of situated forces? Basically, it is an analogy to physics, where one can find numerous forces that interact in space and act in combination to shape the behavior of space.

Consider the example of air flight: why do airplanes fly? This question can only be answered if we look at least at three interacting forces:

— The gravity that causes the plane to move towards the ground
— The change of speed caused by drag or acceleration that is created by the air slowing the airplane down or by the engines speeding the airplane up
— The lift that is created by the shape of the wing that keeps the plane in the air

If these forces are unbalanced, the plane will in the worst case fall to the ground. You can increase the lift by accelerating the airplane, or by changing the angle of the wing so that it interacts differently with the air. These forces interact during flight. If you remember the last time you flew, you might remember that the airplane increases the angle of the wings relative to the direction of movement shortly before the landing. This is done to ensure enough lift even when the speed is low. If the wings did not change their angle, the plane would not have enough lift at low speeds, and as a consequence would need to land at high speed. Landing at very high speed would in turn make it more difficult to stop the plane once on the ground. This problem is solved by increasing the angle of attack of the wings. Some airplanes also increase the area of their control surfaces, which emphasizes the lift. Another solution, which is often used by military aircraft landing on carriers, is to use tailhooks to catch a cable stretched across the deck of the carrier. The cable stops the aircraft after a few hundred feet.

What this example shows is that a change to, or the insertion of an artifact in, the space occupied by the forces re-balances their interaction. Depending on the problem (for example the problem of landing large planes at low speed without crashing), different strategies for changing the artifacts in space are appropriate to a greater or lesser degree. Experts know how to play with the various forces in their area of expertise. An experienced pilot knows what to do with the wings and the engines of the airplane in order to move the plane in the air, while a pilot of a military aircraft knows how to approach the aircraft carrier.

After a solution is put in place, the whole set of forces will change as an effect of the solution. In the example of a military aircraft, the process of being slowed down by the arrestor cable adds new forces to the pilot and to the whole aircraft. It is obvious that in such cases the plane needs additional features (for example with respect to stability) that were not previously in the design focus. In general terms, we can state that the applications of a specific solution often changes the set of forces again. Rittel and Webber (1973) called such problems *wicked problems*. The authors' basic assumption is that in such problems the forces change whenever a design step is performed. Since the design action itself changes the context of a problem, it is very likely that the context needs to be reanalyzed before applying the next design step. During each analysis step, new forces may evolve that can be stronger than the strongest force seen in the previous analysis phase.

In the context of computer-mediated interaction, the forces are not as well studied as in traditional physics. While we can make use of elaborate scientific models to describe the process of flying an aircraft, we can often not explicitly name all the forces that exist in human interaction. What we can do, however, is to describe forces that result in stress for the participants. An example could be that users only interact by means of a textual communication channel and that this channel blocks non-verbal elements of the communication. Another force could be that negotiations often reach a consensus by means of non-verbal clues. Many resulting problems emerge from these forces: one could be that users can no longer distinguish irony from serious utterances.

As in the airplane setting, we can also count on best practices in human interaction. Trained facilitators, as well as successful support technology, can guide us to good solutions that help to balance conflicting social or technical forces.

Patterns are an important tool to understand such design problems better, the forces of the context, and the solution space of the problem. This is why a pattern language for computer-mediated interaction is needed.

2.1.2 Representations of Patterns

In *The Timeless Way of Building*, the architect Alexander (1979) proposed a new way of addressing connected requirements that puts an emphasis on the context of the problem—the *pattern*. Early forms of patterns were formulated as a mathematical description of problem spaces introduced in Alexander's *Notes on the Synthesis of Form* (Alexander, 1964). The first reference to patterns can be found in an essay describing the construction of multi-level service centers in which Alexander et al. (1968) defined a pattern as a rule with two parts:

"the PATTERN statement itself, and a PROBLEM statement. The PATTERN statement is itself broken down into two further parts, an IF part, and a THEN part. A pattern reads like this:

IF: X THEN: Z / PROBLEM: Y

X defines a set of conditions.
Y defines some problem which is always likely to occur under the conditions X.
Z defines some abstract spatial relation which needs to be present under the conditions X, in order to solve the problem Y." (ibid., page 15)

Alexander later moved away from the above understanding of patterns. In *A Timeless Way of Building*, he defined it as a morphological law that explains how to design an artifact in order to solve a problem in a specific context. A pattern is a

> A pattern is a "general planning principle, which states a clear problem that may occur repeatedly in the environment, states the range of contexts in which this problem will occur, and gives the general features required by all buildings or plans which solve this problem." It "describes a problem, in such a way that you can use this solution a million times over, without ever doing it the same way twice" (Alexander et al., 1977).

This definition led to the *Alexandrian pattern* form as they were used in *A Pattern Language* (APL) (Alexander et al., 1977). These patterns are natural language descriptions and include the following elements:

Name. Patterns start with a name that describes the solution. Each name is attributed a confidence rating in the form of zero to two asterisks. A pattern having two asterisks states a "true invariant." Such patterns can, in the view of Alexander et al., be found in all possible solutions to the described problem. If a pattern name has one asterisk, it describes a pattern that presents a good solution that is close to such an invariant. However, the authors still assume that one can improve the solution. While patterns with two asterisks should be mapped to the solution space, patterns with one asterisk should be treated with "a certain amount of disrespect." Finally, patterns having no asterisks describe one possible solution to the problem. The authors actively ask readers to improve these patterns and to experiment with the solution provided to find a true invariant of a solution to the problem.

Sensitizing photography. This element contains photography of an environment in which the pattern occurs. Photographs fulfill two purposes: (1) they give the reader an initial idea of how the solution might look, and (2) they help the reader to remember the pattern better.

Context description. The context of a pattern describes the space in which the pattern can be embedded. It often includes references to patterns at a higher level of granularity that have been considered before.

Problem statement. The problem statement marks the start of the pattern's body. It is first expressed in a short boldface paragraph and continues with the discussion of forces.

Discussion of forces. The discussion of forces helps the reader to understand the problem and its relation to the context better. In the Alexandrian pattern form forces are discussed and resolved in the text between the problem statement and the solution statement.

Solution statement. The solution statement summarizes how the forces described in the forces discussion were resolved. Again, it is a short boldface paragraph. Together with the problem statement, the solution statement forms a thumbnail of the pattern that communicates its most important aspects. This allows readers to get a quick overview of the pattern without reading too much. If the pattern looks relevant, a reader can read the forces section.

Diagram. In the context of architecture, patterns should, according to Alexander, be drawable. If the pattern author is not able to draw a picture, then the solution described is not a pattern. This extreme criterion for patterns is not necessary in other problem domains where the solutions help to model dynamics, such as social interaction patterns

Related patterns. The final part of the Alexandrian pattern form is the related patterns section. This lists other patterns that are intended to be considered in association with the current pattern. This section often includes references to patterns at a lower level of granularity.

Instead of being mathematical algorithms for resolving forces, the Alexandrian patterns focus on educating the users of the patterns so that they can act like experts. By using a rather informal style, people should be enabled to design and build their own houses and influence their local environment, such as the process of growth in cities. The following three examples for problems and solutions illustrate the level of abstraction used in the Alexandrian format.

---

10. MAGIC OF THE CITY
Problem. There are few people who do not enjoy the magic of a great city. But urban sprawl takes it away from everyone except the few who are lucky enough, or rich enough, to live close to the largest centers.
Solution. Therefore: Put the magic of the city within reach of everyone in a metropolitan area. Do this by means of collective regional policies which restrict the growth of downtown areas so strongly that no one downtown can grow to serve more than 300,000 people. With this population base, the downtowns will be between two and nine miles apart.

11. LOCAL TRANSPORT AREAS**
Problem. Cars give people wonderful freedom and increase their opportunities. But they also destroy the environment, to an extent so drastic that they kill all social life.
Solution. Therefore: Break the urban area down into local transport areas each one between 1 and 2 miles across, surrounded by a ring road. Within the local transport area, build minor local roads and paths for internal movements on foot, by bike, on horseback, and in local vehicles; build major roads which make it easy for cars and trucks to get to and from the ring roads, but place them to make internal local trips slow and inconvenient.

20. MINI-BUSES*
Problem. Public transportation must be able to take people from any point to any other point within the metropolitan area.
Solution. Therefore: Establish a system of small taxi-like buses, carrying up to six people each, radio-controlled, on call by telephone, able to provide point-to-point service according to the passengers' needs, and supplemented by a computer system which guarantees minimum detours, and minimum waiting times. Make bus stops for the mini-buses every 600 feet in each direction, and equip these bus stops with a phone for dialing a bus.

The examples show how different design problems relate to each other. Starting from the goal of creating vivid city centers that places the MAGIC OF THE CITY within the reach of everyone, the question of how to organize transportation in such environments arises. The solution of LOCAL TRANSPORT AREAS then leads to a network of interconnected carriers that are highly flexible and that adapt to the people's transportation needs, for example by means of MINI-BUSES. The problems as well as the solutions of Alexandrian patterns are kept at a level that is easy to understand for everyday inhabitants. Although these users are often not under control of their environment—it is difficult for a citizen to influence the transportation system—they still create a vision of a future in which the different forces are well balanced.

The pattern descriptions in *A Pattern Language* have inspired experts in the field of software design to describe recurring problems and their best known solutions as patterns as well. The most influential publication in this area was *Design Patterns: Elements of Reusable Object-Oriented Software*, published by Gamma et al. (1995), known as the *Gang of Four (GoF)*.

The rationales behind design patterns for the GoF were to:

— Provide designers with a shared vocabulary to discuss and comment on design alternatives

— Provide designers with micro-architecture building blocks that they can compose to generate more complex architectures

— Ease learning of frameworks by referring to design patterns in the framework's description

— Most importantly, discuss the trade-offs that are related to a specific design decision (Gamma, 2002)

With this in mind, it is obvious that the GoF patterns were written in a more formal style, including sections for implementation-specific aspects, as well as technical diagrams that visualize the object structure imposed by the pattern.

A good explanation of why object-oriented design patterns should be formulated in a more technical way was given by Gabriel (1996):

> "The first place where I think I differed with others' interpretation of Alexander's work was in defining the users or inhabitants of a piece of software as its coders or maintainers. At least one computer scientist identified the 'user' of a piece of software as the end-user. This appears to make sense at first, but when you read Alexander, it is clear that a 'user' is an inhabitant—someone who lives in the thing constructed. The thing constructed is under constant repair by its inhabitants, and end-users of software do not constantly repair the software, though some might want to."

While Gabriel is right for low-level technology issues, his interpretation needs to be questioned for high-level issues that should be of relevance both for the developer and the end user. Borchers (2000), who uses Alexandrian patterns in the context of human computer interaction design, goes so far as to state that the GoF patterns were not patterns, since they did not bridge the gap between lay people and professionals. If we consider environments that are tailorable, the inhabitants are end users. For that reason, high-level aspects of software that address requirements and user interface issues need to be explained with patterns that have the developers *and* the end users as target audience.

We do not follow Borcher's extreme position. Instead, when talking about patterns for computer-mediated interaction, we see the need for patterns at different levels of abstraction:

— Patterns at a high abstraction level usually target at the end user. They describe problems that occur in the social part of the socio-technical system. Often, these patterns can be "implemented" by changing the way in which users use a given set of tools in their group processes.

— Patterns at a medium level of abstraction address the human-computer-interaction part of the group interaction setting. They define how specific parts of the application should be built in order to balance forces that emerge in contexts of computer-mediated interaction.

— Finally, patterns at a low level of abstraction deal with technical aspects like network communication issues. The target audience for these patterns are developers that help end-users in implementing the groupware system.

Considering the GoF patterns, we would place them at an even lower abstraction level. While our technical patterns resolve specific design issues at an application level, the GoF patterns help to shape the internal structures of objects in the design. They are the basic building blocks in the toolbox of a software developer, while our technology patterns describe groupware-specific solutions used by a specialized groupware developer.

2.1.3 A Pattern Style for Computer-Mediated Interaction

A pattern form for computer-mediated interaction also needs to reflect the sociotechnical nature of the problems that patterns resolve. For that reason we will describe our patterns in a less formal way than the GoF patterns. However, we borrow some of the implementation specific aspects from the style used in the GoF book. They are composed of the following sections:

Name. The name of the pattern serves as a handle for the pattern. You should be able to use the name in your daily communication within a project.

As in the Alexandrian form, we use stars to express the maturity of the pattern. Since the field of computer-mediated interaction is still evolving, we have included patterns that describe good current solutions. However, some of these are preliminary solutions that reflect the current state of the art of computer-mediated interaction. Such patterns receive no asterisks. Patterns with one asterisk represent solutions that are close to invariants. They can describe one solution among others of which we are however convinced, and for which we could find numerous known uses as proof that the solution really works. Finally, patterns with two asterisks capture a solution that will be used whenever the problem is to be solved.

The pattern name is complemented with other well-known names by which it is know if such exist. The patterns from the GoF collection call this section *Also known as*.

> *An example is the* BUDDY LIST ** *pattern with the alias names roster (in Jabber), contact list (in MSN or ICQ), and address book.*

We use SMALL CAPS to denote pattern names. The chapter in which the referenced pattern can be found is shown as a subscripted index number after the pattern. BUDDY LIST$_{\rightarrow 3.1.7}$, for example, means that the BUDDY LIST pattern can be found in Section 3.1.7.

Sensitizing picture. As in the Alexandrian pattern form, we add a sensitizing picture to each pattern. You should be able to use the picture to remember an aspect of the pattern. Most pictures tell a story that we do not explicitly explain in the text. You can think of the pictures as tools to remember the pattern better: for example, you might find yourself in discussions with your colleagues when you refer to the pattern with the *elephant's head* (the ACTIVITY LOG$_{\rightarrow 4.5.1}$ pattern, which advocates remembering activities forever, like elephants).

The picture is complemented by a dictionary definition of parts of the name. This definition helps you to approach the name from a different perspective.

The picture is illustrative of the pattern. Our intention is that you take time to reflect on the name so that you capture the essence of the metaphor used, and better remember the pattern in your design activities.

Intent. The intent section of the pattern captures the core of the pattern's solution in one sentence. You will find the catalog of intents at the beginning of each chapter. In the case of the BUDDY LIST, for example, the intent is:

Show only selected known users.

Context. The context describes the situation in which the pattern is intended to be used. It may refer to other patterns that use the current pattern in its solution. The goal of the context description is to help you to understand for which context the pattern was *designed*. Nevertheless, it does not restrict the application to such a context. You can decide to apply the pattern in other contexts as well, although this may complicate the process of adapting the pattern to the new context. For example:

You are using an interaction space like a communication channel, a groupware application or a collaborative virtual environment together with many other users.

Problem. The problem description describes the most important aspects of the problem that occur over and over again. To gain a quick overview of the pattern, you should start by reading the problem statement. In the case of the BUDDY LIST the problem is:

When many users are able to interact in the interaction space it is hard to maintain an overview of relevant interaction partners, since the number of users exceeds the number of relevant contacts for a specific user. User lists grow very large and it is hard to find people who the local user knows. On the other hand, the local user is often only interested in those people they already know.

Scenario. The scenario situates the pattern's problem in the context of our example setting, the collaborative game engine development community. You will probably be able to draw parallels to scenarios of your organization or community. We have noticed that the scenarios are especially valuable when interacting with end users. If you are a developer who wants to introduce the patterns in an organizational context, you should consider using the scenarios as scene-setters to give a handle on the patterns.

The scenario for the Buddy List tells a story about Paul who is bad at remembering the names of his interaction partners and therefore has problems finding Charley, with whom he interacted some days ago, again.

Symptoms. This section describes ways in which to detect conflicting forces. It has the form of a list of sentences that start with the phrase "You should consider applying this pattern when...". For each design problem that you face in your context, you can tick the symptoms to find out if you have also experienced them in your problem setting. An example symptom of the BUDDY LIST pattern is:

— *Users spend a long time searching for another user.*

Solution. The solution resolves the conflicting forces mentioned in the problem statement and the symptoms section. If you are quickly browsing the pattern language, you should always look at this part and the problem statement.

Provide buddy lists where a user can enter other users who are of interest. Whenever the local user browses other users, initially show only users from the buddy list.

Dynamics. This section names the actors and components of the pattern and explains how the different parties interact to resolve the pattern's forces. Since most patterns are socio-technical patterns, you will often find group processes described in the dynamics section, together with a brief description of artifacts that need to be managed by the groupware system. For patterns with a greater technical focus, this section can also contain diagrams that describe the interaction of software components. In most cases these are not needed.

Whenever the local user interacts with another user the local user can add the other user to his buddy list. The buddy list is a set of user objects. Users can be added to the buddy list by selecting their representation in the user interface and executing a command, such as a menu item associated with the individual user objects.

Rationale. The rationale section provides the first part of the pattern's "proof." It explains how the pattern supports its objectives, gives an explanation of why the whole pattern works, and shows why it is appropriate in the given context.

The first part of the BUDDY LIST's rationale reads as follows:

> *The main reason why this pattern works is that it eases the process of finding other users by storing these users in a personal list. Compared with public directories of users, the personal list only contains the users that are important for the local user.*

Check. When applying a pattern, you have to map the abstract definition of the pattern to your concrete context. This means that the pattern serves as a generic template that needs to be filled with details from your application domain. If the pattern, for example, speaks of users, you will have to work out how the user is represented on a technical level. The check section poses questions that need to be answered when the pattern is applied. In the case of the BUDDY LIST, for example, these are:

— Can the user representation be associated with a context-sensitive command to add the user to a buddy list (and how)?

— How does a user select other users in the application?

Danger spots. When applying a pattern, you modify the set of forces that can currently be found in your problem context. This can result in a new conflict of forces, or introduce new forces (remember that most problems here are wicked problems). The danger spots section identifies prominent new forces explicitly that can emerge from the application of the pattern, and points to possible solutions.

For example, a danger spot of BUDDY LIST is:

> *If users only consider buddy lists for maintaining contacts to other users, they will rarely find new users in the system. Thus, you should ensure that users can also browse other users who are not on their buddy list, for example by providing a USER GALLERY$_{\rightarrow 3.1.6}$.*

Known uses. The known uses section is the second part of the pattern's proof, and provides examples of systems that implement the pattern. The example below shows an excerpt from the description of one of several known uses of the BUDDY LIST pattern.

> *XING (https://www.xing.com/) uses BUDDY LISTS to create social networks. Users can ask other users if they can add them to their BUDDY LIST. If the other user agrees, they appear in the first user's set of confirmed buddies. Users can then browse through their*

confirmed buddies, and through the BUDDY LISTS *of the confirmed buddies. They can thus move through a social network of contacts.*

Related patterns. Just as forces are connected to relate the different needs of different stakeholders, patterns are connected that address comparable forces, or that may complement one another. The related patterns section lists such patterns and explains why the patterns are related.

USER GALLERY$_{\rightarrow 3.1.6}$ *provides a means of browsing all users in a system. As outlined in the safety rules, a* USER GALLERY *complements a* BUDDY LIST *by offering an opportunity to meet new community members.*

After presenting our pattern format, we will now take a closer look at the effects that the application of a pattern has in a socio-technical system.

2.1.4 How Patterns should be Applied

To understand the theory behind the application of patterns better, we will look at three concepts discussed in the most recent works of Alexander (2003a): the *concept of wholeness*, the *concept of centers*, and the idea of *sequences*.

— *Wholeness* defines how well the different parts of a domain space interact. If a space is whole, the different parts of the space help each other instead of imposing conflicting requirements on the space. Each part in the domain space is connected to other parts by a field of forces.

— *Centers* represent areas of attention in the domain space. They emerge when semantically related parts of the space reinforce one another, and vanish if the forces connecting the different points in the domain space are in conflict.

— *Sequences* describe how strong centers emerge over time by the application of patterns. They relate the patterns to each other so that the resulting context gradually improves its wholeness with each pattern.

The level of wholeness of any given solution space can be understood as the strength of the centers that can be found in the space. According to Alexander, all design activities should focus on improving wholeness. While for Alexander, wholeness is always bound to spatial structures, we consider it as applicable to any structure regardless of its spatial properties. The only important property is that the structures are semantically related and that you can define a distance between the elements. This is why we consider the concept of wholeness applicable for socio-technical systems (like groupware) as well.

In socio-technical systems, the wholeness is composed of technical and social components: technical artifacts and users. A user can, for example, play a specific role in a group process. The role defines the user's actions that shape the socio-technical system. At the same time, the role is defined by the socio-technical system. Users interact with artifacts, and artifacts in turn suggest specific actions. Considered as a design space, this observation leads to an interrelated map of users, artifacts, and actions. Each of these elements can act as centers and each element imposes forces on every other element.

If the forces of such a socio-technical system are compatible—for example, if one user of the system has the goal of teaching another user, and the other user in turn has the goal of learning from the first user—then structures supporting the users, artifacts, or actions also support each other and thereby create strong centers and wholeness. On the other hand, if the forces are conflicting, the structures supporting the forces do not support each other and can even destroy the different centers.

In *The Phenomenon of Life*, Alexander (2003a) proposed fifteen fundamental properties that help the set of centers to constitute the whole. A solution can be judged by the level to which it supports the different properties. A solution that intends to support the requirements of a subregion in the map of requirements can be considered a coherent solution if many of the fundamental properties can be found in this region. Examples from spatial systems are:

LEVELS OF SCALE that help to perceive the center as part of a larger whole. Each part contains different parts that are related to elements of a comparable size. In order to perceive the coherence of the whole, the difference in scale must not be too large.

STRONG CENTERS that help to identify the most important parts in a design. Alexander provides the example of a fireplace, which serves as a strong center in ancient buildings. It brings together the inhabitants, since it is the center for various purposes: getting warm, preparing food, telling stories, and so on. In modern societies it is much more difficult to identify strong functional centers.

BOUNDARIES that help to identify the center better. These focus attention on the bounded part and situate the center in the context.

DEEP INTERLOCK AND AMBIGUITY, which suggests creating centers that share parts of their surroundings. The intersections of the surroundings form a new intermediate center that helps to strengthen the two original centers.

CONTRAST that stresses the need for differentiation. A center has to differentiate itself from its surroundings and from other centers.

ALTERNATING REPETITION describes how structures repeat themselves over time and space and how there is an alternate structure that fills the space when the initial structure is not present.

GRADIENTS that explain how centers with different goals can be connected. The solution is to establish intermediate centers that help to change one quality to another slowly across space.

SIMPLICITY AND INNER CALM, which suggests removing all centers that do not actively support others. This could be considered as a demand for creating the simplest solution that could possibly work.

NOT-SEPARATENESS, which reminds the designer to consider the designed artifact as a situated artifact. The goal is to create a design that lacks abruptness or "sharpness." Such a design minimizes the probability of discontinuities that distract the user of the space from his initial task. This is the reason why Alexander considered this as the most important of the fifteen properties.

ECHOES describe the fact that built structures mirror their shapes in substructures.

Other properties are POSITIVE SPACE, GOOD SHAPE, LOCAL SYMMETRIES, ROUGHNESS and THE VOID. Alexander argues that the fifteen properties constitute living structures in diverse sciences like architecture, biology, or physics.

When applied to socio-technical systems, the above properties can be interpreted as follows (extended from (Schümmer and Lukosch, 2006)):

LEVELS OF SCALE affect the different levels of interaction, ranging from single user actions (without considering other users), over small group interaction, up to the interactions in a large community.

STRONG CENTERS, for example, can be things that are considered as important events by all group members, such as kick-off meetings.

BOUNDARIES help to shield group members from other group members and thus support better interaction in the group.

DEEP INTERLOCK AND AMBIGUITY are omnipresent in group processes, since group members never belong to only one group. Instead, each person is a member of many groups in different social contexts.

CONTRAST can be observed when a group creates an identity that makes them different than other groups.

ALTERNATING REPETITION comes into play when different phases in the group process require a different level of involvement. Group members will follow a rhythm of participation and passivity, which is then used to participate in other social contexts.

GRADIENTS are important, for example, if group members gradually take responsibilities or build up trust within the group.

SIMPLICITY AND INNER CALM argues for group processes that attain the group's goal without much distraction.

NOT-SEPARATENESS reminds group members that the group is part of a larger social system and that exchange with this system is important for the group's success.

ECHOES point to the fact that we can find the same patterns of social interaction at various levels of scale. Problems like membership and interest arise equally at a community level with thousands of potential members as at a small group level where two to ten members might interact.

As we mentioned before, any design in the space leads to a transformation of the field of forces. Each modification of the designed space should focus on strengthening the wholeness of the addressed subregion in space. And since the fifteen properties contribute to wholeness, each transformation should focus on making one or more of the properties stronger. Alexander calls these modifications *structure preserving transformations*.[1]

Theoretically, you could try to identify all forces in your design space at each point in time. The problem is that the number of interrelating forces in the design space grows exponentially with the number of actors, artifacts, or actions. It is thus more realistic to consider a small subset of forces, namely the forces that can create a large conflict in the system at any one time. Note that this does not mean that you can consider a subset of your design space without its context. Instead it means that you only consider the most relevant parts of the context, but remain aware of other forces that can become more important when the configuration of your solution space is changed.

In *The Process of Creating Life*, Alexander (2003b) discussed why design can lead to configurations with greater or lesser wholeness. According to Alexander,

---

[1] Alexander is convinced that his fifteen fundamental properties completely define the nature of good design. In our context of socio-technical systems, we are less confident. The properties discussed above do help to describe good socio-technical designs, but we are sure that there have to be more fundamental properties in the socio-technical fabric of group interaction. Actually, it took Alexander several decades before he could name the properties. Before that, he was referring to the properties of good design in architecture as *the quality without a name*. For the time being, we assume that such a quality without a name is also present in socio-technical designs and we only claim that the properties are a first step in describing such a quality.

the key factor lies in the sequence of structure-preserving transformations that are applied to the system: if the transformations unfold in a way that relevant centers are empowered and unimportant centers are reduced, it is very likely that the resulting design creates a living structure.

In the sense of Alexander, the process for creating good sequences can be defined at an abstract level as follows:

1. The process starts by paying attention to the current state of wholeness of a focal region.
2. The weakest subregions, those that lack wholeness, are detected.
3. These subregions are scanned for latent centers. One of these centers is the focus for the following steps.
4. The region is now transformed by applying a structure-preserving transformation.
5. This results in the strengthening of centers and the birth of new latent or matured centers. Specifically, larger existing centers should be strengthened and the overall coherence of the region should be improved.
6. A first test checks whether or not centers are really improved.
7. A second test checks whether the improvement was the simplest solution that could possibly work.
8. If one of these two tests fails, the modification is undone.
9. The process continues in a further cycle by looking at weak centers again.

How does this relate to patterns? Considered in the context of wholeness, patterns are concrete instances of structure-preserving transformations in a specific context. They describe how centers can emerge in a system of wholeness, and therefore serve as *generic centers*.

From this perspective, patterns can be considered as strong generative rules that play a comparable role, just as memes do. Richard Dawkins, who coined the term, explained it as a replicator for ideas:

"Just as genes propagate themselves in the gene pool by leaping from body to body via sperms or eggs, so memes propagate themselves in the meme pool by leaping from brain to brain via a process which, in the broad sense, can be called imitation. If a scientist hears, or reads about, a good idea, he passes it on to his colleagues and students. He mentions it in his articles and his lectures. If the idea catches on, it can be said to propagate itself, spreading from brain to brain." (Dawkins, 1989)

As Gil-White (2005) argues, memes mutate in every act of transmission, since they are combined with the receiver's current set of memes—his mental state. Transferred to the concept of patterns, a pattern is interpreted by the user who reads (or learns) the pattern. This user combines the practices proposed in the pattern with his own mental state, thus creating a mutated version of the pattern. It is in this sense not intended that each solution is an exact replication of the pattern. Instead, the solution has to have adaptations to the concrete context and the designer's views (for example, of aesthetics). You, as a user of patterns, are requested to adapt the pattern to your own context before you can apply it. In contrast to other approaches, like the instantiation of components of a framework, you are invited to transfer the idea of the pattern so that it best fits your forces. But the transfer should not be too large, otherwise the statements made by the pattern may become invalid.

Gil-White (2005) pointed out that memes can only survive in the context of other supportive memes. He provided the example of the meme of *Beethoven's Fifth symphony*, which requires that the memes of *playing musical instruments like the violin or the trombone* are passed on. The same is true for patterns. They require that supportive (and more widely accepted) patterns are passed on as well. The full set of required patterns then forms a pattern language.

Alexander proposes that each project constructs its own pattern language. This language can be invented from scratch (but still founded on an empirical basis), composed from existing pattern languages, or constructed by appropriating patterns to the context of the project. It can even be valid to invent patterns without an empirical basis. In this case, the application of the patterns (in different sequences) has to prove the validity of the patterns *a posteriori*.

A knowledge of pattern sequences helps when learning how to speak a pattern language. Compared to natural language, pattern sequences are examples of great literature that makes the best possible use of the language.

2.1.5 Relationships among Patterns in a Pattern Language

The patterns in *A Pattern Language* form a network of 253 interconnected patterns. As we pointed out in the previous section, the connections between the patterns may help to define sequences of structure-preserving transformations. These relations constitute the grammar for talking about a pattern language. It is up to the user and the developer of a system to agree on sequences that address their current needs. Explicit relations among the patterns that represent frequently selected sequences in the pattern language can help in this process.

For that reason it is quite common that authors of a pattern language arrange their patterns on a pattern landscape. Figure 2.1 shows a small subset of the patterns in our language, together with their connections.

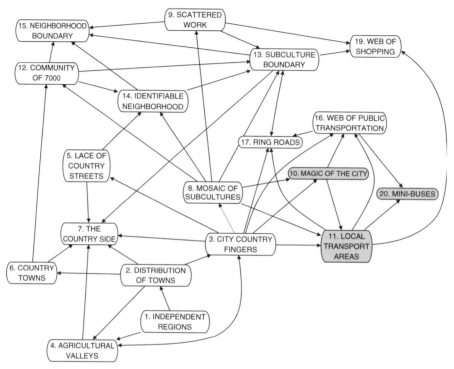

Figure 2.1 The first twenty patterns in *A Pattern Language* and their interconnections

The example patterns from Section 2.1.2 are shown as shaded nodes in Figure 2.1. The diagram shows the connections between the first twenty patterns of the pattern language.[2] It can be read as follows: assuming that you want to create the MAGIC OF THE CITY, you should think about building the downtown areas of the small cities, so that only few cars disturb the life that evolves on the streets. One solution for this is to create LOCAL TRANSPORT AREAS that cannot easily be transited by cars. However, this requires that you consider other means of bringing people from point A to point B. MINI-BUSES are one way to offer public transportation that quickly adapts to pedestrians' needs.

---

[2]Pattern 18, NETWORK OF LEARNING was omitted, since it is not connected to any of the first twenty patterns in the pattern language.

Initial pattern languages in the area of computer science, such as the influential GoF pattern language, were often less connected than Alexander's pattern language.

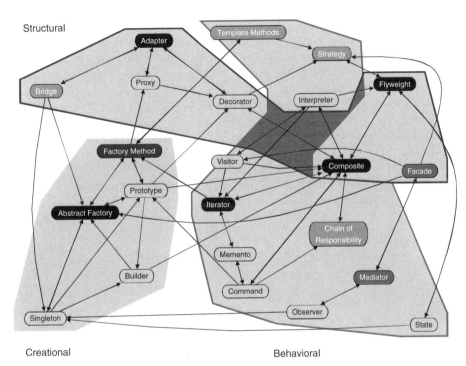

Figure 2.2 Patterns and their connection in the *Gang of Four* pattern language

Looking more closely at the relations in this pattern language, we can map the picture shown in Figure 2.2[3]. The picture has several properties that are interesting for the design of our pattern language as well. Most importantly, the authors decided to cluster their patterns with respect to their purpose:

> "Creational patterns concern the process of object creation. Structural patterns deal with the composition of classes or objects. Behavioral patterns characterize the ways in which classes or objects interact and distribute responsibility." (Gamma, 2002)

---

[3] Note that the original publication included a less comprehensive map of the patterns that however showed additional labels for each connection. The problem with labels is that they can be easily included in a pattern language diagram with a low degree of connectivity, but that there will not be enough space to show them when all relations between the patterns should be shown.

In general, we can observe that smaller pattern languages can make it easier to create a pattern language if related patterns are only considered from within the language. On the other hand, the relations become more important in larger pattern languages, since one can in this case no longer assume that the reader knows all potential relations in the language.

A high level of connectivity is thus both a strength and a weakness of a pattern language. Higher connectivity implies that the patterns in the language can form a larger set of pattern sequences. However, such languages are harder to grasp and users may get lost in the language.

The pattern language included in this book consists of seventy-one patterns. Relying only on pattern relations for providing guidance to the reader is thus inappropriate. As in the GoF collection, we therefore distinguished between different pattern categories and introduced abstraction levels to show which patterns will be used by whom in the development process.

We provide an overview of the whole language in the next section, and explain how you can best access the patterns.

2.2 An Overview of our Pattern Language for Computer-Mediated Interaction

A simplified view of our pattern language for computer-mediated interaction is shown in Figure 2.3. We have already touched on the basic structure of the language in the introduction. Now that you are aware of patterns and pattern languages, we will provide a more comprehensive overview of the patterns that will follow in Chapters 3 to 5. The basic structure of the language is made up of three layers, each of which addresses different questions, namely:

— Questions that arise during the design of *community support*
— Questions that address issues that relate to *group support* for specific tasks
— Questions related to the *base technology*

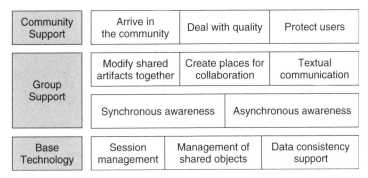

Figure 2.3 Clusters in our pattern language for computer-mediated interaction

In the following sections we first give a brief summary of the individual layers. We then go through the individual themes covered by the layers. Finally, we situate our pattern language in the global context of existing pattern languages and provide pointers for further reading.

2.2.1 The Three Layers of our Pattern Language

At the highest layer are *patterns for establishing a community* (see Chapter 3). You should consider these patterns if you have not yet created a group and you plan to use a collaborative system in a large organizational context. The patterns in this layer mainly describe social processes and propose minor changes of, or extensions to, the technology support. The main target audience is the end user and not the developer, although their technical implications make these patterns interesting for developers as well. In many cases you could implement the patterns at this level without writing any lines of code by tailoring your use of existing group support technology.

An example is the WELCOME AREA pattern. This pattern states that new members of a group or community should be listed in a prominent place and introduced to other members. Although we point to a well-integrated solution in the pattern, you could also implement this pattern using existing technologies such as discussion groups. In this case, you could send a new message to the discussion group in which you ask new members to identify themselves. In a second step, you would ask existing members to reply to the introduction of new members.

The middle layer contains *patterns for supporting small groups in their interaction* (see Chapter 4). We now assume that users have found a collaboration context and that they want to perform tasks that advance the group towards its collective goal. Most of the patterns are as much technical as social. You should use these patterns in interaction between developers and end users to inspire your design task.

In most cases these patterns require that some parts of your environment are adapted to the needs of group collaboration. However, all the patterns describe aspects of the groupware application that will be visible by the end user. If you are a developer, you should use these patterns when discussing the opportunities of collaborative systems with the end users. If you are an end user, you may want to take these patterns with you when you next meet your development team.

The lowest layer includes *patterns for designing the infrastructure that is needed by the groupware tools* (see Chapter 5). These patterns are mainly targeted at developers who have to work out how shared objects should be managed and how information exchange is mediated by the computer system.

2.2.2 Topic Clusters in the Different Layers

We can further organize the clusters in subclusters, each addressing a specific theme or type of need in your group process. You will find these subclusters as section headers in the chapters that follow. At this point, we would like to give a brief overview of the patterns that you can find in these smaller clusters.

When *establishing a community*, you will have to think about the relation of your group with its surrounding environment.

Assuming that you have not yet established a community, you will first need to think about how a community might emerge given an initial environment or context (see Section 3.1). Starting with the LOGIN$_{\rightarrow 3.1.2}$ pattern, you will be able to identify the members of your community. They will do a QUICK REGISTRATION$_{\rightarrow 3.1.1}$ and turn themselves from passive recipients of information (perhaps perceived from web pages) into active contributors. But becoming active is not always easy for new members. In an initial step, they might describe themselves by using the VIRTUAL ME$_{\rightarrow 3.1.5}$ pattern, but there may be hindrances like social barriers, a lack of trust, or simply a missing overview of the community's topics and goals that will make

2.2 Pattern Language for Computer-Mediated Interaction

users reluctant to become active. Techniques like the WELCOME AREA$_{\rightarrow 3.1.3}$, the MENTOR$_{\rightarrow 3.1.4}$, or a USER GALLERY$_{\rightarrow 3.1.6}$ all share the goal of easing the initial steps in a community. They describe how you can shape your social processes such that new users do not get lost in the community, quickly learn more about the community's spirit, and soon have a BUDDY LIST$_{\rightarrow 3.1.7}$ of their own.

In the next stage, you can assume that users are interacting in the community, for example exchanging messages or publishing documents. At this stage it becomes important to *deal with quality* issues in the community (see Section 3.2).

As an example, imagine a medical community. The funders of the community did not assume that it would grow much. However, it attracted more and more people. But what do the members expect from the community? Members with specific diseases, for example, try to find BIRDS OF A FEATHER$_{\rightarrow 3.2.3}$ who share their ailment and who are interested in exchanging experiences. What they seek is an interaction of high quality, where "quality" is defined as the relevance of the topics and the involvement of each user in them. Other members are looking for qualitatively good explanations of a specific disease. Quality of content is important in this domain, which is the reason that the QUALITY INSPECTION$_{\rightarrow 3.2.1}$ carefully checks all contributions. After having found helpful information, members look for ways to thank the original authors. They could for example write a LETTER OF RECOMMENDATION$_{\rightarrow 3.2.2}$, or REWARD$_{\rightarrow 3.2.6}$ the top experts in the HALL OF FAME$_{\rightarrow 3.2.5}$. As well being flattered, the experts may also be more motivated to be found by the EXPERT FINDER$_{\rightarrow 3.2.4}$.

But what do you do when users no longer want to participate in a community? How do you prevent other users from contacting former members of the community? Such questions point to the importance of *protecting users* in your community (see Section 3.3). You should for example prevent leaving users from being bothered by messages that are no longer of interest to them. Patterns like QUICK GOODBYE$_{\rightarrow 3.3.5}$ or ATTENTION SCREEN$_{\rightarrow 3.3.4}$ help users to control information that can reach them. AVAILABILITY STATUS$_{\rightarrow 3.3.3}$ addresses the same problem on a less technical level: instead of defining *a priori* on a system level what information can reach the users, they individually signal whether or not they are available for collaboration. Other users are still able to contact a user who signalled unavailability, but they know by means of a social protocol that this will be considered as an interruption. MASQUERADE$_{\rightarrow 3.3.2}$ allows users to act anonymously in the community. This can become very important, especially for sensitive topics like the health example above. When thinking about privacy, you should ensure that RECIPROCITY$_{\rightarrow 3.3.1}$ is guaranteed.

The patterns in the chapter on *group support* describe how interaction in a GROUP$_{\rightarrow 4.1.1}$ can be better supported by means of technology (see Chapter 4). The basic assumption of this chapter is that you have identified the members of the community and that you now have the goal of accomplishing a task within the community.

This is why we first focus on *how to modify shared artifacts together* (see Section 4.1). In any collaboration setting in which you have the goal of collaboratively creating artifacts, you will have to think about how users can access these artifacts. A frequently found solution is to use a SHARED FILE REPOSITORY$_{→4.1.2}$ where users can exchange their files. While this provides the basic support for collaborative work, it is often just the first step before thinking about means for tighter collaboration. You could allow users to perform SHARED BROWSING$_{→4.1.3}$. A group could then explore an information space together and VOTE$_{→4.1.4}$ on the route that they should take in the information space. Or you could allow group members to collaborate with existing domain-specific applications by means of APPLICATION SHARING$_{→4.1.5}$. The more synchronous your interaction becomes, the more important becomes the question of how FLOOR CONTROL$_{→4.1.7}$ is organized. Will you create a group process that has specific roles that define who is allowed to work on shared artifacts at a specific time? Or will you provide a SHARED EDITOR$_{→4.1.6}$ in which all users can interact concurrently?

All these patterns help to support the collaboration process. In many cases it makes sense to complement this view with the view of a collaboration space. The question is then *how to shape places for collaboration* (see Section 4.2). We understand *places* in the sense of Harrison and Dourish (1996), who pointed out that:

"Physically, a place is a space which is invested with understandings of behavioral appropriateness, cultural expectations, and so forth. We are located in *space*, but we act in *place*. Furthermore, *places* are spaces that are valued." (page 69)

In the context of places for collaboration, you can often find a ROOM$_{→4.2.1}$ in which a group meets for communication and collaboration. In larger environments, the rooms are connected to form virtual worlds. To orient themselves in these worlds, users can look up their current position, the position of relevant rooms, and the position of their group members in an ACTIVE MAP$_{→4.2.2}$. In cases where the arrangement of the rooms is less important (for example, if the rooms are less related), you can often find an INTERACTION DIRECTORY$_{→4.2.3}$ instead of an ACTIVE MAP$_{→4.2.2}$. In the sense of Alexander (2003a), these three patterns help to create STRONG CENTERS and STRONG BOUNDARIES. A ROOM$_{→4.2.1}$, especially, creates a private place for interaction that gives the group a virtual home.

In order to support more flexible group settings, we have to complement this view with some means for entering and leaving a place for collaboration. You might have noticed that we now face the same issues at the group support level that were introduced before at the community support level. Users may be asked to join a group following an INVITATION$_{→4.2.5}$, or they may actively request entrance by pressing a virtual door BELL$_{→4.2.4}$. In a third case, users might just be interested in collaborating at a specific place, but not care about the collaborators. A BLIND DATE$_{→4.2.6}$ could be most appropriate in these cases.

Complementary to the collaboration-centered view of the patterns mentioned above, a communication-centered view should always be considered when designing computer-mediated interaction. In Section 4.3 we present eight patterns that help to shape *textual communication*. Prominent techniques are to integrate synchronous communication by means of an EMBEDDED CHAT$_{\rightarrow 4.3.1}$, or asynchronous communication as found in a FORUM$_{\rightarrow 4.3.2}$. Just as for collaboration support, orientation becomes an important aspect for communication in distributed groups. The groups have to understand the references between utterances, for example in THREADED DISCUSSIONS$_{\rightarrow 4.3.3}$, and they may need to FLAG$_{\rightarrow 4.3.4}$ important messages for future reference. Often, feedback is very important: users should be encouraged to comment on messages from other users by attaching a SHARED ANNOTATION$_{\rightarrow 4.3.5}$, and should close the FEEDBACK LOOP$_{\rightarrow 4.3.6}$ so that a dialogue emerges between authors and readers of messages. In traditional face-to-face communication, additional feedback is often given by non-verbal clues. Users may look amused, or they may stare at their communication partner with a look of incomprehension. The DIGITAL EMOTIONS$_{\rightarrow 4.3.7}$ pattern describes how this sort of communication is mapped to a textual communication channel. Finally, FAQ$_{\rightarrow 4.3.8}$ describes how recurring questions can be avoided so that communication becomes more efficient.

The model of Gerosa et al. (2004) (see page 8) related communication, collaboration, and coordination to an orthogonal dimension of groupware applications: the provision of *group awareness*. Our pattern language addresses awareness from two perspectives: *synchronous awareness* presents patterns that help to stay aware of collocated users in a workspace, while *asynchronous awareness* describes how absent users can stay informed about group process, and how the group can in turn stay aware of absent users.

In the *synchronous awareness* cluster (see Section 4.4), users usually first become aware of others who work at the same place and appear in a USER LIST$_{\rightarrow 4.4.1}$. For large interaction spaces, it can also be important to stay aware of ACTIVE NEIGHBORS$_{\rightarrow 4.4.3}$ who work on related artifacts. An ACTIVITY INDICATOR$_{\rightarrow 4.4.9}$ can further help in an understanding of what other users currently do. Seeing such users is the first step to initiating SPONTANEOUS COLLABORATION$_{\rightarrow 4.4.2}$ among them. Users activate commands on INTERACTIVE USER INFO$_{\rightarrow 4.4.4}$ to send an INVITATION$_{\rightarrow 4.2.5}$ to other users so that they can start a COLLABORATIVE SESSION$_{\rightarrow 5.1.1}$.

Once involved in a collaboration, it becomes important to understand what happens to the more fine-grained artifacts that are in the focus of all group members. It is important to understand the REMOTE FIELD OF VISION$_{\rightarrow 4.4.5}$ and the REMOTE SELECTION$_{\rightarrow 4.4.6}$ as they are experienced by a remote user. For tight interaction, users can even use a REMOTE CURSOR$_{\rightarrow 4.4.7}$ that visualizes remote users' mouse pointers.

One drawback of distributed collaboration is that communication about things seen on the screen becomes more difficult. In a collocated setting, users use their fingers to point to regions of the screen to which their communication refers. In remote settings, a TELEPOINTER$_{\rightarrow 4.4.8}$ can compensate for this problem.

The *asynchronous awareness* cluster complements the patterns from the cluster above with patterns that help to stay aware of collaboration partners over longer periods (see Section 4.5). Activities are persisted in an ACTIVITY LOG$_{\rightarrow 4.5.1}$ and can be visualized in different forms: a TIMELINE$_{→4.5.2}$ creates a diagram with events that take place on documents over the lifetime of the collaboration. A PERIODIC REPORT$_{→4.5.3}$ informs absent users about activities that have taken place. This report is sent to the users on a regular basis, so that the delay between the event and the notification does not become too long. However, it is not always the case that the events are important when the report is received. Instead, they can become important the next time the user is interested in the modified artifact. They then need to know that the artifact is different from what they remember it to be. A CHANGE INDICATOR$_{→4.5.4}$ explains how this can be communicated to the user.

Two more patterns in this cluster address the absence of users by addressing the problems that arise when users wait for the actions of other users who are unavailable. An ALIVENESS INDICATOR$_{→4.5.5}$ shows when a user was last active, while an AWAY MESSAGE$_{→4.5.6}$ responds to interaction requests directly with an explanation of the user's absence.

All the patterns mentioned so far require that objects are shared between distributed users, which is subject of Chapter 5.

The basic support can in turn be split in two layers. At a higher level, *Session Management* has to be considered (see Section 5.1). At lower levels, you have to design how shared objects are managed and how modifications to shared objects are kept consistent.

The first pattern cluster on session management assumes that collaboration episodes are embedded in a COLLABORATIVE SESSION$_{→5.1.1}$—a technical representation of users, the computer systems on which they act, and the artifacts used. By means of a PERSISTENT SESSION$_{→5.1.2}$, users can pause their work and continue it later, even from another computer system. In this case, and in the case of late-joining users, the state of the session has to be communicated to all participants using either a STATE TRANSFER$_{→5.1.3}$ or a REPLAY$_{→5.1.4}$.

The patterns for session management rely on the fact that users can access *Shared Objects* (see Section 5.2). The easiest paradigm for sharing data is to store the data on a central server as CENTRALIZED OBJECTS$_{→5.2.1}$. The clients use the data and receive change notifications because of their REMOTE SUBSCRIPTION$_{→5.2.2}$. They can then access the new state from the server. This works well for applications in which objects are changed infrequently, especially in asynchronous collaboration settings. Synchronous settings, on the other hand, require rapid feedback to the user. One technique that is often used in this context is to perform changes on local copies called REPLICATED OBJECTS$_{→5.2.3}$. Note that replication is not always done for speed reasons. The other most important reason is that users may disconnect from the server for a long period and work with the objects in the meantime. In this case, we call the replicas NOMADIC OBJECTS$_{→5.2.4}$.

Changes to REPLICATED OBJECTS are communicated back to the server from which the object was initially retrieved, then sent to all other clients that hold a replica of the object. We call this mechanism MEDIATED UPDATES$_{→5.2.5}$. An alternative to this is to allow the client that originated the modification to inform all other clients directly

2.2 Pattern Language for Computer-Mediated Interaction

using DECENTRALIZED UPDATES$_{\to 5.2.6}$. The updates can include the new state of the object. In many cases we find another strategy, in which an explanation of how the change was achieved is transferred. Such a DISTRIBUTED COMMAND$_{\to 5.2.7}$ can be re-executed at remote sites to change the replica in the same way as the original or another replica.

If we allow users to change shared objects in a distributed context, we have to ensure that changes are performed in a consistent way. The *data consistency support* cluster describes different strategies for this (see Section 5.3). The simplest but most inconvenient method is to allow only one user at a time to change a shared artifact. This PESSIMISTIC LOCKING$_{\to 5.3.1}$ works best in environments with a low level of concurrency. Other contexts may require a faster response time. OPTIMISTIC CONCURRENCY CONTROL$_{\to 5.3.2}$ assumes that changes will be correct in most cases, but identifies potential problems using a CONFLICT DETECTION$_{\to 5.3.3}$ technique.

Such conflicts emerge from different changes to the same shared object by different users. You could simply restore the old state in conflict situations, so that the users have to perform their modifications again. However, there are better techniques: two changes can be transformed in a way such that they have the same effect if they are executed in a different order. How this can be done is discussed in the OPERATIONAL TRANSFORMATION$_{\to 5.3.4}$ pattern. A completely different approach is to structure the shared data in a way that no or only very few conflicts can take place. LOVELY BAGS$_{\to 5.3.5}$ and IMMUTABLE VERSIONS$_{\to 5.3.6}$ are two approaches to this problem.

In summary, the patterns form the network shown in Figure 2.4. This network is embedded in the context of other pattern languages, which is the topic of the next section. It is not important for now that you read all the details of the figure. Consider it rather as an introduction to the connectivity and overall structure of the language. You will find enlarged selections from the figure at the beginning of each section.

2.2.3 Related Pattern Languages

Just as the patterns in our pattern language form a densely connected network, our pattern language as a whole is part of a larger network of pattern languages. When describing the language, we have already mentioned areas like security or workflow management that would well fit into the pattern language but which are not part of this book.

Figure 2.5 extends the layers of our pattern language with complementary pattern languages. In this section we give an overview of other pattern languages that can provide guidance in related problem domains.

Fearless Change by Manns and Rising (2005) describes patterns for introducing new ideas into organizations. The common background of these patterns is that change in an organization requires social practices that establish trust in new goals and rely on existing social structures. The patterns provided in Fearless Change can often be transformed into a computer-mediated environment. As in

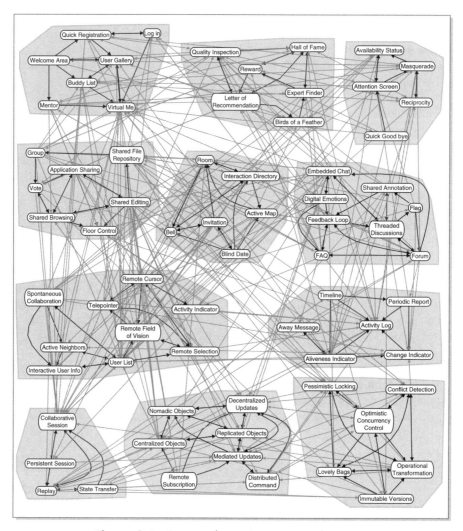

Figure 2.4 Patterns clusters in our pattern language

traditional settings, trust is an essential prerequisite for changing social interaction in a computer-mediated setting.

Team interaction in software projects is the focus of the *Organizational Patterns* language (Coplien and Harrison, 2004). Our pattern language again provides means for supporting the patterns mentioned in Organizational Patterns in a computer-mediated setting. Although Organization Patterns was designed for the context of software development, we consider it just as applicable in many settings in which a team solves a design task collaboratively.

2.2 Pattern Language for Computer-Mediated Interaction

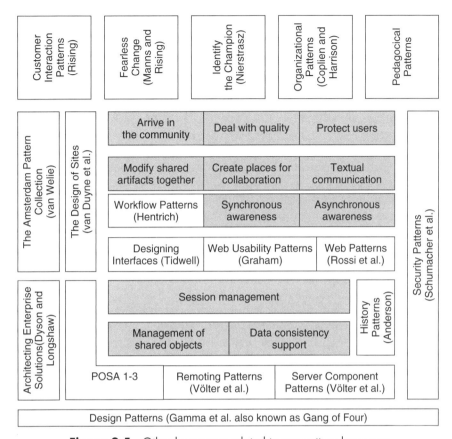

Figure 2.5 Other languages related to our pattern language

Other important domains in pattern languages that have emerged which build on the idea of group interaction are pedagogy and customer interaction. Pattern languages in these domains are probably relevant for you if you are professionally involved in such areas. If you are a teacher and are seeking better support for group-based learning with collaboration technology, you should look at the *Pedagogical Patterns Project* (Eckstein, 1999), as well as at the TELL project, a European-Union funded project in which the first patterns for computer-supported learning were collected (TELL Project Consortium, 2005). The *Customer Interaction Patterns* collected by Rising (2000) describe how the interaction between a product developer and a customer can be enhanced. Collaboration technology can augment this and comparable group processes.

In the area of business process management, the *Workflow Pattern* collection by Hentrich (2004) is an initial attempt to better describe socio-technical systems that follow strict business processes. While these are not necessarily cooperative, we consider the approach started by the Workflow Pattern collection as an interesting initial step to understand the mechanics of workflows better. We are not aware of a comprehensive pattern language in this area.

Several pattern languages have emerged in recent years that describe best practices for designing user interfaces. *Design of Sites* (Duyne et al., 2002), the *Amsterdam Pattern Collection* (van Welie, 2005), *Web Usability Patterns* (Graham, 2002a), and the *Web Patterns* collection (Rossi et al., 1995) all focus on the design of web-based user interfaces. Questions relating to navigation and content management are important issues in these languages. As regards collaborative aspects, some of the pattern languages mentioned provide guidance on how to design community websites, but the main focus is on traditional websites that make a clear distinction between content producers and content consumers.

In most projects you will probably need a good mix between community aspects and traditional content provision. We see the role of our pattern language as making the community experience a better one, and providing support for tighter collaboration among the users of a website. This means that the web pattern languages are probably valuable for you as an additional resource if you plan to design a web-based community.

In the context of non-web-based applications, *Designing Interfaces* (Tidwell, 2006) is currently the most comprehensive pattern language for computer-mediated interaction. It discusses usability issues that are also relevant to groupware development. We have linked our patterns to patterns from the *Designing Interfaces* language wherever the style of interface is important for better support of computer-mediated interaction.

You may also consider looking at Jan Borcher's *Pattern Approach to Interaction Design* (Borchers, 2001). This book explains how patterns can support the construction of interactive devices. An example of such a pattern is AUGMENTED REALITY, in which the author describes how interactive devices such as large displays can be embedded in a meeting space to support the user experience better. Remarkably, the example provided by the author was based on research made in the context of improving support for groups in "intelligent buildings" in which computer technology merges with traditional office furnishings such as tables or chairs (Streitz et al., 1999). All the embedded computers in this environment used software that was intentionally designed as groupware, based on the COAST framework (Schuckmann et al., 1996a), which will also serve as a known use for our patterns. In most cases, however, you will be confronted with traditional user interfaces. For this reason we do not address hardware design issues in our pattern language.

This brings us to pattern languages that address technical problems related to the creation of collaborative systems. The *History Patterns* collection (Anderson, 2000) describes practices for logging and restoring previous states of a system. Logging is an aspect that is relevant for the provision of awareness in collaborative systems. Users have to understand how a collaboration space evolved over time to be able to situate their own actions in the current context. On a more technical level, it is often required that the state of an object used by more than one user be reverted to an older version. We will return to these patterns when discussing the need for logging activities in groupware contexts (ACTIVITY LOG$_{\to 4.5.1}$).

Several pattern languages discuss the design of distributed systems:

— *Server Component Patterns* by Völter et al. (2002) show how components in a component-oriented architecture can be connected to enable the collaboration of components over a network. The language explains the basic building blocks that are used, for example, in the Enterprise JavaBeans (EJB) architecture. In some contexts it can be adequate to use such an infrastructure for the development of collaborative systems. In most contexts you will only need to consider some of the basic principles. In Section 5.2 we connect our patterns to patterns from this language.

— In the same vein, *Remoting Patterns* (Völter et al., 2004) describes the internal structures of distributed object middleware. Middleware in this context is an infrastructure that enables the communication between two or more distributed clients. In the context of collaborative applications we face the same problems: the applications of individual users have to communicate in order to support the user's collaboration. In Chapter 5 we provide patterns that are closely related to the remoting pattern language, but which have a special focus on concurrent modification of shared objects.

— *Architecting Enterprise Solutions* (Dyson and Longshaw, 2004) addresses issues that arise when systems should be stable and scalable. This is often a critical issue for interactive collaborative applications, since many users require the application to respond as fast as a single-user application. The patterns from (Dyson and Longshaw, 2004) therefore relate to the base technology chapter of our pattern language.

The collection in *Security Patterns* (Schumacher et al., 2005) is orthogonal to the aspects mentioned so far. These patterns are relevant to user authentication and securing the exchange of objects between members of a group. Since we assume that a group will always interact over a network, security questions become important. We do not discuss these aspects in our pattern language, but recommend that you study the security pattern language.

Finally, several volumes discuss *Pattern-Oriented Software Architecture* (Volume 1: (Buschmann et al., 1996); Volume 2: (Schmidt et al., 2001); Volume 3: (Kircher and Jain, 2004b)) and software design in general (*Design Patterns* (Gamma et al., 1995)). We assume that you are at least superficially familiar with these pattern collections if you develop software. In cases where we believe that a specific class design is beneficial for the implementation of our patterns, we will highlight this relationship.

2.3 The Oregon Software Development Process (OSDP)

Patterns and pattern languages are normally applied in the context of a software development project or process. There is no specific process that has to be used to apply patterns. However, many processes show a lack of end user participation when designing software. This can be the source of invalid requirements resulting in low end user acceptance and inadequate systems, especially for groupware design.

Fostering interaction between end users and developers should be an essential part of the selected development process. The Oregon Software Development Process (OSDP) argues for end user participation, pattern-oriented transfer of design knowledge, piecemeal growth of the system under development in the form of short iterations, and frequent diagnosis or reflection that leads to an improved application (see (Schümmer and Slagter, 2004), (Schümmer et al., 2005), and (Schümmer, 2005)).

The use of patterns is an essential part of this development process. Patterns are used both as a means of capturing and representing design knowledge, as well as a means of communication between end users, designers, and other stakeholders. Given these different types of use, OSDP makes use of the different layers in the pattern language and the corresponding target audience (see Section 2.2.1).

OSDP incorporates three different types of iterations:

1. In *conceptual iterations* users envision future concepts of system usage.
2. In *development iterations* users and developers collaborate to build the required groupware infrastructure.
3. In *tailoring iterations* users appropriate the groupware system to changed needs.

Note that the original Oregon Experiment focused on modifying existing structures of buildings (Alexander et al., 1980). Transferred to software development, it focuses on tailoring iterations. Alexander's Oregon Experiment relied on the existence of buildings that were already inhabited by users. In software development, on the other hand, one often seems to start a new project from scratch. This is comparable to the development of a building in empty countryside. In the OSDP, we extend the phases of the Oregon Experiment to the early stages of product development, because the role of the customer cannot be perfectly filled at that stage.

In addition, the Oregon Experiment did not focus on product retirement: its assumption was that a planning office would exist as long as the building remained in use. Transferring this to the domain of software development poses new problems over the practice of how contracts are handled. A user community, for example, has to agree to continue development and not think of the application as completed.

2.3 The Oregon Software Development Process (OSDP)

During a project lifecycle, the different types of iterations will have different importance, as indicated in Figure 2.6. At the beginning of the project the team will start with conceptual iterations. When initial requirements emerge, development iterations will start, while conceptual iterations become less important. When the development has resulted in a product that can actually be used, tailoring iterations can be started as well. Figure 2.6 also shows that product development typically decreases over time (because bugs are fixed) and that the majority of tailoring iterations take place in the first period after the groupware system is introduced. Tailoring iterations end when the product is replaced.

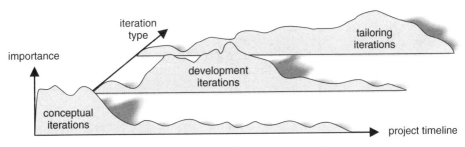

Figure 2.6 Frequency of iterations during the project

As OSDP is an iterative approach, each iteration may actually be performed multiple times: in fact, designers and users may even choose to go back to a previous iteration type. Since more than one group can work on the future concepts in parallel, tasks can emerge concurrently. The groups use *backlogs* to coordinate their development activities. A backlog is a set of task cards—in the simplest case a set of paper-based index cards—that describe activities that have to be done in order to satisfy a functional requirement. Each group creates one backlog on which the tasks for their specific concept are outlined. One member of the project team fills the role of the *gardener*(Rittenbruch et al., 2002), collecting all the task cards from the different backlogs and sorting them according to their relevance as indicated by users.

A more detailed description of the iterations is provided by Figure 2.7: the three concentric circles represent the three different iteration types. The following sections explain activities in the iteration in detail.

2.3.1 Conceptual Iteration

The role of conceptual iterations is twofold: they should help the users to form a project group and *norm* (see below) their goals in the participatory process.

The first conceptual iterations will have a special focus on group formation, as proposed by Tuckman and Jenson (1977). They suggested that a group's life cycle

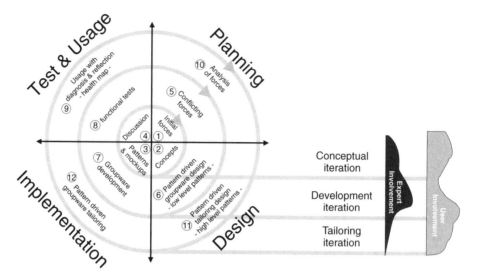

Figure 2.7 The Oregon Software Development Process

runs through different stages, beginning with the first meeting of the group and running to the end of group work. The first three stages describe how the group lays the foundation for future collaboration. These three stages are:

Forming is the stage at which group members become aware of the other's identities and get an idea of the group's goals and activities.

Storming is the stage at which initial conflicts are fought out. Examples for such conflicts can be an unequal participation in the group or the fight for group leader roles.

Norming represents the stage of the group process at which group members have found their position in the group. Group members start to design their group interaction constructively and define group goals.

Conceptual iterations are initiated from within the organization. Users or management bring in ideas for changing social practices in the organization. This often implies changing the groupware technology used so far as well. The ideas serve as seeds for the interaction between end users and developers in conceptual iterations. The ideas should evolve from concrete needs, but still leave an open area for user participation. Examples might be support for computer-mediated distance education in a traditional university, the creation of a support community for users of an industrial product, or a community support system for teenagers.

The extent to which real users can be involved in early conceptual iterations depends on the existence of the user community. If the goal of the project is to establish a user community that did not exist before, it may be difficult to find initial users who can be involved in the group process. In this case, it is reasonable to look for people who are close enough to future users. Consider a university aiming at computer-mediated cooperative distance education. In this example it makes sense to find users from the following groups: students studying at a traditional university, students from distance teaching universities, teaching staff, and employed people who cannot attend a traditional university due to time constraints, but who feel the need for additional training.

These users are invited to participate in a focus group that runs the conceptual iterations. Such an iteration consists of four main activities (numbers in the text refer to the numbers in Figure 2.7): 1) collection of forces, 2) envisioning of future concepts, 3) selection of patterns and creation of low-fidelity prototypes, and 4) reflection on the concepts and prototypes created.

In the first step, users exchange stories from their workplace that are related to the seed ideas. In the example of an industrial support community, a technician might for example describe how he manages a phone call from a user. A user, on the other hand, would describe a situation in which they need support and how they normally request help. The stories are an important source for *finding initial (high-level) forces* (1).

Special attention is put on break situations[4]. Two questions are asked: What is difficult in the current form of interaction? What are the reasons for these difficulties? The first question focuses on reflection and the detection of a break, while the second focuses on better understanding the break and detecting the forces that led to the break.

For each story, a *concept interest group* (CIG) is formed that includes the users who originated the story and the development team. The CIGs transform the stories to a *future concept* (2). This concept envisions the future structure of interaction at a very high level of abstraction. CIG members then relate the concepts to forces and discuss which forces are addressed. The extent to which the forces can be made explicit depends on the certainty that users have about the domain task. In most cases this will still be very vague.

In the *implementation phase of conceptual iteration* (3), the users look for patterns that can support the future concepts. The patterns in return reshape the concepts, since they can bring up related or new aspects of technology use that were unfamiliar to the participants who created the initial future concept. The special focus is on the scenario part of the patterns, since it tells a related story to the user (see Section 2.1.3). The pattern scenarios are at the same level of abstraction as the stories created by the users in the first phase.

---

[4] According to Heidegger (1927), the design of a tool can only take place *in situ*, as users are in most cases not aware of the tool. When using a car, for example, the driver is focusing on the context, namely the road and the destination. They start to become aware of the car as a tool when their expectations of the car do not match its real behavior, perhaps because of an unexpected noise. Heidegger calls such a situation a *break*.

The scenarios of the patterns inform the design of the future concepts of sociotechnical interaction. Through analogy with their stories, the users may detect that additional forces are addressed by the pattern. Thus, adding the pattern solution to the design of the future concept can help to address previously ignored forces. The patterns also suggest a concrete solution. Users consider the solution and think about how the solution matches the envisioned interaction. The individual steps found in the use cases of the future concepts are finally associated with the relevant patterns. In addition, these patterns are added to the group's pattern language, together with any additional patterns that are closely related.

The patterns and the future concepts are used to create *low-fidelity prototypes* of the system. Users are supported by examples provided in the patterns that illustrate how the individual patterns have been reflected in the user interface of some applications.

The prototypes and the pattern-attributed future concepts are then *discussed* (4) in the whole group. The group performs a ranking of the concepts and selects a specific number of concepts that should be implemented in subsequent development iterations.

Besides the detection of initial functional forces, conceptual iteration will set the stage for future development. This includes finding a system metaphor, as demanded by eXtreme Programming (Beck, 1999), and using it in the future concepts. It also requires that the users form an initial impression of effort and possibilities in the new or changed system. The prototypes provide a very vivid idea of how the system could be changed. The methods used in conceptual iterations are related to methods employed in traditional participatory design, complemented by the use of patterns from higher layers in the pattern language.

2.3.2 Development Iteration

In development iterations the future concepts are further refined by the CIGs. All CIG members meet for a *planning game* (5). They discuss the most obvious forces that appear in the concept. These forces are written on story cards together with the specific part of the concept that is in conflict with, or supporting, the force. The result is a set of user story cards, as in eXtreme Programming (Beck, 1999).

Users again refer to patterns in the higher layer to inform their process of decomposition and solution design. They provide answers to the questions stated in the pattern. As long as the pattern language is, as in the original Alexandrian example, organized using different levels of scale, the decomposition can follow the connection between the different levels of scale. At the same time, developers refer to patterns at the lower layer of our pattern language to answer more technical questions raised by the *user story* (6). Users and developers can propose additional patterns at this stage of the process. These will be considered as preliminary patterns that have not yet shown their validity. However, they should be documented by means of patterns, since the pattern language serves as the community's design memory and vocabulary.

The patterns are connected to the story cards in order to inform later implementation of the story. Developers further attribute the stories with a rough effort estimate in pair-programming hours.

As in eXtreme Programming, users can then *go shopping* and *buy* user stories. At each shopping step, they are only allowed to buy a fixed, but small, number of hours. This results in an ordering of the user stories in a backlog.

At any time in the process, users are encouraged to provide feedback about stories that are on the backlog and reorder or modify the stories. The users can modify stories until a developer begins to implement them. This has the effect of giving users continuous control over the direction of development actions taken by the developers. On the other hand, it has the drawback that fixed milestones (containing functional and temporal fixtures) are no longer possible. The users thus have to agree with the development team that functionality will always be developed according to the stories on the backlog. The order of the backlog determines the order of the implementation. The development team is paid for the real effort they spend implementing the stories. Trust between developers and users is an important factor when working together on this basis. The developers have to trust the users to voice their most urgent requirements. Users in return have to trust the developers to create a system that exactly satisfies their urgent requirements, and that the effort they put into resolving these requirements is worth paying for.

Since different CIGs can work on different future concepts in parallel, the creation of different backlogs has to be coordinated. The ODSP distinguishes four different types of backlogs: *project backlogs*, *CIG backlogs*, *end-user backlogs*, and *non-functional requirements backlogs*. They are discussed below.

The most important backlogs are the CIG backlogs. These hold the task cards from the CIGs that were formally appointed by the user community. One problem with eXtreme Programming is that it may be difficult to convince the customer of the need for refactoring. This is the reason why the OSDP adds an artificial CIG, the system maintenance CIG, which is responsible for detecting design smells in the system. The system maintenance CIG has the same rights as the other CIGs: its members collect and prioritize tasks in the system maintenance CIG backlog.

Stories that are brought up by users without the context of a special CIG are collected in an end-user CIG backlog. These are difficult to prioritize, since they emerge from different users with potentially different goals. The end-user backlog is therefore addressed on a first-come first-served basis.

As proposed by Rittenbruch et al. (2002), the team member with the role of the *gardener* is responsible for coordinating the different backlogs. They observe the different backlogs created by the teams and create a scheduling that is comparably fair for all CIGs (a round robin strategy can be sufficient). The CIGs are informed of the merged schedule for story cards and can comment on this schedule, for example to convince the gardener that two cards of the merged schedule should be swapped.

Figure 2.8 shows an example of a project with two future concept CIGs, the artificial system maintenance CIG, and the end-user CIG. All CIGs have their

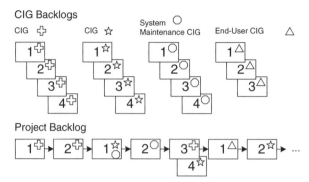

Figure 2.8 Different backlogs in the OSDP

backlogs. The two future concept CIGs have created the backlogs with the cross symbol and the star symbol. The system maintenance CIG is shown with circle symbol and the end-user CIG with the triangle symbol. The gardener takes cards from these backlogs and adds the cards to the project backlog, which is shown at the bottom of the figure.

Instead of adding all stories to a set, the gardener can look for comparable stories or overlaps in stories. Cards can be rewritten whenever the gardener detects redundancy. The CIGs and the gardener then propose a new set of merged stories. In Figure 2.8, the first task of the star CIG overlaps with the first card of the system maintenance CIG. The gardener therefore takes both cards and creates one merged card. The third task of the star CIG turns out to be identical with the fourth task of the cross CIG. Even though the cross CIG's previous cards are not yet scheduled, the gardener can decide to combine a less important cross task card with a star task card rated as important by the star CIG.

As long as no stakeholder disagrees, the development team will implement the most urgent task from the backlog.

In the *implementation step* (7), developers provide a software solution for the first card from the backlog and an *automated test* (8) to confirm the solution's conformance to the users' wishes. Developers typically implement a pattern by means of application frameworks or developer-centered component frameworks. This may involve the development of new software components. Such components can be built using frameworks or other base technologies. The developer uses the answer to the questions provided in the check section and the information provided in the dynamics section to inform their design. Note that the order of testing and implementation can be reversed, as in eXtreme Programming.

After the first user story is implemented users get access to the system and start using it, as far as the system supports their tasks. This system use will result in modifications of the backlog as well as in tailoring iterations. These are described in the next subsection.

2.3.3 Tailoring Iteration

In *tailoring iterations* end users use the application for its intended purpose. While using the system, users with pattern-based design knowledge are encouraged to reflect on their activities whenever they encounter a *break* (9). A break leads to an entry in the groupware's health map—in the simplest case, a note that a specific group need could not be satisfied with the groupware system. In cases in which the user does not detect the break (perhaps the user just feels uncomfortable), another, evaluation, user can expose the break, discuss it with the first user, and initiate a reflection process.

Users then take a closer look at the shortcoming they have detected. First, they *analyze the forces* that are in conflict (10). High-layer groupware patterns help in this process by describing frequently occurring issues, the various forces, and a proven solution in a way that is appropriate for end-user tailoring. The term *end user tailoring* is frequently used to describe the process of customizing an application to the end users' needs (Mørch, 1997). Note that the end user is doing this tailoring or customization without developer support.

The solution provided by the patterns in the higher layers informs successive *groupware tailoring design* (11) and execution of the *tailoring* (12). Tailoring actions can take place at different levels. In content-level tailoring, users change the artifacts that are managed by the groupware system in order to solve the problem. At this level, patterns in the higher layer assist the user in using a tool. At the functional level, users appropriate the functionality provided by the tool. They activate required functions and deactivate functions that are in their way. At the component level, users perform more extensive tailoring actions: they compose functional groupware components to create new configurations of applications that support the team in a previously unanticipated way.

To support tailoring at the group level, a pattern scout looks for solutions that work well. As with evaluation users, the pattern scout observes users' interaction with the system with the goal of finding recurring successful system use. The best practices found are then discussed with the users and documented in the pattern format. Such new best practices then find their way in the pattern catalogue. Note that these patterns are in most cases very domain-specific—for example, patterns for supporting customer relationship management in the context of a support system. On the other hand, the patterns will be used most frequently in the user community, since they are most relevant for interactions that typically take place in the community.

2.3.4 Applicability of OSDP

An important issue for the applicability of OSDP is the availability of users and developers in the process. As is the case for most agile methods, such as eXtreme Programming (Beck, 1999), OSDP originally relies on the fact that groups, users, and developers can meet in person and are aware of each other. In fact, many of the tasks rely on intensive communication between users and developers.

However, two situations complicate such interaction: the development of mass-market groupware (off-the-shelf groupware) and the situation in which groupware systems are in use. As Figure 2.9 shows, these types of systems vary with respect to the availability of either members of the software development team or members of the user community (Schümmer et al., 2006). The main problem with such application contexts is that a smooth transition between the different iteration types is no longer possible.

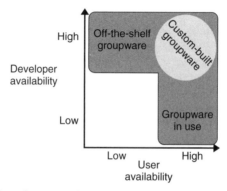

Figure 2.9 Availability of users and developers in different types of groupware development projects

In off-the-shelf groupware the percentage of users who are available during development iterations is relatively small. Although customer representatives can be part of the development project, the real situations of system use (in the sense of Heidegger's situated actions) will not provide new tasks for the development team in development iterations. Customer representatives have to be carefully selected by analyzing the target market. They will participate in pre-release testing and provide user feedback. In any case, the test phases will run the potential risk of creating artificial contexts of interaction, since users will not normally use pre-release software in their daily work. Before the system is used in the field, its functionality will be fixed and the commitment of the development team will be reduced to bug fixing. The main focus therefore lies in development iterations that interact with relatively few conceptual iterations.

While the case of off-the-shelf groupware involves the problem of unavailable users, the use of such groupware, or the use of any other completed groupware system, raises the problem of unavailable developers. Users can still perform conceptual iterations, although they no longer have the choice of all possible groupware technologies. Users are free to reshape group processes as long as the changed processes are still supported by the groupware in use. Tailoring iterations can still be performed as long as the groupware system provides hooks for tailoring and creative system use. But since end users can no longer escalate problems from tailoring iterations to development iterations, they will not be able to incrementally improve the system.

Another important dimension comes into play when considering the use of off-the shelf groupware: different groups using the groupware in different organizational contexts are in most cases not connected. Users from company A will probably not notice improvements done by users in company B, even if the users would otherwise like to learn from each other. This is the reason why the use of off-the-shelf groupware requires a more sophisticated process of collecting and sharing user-made customizations of the groupware system. This problem also arises if a groupware application was originally custom-built and is now used in different organizational contexts.

To overcome such problems, you should establish a virtual user community. Users should contact the development team before, during, and after the main development activities. Developers, on the other hand, should stay informed about how the system is used by end users, to repair the current release and gain insights for the next major release.

In the ideal case, the members of the user community would interact using a repository of best practices for groupware customization. The groupware application should link to this community repository and ease the process of publishing best practices of customizations in the repository.

However, the technical part of providing the interaction space for the user community only solves parts of the problem. The more difficult part is encouraging users to contribute their practices to the community and to detect practices that are worth sharing. To overcome this issue, the pattern scout observes the users and looks for best practices. These best practices are captured as new high-level patterns and added to the user community's pattern collection. By this method the pattern collection evolves to form a group memory of design and tailoring knowledge for the specific groupware application.

CHAPTER 3

Community Support

A famous discussion of the term "community" originates in the work of the German sociologist Ferdinand Tönnies, who in 1878 compared the meaning of community (German: *Gemeinschaft*) with the meaning of society (German: *Gesellschaft*). Humans acting in a society, according to Tönnies (1997), consider the society as a system that imposes social rules. They utilize the society to get most personal benefit. The member of the society *makes use* of other members so that their personal goals can be reached. In a society, humans coexist with weak social bonds.

His definition of communities contrasts with the understanding of societies, so that the community focuses on benefits for the whole community. Members of a community serve the goal of the community. The goals of the community members form a unity that creates a natural incentive for serving the community. Strong social relations between the community members are a characteristic that emerges from the unity of goals and actions.

In reality, communities decay to societies when a strong social bonding no longer exists. The personality of the individual becomes a "pastiche of personalities" (Gergen, 1991). Gergen argued that "for the pastiche personality, there is no self outside that which can be constructed within a social context." (page 154). The individual chooses roles according to the behavior expected within a specific social context. When creating a community, it is important to shape the social context so that it supports social bindings. Communities can then become strong centers (in the sense of Alexander) and membership of the community becomes an integral part of each individual's pastiche of personalities.

Conceptually, this can be understood as shown in Figure 3.1. The individual is part of the society, as are all other individuals. In addition, the individual acts in different social contexts. Some of these social contexts can be identified as communities. The individual maintains bonds to the different communities in which they act. These bonds can be strong or weak and the bonds can influence one another. In Figure 3.1 the user is strongly involved in community B (thick arrow) while his involvement in community C is only weak. If two communities share common subgoals, the bonds of the individual to each community can reinforce each other. If the goals are contradictory, membership of both communities creates a conflict in the members selves. The bonds threaten to tear the member apart, and to maintain self-integrity the member must weaken one of the bonds and strengthen the other.

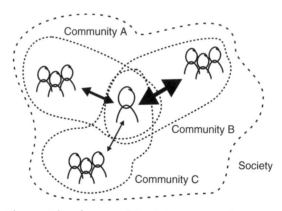

Figure 3.1 The pastiche of personalities in the context of community and society

Applying the concepts of communities to the COGE project, we come to the next part of our story with Paul Smith:

Since the collaborative game engine (COGE) has moved to an open source project, the number of users has dramatically increased. The initial development team at Paul's company has therefore decided to bring the users and developers together by establishing an online community.

Preece (2000) defines online communities as a set of "people, who interact socially as they strive to satisfy their own needs or perform special roles, such as leading or moderating." These people share interests or needs, which make up the purpose of the community. They use group policies such as rules and assumptions to guide social behavior, and computer systems to mediate the interaction.

To set up an online community, you have to assist potential members in finding common goals or purposes and feeling part of the community. You have to design how interaction should take place in your community, and you have to think about incentives and motivational aspects to make your members return to the community.

There are different classifications of communities. Most classifications distinguish at least *communities of interest*, *communities of purpose*, and *communities of practice* (see (Marathe, 1999; Chapman, 2001; Carotenuto et al., 1999)).

Members of a *community of interest* share the same interests in a topic, and often a common background. Examples of such communities might include discussion groups for a television show, or people interested in astronomy. Some authors (for example (Carotenuto et al., 1999)) also define *communities of passion*, which are very close to communities of interest. The difference is that their members are involved in the community's topic to the point where they become passionate advocates. A community of interest can become a community of passion, such as the discussion group for a TV show that becomes a fan club of the show's host.

Communities of purpose consist of members who share a common short-term goal. For example, customers at a virtual bookstore share the goal of finding and buying books. They all have to go through the same process (selecting the item and checking out) and they can help one another in reaching the goal. Thus a community of purpose has a functional purpose and may dissolve after the goal is reached. In contrast to communities of interest, its members don't necessarily share the same interests, and therefore are not likely to start activities that exceed the community's purpose (Carotenuto et al., 1999).

If the members of a community share a common profession, they are called *communities of practice*. Their members reflect on how they perform their tasks and enhance their ways of working in a community learning process. Since the community's topic is the member's profession, members are normally highly involved in such communities. A concrete community of practice, for example, might consist of Smalltalk programmers who meet in a user group to shape the process of programming.

Marathe (1999) adds another type of community: a *community of circumstances*, which is defined by common circumstances such as current life situations. Interaction in these communities is often personally focused and third parties are not involved in the community.

We can depict the process of becoming involved in a community as a graph showing the member's interest compared to their involvement (Figure 3.2). By interest, we subsume the topics, the goals, and the practices shared by the community—all the aspects that are relevant to the different types of communities. When a user first notices a community, they start to observe the community and—after a threshold of interest is passed—becomes active in the community. In an ideal community

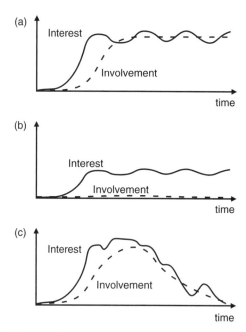

Figure 3.2 Involvement compared to interest in a community

(Figure 3.2–a), involvement would stay at a more or less constant and high level. The user quickly establishes strong bonds with the community and maintains these bonds forever, even if their interest varies slightly over time.

Reality, however, often is different. The initial interest level may often not pass the interest threshold that is required to become active (Figure 3.2–b). In this case, involvement will never be significant, or may not even take place at all. In cases in which the initial interest threshold is passed, it often happens that interest in the community's actions vanishes over time as both the community and the member evolve and shift their interests over time. Figure 3.2–c shows such a case.

As you can see from these diagrams, maintaining the interest of users and keeping their involvement high is an important force in an online community. Since initial involvement requires a specific level of interest, it is important to keep this interest as high as possible and make the threshold for entering the community as low as possible. The next section provides patterns that focus on this initial effort. In Section 3.2 we then show how the interest and the effort of existing members can be kept high, and in Section 3.3 we present patterns for the phase in which users want to temporarily or permanently move away from a community.

3.1 Welcome me... or how to arrive in the community

In our considerations on online communities, we have already stressed the issue of the involvement hurdle: before users will participate in a community, it has to be of interest to them. In this section we look at this aspect in more detail.

The involvement hurdle is strongly related to the principle of BOUNDARIES, as we discussed in Section 2.1.4. For the understanding of groupware, BOUNDARIES play an important role, as Peter and Trudy Johnson-Lenz, the inventors of the term *groupware*, discussed in their paper *Rhythms, Boundaries, and Containers: Creative Dynamics of Asynchronous Group Life* (Johnson-Lenz and Johnson-Lenz, 1990):

> The functions of boundaries include defining group membership; delineating group identity; and marking group rhythms, beginnings, and endings. [...] An appropriately permeable boundary retains the identity of the group while allowing enough flow in and out to keep it alive. If a boundary is too permeable, it's too easy to join or leave a group, or if the beginning or ending is unclear, energy may leak away. If a boundary is not permeable enough, if joining or leaving is difficult, or if beginnings and endings are too rigid, some individuals may resist or break the boundaries anyway. The right balance depends on the situation.

Involvement hurdles are representations of non-permeable boundaries. As described here, they hinder the participation of future members that are interested in the community.

Figure 3.3 shows the relation between interest and involvement. In the Figure 3.3–a we show an interest hurdle that needs to be exceeded by the

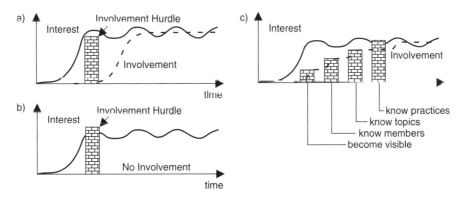

Figure 3.3 Involvement hurdles

perceived interest level. After this occurs, the user becomes active in the community. Figure 3.3–b shows a different situation. In this diagram, interest in the community never exceeds the interest hurdle, and the user does not become involved in the community.

In reality, we do not just find one hurdle, but a staircase of increasing hurdles (Figure 3.3–c). Considered from the perspective of boundaries, this means that a community can be defined not only by one boundary, but by a set of concentric boundaries of differing radii. The more intensive an involvement is desired, the more boundaries have to be crossed. Alexander et al. (1977) have captured this insight in the INTIMACY GRADIENT pattern[1] in which they propose to:

"Lay out the spaces of a building so that they create a sequence which begins with the entrance and the most public parts of the building, then leads into the slightly more private areas, and finally to the most private domains." (Page 613)

For computer-mediated interaction and online communities, you will find exactly this scheme: depending on the quality of involvement, users have to cross different hurdles of increasing heights. Figure 3.3 top right shows four archetypal hurdles that can be found in every community. The lowest hurdle is that of becoming visible in the community. Users become members of the community after undergoing a registration procedure. They thereby give up their anonymity. They have moved from the outside world to the public entrance space of the community. The next hurdle is to find out more about the members of the community. Who is participating and how can the relation between the new member and the existing participants be defined? The hurdle of comprehending the community's goals and topics is at a comparable level. This however is a prerequisite for understanding the community's practices. Each hurdle puts an effort on the user that has to be in balance with the perceived interest in the community. As you can see in the involvement curve of the third diagram, the level of involvement remains limited after passing a hurdle. It often relates to the investment that is required to pass the hurdle.

For the designer of an online community, the hurdles should be lowered and interest should be increased. This combination helps to get more users involved in the community. How to shape the initial phases of community interaction is thus a very important aspect of community design.

In our scenario of the COGE project (see Section 1.2), consider the following situation:

It is now time to motivate users to participate in the community. This means that Paul and his colleagues structure the way in which new users can arrive in

---

[1] See also the GRADIENTS property in Section 2.1.4.

3.1 Welcome me... or how to arrive in the community

the community. They decided to be as open as possible, which means that they would like to attract many new members, help these members to understand the community's culture better, and establish relations in the community.

The patterns in this section, which are also shown in Figure 3.4, provide examples of how this can be done. They are:

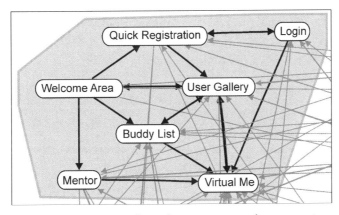

Figure 3.4 Patterns for welcoming users in the community

QUICK REGISTRATION→3.1.1 Make it as easy as possible for a user to join a community while still protecting the members of the community of strangers.

LOGIN→3.1.2 Let users identify themselves before they can use an application.

WELCOME AREA→3.1.3 List new members of a group or community at a prominent place and introduce them to other members.

MENTOR→3.1.4 Pair a novice with an experienced member to ease the novice's integration.

VIRTUAL ME→3.1.5 Create a virtual representation of the user's self that is seen by other users before and during interaction.

USER GALLERY→3.1.6 Show who is using a collaborative application

BUDDY LIST→3.1.7 Show only selected known users.

3.1.1 Quick Registration **

quick (kwĭk), ADJECTIVE: **1.** Moving or functioning rapidly and energetically; speedy. **2.** Learning, thinking, or understanding with speed and dexterity; bright: *a quick mind*. **3a.** Perceiving or responding with speed and sensitivity; keen. **b.** Reacting immediately and sharply: *a quick temper.* **4a. Occurring, achieved, or acquired in a relatively brief period of time: *a quick rise through the ranks; a quick profit*. b. Done or occurring immediately: *a quick inspection*.**

Intent

Make it as easy as possible for a user to join a community while still protecting the members of the community of strangers.

Context

You have established a community that is open to welcome new users. From a community perspective, you envisage that many users become active members and thereby help to mature the community. From a user's perspective, new users who are not yet members of the community are interested in finding out more about the community.

Problem

From a community point of view, it would be good if new users could commit to all group goals and norms and become a mature user of the community as soon as possible. But users fear a high commitment because they have not yet established trust with the community. They are not yet sure if they want to be strongly involved in the community.

Scenario

Giana has just downloaded the collaborative game engine. She has also noticed that there is an online community for users and developers of the game engine. She moves to the registration page and is confronted with a long questionnaire that she has to answer before she can apply for membership. She has to print the questionnaire, sign it and send it to a fax number in the US. Giana hesitates on being faced with this procedure, and finally decides that she does not want to reveal that much of private data just to become a member of the game engine user community.

Symptoms

You should consider applying this pattern when ...

— Users are reluctant to reveal personal information when they enter a community.
— The community is open for new users and wants to grow quickly.
— Users enter a registration workflow but do not complete it.

Solution

Therefore: allow users to register with as little information as possible. Mark their accounts as unconfirmed accounts and restrict the actions that can be performed using the unconfirmed account to those that you would allow strangers to perform. Convert their user accounts to full accounts after they and a potential QUALITY INSPECTION$_{\rightarrow 3.2.1}$ **have confirmed their account.**

Dynamics

When launching the collaborative system, the user can choose to use either an existing LOGIN$_{\rightarrow 3.1.2}$ or request a new login.

In the simplest case, a login is requested by using a random name. The user will then be connected to the system with this random name, which lasts for one session. This is the quickest way of entering the system.

In most cases, the user must keep an identity that lasts longer than one COLLABORATIVE SESSION$_{\rightarrow 5.1.1}$. In this case, the request for the login should ask for a name and a password. If the name is not yet used, you should grant access with this name-password combination.

In other cases, it can be sufficient to ensure that the login is unique for the concrete COLLABORATIVE SESSION$_{\rightarrow 5.1.1}$. Passwords are then not necessary as long as the session is not a PERSISTENT SESSION$_{\rightarrow 5.1.2}$. Otherwise, a password at least is needed, so that the account can be reused when entering the session again.

In systems in which users can share content, legal issues often require that a user can be associated with a real identity. Requesting an e-mail address is one step in this direction.

From that point in time the users can—if no higher level of security is required—enter the system. Their user representation can be marked as unconfirmed (for example by adding a note to the user name). With such a user account the user can only perform operations that are not critical for the community, such as reading community news.

To change an account status from unconfirmed to confirmed, the system needs to verify that the contact details provided are correct. Many systems require at least a correct e-mail address. To confirm the address, the system sends an e-mail message in which a verification code is provided to the address. The requesting user uses the verification code, together with the previously generated or chosen login, to prove that the e-mail address belongs to the user who has requested the account.

Wherever greater security is required, more sophisticated verification schemes can be used. If the postal address should be verified, the community owner can send an unconfirmed user a physical letter that includes a secret verification code.

If the identity also needs to be confirmed, the user is normally asked to submit a signed application form, together with a letter from a trusted third party that confirms that the letter was signed by the right person. An example is the identity verification made by post offices in which a human checks the passport of a user. Such a model is often used by banks to ensure that new account owners are really who they pretend to be.

After successful confirmation, the user can access resources that are only available to confirmed users.

Rationale

Users should be able to decide for themselves how much information they wish to pass to the community or to the owner of the community site. If information is not required to fulfill a service, it should not be requested, or should be explicitly marked as optional data.

The less information is required from the users, the more likely will they pass this information to the system. In systems where no authentication is required, users can sneak in and get an idea of the content shared in the system. This helps them to decide whether or not they want to participate later on.

The community is still quite safe, since unverified users are explicitly labeled. It is clear that such users are new to the community and that one might not trust them. Reducing the capabilities of unverified users further saves the verified users from destructive behavior.

Check

When applying this pattern, you should answer these questions:

— How will the verification process work? Can you create an e-mail based process as described in the collaborations section?

— What operations should unverified users be allowed to perform?
— How do you label unverified users?
— Are you going to allow each user to register, or are you going to restrict the users that are allowed to register?
— What information are you going to request for registration?

Danger Spots

Beware of the bots. If the registration dialog does not require any verification, it is quite easy to write a web crawler that submits random account information to enter your community. One way to overcome this is to rely on the intelligence of the human user: as part of the registration procedure, the user is asked a question that is easy to answer for a human but difficult to solve for a computer program. An example from the PayPal registration site is shown in Figure 3.5.

Figure 3.5 Bot protection at PayPal

The system shows the user a bitmap containing some distorted text. The user is then asked to re-enter the text in a text box. This is an easy task for most people. Computers however fail to recognize the characters because the image contains enough noise to make current recognition mechanisms fail. For users with limited vision, PayPal offers an option that reads the text aloud. In this case, an audio file is transmitted to the user's browser that contains a spoken version of the characters. Again, the file contains noise that prevents speech recognition mechanisms understanding it.

The selected account name may already be in use. When users are able to select their account name on their own, they often tend to use their real name. However, it is very probable that there is more than one user called *Paul* in your community. You therefore have to verify that the account name is not yet in use. If the name has been taken by another user, you should propose an alternative account name that is close to the name that the user selected.

Known Uses

Google (https://www.google.com/accounts/NewAccount), as well as many other online community systems, provides an easy registration process (see Figure 3.6).

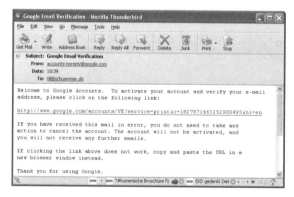

Figure 3.6 The registration process at Google.

Users first provide minimal information: an account name, a password, and an e-mail address. After submitting the information, a user can enter the system. However, they are not allowed to perform all operations.

At the same time, the server sends an e-mail message to the e-mail address provided. This message contains a link to a verification site. After the registering user clicks on this link, his account is activated.

SpinChat (http://www.spinchat.com) is a chat system that provides numerous chat rooms. It implements a quick registration in which only a nickname and gender are queried from the user (see Figure 3.7-left). After providing this minimal information, the user can enter the system and the chat rooms provided. However, the system remembers that the account is still unconfirmed. On the welcome page, it reminds the user that additional functionalities are available after a full registration.

Figure 3.7 Quick registration at SpinChat

For full registration users have to provide their e-mail address (Figure 3.8). This address is confirmed by sending an e-mail message that contains the password of the user to the address they provided. SpinChat assumes that only the owner of the e-mail address can access the password. Even if other users can access the contents of the e-mail, they would only see the password, not the account name.

SpinChat suggests alternatives for the account name if a user tries to register with a name that is already in use (Figure 3.9). It takes the user's original name and creates popular variations by adding attributes or memorable numbers.

PayPal (http://www.paypal.com) is a service that offers bank transfers between individual users in different countries. Although the registration procedure is not a quick registration—PayPal requests a lot of information—one can find

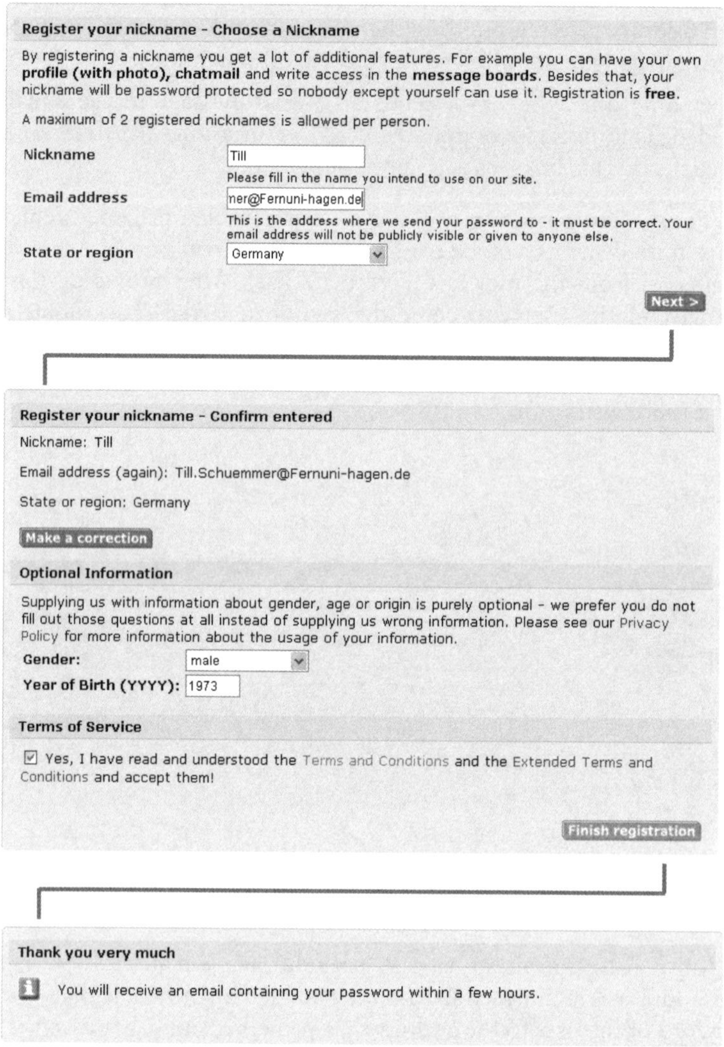

Figure 3.8 Account creation at SpinChat

an interesting account verification method at PayPal. Since the system relies on the existence of a bank account for an individual user, this account is also used for verification purposes. The idea behind this procedure is that only the owner of a bank account will have access to the account statements. After registering at PayPal the system transfers two small amounts of money to the

Figure 3.9 Alternative names for an account that is already in use at SpinChat

new user's bank account. When entering the system, the user is asked to tell PayPal which amounts were received. If the information is correct, PayPal can assume that the user is really the owner of the bank account provided.

Related Patterns

BELL$_{\rightarrow 4.2.4}$ is used in cases where the group has to agree to welcome the new member.

QUICK GOODBYE$_{\rightarrow 3.3.5}$ suggests making leaving a group as easy as joining it.

USER GALLERY$_{\rightarrow 3.1.6}$ Ensure that new users appear in a USER GALLERY even though they have not yet confirmed their account or provided information about themselves, otherwise they could stay unnoticed and act destructively.

QUALITY INSPECTION$_{\rightarrow 3.2.1}$ Unconfirmed users should be observed by experienced users and their actions should be checked against the community's rules. If unconfirmed users continue to behave contrary to the community's rules even after a warning, they should be banned from the system.

LOGIN$_{\rightarrow 3.1.2}$ discusses how authenticating to a system is perceived by the user. It assumes that the user already has an account, or that it can be created by simply using a new login. It also suggests requesting as little information as possible when creating a user account. The QUICK REGISTRATION pattern in addition puts special focus on the distinction between verified and unverified accounts and the verification procedure.

GUEST ACCOUNT (Duyne et al., 2002) allows users to identify themselves for a single session only.

3.1.2 LOGIN **

log·in (lôg'ĭn), NOUN: The process of identifying oneself to a computer, usually by entering one's username and password.

Intent

Let users identify themselves before they can use an application.

Context

Users are interacting anonymously, but now wish to interact personally.

Problem

Users want to interact as personalities, but the interaction space does not recognize them as individuals.

Scenario

Paul has established a collaboration portal on the web where everyone can contribute to the release plan of the next version of the game engine. Unfortunately, it is not only the members of the game engine community who contribute to the plan, but also some more destructive users. After some weeks of operation, the website is full of spam, such as advertisements for Viagra, suggestions for bank transfers to suspicious countries with potential profits of several billion dollars, and other content that is irrelevant to the game development community.

Symptoms

You should consider applying this pattern when ...

— Users want to distinguish private from public interaction.
— Users need to restrict and grant access to specific shared data.
— Users are annoyed about not knowing with whom they are interacting.
— Users want to interact over a longer period.
— Users want to access the community from different locations.

Solution

Therefore: Prompt users for a username and a password before allowing them to enter the shared collaboration space.

Dynamics

Users have to enter their account information—their username and the corresponding password—on a login screen before they can start interacting in the shared collaboration space. The login screen provides at least two text fields in which users can enter their username and their password. The password field uses a password input field component to ensure that the characters typed are not visible. Once a user has entered this information, a button on the login screen allows the user to transfer their username and password to the shared collaboration space. The collaboration space checks whether the information entered is correct. For that purpose, the collaboration space maintains a list of usernames and the associated passwords, or encrypted versions of the passwords.

Upon successful LOGIN, the collaboration space returns a token to the user's client application that the application can use to identify the user in subsequent interactions with the collaboration space. This prevents the user from having to log in for every interaction.

As the user is now uniquely identified, the collaboration space can associate every interaction with the user, as is necessary for the ACTIVITY LOG$_{\to 4.5.1}$. If the information provided was not correct, the login screen displays a message telling the user and giving a hint on how to recover their password.

The system from then on visualizes the account into which the user is logged. It also enables an action by which the user can log out again. By logging out, the system discards the information about the user currently connected and acts as if the user is not logged in.

The login screen links to a registration screen for users without an account, as well as to a password recovery system for users that have forgotten their username or password. To motivate users to request a login, the screen briefly describes why a login is necessary.

Rationale

As users have to provide a valid username and associated password before they can enter the shared collaboration space, the shared collaboration space is restricted to a specific user group. The collaboration space knows who is acting from a specific computer in a specific session from then on.

As the collaboration space can use the information provided to associate each activity with a user, non-anonymous interaction is enabled. This is a prerequisite for identifying other users and creating social bonds. The collaborative application can also tailor the information to the specific user and show the user's VIRTUAL ME$_{\rightarrow 3.1.5}$ in the collaboration space.

Since the list of registered users is known in the community system, one can state clearly who is a member of the community and who is not a member.

Check

When applying this pattern, you should answer these questions:

— Are you going to allow users to change their password? Are you going to request users to change their password periodically?

— Are you going to set up rules for the password to increase security, such as at least eight characters, of which at least two are symbols or numbers?

— How are you going to transmit the username or password? Are you going to use an encrypted channel?

— Where will the user be located after logging into the system? Will they always start at a personalized start screen, or is there a common place for all users?

— Where can you show the account information under which a user is logged in? Can you link it to a button or link that can be used to log out from the system?

— How are you going to allow password recovery? Are you going to provide a central address that can be contacted for password recovery? Are you going to return a new password just by answering a question and entering the correct e-mail address? Some concrete examples are given in the danger spots section.

Danger Spots

Having to enter the password with each login may irritate users, especially if they log in frequently. In this case, you could think about storing the username and the password locally and automatically transmitting it to the system whenever the user wants to access the community.

Users might forget their password. Therefore, include mechanisms to recover lost passwords or reset the password. Well-known mechanisms for password recovery are:

— The use of a safety question: in this case, a user provides a question like "What is the color of my cat?" and a corresponding answer. When the user forgot the password, the system prompts the question and the user enters the (hopefully still known) answer. The system then takes the user to a dialogue in which they can enter a new password.

— E-mail the password: after forgetting their password, users can provide their username. The password is then reset by the system and sent to the user by e-mail. The user can use this password to log into the system, but will be prompted to change the password after the login. Ensure that you do not send username and password in the same message.

— Reset token: this mechanism works like the previous one but does not transmit a password. Instead, an entry address that can be used exactly once is sent. After following the link in the e-mail message, the user is prompted for a new password.

All these mechanisms help to reduce the risk of strangers invoking the recovery mechanism with the goal of stealing account information.

Known Uses

Ebay (www.ebay.com) shows users a sign-in screen that deals with new and registered users (see Figure 3.10). New users can register in the left part of the dialog. The right part allows already registered users to log in, and also to recover their username or their password. Additionally, it is possible to store the username and the password locally, so that it is not necessary to enter the login information every time. After users have identified themselves, they can start interacting with other users, such as placing bids on their goods.

Figure 3.10 ebay login dialog

Planeshift (http://www.planeshift.it) is a massive multiplayer online role-playing game. Players have to log in at a server and authenticate themselves (see Figure 3.11).

ICQ, Yahoo Messenger, MSN Messenger, or **Skype** ask new users to register before they can interact and communicate with other users. Once users are registered, they can store their login information locally and allow the application to log them in automatically whenever it is started.

HTTP Authentication (HTTP-Auth) (Berners-Lee et al., 1996) is a protocol that describes how clients can log in to an HTTP server. The advantage of this login method is that it is supported by all modern web browsers. Therefore,

Figure 3.11 LOGIN screen of the MMORPG Planeshift

it is often used in web-based community systems. If a user tries to access a protected area on a web server, the server answers with a response indicating that authorization is required. This has the effect of causing the web browser to ask the user for a username and a password. In Basic Authentication, which is the simplest but most insecure version of HTTP authentication, the password and the username are simply base64-encoded, which means that anyone monitoring the communication channel can read the password in plain text. The client uses the same information for subsequent requests to the server.

Forcing a browser to forget about a connected user is problematic. One mechanism that can bypass this problem is to simulate the log-out procedure with the login of an anonymous user. This overwrites the session information and ensures that the connection to the user is lost.

Related Patterns

QUICK REGISTRATION$_{\rightarrow 3.1.1}$ describes how a user can request a login quickly.

SECURITY SESSION (Schumacher et al., 2005) defines how a secure session spanning successful authentication to successful log-out can be represented in the system.

HANDLES (Björk and Holopainen, 2005) discusses the need for a unique login in the context of multi player games.

SIGN-IN/NEW ACCOUNT (Duyne et al., 2002) discusses issues related to user accounts. In one section, it also discusses how to handle lost accounts.

LOGIN (van Welie, 2005) discusses the same pattern in a web context. This version of the pattern gives special attention to the login screen design.

PASSWORD DESIGN AND USE (Schumacher et al., 2005) discusses security issues related to the content and use of passwords. The authors suggest that users should be urged to change their password frequently (at least once a year), and how unsuccessful login attempts affect the possibility of logging in again.

SINGLE ACCESS POINT (Schumacher et al., 2005) describes how entry to a system can be shielded by means a single point of entry. Whenever users want to access a resource in the system, they are routed through the single access point, which is secured by a LOGIN.

AUTHENTICATOR (Schumacher et al., 2005). The LOGIN pattern plays the role of an AUTHENTICATOR, since it checks the identity of the requesting user.

3.1.3 WELCOME AREA *

Alternative name(s): Hello Hello

wel·come (wĕl′kəm), ADJECTIVE: **1. Received with pleasure and hospitality into one's company or home:** *a welcome guest.* [...] NOUN: **1.** A cordial greeting or hospitable reception given to an arriving person. **2. A reception upon arrival:** *gave the stranger an unfriendly welcome.* **3.** The state of being welcome: Don't overstay your welcome.

Photo: Photo Library of Congress, free at www.visipix.com

Intent

List new members of a group or community at a prominent place and introduce them to other members.

Context

You have established a group and initial users have created social bonds. This has allowed the group to find its identity. Group members distinguish themselves from people who are not part of the group.

Problem

If the group wants to progress it often needs to attract new members. But group members focusing on internal interaction may fail to notice potential new members and ignore their possible contribution.

Scenario

Mario is new to the community. He sees that there is an ongoing discussion between Paul and Ana but, to be honest, he has not understood a word so far. Paul and Ana seem to be old stagers and they use conventions and terms that are not used outside the community. Mario does not know how to approach Paul and Ana. On the other hand, Paul and Ana have not noticed that Mario has joined the community.

Symptoms

You should consider applying this pattern when ...

— Long-time members share a large collective history, in which new members have not played a role.

— The community is large enough to allow the formation of sub-groups so that long-time community members form a closed group.
— New members find it hard to enter the community.
— Fresh ideas that move the community forward are provided by new members but ignored by existing members.

Solution

Therefore: Provide a prominent place in the community's interaction space where new members and their ideas are introduced, such as a special section on the group's home page in a computer mediated group. Whenever a new member joins the community, ensure that the existing group members notice the new member.

Dynamics

The *newcomers* join the community. They introduce themselves in the welcome area and explain why they want to be a part of the community.

The *welcome area* is a prominent region of the community's interaction space. It can be a special spatial area in a physically collocated community, a special page in a virtual web-based community, or a special topic or thread on a discussion board. While the first two examples are bound to a spatial dimension, the last example is bound to a temporal dimension. It denotes a specific time span during which community members use their interaction space as a welcome area.

Veterans share a long interaction history within the community. They are accepted members and maintain many social links to other people. Veterans commit to visit the welcome area frequently. In cases in which the welcome area is a specific point in time, the veterans commit to participate in the community at this time.

Rationale

Since newcomers are asked to introduce themselves, they are provided with a forum in which they can articulate their ideas and thoughts that drove them to join the community. Since all newcomers act in this way, individual newcomers do not have to fear that their introduction could disturb existing members.

Due to the commitment of the veterans, they will notice when the newcomers introduce themselves. The newcomers will therefore be recognized by existing community members.

The benefit of using a designated welcome area is that introductions do not interfere with other group interaction. Veterans can decide consciously when to visit the welcome area—in cases where it is a special place—or the whole group can focus on the welcome area at the same time in cases where the welcome area is a specific timeframe.

Check

When applying this pattern, you should answer these questions:

— How can you technically detect newcomers? Is there a registration procedure?

— How long should newcomers be part of the group before they are asked to introduce themselves in the welcome area?

— Does it make sense for users to decide on their own when they should introduce themselves. If yes, how do they decide?

— Does it make sense to introduce users who have not yet provided personal information?

— Can you connect the welcome area with other interaction areas that are of high relevance for the veterans, for example by interleaving the welcome area and an alumni event?

Danger Spots

Newcomers might not wish to attract much interest when they initially join the group. They may need some time to look passively at the group and see how group members interact. In this case, you should move the welcoming ceremony to a time when the member actively decides to participate in the group. Until then, newcomers can act as unconfirmed users (QUICK REGISTRATION$_{\to 3.1.1}$).

Another problem can be to convince veterans to commit themselves to pay attention to the welcome area. Veterans might not see the need for investing efforts in newcomers. This is an indication that the community is resistant to growth. Considering participation in the welcome area as part of the metric that calculates the users' ranking in a HALL OF FAME$_{\to 3.2.5}$ can help to resolve this issue.

Known Uses

www.visualbuilder.com is a community of software developers. New members are listed in a designated welcome area on the entry page (shown in the left side of Figure 3.12). Clicking on the user's login opens another page that shows the user's profile (right side of Figure 3.12).

www.communities.com (see also the known uses section of USER GALLERY$_{\to 3.1.6}$) allows members to be queried by clicking on the "New Members" link, shown on the right-hand side of Figure 3.13. This shows the list of new users that is shown on the left of Figure 3.13. By clicking on the user's login, the information provided by the new member is listed.

XING (https://www.xing.com/) is a collaborative environment for maintaining relations with other people. Users can add known users to their BUDDY LIST$_{\to 3.1.7}$ (see also the discussion of XING in the BUDDY LIST pattern).

3.1.3 WELCOME AREA

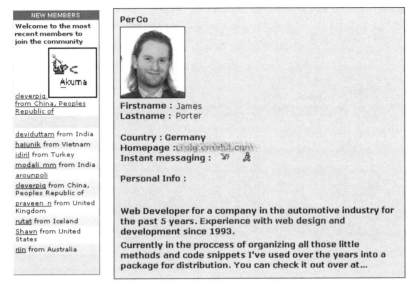

Figure 3.12 New users at www.visualbuilder.com and a user profile

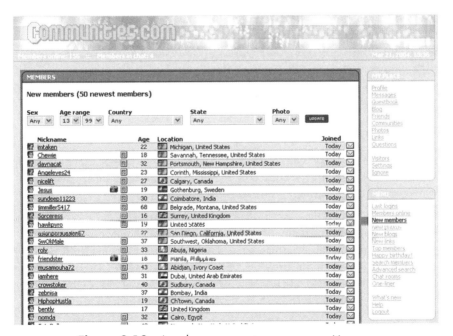

Figure 3.13 A welcome area at www.communities.com

In addition to known users, the system presents users who recently registered (see Figure 3.14). The idea is that newly registered users should be recognized by old friends and be added to their network of contacts.

Figure 3.14 A welcome area in XING

Games at EuroPLoP are special slots in the conference schedule where the participants meet for cooperative games. The games have the purpose of getting in touch with each other. Name games help to learn the participants' names and other games help to find similarities between participants.

Related Patterns

MENTOR$_{\rightarrow 3.1.4}$ Newcomers, who introduced themselves in the welcome area, can be paired with a mentor who accompanies the newcomer in his first steps and personally introduces him to relevant veterans.

MASQUERADE$_{\rightarrow 3.3.2}$ To allow newcomers to interact within the community without exposing themselves, they can move through the community anonymously. The MASQUERADE pattern discusses this form of interaction in depth. In general, you should think about providing anonymous access to the community for a specific amount of time before exposing the user in the WELCOME AREA.

HALL OF FAME$_{\rightarrow 3.2.5}$ WELCOME AREA focuses on the introduction of newcomers to veterans. The opposite is done in the HALL OF FAME: here, honorable community members are presented to the community to provide newcomers with an orientation, who influenced the community most.

USER GALLERY$_{\rightarrow 3.1.6}$ The welcome area is often a special section of the USER GALLERY.

BIRDS OF A FEATHER$_{\rightarrow 3.2.3}$ addresses the opposite problem of how to keep connected with close contacts without being disturbed by newcomers and other users.

BIG JOLT (Manns and Rising, 2005) suggests inviting a knowledgeable expert to the community to talk about their experience in the field. Inviting the expert to the welcome area can serve two purposes: first, the welcome area gets a better reputation, since it is not only a place to meet newcomers, but also to get in touch with experts. Second, newcomers will learn more about the ideas that the community propagates. Experts who are also community members will probably be among the top members in the HALL OF FAME$_{\rightarrow 3.2.5}$.

INTRODUCTION SESSION (Fricke and Völter, 2000) suggests a welcoming phase at the beginning of a seminar. It shows how the problem of learning more about newcomers (in this case all seminar participants are considered as newcomers) can be resolved in a collocated seminar. The solution is to "take time at the beginning of the seminar to let everyone introduce him-/herself to the others."

FACE TO FACE BEFORE WORKING REMOTELY (Coplien and Harrison, 2004) points out that socializing remotely may be insufficient for distributed teams. The problem of remote interaction in the context of socializing is that it often lacks opportunities for casual unfocussed interaction. Such interaction is, however, important for becoming aware of other users' identities. In the context of our pattern language, we should take this pattern as a reminder that remote team building is only a solution if a collocated session is not possible. If you know who the team members will be and you can arrange a common place and time to meet them, you should design your WELCOME AREA as a real location.

3.1.4 MENTOR

Alternative name(s): Master and Apprentice

men·tor (mĕm'tôr), NOUN: **1. A wise and trusted counselor or teacher. 2.** Mentor Greek Mythology Odysseus's trusted counselor, in whose guise Athena became the guardian and teacher of Telemachus.

Intent

Pair a novice with an experienced member to ease the novice's integration.

Context

You are designing an environment for a large group or community. Membership changes over time. Now you are thinking about ways to better integrate new members.

Problem

Newcomers do not know how community members normally act in specific situations. They are not used to practices that are frequently applied in the community.

Scenario

Each Friday afternoon, all members of the community meet to discuss the results of the week. Mario is new to the community and as nobody told him about the weekly meeting, he does not join the discussion. This is irritating for the community.

Symptoms

You should consider applying this pattern when ...

— Newcomers attract attention because their behavior is recognized.
— Newcomers have problems in understanding the best practices of the group entered.
— Veterans have established a common practice for interacting in the group.
— It is difficult to explain the practices of interaction in a textual way, such as in a FAQ$_{\rightarrow 4.3.8}$.
— You experience wide differences of expertise among the group members.

Solution

Therefore: Pair newcomers with experienced group members who act as mentors. Initially let newcomers observe their mentors, and gradually shift control to the newcomer.

Dynamics

A veteran agrees to act as a mentor.

When newcomers enter unknown terrain, they are informed about the opportunity of having a mentor. There are basically two ways to assign a mentor:

1. The newcomer asks for a mentor. This request is then forwarded to all potential mentors automatically or manually. Mentors interested in the newcomer volunteer to interact with them.

2. The newcomer sees a list of mentors. This requires that the mentor's expertise is made explicit, either by a self-description from the mentor, or by automatic extraction of expertise, and published in a list of mentors (comparable to a HALL OF FAME$_{\rightarrow 3.2.5}$). The newcomer can then pick the mentor who looks most promising for his current needs.

Depending on who pairs a mentor with a newcomer, one of them gets in contact with the other. The newcomer then starts watching the mentor act in the community. Whenever newcomers have a question, they can ask their mentors. The mentors observe how well the newcomers understand their current actions, and gradually ask the newcomers to perform those actions that they can master.

After the newcomers have shown that they can perform most actions, the mentors set the newcomers free. The newcomers in return express how well the interaction with their mentors worked: these statements can then be considered as LETTER OF RECOMMENDATIONS$_{\rightarrow 3.2.2}$.

Rationale

Benjamin Franklin coined the saying "Tell me and I forget. Teach me and I remember. Involve me and I learn." The mentor pattern targets the third way of passing on knowledge. Experts pair with novices and solve a problem together. The mentor has the goal of empowering the novice to gradually perform more parts of the task.

Check

When applying this pattern, you should answer these questions:

— How can mentors express their willingness to help newcomers?
— Will you show mentors in a mentor list?
— Can newcomers select their mentor on their own, or are they assigned?

— How long should a mentor-facilitated session last?

— How will mentor and novice interact? Can you provide synchronous editors that let them manipulate group artifacts together?

Danger Spots

Finding the right group member to act as a mentor may be difficult, especially if group members can voluntarily act as mentors. The mentors may overestimate their own expertise, or can lack educational expertise, so that they have problems in providing background information on what they are doing. To compensate for these problems, you could think of recommendation mechanisms for mentors—a LETTER OF RECOMMENDATION$_{\to 3.2.2}$—or automatic detection of knowledgeable users, an EXPERT FINDER$_{\to 3.2.4}$.

As Manns and Rising (2005) point out, the mentor can be hard to find. Outstanding experts are often rare, and it can be difficult to motivate experts to help newcomers.

During the interaction, it is important that mentor and novice can watch their actions. You should consider the APPLICATION SHARING$_{\to 4.1.5}$ pattern if the use of an application is part of the practices that the novice should learn.

Known Uses

MSN Messenger (cf. http://groups.msn.com/MessengerTreff/buddyscoutteam.msnw) The German version of the MSN Messenger provides a pool of buddy scouts (see Figure 3.15).

Users can apply to become mentors, called "buddy scouts", by revealing some personal details and describing why they want to become a buddy scout. If their application is approved, they are listed in a mentor list. More detailed information for each buddy scout can be found in their personal description (see VIRTUAL ME$_{\to 3.1.5}$). Other users can contact buddy scouts when they begin using MSN Messenger. The buddy scout assists new users with questions about tool usage and about the various communities in MSN.

Pair Programming in XP While the activity of pair programming (Beck, 1999) was initially considered as a collocated face-to-face activity, attempts have been made to support virtual pair programming in distributed teams. The Sangam system (Raha, 2004) is one example of such an approach. The idea of the group process stays the same as in collocated eXtreme Programming: one user acts as the "driver" and the other user is a "navigator". The driver creates code while the navigator comments the driver's actions. In the context of the MENTOR pattern, the driver acts as a MENTOR at the beginning. As soon as the navigator gets a promising idea, the navigator takes over. During the process of learning, this will happen more frequently as the less experienced developer learns more and more from their mentor.

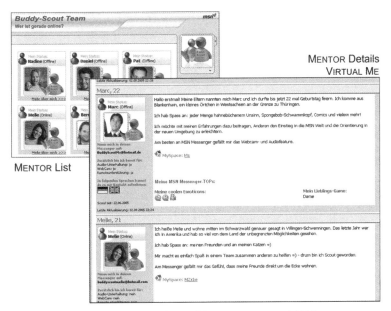

Figure 3.15 The Buddy Scout team at MSN

During the session developers are provided with a shared text editor that supports two different roles. The driver gets a token (see Floor Control$_{\to 4.1.7}$) that allows them to modify the text. The other user's editor is informed about the driver's actions, for example by using a Distributed Command$_{\to 5.2.7}$.

GestureMan (Kuzuoka et al., 2000) is one example of how the Mentor pattern can be used in a real workplace setting—although it's important to add that it's a setting that was augmented with much computer technology. The idea is that the remote mentor assists a local worker in performing tacit tasks (see Figure 3.16).

Figure 3.16 Supporting mentor-novice interaction using the GestureMan

The mentor can control a robot—the GestureMan—to point to important areas in the remote environment. Novices act at the remote site and perform the operations with their hands. Gradually, the mentor reduces the amount of advice and finally only follow the novices in their actions.

Related Patterns

SHARED BROWSING$_{\rightarrow 4.1.3}$ is one way to experience a group with a MENTOR and explore the information space created or used by the group using a shared browser. SHARED BROWSING$_{\rightarrow 4.1.3}$ discusses different ways in which such interaction can be shaped.

LETTER OF RECOMMENDATION$_{\rightarrow 3.2.2}$ can be used to rate the mentor's job. Novices are asked to rate their interaction with the mentor after they have finished the interaction. New potential novices can browse a mentor's LETTERS OF RECOMMENDATION in order to learn what to expect from the mentor.

EXPERT FINDER$_{\rightarrow 3.2.4}$ is an alternative to find help for a specific topic. As in the MENTOR pattern, it brings together an expert with a less experienced person. However, care is required to avoid overloading experts with too many requests from novices.

MASTER AND APPRENTICE (Coldeway, 2003) focuses on the role of documents—or better the absence of documents—for knowledge transfer. The idea is that one should pair an expert in a specific area of a project with a novice and let them work together. They should stay together until the novice feels confident to do the work without the mentor.

MENTOR (Manns and Rising, 2005) discusses how an external expert can help a group during the launch of a new project. The main difference is that their version of the mentor pattern assumes that the expertise will be reached in the project and that from then on there will no longer be a need for an external mentor.

ACTIVITIES THAT SHAPE (May, 2001). The act of mentoring can be considered as an ACTIVITY THAT SHAPES. Both patterns share the idea that the community's culture should be reinforced by cooperate activities involving newcomers and "old stagers". However, the MENTOR pattern suggests one concrete instance of interaction and discusses the means for enacting this instance in a computer-mediated environment.

3.1.5 VIRTUAL ME **

Alternative name(s): Avatar

vir·tu·al (vûr'choo-əl), ADJECTIVE: **1.** Existing or resulting in essence or effect though not in actual fact, form, or name: *the virtual extinction of the buffalo.* **2.** Existing in the mind, especially as a product of the imagination. Used in literary criticism of a text. **3. Computer Science Created, simulated, or carried on by means of a computer or computer network: virtual conversations in a chatroom.**

Intent

Create a virtual representation of the users' self that is seen by other users before and during interaction.

Context

Users are interacting with each other in a collaborative system.

Problem

In a large user community, account names look similar. But users need to communicate their identity to interact with other users.

Scenario

Rodrigo is a new member of the game engine community. He has chosen his name as a login and now sees that three more users are currently participating in the discussion of the graphics engine. These are Marc, Juan, and Carla. But what are the goals of these users? How are they related to the collaborative game engine? Rodrigo has no idea and therefore hesitates to get in closer contact with them.

Symptoms

You should consider applying this pattern when ...

— Users identify themselves in a collaborative system using a short textual login, such as a seven-character Unix account name.

— The user community is too large to allow all users to get to know one another personally.

- The user community changes over time as users leave the community and new users join.
- Users should interact with new contacts.
- Personal involvement is important.

Solution

Therefore: Allow users to create and perform a role. Provide them with means of creating a virtual identity that represents them while they act in the system. Show the virtual identity when the user is active.

Dynamics

After users have logged in to the system, the system presents them with a reference to their individual information area. In this information area, the users can provide information describing themselves.

Relevant information contains the user's full name, a picture of the user, and a textual description of the user. If the community is topic-centered, the textual description should in addition ask for information that is related to the community. In the case of a software development community, this could be a list of programming languages that the user knows. In a movie fan club, it could be a description of the user's current favorite movie.

When visualizing the user in the user interface, the system shows the full name instead of the user's login. Wherever possible, it also shows the picture. By clicking on the user's name, other users can open the user's self-description and learn more about the user.

Rationale

To understand the importance of this pattern you need to look at the concepts of identity. In sociology, one speaks of *impression management* to describe the efforts undertaken by an individual to control the impression that others have of them. It is an important part of developing a personal identity.

Different theories have been developed to describe how humans create a self-image, but it goes beyond the context of this pattern to elaborate on this topic in depth (see Weigert et al. (1986) for a comprehensive elaboration of self-images). We simplify the subject and say that the self-image is influenced by:

- The internalization of external expectations (Mead)
- The reflection of the person's current interaction partners (Strauss)
- The expectations that a group has of an individual and the degree to which the expectations can be harmonized with the identity (Habermas)
- The self-presentation of the self (Goffmann)

The last two aspects especially explain the core of the VIRTUAL ME pattern: the users need to be empowered to adapt themselves to a specific social context such as the community in which they are currently participating. They also need to present themselves in that role.

Making the self explicit to other users is therefore an important aspect of the evolution of an online participation. It helps other users to adjust their expectations of a specific user. Döring (1999) discusses how impression management is influenced by several factors (pages 261–262). Among others, these factors are:

Publicity. Users consider impression management as more important if the interaction space is public.

Audience. Users adapt their presentation to match the audience's expectations.

Intention. Users follow specific goals when they present themselves in public spaces. These can be defensive goals—for example, that users don't want others to have a negative impression of them—or more offensive goals like self-promotion. Importantly, they have specific ideas of possible interaction within the environment.

By filling out their own profile, users can construct a virtual identity that emphasizes the audience and the user's intentions in the community. The profile describes their virtual identity and their expectations of the community. Visual clues can additionally support the process of obtaining an impression of other users.

The structured description enforced in the personal information area helps to keep these factors in mind. In contrast to Goffman's understanding of a "staged self" (Goffman, 1959), it can be important to limit the extent to which users can create/imagine their personality. Users should for example use a photograph of themselves if the system aims at providing an authentic interaction. This means that playing theater is more like describing oneself.

Even short logins could serve as means for impression management, but they fail in most cases. Logins like "schuemm" or "schummer" that were assigned to me in recent years rather encrypt my identity. A good example is the login of a former colleague: he has the login "casco", which is the Spanish word for helmet. He had this nickname since he was a small child because his hair was often dressed like a helmet. Knowing this story helps to build up an impression of the user by only seeing the login, although this is an exception.

Check

When applying this pattern, you should answer these questions:

— What questions should you ask users in order to structure their self-description?
— Is it possible to show a picture of the user?

— Can you link the users' short representations (their full names) to their presentation, for example by using a hyperlink?

Danger Spots

Users often hesitate to provide a photograph. If your community design could benefit from showing photos of users, you should consider using a default picture for users who have not yet provided a photograph. The worse this picture looks, the more users will want to provide a custom picture soon!

Users can also provide wrong information. Again, it depends on the type of groupware system that you are designing. If interaction needs to be honest and authentic—as it is often the case in learning settings—you should make an authentic photo mandatory, since this will make it less likely for other users to imagine a totally different self.

You need to keep privacy concerns in mind. If the collaboration space is open to the public, you should provide less information than if it was restricted to registered users.

User profiles can soon become outdated. One possible solution for this problem is that you ask users to update their virtual identity regularly.

Known Uses

E-Mail Signatures. Most e-mail clients allow the user to attach a signature to each message. For each account, the user can create a different signature, as shown in Figure 3.17.

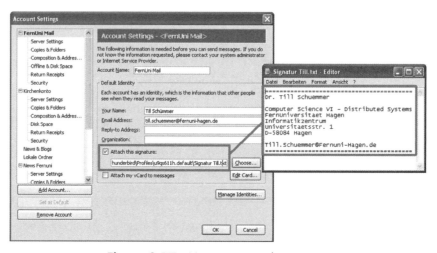

Figure 3.17 Managing e-mail signatures

The signature is a short text file that in most cases contains additional contact information such as the user's address or their affiliation. Some users make use of longer signatures that contain ASCII art. These are collections of characters that can be interpreted as pictures (see DIGITAL EMOTIONS$_{\rightarrow 4.3.7}$).

CHIplace (Girgensohn and Lee, 2002) was used at the CHI2002 conference to foster networking between attendants before the conference took place. Users could provide a description of themselves. When entering the people page (see the left-hand side of Figure 3.18), a selection of the users was shown, so that one randomly met new users. A click on the user name lead to a user profile (see the right-hand side of Figure 3.18). This included personal data such as the user's name, their job title, and their affiliation, a photograph, and information related to the user's CHI participation, such as how the user was involved in CHI and their current research interests.

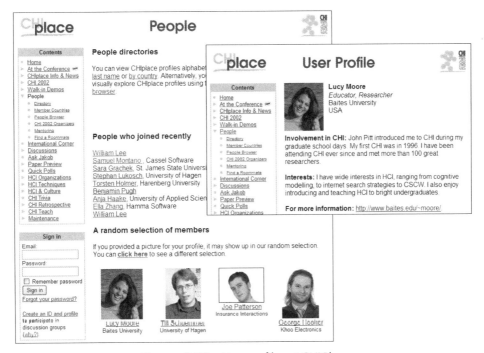

Figure 3.18 User profiles at CHI-Place

Drehscheibe (Koch, 2003) is a community support system for the department of informatics at the technical university of Munich. It allows users to create their own user information pages. These information pages are linked to all the information the user publishes in the community system.

XING (https://www.xing.com/) is a community with the goal of forging links between professionals. Members create a structured description of themselves in order to attract other members who are searching for specific services.

Figure 3.19 Structured home page at XING

Figure 3.19 shows such a structured page. It includes personal contact details, services the user wants or has,—to support professional interaction—interests (to find people for social interaction), and companies or universities with which the user is associated.

Other community systems are comparable, but tailor the structure of the page according to the community's goals. At www.communities.com users meet primarily for social interaction and dating. The profiles include fields like their dating status.

Note that, compared to the private home pages that can be found frequently on the web, approaches to user profiles on community sites such as these are always more structured.

Related Patterns

USER GALLERY$_{\rightarrow 3.1.6}$ All user profiles should be listed in a USER GALLERY if users are allowed to search for other users.

USER LIST$_{\rightarrow 4.4.1}$ or REMOTE CURSOR$_{\rightarrow 4.4.7}$ provide information about who is currently performing activities or has been active in the system. They both need to reference the active user. Using the user's picture here can make a site livelier.

INTERACTIVE USER INFO$_{\rightarrow 4.4.4}$ explains how a visual representation of a user can be used to support contact facilitation and initiate tighter collaboration.

MASQUERADE$_{\rightarrow 3.3.2}$ discusses how information in a user's profile can be protected from unwanted readers.

NAMEPLATE (Fricke and Völter, 2000) discusses the need for identifiable users in collocated seminars. Users should wear nameplates so that people can relate their name to their visual appearance. Compared to VIRTUAL ME, this is the opposite problem: here, the name is the most visible part and the users need to associate the actual visual appearance.

3.1.6 USER GALLERY   *

Alternative name(s): User Directory; Member Directory

gal·lery (găl'ə-rē), NOUN: **1.** A roofed promenade, especially one extending along the wall of a building and supported by arches or columns on the outer side. [...] **8a. A building, an institution, or a room for the exhibition of artistic work. b.** An establishment that displays and sells works of art. **c.** A photographer's studio. **9. A collection; an assortment: The trial featured a gallery of famous and flamboyant witnesses.**

Intent

Show who is using a collaborative application.

Context

You are building a system in which users should actively participate in a community. The users are identifiable by their real name or a nickname.

Problem

If more than one user interacts with shared data, it is hard to coordinate the interaction—especially with strangers. Without knowing who is using the system, it is hard to establish collaboration or become aware of other users' activities.

Scenario

After a few month of existence the game engine community has grown to 200 members. This is quite a success, but it has the negative side effect that individual members no longer know all the others. Mario is for example looking for a member living nearby with whom he can meet for a drink and discuss the game engine's graphics engine. Paul is looking for an experienced developer for the security part of the game engine, but since this is not his main area of interest he is unaware of colleagues working in this area.

Symptoms

You should consider applying this pattern when ...

— New users hesitate to get in contact with other users of the community.

- Users find it hard to remember who is a member of the community.
- Users know the names of other users and want to find out more about them.

Solution

Therefore: Provide a list of all users who are members of the community. Design this list in a way that makes it interesting to browse.

Dynamics

Users register with the system and construct their VIRTUAL ME$_{\rightarrow 3.1.5}$. The information about all registered users is displayed in a user gallery. This gallery includes the user's name or pseudonym, and in many cases a picture of the user.

Rationale

Since users can browse through the list of community members, they can establish a sense of the community. They can compare other users' descriptions with their own preferences and find users who share their goals or preferences, which eases the process of getting in contact with other users. Note that this search process can be automated, which is described in the BIRDS OF A FEATHER$_{\rightarrow 3.2.3}$ pattern.

If the gallery uses pictures or provides interesting personal information, it will be fun to read. This has the effect that users will return to the gallery and stay up to date with current community members.

Check

When applying this pattern, you should answer these questions:

- Does it make sense to provide a search interface because of the number of users?
- Should you distinguish between public and private information in the USER GALLERY?
- Do you want to include pictures of users?

Danger Spots

In large communities you should make the user gallery searchable, otherwise it is hard to find interesting contacts.

When designing a USER GALLERY, you need to carefully balance the amount of information a user has to provide with the benefits of anonymity. For example, it can be advisable not to include user pictures when visual attraction should not influence the discussion.

Known Uses

CHIplace (Girgensohn and Lee, 2002) lists people in the CHI community in a people browser. They are arranged according to the interests they provided in their USER PROFILE.

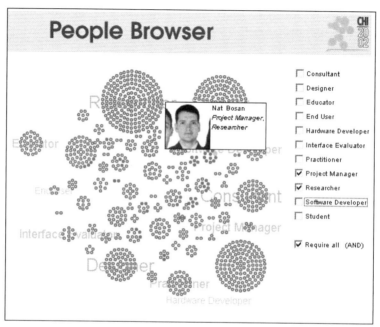

Figure 3.20 Clustered users in the CHI-Place People Browser (http://chiplace.fxpal.com/people/browser.jsp)

Figure 3.20 shows the user interface of the people browser. A visitor can tag different professions to narrow the set of relevant members. The relevant members will be shown with dots of a different color. When mousing over a dot, the related user information appears as a pop-up window[2]. If users want to find other users, they have to move the mouse over various dots. By doing so, they also see the picture and classification of users they probably have not seen before.

Drehscheibe (Koch, 2003) is a community support system for the Department of Informatics at the Technical University of Munich. Users can add a photograph

---

[2]Note that this interface technique has been described as MINESWEEPING (http://www.welie.com/patterns/showPattern.php?patternID=minesweeping).

to their personal information. These photographs are collected in a USER GALLERY that allows searching for other users by picture (see Figure 3.21).

Figure 3.21 USER GALLERY in the Drehscheibe project

Community websites such as www.communities.com often list their members in a USER GALLERY. During the registration process, members are asked for personal information in a structured profile. Parts of the personal information and the photo of the member are shown in the USER GALLERY.

Related Patterns

WELCOME AREA$_{\rightarrow 3.1.3}$ In cases where the community is large, it can be difficult to find new users in a user gallery. Therefore, provide a special area in the community where new members are introduced. In combination with a user gallery, this could for example mean that new members are shown at the beginning of the user gallery.

HALL OF FAME$_{\rightarrow 3.2.5}$ Some members may be more important to the community than others. These can be collected in a special user gallery, the HALL OF FAME. In combination with the user gallery, important members can be displayed at the beginning of the user gallery.

BUDDY LIST$_{\rightarrow 3.1.7}$ Another way of keeping the user gallery manageable in a large user population is to show only those members that the local user knows in a BUDDY LIST. Note that this preselection of buddies no longer supports the forging of new links with previously unknown users.

USER MODEL DEFINITION (Vogiatzis et al., 2005) provides means for structuring the user's self-description. Users are asked to tag their main interests, which makes it easier to find users with specific interest profiles, especially users with comparable interests—see BIRDS OF A FEATHER$_{\rightarrow 3.2.3}$.

VIRTUAL ME$_{\rightarrow 3.1.5}$ discusses how users can create the self-description that is shown in the USER GALLERY.

USER LIST$_{\rightarrow 4.4.1}$ solves a comparable problem at a smaller level of scale. While the USER GALLERY shows all users who are registered in a community, the USER LIST shows users with whom the local user currently interacts.

3.1.7 BUDDY LIST **

Alternative name(s): Roster (in Jabber), Contact List (in MSN or ICQ), Address Book

bud·dy (bŭd'ē), NOUN: **1. Informal A good friend; a comrade. 2.** A partner, especially one of a pair or team associated under the buddy system. **3. Friend or comrade; chum. Used as a form of familiar address, especially for a man or boy: Watch it, buddy.**

Intent

Show only selected known users.

Context

You are using an interaction space such as a communication channel, a groupware application, or a collaborative virtual environment, together with many other users.

Problem

When many users are able to interact in the interaction space, it is hard to maintain an overview of relevant interaction partners, since the number of users exceeds the number of relevant contacts for a specific user. User lists grow very large and it is hard to find people that local users know. On the other hand, local users are often only interested in people they know.

Scenario

Paul has found a security expert after browsing the USER GALLERY$_{\to 3.1.6}$. This is Charley, who specializes on simulating attacks on security systems. Together with Charley, Paul spent some time securing the graphics engine. This was a very enjoyable episode. A week later, Paul has some follow up questions, but since he is very overloaded with work, he already forgotten the name of this brilliant security expert. He therefore starts searching again in the USER GALLERY.

Symptoms

You should consider applying this pattern when . . .

— Users are interested only in a small set of other users.
— Users spend a long time searching for another user.
— The system may be used by more than one user with a specific name who only differ in their address or login.

Solution

Therefore: Provide BUDDY LISTS where a user can bookmark other users who are of interest. Whenever the local user browses other users, initially show only users from the BUDDY LIST.

Dynamics

Whenever *local users* interact with *other users*, they can add the other users to their BUDDY LIST. The BUDDY LIST is a set of user objects. Users can be added to the BUDDY LIST by selecting their representation in the user interface and executing a command, for example a menu item associated with the user object.

Rationale

The main reason why this pattern works is that it eases the process of finding other users by storing them in a personal list. Compared to public directories of users, the personal list only contains those users that are important to the local user.

Connecting the means of adding users to the BUDDY LIST with the user's representation, or the interface elements that are used to interact with the other user, makes the process of adding a user to the BUDDY LIST obvious and intuitive.

Check

When applying this pattern, you should answer these questions:

— How do users add other users?
  - Can you add a button to the user interface that adds the current interaction partner to the BUDDY LIST?
  - Can you use a context menu on the user's VIRTUAL ME$_{\to 3.1.5}$?
— Does a user need to agree to be added to a BUDDY LIST?

Danger Spots

If users only consider BUDDY LISTS for maintaining contacts with other users, they will rarely find new users in the system. You should therefore ensure that users can browse other users who are not on their BUDDY LIST, for example by providing a USER GALLERY$_{\to 3.1.6}$.

If the users of your application enter the application from many different computers and therefore need their BUDDY LIST at many different computers, do not store the BUDDY LIST locally. Instead, use a server to maintain the BUDDY LISTS, for example by using CENTRALIZED OBJECTS$_{\to 5.2.1}$.

Known Uses

Instant Messaging Systems like MSN Messenger, ICQ, AIM, or Jabber all provide BUDDY LISTS. Presence information is retrieved from the presence server only for those users who are in the BUDDY LIST.

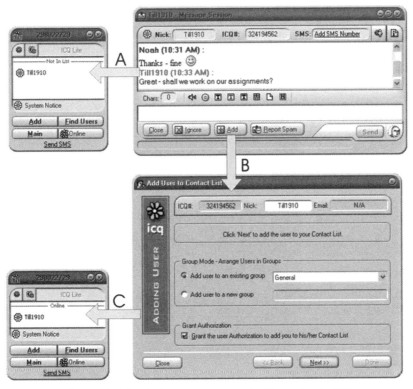

Figure 3.22 Adding a contact to the BUDDY LIST in ICQ

Figure 3.22 shows how a contact can be added during a conversation with ICQ. If local users allow other users to contact them, they can talk directly to the local users by sending a message. Note that the remote user has to retrieve the address of the local user by other means than the BUDDY LIST, since the local user is not yet on the remote user's BUDDY LIST. The remote user will be shown as a user "Not in List" (see Figure 3.22-A) on the BUDDY LIST for the duration of the chat. If the local user feels that the contact is valuable, they can add the remote user to the BUDDY LIST by pressing the Add button, which will open the Add User dialog (see Figure 3.22-B). The local user can provide a nickname for the remote user under which the remote user will appear in the BUDDY LIST. Note that by default the Add User dialog checks an option to allow remote users to be able to add the local user to their BUDDY LIST as well. This is important to maintain RECIPROCITY$_{\rightarrow 3.3.1}$, although it can be bypassed by unchecking the option.

From then on the current status of the remote user will be shown on the BUDDY LIST (see Figure 3.22-C). The local user can thus get in contact with the remote user easily without having to look up the remote user's ICQ number.

World of Warcraft (Blizzard Entertainment, (europäische Server), as well as many other multiplayer online games, provide buddy lists to keep track of other players with whom a user has previously interacted.

Figure 3.23 A BUDDY LIST in the game World of Warcraft

An example buddy list is shown in Figure 3.23. It lists all the players that a player has previously added to the buddy list. For all players it shows the role of the player and their current level in the game. It also shows whether or not the player is connected to the system.

XING (https://www.xing.com/) uses BUDDY LISTS to create social networks. Users can ask others if they can add them to their BUDDY LIST. If the other user agrees, they appear in the first user's set of confirmed buddies. Users can then browse through their own buddies and also through the BUDDY LISTS of their buddies. They can thus move through a social network of contacts.

In XING's user interface, users can examine the paths of this social network graphically, as shown in Figure 3.24.

Figure 3.24 Browsing through connected Buddy Lists at XING

Drehscheibe (Koch, 2003) is a community support system for the Department of Informatics at the Technical University of Munich. Each registered user in the community system can create a new community space and add it to the hierarchy of defined community spaces. Such a community space has a name and can have members. Since every member of such a sub-community space can edit the list of members, (Koch, 2003) refers to this a SHARED BUDDY LIST.

e-Mail address books. E-mail clients allow the local user to interact asynchronously with remote users by reading messages from them or sending messages to them. Together with the message, most systems show information about the sender of the message (see Figure 3.25). The sender can be selected and added

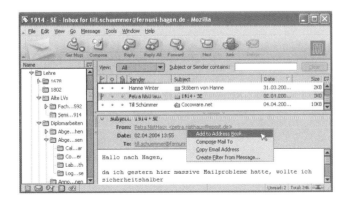

Figure 3.25 Adding a user to an e-mail address book

to an address book, which makes future interaction easier, since the local user does not have to remember the remote user's address.

Related Patterns

USER GALLERY$_{\rightarrow 3.1.6}$ provides a means of browsing all users in a system. As outlined in the danger spots section, a USER GALLERY complements a BUDDY LIST by offering the opportunity to meet new community members.

RECIPROCITY$_{\rightarrow 3.3.1}$ is important if BUDDY LISTS reveal a lot of personal information. In this case, users should be able to control who can put them on their BUDDY LISTS. On the other hand, if local users add a remote user to their BUDDY LIST, remote users should also be allowed to add the local user to their BUDDY LISTS.

USER LIST$_{\rightarrow 4.4.1}$ provides another filtering for the set of all users: it shows only those users who are currently logged in, whereas the BUDDY LIST shows only known users regardless of their current status. Both patterns are often combined to provide awareness of buddies.

VIRTUAL ME$_{\rightarrow 3.1.5}$ should be used to visualize the members of the BUDDY LIST.

CENTRALIZED OBJECTS$_{\rightarrow 5.2.1}$ allows the BUDDY LIST to be maintained on a central server.

3.1.8 Welcome me... applied

Paul initially planned to establish a site for sharing information about the game engine. The more contacts he made with other developers, however, the more interesting became the idea of turning them into an active community. Paul therefore set up a web-based community system for the COGE project. As Paul felt that the activities within the community should stay private, he added a LOGIN$_{\rightarrow 3.1.2}$ to the COGE community site.

He initially added all the users that he was aware of to the community system and created accounts for them. He sent the passwords out by e-mail and the group started to explore the content together. What Paul did not consider was that friends of the members would like to become members themselves. These friends sent Paul e-mails and asked him if they could have accounts to allow them to access the community resources. After the first press release featuring the community, more and more people asked Paul for accounts. This was the point at which Paul decided to let users register on their own using a QUICK REGISTRATION$_{\rightarrow 3.1.1}$, as shown as a the mock up in Figure 3.26.

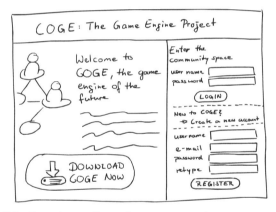

Figure 3.26 Providing a QUICK REGISTRATION to become a member easily

Paul placed a link to the registration form next to the download area of the game engine. This was a good decision, since people interested in the game engine also saw that there was an active community. The community itself had two presentation areas: in a web-based area, users could browse basic community content, and in the Eclipse-based[3] view the users could create and manipulate content. Paul used Eclipse as a thick client to create a rich experience from within the environment

---

[3]Eclipse (http://www.eclipse.org) is a Java integrated development environment (IDE) and platform for rich client applications. It was originally created by IBM.

that the COGE community's developers used on daily basis. (Section 4.4 provides more details about why the integration provides special benefits for the community members.)

Many new members joined the community, partly because they wanted to help to implement the next version of the game engine, and partly because they were looking for assistance in developing products on top of the game engine. After a while, even Paul lost his overview of the community. Other members therefore suggested adding a USER GALLERY$_{\rightarrow 3.1.6}$.

In the process of designing the USER GALLERY, Paul and some other members of the community thought about what was the most unique aspect of the community. Suzan suggested that it could be the global distribution of the team. The other members involved agreed to this, and the idea was born to design the USER GALLERY using a world map and connect it to representations of the members.

Users could browse the USER GALLERY in two different ways: they could select a point on the map that would scroll the list of users to the member located at that point. They could also select a user in the list shown at the bottom of Figure 3.27, which would show an arrow from the selected user to this user's home location.

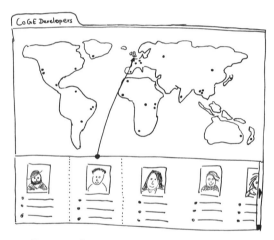

Figure 3.27 Collecting information on community members in a USER GALLERY

The USER GALLERY was combined with ideas from the WELCOME AREA$_{\rightarrow 3.1.3}$: when opening the USER GALLERY view, new users were shown as the initial users in the list. This ensured that new users became visible when others browsed the community. However, there was no technical solution that forced current members to look for new members on a regular basis.

The descriptions of the users in the USER GALLERY were actually instances of the VIRTUAL ME$_{\rightarrow 3.1.5}$ pattern. They showed part of the self-description that users were asked to enter when editing their profile (see Figure 3.28).

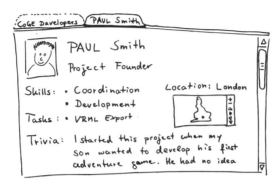

Figure 3.28 Structure the self-description using a VIRTUAL ME

Paul and some other old-stagers in the community decided to structure the self-description in the VIRTUAL ME in such a way that the most important information for the community was provided. Beside the details of the person described, users could add information about their programming and project skills, their current tasks in the community, and their current location. They could select their location by pointing at a specific region on the map shown at the right of the profile editor in Figure 3.28. Finally, they could provide some items of trivia.

After inspecting the information in their USER PROFILE, the user could be added to a BUDDY LIST$_{\rightarrow 3.1.7}$, as shown in Figure 3.29.

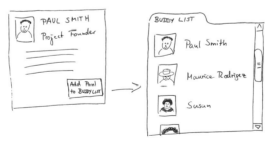

Figure 3.29 Collecting users in a BUDDY LIST

3.2 Guide me... or how to deal with quality

One of Alexander's fundamental properties is that of ALTERNATING REPETITION (see Section 2.1.4). At the community level, this points us to the rhythmic nature of group membership and binding.

As shown in Figure 3.30, interest in participation will vary over time. The interaction follows a rhythm that significantly shapes our social life. "Rhythms, boundaries, and containers are primitives—universal, fundamental patterns from which all life is built—including our social life. Our face-to-face contacts often occur in regular rhythms." (Johnson-Lenz and Johnson-Lenz, 1990).

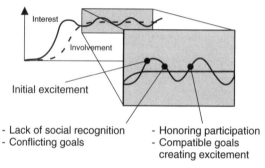

Figure 3.30 Involvement hurdles

At the time when users decided to join a community, they exhibit a peak of interest, their motivation to join the community's space. However, several factors decrease the interest of the individual in the community's actions. The goals of the community might shift in a direction that is less relevant to the specific member, or the efforts expended by the member might not be visible enough in the community, so that the individual experiences a lack of social recognition.

If there were no counter-forces to the forces that reduce the individual's interest in the community, they would probably leave the community after a short time. The community would eventually die unless it was capable of creating an alternative cycle: a lack of social recognition should be followed by a phase during which the participation is honored, while a shift of topic into an uninteresting direction should be followed by detection of relevant interaction partners and topics in the community.

> *Paul has reached his first goal in establishing a community around the COGE project. Initial developers and users of the engine have registered and started to discuss various aspects of the engine. After the first excitement is over, however, many of the community members decrease their activity level, and*

3.2 Guide me... or how to deal with quality

the community is in danger of becoming a dead site. Paul therefore thinks about means for motivating long-term members to maintain a high level of involvement and make the community more attractive for newer members who have not yet made many contacts.

This scenario sets the stage for the patterns that are presented in this section: patterns for decreasing loss of interest and social isolation by providing pointers to active areas of the community and by offering additional mechanisms that lead to social recognition.

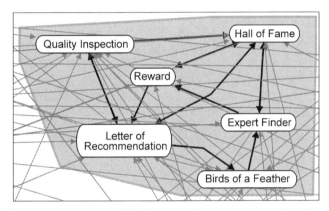

Figure 3.31 Patterns for finding relevant contacts and artifacts

The patterns in this section, which are also shown in Figure 3.31, are:

QUALITY INSPECTION$_{\to 3.2.1}$ Raise the quality of interaction by removing bad content and destructive members.

LETTER OF RECOMMENDATION$_{\to 3.2.2}$ Let users rate each other on their reliability or expertise.

BIRDS OF A FEATHER$_{\to 3.2.3}$ Find others who have most in common with the user.

EXPERT FINDER$_{\to 3.2.4}$ Contact the user who is most likely to be able to help with a specific artifact.

HALL OF FAME$_{\to 3.2.5}$ Honor the most helpful participants in the system by showing them in a HALL OF FAME.

REWARD$_{\to 3.2.6}$ Reimburse positive participation of individuals or groups.

3.2.1 Quality Inspection   *

Alternative name(s): Editorial Board

qual·i·ty (kwŏl'ĭ-tə), NOUN: **1a.** An inherent or distinguishing characteristic; a property. **b.** A personal trait, especially a character trait: "The most vital quality a soldier can possess is self-confidence" (George S. Patton). **2.** Essential character; nature: "The quality of mercy is not strain'd" (Shakespeare, The Merchant of Venice IV.i.184) **3a. Superiority of kind: an intellect of unquestioned quality. b. Degree or grade of excellence: yard goods of low quality. 4a.** High social position. **b.** Those in a high social position.

Intent

Raise the quality of interaction by removing bad content and destructive members.

Context

You have created a communication space for your community. Now you are concerned about the quality of the contributions.

Problem

Members participate in a community to enjoy high-quality contributions from fellow members. However, not every contribution has the same quality. Low-quality contributions can annoy community members and distract their attention from high-quality gems.

Scenario

Mario turned out to be a rather destructive community member. He modified the game engine's source code so that it fitted his own context and published the modified code in the project's central code repository. He did not care about testing and ignored the needs of other developers and users of the game engine. So, each evening after Mario uploaded changes, Paul and Ana spent a lot of time restoring the original content of the repository, because Mario's changes were not really suitable for the whole project.

Symptoms

You should consider applying this pattern when . . .

— Some community members provide low-quality or offensive content.
— Community members complain that they receive too many disturbing messages.
— Even after being warned, destructive members do not stop being destructive.

Solution

Therefore: Select users as moderators and let them release only relevant contributions into the community's interaction space. Give moderators the right to remove any contribution and to expel users from the community.

Dynamics

Experienced users can apply for membership of the moderation team.

Community members contribute to the collaboration space. The contribution is initially only visible to members of the moderation team, who are informed about new contributions. If the contribution is appropriate, a moderation team member releases the contribution to the community so that it is visible to everyone. If it is inappropriate, the moderator contacts the author of the contribution and explains why the contribution cannot be released. If members continue with destructive behavior, the moderator can close their account so that they are expelled from the community.

If more than one user acts as a moderator, the contribution can either be permitted by any of the moderators or require negotiation between the moderators.

Rationale

Since the moderators filter out low-quality contributions, the quality of interaction in the community will increase. If the moderators handle their role responsibly, they will ban destructive users so that they can no longer disturb the community. Having a group of moderators further helps to make the moderation process fast and relatively effortless.

Check

When applying this pattern, you should answer these questions:

— Who will be the initial moderator, and who decides whether or not applications to becoming a moderator are accepted? Does it make sense to VOTE$_{\rightarrow 4.1.4}$ for moderators?
— How will you inform users about the progress of moderation? Does it make sense to send them a message when their contribution is received by the moderation team, when it is assessed, and when it is finally released or rejected?

— How do you handle moderators who no longer perform the moderator role? Will you automatically reject a contribution after a specific time? Or will the inactivity of a moderator trigger the assignment of a new moderator?

— Are there other tasks that should be the moderator's responsibility? Should moderators be responsible for allowing users to enter the community, for example?

— Does it make sense for moderators to order contributions before releasing them to the group?

— Is a single assessment sufficient, or do you need multiple views about a contribution to ensure balanced assessment? If the latter is the case, how do you coordinate interaction between peer moderators? Will you allow them to discuss different viewpoints?

— Will different users be handled differently by moderators? Does it for example make sense to have a "white list" of users who normally contribute valuable information, so that their contributions can be assessed more quickly, or even released without manual inspection? Does it make sense to have a "black list" of users who normally provide low-quality contributions, so that their contributions are inspected in more detail?

Danger Spots

The task of moderation can soon become time-consuming. Therefore, you should balance the size of the moderator team with the volume of messages moderated by the team.

Moderators fill a responsible position. If their moderation is too rigid, they can hinder the growth of a community. In cases in which this is a problem, you should think about allowing members to present their message to another moderator. In general, you should think about a QUALITY INSPECTION for the process of moderation itself, to keep the quality of moderation high.

Since moderation takes time, members can be offended if their contributions do not appear in the community fast enough. Synchronous collaboration between community members becomes impossible. Therefore, you can think about a variation in which contributions are immediately visible to everyone. These contributions should be marked, so that everyone can see that quality inspection has not been carried out on the contribution yet. Instead of releasing suitable contributions, the moderators are now in the role of finding inappropriate contributions and deleting them.

Known Uses

Slashdot.org (Lampe and Resnick, 2004) is a news community with an elaborated group moderation policy. Users can post their contributions to the moderation team. The moderation team will then decide which articles will be release prominently.

Yahoo groups provide mail-dispatching forums. Each group has a moderator. The moderator can decide whether or not submissions need a moderator's approval before they are delivered to the group members. If moderation is activated, the moderator receives all participants' submissions and can release or block individual submissions.

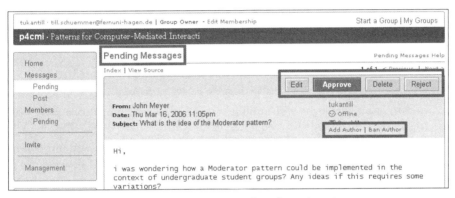

Figure 3.32 Moderator interface for Yahoo Groups

Figure 3.32 shows the interface used to approve messages. Whenever a message is sent to the group, it is listed in the set of pending messages to which moderators have access. The moderator can approve or reject a message. In addition, the moderator is also able to edit a message and to delete messages from the group's message forum.

Besides a responsibility for content, moderators of Yahoo Groups are also responsible for approving group membership.

Rate my Professor (http://www.ratemyprofessors.com) is a system that allows students to post comments and ratings on their professors. The goal of the system is to give new students an idea of who the professor is. However, since all professors have enemies, there is a high probability of unfair ratings and offensive comments. All users are asked to flag such offensive comments, using a flag button that is shown with every comment. When this occurs, a group of moderators, called *screeners*, is informed who will look at the comment and remove it if it is inappropriate.

Wikipedia (http://wikipedia.org), the Wiki-based online encyclopedia, follows the approach of releasing contributions immediately. Due to the high number of contributions, it would be difficult for a moderation team to check all contributions before they can be released. However, Wikipedia has installed a community of patrols who observe recent changes and/or new pages and identify bad edits (see http://en.wikipedia.org/wiki/WP:RCP). If patrols detect an inappropriate page, they:

— Restore an old version of the page or correct the flaws in the author's contribution

— Warn the author or editor of the page, so that they can learn from their faults

— Check other contributions by the same author, since these may also be faulty

— Inform the administration team if the inappropriate behavior of the contributor persists

In case of an escalation, the administration team will follow a banning policy (see http://en.wikipedia.org/wiki/Wikipedia:Banning_policy).

The administration team can impose several punishments on problematic users. They can ban users for a specific amount of time so that they cannot edit any pages. However, the concept of banning is only a social construct. Banned users are shown on a list of banned users. If they continue to modify content, the Wikipedia administrators can decide to block those users. In this case, the users can no longer use their account, or connect from their computers if their IP addresses are blocked.

Related Patterns

LETTER OF RECOMMENDATION$_{\to 3.2.2}$ also deals with the quality of contributions (or users). However, the impact of the rating is different. If a moderator discards a contribution, it will not be shown to other users. In the case of the LETTER OF RECOMMENDATION, all users are allowed to rate a contribution and bad contributions are still shown, together with a low score. In combination with the QUALITY INSPECTION, it can allow users to rate the moderation process as well and thus to provide feedback on the moderator's capabilities.

MENTOR$_{\to 3.1.4}$ Moderators to some extent fill the role of mentors: they inform problem users of their faults with the goal of communicating a sense of the community spirit to them. However, MENTORS have a closer interaction with a new user, since they accompany the new user.

ATTENTION SCREEN$_{\to 3.3.4}$ also protects recipients of information from irrelevant behavior. The difference is that an ATTENTION SCREEN protects an individual user, while a QUALITY INSPECTION protects the whole community.

HALL OF FAME$_{\rightarrow 3.2.5}$ It is important for the members of the moderation team to be accepted by other community members. You could think about recruiting moderators from the HALL OF FAME. Such members have significantly helped the community, so their judgement is likely to be in line with the community's rules and goals. However, it can also lead to a narrow focus if the members of the HALL OF FAME do not accept new ideas into the community.

VOTE$_{\rightarrow 4.1.4}$ An alternative criterion for assessing the quality of content is to let users vote on accepting the contribution. This, however, only works when there isn't a high volume of traffic in the community.

ENGAGE QUALITY ASSURANCE (Coplien and Harrison, 2004) provides an example setting in which quality assurance plays a central role: in software projects, appointed members of the team should start to test artifacts as soon as they are produced to ensure that the result of the team maintains a high standard.

3.2.2 LETTER OF RECOMMENDATION *

Alternative name(s): Rating, User Experience Feedback

rec·om·men·da·tion (rĕk'ə-mĕn-dā'shən), NOUN: **1.** The act of recommending. **2. Something that recommends, especially a favorable statement concerning character or qualifications. 3.** Something, such as a course of action, that is recommended.

Intent

Let users rate each other on their reliability or expertise.

Context

Your system allows users to select their interaction partners. It assists them by allowing each user to provide detailed information about themselves, for example in a USER GALLERY→3.1.6.

Problem

When users do not know any potential interaction partners they may fear interaction, because they do not trust a partner. This may result in a high inhibition threshold and impair or prevent interaction.

Scenario

James found several experts with experience in speech recognition. One of them is Susan, the other is Wil. James does not know either of them and randomly picks Wil as a collaboration partner for clarifying internationalization aspects. Unfortunately, Wil is far less supportive than Susan would have been. He simply points James to the manuals and ignores specific questions. This did not really help James.

Symptoms

You should consider applying this pattern when . . .

- There has been no prior interaction between the interaction partners, which means that the partners could not collect prior experience of the quality of interaction.
- The interaction consumes resources and it takes time before a user can judge the quality of the interaction.
- Investing resources in interaction is not desirable if a satisfying result cannot be guaranteed.
- An interaction requires trust in the interaction partner or the content.

Solution

Therefore: **Provide a method of rating interactions and display an analysis of all users' ratings together with the users or artifacts with which the users interacted.**

Dynamics

The user interacts with an interaction partner. The interaction partner can be another user or an artifact. Interaction with an artifact represents indirect interaction. This means that one user created an artifact that is later noticed by the local user. Interaction between users can for example be the exchange of information or goods.

After an interactive episode users rate the quality of the interaction. They express how well their requirements for the interaction were met. The rating is expressed on a scale, for example from *poor* to *excellent*. It can also include a textual description of why the interaction was rated as it was. The ratings are collected in a central repository or as an attribute of the rated artifact or user.

Whenever an artifact or a user is shown to other users, the system also shows the average of other users ratings.

Rationale

The basic assumption of this pattern is that users will act in a comparable way if they face comparable situations. Thus, if a user had bad experiences with an interaction partner, a third user will probably also have bad experiences with the same interaction partner if the situations are comparable. On the other hand, if other users were able to interact with the interaction partner successfully, a third user will also probably have a successful interaction.

If the rating is performed on the level of artifacts, it means that an artifact that was helpful to other users will very likely be helpful to a new user.

A knowledge of the quality of former interaction episodes can strengthen or weaken the trust in a potential interaction partner. Increased trust lowers the inhibition threshold and thus eases the start of an interaction.

This pattern does not reduce the time that is needed before users have made their personal judgement of the interaction quality, but it reduces the risk of investing too much effort in failing interactions.

Check

When applying this pattern, you should answer these questions:

— What are your interaction scenarios? Is there an action that constitutes the end of an interaction episode (for example, when a user leaves a chat room or when a collaborative task is marked as finished)?
— What rating scale will you use?
— Will you rate users or artifacts?
— How will you display the rating? Can you extend the artifact's or the user's visualization for this? Are you able to provide views that sort artifacts and users according to their average rating?
— How will you display textual parts of the recommendation? Does it make sense to show only the worst and the best recommendations?

Danger Spots

Whether the ratings will rate users or artifacts depends on the application domain. In cases in which the artifacts are not relevant to a large user group, it can be more helpful to rate the users associated with the artifacts instead. Although this transfer from an artifact experience to the user who created or offered the artifact can work in many cases, it can also lead to incorrect assumptions, such as that others had rated a user and not an artifact. Systems should therefore carefully explain any transformations applied to ratings.

Ratings of users can be offensive to the rated user. Since a rating is always a personal opinion, it can hurt the rated user unjustly. You should therefore give rated users the option of commenting on their rating. Additionally, you should consider moderating ratings if destructive ratings are a problem.

A related issue is the fact that users can learn from prior mistakes. If a user received a bad LETTER OF RECOMMENDATION, it is possible that they will change their interaction style so that the reported problems are fixed. Users should therefore be able to rehabilitate themselves.

It can be difficult to detect the end of an interactive episode. In systems in which interaction follows strict workflows, the episodes may last from the first to the last appearance of the user. In systems with no strict workflow, interaction episodes may start and end at any time.

The rating can distract the user from their task. The means for providing ratings should thus be unobtrusive.

Known Uses

eBay uses recommendations to indicate the reliability of a user. Since trade interactions at eBay include the transfer of money, trusting the interaction partner is a crucial issue. After each transaction, purchasers are asked by e-mail to rate their interaction partner. The rating consists of a number (−1 for negative rating, 0 for neutral rating, and 1 for a positive rating) and a textual comment.

The numbers are used to calculate an overall rating for users, which is then displayed together with their user name with each product that the user sells (see Figure 3.33-left).

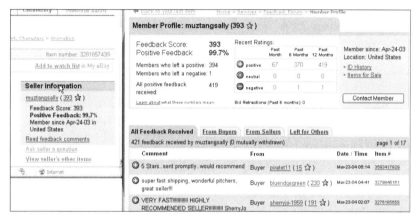

Figure 3.33 Rating transactions on eBay

The overall rating computation counts all users who rated positively and subtracts all users who rated negatively. A user's opinion is counted only once even if the user provided more than one recommendation. This ensures that the overall rating cannot be distorted by an individual user's voting. If a user made more positive than negative recommendations, then the recommendation will be counted as a positive recommendation. If negative recommendations prevail, than a negative recommendation is counted.

SETI@home is a distributed application that looks for signs of extraterrestrial intelligence. Clients download raw data for later off-line analysis.

While this website started as a community of purpose (for finding extraterrestrial intelligence), it is possible to observe a shift to a community of interest. The site designers encourage users to create a personal home page where they can describe themselves and share their thoughts about SETI@home (see Figure 3.34).

Figure 3.34 Recommending a profile at SETI@home

Other users can browse home pages and rate the information provided: they can decide to recommend it to the community—the buttons labeled "Recommend" in Figure 3.34. Users with positive recommendations are selected to become a "user of the day", who is shown on the SETI@home entry page.

Rate my Professor (http://www.ratemyprofessors.com) is a system that allows students to share experience of their professors. After participating in a class, the students can post a comment and give grades to the professor. The grades can be given based on different criteria like helpfulness, clarity, or the easiness of the class. The system takes the grades and calculates averages for each individual grading student, as well as a global average where all ratings of the students are combined.

Amazon.com provides various means of rating information. First, users can rate items and create a review, for example for a book. Each item is shown with a link labeled "Write a review". Users are encouraged to share their thoughts whenever they browse an item. Reviews contain a textual comment on the item and a star rating (1–5). The average of all star ratings is displayed with the item. Items can be sorted according to the number of stars they have, which eases the process of finding popular items.

The second means of providing feedback is a rating of other users' reviews. Each review is shown with buttons asking whether or not the review was helpful, as shown in the lower part of Figure 3.36. In each review's heading, the system shows how many users found the review helpful. The reader is thus able to skip reviews that were not considered as useful by other users.

The rating of the review is also used to calculate a score for the reviewer. A user who creates many helpful reviews is considered as a popular user, and

3.2.2 Letter of Recommendation

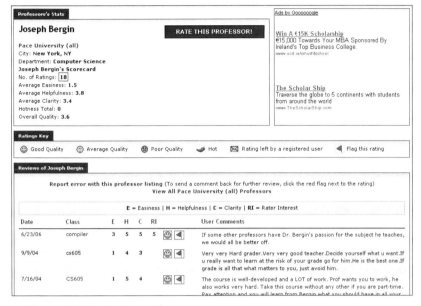

Figure 3.35 Rating professors at http://www.ratemyprofessors.com

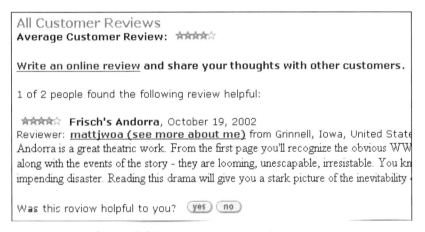

Figure 3.36 Rating a review at Amazon.com

receives a place in the HALL OF FAME$_{\to 3.2.5}$. As mentioned in the danger spots section, however, this can be problematic: it is important that users understand that famous reviewers became famous because other users liked their reviews and not for any other reason.

A third means for providing recommendations is the rating of external merchants. As with trade on eBay, trust is an important issue when buying items from external merchants. Users can rate their experience—again on a star scale from one to five stars. The ratings are then translated to -1 (one and two stars), 0 (three stars), and 1 (four and five stars) and a merchant's rating is calculated in the same way as at eBay.

Related Patterns

HALL OF FAME$_{\to 3.2.5}$ accumulates recommendations for users in a HALL OF FAME. If users receive many positive recommendations, they will have a prominent ranking in the HALL OF FAME.

QUALITY INSPECTION$_{\to 3.2.1}$ also discusses rating of artifacts. The difference is that in QUALITY INSPECTION only specific users are allowed to rate an artifact, and their rating can influence the visibility of the artifact.

VOTE$_{\to 4.1.4}$ models the LETTER OF RECOMMENDATION as a vote. The *SETI@home* example follows this approach. The VOTE pattern does not restrict the theme of the election to users or artifacts. It is possible to elect on any question.

BIRDS OF A FEATHER$_{\to 3.2.3}$ LETTER OF RECOMMENDATION is often combined with the BIRDS OF A FEATHER pattern. This is then referred to as *collaborative filtering*.

The basic idea behind collaborative filtering is that one should first look for users who share opinions. If we consider the ratings performed by a user as expressions of opinion, we can treat them as activities on the artifact rated. Rating the activities of different users can then be analyzed to find BIRDS OF A FEATHER, those who assessed many artifacts in the same way. The recommender system next looks for artifacts rated by one user that have not yet been rated by another user. These artifacts are—in the case of good ratings—recommended to the other user.

PARTICIPANT'S FEEDBACK FORM (Fricke and Völter, 2000) suggests providing participants in a seminar with a feedback form at the end of the seminar. Students should be encouraged to rate their teachers so that the teachers can refine their teaching. The LETTER OF RECOMMENDATION pattern goes beyond this approach, since the results of the feedback forms are returned to both existing and potential new participants.

RECOMMENDATION COMMUNITY (Duyne et al., 2002) discusses how customers can rate products in e-commerce sites. It suggests a two-phase recommendation process: first, users should comment and rate a specific product. Next, a QUALITY INSPECTION$_{\to 3.2.1}$ should scan the review for its appropriateness. After this, the review becomes visible and other users can comment on it, as described in the Amazon known use of this pattern.

JUST SAY THANKS (Manns and Rising, 2005) argues for paying special attention to the expression of gratitude for help received from other people. A LETTER OF RECOMMENDATION is a computer-mediated way to do this.

3.2.3 BIRDS OF A FEATHER

Alternative name(s): Expertise selection (Yiman, 2000)

feath·er (fĕth'ər), NOUN: **1.** One of the light, flat growths forming the plumage of birds, consisting of numerous slender, closely arranged parallel barbs forming a vane on either side of a horny, tapering, partly hollow shaft. **2.** feathers Plumage. **3.** feathers Clothing; attire. **4.** A feathery tuft or fringe of hair, as on the legs or tail of some dogs. **5. Character, kind, or nature: Birds of a feather flock together.**

Intent

Find others who have most in common with the user.

Context

Many users interact with artifacts in a shared information space. The artifacts refer to specific topics. The user community is quite large and the community members don't know one another well.

Problem

The larger is a user community, the higher the probability that a perfect teammate is part of the community. However, these are very hard to find in large user communities.

Scenario

James has noticed that many developers are interested in dialogue interpretation. He has the idea of adding speech recognition to the game engine. James knows that Rodrigo has been working on the dialogue interpretation code recently, but he has the vague impression that many other community members would be interested in discussing speech recognition. Since he does not know these people, it is hard for him to reach them and encourage them to share their thoughts.

Symptoms

You should consider applying this pattern when . . .

— Users complain that it is difficult to find suitable collaboration partners.
— Successful collaboration depends on an overlap of shared interests, because there is little time to norm the group.

Solution

Therefore: **Compare user profiles or interaction histories to identify two users who share large parts of their history. Suggest these users as collaboration partners.**

Dynamics

Users perform activities on artifacts in the community. These activities are logged and used to create a profile of important artifacts for the user. Artifacts that are accessed frequently or recently are considered to be the user's interests.

When a local user is seeking a collaboration partner, the system compares the user profiles of all remote users to find those profiles that correlate best, that is, that share many similar interests. "Birds of a feather" are users who have the best matching profiles. They are recommended to the local user as possible collaboration partners.

Rationale

Psychology suggests that one strategy for successful team building is to bring together users with the same background. Byrne (1971) showed that people who share many attributes more often like one another and consider each other as more intelligent and knowledgeable. As a result, such peers will respect each other and enjoy communicating and interacting with each other. Better group interaction is the result. Tasks that focus on exploiting and implementing existing knowledge can particularly benefit from homogenous groups (Mannix and Neale, 2005).

If the users share a large overlap in their interaction history, they will also have a shared language and sometimes also a shared understanding of the artifact with which they interacted in the past. This eases the initial phase of goal alignment and lets the group achieve effective working more rapidly.

Check

When applying this pattern, you should answer these questions:

— Does it make sense to show how well the profiles of discovered users correlate? If yes, how will you visualize them? You could for example use a number or a star rating.
— Will you present more than one result at a time, or are users only interested in the best match?
— Does it make sense to initiate interaction between the users automatically?

Danger Spots

Not all goals benefit from users with the same interaction history. Tasks that require creativity gain particular benefit from diverse teams. Mannix and Neale (2005) provide a good summary of diversity research and the positive and negative impact of diversity on work groups.

The current context of a user who seeks collaboration partners may be mainly independent of large parts of their detected interests. An expert in the history of art may for example seek a person interested in classical music. Although they have quite a large activity history in classical music, it is dominated by a much larger history in classical art. The system will, therefore, not recommend users with a music background, although these are the ones that the user seeks. A solution is to allow the requesting user to filter their interest profile so that it matches their current interests. What such filtering interfaces might look like is, however, very application-dependent.

Known Uses

MEMOIR (Pikrakis et al., 1998) is a system that monitors web browsing activities to recommend other users with related browsing histories. For each user, the addresses of all web pages visited are stored in a web trail. These web addresses form the user's interests. Whenever a user is interested in others with comparable interests, the system calculates BIRDS OF A FEATHER that have a large overlap in their browsing history. These users are then recommended for collaboration.

Autonomy CEN (Autonomy, 2002) is a knowledge-management portal that manages collaboration and expertise networks. Users are monitored for the documents they read or author within the document repository. These documents form their interests in the user's profile. If users feel the need to collaborate with others, they can query the system for users with close interests. Closeness in this case means a close semantic relationship of the relevant documents.

Yenta (Foner, 1996) is an agent-based system for supporting matchmaking. An agent observes the local user's e-mail, news and file consumption and creates user profiles based on these artifacts. As in the case of *Autonomy CEN*, similarity is calculated as a semantic distance between the two artifacts. Since all artifacts are textual, this distance can be calculated using linguistic approaches.

The unique part of Yenta's architecture is the way in which profiles are compared, since each profile resides under the local user's control. Yenta uses the concept of autonomous agents. Each user provides 'their' agent with a profile for the matching user they wish to find. The agent then contacts other agents at other clients. Both agents compare their profiles and see if they could match. The agent finally presents to 'its' user the set of other agents that match well.

BoF-Sessions at Conferences are events where people with the same interests can come together to discuss a specific topic. They are in most cases announced by stating the theme or the attribute, so that other conference attendees who identify with the theme can join the event. Although matchmaking is not supported by any technology, BoFs share the same flow of interaction as described in the solution of this pattern.

Related Patterns

ACTIVE NEIGHBORS$_{\to 4.4.3}$ extends the interests of a user to related artifacts. The ACTIVE NEIGHBORS pattern is intended to detect co-present users, but can also be used to find users with related interests in their histories.

ACTIVITY LOG$_{\to 4.5.1}$ logs users' activities and thus provides the information needed to calculate similarities between users' interaction histories.

EXPERT FINDER$_{\to 3.2.4}$ considers the local user's current artifact in order to find other users who share a long history with the same artifact. While BIRDS OF A FEATHER finds people who share a common interaction history across many artifacts, EXPERT FINDER in most cases finds people with different interaction histories and an expertise in a specific area, in which the requesting user is a novice. BIRDS OF A FEATHER thus focuses on users' interests and backgrounds to bring users together, while EXPERT FINDER$_{\to 3.2.4}$ focuses on interaction histories with a specific artifact regardless of the history of the local user.

DIVERSE GROUPS (Coplien and Harrison, 2004) describes the opposite of this pattern by requesting heterogeneous teams in the context of design tasks. The rationale behind this is that tasks where change is needed require differing opinions and backgrounds. This is more difficult in teams that share a large common background.

SUBSYSTEM BY SKILL (Coplien and Harrison, 2004) argues in favor of composing teams in such a way that people with comparable skills collaborate. Compared to BIRDS OF A FEATHER, which focuses on knowledge about artifacts, SUBSYSTEM OF SKILLS focuses on experience in practices.

3.2.4 EXPERT FINDER

Alternative name(s): Find the Guru, Expert Recommender, or Expertise Recommender (Yiman, 2000).

ex·pert (ĕk'spûrt'), NOUN: **1. A person with a high degree of skill in or knowledge of a certain subject. 2a.** The highest grade that can be achieved in marksmanship. **b.** A person who has achieved this grade.

Intent

Contact the user who is most likely to be able to help with a specific artifact.

Context

You provided an environment in which users can interact with artifacts. However, users need more detailed information than that which is provided within the artifact. You are therefore thinking about providing users with personal help for specific artifacts.

Problem

You know that other users have more expertise with a specific artifact but you do not know who they are.

Scenario

Rodrigo becomes more and more active in implementing his first package for the game engine. He has chosen to contribute to a dialog interpretation unit that can be used for modeling dialogues between human and artificial players. While implementing the interpreter, he comes across code that seems to be used for modeling roles in the role-play engine. However, he does not understand the role concept at all. Since he is new in the COGE project, he does not know that Susan implemented this part of the engine and that he needs to ask for her help.

Symptoms

You should consider applying this pattern when ...

— Users are not making their expertise explicit and thus there is no directory of expertise (Yiman (2000)).
— There are no global experts, for example in a HALL OF FAME$_{\rightarrow 3.2.5}$, that can answer a specific question, or the global experts are tired of answering questions because they are asked too often.
— Different users make the same mistakes because there is no way of sharing experiences.

Solution

Therefore: Find the user who has a long history with the artifact. Use the ACTIVITY LOG$_{\rightarrow 4.5.1}$ to see who performed activities on the artifact. Sort the list of people according to the number and type of activities and/or the time that has elapsed since their involvement. Make this list available to other users.

Dynamics

Users perform activities on artifacts that are tracked in an ACTIVITY LOG$_{\rightarrow 4.5.1}$. Whenever uses are working with an artifact for which they need personal assistance, they start a query to find the user who is most likely to provide more information on the artifact. This user can be found using different strategies:

1. It can be the user who looked at the artifact most recently. In this case, it is probable that the user found shares a common context with the requesting user. See SPONTANEOUS COLLABORATION$_{\rightarrow 4.4.2}$ for more details of this strategy.
2. It can be the user who has modified the artifact most recently. This implies that the user actively interacted with the content and detected a reason to change the artifact, which requires at least some experience.
3. It can be the user who performed the largest number of activities with the artifact. This case can again be distinguished from reading and changing activities.
4. If the effect of the activity can be measured in the sense of an activity size, it can be the user who performed the largest activities on the artifacts. This can be combined with the two last strategies.

Basically, the strategy should reflect how much the artifact changed due to a user's action and how much of this change survived in the latest version of the artifact.

Rationale

McDonald and Ackerman (1998) performed an ethnographic study of how team members use artifacts to locate expertise on the artifacts. The authors interviewed team members in a software development team to find out how they act when they have a question:

> "When a programmer makes a change in a program he is supposed to add his mnemonic to the line and update the date. This is how we know who last changed the program. Whoever made the last change in the program is the default expert on that program ... It's close enough. The logic is that the person who spent time on it has it freshest in memory and so they are the best person to ask a question". (A user called Brad in (McDonald and Ackerman, 1998)).

From this quote one can see that there are traditional means for assessing a user's expertise. The authors discovered one problem that can make the above approach fail: if users only performed small changes, they are often not experts on the artifact.

This motivates a means for finding experts that is based on the number or the impact of changes (strategies 3 and 4).

Regardless of the strategy chosen, the system will provide the requester with another user who has experienced the artifact before. This user can be considered as an expert who shares their experience with the requesting user.

Check

When applying this pattern, you should answer these questions:

— How do you calculate a user's expertise level?
— Which artifacts and activities do you consider for calculating a user's expertise level?

Danger Spots

It can be very complicated to find a valid means of measuring the size of a contribution (in strategy 4). It may require the effects of a contribution to be traced back from the latest version to the first version of the artifact. Contributions that are still visible in the current version of the artifact can often be considered as important contributions.

Known Uses

Expertise Browser (Mockus and Herbsleb, 2002)[4] is a tool to support software development teams.

---

[4] A demo version is available at http://www.research.avayalabs.com/user/audris/ExV/ExV2.html.

3.2.4 Expert Finder

Expertise is determined from the change history of a software artifact. When a developer performs a change, this change is recorded in a version management system. Each change is weighted according to the number of lines that were changed.

Figure 3.37 shows the user interface for finding an expert. A project artifact can be selected on the right-hand side of the figure. The system then looks up all changes to the artifact and calculates expertise levels for all participants considering all weighted changes (strategy 3 considering only write activities and weighting the activities according to strategy 4). The result of this query is shown on the left of Figure 3.37. The center column shows the contributing users sorted by their expertise, and the font size represents the level of expertise. A user can contact another expert by selecting the user's name in the middle column and clicking on the corresponding e-mail address shown at the bottom of the window.

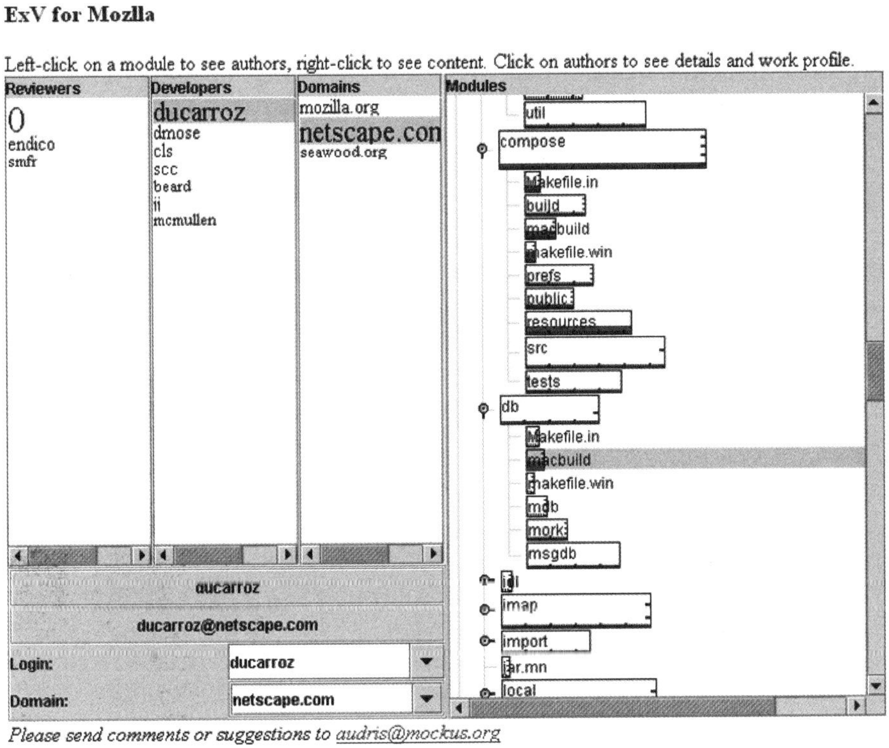

Figure 3.37 The Expertise Browser

MEMOIR (Pikrakis et al., 1998) collects trails of users' web browsing behavior. When users need to find an expert for a specific topic, the system collects all trails that contain pages on the topic. Experts are listed by the quantity of keyword matches in the user's trails.

Related Patterns

ACTIVITY LOG$_{\to 4.5.1}$ stores all activities performed by users.

USER LIST$_{\to 4.4.1}$ considers only active activities of other users to show who else is currently interacting with an artifact. Although these users may have less expertise than the users recommended by an EXPERT FINDER, they have the advantage of being available and sharing the same focus as the local user.

HALL OF FAME$_{\to 3.2.5}$ An EXPERT FINDER can be interpreted as a variant of HALL OF FAME in which the focus of hall of fame is restricted to a specific artifact.

MENTOR$_{\to 3.1.4}$ also describes how experts should pair with novices. The difference is that MENTOR is open for any question and expects questions mainly from novices, while EXPERT FINDER primarily concentrates on the topic of their expertise.

REWARD$_{\to 3.2.6}$ You should think about ways to thank an expert for the assistance. The REWARD pattern suggests ways in which an effort for the community can be compensated.

ASK FOR HELP (Manns and Rising, 2005) reminds people who are trying to introduce change in their social environment to not make the change alone. Instead, one should ask many people for help, so that the effort of change is distributed among the group that is interested in the change.

3.2.5 Hall of Fame *

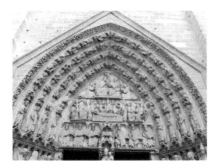

Hall of Fame (hôl ŏf fām), NOUN: **1. A group of persons judged outstanding, as in a sport or profession.** 2. A building housing memorial items honoring illustrious persons.

Intent

Honor the most helpful participants in the system by showing them in a HALL OF FAME.

Context

Your community system allows users to contribute their capabilities to the community. You now want to encourage active users to even greater efforts.

Problem

Motivation for participation in a community is often related to the feedback that participants receive from the community. Often, however, even very active participants are insufficiently recognized by community members.

Scenario

Susan has been an active member of the community from its earliest days. It was she who implemented the role-play engine that makes the collaborative game engine so successful. However, new members do not know this. Susan has also been very supportive to new members. However, in recent months her interest has faded and the community has started to ignore her, even though losing her would be a big problem for the community.

Symptoms

You should consider applying this pattern when ...

— The number of passive participants is much higher than the number of active participants, and the ratio between benefit and effort is better for passive

participants than for active participants. This means that RECIPROCITY$_{\rightarrow 3.3.1}$ is violated.
— Participation is unequally distributed, which results in frustration for very active participants.
— Participation decreases over time, although the subject is still interesting for the participants.

Solution

Therefore: Provide a list of those participants who contribute most. Calculate the participants' contribution level with respect to the degree that they have helped others. Let participants compare themselves to those participants shown in the HALL OF FAME.

Dynamics

A participant contributes to the community. A participant can either be a member of the community or a group of users (see GROUP$_{\rightarrow 4.1.1}$). The participant's contributions are rated by other users or by means of a contribution metric. A contribution metric can be something like the number of posts on a discussion board.

Participants who receive the highest ratings are listed in a HALL OF FAME. All members can browse the HALL OF FAME and see information about the participants with high ratings. They can also see how much more the members of the HALL OF FAME have contributed by comparing their personal rating or position with their own rating.

Ensure that the HALL OF FAME is positioned in a prominent place in the community.

Rationale

The HALL OF FAME adds a competitive element to the community. Only participants who contribute to the community will gain a place in the HALL OF FAME. If participants stop contributing they will be outdone by others, assuming that at least a small set of participants contributes.

How well a HALL OF FAME works depends greatly on the community's culture. If community members are eager to know who is the best participant in the community, it will also encourage participants to outdo other participants in the HALL OF FAME. This helps to convert relatively passive participants into active ones.

Check

When applying this pattern, you should answer these questions:

— How can you calculate the participation level?

- How can you recognize valuable participation? Can the users comment on the participation, for example by using a LETTER OF RECOMMENDATION$_{\rightarrow 3.2.2}$?
- Where should you place the HALL OF FAME?

Danger Spots

The difference between a newcomer and a participant shown in the HALL OF FAME can make it discouraging for new users to work at being included in the HALL OF FAME. One solution to this is to ensure that fame vanishes over time. Otherwise, participants may have become famous because they participated a lot in the past, but have since stopped participating in the community. For the same reason, newcomers will have to invest much before they are recognized in the HALL OF FAME if fame does not fade with time.

Fading fame can for example be achieved by dividing the perceived value of the contribution by the elapsed time that has passed since the contribution.

Participants can try to trick the metric in order to reach a better position in the HALL OF FAME. Consider, for example, a HALL OF FAME for software development projects as is modeled at freshmeat.net presented in the known uses section. Since the vitality of a project is measured by counting contributions to the project's discussion board, project members can simulate high vitality by generating noise in the form of meaningless messages on the discussion board.

Known Uses

software-engineer.org was a community web site for software developers. To encourage participation, the designers grouped activities by their helpfulness to others. Participants could earn fifty points by submitting job offers or links, a hundred points by submitting news or downloads, and 150 points by submitting an article to the site. The top contributors to the site were shown in a HALL OF FAME.

freshmeat.net hosts an open-source community and lists the most popular and vital projects. Besides overall popularity, it also shows those projects that have improved their popularity within the last month, shown as *projects on the horizon* in Figure 3.38. This solves the problem seen in the previous example of newcomers having to invest a great deal of effort before they are recognized by the community. By showing the *tendency* of participation, active newcomers can be honored in this section of the HALL OF FAME.

Amazon.com lists all top reviewers, as shown in Figure 3.39.[5] Reviewers are not ranked according to the number of reviews they have written, but using the volume of positive feedback from other users in response to their reviews.

---

[5] http://www.amazon.com/exec/obidos/tg/cm/top-reviewers-list/-/1/

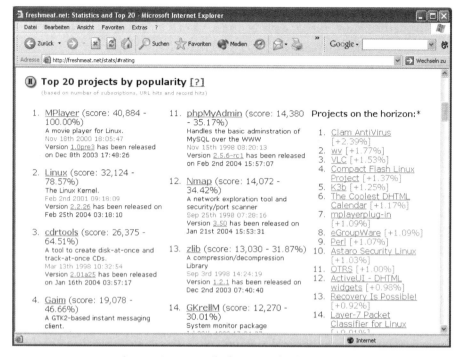

Figure 3.38 Hall of Fame in freshmeat.net

Related Patterns

EXPERT FINDER→3.2.4 reduces the focus of the calculation of prominent users to interaction with one specific artifact. The guru for an artifact is the first in the artifact's HALL OF FAME.

REWARD→3.2.6 can be used to emphasize important groups instead of individuals. One example is the *freshmeat.net* community in the known uses section, where projects are listed instead of single developers.

LETTER OF RECOMMENDATION→3.2.2 can be used to determine how much a user has helped others. A user with many letters of recommendation will achieve a higher position in the HALL OF FAME.

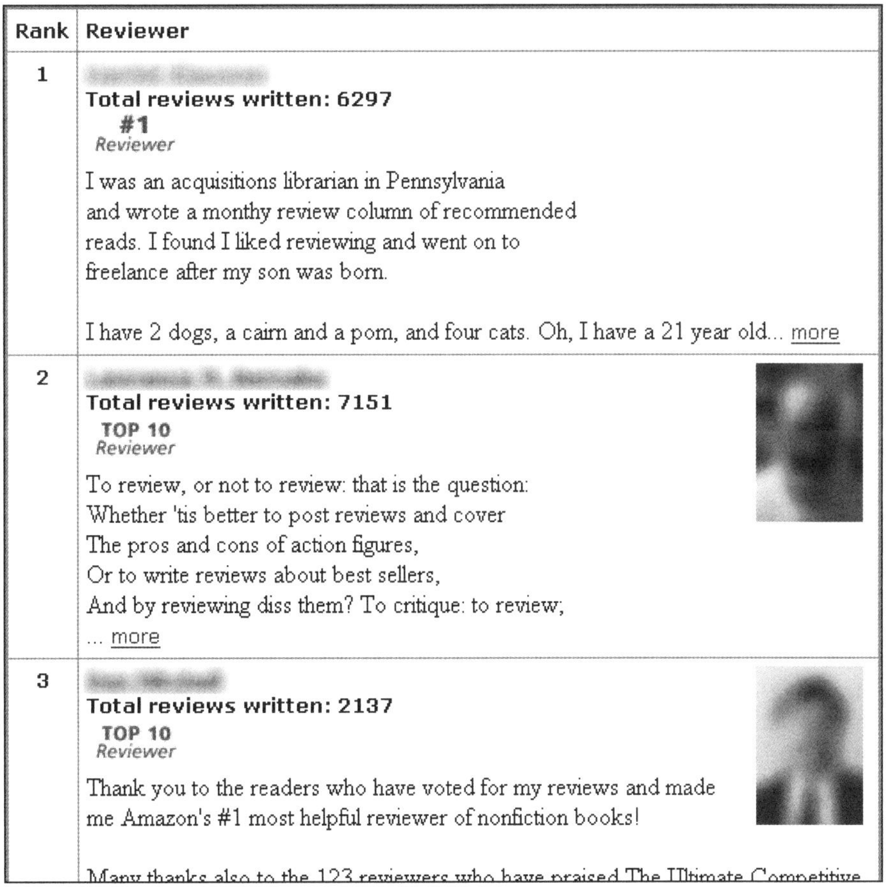

Rank	Reviewer
1	**Total reviews written: 6297** **#1** *Reviewer* I was an acquisitions librarian in Pennsylvania and wrote a monthy review column of recommended reads. I found I liked reviewing and went on to freelance after my son was born. I have 2 dogs, a cairn and a pom, and four cats. Oh, I have a 21 year old... more
2	**Total reviews written: 7151** **TOP 10** *Reviewer* To review, or not to review: that is the question: Whether 'tis better to post reviews and cover The pros and cons of action figures, Or to write reviews about best sellers, And by reviewing diss them? To critique: to review; ... more
3	**Total reviews written: 2137** **TOP 10** *Reviewer* Thank you to the readers who have voted for my reviews and made me Amazon's #1 most helpful reviewer of nonfiction books! Many thanks also to the 123 reviewers who have praised The Ultimate Competitive

Figure 3.39 Top reviewers at amazon.com.

ACTIVITY LOG$_{\rightarrow 4.5.1}$ can be used to keep track of users' activities. In most cases it is not necessary to keep track of all activities in order to calculate an expert rating. Instead, users can collect points with each activity and thus always know their current expert rating.

USER GALLERY$_{\rightarrow 2.1.6}$ shows all the users of a community instead of only the most prominent ones.

3.2.6 REWARD

Alternative name(s): Compensation, Fringe Benefit Remuneration

re·ward (rĭ-wôrd'), NOUN: **1.** Something given or received in recompense for worthy behavior or in retribution for evil acts. **2.** Money offered or given for some special service, such as the return of a lost article or the capture of a criminal. **3.** A satisfying return or result; profit. **4. Psychology The return for performance of a desired behavior; positive reinforcement.**

Intent

Reimburse positive participation of individuals or groups.

Context

Your environment supports users or groups of users who actively contribute to the community. Now you are thinking about how to better motivate contributors and how to strengthen the incentives of groups to collaboratively create value in the community.

Problem

Community actors—individual users or small GROUPS$_{\rightarrow 4.1.1}$—participate at different levels. Very supportive actors may not see a direct benefit of their contribution. As a result, motivation and participation declines.

Scenario

Janet is the expert on visualization algorithms. Many users of the game engine appreciate her advice whenever it comes to a graphics question. However, Janet gets bored by the recurring questions and, in the rare cases when she has a problem, nobody want to help her. For example, she recently had a problem related to security, but Charley had no time to talk about the problem even though Janet has helped Charley many times before when he struggled with graphics questions.

Symptoms

You should consider applying this pattern when . . .

— Actors have diverse capabilities.

- Actors do not need assistance in areas in which they perform well, but could benefit from assistance in other areas.
- The fact that actor A can help actor B does not imply that actor B can provide any benefit for actor A.
- The community needs some actors who are prepared to perform unpopular tasks.
- Actors are unmotivated because other actors harvest the fruits of their work.
- Some users in a group are publicly announced while others remain unrecognized.

Solution

Therefore: Create tokens in your community that can be passed on to users who contributed positively to the community's goals. Enable users to trade their tokens if they want to persuade other community actors to support them.

Dynamics

All users have an account that stores their current balance of community tokens. Users can act as *service providers* or as *service consumers*. When a service consumer wants to use a service from a service provider, the service provider may ask for the transfer of a fixed or negotiated number of tokens.

The community as a whole can act as a service consumer for services that are of common interest. In this case, the service provider receives newly generated tokens.

In cases in which a group receives tokens for a shared contribution to the community, the tokens are distributed fairly within the group.

Rationale

Users no longer base their exchange of services on direct exchange, but use a token that is not related to the specific task.

By using tokens instead of concrete reimbursements, users are eager to provide services to other users because they can accumulate credit that can be used when they need the services of others.

Allowing users to transfer tokens to a group encourages the group as a whole to achieve the group goal.

Check

When applying this pattern, you should answer these questions:

- How should you set the price for a specific service? Is the market of services large enough to negotiate prices?

— How can you prevent inflation? Does it make sense to limit the credit of the community where the community acts as a service consumer?
— How will the group negotiate the distribution of tokens received for a group result?
— What can users do with their tokens? Will there be special events for users with a lot of tokens? Will users with a lot of tokens be listed in a HALL OF FAME$_{\rightarrow 3.2.5}$?

Danger Spots

Ensure that every user can earn tokens by defining a large set of positive contributions. Otherwise, new members can be discourage from participation.

Users can become addicted to collecting virtual money, with the effect that all interaction is only performed in return for the highest possible benefit. The benefits that were initially thought of as motivational factors become the reason for interaction. The initial intention of the community—the problem that should be addressed by the community—becomes a secondary issue.

Stenmark (2002) compared different systems for idea generation and found that systems that offer rewards decrease the willingness to share ideas. Users instead fear that their ideas could be sold by other users and that the others would be rewarded instead of them. Stenmark thus proposed that users should be rewarded collectively. In the context of this pattern, you should be extremely careful to balance individual rewards and group awards so that the fear of loosing benefits by acting as a group is reduced.

If a group agrees to share the group's rewards equally, some users may stop feeling responsible for the group result if they see that other users perform well. The main problem in this case is that different group members can have different expectations of the group result. Group members with low expectations may start to act as "free riders".

One way to cope with this problem is for the group to receive a group award and for individual group members to receive additional rewards for outstanding contributions, according to the REWARD pattern.

Not everything should be rewarded. Instead, it is important to create a good balance between activities performed for the group and activities that are reimbursed by a reward.

Known Uses

Experts-Exchange is an online help forum that rewards users who provide an answer to a question. Whenever users pose a new question, they have to define how many expert points they will transfer to the user who provides a satisfactory answer. The expert points will be taken from the requesting user's account immediately and stored for the user who provides a satisfactory answer. The "price" is shown against each question in the list of open questions: other users can select which questions that they want to answer.

If an user provides an answer that satisfies the requesting user, the answer is formally accepted. The requesting user can then grade the answer. The higher the grade, the more points are added to the answering user's account. Extremely satisfied requesting users can for example grade the answer with an A and the answering user will receive four times the question's points.

Figure 3.40 shows the profile of a user (left) who has provided an accepted answer to a question (right). The original points for the question (250) are shown on the right, together with the grade the requesting user gave the answer (B). That means that the user who provided the answer receives $3 \star 250 = 750$ points for it.

Figure 3.40 Earning expert points at expert-exchange.com

eMule is a peer-to-peer file-sharing system that introduces a credit system for transactions between peers. Whenever a peer acts as a server for another peer, it receives credit points. These credit points can be used when the peer is acting as a client: the more credit points a client has, the better will be its ranking in the download queue of the requested server.

Mojo Nation (no longer available, but described by Leuf (2002, page 215)) was another peer-to-peer file-sharing environment that honored users with a virtual currency called "Mojo". New users entered the community with a credit of one million Mojos. Every time users consumed content in the network they had to pay some Mojo. The price controlled how fast users could access specific content depending on supply and demand for the desired content. Every time users donated server capabilities such as disk space, computing power, or network bandwidth, they earned some Mojos.

SourceForge.net is a community site for open source projects. Every month one project receives special attention and is presented as the project of the month (see Figure 3.41).

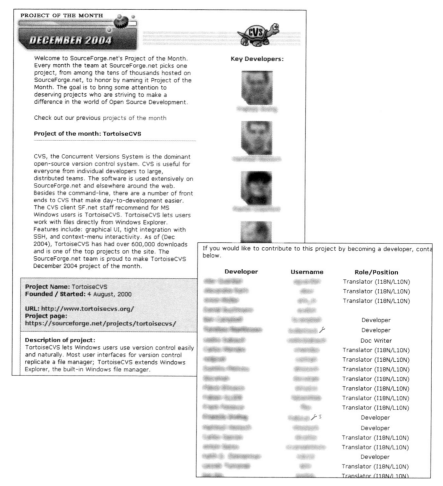

Figure 3.41 The project of the month at sourceforge.net

Instead of only introducing the project lead, SourceForge.net lists all the key developers on the *project of the month* page. These are the developers who have made the largest contributions in the group. Other members are listed on the project's detail page. The project itself is always shown as a group result. Individual contributions are not especially marked, other than by comments in the source code that help to find the developers of a specific component.

Mindpool (Stenmark, 2001) is a system that combines asynchronous brainstorming with an idea-proposal system. Although it does not implement a REWARD pattern, Stenmark observed the problem of rewards during a formal system evaluation. He then added a collective reward scheme for groups, as described in the *danger spots* section.

Related Patterns

LETTER OF RECOMMENDATION$_{\rightarrow 3.2.2}$ One way to pay back helpful behavior can be to write a LETTER OF RECOMMENDATION.

HALL OF FAME$_{\rightarrow 3.2.5}$ Being listed in a HALL OF FAME can be another incentive to provide help to others.

RECIPROCITY$_{\rightarrow 3.3.1}$ can often be considered as a better alternative. If users can provide mutual benefits for one another you should avoid installing an additional REWARD system.

PLAYER-DECIDED DISTRIBUTION OF REWARDS & PENALTIES (Björk and Holopainen, 2005) discusses distribution schemes for rewards in the context of game play. The main message of the pattern is that the mode of distribution should be negotiated between group members. The group can for example decide that the team leader receives a larger percentage of the group's award.

ONE GRADE FOR ALL (Eckstein et al., 2002) also discusses the distribution of awards, but in an educational setting. The authors suggest that all group members should receive a grade based on a presentation given at the end of the project.

HONOR QUESTIONS (Fricke and Völter, 2000). In educational contexts it can be counterproductive if just the answers to questions are rewarded. Instead, you should also consider honoring students who have raised questions in the community, because the question itself is an important step towards understanding new concepts.

COMPENSATE SUCCESS (Coplien and Harrison, 2004) assumes that successful teams stay successful if their success is rewarded. The authors distinguish between rewarding individuals who have helped the group to succeed, and rewarding the whole group. The stronger you focus on individual rewards, the more envy may build up within the team. However, fewer individual rewards may lead to free riders, people who benefit from a group result without investing effort. In the same context, a major body of literature has discussed the relation between individual and team compensation (for example (Gross, 2000)).

3.2.7 Guide me... applied

Paul wants to increase motivation for participation. He therefore conducts a survey among community members to find their initial incentive for becoming a member. The result of the survey shows that one of the most important reasons was to get additional support on parts of the game engine. In contrast to this, new members also report that they have no idea who they should contact if they have a problem with a specific source document about the game engine.

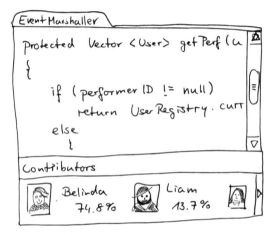

Figure 3.42 Expert Finder

So Paul decides to add an EXPERT FINDER$_{\rightarrow 3.2.4}$ (see Figure 3.42). The second question posed by the pattern, namely which artifacts and activities should be considered for calculating a user's expertise level, leads to an interesting decision: since users mainly search for experts on a specific class or method, Paul decides to use the Java source files of the game engine as artifacts. Further, he looks at the actions that are typically performed with the source files: developers read code and they manipulate code. Code manipulation implies deeper knowledge of the code. So Paul decides to only use modification of the code as a relative activity for the EXPERT FINDER.

After these decisions are made, the implementation of the pattern is straightforward: Paul logs all commit activities and shows the percentage of activities per user together with the source code. So, when opening the source file, the developers can instantly see who has contributed to the file. Note that Paul also decides to integrate this information in the development environment of the community members. Compared to a purely web-based solution, where the users would be listed next to a static view of the classes, this enables the developers to find experts more quickly.

The next incentive for members to participate in the community is to provide code. However, they explicitly mentioned that they did not want to create code in isolation. Instead, most members prefer to find other developers who share comparable interests.

Using the BIRDS OF A FEATHER$_{\rightarrow 3.2.3}$ pattern, users can search for other community members with comparable expertise. Internally, this is done by comparing the expert data that was collected for the EXPERT FINDER pattern. To find a group of relevant collaborators, the developer selects a set of packages and asks the environment to suggest birds of a feather for the package. The system then compares the part of the user's expertise profile that is related to the selected packages with corresponding parts of other users' profiles, and suggests any users found as collaboration partners.

Alternatively, users can decide to find complementary birds of a feather. In this search mode, the system searches for users with a high level of expertise in packages where the local user has low expertise, and vice versa. This example illustrates an interesting point about using the patterns in general: some patterns give you the freedom to experiment and create variations of the original idea proposed by the pattern.

After finding some users, the system offers to show the potential partners' VIRTUAL MES$_{\rightarrow 3.1.5}$ (already shown in Figure 3.28) and reveal how others have experienced interaction with specific partners by looking at their LETTER OF RECOMMENDATIONS$_{\rightarrow 3.2.2}$ (see Figure 3.43).

Figure 3.43 Letter of Recommendation

The information for the LETTER OF RECOMMENDATION is provided by users after an interaction with a collaboration partner. Each user can rate the partner and give them stars. The system will show an average number of stars for any user by aggregating the individual ratings. Clicking on the stars shows the full list of comments.

After the teams form and start to create code, Susan becomes a little worried about the code quality. Together with the other members of the project's steering board, she designs a mechanism for inspecting code based on the QUALITY INSPECTION$_{\to 3.2.1}$ pattern (see Figure 3.44).

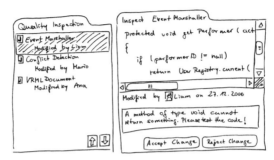

Figure 3.44 Quality Inspection

Whenever a user creates a new version of some code, the code is sent to the project's steering board. Technically, this is implemented by using two different branches of the code base: the main branch contains all code elements that are quality approved. The contribution branch can be used by all project members to submit new versions of their files.

To start an inspection session, the system looks up all changes in the contribution branch and shows the inspector what has been changed. The inspector can then accept or reject the submitted code. If code is rejected, the inspecting user is also asked to add a reason for rejecting it. In this case, the submitting user is notified and can rework the change accordingly. If the contribution is accepted, the system automatically moves it to the main branch.

3.3 Save me... or how to protect users

In previous sections we have seen how the community around Paul and his game engine evolved. Many developers currently contribute to the project and even more users provide suggestions.

We can see this as a successfully created community. However, having so many active members can raise new problems. There is a saying that "too many cooks spoil the broth." The reason for this is that many people have to coordinate their activities and respect each other's wishes.

> *The large number of users became a problem in the game engine development community after Paul added support for direct communication and interaction. He added an instant messaging feature that allowed users to send short chat messages to other users, as an* EMBEDDED CHAT$_{\rightarrow 4.3.1}$. *Paul also added a feature that allowed the users to see who else was currently online using a* USER LIST$_{\rightarrow 4.4.1}$. *In combination, these features allowed other users to see remote users' current statuses and drag them into an interaction. Since many users did not know one another, the establishment of an interaction sometimes became annoying for the users who were drawn into the interaction.*

This episode from our scenario is just one example of the general problem of privacy and self-control in online communities. There is always the dilemma that members of the community, on one hand, have to reveal their identity, but on the other hand often feel a need to control how this information is used. Far too often, community designers focus only on the first part, namely how to convince people to become visible in the community. The reason for this is obvious: the success of an online community is often measured by counting the number of members and the total number of activities in the community. High numbers suggest that the community is a successful social structure, since many members can create high community value—if measured by terms of the captured knowledge—with rather low personal effort.

However, the size of the community makes it more difficult to establish trust between all community members. The probability that a member does not want to interact with all community members increases the larger the community gets. The same is true for the probability of irrelevant content. The more people participate in a community, the more likely is the involvement of a user who does not respect the community's rules. All these factors create "noise" that disturbs individual community members.

Figure 3.45 illustrates the relationship between personal (active) involvement, personal interest, and passive contribution (desired and unwanted content) in a community. Assume that a user initially shows a high level of interest in the

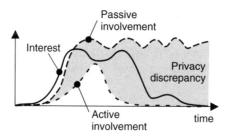

Figure 3.45 Privacy discrepancy

community. They start to contribute content to the community and interact with other community members. It is also not a problem for the user to be passively involved, for example by receiving news feeds from the community. As long as the contribution, the interest, and the passive contribution are in balance, everything works well. At some point, however, the user stops contributing actively. They continue to show a little interest in passive contribution, but as soon as this interest also vanishes, they will perceive the passive contribution as an annoyance that we call *privacy discrepancy*.

A concrete example is membership of a mailing list: users subscribe to the mailing list because they want to find out more about a topic. They receive messages from the list and post their own messages. However, after a while they lose interest in the list and see messages from the list as annoying unwanted material. These messages reach uninterested users and thus limit the extent to which the users are under control of their privacy in terms of the information they must process.

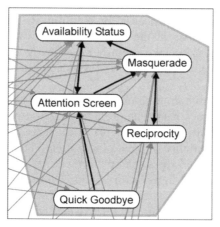

Figure 3.46 Patterns for ensuring privacy

Another form of privacy discrepancy emerges from the conflicting forces of awareness and privacy: to collaborate users have to agree to be observed, and thus give up parts of their privacy. What is needed is a good balance between the drawback of being observed and the benefit received from other users or their contributions.

The patterns in this section, which are also shown in Figure 3.46, suggest ways of minimizing the privacy discrepancy:

RECIPROCITY$_{\to 3.3.1}$ Ensure that users benefit if they contribute to the system. Let the benefit grow when the user contributes more.

MASQUERADE$_{\to 3.3.2}$ Control how much private information you reveal to other users when interacting in a collaborative environment.

AVAILABILITY STATUS$_{\to 3.3.3}$ Indicate to what extent you may be interrupted.

ATTENTION SCREEN$_{\to 3.3.4}$ Define who and what may take the user's attention.

QUICK GOODBYE$_{\to 3.3.5}$ Make it easy for a user to leave a group.

Note that we do not go into details of cryptographic security. We instead assume that basic security has already been established using other patterns, for example those from the security pattern collection (Schumacher et al., 2005).

3.3.1 Reciprocity *

Alternative name(s): Fair Distribution of Efforts, Win-Win Situation

rec·i·proc·i·ty (rĕs'ə-prŏs'ĭ-tē), NOUN: **1.** A reciprocal condition or relationship. **2. A mutual or cooperative interchange of favors or privileges, especially the exchange of rights or privileges of trade between nations.**

Intent

Ensure that users benefit if they contribute to the system. Let the benefit grow when the user contributes more.

Context

Your system uses the user's input to produce the group result. To facilitate collaboration, ideally all group members should participate in the group process to reach a goal.

Problem

It is easy to agree on participation if the goal is lucrative for everyone. In many work situations, however, some people benefit more than others from an attained goal. This may frustrate active users.

Scenario

Charley is worried about the stability of the game engine. In the early days, developers agreed to provide test cases for all the code they submitted for the game engine. However, more recently many of the new developers do not provide test cases: for example, Mario, who doesn't care about test code for his new polygon calculation because he is convinced that it works.

Symptoms

You should consider applying this pattern when ...

— Users are not comparably involved, although the group process demands that all users participate to the same extent.

— Individual group members have a feeling that they do all the work and that others only act as lurkers or free riders.

Solution

Therefore: Establish reciprocity. Ensure that all group members' activities result in an improved group result that is beneficial for all group members. Prohibit people from benefitting from group results if they are not willing to help the group in return.

Dynamics

Users can interact with the groupware system using specific *functionality*. In the design phase all stakeholders decide, for each functionality, who benefits from the functionality and who has to expend effort. This means that they also determine who gains freedom if the functionality is present, and whose freedom is reduced.

Identify benefits and drawbacks for any group of stakeholders that are functionally related and combine them in one collaboration mode. This means that if users want to use a functionality that they find beneficial, they also have to accept or commit to the corresponding functionality that results in additional effort.

Rationale

The RECIPROCITY pattern mainly solves a problem that is imminent in any interaction: "actions taken by one party in an exchange relationship will be reciprocated in kind by the other party." (Carr, 2006). Carr (2006) studied this phenomenon in the context of the interaction between information systems departments and information system users. They stated that the idea of reciprocity would mean in this context that "IS departmental actions will be evaluated and reciprocated by IS users based on evaluations of what they receive from the IS department."

In the extreme case in which RECIPROCITY is missing, or users are not aware of potential reciprocal actions, the beneficiaries of an attained goal do not have to participate in the group efforts at all. This leads to a situation in which the people who have to expend effort on the group result no longer see the need to participate, because the results are not valuable for them.

An early reference to this problem was made by Grudin (1994), who stated that *"groupware applications often require additional work from individuals who do not perceive a direct benefit from the use of the application."* Even earlier contributions such as the seminal work of Grudin (1988) as well as more recent studies like Pipek et al. (2003) have shown that a lack of equally distributed benefit will be a reason why groupware applications fail.

To overcome this problem, motivating people to participate is the key issue in most collaborative systems. Without the participation of the users, the user community soon becomes inactive and a feeling of lack of fairness spreads between those who contribute to the system and those who just consume group results.

This problem of "social loafing", where only parts of the group contribute to the group result, has been widely discussed in the field of social psychology, for example Wilke and van Knippenberg (1996), who discussed the relationship between group performance and individual participation. It is known to be especially visible in systems that provide common goods that can be used by anyone. Community systems on the other hand are based on the idea of common goods that are shared in the community.

By identifying the beneficiaries of a specific service and combining this service with other services that are beneficial for other users, you re-establish the equilibrium of benefits and required work for the users involved.

Check

When applying this pattern, you should answer these questions:

— What are the benefits that each class of individuals will draw from the groupware system?
— Are there causal relations between the actions required to gain the benefits?
— Which groups of users benefit from the activities others perform? Are there complementary benefits that can be related in a reciprocity relationship?

Danger Spots

This pattern is mainly needed in situations in which the critical mass of participation can only be reached when most users participate. If the community is very large (such as a news group), it can nevertheless succeed with a small number of active participants and a larger number of inactive participants (free riders, lurkers).

Known Uses

TUKAN. The collaborative programming environment TUKAN combines a specific level of privacy (see MASQUERADE$_{\rightarrow 3.3.2}$) with the right to receive information about other users to ensure reciprocity. The combination is called *Mode of Collaboration (MoC)*. A user can only utilize information from other users at an interaction level on which the user is also willing to reveal personal information.

The different MoCs are shown in Figure 3.47. The left-hand side of the diagram shows the drawbacks or limitations in the user's privacy. The right-hand side shows the corresponding benefits gained from other users. The middle of the figure shows the mode of collaboration that combines the drawbacks and the benefits.

Figure 3.48 shows how the dependency between modes of collaboration is reflected in the user interface. The slider on the left of the window can be used

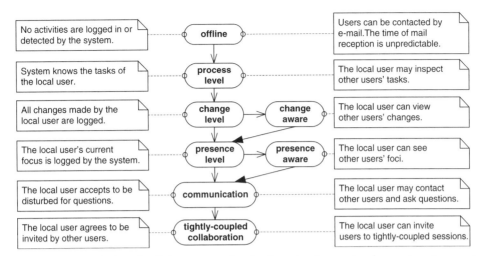

Figure 3.47 Modes of collaboration in the distributed software development environment TUKAN

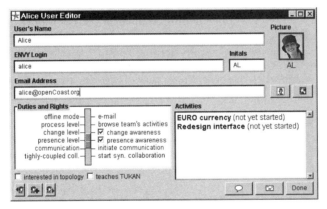

Figure 3.48 Reciprocity reflected in TUKAN's user interface

to select the appropriate mode. The legend against the slider explains which duties and rights are associated to the mode. In the case of change awareness and presence awareness, users can explicitly activate benefits if they decide to be monitored in exchange.

BUDDY LISTS$_{\rightarrow 3.1.7}$ **in instant messaging systems.** When a remote user should be added to the local user's contact list, the system first asks the remote user for permission. If the remote user rejects this, the local user will not be able to see the remote user's online status.

Together with this request for permission, the remote user can decide to add the local user to their contact list.

Bulletin board systems. Early bulletin board systems limited access to information based on the amount of information that a user provided. To access more data, users had to provide more files to the system. One problem that often occurred in these settings was that users provided *useless* information just to improve their download account, such as personal artwork that was not valuable for others, or randomly generated text files. These examples show that the metric for measuring contributions needs to be carefully designed.

Related Patterns

HALL OF FAME$_{\rightarrow 3.2.5}$ can serve as an alternative motivator. If users are rewarded prominently in the community space, they can be motivated to participate in interactions that are of no direct value to them.

REWARD$_{\rightarrow 3.2.6}$ argues in favor of providing compensation that is potentially unrelated to a specific service. This means that it can be used in contexts in which no cluster of related services can be identified.

USER LIST$_{\rightarrow 4.4.1}$ establishes reciprocity, because everyone can see who else is present.

3.3.2 Masquerade   *

Alternative name(s): Anonymous Interaction, Control your Privacy

mas·quer·ade (măs'kə-rād'), NOUN: **1a.** A costume party at which masks are worn; a masked ball. Also called masque. **b. A costume for such a party or ball. 2a.** A disguise or false outward show; a pretense: *a masquerade of humility*. **b.** An involved scheme; a charade.

Intent

Control how much private information you reveal to other users when interacting in a collaborative environment.

Context

You are working in a monitored environment in which personal information such as e-mail addresses, current activities, work status or discussion fragments are visible to all users of the environment.

Problem

Your application monitors the local user. The information gathered is used to provide awareness information to remote users. While this is suitable in some situations, users often do not act as confidently if they know they are monitored. Users may feel a need to avoid providing any information to others.

Scenario

Paul and Ana have both established their VIRTUAL ME$_{\rightarrow 3.1.5}$ *in the community. They have managed to communicate a clear picture of their expertise. In recent weeks, however, they have noticed that some actions in the community did not correspond with their wishes. Normally, they just tell other members about problems, so that the whole community can look for a solution. Now, however, neither Paul nor Ana have the heart to tell the truth, because this will probably offend other members. As a result they don't say anything, and just hope that someone else will discuss the community's problems.*

Symptoms

You should consider applying this pattern when ...

— Personal information is abused by some users.

— After personal information was abused for the first time, users drastically reduced the amount of information that they provided to the system. This resulted in a lack of collaboration.

— Potentially secret information can be related to specific work packages and users know that they don't want to be recognized before they enter the work package.

— Users are willing to provide personal information to collaborating colleagues, but not to managers or strangers.

— Users hesitate to participate because they fear that their contributions will be criticized.

Solution

Therefore: Let users control what information is revealed from their personal details in a specific interaction context. This means that users must be able to filter the information that is revealed from their personal information. Remember to consider RECIPROCITY$_{\rightarrow 3.3.1}$.

Dynamics

While interacting within a collaborative environment, a user can enter a desired level of publicity or a publicity profile. The difference between a publicity level and a profile is that the publicity level arranges all the information that can possibly be revealed on a scale. Selecting a specific publicity level implies that all the information with lower publicity levels will also be revealed. In contrast, a publicity profile allows users to select each aspect they want to reveal.

Monitoring systems such as sensors or state trackers in client-server systems reduce the information revealed according to the user's publicity settings. This reduced information is then forwarded to a central ACTIVITY LOG$_{\rightarrow 4.5.1}$ or to other interested clients so that the information can be made visible to other users.

Rationale

Since users can control how much personal information they provide to other users explicitly, they no longer have to fear that their personal information is misused by strangers. This provides them with an environment that is as private as the situation demands. Users can decide to discuss private matters without the possibility of being monitored by others by simply changing their privacy profile.

Systems that support creative processes like electronic brainstorming systems, or systems that support critical discussions for example in a FORUM$_{\rightarrow 4.3.2}$, often benefit from the anonymity of contributions. Studies in such system contexts have shown that participants create more critical comments and contributions when acting anonymously (Nunamaker et al., 1991).

The RECIPROCITY$_{\to 3.3.1}$ pattern on the other hand can force users to reduce their privacy level when the need for privacy is no longer present. This is done by connecting privacy levels with permissions for interaction. Activities that affect common artifacts will for example demand that the user reveals some personal information to the community. Examples are provided in the RECIPROCITY pattern.

Check

When applying this pattern, you should answer these questions:

— What information can the user control and what information must another user reveal to enable the core functions of the application?
— What levels of publicity are you going to offer?
— Do you want to allow anonymous interaction?

Danger Spots

If you allow anonymous interaction with the system it may lower the inhibition threshold for destructive behavior, because users do not have to fear that destructive activities will be associated with their identity. You should therefore provide only limited functionality for anonymous users, such as read access or moderated postings only to a discussion board.

Known Uses

Video Systems. NYNEX Portholes (Lee et al., 1997) is a video system in which users can blur their video image to communicate less detail.

Zhao and Stasko (1998) evaluated different video filters for video awareness systems. Users were able to decide which filter should be applied to their video image. One example of such a filter is the pixelize filter (Figure 3.49) that reduces the resolution of an image. This enabled users to provide less information about themselves. The authors found out that users who interacted often were still able to draw presence information from very distorted images, while others could not make much sense out of such images.

Boyle et al. (2000) present a video link awareness system that allows users to blur their images using filtered video streams, or to block their image totally by projecting an image of the palm of a hand in front of the video.

TUKAN (Schümmer and Haake, 2001) is a collaborative software development environment that lets the user decide how much awareness information they

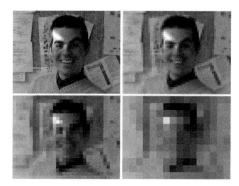

Figure 3.49 Different levels of distortion in a pixelated video image

want to provide to other users. The options range from *process awareness*, where developers publish information about their current programming task, over *change awareness*, where developers inform others about changes they have performed in the project, up to *presence level*, where the current position in the project—the software method a developer is browsing—is published to other users.

XING (https://www.xing.com/) allows users to manage a network of contacts by allowing them to configure their privacy. Figure 3.50 shows the configuration dialog in which users can decide what information they reveal to others.

Figure 3.50 Privacy configuration in XING

XING distinguishes different degrees of contact, ranging from direct contacts up to contacts of the fourth degree. Users can enable communication possibilities according to this degree, which is shown in the upper right corner of Figure 3.50. XING can therefore establish different levels of publicity using different degrees of separation.

TeamSpace (Geyer et al., 2001) distinguishes different *working modes*—the individual, the social, and the meeting mode. In the individual mode, team members work alone at a computer using general office products or tools specialized for their engineering discipline to capture information on their work. In the meeting mode, they can review and discuss their progress against their schedule. The individual and meeting modes are often interrupted for informal work or communication in a social mode. Transitions between the different modes and the information revealed as a result are modeled to allow the user to select the mode that is appropriate for their current task.

Drehscheibe (Koch, 2003) is a community support system for the Department of Informatics at the Technical University of Munich. In this community support system users can represent themselves by creating a VIRTUAL ME$_{\to 3.1.5}$. Since this user information is not just used within the system, users can specify who can access it, for example nobody, everybody, or only users of the same community space.

Related Patterns

AVAILABILITY STATUS$_{\to 3.3.3}$ shields a user from being contacted by others. MASQUERADE can fulfill the same purpose if it is used such that a user interacts with the system anonymously and users can only be contacted if they are registered with an identity.

ACTIVITY LOG$_{\to 4.5.1}$ MASQUERADE can be used to control what information will be logged by information trackers.

RECIPROCITY$_{\to 3.3.1}$ is very important if users can perform secret actions. Without reciprocity, users may consume presence information from others without revealing this information personally. One could imagine a user who always acts in a MASQUERADE, which would prevent the user establishing relationships to others.

QUICK REGISTRATION$_{\to 3.1.1}$ describes how users can join a community quickly. In some cases, however, users are not sure what they can expect as a member of the community. Consider allowing such users anonymous access to the community for a limited time before they have to register formally.

3.3.3 AVAILABILITY STATUS **

Alternative name(s): Don't Disturb, Interruption Gradient (Goldman et al., 2002)

a·vail·a·ble (ə-vā'lə-bəl), ADJECTIVE: **1.** Present and ready for use; at hand; accessible: *kept a fire extinguisher available at all times*. **2.** Capable of being gotten; obtainable: *a bedspread available in three colors*. **3. Qualified and willing to be of service or assistance: a list of available candidates; was not available for comment. 4a.** *Chemistry* Capable of being used in a chemical reaction: *available electrons*. **b.** *Botany* Present, as in soil, and capable of being used by plants as a nutrient: *available water; available minerals*. **5.** *Archaic* **a.** Capable of bringing about a beneficial result or effect. **b.** *Law* Valid. Used especially of a plea.

Intent

Indicate to what extent you may be interrupted.

Context

Your environment encourages spontaneous interaction between users.

Problem

To allow spontaneous interaction, users have to be open to contact requests. Each request disturbs the user or group contacted in their current task, however. In addition, the importance of a contact request may make it vital that the contact takes place.

Scenario

Susan is normally very supportive. After Rodrigo found that out, he stopped bothering Wil and directed all his questions to Susan. Even Susan has times when she wants to concentrate on one task, however. If she could find a way to lock Rodrigo out when she is concentrating on an important task, she could drastically reduce the volume of interactions.

Symptoms

You should consider applying this pattern when . . .

— Users like the possibility of spontaneous communication and collaboration, but also complain about being disturbed during important activities.

Solution

Therefore: Include an indicator in the application that signals the user's availability and how the user would react to an interaction.

Dynamics

Any user who is connected to the system can select a level of availability. This level in most cases ranges from *Available* to *Don't disturb*. Intermediate levels could for example be *On the phone* or *Busy*.

It is not necessary for levels of availability to be ordered. For example, the user could select between *Busy* and *On the phone*: both indicate that the user is currently not interruptible, but there is no natural order between these two levels.

In cases in which a group can be contacted as a whole, the group can also have a level of availability.

The level of availability is shown together with the user representation, but has no effect on possible contact establishment.

Remote users perceive the availability of the local user or group and decide whether or not contact should be established.

In cases in which additional information about status is required, you should consider allowing users to enter a free text description of what they are doing. A user could switch their AVAILABILITY STATUS to *Don't disturb* and complement this information with some text like *I am preparing my talk for next week*. This allows other users to estimate the impact that an interruption would have.

Rationale

The main problem addressed by this pattern is the difference between planned interruptions and the concrete demands of the current situation. If a user simply blocks all contact requests, their own needs over interruption are met. Since a context can demand that the user is contactable, however, this solution is in conflict with the context. On the other hand, if all requests are allowed, interruptions will be too frequent.

The availability indicator has the effect of making the contacting user reflect on their request. They may decide to contact the user, but will also aware of the fact that they will be the reason for the interruption.

This pattern relies on social norms for interaction. It is not considered polite to interrupt a user who does not want to be disturbed.

Check

When applying this pattern, you should answer these questions:

— How do you represent the availability status? Can you show it with each user's name?

— What levels of availability make sense in your application context?

— Should the availability take the user's context into account, for example by having availability states like 'On the phone' or 'Traveling'?

— Do users require additional information that explains more about their status using a text annotation?

Danger Spots

Ensure that users switch their status when they become available. Since they often forget to do this, it can be helpful to limit the validity of non-availability levels to specific time spans. After the specified time has passed, availability can increase.

Known Uses

Expertise Recommender (McDonald and Ackerman, 2000) is an infrastructure that supports the retrieval of experts for specific questions. Discovered experts can be contacted directly using an integrated synchronous chat system. To ensure privacy, the system provides *expert face management*: experts can enter their level of availability on a scale from *Available* to *Do not disturb*. The recommender software takes this information into account when selecting possible experts.

The expert face manager also includes a decay mechanism: users can control how long elapses before they become available again. This ensures that users do not forget to remove the "Don't Disturb" sign from their user representation.

MSN Messenger maintains a list of users who are connected to the system. Others can normally contact connected users, which results in a popup-message on the contacted user's screen.

Since this can be disturbing, for example when a user is giving a presentation using his connected computer, users can set their status to busy. All other users will see this by means of a small icon in the buddy list (Figure 3.51, right). However, other users can still contact the user who does not want to be disturbed: this can be important if the conversation cannot wait. The requesting user is informed that they should not expect an immediate reply (see the left-hand side of Figure 3.51), but interaction with the other user is still possible.

Online Games like Star Wars Galaxies (Sony Online Entertainment, 2003) allow the players to indicate that they are unavailable by typing the abbreviation *AFK*. The user will then be shown as *away from keyboard* (Figure 3.52).

The status is reset after the user again becomes active in the game.

Figure 3.51 MSN Messenger: Casco has indicated that he does not want to be disturbed

Figure 3.52 Unavailable user in Star Wars Galaxies.

Related Patterns

ATTENTION SCREEN$_{\rightarrow 3.3.4}$ solves a comparable problem, but filters requests for attention automatically before they can reach the local user.

AWAY MESSAGE$_{\to 4.5.6}$ provides information on the availability of another user after the first step of interaction has taken place. In contrast, AVAILABILITY STATUS provides this information before the user tries to contact the potentially unavailable user.

ALIVENESS INDICATOR$_{\to 4.5.5}$ shows when users are unavailable because of their absence.

COLLABORATIVE SESSION$_{\to 5.1.1}$ can use the availability indicators of AVAILABILITY STATUS to indicate a closed session or group.

3.3.4 ATTENTION SCREEN   *

Alternative name(s): Message Filter, Go Away (Goldman et al., 2002).

screen (skrēn), NOUN: **1.** A movable device, especially a framed construction such as a room divider or a decorative panel, designed to divide, conceal, or protect. **2. One that serves to protect, conceal, or divide: Security guards formed a screen around the President. A screen of evergreens afforded privacy from our neighbors. 3.** A coarse sieve used for sifting out fine particles, as of sand, gravel, or coal. **4.** A system for preliminary appraisal and selection of personnel as to their suitability for particular jobs.

Intent

Define who and what may take the user's attention.

Context

Other users provide information to a shared environment and users are consuming this information. Other users may feel the need to get in contact with a local user. To do so, they send information to the local user that catches their attention.

Problem

Every request for attention needs to be processed by the users, so it already takes some of their attention. In situations in which users need to focus their attention on other things, this is disturbing.

Scenario

Rodrigo really appreciates the new features for establishing quick sessions with other users who are connected to the community system. He now contacts the speech recognition expert Wil frequently and asks him questions about dialogue comprehension. This however disturbs Wil, especially when he is working on complex signal processing algorithms. Wil gets angry over the new features and asks Paul to remove these features from the system.

Symptoms

You should consider applying this pattern when . . .

— Information that is unrelated to the user's current task is pushed into the foreground.

— Meetings are interrupted by unrelated topics like a ringing telephone, or a colleague dropping in for a social chat.

— Users are disturbed by requests for attention and have problems focusing on their original topic again.

— Users are contacted by people that they don't want to interact with in the current situation.

Solution

Therefore: Allow users to filter the information that reaches them. Use meta-information such as sender details, or content information such as important keywords, to distinguish between important and unimportant information. Collect less important information at a place where the user can process it on demand and forward relevant information directly to the sender.

Dynamics

A *local user* defines *rules* for *incoming attention requests* (incoming messages or events). The rules define which attribute of the incoming request should be considered. A rule also defines which values lead to which level of attention. A rule could for example check the sender field of an e-mail message and calculate an importance value based on the sender's address. Methods for calculating the importance value include for example the comparison of an address with addresses stored in a BUDDY LIST$_{\rightarrow 3.1.7}$. In the simplest case the importance value is binary and indicates whether or not an action should take place.

Whenever an attention request is received, the local user's system checks the rules and weights the received request against the corresponding importance value. Based on the importance value, the local user's system decides what action needs to be performed in response to the attention request. Again, the simplest decision is to decide whether or not any action should take place. Examples of actions that can be associated to an importance level are:

— Specific audio signals or other ambient awareness information (Wisneski et al., 1998)

— Less or more obtrusive ways for propagating the message to the user

— Storage of the message in specific storage areas that can be displayed when the user has no other important task

— The removal of the request

Rationale

DeMarco and Lister (1999) pointed out that interruptions can drastically reduce productivity. They claimed that it takes approximately fifteen minutes to reach an ideal productivity level. A five-minute interruption therefore results in twenty minutes of reduced productivity. Jackson et al. (2003) studied the effects of interruptions by e-mail messages. They observed the e-mail behavior of sixteen employees and found out that the recovery time was much lower for e-mail interruptions (an average of 64 seconds). Even with such a short recovery time, this is still a significant factor.

Rules reduce the number of messages that are propagated directly to the user. This leads to fewer interruptions and keeps the local user focused to their current task unless there is an important event that requires immediate attention. The effect of the recovery time is reduced because users can actively decide to receive messages when they are unoccupied.

On the other hand, important messages are not delayed. This reduces the chance of missing an important request.

Check

When applying this pattern, you should answer these questions:

— What rules make sense in your context? Should the rules consider artifacts, users, or both?
— How should your users describe the rules? Will it be a simple dialog asking for properties of events, or will it be a more complex variant in which users *program* rules using a domain-specific language?
— Can you provide predefined rules that can be shared between all users?
— Where should you store the rules? Can you place them on a central server to allow use of the same rules independent of current client configuration?
— Can you provide users with a list of currently defined rules?

Danger Spots

The definition of rules can become too complicated for naive users.

Rules may classify important information incorrectly, resulting in it being ignored by the user. You should therefore not be too rigid when filtering the information. If for example only requests from users that are on the local user's BUDDY LIST$_{\rightarrow 3.1.7}$ are reaching the local user, they will no longer be able to establish new contacts. This would be crucial in a community system, because members are required to be open to other members.

Known Uses

Mozilla Junk Mail Filter. The junk mail filter in Mozilla[6] blocks incoming e-mail messages. Whenever a message is received by the Mozilla e-mail client, it is

---

[6]The source files for the junk mail filters are available at `http://lxr.mozilla.org/mozilla/source/mail/base/content/mailCommands.js#474` and `http://lxr.mozilla.org/mozilla/source/mailnews/extensions/bayesian-spam-filter/src/nsBayesianFilter.cpp`. The basic concept of the algorithm is a Bayesian Filtering approach. More information is provided by Graham (2002b).

analyzed using a user-trained junk mail filter. The result of this analysis is a decision over whether or not the message is a junk message. The user can control aspects of the filter by specifying attributes that should be considered during the analysis (see Figure 3.53). If the user for example provides an address book of trusted contacts, e-mail messages from these contacts are never considered as junk. Such an address book is called a *white list* in Mozilla, and is an implementation of the BUDDY LIST$_{\to 3.1.7}$ pattern.

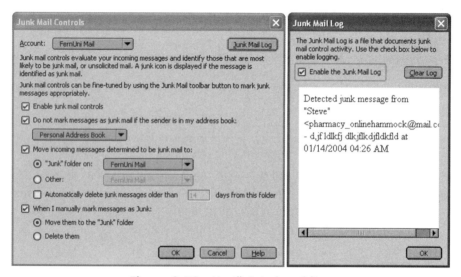

Figure 3.53 Mozilla's junk mail filter

Within the junk mail configuration dialog the user can also define an action that should take place if a message is classified as junk. Options include the removal of the message, moving the message to a specific folder, or marking the message as junk.

Instant messaging systems such as MSN Messenger, ICQ, AIM, or Jabber provide modes in which only messages from users who are on the BUDDY LIST$_{\to 3.1.7}$ are accepted. If other users not on the buddy list of the local user try to contact them, the local user is notified that an unknown user wants to get in contact with them. They can respond to the chat request in different ways:

— They can accept the request for the current session and allow the other user to communicate with them
— They can add the other user to their buddy list and thus allow the user to get in contact with them in the future

— They can add the other user to a block list, which contains those users who are not allowed to contact the local user. In this case, no more chat requests from this specific user will be transmitted to the local user.

WebWasher (https://www.webwasher.com/) is an example of a system that blocks specific content from the web, such as links to offensive content, banner advertisements, or specific media types like MP3 files. The user or the administrator first has to select the filtering criteria. WebWasher then filters specific responses according to these criteria and prohibits disturbing content from being transmitted to the user.

Online games often provide a means of filtering requests from other players. Examples are Guild Wars (ArenaNet, 2005), Star Wars Galaxies (Sony Online Entertainment, 2003), or World of Warcraft (Blizzard Entertainment, (europäische Server)). In each of these games the user can configure an "ignore list" to tell the game which of the other players should not be allowed to contact the local player. In Star Wars Galaxies the players can in addition block specific kinds of requests globally, such as an *invitation to trade*. This helps players to concentrate on their current mission in the game.

Related Patterns

AVAILABILITY STATUS$_{\to 3.3.3}$ also allows a user to express the fact that they do not want to be disturbed. Instead of filtering requests, however, the AVAILABILITY STATUS pattern relies on a social protocol and the status awareness of the user. If the local user does not want to be disturbed, they signal this to other users and the contacting user can decide whether or not they want to act against the local user's wishes.

BUDDY LIST$_{\to 3.1.7}$ defines the number of users who are considered as valuable communication partners by the local user.

BIRDS OF A FEATHER$_{\to 3.2.3}$ can be used to extend the list of allowed communication partners. If two users share many preferences, they are more likely to give their attention to each other.

MASQUERADE$_{\to 3.3.2}$ provides a means of interacting invisibly in the system. Whenever attention requests are based on the notion of co-presence (for example in instant messaging systems), other users will not be able to ask for the local user's attention, because they assume that the local user is not present.

FIREWALLS (Coplien and Harrison, 2004) argues for a specific role to shield members of a project team from external interaction partners. The rationale behind this is that at specific times the team should have a realm in which they can work on the group task at a high level of concentration and at a high pace.

3.3.5 Quick Goodbye *

Alternative name(s): Easy to Unsubscribe (Goldman et al., 2002)

good·bye (go͝od-bī'), NOUN: **1. An acknowledgment at parting, especially by saying "goodbye." 2.** An act of parting or leave-taking: *many sad goodbyes.*

Intent

Make it easy for a user to leave a group.

Context

Users are engaged in long-term group interaction.

Problem

The time span between a user's commitment to participate in a group interaction and their wish to terminate the commitment can be very long. Users can therefore forget how to leave the group.

Scenario

Gianna has been a member of the game engine community for some months now. She initially planned to find out more about game design, but now she sees that the technical discussions of the game developers are focusing more on software development in general. Unfortunately she has forgotten how to leave the community, and so she still receives messages from the community and propositions from other members to join collaborative sessions.

Symptoms

You should consider applying this pattern when ...

— Users contact other group members and ask them how they can leave the group.

— After an initial peak of activity, users become inactive and do not respond to requests. (Note that such users can be both lurkers and people who have forgotten how to get out of the group).

Solution

Therefore: Keep in mind that a user may leave a group at any time. Make it easy for them to leave the group and provide easy access to the required procedures. Do not require users to know the details of how the community system handles registrations.

Dynamics

The most important message of this pattern is that you should keep the unsubscription procedure simple and easy to find. When users are involved in group interaction, the information that they use during their interaction should include a reference to the unsubscription procedure. If the users communicate by e-mail, for example, you can add a link to the unsubscription procedure to the e-mail's footer. If they interact using a web-based system or a thick client, you should consider providing a menu button for leaving the group. This should not be hidden in sub-menus, but be accessible from the top level.

Leaving the group should not take any more effort than clicking on a single link or button. Do not ask for any information that the user provided a long time ago, such as a special password: they will in most cases no longer know this information. After the user initiates the exit procedure, the system should ask the user to confirm their wishes. If confirmed, the user is removed from the system, or marked as a former user in cases where their contributions and identity should remain visible to the rest of the group.

Rationale

Providing an easy way to leave the group will help to reduce the number of uninterested members. These are inactive people who will not respond to any actions and who—in contrast to lurkers—are no longer interested in what the group does. Providing a simple way for uninterested members to leave the group will make it easier for active group members to identify potential interaction partners.

At a technical level, the efforts wasted keeping uninterested group members updated will be reduced.

The group will no longer irritate uninterested group members. Knowing that you can leave a group easily may increase motivation to join the group in the first place.

An alternative to providing an easy way to leave the group could be to automatically remove user accounts after a specific period of inactivity. However, this is a bad idea, because inactive users may have good reasons for their inactivity.

Check

When applying this pattern, you should answer these questions:

— What steps are required in your process for leaving a group?
— Where should you put the information describing how to leave a group?
— Will you delete a departing user's account completely, or will you only mark it as inactive? If the former, what will happen to the places where the VIRTUAL ME$_{\rightarrow 3.1.5}$ of the departed user was previously shown?

Danger Spots

Even when unsubscription information is provided as part of every interaction in the community, it may still be too complicated for users to leave the community. For example, consider a mailing list that attaches a footer to each message in which the commands for unsubscription are mentioned. Many users will send the command to the wrong address, such as to the mailing list itself. Ron Goldman witnessed a huge number of such unsubscribe messages that were sent to the forum by mistake: "It is somewhat comic to receive a message from someone clearly trying to unsubscribe that includes directions on what they should have done." (Goldman et al., 2002) So, try to keep the unsubscription mechanism *really simple*.

Deleting user accounts from the system may be complicated because there may still be active references to the account. A user may, for example appear as the author of an artifact. Handling this sort of issue for users who leave the system is complicated. The system may either still show the user's name but state that the user is no longer a member, or it may show a null user.

It is difficult to allow a user to rejoin a group if their account has been deleted. If rejoining is important, you should only mark a departing user's account as deleted and restore it with full rights if the user decides to rejoin the community.

Known Uses

Yahoo Groups adds a link to each message that can be used to leave the group. Clicking the link opens a new e-mail with a predefined subject. After the user sends this e-mail, they receive a confirmation message. Replying to the confirmation message removes the user from the group. The reply is directed to a request- specific reply address by which the Yahoo Groups server can map the reply to the original request of the user.

Although it looks easy, this approach still has one pitfall: if the e-mail client of the user is configured to send e-mails from a different account, the Yahoo group will not be able to map the request to the requesting user. Unsubscription will fail in this case.

3.3.5 Quick Goodbye

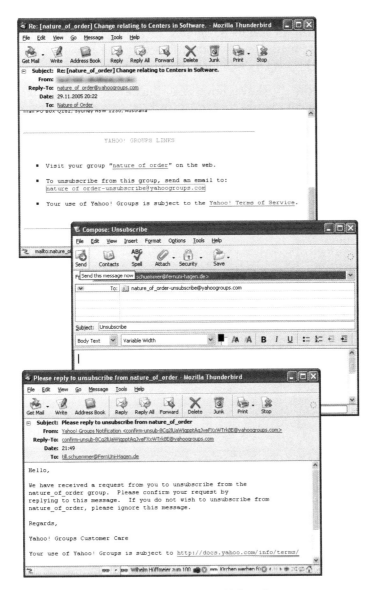

Figure 3.54 Leaving a Yahoo Group

Related Patterns

QUICK REGISTRATION$_{\to 3.1.1}$ explains how a user can easily enter a community.

QUALITY INSPECTION$_{\to 3.2.1}$ describes how users can be forced to leave a group.

ATTENTION SCREEN$_{\rightarrow 3.3.4}$ is an alternative if the user simply does not want to be disturbed by group members. In this case, they can shield themselves so that no further messages reach them but they still remain a member of the community. This makes "rejoining" the community easier.

ALIVENESS INDICATOR$_{\rightarrow 4.5.5}$ shows how to distinguish active from inactive users. From a community perspective, this can be sufficient to handle uninterested users.

3.3.6 Save me... applied

Paul identified two contexts in which users should be protected in the COGE community. According to the AVAILABILITY STATUS$_{\to 3.3.3}$ pattern, the users should be able to signal when they are unavailable for contact requests, and according to the QUICK GOODBYE$_{\to 3.3.5}$ pattern they should be free to quit their participation in the community at any time.

The implementation of AVAILABILITY STATUS was straightforward. Paul added a context menu to the user's VIRTUAL ME$_{\to 3.1.5}$ from which the user could select a status (Figure 3.55).

Figure 3.55 Availability Status

The implementation of the QUICK GOODBYE pattern was a bit more complicated. The pattern's danger spots became important in the context of the COGE community. Since users are visible as authors of source code, it is complex to completely remove a user's account. Even if Paul had decided to substitute a pseudonymous account, the stored information would no longer make sense. Remember that the authors' contributions are used as indicators for finding experts and that the authors also appear in the LETTER OF RECOMMENDATION$_{\to 3.2.2}$.

Therefore, Paul decided to follow another strategy: whenever a user left the community, their account was marked as deleted. In addition to this, another user was assigned as representative for the account, as demonstrated in Figure 3.56, which shows Paul as representative for Wil. This representative user takes over all rights and responsibilities for the departed user. To make the process of leaving the

Figure 3.56 Visualizing a user who has closed their account

community quick, the assignment of the representative is done initially by assigning a member of the project board. The board members can then look for BIRDS OF A FEATHER$_{\to 3.2.3}$ of the departed user and ask them to take over the responsibility.

From then on, whenever a user is shown who has left the community, the system also shows the representative, and contact requests to the user who has left are automatically redirected to the representative.

CHAPTER 4

Group Support

The previous chapter discussed the wide context of community interaction: we now focus on interaction in small groups. We have already discussed how membership of different communities results in rhythms of participation in a community. We can see the same properties at the group level: users arrive in a group and need to adapt their activities from single-user actions to group actions. They will then interact with the group and create or modify content collaboratively. This interaction takes place in rhythms that vary between close interaction and more independent work. The same is true for communication, which varies from ad-hoc short-term communication to long-term discussions. As pointed out by Gerosa et al. (2004), awareness is the essential glue for group interaction (see Figure 1.2 on page 8).

To approach the difference between single-actor and group-based actions, look at Figure 4.1. Humans are accustomed to use tools for achieving a specific goal. On the left of Figure 4.1, a single person has the goal of driving a nail into a piece of wood. The artifact of attention is the nail, the actor is the human. To achieve the goal, the actor makes use of a tool, the hammer. However, in the case of a professional actor, the tool will remain unnoticed Instead, the tool extends the capabilities of the actor

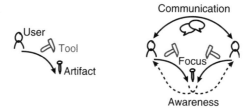

Figure 4.1 Single actor tool use versus group tool use

to drive nails into wood. The tool becomes part of the actor, or as the philosopher Martin Heidegger (1927) termed it, the tool becomes the *ready-to-hand*.

In group contexts we have to consider more than one actor. A group of actors uses tools to manipulate shared objects. The right hand of Figure 4.1 provides an example: both actors want to manipulate a nail. One could assume that the manipulation would take place in the same way as it took place in single-actor actions. However, this will in most cases not work: the group members have to communicate in order to coordinate their actions. They have to agree on a rhythm in which they manipulate the material. They also have to stay aware of the manipulations that other group members perform while they are not active. While the tool becomes invisible in single-actor actions, it has to be carefully observed in group interaction, and can no longer be used in the same way as it was used in single-user work. Probably more important, the feedback obtained from use of the tool before is no longer the only means of feedback. The nail in our example becomes a moving target and actors have to carefully observe this target.

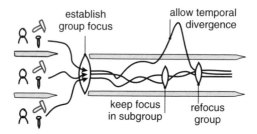

Figure 4.2 Interaction during the life cycle of a small group

If we extend this understanding of inter-actor interaction, we arrive at the model shown in Figure 4.2. Group members come from a context in which they work more or less independently of one another with their own tools and artifacts. In a group formation phase, the group members agree on the use of suitable tools and contribute initial artifacts to the group process. The lens in Figure 4.2 is a metaphor for this phase. Group members arrive from different directions and the lens aligns their paths such that collaboration can take place.

Users then start to interact. We show this as a set of intertwined paths in Figure 4.2. The vertical position on each path corresponds to the current focus, while the horizontal axis represents the temporal progress of the group. Group members will work with different coupling modes over time: tightly coupled synchronous work will interleave with loosely coupled asynchronous work. From time to time, the group needs to re-focus in order to confirm its current goals. It may also happen that group members leave the group for a while and return later.

Although this description is rather abstract, we see exactly these patterns in real-world computer-mediated interaction. As an example, consider the interaction diagram shown in Figure 4.3. It shows the strength of interaction between students in a three-month group project, which we were able to mine from interaction logs. (Details of the computation of the interaction strength can be found in (Schümmer et al., 2005)). The students collaborated over distance using a SHARED FILE REPOSITORY$_{\rightarrow 4.1.2}$ to share intermediate results.

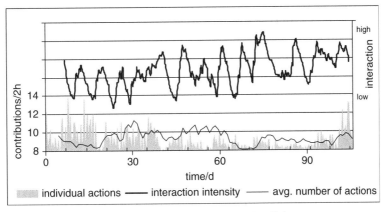

Figure 4.3 Interaction strength in a typical collaboration setting

The gray area in the diagram shows how many activities were performed within two hours. The thin curve in the lower part shows the floating average number of activities within an interval of 10 hours. The interesting fact that we can read from the diagram is the thick curve in the upper part. It shows that the group has found a regular rhythm of interaction. Peaks in the curve represent collaboration between different team members on semantically related artifacts at points close in time. Such activities relate to each other. These peaks alternate with local minima indicating that group members have worked on independent artifacts. We can also see that the group worked more intensively when milestones had to be reached. An example is the time period shortly after day 30, where the group had to deliver a first draft of their group result to the teacher.

In this chapter we will refine this model of computer-mediated interaction in small groups. We will look first at how interaction can take place in shared environments. This includes the discussion of tools for collaboration and the support of a few typical group processes. Section 4.2 focuses this discussion on places for collaboration, while Section 4.3 discusses communication support requirements. Finally, Sections 4.4 and 4.5 provide patterns for adding the *social glue* to the interaction: synchronous and asynchronous awareness mechanisms.

4.1 Touch me... or how to modify shared material together

Consider a typical part of our scenario, the COGE project, where tighter collaboration among community members becomes relevant:

> *Paul and Maurice have agreed to develop the virtual reality driver for the graphics engine together. Now they are looking for an environment that supports their work.*

From the model of group interaction that we described above we can assume that Paul and Maurice have so far been using their individual tools. They may also have created some artifacts that they will now bring into their collaboration.

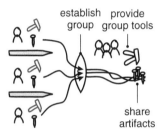

Figure 4.4 Collaborative actions on artifacts

Figure 4.4 provides more details of this phase. Individual users establish a common focus by contributing their background on tools and artifacts. They have identified coworkers and outlined the goals of the GROUP$_{\rightarrow 4.1.1}$. The artifacts are added to a shared artifact space so that all group members can potentially see and manipulate the artifacts.

The extent to which tools are added to the collaboration context depends on the desired strength of interaction. For loosely coupled (asynchronous) work, if is often sufficient to support the exchange of artifacts. Users retrieve a shared artifact from a SHARED FILE REPOSITORY$_{\rightarrow 4.1.2}$ and manipulate the artifact with their private tools. Afterwards, they share the results with the group. For tightly coupled interaction, users may need specialized tools that support synchronous exploration and manipulation of shared artifacts. Note that the need for loosely coupled and tightly coupled interaction will vary over time. In general, we can distinguish different modes of collaboration (Schümmer and Haake, 2001) in which the interaction is closer or looser (see the description of the TUKAN system on page 162).

These modes of collaboration map directly to the paths in Figure 4.4. They cross from time to time, which means that the users collaborate synchronously. In such situations the need for specialized group tools arises, symbolized by the hammer with two handles in Figure 4.4, which enables two group members to move the hammer together. Obviously, it is not the best possible tool for group support, but it shows that different levels of support can be imagined.

In general, the most important reasons for providing specialized group tools can be summarized as the:

— Need for working together on the same artifacts
— Need for exchanging artifacts in a group process
— Need for concurrent access to the artifacts
— Need to establish a common focus
— Need for sharing work in a group and structuring the individual participants' tasks in a group process

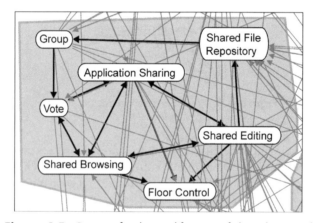

Figure 4.5 Patterns for the modification of shared material

The patterns in this section, shown in Figure 4.5, introduce the mechanics of the most widely used forms of collaboration used to inspect or manipulate shared artifacts. They are:

GROUP$_{\to 4.1.1}$ Allow users to manage groups and interact with a group in the same way in which they would interact with a user.

SHARED FILE REPOSITORY$_{\to 4.1.2}$ Allow users to collaborate over the use of files.

4.1 Touch me... or how to modify shared material together

SHARED BROWSING$_{\to 4.1.3}$ Explore an information space together with a teammate.

VOTE$_{\to 4.1.4}$ Quickly test the group's views on a specific question.

APPLICATION SHARING$_{\to 4.1.5}$ Enable synchronous interaction in single-user applications by replicating their user interface.

SHARED EDITING$_{\to 4.1.6}$ Allow users to edit shared data simultaneously.

FLOOR CONTROL$_{\to 4.1.7}$ Let only one user at a time act in the shared collaboration space.

4.1.1 GROUP *

Alternative name(s): Team

group (groop), NOUN: **1.** An assemblage of persons or objects gathered or located together; an aggregation: *a group of dinner guests; a group of buildings near the road.* **2.** Two or more figures that make up a unit or design, as in sculpture. **3. A number of individuals or things considered together because of similarities: a small group of supporters across the country. 4.** *Linguistics* A category of related languages that is less inclusive than a family. [...]

Intent

Allow users to manage groups and interact with a group in the same way in which they would interact with a user.

Context

Users interact in a community.

Problem

Interaction takes place among a set of users, but users are treated as individuals by the collaboration infrastructure. This makes it hard to develop group awareness.

Scenario

James and Rodrigo have become real gurus in dialogue interpretation. They implement most of the tricky speech recognition together, but it is only James who submits results to the version control system. Susan wants to invite the dialogue interpretation gurus to a meeting, but she only invites James. Rodrigo is disappointed.

Symptoms

You should consider applying this pattern when ...

— Participants for a COLLABORATIVE SESSION$_{\to 5.1.1}$ must be selected manually each time a session is planned.

— Users want to collaborate frequently with the same set of people.

— Users do not clearly know with whom they interact.

Solution

Therefore: Compose users into groups and name the group. Visualize the group composition. Allow users to manage groups and interact with a group in a same way in which they would interact with a single user.

Dynamics

Allow users to manage user groups. For that purpose, offer the following operations:

— Add users to a GROUP
— Remove users from a GROUP
— Create GROUPS
— Name GROUPS
— Remove GROUPS

Once a GROUP is created, it can appear in BUDDY LISTS$_{\to 3.1.7}$ or in USER LISTS$_{\to 4.4.1}$. In most cases, GROUPS are only visualized in BUDDY LISTS, while USER LISTS show individual users.

Offer all operations to GROUPS that are available for individual users.

Rationale

As GROUPS can be treated in the same way as users, it is possible to INVITE$_{\to 4.2.5}$ them to a COLLABORATIVE SESSION$_{\to 5.1.1}$. Furthermore, as GROUPS are visualized in the user interface, users always know with whom they are interacting.

Check

When applying this pattern, you should answer these questions:

— At which places will you visualize the GROUP and at which places will you show individual users?
— Will the GROUP be visible to non-group members, or will it be invisible to the rest of the community?
— What operations will you allow on GROUPS?
— Who will decide on group membership? Will you have a moderator, as in QUALITY INSPECTION$_{\to 3.2.1}$, or will group members be allowed to VOTE$_{\to 4.1.4}$ on group membership?

Danger Spots

The management of GROUPS may create additional workload for users.

GROUPS create strong borders which may isolate group members from the rest of the community.

As in the broader context of communities, you should think about implementing a means of expelling group members (see QUALITY INSPECTION$_{\rightarrow 3.2.1}$).

Known Uses

Skype, as well as most other communication tools like Microsoft Messenger, allows users to organize the users in their BUDDY LIST$_{\rightarrow 3.1.7}$ into groups. Just as for individual users, GROUPS can be selected as the recipients of actions.

Figure 4.6 Interacting with a GROUP in Skype

Figure 4.6 shows a list of groups in the Skype BUDDY LIST, with a group called "MAPPER e-team" selected. Users can start a conversation with all group members, or send a file to all group members.

Yahoo Groups allows users to create FORUMS$_{\rightarrow 4.3.2}$ for group communication. For group management, users can subscribe and unsubscribe to these FORUMS.

Related Patterns

ACTIVITY LOG$_{\rightarrow 4.5.1}$ A GROUP can be the actor in an activity that is stored in a ACTIVITY LOG. However, you should think carefully about whether it makes more sense to add multiple log entries for all group members whenever a group performs an activity.

COLLABORATIVE SESSION$_{\to 5.1.1}$ and INVITATION$_{\to 4.2.5}$ GROUPS can be invited to a COLLABORATIVE SESSION, with the effect that all group members join the session.

ROOM$_{\to 4.2.1}$ GROUPS can be associated with a ROOM where they meet for interaction. This gives all group members access to the room.

FORUM$_{\to 4.3.2}$ Group communication often takes place in a FORUM.

USER GALLERY$_{\to 3.1.6}$ GROUPS can appear in the USER GALLERY, which gives all members a better understanding of the community's social network.

BUDDY LIST$_{\to 3.1.7}$ and USER LIST$_{\to 4.4.1}$ GROUPS are visualized in these lists.

VIRTUAL ME$_{\to 3.1.5}$ GROUPS can present themselves to the community by creating a self-description. This self-description should provide pointers to all group members.

REWARD$_{\to 3.2.6}$ If you use a reward scheme, you should ensure that rewards can also be given to GROUPS.

COMPOSITE (Gamma et al., 1995). On a technical level, GROUPS can be treated as a COMPOSITE of users.

GROUP IDENTITY (Manns and Rising, 2005) argues that groups should become visible in order to raise the awareness of the groups' goals. The authors provide examples of how such a visibility can be achieved, for example by establishing a group FORUM, or by giving the group a website on which it is described (comparable to a VIRTUAL ME).

TEAM PRIDE (Coplien and Harrison, 2004) argues that teams should show a certain level of elitism, because such teams work harder to achieve a common goal.

4.1.2 SHARED FILE REPOSITORY **

Alternative name(s): Shared File System, Shared Workspace

re·pos·i·to·ry (rĭ-pŏz'ĭ-tôr'ē), NOUN: **1. A place where things may be put for safekeeping. 2.** A warehouse. **3.** A museum. **4.** A burial vault; a tomb. **5.** One that contains or is a store of something specified: *"Bone marrow is also the repository for some leukemias and lymphomas"* (Seth Rolbein). **6.** One who is entrusted with secrets or confidential information.

Intent

Allow users to collaborate over the use of files.

Context

Users collaboratively produce files.

Problem

Users share intermediate results by passing files to one or more users. Ensuring that every user stays in the loop is error-prone.

Scenario

The first approach for organizing the interaction between Paul and Charley was to agree on a common project structure. Each of them created folders on their computer where they stored their files. At regular intervals, Charley compressed the folders to a single archive and e-mailed this to Paul. Paul then compared this archive with his local files and updated them accordingly. However, Paul is tired of updating his files based on e-mail exchange.

Symptoms

You should consider applying this pattern when . . .

— Users exchange large e-mails with megabytes of attachments.
— Not all collaborating users have the most recent documents and thus collaboration is based on inconsistent documents.
— Files used for collaboration get lost.

Solution

Therefore: Provide a SHARED FILE REPOSITORY where users can place and retrieve files. Allow users to organize the files in folders.

Dynamics

The place for the SHARED FILE REPOSITORY can for example be a central server, or be based on a peer-to-peer architecture. Allow users to perform at least the following basic operations in the repository:

— Create files and folders
— Remove files and folders
— Rename files and folders
— Move files and folders
— List files and folders

Before changing a file, users create a local copy by downloading it to their own system. Then they use local tools to modify the file. When they have finished, they save the file locally. Before uploading the modified file to the repository, users or the system check whether another user has changed the file in the meantime. In the case of a changed file, the user compares the local version with the version in the repository to create a merged version that includes all changes. Finally, the user uploads the modified file.

Allow users to restrict and grant rights for performing the above operations on files and folders in the repository to individual users or GROUPS$_{\rightarrow 4.1.1}$. Store this information for each file and folder.

Rationale

As users can share the files that are necessary for collaboration via the SHARED FILE REPOSITORY, users no longer have to exchange large e-mail attachments and the files cannot get lost. If all users follow the process of downloading a file before changing it, a SHARED FILE REPOSITORY can also ensure that users have the most recent version of the file.

Check

When applying this pattern, you should answer these questions:

— What distribution architecture are you going to use for the SHARED FILE REPOSITORY, for example a central server or a peer-to-peer architecture?
— How are you going to control access to the repository?
— Are you going to manage multiple versions of files?

— Are you going to provide tools that support users when synchronizing the local copies with the files in the repository?

Danger Spots

Keeping local copies of files up to date is difficult and time-consuming. The system can support users in this task by offering a means of synchronizing local copies with the copies in the repository. For that purpose, the system can store meta-information about the file version in the repository as well as locally at the user's site and compare this meta-information for synchronization. When only the local file has been changed, the file is uploaded to the repository. When the file in the repository has been changed, the local copy is replaced with the most recent version. When the local file and the file in the repository have both been changed, the user has to resolve the conflict manually.

If different users modify the same file, this can lead to conflicts when uploading a modified file if another user has also already uploaded a newer version of the file. Such conflicts can be detected by using CONFLICT DETECTION$_{\rightarrow 5.3.3}$. However, resolving such conflicts manually can be difficult and time-consuming. To overcome this issue, the files in the repository can be locked for exclusive access (cf. PESSIMISTIC LOCKING$_{\rightarrow 5.3.1}$).

Users might need to know the evolution of a file. To allow users to retrieve the history of a file, use IMMUTABLE VERSIONS$_{\rightarrow 5.3.6}$.

Users may find it difficult to find new and updated files. To overcome this, integrate CHANGE INDICATORS$_{\rightarrow 4.5.4}$.

Known Uses

CVS (Concurrent Versioning System) (http://www.nongnu.org/cvs and **SubVersion** http://subversion.tigris.org) are SHARED FILE REPOSITORIES that offer a central server on which users can manage and organize files. In addition to the repository, both systems store all versions of the files and offer a means to manage and access the different versions.

FTP (File Transfer Protocol) (Postel and Reynolds, 1985) describes how to transfer files via the network and how to manage these files on a central server. FTP does not manage different versions of file, but allows access rights to the managed files to be granted or restricted. .

WebDAV (http://webdav.org) stands for **Web-based Distributed Authoring and Authoring**. Technically, WebDAV extends HTTP/1.1. (Fielding et al., 1999) with the aims of making the World Wide Web a readable and writable medium. For that purpose, WebDAV adds a set of methods to HTTP to allow file management (Goland et al., 1999). To avoid conflicts, WebDAV supports shared as well as exclusive locks.

Google Docs (http://docs.google.com/), as shown in Figure 4.7, is a web-based repository for sharing files. Users can upload their files and invite other users to collaborate on individual files or a set of files.

Figure 4.7 Sharing files in Google Docs

Google Docs does not support folders. Instead, files can be tagged with different keywords and the keywords can be used to filter the set of files shown.

Related Patterns

CENTRALIZED OBJECTS$_{\to 5.2.1}$ Files in the repository can be treated as CENTRALIZED OBJECTS.

CONFLICT DETECTION$_{\to 5.3.3}$ allows conflicts between a file in the repository and a local copy to be detected.

INTERACTION DIRECTORY$_{\to 4.2.3}$ allows users to look up SHARED FILE REPOSITORIES in which they might be interested.

LOGIN$_{\to 3.1.2}$ identifies users and determines their access rights.

USER LIST$_{\to 4.4.1}$ can be used to associate the files in the file repository with the users who currently use the files. A USER LIST can be applied to different levels in the folder hierarchy of a SHARED FILE REPOSITORY to show participation, not only for individual files, but also for a group of files.

PESSIMISTIC LOCKING $_{\to 5.3.1}$ can be used to ensure that only one user at a time can modify a file in the repository, avoiding conflicts.

FILE AUTHORIZATION (Schumacher et al., 2005) describes how access control can be implemented on a shared file repository.

LIMITED ACCESS (Schumacher et al., 2005) argues that only those operations that can be performed by a user should be shown in a graphical user interface. The pattern provides an example of a SHARED FILE REPOSITORY in which only the owners of a file can modify the file.

4.1.3 SHARED BROWSING *

Alternative name(s): Collaborative Browsing, Travel Together

browse (brouz), INTRANSITIVE VERB: **1a.** To inspect something leisurely and casually: *browsed through the map collection for items of interest.* **b.** To read something superficially by selecting passages at random: *browsed through the report during lunch.* **2.** To feed on leaves, young shoots, and other vegetation; graze.

Intent

Explore an information space together with a team mate.

Context

Users of your application have different degrees of knowledge about the data or the virtual environment that is presented in the application. Now you are thinking about ways to ease their orientation in the environment.

Problem

Users have problems finding relevant information in a collaboration space. They often get lost.

Scenario

Michelle is a PhD student interested in document exchange formats. She became interested in the game engine project after she heard that Ana and Maurice were working on Virtual Reality Modeling Language (VRML) export features. She asks Ana if she can join her and Maurice in the development. Ana and Maurice are happy to welcome Michele as a new developer, but on the other hand regret that Michele cannot really help, because she often gets lost when browsing through the project documents and source code.

Symptoms

You should consider applying this pattern when ...

— Users take a long time to find the information that they are looking for.

- Different users have different degrees of previous knowledge of the information environment. This leads to different orientation skills in specific parts of the collaborative environment, and users with less skill get lost.
- The goal is to find the information as a group, but several group members duplicate efforts to reach this goal.
- Navigation demands creative decisions in selecting the right trails but single users do not have the creativity they need to tell them where to search for the desired information.
- Users want to talk about shared artifacts, but do not know how to ensure that their peer user sees the same artifact.

Solution

Therefore: Browse through the information space together. Provide a means for communication, and collaborative browsers that show the same information at each client's site.

Dynamics

User collaborate in a shared information space. This can be a document (with a spatial layout) or a set of documents that are distributed in a collaborative information space. When interacting with a specific chunk of information, users position themselves at this chunk. If it is a document, they see a specific part of the document. In the case of a larger information space, they focus their interest on one specific document or artifact in this information space.

The position of each user can be described as a location. This can be a URL in the case of the web, it can be a file name in the case of a shared workspace, it can be a point in case of a two-dimensional document, for example a drawing, or it can be an index in a linear document, for example the 1769th character of a text document.

The collaborative browser communicates and shares the viewing positions of each user in the group. How this information is processed depends on the navigation strategy of the collaborative browser. Examples of different navigation strategies in collaborative browsing are:

Master-slave browsing in which one user "drives" and the other users follow. Whenever the master user updates the position, this position is also set for all slave users. This method of collaborative browsing is suitable in situations such as those in which newcomers should be guided through the information space by an expert.

Anarchistic browsing that does not have any roles. Whenever one user moves to a new location, all other users follow. This is suitable when a group is seeking for information together and all group members have the same level of knowledge of the information space. It is also a strategy that is often used in collaborative diagram editors where the users share the scroll position.

Democratic browsing in which the group has to form a collaborative opinion first before its members move on to the next artifact (VOTE$_{\rightarrow 4.1.4}$). This strategy is only suitable for contexts in which navigation is a heavyweight activity. An example could be a collaborative web browser: whenever a user follows a link, the remainder of the group has to agree on whether to follow. If you contrast the case of a shared diagram, it would not make much sense to vote on a new scroll position after one user drags the scroll bar.

Rationale

In a study of traditional libraries, Twidale et al. (1997) showed that browsing should be a collaborative action. Although many searches for information is carried out alone in such places, Twidale et al. (1997) show that interaction between users also takes place.

Since collaborative browsers always show the same artifacts, their users will be able to communicate about the content shown. This helps them to understand the artifacts better. When a user navigates to another artifact, all other users follow, which ensures that the group remains focused on the same artifact.

By discussing the route, the team will choose the most appropriate path. Since many users traveled together, there is a better history of the steps taken.

In the case of SHARED EDITORS, as well as in the case of more coarse-grained information spaces, coupled navigation makes it easier to talk about the information that is shown on the screen.

Check

When applying this pattern, you should answer these questions:

— How should you represent the view location? Can you use a URL or a coordinate?
— Which browsing strategies will you offer the users?
— If you are using a master-slave browsing approach, how will you decide on who is the master?

Danger Spots

Since all browsers are coupled, the group will always travel at the same pace. This can be a problem if the various users' comprehension speed of the browsed artifacts differs significantly. In this case, fast users can feel obstructed by slower users.

Users may also be annoyed by not being able to leave the group's location for a personal detour. You should therefore make it easy to leave the COLLABORATIVE SESSION and re-enter it after such a detour.

Known Uses

TUKAN (Schümmer, 2001) is a collaborative software development environment. It informs programmers of the presence of other programmers to support dynamic group formation. After users have met, they can navigate through the source code using a tightly coupled browser. Whenever one user selects a class or a method, the browsers of all connected users are also directed to the selected class or method. Within the method, the users can read independently—that is, the scroll positions of the text panes are not coupled.

During collaborative exploration of the source code, developers can communicate about the code fragments shown using an integrated chat tool.

CobWeb (Stotts et al., 1998) allows a group of users to browse web pages together. It uses two frames in a standard web browser: the content is shown in one frame of the browser, while the other frame is used to control the browsing. This frame also includes a means for requesting the floor (see FLOOR CONTROL$_{\to 4.1.7}$).

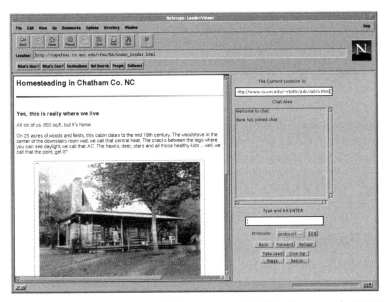

Figure 4.8 Collaborative web browsing in CobWeb (Stotts et al., 1998)

A special feature of CobWeb is that it allows the system developer to model interaction models for collaborative browsing. This approach provides a flexible means for designing all interaction processes discussed above.

GroupScape (Graham, 1997) and CoWeb (Jacobs et al., 1996) are comparable to the CobWeb system. Both systems also support collaborative synchronous browsing of the web.

efa (Lukosch and Schümmer, 2006) is a web-based presentation system in which students can rehearse seminar talks over distance. Talks are prepared asynchronously using the built-in Wiki authoring features of the system.

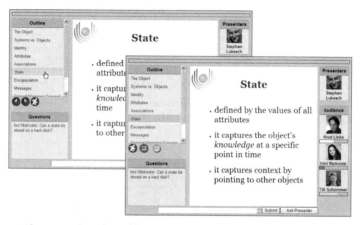

Figure 4.9 Shared browsing in the presentation system efa

In a synchronous session, one user takes the role of the presenter. The presenter can select slides from the outline of the presentation or by means of the navigation buttons (on the left of Figure 4.9). After selecting the page, the views of the participants are updated accordingly so that all users see the same slides. The right-hand side of Figure 4.9 shows the participant's view of the presentation. Note that the participant does not see navigation buttons.

Related Patterns

APPLICATION SHARING$_{\to 4.1.5}$ is the general concept of using an application together with another user and seeing exactly the same application state at each point in time.

SHARED EDITING$_{\to 4.1.6}$ When modifying a shared document collaboratively, you should consider applying SHARED EDITING, in which the scroll bars are coupled using the SHARED BROWSING pattern.

REMOTE FIELD OF VISION$_{\to 4.4.5}$ is an alternative for sharing the positions of other users in a shared document. Instead of coupling the locations of the different users, they are visualized such that each user can always see which parts of other users' fields of vision overlap their own view.

COLLABORATIVE SESSION$_{\rightarrow 5.1.1}$ Browsing takes place in a COLLABORATIVE SESSION that defines who is currently participating in the group.

FLOOR CONTROL$_{\rightarrow 4.1.7}$ can be used to define who is currently allowed to move through the information space, especially in master-slave browsing.

VOTE$_{\rightarrow 4.1.4}$ is used in democratic browsing to decide on a change in location.

EMBEDDED CHAT$_{\rightarrow 4.3.1}$ supports users in discussions about shared information.

REPLAY$_{\rightarrow 5.1.4}$ The trails of a group can be important for understanding group activities later. You could think about recording the different browsing activities in an ACTIVITY LOG$_{\rightarrow 4.5.1}$ and REPLAY them to other users. This would make it possible to create guided tours through the information space.

JIGSAW (Asensio et al., 2004) is comparable to collaborative browsing in that a group wants to explore a collaborative information space together. The difference is that each group member explores parts of the space individually and then shares the relevant results with the group.

4.1.4 VOTE *

Alternative name(s): Poll, Election, Ballot

vote (vōt), NOUN: **1a.** A formal expression of preference for a candidate for office or for a proposed resolution of an issue. **b.** A means by which such a preference is made known, such as a raised hand or a marked ballot. **2.** The number of votes cast in an election or to resolve an issue: *a heavy vote in favor of the bill.* **3.** A group of voters alike in some way: *the Black vote; the rural vote.* **4. The act or process of voting: took a vote on the issue. 5.** The result of an election or referendum. **6.** The right to participate as a voter; suffrage.

Intent

Quickly test the group's views on a specific question.

Context

You have established a community and equipped them with an environment in which community members can share their thoughts.

Problem

It is hard to work out the distribution of opinions in the community. However, good understanding of other users' attitudes can be important when making decisions.

Scenario

Liam, Paul, and Ana are not sure whether or not they should upgrade the game engine core to a new operating system version. The problem is that this upgrade would make it incompatible with older machines. On the other hand, it would speed up the game engine tremendously. What shall they do?

Symptoms

You should consider applying this pattern when ...

— Uncertainty of users' experiences lead to repetitive actions.

— Users are unsure about the most appropriate strategy for a community action.

— Decisions made in the community are discussed controversially and shown to be wrong after the discourse took place.

Solution

Therefore: Provide an easy means of setting up and running a poll. Show a virtual ballot in a prominent place in the community. After the vote is over, present the result.

Dynamics

One user sets up an election by stating a question and a set of possible answers. The creator of the election also defines when users can vote and whether users can see intermediate results of the election. The time frame for voting can be defined using explicit dates or quorum information. In the latter case, the election ends when a required quorum is reached, for example when 50% of all eligible voters have voted *yes* or *no*.

The question is sent to all participants in the community or shown when users enter the community's workspace. Users can place their vote by selecting the most appropriate alternative. This vote is counted and the system tracks the fact that the specific user has voted. If users are allowed to see intermediate results, they are directed to a results page directly after they submit their ballot.

In cases in which it is important who voted for which option, you should track the voters' identities whenever a vote is placed. This will make the object structures used to represent the election model more complicated. Instead of just counting the votes for each option, you then have to store the user objects in a set of voters for each option.

When the election is finished, the result is shown to all users in the same way as it was announced.

Rationale

When asked to vote, users will reflect on their own attitude to the question. If the process of voting is kept simple (for example a single mouse click), they will be eager to place their vote in most cases. By comparing their own decision with the community's decision, the users will better understand their position in the community and how other users judge the question.

Check

When applying this pattern, you should answer these questions:

— Do you have different quorums in your community culture, or is there a well-defined quorum for all elections?

— Are all registered users eligible? If not, how do you calculate the set of eligible voters?

— How should you announce an election? Do you know all your users and can you send them all a message?

— Does it make sense to remind users to vote shortly before the election is finished?

— How should you present intermediate results? Can you use a graphical visualization such as a bar chart?

— Are there any actions that should be triggered at the end of an election? If yes, can these actions be automated?

— How should you handle users who do not vote? Will you terminate the vote at a specific point in time? If yes, ensure that you tell users who have not yet voted how much time is left to submit a vote.

Danger Spots

Allowing users to see intermediate results can influence the voting behavior of users who have not yet voted.

The automatic termination of an election after a specific quorum is reached also can be problematic. Small nuances can be important for future decisions, particularly when the election should shed light on the community's feelings.

Users might not really understand what they are voting for or how important the VOTE is. However, the VOTES of such users influence the final result.

Known Uses

The starcraft community site (http://starcraft.org/) has a weekly poll on the community's entry page, There is a menu bar next to the daily news that includes a question and possible answers. After selecting an answer, the user can see the intermediate result of the poll (see Figure 4.10).

The results of the poll sometimes provide the headlines for the news shown on the entry page, as was the case in Figure 4.10.

PoliTeam (Stiemerling and Wulf, 2000) uses votes to negotiate access permissions to artifacts in groupware systems. Whenever users want to access an artifact for which they have no explicit access rights, they can create a poll. All users who *can* access the artifact are asked whether or not they want to grant access to the requesting user. As soon as a majority is reached, the requesting user is informed and the access rights are granted. All voting users can be informed of the result of the poll.

efa (Lukosch and Schümmer, 2006) is a web-based presentation system in which users can collaboratively rehearse seminar presentations.

efa makes use of elections at two different points in the presentation process:

— Before the presentation, users can elect the presenter from users that volunteered for this role. All users see an election screen, shown on

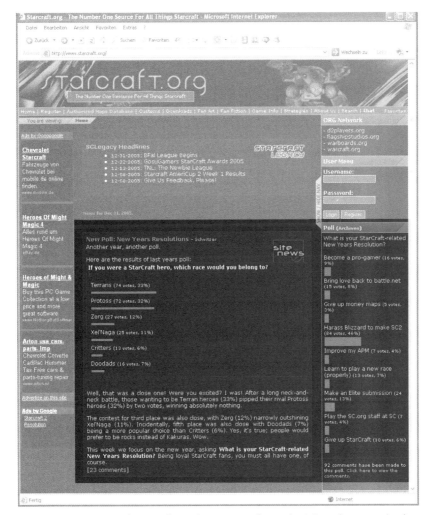

Figure 4.10 An intermediate poll result at starcraft.org (right) and an article discussing the result of the previous week's poll

the left-hand side of Figure 4.11. After a majority is reached, the user will become a presenter. This example shows how votes are used for coordinating the group process.

— During a presentation, users can express their level of understanding by pressing the smiley buttons, shown in the centre of Figure 4.11. This decreases or increases the personal level of understanding, which is shown below the user names in the user list on the right of Figure 4.11.

 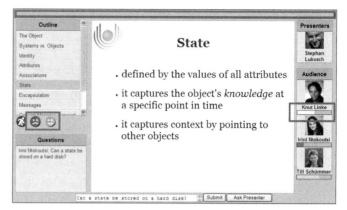

Figure 4.11 Voting in the collaborative presentation system efa

The average of all users' understanding levels is shown as a vote on the current quality of the presentation, the bar at the top border in Figure 4.11.

Lotus Sametime (http://www.lotus.com/sametime) includes a conferencing tool in which users can discuss content, collaboratively construct diagrams using a SHARED EDITOR, or shared proprietary applications using APPLICATION SHARING$_{\rightarrow 4.1.5}$ mechanisms. At any point in time, the moderator can initiate a poll by simply providing a question. This question can then be sent to all participants of the current COLLABORATIVE SESSION$_{\rightarrow 5.1.1}$, which displays a pop-up window to participants for providing an answer to the poll. Answers can either be collected anonymous or with the user's identity.

Digital Moderation (http://digital-moderation.com) is a system for supporting group facilitation, from small workshops with five people up to large events with more than 500 participants, and for both collocated and virtual meetings. Digital Moderation offers a wide range of facilitation tools, including a range of voting tools.

The simplest voting tool is a "discrete vote": users can select one answer from the given set. A matrix can be used for voting on two interdependent criteria. Voting can also be used on a list of ideas, generated during a preceding brainstorming session, to rank the ideas according to a given criterion.

Before the meeting, the facilitator uses an editor to select and configure the tools that will be used in the meeting, and for preparing the meeting script (see the top of Figure 4.12). If necessary, the configuration can be adapted during the session, and also new tools inserted, for example if a decision needs to be made that was not foreseen when the meeting was planned.

4.1.4 Vote 213

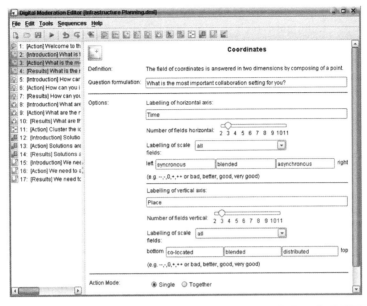

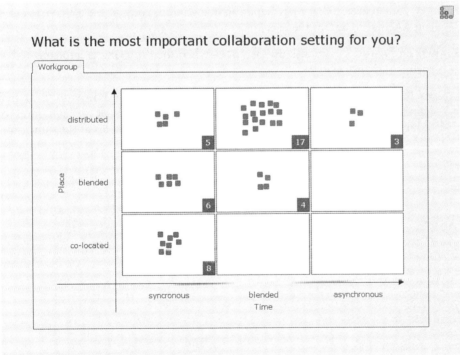

Figure 4.12 In *Digital Moderation*, participants can place virtual dots to vote. The image shows the vote set-up (top) and the casting of votes (bottom)

In general, voting is based on the metaphor known from paper-based facilitation techniques such as the *Metaplan* method, which is well-known in Germany: to cast a vote, participants place a virtual *dot* on the item they choose (see bottom of Figure 4.12). Depending on the tool and its current configuration, participants are allowed to place one or more dots. In collocated meetings several people can share a single computer to enter their answers. In this case—depending on the situation—people are asked to agree on a common vote, or, if the system is so configured, can take turns to each submit their own vote.

To avoid distraction during voting, the results are shown after all participants have submitted their votes.

Related Patterns

LETTER OF RECOMMENDATION$_{\to 3.2.2}$ is a vote on the interaction qualities of a specific user, since all ratings are accumulated as an overall recommendation level.

COLLABORATIVE SESSION$_{\to 5.1.1}$ A vote can be modeled as a collaborative session.

BELL$_{\to 4.2.4}$ When users ask for participation in a session, you can use a VOTE to agree on whether to accept the user.

SHARED BROWSING$_{\to 4.1.3}$ makes use of VOTES when the browsing is implemented as democratic browsing.

LOVELY BAGS$_{\to 5.3.5}$ The choice of each vote can be stored in a LOVELY BAG that contains vote objects for each user in order to provide a high level of concurrency—that is, users should be able to cast their votes at the same time.

4.1.5 Application Sharing **

ap·pli·ca·tion (ăp'lĭ-kā'shən), NOUN: **1.** The act of applying. **2.** Something applied, such as a cosmetic or curative agent. **3a.** The act of putting something to a special use or purpose: *an application of a new method*. **b.** A specific use to which something is put: *the application of science to industry*. **4.** The capacity of being usable; relevance: *Geometry has practical application in aviation and navigation*. **5.** Close attention; diligence: *shows application to her work*. **6a.** A request, as for assistance, employment, or admission to a school. **b.** The form or document on which such a request is made. **7. Computer Science A computer program with a user interface.**

Intent

Enable synchronous interaction in single-user applications by replicating their user interface.

Context

Users are geographically distributed and want to collaborate on data that can only be edited with domain-specific single-user applications.

Problem

Users are working with a domain-specific single-user application. The need for synchronous collaboration emerges, but the single-user application does not support this.

Scenario

Maurice lives in Brazil and thinks that he has found a bug in the VRML export routines. He has tested the defective part of the export driver but is not totally sure about its behavior. It would be good if George, one of the test experts in London, could have a look at Maurice's test application. London is a long way from Brazil, however.

Symptoms

You should consider applying this pattern when . . .

— Users want to collaborate using proprietary single-user applications.
— Users want to discuss what they see on their screen with others.

— Users need help with using a single-user application, but a helpful user is far away.

Solution

Therefore: Observe user interface output and input streams and replicate these to the remote users' machines.

Dynamics

One user decides to share an application, or his complete desktop, with another user. At the sharing user's site an application-sharing server captures the user interface output and input streams. The output stream is typically the graphical rendering of the views and the input stream is a sequence of mouse and keyboard events. Other users can connect to this application-sharing server by using an application-sharing client. From then on the application-sharing server sends the output stream to all connected users. At the sites of the connected users the application-sharing client uses this information to visualize the user interface captured in the output stream.

When the remote users connected to the application-sharing server want to change any content in the application, they first have to request the right to modify it. This can be implemented by using FLOOR CONTROL$_{\rightarrow 4.1.7}$. As soon as a user is allowed to modify the content, the application-sharing client captures the remote user's input stream and sends it to the application-sharing server. When the application-sharing server receives the remote input, it applies it locally. The effects of the input are again captured and replicated.

Rationale

As any application can be shared using the APPLICATION SHARING approach, users can interact synchronously in their proprietary single-user applications and share the user interface of their application to enable discussion.

Check

When applying this pattern, you should answer these questions:

— Will you share individual applications or the complete desktop?
— How are you going to capture the output stream of the user interface for replication?
— Are you going to update the whole user interface whenever a change occurs, or are you going to distribute the change only? In the latter case, how are you going to identify the changes in the shared user interface?
— How are you going to apply the remote input to the shared application?

Danger Spots

Replicating the output stream of a user interface requires a lot of network bandwidth. If the available bandwidth is too small, reduce the screen resolution and the color depth when replicating the output stream to save bandwidth.

Some users might not want to share their whole desktop, for example because of privacy issues. Therefore, distinguish between sharing a single window and sharing the whole desktop.

The model of the shared application is only available to the user that is sharing their user interface. At the end of the collaboration the result is only available to this user. Therefore think about mechanisms for distributing the results to all participating users.

As only the user interface of one user is replicated, the application cannot offer any special group services that support collaboration or make users aware of each other's actions. Such applications are called *collaboration-transparent* (Lauwers and Lantz, 1990). To better support group process and collaboration, think about implementing a collaboration-aware application, for example by enabling SHARED EDITING$_{\rightarrow 4.1.6}$.

When using APPLICATION SHARING only one user can modify the shared content at a time. SHARED EDITING$_{\rightarrow 4.1.6}$ describes how to overcome this issue and allow concurrent interaction.

Known Uses

HP SharedX (Garfinkel et al., 1994) allows sharing of applications between remote users and displays by extending the X Window System (Gettys et al., 1990). HP SharedX consists of the HP SharedX user interface, known as the *connector*, the HP SharedX receiver service, and the HP SharedX extension to the X server. The connector allows the user that shares an application to control which windows are shared or which users are allowed to generate input. The receiver service simplifies sharing windows and increases security. The HP SharedX extension is a low-level mechanism that is responsible for sharing windows, keeping them up to date, and merging input from interacting users.

Microsoft NetMeeting (Summers, 1999) allows sharing of applications that are running under Microsoft Windows. NetMeeting conforms to the ITU T.128 recommendation for Multipoint Application Sharing, which was proposed by Microsoft and PictureTel. The ITU T.128 facilitates display broadcasting: the protocol used is similar to the X protocol used in the X Window System (Gettys et al., 1990).

Figure 4.13 shows the view that a user who is using another user's spreadsheet application remotely sees. Netmeeting only transmits the display data from the local user to the remote user. Elements currently not visible on the local user's

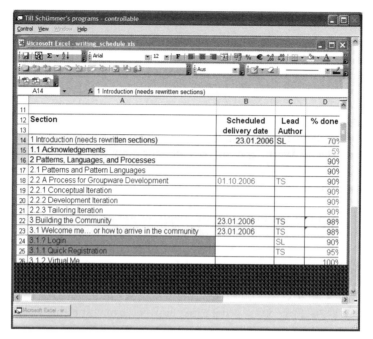

Figure 4.13 Application sharing in Microsoft Netmeeting

screen will not be shown to the remote user either. Instead, Netmeeting shows a default pattern to signal to the remote user that the the shared application window has invisible parts, shown in the lower part of Figure 4.13.

RealVNC (Richardson et al., 1998) (http://www.realvnc.com/) stands for real virtual network computing. RealVNC was developed as remote control software that allows you to view and interact with one computer (the *server*) from another computer using a simple program (the *viewer*). RealVNC also allows a group of users to connect to the VNC server and to collaborate.

Related Patterns

SHARED EDITING$_{\to 4.1.6}$ and SHARED BROWSING$_{\to 4.1.3}$ describe more sophisticated ways to interact synchronously and keep users aware of working in a group.

FLOOR CONTROL$_{\to 4.1.7}$ describes how the right to modify the content can be passed between interacting users.

REPLICATED OBJECTS$_{\to 5.2.3}$ and MEDIATED UPDATES$_{\to 5.2.5}$ describe how to replicate the output stream.

4.1.6 SHARED EDITING **

ed·i·tor (ĕd´ĭ-tər), NOUN: **1.** One who edits, especially as an occupation. **2.** One who writes editorials. **3.** A device for editing film, consisting basically of a splicer and viewer. **4. Computer Science A program used to edit text or data files.**

Intent

Allow users to edit shared data simultaneously.

Context

Users are geographically distributed and want to collaborate synchronously on shared data.

Problem

Users are sharing data for collaboration. The need to edit the shared data simultaneously emerges, but the shared single-user application (see APPLICATION SHARING$_{\rightarrow 4.1.5}$) does not allow concurrent editing.

Scenario

Maurice is continued his work on the VRML export driver of the virtual reality engine. Most of his tasks are straightforward so he can implement them over a cup of coffee. He suddenly comes across a difficult triangulation problem, however. He would like to solve this problem in collaboration with Paul, but Paul is currently on a business trip and can only be reached via the Internet. So Maurice sends Paul an e-mail with his questions and proposes some edits. Paul has different ideas and proposes additional edits. After several dozen such iterations, they agree on a solution. How much easier would it have been if they could have interacted in a pair-programming style as if they were both located in front of the same computer with joint access to the keyboard.

Symptoms

You should consider applying this pattern when . . .

— Users want to modify shared data synchronously.
— Users do not feel as if they are collaborating with a group.
— APPLICATION SHARING$_{\rightarrow 4.1.5}$ is inappropriate because

- Users want to interact synchronously
- Users are complaining that they are not aware of the group
- The performance of the shared application is too low

Solution

Therefore: Provide a shared editor in which users can manipulate the shared artifacts together. Ensure that state changes are instantly reflected in all other users' editors, and provide mechanisms that make users aware of each other.

Dynamics

The shared editor allows shared artifacts to be manipulated. Assuming that the shared editor is using the MODEL-VIEW-CONTROLLER pattern (Krasner and Pope, 1988; Buschmann et al., 1996), the model represents the shared artifacts of the application. To share the model among collaborating users it can be implemented as CENTRALIZED OBJECTS$_{\rightarrow 5.2.1}$ or REPLICATED OBJECTS$_{\rightarrow 5.2.3}$. The shared editor provides controllers for performing actions on the shared objects and views to visualize the effects of actions in the user interface.

State changes are instantly reflected in all shared editors to enable synchronous editing of the model. In the case of CENTRALIZED OBJECTS$_{\rightarrow 5.2.1}$, the shared editor has to use REMOTE SUBSCRIPTION$_{\rightarrow 5.2.2}$ to invalidate the view and display the most recent state of the application (see Figure 4.14 a). In the case of REPLICATED OBJECTS$_{\rightarrow 5.2.3}$, a state change results in an update message that is transferred via the network by either DECENTRALIZED UPDATES$_{\rightarrow 5.2.6}$ or MEDIATED UPDATES$_{\rightarrow 5.2.5}$. These update messages trigger an invalidation of the view to display the most recent state of the application (see Figure 4.14 b).

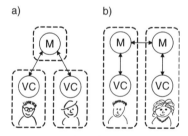

Figure 4.14 Distributed MODEL-VIEW-CONTROLLER

One problem with shared editors is that the users have their own input control flow. This means that the user interface at each local user's computer receives input events such as mouse movements, clicks, or keyboard events. These events are traditionally handled by an input controller that interprets the events and modifies the corresponding model objects. The modified model object results in the need to invalidate the visualization of the model on the screen. This behavior can be found in all modern user interfaces that follow the MODEL-VIEW-CONTROLLER pattern.

In the case of the shared editor, there can be more than one input event at the same time. Because the events need to be distributed by a network, they can reach different computers in different orders. When implementing a shared editor, you therefore have to structure the input and avoid inconsistencies in the shared data by one of the following:

— Only allowing sequential input (see FLOOR CONTROL$_{\to 4.1.7}$)
— Only allowing one user at a time to modify specific, but not all, shared artifacts (see PESSIMISTIC LOCKING$_{\to 5.3.1}$)
— By reordering and restoring conflicting input after it is detected (see OPTIMISTIC CONCURRENCY CONTROL$_{\to 5.3.2}$ and CONFLICT DETECTION$_{\to 5.3.3}$)

Once you have ensured consistent behavior, you should let users feel that they are collaborating in a group. For that purpose, special user interface widgets can be added to the shared editor: see REMOTE CURSOR$_{\to 4.4.7}$, TELEPOINTER$_{\to 4.4.8}$, REMOTE SELECTION$_{\to 4.4.6}$, and REMOTE FIELD OF VISION$_{\to 4.4.5}$.

Rationale

By sharing the model of an editor and structuring the input to ensure consistency, users can edit shared data in parallel. Compared to APPLICATION SHARING$_{\to 4.1.5}$, it is possible to design the user interface so that it fosters group awareness and gives users the feeling of working in a group. Additionally, the performance of the shared editor is increased compared to shared applications. This is due to the fact that only update messages about changes to the model need to be distributed, instead of complete updates of the view, which requires much more network bandwidth. Implementing the model as REPLICATED OBJECTS$_{\to 5.2.3}$ further improves the response time of the shared editor, as read operations can be performed locally, allowing the local view to be updated without accessing the Internet.

Danger Spots

When sharing the complete model of the editor, each user has an identical view, including the window size of the editor, the scroll-bar position, and so on. Stefik et al. (1987) consider this as *strict* WYSIWIS (what you see is what I see). In some cases, strict WYSIWIS cannot be achieved, for example when the maximum screen resolution is not the same at each participating site, so that some users might not be able to see the full editor window. Additionally, users often want to configure their workspace or application individually. In the case of strict WYSIWIS this can lead to so-called *scroll-wars* or *window-wars*. To overcome these issues, Stefik et al. (1987) introduced the concept of *relaxed WYSIWIS*. This kind of WYSIWIS allows users to have private models aside from the shared model. Figure 4.15 illustrates this for two collaborating users. Each user has a shared model and also some private model objects.

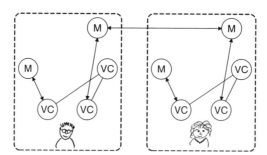

Figure 4.15 Distributed MODEL-VIEW-CONTROLLER with relaxed WYSIWIS

Users might be used to their single-user applications. Before implementing and introducing a shared editor to enable synchronous editing of shared data, it should be absolutely clear that users want to use this editor permanently. If not, enabling collaboration by applying APPLICATION SHARING$_{\to 4.1.5}$ should be considered.

Check

When applying this pattern, you should answer these questions:

— Are you going to use CENTRALIZED OBJECTS$_{\to 5.2.1}$ or REPLICATED OBJECTS$_{\to 5.2.3}$?
— How are you going to structure the input and avoid inconsistencies in the shared data?
— How are you going to support group awareness?
— Are you going to implement strict or relaxed WYSIWIS?

Known Uses

GroupDesign (Karsenty et al., 1993) is a multiuser drawing tool and one of the first editors to allow SHARED EDITING. GroupDesign is based on a purely replicated architecture—a replica of the application runs at each site participating in the COLLABORATIVE SESSION$_{\to 5.1.1}$.

Shared Whiteboards like the shared whiteboard of the NetMeeting Conferencing system (Summers, 1999) (Figure 4.16) support a group in creating drawings together. Each user can select the tool that they want to use individually, create drawing elements using the tool, or manipulate existing drawing elements.

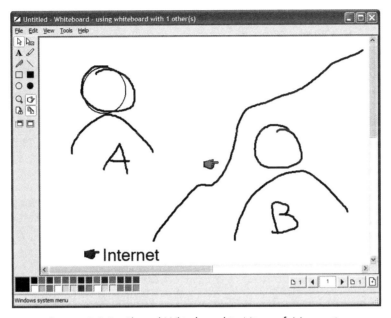

Figure 4.16 Shared Whiteboard in Microsoft Netmeeting

The COAST Puzzle (Schümmer et al., 2005) (http://www.opencoast.org/download/puzzle/) shown in Figure 4.17 is an example of how the shared editing principle can be implemented for tasks other than diagram editing or text editing.

The shared artifacts are the pieces of a jigsaw puzzle. A picture is presented to the user for a short interval (five seconds). It is then cut into thirty rectangular pieces that are scrambled. The players have to restore the original image in a special image area. They can move pieces by dragging them with the mouse.

Whenever a user moves a piece, it is moved at the other machines as well. To show who has moved the piece, a little hand icon is shown against the piece that is moved. Besides the cooperation aspect, users can select which picture they want to use as a puzzle and how many pieces the puzzle should have. A special settings allows the users to solve the same puzzle with different pictures. In this setting, one user tries for example to reassemble a scrambled picture of a Polar Bear, whereas his peer reassembles a scrambled sunflower. Both

Figure 4.17 The COAST puzzle

solve the same puzzle as far as the correct destination position of the pieces is concerned. The top-right piece of the Polar Bear is also the top right piece of the sunflower—they just have different pictures mapped onto the piece.

The COAST Puzzle is an extreme example of relaxed WYSIWIS: the users only share the geography of the puzzle, but they see different images.

Related Patterns

APPLICATION SHARING$_{\to 4.1.5}$ describes how the view and the controller of single-user applications can be replicated to enable synchronous interaction. Compared to SHARED EDITING, users cannot work in parallel.

CENTRALIZED OBJECTS$_{\to 5.2.1}$ or REPLICATED OBJECTS$_{\to 5.2.3}$ allow sharing of the model, view, and controller of the shared editor.

COLLABORATIVE SESSION$_{\to 5.1.1}$ The SHARED EDITING takes place in a COLLABORATIVE SESSION that defines who is currently participating in the group.

FLOOR CONTROL$_{\to 4.1.7}$, PESSIMISTIC LOCKING$_{\to 5.3.1}$, and OPTIMISTIC CONCURRENCY CONTROL$_{\to 5.3.2}$ provide different ways to order and structure the input to the shared editor and, thereby, ensure consistent behavior.

SHARED BROWSING$_{\to 4.1.3}$ describes how an information space can be explored with a teammate. Thus SHARED BROWSING supports collaborative interaction, but not collaborative editing.

SHARED FILE REPOSITORY$_{\to 4.1.2}$ and ROOM$_{\to 4.2.1}$ describe how users can share files and documents that are necessary for collaboration, but do not describe how users can manipulate the shared files simultaneously. SHARED FILE REPOSITORIES or ROOMS can be used as meeting points to initiate SHARED EDITING.

REMOTE CURSOR$_{\to 4.4.7}$, REMOTE SELECTION$_{\to 4.4.6}$, and REMOTE FIELD OF VISION$_{\to 4.4.5}$ can be used to make collaborating users aware of the working focus of their peers.

TELEPOINTER$_{\to 4.4.8}$ can be used by collaborating users to point to a specific artifact in the collaboration space.

MODEL-VIEW-CONTROLLER (Krasner and Pope, 1988; Buschmann et al., 1996) describes how to split up an application into model, view, and controller components. Model components contain the data structures and the necessary algorithms to deal with the data. View components encapsulate all functions that are necessary to visualize the model. Controller components receive and handle user input events, which include modifications to the model and triggering view updates.

4.1.7 FLOOR CONTROL **

floor (flôr), NOUN: **1a.** The surface of a room on which one stands. **b.** The lower or supporting surface of a structure. [...] **5a.** The part of a legislative chamber or meeting hall where members are seated and from which they speak. **b. The right to address an assembly, as granted under parliamentary procedure. c.** The body of assembly members: *a motion from the floor.* **6.** The part of a room or building where the principal business or work takes place, especially: **a.** The area of an exchange where securities are traded. **b.** The part of a retail store in which merchandise is displayed and sales are made. **c. The area of a factory where the product is manufactured or assembled.** [...]

Intent

Let only one user at a time act in the shared collaboration space.

Context

Users interact synchronously in a collaboration space.

Problem

Synchronous interaction can lead to parallel and conflicting actions that confuse the interacting users and makes interaction difficult.

Scenario

Paul would like to create some project flyers for potential sponsors of the game engine. He starts a shared editor on a text document and invites ten more members from the team to a collaborative authoring session. However, their work is quite unstructured, because all of them edit at different places in the shared editor. Consistency soon gets lost.

Symptoms

You should consider applying this pattern when ...

- Conflicting and parallel actions confuse interacting users.
- Parallel use of a shared resource such as a communication channel is not possible.

Solution

Therefore: Model the right to interact in the shared collaboration space by means of a token and only let the user holding the token modify or access the shared resources. Establish a fair group process for passing the token among interacting users.

Dynamics

A user holding the token is said to hold the floor. The user holding the floor is the only one who can manipulate or access a set of shared resources in the collaboration space associated with the floor. There can be different floors in a collaboration space that are associated with different sets of shared resources. As this only depends on the collaboration process that has to be supported, we assume in here that there is only one floor.

Many different possible group processes exist for passing the floor among collaborating users. These group processes have to ensure that the floor is passed among the users in a fair—or at least an accepted—way.

A common group process is based on users explicitly requesting and releasing the floor via the user interface. To implement the floor and ensure a fair selection process among the users requesting it, the token can be modeled as a queue using CENTRALIZED OBJECTS$_{\rightarrow 5.2.1}$. Every floor request is added to the queue: as soon as the current floor owner releases the floor, it is granted to the next user in the queue. To support group awareness, the current floor holder and the position of other users in the queue can be displayed in the USER LIST$_{\rightarrow 4.4.1}$.

If it is impossible to provide a central site to manage the queue of floor requests, the floor can implemented as a distributed token by using token-based algorithms for mutual exclusion. Chang (Chang, 1996) provides a classification of existing algorithms for distributed mutual exclusion.

Apart from the basic request policy, Dommel and Garcia-Luna-Aceves (Dommel and Garcia-Luna-Aceves, 1997), for example, discuss several further possibilities for passing the floor between collaborating users.

— *Chair guidance*. The chair of a session is the arbiter of the floor.
— *Agenda orientation*. The floor is assigned according to a special schedule or task.
— *Time orientation*. The right to own a floor is based on a timeout.
— *Predefined ordering*. The floor is passed among the participants according to a specific order.
— *Election*. The participants vote on the next floor holder.
— *Lottery scheduling*. The floor is assigned to the participants according to a probabilistically fair scheme.

Rationale

As only one user at a time can access or manipulate the shared resources, there cannot be any conflicting changes or parallel use of the shared resources.

Check

When applying this pattern, you should answer these questions:

— How are you going to pass the floor between the interacting users?
— Are you going to manage the floor using a central site?
— Are you going to visualize the current floor holder and users requesting it in the user interface?

Danger Spots

Ensure that the floor is released when the user holding the floor disconnects.

Some collaboration processes might afford a greater degree of concurrent interaction. In that case, shared resources either have to be split into different sets, for which multiple floors are necessary, or OPTIMISTIC CONCURRENCY CONTROL$_{\rightarrow 5.3.2}$ has to be used.

Known Uses

NetMeeting (Summers, 1999) uses FLOOR CONTROL for APPLICATION SHARING$_{\rightarrow 4.1.5}$. Only one user at a time, the one owning the floor, is allowed to interact with the shared application. The other users are only allowed to watch the floor owner's actions. Users have to explicitly request the floor from the floor owner, who can either pass the floor to the requesting user or keep it.

VITERO is a conferencing system that puts the responsibility for FLOOR CONTROL in the hands of up to two moderators. To talk, users have to signal their intent by raising their "hand"—changing the status of their VIRTUAL ME$_{\rightarrow 3.1.5}$ so that it is visualized with a raised hand icon. The moderators can then pass a microphone icon to the user. The microphone is shown to all other users as well so that they stay aware of who is currently able to speak. If a user holds the microphone, the system establishes an audio channel from this user to the rest of the group.

FlashMeeting (http://www.flashmeeting.com/) is a web-based audio/video conferencing tool. In FlashMeeting, users that want to speak have to request the floor explicitly. Their request and their position in the queue is visualized in the USER LIST$_{\rightarrow 4.4.1}$ of the FlashMeeting (see Figure 4.18). Additionally, FlashMeeting shows the next floor holder in a status bar. The next floor holder is granted the floor as soon as the current floor holder stops broadcasting.

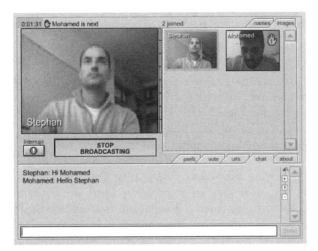

Figure 4.18 FlashMeeting audio/video conference

Related Patterns

OPTIMISTIC CONCURRENCY CONTROL→5.3.2 describes how a greater degree of concurrent interaction among the participating users can be supported while still ensuring shared data consistency.

PESSIMISTIC LOCKING→5.3.1 shows how the right to participate can be managed at a very fine-grained level. It uses short-term locks that are requested each time the application needs to update data, for example when moving an object in a shared drawing editor, and thereby relieves the user from explicitly managing locks. However, it does not help the group to structure turn-taking in the group process.

TURN TAKING (Björk and Holopainen, 2005) motivates a comparable solution in the context of game design. The authors suggest that only one player should be able to act at a time while the others are spectators. How the token to act is passed on depends on the game strategy—for example, random player selection.

4.1.8 Touch me... applied

The patterns in this section are the most relevant for the COGE community. Paul and Susan had the vision of supporting distributed development using techniques like distributed pair programming. While he has heard doubts about the practicability of pair programming over distance, he has also heard of research into approaches for better supporting distributed XP[1]. He therefore thinks about how the patterns in this section can be used to make the Eclipse development environment into an environment for distributed pair programming[2].

The first step towards this vision was to create a SHARED FILE REPOSITORY$_{\rightarrow 4.1.2}$ for storing and accessing the source documents. Paul decided to use an off-the-shelf component, CVS, for this. Its integration with user accounts was relatively straightforward. Paul implemented a mechanism that automatically creates a CVS account for users after they register. Passwords are also automatically registered. By having synchronized accounts, the Eclipse system could then use the user's LOGIN information to access the source code repository.

SHARED BROWSING$_{\rightarrow 4.1.3}$ and SHARED EDITING$_{\rightarrow 4.1.6}$ were implemented by adding a pair-programming editor to the Eclipse environment. Users could join a COLLABORATIVE SESSION$_{\rightarrow 5.1.1}$ and decide which role they wanted to have in the session. From their collocation experience it was clear to them that at least two roles should be supported: the role of the driver, who is allowed to navigate through the code and change it, and the role of the navigator, who comments on actions performed by the driver.

Depending on their role, the users would then see another user interface. The driver can use this Eclipse as if it were a single-user installation. However, Eclipse monitors all the actions that the user performs and replicates them at the remote instances of all connected users. This means that all browsing activities are synchronized within the team. For the navigator, the scroll bars and other navigation mechanisms are made passive, which means that they can see these elements but cannot use them.

Note that the user interface mock-up shown in Figure 4.19 already includes the most relevant awareness widget, namely a USER LIST$_{\rightarrow 4.4.1}$ that informs users about the presence of their colleagues. From our experience, such an awareness widget is the minimum needed for SHARED EDITING. We extend the editor with additional awareness support in Section 4.4.

---

[1]For example (Schümmer and Schümmer, 2001; Kircher et al., 2001; Cheng et al., 2003; Reeves and Zhu, 2004).

[2]The tools described in this section are currently under development in our research department. This background was the main reason why we created the scenario around Paul and the COGE project. Please contact us if you are interested in using the tools or have ideas for contributing to their further development.

4.1 Touch me... or how to modify shared material together

Figure 4.19 Shared editing of source code and diagrams

As in the collocated pair-programming setting, the navigator can ask to switch roles at any time. This is implemented as an instance of the FLOOR CONTROL$_{\rightarrow 4.1.7}$ pattern. The navigator can press the "Drive" button shown in the top-right corner of Figure 4.19, which opens a request dialogue at the driver's site, as shown in Figure 4.20. If the driver accepts the role change, the views are updated accordingly in both clients.

Figure 4.20 Shared editing of source code and diagrams

As the developers also asked for diagram support, Paul implemented a shared diagram editor, shown on the left of Figure 4.19. This was built as a fully synchronous editor, which means that users can all modify the diagram at the same time and immediately see modifications made by other users.

Finally, developers asked to be able to test source code remotely. The driver should be able to start the test and all clients should see its screen output. Since this task involves proprietary applications, namely the game engine that is currently being developed by the community, Paul decided to support this request by means of integrated application sharing.

From a user's perspective, this is implemented by adding a *Share Application* button to the driver's perspective of the Eclipse environment. When pressing this button,

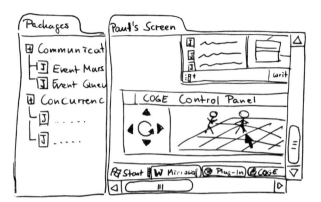

Figure 4.21 Application sharing as an embedded Eclipse view

the system automatically initiates a RealVNC session (http://www.realvnc.com/) to implement APPLICATION SHARING$_{\rightarrow 4.1.5}$. The driver's computer then launches a VNC server and notifies the navigator's Eclipse environment about the address to which a VNC client can connect. The navigator's client then automatically connects to the driver's system and displays the screen in an additional Eclipse window, as shown in Figure 4.21.

4.2 Meet me... or how to create places for collaboration

The patterns in Section 4.1 showed how specialized tools can support collaboration in small teams. We have opened the computer-mediated interaction space up for the team. However, instead of talking about spaces, Harrison and Dourish (1996) argue that we should rather talk about *places* when we consider collaboration.

"Physically, a place is a space which is invested with understandings of behavioral appropriateness, cultural expectations, and so forth. We are located in space, but we act in place. Furthermore, places are spaces that are valued." (Harrison and Dourish, 1996, page 69)

The goal should thus be to create virtual places in the computer-mediated interaction space. We visualize three levels, ranging from spaces to living places:

— A space is a region in the world. It has attributes like dimensions, connections to other regions in the space, or spatial properties like walls.
— If a space is configured for a specific purpose, we transform it to a place.
— A place becomes a living place if people start to use the place. They enter the place and make use of the facilities provided by the configuration.
  Each living place tells the users its story. It is the fixed point with which users relate their memories about activities that took place at the place. It shows traces of activities that previously took place at this place.

As in the physical world, virtual places for interaction exhibit several fundamental properties that help us to see them as a suitable context for computer-mediated interaction. A place first of all has a STRONG BORDER. We have already addressed this property with respect to communities. However, when we consider it in the context of small group interaction, the need to establish privacy becomes more urgent. Figure 4.22 emphasizes this aspect of a place. Compared to Figure 4.4 in the introduction of Section 4.1, the borders of the space shield it from the rest of the community.

If we create such strong borders, we also have to think about creating a means of passing this border. Otherwise, there will be no DEEP INTERLOCK between different places, which makes it extremely hard for participants to be active in more than one place.

These two properties have already been relevant on a community level. In Section 3.1 we argued that users from outside the community should be able to gain easy entrance to the community (QUICK REGISTRATION$_{\rightarrow 3.1.1}$ and LOGIN$_{\rightarrow 3.1.2}$). Once they are part of the community, they should be able to control their privacy

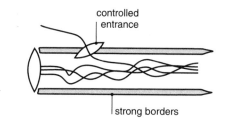

Figure 4.22 Creating places for interaction

and create realms for concentrated work (AVAILABILITY STATUS$_{\to 3.3.3}$ and ATTENTION SCREEN$_{\to 3.3.4}$).

When discussing places for group interaction in this section, we will transfer comparable principles from the level of community interaction to the level of workgroup interaction. This results in the patterns shown in Figure 4.23.

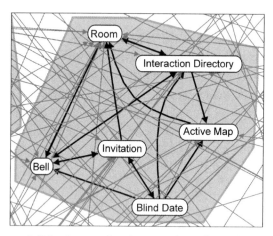

Figure 4.23 Patterns for shaping places for collaboration

The strong borders are provided by a ROOM, which can be listed in an ACTIVE MAP or an INTERACTION DIRECTORY. Deep interlock is achieved by allowing community members to enter the room after they receive an INVITATION$_{\to 4.2.5}$, or after their request via the BELL is answered positively. Finally, we will describe how places can also be used for establishing new contacts and collaborating with strangers on a common topic in a BLIND DATE.

This section presents the following patterns:

ROOM$_{\to 4.2.1}$ Provide the group with a place where they can meet for collaboration.

4.2 Meet me... or how to create places for collaboration

ACTIVE MAP$_{\to 4.2.2}$ Show a graphical and scaled representation of the space and enrich this with awareness information.

INTERACTION DIRECTORY$_{\to 4.2.3}$ List potential interaction contexts.

BELL$_{\to 4.2.4}$ Inform session participants that a user wants to join.

INVITATION$_{\to 4.2.5}$ Allow users to plan interaction with others.

BLIND DATE$_{\to 4.2.6}$ Ease group formation for task-oriented groups.

4.2.1 Room **

Alternative name(s): Area, Place

room (rōōm), NOUN: **1.** A space that is or may be occupied: *That easy chair takes up too much room.* **2a.** An area separated by walls or partitions from other similar parts of the structure or building in which it is located: the first room on the left; an unpainted room. **b.** The people present in such an area: The whole room laughed. **3.** rooms Living quarters; lodgings. **4.** Suitable opportunity; occasion.

Intent

Provide the group with a place where they can meet for collaboration.

Context

Users are distributed and want to work together using communication channels and documents.

Problem

Users use different tools for communication, file transfer, application sharing, and other tasks that are needed in group interaction. In most COLLABORATIVE SESSIONS$_{\rightarrow 5.1.1}$ these tools are used together. However, setting up the tools is difficult and time-consuming.

Scenario

Since Paul is still on his business trip, Maurice has the idea of inviting Noah for a pair programming session. Noah has not yet participated in the development of the virtual reality engine. Maurice grants Noah access to their SHARED FILE REPOSITORY$_{\rightarrow 4.1.2}$, *but this still means that Noah can only see a small part of the project. For example, Maurice has a long e-mail history with Paul that contains valuable information, but which Noah cannot access. Paul and Maurice also exchanged phone numbers so that they could establish an audio communication channel in their session. All this setting up now has to be performed for Noah as well, and Maurice is sure that he will nevertheless forget some important information.*

Symptoms

You should consider applying this pattern when ...

— Users find it difficult to join a COLLABORATIVE SESSION$_{\rightarrow 5.1.1}$.

— Documents are edited in parallel and users have to distribute new versions to the group frequently.

— Users use several tools that need to be started and controlled separately, but they always want the existing group to use the tools together.

— Users complain that the management of tools and communication channels is too difficult.

Solution

Therefore: Model a virtual place for collaboration as a room that can hold documents and participants. Ensure that users who are in the same room can communicate by means of a communication channel that is automatically established between all the users in the room. Make sure that all users can access all documents that are in the room and make these documents persistent. Changes to the documents should be visible to everyone in the room.

Dynamics

The *room* contains *users* and *documents* and provides a *communication channel* as well as *shared editors*. Each room has a well-defined border that defines what is in the room and what is outside the room. A room has an identification that allows users to find it. This can be either a name or a position in a set of connected rooms.

Users can enter a room, which has the effect of allowing them to access the room's communication channel and participate in collaborative activities. Note that the communication channel can be synchronous, such as an EMBEDDED CHAT$_{\rightarrow 4.3.1}$, or asynchronous, such as a FORUM$_{\rightarrow 4.3.2}$.

Users can add documents or artifacts to a room. This means that the document becomes visible to all other users of the room. When users work with a document, they can often do this together with all the room's other participants, by using shared workspaces, or sharing the results by accessing the same document in the room.

When users leave the room, the content stays there, to allow users to come back later and continue their work on the room's documents.

Rationale

All users who are present in a room automatically share communication channels and documents that they place in the room. This ensures that users do not have to deal with complex establishment of communication channels. The only thing that a user does is enter the room: being in the room triggers all connection management.

The same is true for the use of shared documents. The system distributes changes to documents to all users in the room. Users therefore no longer have to cope with establishing application-sharing connections.

Documents no longer need to be sent to the group members via external communication media, but just placed in the room, where the collaboration on the documents can then take place.

Note that rooms are attractive metaphors for single-user applications as well. Henderson, Jr. and Card (1986) evaluated the metaphor of rooms compared to that of a desktop.

Check

When applying this pattern, you should answer these questions:

— How can you make the boundary of the room perceivable?
— How will you support the configuration of tools and documents in your room?
— What communication channels do you need in your room?
— How should you place rooms in space? Will the user be able to define a position? Is this position important?

Danger Spots

The benefit of the pattern, the automatic creation of communication channels, can be problematic, since this requires computing power and bandwidth. If users are too disturbed, you should consider allowing them to deactivate the communication channels. However, this can lead to invalid assumptions on the part of other users, since they still think that all room members are participating in communication.

Known Uses

Collaborative virtual learning environments like VITAL or Lecture2000. In VITAL—Virtual Teaching And Learning—(Pfister et al., 1998), rooms were used to structure virtual learning. In both systems the rooms held hypertext documents that groups could work on collaboratively. The learners had their personal room that modeled their home. This is the room that they enter when they start using the system, and normally they are alone in it. They can invite other learners to their home, as was outlined in the scenario, or they can go to special group rooms that can be used for group learning.

Both homes and group rooms provide an audio channel that can be established automatically for all users in the room. Other rooms imply special social interactions, such as the auditorium, (see Figure 4.24), where the trainer can

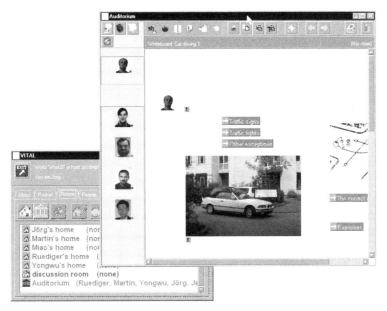

Figure 4.24 A group room in the VITAL environment for collaborative learning

control the interaction by allowing users to speak or to act on a shared document.

A comparable room structure is used in the Lecture2000 prototype (Schlichter et al., 1998a). Users enter the system via a entrance hall and can move to group rooms or tutoring studios from the hall.

MOOs. MOO is an acronym for "MUD[3], object oriented". For an example, see LambdaMOO (Curtis, 1998). MOOs are general-purpose virtual environments. Early MOOs were used for recreational purposes, such as adventure or other role-playing games, but later other application areas were addressed by MOOs, such as collaborative learning or collaborative work.

CollegeTown (Guernsey, 1996) is one example of an educational MOO. Users can move through a virtual campus. Whenever they enter a room, they get a description that describes the room, objects inside the room, and other users who are present in the room (see Figure 4.25).

TeamWave. The TeamWave Workplace groupware platform (Greenberg and Roseman, 2003) organizes all collaborative activities in rooms. After users enter the collaboration server, they can decide which room they want to enter. In

---

[3] Multi-User Dungeon.

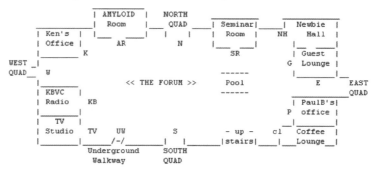

Figure 4.25 The forum in the CollegeTown MOO, explaining the room, the objects inside the room, and co-present users

the rooms they find documents and tools to manipulate them. If users decide to manipulate a document, they do this using a tool that they find in the room. The tool opens for all other users as well, so that they can do the manipulation cooperatively. Communication with other room members can take place via a chat or a paging channel that creates little pop-up messages for all users who are present in the room.

Lotus Quickplace (http://doc.notes.net/uafiles.nsf/docs/QP70/$File/qp7user.pdf) is a web-based collaboration support system that organizes topic-based interaction in team rooms. Rooms can contain pages and provide the required tools to interact with the pages in the room. Users can invite other users to a room and give different access permissions to each user of the room.

DIVA (Sohlenkamp and Chwelos, 1994) models rooms to support virtual interaction in work contexts. The rooms can be equipped with desks that hold documents. In addition, they are populated with users, who are currently on line.

Related Patterns

BELL$_{\to 4.2.4}$ In the event of locked doors, users need a means of attracting attention if they want to join the members in the room. The BELL pattern provides a solution to this requirement.

COLLABORATIVE SESSION$_{\to 5.1.1}$ A collaborative session represents a group of people who work together synchronously. In contrast, a ROOM can be used synchronously and asynchronously. In addition, it keeps track of documents used in the room.

INTERACTION DIRECTORY$_{\rightarrow 4.2.3}$ allows users to look up ROOMS in which they might be interested.

PERSISTENT SESSION$_{\rightarrow 5.1.2}$ A room stores the documents used in it in the same way that a PERSISTENT SESSION stores the results achieved in a COLLABORATIVE SESSION$_{\rightarrow 5.1.1}$.

SHARED FILE REPOSITORY$_{\rightarrow 4.1.2}$ allows users to share files. Often a SHARED FILE REPOSITORY forms the document interface of a ROOM.

USER LIST$_{\rightarrow 4.4.1}$ The user list represents the presence and status of users in a ROOM.

PHYSICAL METAPHORS (Barr et al., 2004) discusses the use of physical metaphors in graphical user interfaces in general. A ROOM is a concrete instance of a PHYSICAL METAPHOR.

GOOD INTEGRATION WITH OTHER TOOLS (Goldman et al., 2002). A ROOM is an example of good integration of different tools. It brings together functions that are often separated because of a technical perspective, but which should collude from the user's point of view.

4.2.2 ACTIVE MAP *

Alternative name(s): Overview Diagram, Radar View

map (măp), NOUN: **1a. A representation, usually on a plane surface, of a region of the earth or heavens. b.** Something that suggests such a representation, as in clarity of representation. **2.** *Mathematics* The correspondence of elements in one set to elements in the same set or another set. **3.** *Slang* The human face. **4.** *Genetics* A genetic map.

Intent

Show a graphical and scaled representation of the space and enrich this with awareness information.

Context

Users interact in a large and complex space containing many artifacts and places for collaboration. You need a means to ease orientation and coordination in the space.

Problem

To orient themselves and interact in space, users have to create a mental model that represents the space and the artifacts and users it contains. This is a difficult task.

Scenario

The idea of using rooms was well accepted in the community. Several working groups have created their own work rooms and built adjacent rooms that are used by subgroups. Michele remembers that she has a date with Noah to continue the VRML export work. She has forgotten in which room they wanted to meet, and they created several rooms for collaborating on different aspects of the VRML export. So Michele "walks" through all their rooms until she finally finds Noah.

Symptoms

You should consider applying this pattern when ...

— Users only see a small part of the very large interaction space, which makes it difficult for them to get an overview.

— Users work on different non-overlapping regions in space, which makes it difficult to become aware of other users' activities, for example by means of REMOTE CURSORS$_{\to 4.4.7}$ or REMOTE FIELDS OF VISION$_{\to 4.4.5}$.

Solution

Therefore: Create a reduced visual representation of the spatial domain model by means of a map. Show other users' locations on the map. Ensure that the map is dynamic for artifacts and users, but static with respect to landmarks.

Dynamics

The creation of an active map requires six steps:

1. *Filter.* The first step is to select only those artifacts for the map that are important to provide an overview. Which artifacts are important depends on the intended audience. In a collaborative learning environment, students may for example only be interested in rooms that are related to their courses. Other rooms for courses from other faculties can be filtered out.

2. *Combine into clusters.* Different artifacts or spatial structures need to be combined into one composite structure to create a map that has a reasonable level of detail. This means that individual rooms may be combined into a "building" and the map may only show the building. This helps to reduce the amount of detail that is shown in the map.

3. *Layout/Arrange.* If the clusters do not yet have a spatial arrangement, they can be arranged using automated layout algorithms such as the graph embedder algorithm (Frick et al., 1995). Any automatic layout should take two aspects into account: first, it should allow the user to enhance the automated layout with manual corrections. This means that an automatically generated map should be editable by the users of the space so that they can rearrange the different parts of the map. Second, it should respect old positions that have already been communicated to users. For example, if a specific room was placed in the upper-left corner of the first version of the map, it should be in the upper-left corner in the second version as well.

4. *Enhance with awareness information.* After defining the spatial arrangement of the artifacts and rooms, activities associated with the artifacts and specific rooms can be related to the positions of the artifacts/rooms in the map. Potential visualizations are USER LISTS$_{\to 4.4.1}$, VIRTUAL MES$_{\to 3.1.5}$, REMOTE CURSORS$_{\to 4.4.7}$, or REMOTE FIELDS OF VISION$_{\to 4.4.5}$.

5. *Scale.* All coordinates have to be scaled down in order to create a miniature version of the virtual environment. If the map can be scrolled, the scale factor should be selectable by the user. Otherwise, the scale factor depends on the size of the map in relation to the size of the space.

6. *Paint.* The map needs to be drawn as a view. This view should be kept valid for all users. Changes, for example where a user moves from one place to another, have to cause an automated update of other users' maps. The SHARED SUBSCRIPTION pattern can be used to enforce such an update.

Steps 1–3 have to be triggered whenever the artifacts that are relevant for the production of the map change. Step 4 will be performed frequently, since it represents the users' activities in the virtual environment. Steps 5 and 6, finally, are the production phase. Whenever information on the map changes, these steps need to be performed.

Rationale

The active map solves the problem by combining two advantages: it reduces details found in the collaboration space, and is therefore an abstraction of the concrete space, including information relevant for finding places and artifacts. It combines this reduced view with information on other users' activities, thereby providing group awareness.

Sensing where other users are located helps them to meet at a concrete place by navigating to the other user's location. It can also help to avoid conflicting work by moving to a place that is currently not inhabited.

The most comprehensive series of studies regarding the usefulness of active maps has been performed by Gutwin and Greenberg (1999). They ran experiments in which participants had to fulfill a construction task in a two-dimensional shared workspace. Teams with active maps performed significantly better in tasks that demanded coordination between the team members, such as guiding team members through the workspace. In their study, Gutwin and Greenberg (1999) also compared the difference between active maps with a REMOTE FIELD OF VISION$_{\to 4.4.5}$ and active maps that only showed the topology of the workspace and the local field of vision (referred to as *overviews*). According to their results, active maps provided greater benefit if remote fields of vision are included.

Check

When applying this pattern, you should answer these questions:

— Which artifacts are relevant if you look at the collaboration space at a high level of abstraction? What would still be important if you were looking at the space from a long distance?

— How should you lay out the parts of the map? Does the application of an automated layout algorithm make sense? If yes, are there characteristics of the space, such as hierarchical room structures, that suggest a specific layout algorithm?

— How can you ensure spatial consistency and durability? Can you apply an incremental layout algorithm that only considers added artifacts in the layout?

— What awareness information should you add to the map? How many users will be shown in one map?

— How should you calculate the scale? Is it fixed or dynamic? Can the user control the scale?

— Can the user interact with the map—for example, will a click on the map move the user to the clicked point?

Danger Spots

The reduction of detail may be too rigorous, for example if doors between rooms are removed. This can result in a situation in which the perceived space no longer matches the model shown in the map.

Automatic mechanisms for filtering, clustering, and laying out artifacts can produce suboptimal maps. They should only be considered as tools for creating the first draft of the map. The final map layout may require manual changes by users.

Known Uses

GIA (Group InterAction) (Manhart, 1999) was a prototypical system used at DaimlerChrysler to support interaction on cooperative websites. The pages currently visited were arranged in a map view together with the current users at each location. It was possible to move between the locations by selecting a user on the map and asking the system to follow them.

CollegeTown (Guernsey, 1996) uses maps to explain the relations between rooms and enhance the perception of spatiality.

COAST UML-Editor The COAST UML-Editor (http://www.openCoast.org) shows diagram nodes in a radar view (see Figure 4.26). Texts and details of the nodes are omitted in this visualization. Instead of a node for a class or an interface, the radar view only shows a colored rectangle.

Each user's field of vision is shown as a rectangle in the user's color.

From a technical perspective, the active map is modeled as an instance of an additional view class that uses the same shared data model as the diagram view. The view recomputes the component's positions and reduces their size to show the whole workspace in a small screen space.

The ACTIVE MAP instance also has a different controller (UMLActiveMap-Controller), which moves the local user's field of vision when they click on a point in the radar view. This eases navigation to another user's field of vision.

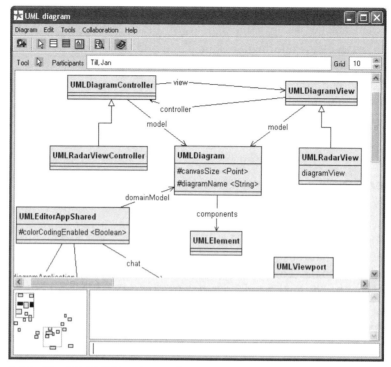

Figure 4.26 The COAST UML editor with an ACTIVE MAP showing a reduced class diagram and other users' viewports

JAMM (Begole et al., 1997) is a platform for transforming single user Java applets into collaborative applications. It includes several awareness widgets that can be added to the applet. One of them is the JRadarPane (http://java.cs.vt.edu/~begolej/classes/JRadarPane/) shown in Figure 4.27.

On a technical level, sharing an applet requires that a Panel object is replaced by a collaborative rJAMM Panel object. This collaborative panel will make all included Swing components accessible by remote applications. Since the panel "knows" the whole shared workspace, it can serve as a model for the radar view.

Related Patterns

REMOTE FIELD OF VISION$_{\to 4.4.5}$ As discussed above, radar views should make use of remote fields of vision to show other user's current working area.

REMOTE CURSOR$_{\to 4.4.7}$ Remote Cursors provide a more focused view of the user's position. In shared workspaces with large overlapping fields of vision, it can

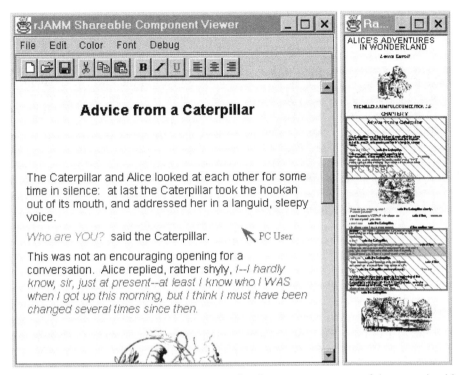

Figure 4.27 A radar view in a rJAMM applet showing a miniature of the text edited by two users and the users' current fields of vision

be better to include remote cursors in the radar view, since they consume less screen space, allowing more users to be shown.

VIRTUAL ME$_{\to 3.1.5}$ An *avatar* is a graphical representation of a user. It eases the task of connecting a user with a specific point in space. Avatars with reduced size can be shown in a radar view instead of remote fields of vision or remote cursors.

ROOM$_{\to 4.2.1}$ An ACTIVE MAP is used to show the position of different rooms in a collaboration space. It should reflect the relationships between rooms and thereby help the user to understand the virtual environment better.

ANNOTATED SCROLLBAR (Tidwell, 2006) discusses how the linear structure of a document can be visualized together with a navigation interface. The scroll bar in this case serves two purposes: it shows a linear map of the content as well as the user's current position. Applied to the context of groupware applications, it should also show the other users' positions (as discussed in the REMOTE FIELD OF VISION$_{\to 4.4.5}$ pattern).

4.2.3 INTERACTION DIRECTORY **

Alternative name(s): Service Directory

di·rec·to·ry (dĭ-rĕk'tə-rē), NOUN: **1. A book containing an alphabetical or classified listing of names, addresses, and other data, such as telephone numbers, of specific persons, groups, or firms. 2.** *Computer Science* **a.** A listing of the files contained in a storage device, such as a magnetic disk. **b.** A description of the various characteristics of a file, such as the layout of the fields in it. **3.** A book of rules or directions. **4.** A group or body of directors.

Intent

List potential interaction contexts.

Context

Users interact in more than one context, involving interaction with different users on different artifacts at different places and using various tools.

Problem

Finding existing contexts to start interaction and memorizing older contexts to continue an interaction is difficult.

Scenario

After the first release of the game engine, Paul has the great idea of hosting a virtual conference to discuss new directions for the game engine synchronously. He points out moderators for special topics, such as sound synthesis or artificial intelligence, and asks them to host sessions. However, nobody comes to these sessions. Paul and the moderators were quite disappointed, until they found out that the other developers simply did not know when and where the sessions took place.

Symptoms

You should consider applying this pattern when …

— Users want to collaborate but do know where or how to find the necessary interaction context.

— Users pause in their interaction and need to continue after they have worked in other contexts.

Solution

Therefore: Provide a shared space that is available to all users in which users can store and retrieve interaction contexts.

Dynamics

Users can enter a shared space that allows them to describe interaction contexts, search for interaction contexts, or browse for interesting contexts. To support browsing, the shared space can classify interaction contexts according to metadata and offer a link to a short description of the context. Both metadata and the short description are provided by the user who created the context.

Rationale

As users now have a shared space that allows them to retrieve information about existing interaction contexts, or describe and announce their own interaction contexts, they have now the possibility of establishing interaction.

Check

When applying this pattern, you should answer these questions:

— What is your context?
— What kind of metadata must users provide?
— How should you generate a user-readable description for the context? Automatically based on the described object, or manually by the user?
— How should you model the shared space?
— Do you want to remove contexts over time?
— Are you going to use access permissions for the shared space?

Danger Spots

In large directories it can be difficult to find interesting interaction contexts, even when the directory is searchable. To overcome this issue, you should categorize the interactions' contexts, and allow users to limit their search to a number of categories in which they are interested.

Known Uses

CURE (Haake et al., 2003b) is a web-based shared workspace system. It is based on ROOMS for organizing collaboration. Users in CURE can find appropriate ROOMS for their interaction in a ROOM directory (see Figure 4.28) or a room

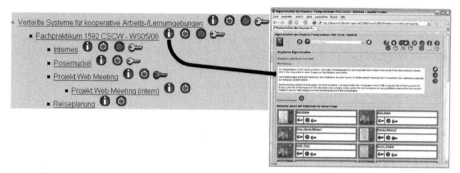

Figure 4.28 CURE room directory

map. Links in the directory allow users to request an information page, or access to the room by knocking at the door (see BELL$_{\rightarrow 4.2.4}$).

DreamTeam (Roth, 2000a) is a development platform for synchronous groupware. Apart from a development environment, DreamTeam offers a runtime environment that allows users to define, announce, and search for COLLABORATIVE SESSIONS. For these purposes, DreamTeam offers a session directory, shown in Figure 4.29, that shows a list of available sessions and their current state.

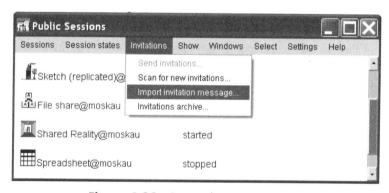

Figure 4.29 Session list in DreamTeam

Yahoo groups allow users to browse all available groups using their favorite web browser. For browsing, Yahoo categorizes the available groups and offers a link to an information page (see Figure 4.30). Users can also search for keywords in the different categories, which makes it easier to find a group that is relevant to a specific field of interest.

4.2.3 INTERACTION DIRECTORY

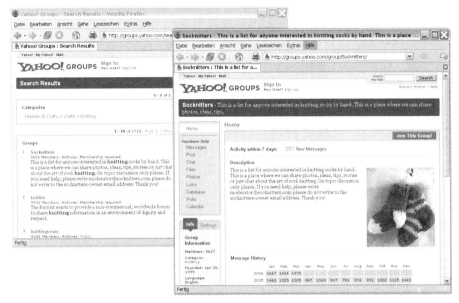

Figure 4.30 Yahoo groups directory

Related Patterns

COLLABORATIVE SESSION$_{\to 5.1.1}$ describes the interaction context for synchronous collaboration.

FORUM$_{\to 4.3.2}$ describes the interaction context for asynchronous textual communication.

ROOM$_{\to 4.2.1}$ describes an interaction context as a virtual place where users can meet for synchronous or asynchronous collaboration.

ACTIVE MAP$_{\to 4.2.2}$ If your collaboration environment has a spatial structure, you should consider linking interaction contexts with places on the map. The INTERACTION DIRECTORY could then have the visual form of a ACTIVE MAP.

SHARED FILE REPOSITORY$_{\to 4.1.2}$ describes an interaction context based on shared files and their organization.

4.2.4 BELL **

Alternative name(s): Door Knocker

door·bell (dôr'bĕl'), NOUN: **A bell, chime, or buzzer outside a door that is rung to announce the presence of a visitor or caller.**

Intent

Inform session participants that a user wants to join.

Context

You have established collaboration among users, for example using the COLLABORATIVE SESSION or ROOM pattern. Now you are concerned about how latecomers can ask to join the collaboration.

Problem

When latecomers want to join a collaborating group they may intrude on the group's privacy. The group could be disturbed by uninvited visitors, or simply not notice that someone wants to join.

Scenario

Paul and Charley collaborate using a SHARED EDITOR *to implement a new version of the Message Digest algorithm that is used for authentication. John, another security expert, would love to join them, but he does not know how to enter their group interaction space.*

Symptoms

You should consider applying this pattern when . . .

— You are modeling group interaction as an access-controlled event.

— You cannot ensure that all users can participate in the group interaction from its beginning.

Solution

Therefore: Provide the meeting place with a bell that allows latecomers to draw attention to their desire to participate in the group.

Dynamics

A group of users meet in a session to discuss or work on shared artifacts. The session ensures their privacy from the rest of the world. One user, a latecomer, knows how to find the session and wants to participate. They therefore ring the bell. The bell is modeled as an interface element that is associated with the representation of the shared space where group interaction takes place. The bell signals its activation to the members of the group and lets them decide whether or not to allow the new user to join the group. In either case the new user is informed and—if possible—guided in entering the session (or staying out).

Rationale

The BELL pattern models an interaction policy that is well known from real life, making it easy to understand.

Check

When applying this pattern, you should answer these questions:
— What should the bell look like? Will it be obtrusive, such as playing loud sounds, or should it be less intrusive, such as an e-mail?
— How long should a latecomer wait for a reaction to ringing the bell?
— How should you display the reactions of the group to the bell request?

Danger Spots

In many cases it is non-trivial to find the entry point to a session. A simple session list can help here by explicitly showing what sessions are currently available or active. A BELL is then attached to each entry in the session list and models a means to request admission to a session.

Known Uses

ISDN. The Deutsche Telekom ISDN telephone system allows users to hold telephone conferences. A latecomer can call the number of the subscriber hosting a conference. The phone system then detects that the host subscriber is currently in the conference (actually in communication). It therefore signals the host subscriber that the latecomer want to speak. This is done by short beeping sounds. The host subscriber can now talk to the latecomer, to identify the new subscriber and find out what they want. If the host subscriber decides that this is compatible with the conference's activities, they can include the latecomer in the telephone conference.

NetMeeting. The Microsoft NetMeeting application-sharing system (Summers, 1999) uses the BELL pattern to signal that another user wants to join the application-sharing session.

FUB (Haake and Schümmer, 2003) (Haake et al., 2003a) lists all COLLABORATIVE SESSIONS$_{\to 5.1.1}$ in a session list. Users can ask participants in a COLLABORATIVE SESSION, whether or not they are allowed to participate, by using a context menu command on the session's entry in the list.

Related Patterns

COLLABORATIVE SESSION$_{\to 5.1.1}$ and ROOM$_{\to 4.2.1}$ use BELLS to request admission.

AVAILABILITY STATUS$_{\to 3.3.3}$ when attached to a COLLABORATIVE SESSION instead of a user, can be used to turn a bell off.

INVITATION$_{\to 4.2.5}$ aims at adding a user to a group. The difference to BELL is that a user wishing to join the group does not take the initiative in INVITATION. Rather, it is the group that decides that a user should be asked to join them. In BELL the roles are exchanged: the user asks the group whether or not they may join.

INTERACTION DIRECTORY$_{\to 4.2.3}$ In many cases it is non-trivial to find the entry point to a group's collaboration context. An INTERACTION DIRECTORY explicitly describes which sessions are currently available or active. Bells are attached to the entries of the session list and model a means for entering a session.

4.2.5 Invitation **

in·vi·ta·tion (ĭn'vĭ-tā'shən), NOUN: **1.** The act of inviting. **2. A spoken or written request for someone's presence or participation. 3.** An allurement, enticement, or attraction. **4.** See altar call.

Intent

Allow users to plan interaction with others.

Context

You want to collaborate.

Problem

One user wants to interact with another. The other user may be unavailable or busy in another context so that an immediate collaboration would disturb them.

Scenario

Maurice would like to interact with Charley on a security feature of the VRML exporter. He thinks that a tight collaboration is appropriate and sees that an application-sharing link is still established with Charley. He therefore just opens the development environment, which pops up on Charley's screen. What Maurice didn't know was that Charley was currently giving a business presentation to one of his most important customers. The window opened by Maurice disturbs Charley's presentation and the result is that the customer is not convinced by Charley's bright ideas. From then on, Charley decides that he will never keep an application-sharing channel open again, and is no longer interested in working with Maurice.

Symptoms

You should consider applying this pattern when ...

— Users want to work synchronously and collaboratively but do not know how to plan a synchronous session.

— A user wants to interact with another user but does not know how to tell them.

- Users cannot be drawn into the interaction directly, since they may have other things to do.
- Unlike short message exchanges, a planned interaction requires users to focus their attention on the interaction for a longer period.

Solution

Therefore: Send and track invitations to the intended participants. Include meta-information on the intended COLLABORATIVE SESSION$_{\to 5.1.1}$**. Automatically add all users who accept the invitation to the** COLLABORATIVE SESSION**.**

Dynamics

The user who is planning to interact creates an INVITATION object. This INVITATION object includes meta-information describing the planned COLLABORATIVE SESSION. The meta-information may include the topic, the intended participants, the scheduled time, and the (virtual) location of the session.

The inviting user submits the INVITATION, which is then sent to a set of invitees. For long-term scheduling this can be achieved using e-mail, for example. For short-term scheduling the INVITATION can be distributed as a short message to all users currently on line. The system shows the INVITATION to each invitee, who can accept or reject it. In both cases, the system notifies the inviting user and updates the status of the INVITATION.

When the scheduled time for the meeting arrives, the system adds all users who accepted the INVITATION to the COLLABORATIVE SESSION and reminds the users of the session's start.

Several variations are common. The inviting user may provide no scheduled time for the meeting. In this case, the INVITATION assumes that the invitee can join the session as soon as they accept the INVITATION. In many cases the INVITATION does not provide the invitee with visible information about the intended participants.

Optionally, the system used for interaction may automatically start the tools that support the meeting. This might not be possible, for example if the mechanisms for joining the meeting are not fully under the technical control of the application.

Rationale

The pattern models a well-known cultural interaction: a user or group of users invites a specific user to interact. The invitee can accept or reject the INVITATION.

Check

When applying this pattern, you should answer these questions:

- Is the session's date important, or will users only send INVITATIONS for sessions that are about to start?

— Can you provide an interface to the user's calendar tools to make it easier for them to keep track of the INVITATION?
— Can you select the communication channel by which the INVITATION is sent based on the user's availability—for example, instant message if the user is connected, e-mail otherwise?
— Are you allowed to reveal the identities of other participants in the INVITATION? How should you display the list of users and how does this scale? (See USER LIST$_{\rightarrow 4.4.1}$).
— Can you include an active reference such as a hyperlink to the meeting's location in the INVITATION?
— What happens if too many users reject the INVITATION? Will you inform the other invitees?
— How should you distribute reminders for the start of the interaction? Is e-mail appropriate, or do you need a more direct notification such as SMS?
— Will you provide support for inviting people that are not yet members of the community? If so, should you think about ways to contact these users, such as by e-mail, and a QUICK REGISTRATION$_{\rightarrow 3.1.1}$ for accepting such new users into your community.

Danger Spots

It can be difficult to predict when a user will notice an INVITATION. The inviting user may assume that the invitee will answer immediately and so wait for a response. Providing presence awareness, for example by means of a system-wide USER LIST$_{\rightarrow 4.4.1}$, can help the inviting user to predict when the INVITATION will be noticed.

Users may be afraid to reject an INVITATION because it could be regarded as impolite. You could consider providing an additional message field for the invitee to explain why they cannot accept an INVITATION.

Known Uses

FUB (Haake and Schümmer, 2003) is a system that supports students in solving collaborative exercises. Since the exercises require synchronous interaction, such as a brainstorming session, users have to coordinate the start of the session.

The inviting user can select a set of users and a topic from the list of possible exercises. At the invitees' screens, a pop-up window appears that informs invitees of the invitation. In the example in Figure 4.31, Juergen sees a window on his screen explaining that Till would like him to participate in the session KE6. Juergen can accept or reject the INVITATION. In the case of acceptance,

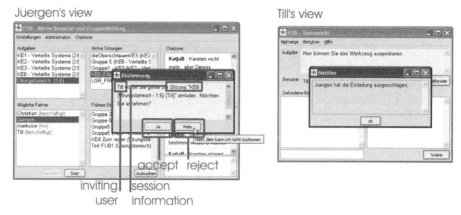

Figure 4.31 An INVITATION in the CSCL system FUB

he would be added to the session KE6, with the effect that he sees the same window as the one that is visible on Till's screen, shown on the right of Figure 4.31.

In the example, *Juergen* has decided to reject the invitation and *Till* is informed by the pop-up window at the right of Figure 4.31.

Google Docs (http://docs.google.com/) allows users to invite other users for collaboration on a specific document or folder. It provides a dialog in which the owner of the document can enter the e-mail addresses of desired collaborators (see Figure 4.32).

One can invite others either as collaborators, which means that they will be able to edit the document, or as viewers, which means that the document cannot be changed by them. After entering the e-mail addresses of the intended people, Google Docs prompts for an INVITATION message that is then sent to the invitees, together with a link that points to the document for discussion. If the user follows this link and enters the correct e-mail address, they will be able to access the document.

DreamTeam provides two different mechanisms, one for a long-term rendezvous and one for a short-term rendezvous (Roth and Unger, 1999). The long-term rendezvous sends an e-mail to other users or puts an announcement in a designated newsgroup. The runtime environment allows users to search for invitation messages (see Figure 4.29 on page 250). The short-term rendezvous uses a decentralized approach to gather information about currently available users.

4.2.5 INVITATION 259

Figure 4.32 An INVITATION to collaborate on a shared document in Google Docs

Related Patterns

BELL$_{\to 4.2.4}$ discusses the problem from the perspective of the invitee. Instead of waiting for an invitation, users in the BELL pattern have to ask the current users of the session if they can participate.

BLIND DATE$_{\to 4.2.6}$ can be considered as a general INVITATION to all users to participate in a specific collaboration context.

COLLABORATIVE SESSION$_{\to 5.1.1}$ or ROOM can use INVITATIONS to invite users to events that take place as a COLLABORATIVE SESSION or in a ROOM.

USER LIST$_{\to 4.4.1}$ allows users who are available for collaboration to be identified.

INTERACTIVE USER INFO$_{\to 4.4.4}$ often provides a menu item for inviting a specific user to a bilateral collaborative session.

QUICK REGISTRATION$_{\to 3.1.1}$ can be combined with INVITATION to assist unregistered users in reacting to an INVITATION. In such cases you can send the unregistered user an INVITATION message that also includes a registration token. The user can use this token in a QUICK REGISTRATION as INVITATION for a specific session. The system then creates a new user account and associates the INVITATION and the resulting session membership to this newly created account.

4.2.6 BLIND DATE

Alternative name(s): Meeting Area

blind date (blīnd dāt), NOUN: **1. A social engagement between two persons who have not previously met, usually arranged by a mutual acquaintance. 2.** Either of the persons participating in such a social engagement.

Intent

Ease group formation for task-oriented groups.

Context

Your system includes tasks that have to be solved by a group of users.

Problem

If tasks have to be solved in collaboration with another user, at least two users have to interact. However, if the users don't know who else is available for the task, it is hard to find appropriate collaborators.

Scenario

Marc wants to start a new task on the visualization engine. He is a fan of pair programming and therefore looks for an appropriate peer. However, this is more complicated than he initially thought: Juan is currently busy on another task, and Carla is on vacation, while Rodrigo cannot be reached. After a third try, Marc does not contact any more potential partners and decides to do something else. What he did not know was that Janet would have been happy to do some pair programming with him.

Symptoms

You should consider applying this pattern when ...

— Your group is fairly homogeneous, which means that several users could form a group to solve a task.

— The need for collaboration is triggered by a specific context of system use, such as when a user gains some specific experience.

Solution

Therefore: Create a meeting area for the task that has to be solved cooperatively and let users express their interest in the task. Inform all interested users when there are enough users at the meeting area, and allow them to start a COLLABORATIVE SESSION$_{\rightarrow 5.1.1}$.

Dynamics

A user navigates to the meeting area, which is a description of the task. It is in most cases related to a specific application context. Examples for such a context could be a specific lesson in a course, or a specific level in a collaborative computer game. In the context of distributed eXtreme Programming support, the task could simply be to continue the development of the system with a peer.

When the users decide to perform the task, they place their VIRTUAL ME$_{\rightarrow 3.1.5}$ at the meeting area. Technically, their user object is enqueued in the list of ready users.

When there are enough users at the meeting area—that is, the list of ready users is of sufficient size—the system initiates a COLLABORATIVE SESSION$_{\rightarrow 5.1.1}$ and adds all ready users to the session.

Rationale

Compared with other means for group formation in which users select their collaborators with respect to their personality or their capabilities, BLIND DATE brings together users based on their ability to participate in a specific task at a specific time. This ensures that the group forms as fast as possible, assuming that all users who are willing to participate in the task add their user representation to the meeting area.

Users don't need to know one another in advance. This encourages them to make new contacts. Since they share a common goal, group formation is eased.

Check

When applying this pattern, you should answer these questions:

— How should you display the meeting area?
— How should you show the users who are interested in the task? Will they be visible to anybody, or will only other interested users be allowed to see who else is interested in performing the task?
— Will you initiate a COLLABORATIVE SESSION$_{\rightarrow 5.1.1}$ as soon as other users are available, or will you just inform the users and leave the decision as to whether or not a group is formed to them?

Danger Spots

If it takes a long time for other users to join the meeting area, a user may forget that they have placed their user representation there. Therefore, you should think about displaying the user's interest in the user interface.

A large time difference between expressing an interest and reaching the critical number of participants can result in a situation in which users have lost their interest in the collaboration. Among others reasons, this can be because the user has started to work in a different context. In this case, they should have removed their VIRTUAL ME from the meeting area. A prominent reminder in the user interface can help users to stay aware of the interest.

There is no guarantee that the group will work well. You should think about providing a means for leaving a group. This may require that the user who is leaving provides a substitute.

Known Uses

World of Warcraft is a multiuser online game in which some tasks can only be mastered collaboratively—a player could try alone, but would probably not succeed. On the left of Figure 4.33 a player approaches a meeting area,

Figure 4.33 A meeting stone as an implementation of the meeting area in World of Warcraft

signified by the obelisk. The player can express their interest by navigating to the meeting stone, which enqueues the player in the list of waiting players. After that, they can continue to explore the virtual environment. The fact that they still seek collaborators for the task is shown using an icon next to the ACTIVE MAP$_{\rightarrow 4.2.2}$, which is shown on the right of 4.33.

L3 (Wessner and Pfister, 2001) models iPOCs (intentional points of collaboration) as part of a collaborative learning environment. When learners have studied specific course material, they reach an iPOC. They can then decide whether to participate in the exercise related to the iPOC. This adds the task to their POC pool (Figure 4.34), a collection of tasks that the learners carry. In addition, their representation is placed at the POC.

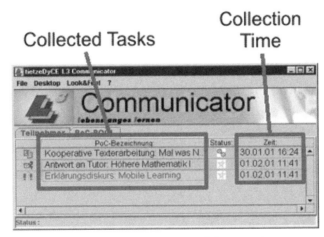

Figure 4.34 The set of collected tasks in the collaborative learning environment L3

When other learner pass the iPOC, they can also decide to participate in the task. After the required number of learner has agreed to participate, they can start the task's group formation and begin to solve the task together.

Related Patterns

BIRDS OF A FEATHER$_{\rightarrow 3.2.3}$ can be used to find potential group members that have most in common with a requesting user, while BLIND DATE can be used to establish cooperation among users that are interested in the same task.

INVITATION$_{\rightarrow 4.2.5}$ can be used to explicitly invite a specific user to a collaborative session.

BELL→4.2.4 can be used to inform users of an active collaborative session that another interested user has arrived in the meeting area. The existing group can then decide whether or not the waiting user should be accepted into the group.

COLLABORATIVE SESSION→5.1.1 The BLIND DATE is used to prepare the membership for a COLLABORATIVE SESSION.

INTERACTION DIRECTORY→4.2.3 also lists potential contexts for collaboration. However, it does not focus explicitly on finding a critical number of participants needed to start an interaction.

4.2.7 Meet me... applied

After the SHARED EDITING$_{\rightarrow 4.1.6}$ functionality was implemented, Paul had to solve the issues related to session management. He could have followed the ROOM$_{\rightarrow 4.2.1}$ pattern to ease the establishment of COLLABORATIVE SESSIONS$_{\rightarrow 5.1.1}$, the communication in the session, and access to shared material. For several reasons, Paul decided not to do this: he thought that it was important for all members of the game engine community to stay aware of all major changes to the code base. Separating the artifact according to the team structure would have made collective code ownership problematic. Collective code ownership is one practice propagated by the eXtreme Programming methodology (Beck, 1999). The idea behind it is that every developer should be allowed to change any code as long as they have a good reason for doing so. If Paul had created isolated work rooms, the material would be created in those rooms. This would mean that the material was owned by the members of the rooms, which contradicts collective code ownership.

What Paul did instead was to provide an INTERACTION DIRECTORY$_{\rightarrow 4.2.3}$ in which all COLLABORATIVE SESSIONS are shown (Figure 4.35). Whenever users start a new collective session, it becomes visible in the INTERACTION DIRECTORY. Instead of creating ROOMS for the subgroups of the community, users start a session and enter or leave a session based on their current interests. Note that a session can have more than two members. In this case, one member plays the role of a driver, while the second plays the role of a navigator who comments on the driver's actions. The remaining users act as spectators: they may ask the driver and the navigator questions, but their main role is to observe the team. The idea for these roles came from Susan, who once tried to teach a class of new game engine users. What she did was to perform a pair programming session with Charley and invite the class to observe the session.

Figure 4.35 A list of XP sessions

To enter a session, users can select a session and press the *join* button in the INTERACTION DIRECTORY. This creates a notification on the driver's screen that prompts the driver to accept the new member (Figure 4.36). Note that this interpretation of BELL$_{\rightarrow 4.2.4}$ gives the driver full responsibility for checking the appropriateness of the new member. An alternative would have been to let all group

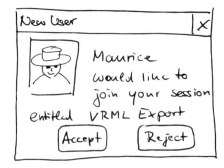

Figure 4.36 Requesting entry to an XP session by means of a BELL

members vote on accepting the new member. However, since the driver is the person who is in control of the session, Paul thought that it would be good to emphasize this in the session management as well.

Consequently, the driver is the only group member who can invite other users to the session. To create an invitation, they can select a set of users and provide an invitation message (Figure 4.37). The users invited see a pop-up window prompting them to join the session. If they accept, they become session members.

Figure 4.37 Inviting users to an XP session

Finally, Paul had a special idea for applying the BLIND DATE$_{\rightarrow 4.2.6}$ pattern (Figure 4.38): since eXtreme Programming argues that all code should be written in pairs, he allowed users to create sessions with empty slots. Users interested in a specific pair-programming session can create a placeholder for the session and

4.2 Meet me... or how to create places for collaboration

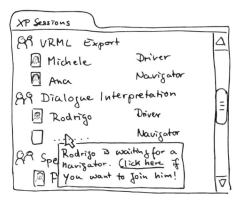

Figure 4.38 Waiting for a peer to start a pair programming session

assign themselves to one of the free participant slots of the session. By this, they express their interest and place it visually in a prominent location in the community (in the INTERACTION DIRECTORY). However, they are not allowed to start the session unless both the driver and the navigator are present. The initiator of the session can continue doing other things and is informed as soon as the session is ready to start.

4.3 Read me... or how to support textual communication

Let's recapture how far the game engine community got with the patterns we have discussed so far:

> *The game engine community has now found a place for collaboration. They meet for collaborative sessions and get a lot of work done. Besides this collaboration, a lot of communication takes place. Users use e-mail to coordinate dates or to make group decisions. They use instant-messaging systems like Skype (http://www.skype.com) to exchange short text messages or to hold an audio conference. However, they feel that their communication could be improved.*

This section presents patterns for computer-mediated communication. We concentrate on textual communication. Though textual communication raises the fewest technical problems, there are many social issues that should be considered when shaping efficient computer-mediated textual communication.

We could have extended the discussion of communication patterns in order to also discuss audio or video communication in this section, but for space and thematic reasons we decided not to do this. The use of audio or video communication has been widely studied in the field of computer-supported collaborative work. The studies consistently mention the benefits of audio conversations over textual conversations, mainly because of the richer media and easier access to the media (talking is faster than typing). However, with respect to video, the studies provide different results over whether or not video really improves group interaction. Comparative studies like (Bos et al., 2002) or (Isaacs and Tang, 1994) mainly concentrated on the value of video in situations in which critical negotiations take place. Such contexts require a very high level of trust and non-verbal cues that cannot be easily communicated in a more restricted media like textual communication.

We foresee major innovation and convergence of media in this area as soon as automatic text recognition and text synthesis improve. An example of a new way of combining the different media in group contexts has been given by Ziegler et al. (2005). In their work the authors created and evaluated a tool that automatically extracted concepts from spoken conversations and realized these concepts as a concept map visible to all participants of a meeting.

Finding best practices to form the basis for patterns in this area is a challenging task: we would like to encourage you to contribute to this task. At the time of writing we do not see many mature practices in computer-mediated audio or video communication that exceed the use of a communication tool and the automatic establishment of an audio channel as proposed in the ROOM$_{\rightarrow 4.2.1}$ pattern, for example. An exception that proves the rule is the use of a headset while being simultaneously involved in audio communication and a shared editing session.

4.3 Read me... or how to support textual communication

Text-based communication has an interesting property that is addressed by many of the patterns of this section: it does not rely on synchronicity of the participants. Figure 4.39 makes use of this fact. Users send text messages to each other while they work on artifacts in the group's interaction space. In the diagram, the messages are represented as small arrows and the users' paths through the group's interaction space are shown as lines. The communication helps to orient the paths of the group members. Parts of the communication will take place while the group shares a common current focus—where the paths follow parallel lines. The flags mark reference points in the communication that are of relevance to the whole group.

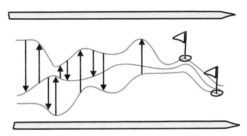

Figure 4.39 Communication between group members

This potential persistence of text messages leads to another interesting property of textual exchanges: participants can use logs of the conversation to search for words in a log, or distill other artifacts from it. Communication can for that reason result in a pool of knowledge that can be shared within the community.

Finally, it is easier to include references in textual messages. While this can also be done in audio communication, it is not nearly as easy to follow an audio reference.

The area of group communication is addressed by the following patterns (Figure 4.40):

EMBEDDED CHAT$_{\to 4.3.1}$ Allow users to communicate synchronously with low technology support.

FORUM$_{\to 4.3.2}$ Provide the means for persistent asynchronous group communication.

THREADED DISCUSSIONS$_{\to 4.3.3}$ Structure contributions to a discussion in an interaction space into threads.

FLAG$_{\to 4.3.4}$ Use a flag to signal important content.

SHARED ANNOTATION$_{\to 4.3.5}$ Provide a means for sharing comments on specific content.

270 Chapter 4 Group Support

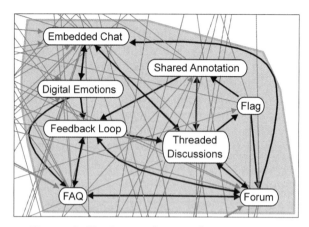

Figure 4.40 Patterns for textual communication

FEEDBACK LOOP$_{\to 4.3.6}$ Support readers in clarifying the author's intention and giving feedback to the author.

DIGITAL EMOTIONS$_{\to 4.3.7}$ Let users express personal feelings.

FAQ$_{\to 4.3.8}$ Reduce the noise produced by repeated questions.

4.3.1 Embedded Chat **

chat (chăt), NOUN: **1.** An informal, light conversation. **2. Computer Science A synchronous exchange of remarks over a computer network. 3.** Any of several birds known for their chattering call, as of the genera *Saxicola* or *Icteria*.

Intent

Allow users to communicate synchronously with low technology support.

Context

Users are collaborating using a groupware system such as a collaborative application or community system.

Problem

Users need to communicate. They are used to sending electronic mail. But since e-mail is asynchronous by nature, it is often too slow to resolve issues that arise in synchronous collaboration.

Scenario

Juan and Carla are still developing the graphics engine. They have met for another pair-programming session and share the same source code, so that both of them can modify the code and see the other developer's modifications instantly. They also need to discuss their changes but they lack any voice communication. Juan uses an instant messaging tool of a well-known messaging service provider. Unfortunately, Carla has an account at another provider. So instant messaging doesn't work so well. Finally they type their messages in the source code, but neither of them is really happy with this solution.

Symptoms

You should consider applying this pattern when . . .

— Turnaround time during asynchronous communication is too long.

— Orally spelling out information such as Web addresses or contact information is difficult and error-prone.
— Users use different tools for collaboration and communication and thereby loose their collaboration context when switching between different applications.

Solution

Therefore: Integrate a tool for quick synchronous interaction into your cooperative application. Let users send short text messages, distribute these messages to all other group members immediately, and display these messages at each group member's site.

Dynamics

To integrate chat in a groupware system, at least three text fields are necessary in the user interface. One of these text fields lets the local user enter a message, another displays the conversation, and the last contains a USER LIST$_{\to 4.4.1}$. The USER LIST shows participating users and thereby makes a local user aware of the communicating group. When displaying the conversation, messages are preceded with the users' names and the time at which they sent the message.

From a technical point of view, an EMBEDDED CHAT can be implemented either by using a central server, or via a peer-to-peer network. In the following we describe an implementation using a central server. For the peer-to-peer solution, refer to REPLICATED OBJECTS$_{\to 5.2.3}$ and DECENTRALIZED UPDATES$_{\to 5.2.6}$.

For a centralized solution, a central server has to be set up and users must be able to LOGIN$_{\to 3.1.2}$ at this server. Information about who has logged in at the server and the messages that were sent to the server are kept in CENTRALIZED OBJECTS$_{\to 5.2.1}$.

The login information is used to identify which user has sent a message. Whenever a user logs in or out of the central server, MEDIATED UPDATES$_{\to 5.2.5}$ are used to distribute this information to the participants of the EMBEDDED CHAT that have already logged in to the server. At the participants' sites this sort of information is reflected in the USER LIST.

Whenever a user enters a new message it is sent to the central server, which uses MEDIATED UPDATES$_{\to 5.2.5}$ to distribute the new message to the participants of the EMBEDDED CHAT. LOVELY BAGS$_{\to 5.3.5}$ are used to manage the received messages at the central server and to avoid inconsistencies. At the participants' sites the newly received messages are displayed in the conversation flow as described above.

Rationale

By embedding chat in a groupware system as described above, users are able to communicate in a textual way and the exchange of textual information is simplified.

As they communicate synchronously, the higher turnaround time of asynchronous communication is eliminated. The integration of chat into a groupware system helps its users maintain their collaboration context.

Check

When applying this pattern, you should answer these questions:

— Are you going to integrate a self-built chat application into your collaborative system, or are you going to connect your system using an existing chat application?
— Where are going to locate the EMBEDDED CHAT in the user interface?

Danger Spots

Users might already use different chat tools for textual communication. This makes it difficult to introduce a new chat tool, as users might not want to lose their established environment and existing contacts. To overcome this issue, establishing a unifying tool may help. Trillian (http://www.ceruleanstudios.com/), for example, unifies different instant messaging systems.

Sometimes the integration and implementation of your own chat application is not possible. In this case, think about implementing a bridge to existing chat applications. Many web-based systems allow their users to provide their ICQ number, Yahoo ID, MSN identification, and so on.

Smith et al. (Smith et al., 2000) identify five core problems with using chat tools for textual communication:

— *Lack of links between people and what they say.* To overcome this issue, you can help to differentiate what individual users are saying by associating an icon or a color with specific users.
— *No visibility of listening-in-progress.* Use awareness mechanisms to show whether users are following a conversation or are unavailable.
— *Lack of visibility of turns-in-progress.* This issue can be addressed by providing awareness of when users are entering messages, for example by means of an ACTIVITY INDICATOR$_{\rightarrow 4.4.9}$.
— *Lack of control over turn positioning.* Often, sub-conversations of the main conversations take place. This makes it hard for users to follow the conversation in which they are interested. Different approaches exist to solving this issue. One popular one is to support THREADED DISCUSSIONS$_{\rightarrow 4.3.3}$.
— *Lack of useful recordings and social context.* Providing a persistent history of chat conversations solves this issue.

Some chat tools limit the size of messages that can be exchanged, for example to 256 characters. This makes it difficult to exchange longer text passages like copied documents or source code. Therefore, do not limit the possible message length.

Known Uses

Eclipse offers an IRC-plugin to enable communication between distributed developers (see Figure 4.41).

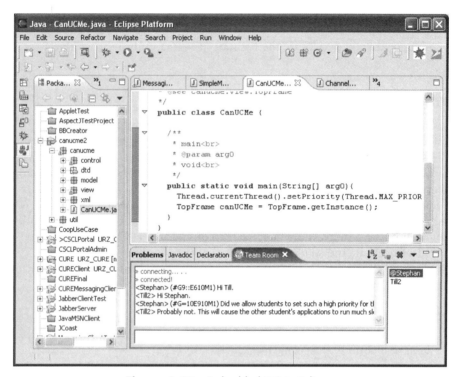

Figure 4.41 Embedded IRC in Eclipse

CURE (Haake et al., 2004b) is a web-based system for collaborative learning. It uses ROOMS$_{\rightarrow 4.2.1}$ as places for virtual collaboration. Users can enable an EMBEDDED CHAT for each room to allow textual communication among all the users in a room.

XING (https://www.xing.com) allows its users to provide their ICQ number, Yahoo ID, or MSN identification to embed textual communication facilities. These facilities can be launched from within XING.

Star Wars Galaxies (Sony Online Entertainment, 2003) is one example of a multiuser online game that integrates chat in the virtual worlds of the game (see Figure 4.42).

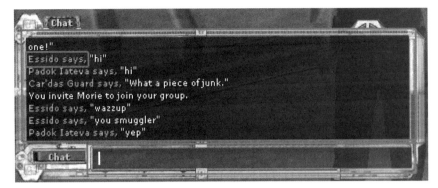

Figure 4.42 An EMBEDDED CHAT in the online game Star Wars Galaxies.

The example shows a conversation between three players. Besides the messages from other players, the chat often also displays status messages. An example of this is the message *"You invite Morie to join your group."* in Figure 4.42.

Related Patterns

DIGITAL EMOTIONS$_{\to 4.3.7}$ allows users to express their current feelings and thereby improve their understanding.

QUALITY INSPECTION$_{\to 3.2.1}$ explains how a chat discussion can be moderated to increase its quality.

FLOOR CONTROL$_{\to 4.1.7}$ is another alternative for achieving moderation in chats. Before users can speak, they have to acquire the right to talk from the person currently speaking. Note that chats often model FLOOR CONTROL on the level of a social protocol. In this case, users enter a specific code (such as **t**) to signal that they want to talk. The person who is currently typing then grants this wish by entering another agreed code (such as **p-Stephan**) to pass the floor to a specific user. Keeping track of the floor can, however, be difficult if it is modeled on the level of a social protocol.

ACTIVITY INDICATOR$_{\to 4.4.9}$ can show when other users are typing a message and thereby support coordination in the chat.

USER LIST$_{\to 4.4.1}$ allows display of the participating users of the chat and makes a local user aware of the listening group members.

PERSISTENT SESSION$_{\rightarrow 5.1.2}$ describes how conversations made in an EMBEDDED CHAT can persist over different sessions. Basically, this implies that chat messages are logged for future reference. The same thing was proposed in the KEEP ARCHIVES pattern (Goldman et al., 2002).

VIRTUAL ME$_{\rightarrow 3.1.5}$ can be used to represent the sender of each chat message.

4.3.2 Forum **

Alternative name(s): Open Discussion, Bulletin Board

fo·rum (fôr'əm), NOUN: **1a.** The public square or marketplace of an ancient Roman city that was the assembly place for judicial activity and public business. **b. A public meeting place for open discussion. c. A medium of open discussion or voicing of ideas, such as a newspaper or a radio or television program. 2.** A public meeting or presentation involving a discussion usually among experts and often including audience participation. **3.** A court of law; a tribunal.

Intent

Provide the means for persistent asynchronous group communication.

Context

Users want to communicate in the context of a community.

Problem

Users want to communicate about a specific topic. Without knowing people interested in the same topic, this is difficult.

Scenario

Martin, an expert in computer-supported collaborative learning, entered the project with the goal of discussing new application areas for the game engine. He is convinced that it can be used to create various games for public education. He also knows that there are other community members like Weigang and Molo who might be interested in such a discussion. Getting in contact with them by e-mail, however, or using a room to establish a task force for the issue, would limit the participants to the people who Martin already knew.

Symptoms

You should consider applying this pattern when ...

— Users receive messages from many communities via the same e-mail address.
— Users can forget to include some group members in the list of recipients.
— Users often have problems relating messages to the group context.

- Users have problems referring to messages in the group interaction.
- You want to allow latecomers to catch up with communication.
- You want to support group building according to themes instead of people.

Solution

Therefore: Create a forum as a central place for communication in which all group members can discuss asynchronously by reading and writing messages. Keep forum messages persistent.

Dynamics

To create a FORUM a central server has to be set up that can easily be accessed by all users. Users must be able to create their own FORUMS on the server. The server has to keep a directory of all available FORUMS and users must be able to browse this list. To enable discussion, users must be able to access the FORUMS via the central server and post messages to their selected FORUM. All messages that are posted to a FORUM are kept persistent (see REPLAY$_{\to 5.1.4}$). When a user accesses a FORUM, the messages that were posted to it are displayed. Users must be able to view single messages and to reply to selected messages, to enable discussion.

Rationale

As users can browse the list of available FORUMS or create a new FORUM, they are able to find interesting discussion partners. Users can read the messages that belong to a discussion, as the central server keeps all messages persistent. New members can understand a discussion that started before they became a member of the FORUM. Finally, as users can post their own messages to a FORUM and reply to messages, users can join or start a discussion.

Check

When applying this pattern, you should answer these questions:

- How are you going to let users access the FORUM?
- How are you going to categorize the available FORUMS?
- How are going to handle communication between the users and the central server that hosts the FORUMS?
- Will you allow strangers to read FORUMS messages?

Danger Spots

Users might not check the FORUM frequently using their community system. If possible, also allow users to access the FORUM with their preferred tool for asynchronous communication, such as their e-mail client, which automatically receives the newest messages.

Users might not want to use additional software to access a FORUM. Instead they want to use their preferred e-mail client. If you cannot support access to the FORUM for e-mail clients, establish a mailing list for the group. For that purpose, collect the e-mail addresses of all group members and create a new e-mail address, the mailing list address. Whenever a user sends a discussion contribution to the mailing list address, distribute this contribution to the collected e-mail addresses of the group members.

When displaying the messages posted to a FORUM using the order in which the messages were received, it might be difficult to find related messages and to follow a specific discussion. This problem can be solved using THREADED DISCUSSIONS$_{\to 4.3.3}$.

Some users might post contributions that do not fit into the topic of the FORUM. To control the content of a FORUM, use a QUALITY INSPECTION$_{\to 3.2.1}$.

Known Uses

USENET is a worldwide compound of discussion FORUMS that are also called "newsgroups". Everybody who has access to the Internet can access a news server and the newsgroups the server hosts and participate in the discussion of the newsgroups. The server persistently stores the discussions and synchronizes its contents with other news servers. Communication among the news servers and between the users and the news servers is described in RFC977 (Kantor and Lapsley, 1986).

Yahoo Groups allow users to browse all available FORUMS using their favorite web browser (see Figure 4.43). Users can read the messages posted to a FORUM and use their web browser, as well as their e-mail client, to post their own messages to the FORUM. In addition, Yahoo groups also allows users to subscribe and unsubscribe to a FORUM, then forwards new messages to these users. Thereby, Yahoo groups also implements a mailing list.

Related Patterns

FEEDBACK LOOP$_{\to 4.3.6}$ describes how users can contact other users if they did not completely understand another user's message.

INTERACTION DIRECTORY$_{\to 4.2.3}$ allows users to look up FORUMS in which they might be interested.

FAQ$_{\to 4.3.8}$ can be used to gather the knowledge of a FORUM community and collect answers to the most frequent questions in the FORUM.

QUALITY INSPECTION$_{\to 3.2.1}$ describes how to ensure the quality of the content in a FORUM.

Figure 4.43 Yahoo groups

THREADED DISCUSSIONS$_{\to 4.3.3}$ helps to find related messages when many different topics are discussed in the same FORUM.

PERIODIC REPORT$_{\to 4.5.3}$ keeps members of a forum informed of new messages. By using a PERIODIC REPORT, users no longer need to actively poll for new messages.

CHANGE INDICATOR$_{\to 4.5.4}$ can be used to highlight new messages in the FORUM.

EMBEDDED CHAT$_{\to 4.3.1}$ should be used instead of a FORUM if there is a need for immediate feedback.

MESSAGE BOARD (Duyne et al., 2002) describes how web-based forums should be designed.

E-FORUM (Manns and Rising, 2005) emphasizes the importance of a FORUM in the context of discussing new ideas and introducing change into an organization.

4.3.3 THREADED DISCUSSIONS *

Alternative name(s): Conversations Threading (Goldman et al., 2002)

thread (thrĕd), NOUN: **1a.** Fine cord of a fibrous material, such as cotton or flax, made of two or more filaments twisted together and used in needlework and the weaving of cloth. **b.** A piece of such cord. [...] **3.** A helical or spiral ridge on a screw, nut, or bolt. **4.** *Computer Science* **a.** A portion of a program that can run independently of and concurrently with other portions of the program. **b. A set of posts on a newsgroup, composed of an initial post about a topic and all responses to it.**

Intent

Structure contributions to a discussion in an interaction space into threads.

Context

Users contribute messages to a textual communication channel such as a FORUM$_{\rightarrow 4.3.2}$.

Problem

Computer-mediated textual communication is often not linear. People refer to contributions made by other users, but between the original contribution and the response other users may have contributed messages that lead the discussion in another direction. This leads to parallel and interleaved conversations that are hard to understand.

Scenario

Martin's initiative for discussing different application areas for the game engine achieved enormous popularity. More than twenty of the test users contribute over eighty new ideas for games. Unfortunately, Martin only used a simple FORUM for the discussion. With such a high level of traffic, it became more and more difficult to separate the discussions of the different ideas. Some ideas got lost because they were started while other ideas were consuming most of the participants' attention.

Symptoms

You should consider applying this pattern when ...

— A conversation space is used to discuss different topics at the same time.
— Users decide for themselves which topics should be discussed.

— Users experience misunderstandings because of wrong references in the conversation.

Solution

Therefore: **Track and visualize the relations between the different messages.**

Dynamics

When a user creates a message, the system tracks the original to which the new message is a response. One way of tracking the original message is for the system to provide a reply button that allows the user to indicate that the new message is a reply to the currently displayed message. In synchronous interaction, the last message that was displayed when the user started to type the reply can be used as reference.

When the user publishes the message to the rest of the group, the message includes a reference to its parent. Other users receiving the message store it as a child of the original message, resulting in a tree structure of messages.

Messages that have no reference are considered as roots for new threads.

In the user interface, the user can browse, collapse, and expand message trees, using a TREE TABLE to display the messages.

Rationale

Threads help to support coherent discussions. Users can concentrate on one thread at a time and filter out messages that are not relevant to the thread.

Check

When applying this pattern, you should answer these questions:

— How can you detect message references? Is there a built-in reference mechanism in the communication protocol?

— How should you allow a user to refer to a message? Will you ask explicitly, or will you infer the message referred to from the user's actions?

Danger Spots

Finding new messages in a thread can become complicated. Therefore, you should ensure that new messages are highlighted, for example by using a CHANGE INDICATOR$_{\rightarrow 4.5.4}$. Alternatively, you could allow the user to switch between thread display and chronological display.

Known Uses

USENET (Kantor and Lapsley, 1986) relies on threaded messages to remain structured. When a client replies to a message in a newsgroup, the news reader normally adds a reference to the parent message in the new message's header.

Figure 4.44 Threaded discussions in newsgroups

As an example, consider Figure 4.44, which shows an excerpt from the comp.lang.smalltalk newsgroup. Unlike the example in our scenario, the news reader used to create this screen shot supports message threading, as is the case for most modern news readers.

The internal representation of the last message includes the following references to previous messages (note that only headers important for threading are shown, and that line breaks have been added for better readability):

```
Date: Sun, 11 Jun 2006 14:13:31 +0200 Newsgroups:
comp.lang.smalltalk Subject: Re: Anyone use Smalltalk to get stock
quotes from Y Finance? References:
<1148531616.866984.253880@g10g2000cwb.googlegroups.com>
        <UpidndCpabopUOjZnZ2dnUVZ_vednZ2d@totallyobjects.com>
        <1148993816.900447.112070@g10g2000cwb.googlegroups.com>
        <1149932985.869205.139490@j55g2000cwa.googlegroups.com>
        <BM-dnXnpo4SscBfZnZ2dnUVZ_s6dnZ2d@totallyobjects.com>
        <1149988495.581139.56440@y43g2000cwc.googlegroups.com>
In-Reply-To: <1149988495.581139.56440@y43g2000cwc.googlegroups.com>
Message-ID: <mbqdnTMgceh2lRHZnZ2dnUVZ_sednZ2d@totallyobjects.com>
```

The most important section is the list of message identifiers stored in the References header (lines 4–6). When creating a reply to a message, the news reader adds the id of the currently shown message to the In-Reply-To header (line 7). It also adds this id to the list of references. The References header thus includes a complete list of messages that preceded the current message in the thread. The message itself gets a new message ID when it is received by the server (the mail server of totallyobjects.com in the example, line 8).

Note that the list of message identifiers in the References header is longer than the list of messages shown in Figure 4.44. The reason for this is that the news server can discard old messages. This means that the earliest messages in the thread are no longer available. Irrespective of missing messages, the news reader can still arrange messages in a thread, since it can merge two parts of the message tree when a root element is no longer present. (The Usenet RFC suggest keeping as many references as possible in the reference line, but allows skipping of old references if the reference line would otherwise get too long.)

E-mail (Crocker, 1982) originally did not require including threading information in a reply. This is one reason why many e-mail clients cannot show the messages in threads. The detection of a thread becomes more difficult in this case (see Lewis and Knowles (1997) for a discussion of text-mining approaches for reference detection). One way to overcome this limitation in groupware systems with embedded forums is to generate subject lines automatically that include a unique message identifier, and to rely on the fact that users don't change the subject line when replying to a message. This works reasonable well in most cases, and changes in the subject line often also signal topic shifts in the discussion.

The CURE forum (Haake et al., 2004a) shown in Figure 4.45 is an example of such an approach. The upper part of the figure shows the messages as they were dispatched to the users' e-mail clients. Each message subject first includes a user-defined part ("Masters Track Discussion" in the example) followed by two program-generated parts. First, the CURE system adds the name of the collaboration space to which the message was directed, then it adds the id of the message (shown in square brackets). When a message is received by the CURE system, it interprets the message number and thereby finds the parent message.

Other relevant research prototypes with a focus on threaded e-mails have highlighted the need for good visualizations of thread relationships. ReMail (Gruen et al., 2004), for example, shows a graphical thread map with each message. The position of the current message is highlighted, so that its relationship to other messages is clear.

KOLUMBUS 2 (Kienle, 2006) (Figure 4.50 on page 296) is a collaborative learning environment that supports content-centered communication with shared annotations.

Communication occurs via annotations that can be linked to material and other annotations. By annotating annotations, discussion threads are developed. To emphasize the communicative character of these contributions, the name of the originator and the date are placed in front of the message, as is

4.3.3 THREADED DISCUSSIONS

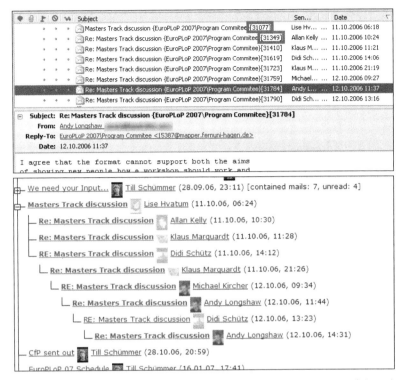

Figure 4.45 Detecting message threads through automated ids as part of the subject line

well-known from discussion forums. You can see an example of a discussion thread at the bottom of Figure 4.50.

Chat Systems. In the context of chat conversation, several systems have explored the use of thread visualization. One of the earliest systems was Threaded Chat (Smith et al., 2000), shown in Figure 4.46.

The problem here is to support an effortless way of creating references between chat messages: to create a new message, users have to select a parent message and start typing. Immediately after this, a message placeholder is shown for all other users indicating that the user is currently adding a new entry to the message thread (as in ACTIVITY INDICATOR$_{\to 4.4.9}$).

The creators of Threaded Chat also pointed out that it can become difficult to keep track of messages that are added to other nodes in the thread tree. The solution that Threaded Chat uses is to highlight new messages using bold font and to add status information on the total number of messages and the number of unread messages to each thread (as in CHANGE INDICATOR$_{\to 4.5.4}$).

Figure 4.46 Threaded Chat (Smith et al., 2000)

Other examples of threaded chats are ThreadChat (Holmer and Wessner, 2005) and HyperDialog (Pimentel et al., 2003).

Related Patterns

FLAG$_{\to 4.3.4}$ can be used to mark relevant threads.

FORUM$_{\to 4.3.2}$ and EMBEDDED CHAT$_{\to 4.3.1}$ Threads are used to structure the communication in a FORUM] or an EMBEDDED CHAT.

CHANGE INDICATOR$_{\to 4.5.4}$ When showing messages as a tree, users can miss new messages that are added to different parts of the tree. You should therefore consider attaching CHANGE INDICATORS to both the new message and the parent nodes in the tree if the message itself is currently invisible (folded).

ACTIVE MAP$_{\to 4.2.2}$ can be used to display the thread structure of a THREADED DISCUSSION and show the parts where activity is taking place.

TREE TABLE (Tidwell, 2006) can be used to visualize message threads.

4.3.4 FLAG

Alternative name(s): Flagged Messages (Goldman et al., 2002)

flag (flăg), NOUN: **1.** A piece of cloth, usually rectangular, of distinctive color and design, used as a symbol, standard, signal, or emblem. **2.** National or other allegiance, as symbolized by a flag: *ships of the same flag.* **3.** A ship carrying the flag of an admiral; *a flagship.* **4. A marking device, such as a gummed strip of paper, attached to an object to attract attention or ease identification; a tab. 5.** The masthead of a newspaper. [...] **8.** *Computer Science* A variable or memory location that stores true-or-false, yes-or-no information.

Intent

Use a flag to signal important content.

Context

Users interact in a collaboration space such as a FORUM$_{\to 4.3.2}$ or a ROOM$_{\to 4.2.1}$. Artifacts in this collaboration space are labeled using text.

Problem

It is difficult to distinguish textual artifacts without processing the meaning of the label. Both important and unimportant artifacts are represented in the same way.

Scenario

Charley is again looking for bugs in the game engine. Whenever he finds a bug, he sends a bug description to all the members of the core development team. Since Charley finds a lot of bugs, Paul no longer has an overview of which bugs need further action and which are already resolved.

Symptoms

You should consider applying this pattern when ...

— Users need to track artifacts.
— The collaboration space includes many artifacts and users have problems rediscovering important artifacts.
— Users spend a lot of time distinguishing spam from important messages.

Solution

Therefore: Provide users with a way to flag important artifacts. Display the flags so that flagged artifacts can be easily found later.

Dynamics

Users select an artifact and place a flag on it. The artifact will be shown as visually distinct from other artifacts that are not marked, for example by using a graphical icon or different color.

Some flags are used to express interaction with the system. One example is the flag for new messages. This will be removed as soon as the user reads the message (although they should be able to place the flag on the message again). Other flags express general importance.

To provide a larger classification power, the system should allow users to create their own flags.

When searching for artifacts, the user can query the system for artifacts with specific flags.

Rationale

The flag serves both as a filter and as a reminder. It helps users to concentrate on important messages by speeding up the process of revisiting important content. It also helps users to remember that there is important content that requires their attention.

Check

When applying this pattern, you should answer these questions:

— How will you store flags? Can you add them to the artifact as an additional attribute, or do you have to create a PROXY OBJECT that stores the flags for a specific artifact?

— Does it make sense to use one shared flag for the whole group, or will you use personalized flags?

Danger Spots

Make sure that artifacts can be highlighted and sorted based on how they are labeled.

Limit the number of different flags, to protect users from creating classification schemes that require complex cognitive processing.

Flagging can be time consuming. Think about a way to flag artifacts automatically, for example by using filters, as described in ATTENTION SCREEN$_{\rightarrow 3.3.4}$.

Known Uses

IMAP Message Flags. The Internet Message Access Protocol (IMAP, (Crispin, 1996)) defines how e-mail messages can be stored on a central server. Each message can be decorated with one or more flags. When users change the flags in their e-mail clients, for example by clicking a button that marks an e-mail message as important, the client informs the server and stores the new flags.

An example client-server interaction for marking a message with a flag could look as follows:

```
Client: M7 STORE 42 +FLAGS (\Flagged)
Server: * 42 FETCH (FLAGS (\Flagged \Seen))
Server: M7 OK STORE completed
```

In this example, the client asks the server to add the flag named \Flagged to the message with id 42. The server performs this operation and returns the new set of flags attached to the message—in this case a flag indicating that the message has already been read and a flag indicating that the message is important.

Users can define new flags, which are passed as user-selected strings. However only few e-mail clients support this function.

ToDo Messages in Eclipse. The Eclipse programming environment (http://www.eclipse.org) allows users to define different labels for tasks. The tasks are tracked and visualized in the code as well as in a task query view (Figure 4.47).

Since Eclipse is a team-programming environment, with integrated source code management, team members share the same source code. This means that they also share the task flags. However, the interpretation of task flags can be tailored for each individual user. In the example in Figure 4.47, there are three different task labels. The FIXME and TODO labels are interpreted by all team members. The FIXME label implies a higher priority, which means that tasks with this label will be shown first in the task query view. The BUG TS label is Till Schummer's personal label He uses this label to mark important personal tasks in the code, while other users interpret this label as an unimportant task.

The task flags also appear on the marked scroll bar, which acts as an ANNOTATED SCROLLBAR (Tidwell, 2006) with group annotations.

290 Chapter 4 Group Support

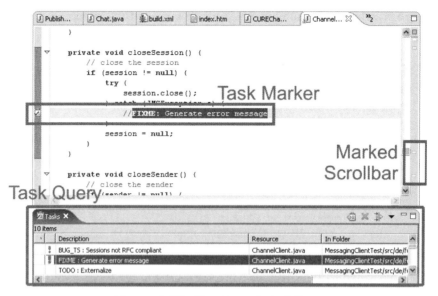

Figure 4.47 Flagging tasks in Eclipse

Related Patterns

FORUM$_{\rightarrow 4.3.2}$ FLAGS are frequently used in FORUMS to mark messages as read.

SHARED ANNOTATION$_{\rightarrow 4.3.5}$ A flag is a special instance of an annotation that can be interpreted by a machine. The main difference is that a flag should only express the relation of an artifact to a specific category, but not communicate additional information. Most flags are private. They are often combined with annotations, as is the case in Eclipse.

CHANGE INDICATOR$_{\rightarrow 4.5.4}$ An automatically generated FLAG is a CHANGE INDICATOR. It is added to a message if it is new or has been modified since last viewed. As the IMAP example shows, users normally remove this flag after they view a specific artifact (or the system tracks the user's actions and removes the flag automatically).

GENTLE REMINDER (Goldman et al., 2002) also addresses the problem that users may forget to process a specific message. The solution is to re-present unresolved messages periodically. However, as the authors state, this does not scale to a situation in which users have large queues of unanswered messages.

4.3.5 SHARED ANNOTATION

an·no·ta·tion (ăn'ō-tā'shən), NOUN: **1. The act or process of furnishing critical commentary or explanatory notes. 2.** A critical or explanatory note; a commentary.

Intent

Provide a means for sharing comments on specific content.

Context

Users share artifacts. Each artifact was created by a specific author or a group of authors that is distinct from the audience for the artifact (the readers).

Problem

Group members want to have the power to influence the way in which artifacts evolve or are perceived by the group. Too often systems limit the users' role to a passive audience.

Scenario

While reading Charley's code, Ana has several ideas and insights. She writes them down on a sheet of paper but is not convinced about the way she's going about this. She has problems relating the comments on paper to the actual source code artifacts, and she regrets that the other group members cannot access her comments.

Symptoms

You should consider applying this pattern when . . .

— Users start to discuss an artifact in THREADED DISCUSSIONS_{→4.3.3} but have problems relating their comments to the artifact.

— Users frequently ask the author the same question. Since the document can no longer be changed, the author cannot express himself more clearly.

— Group members have different opinions on a specific topic, but the two opinions are not linked in the collaboration space, which makes finding alternative viewpoints difficult.

Solution

Therefore: Provide a means for entering comments on specific messages or parts of a document. Collect all users' comments and display them with the content.

Dynamics

The pattern can be described by looking at the two different phases that need to be supported: the creation of an annotation and the display of an annotation.

To create an annotation, the user selects the part of the document or message to be commented. Then the user selects the "add comment" command, which opens an input field for the comment. The comment can be saved and is stored in a shared repository (that is, as CENTRALIZED OBJECTS$_{\to 5.2.1}$).

Each comment needs to include the target reference of the commented object (for example the URL of a web page), a more detailed pointer to the parts of the referenced object that are of interest (such as the position of the selection in the web page), the comment itself, and the identity of the user who wrote the comment. In most cases, comments also include time stamps.

When viewing the document, the application first retrieves the document from its original location. It then requests the set of annotations that have the document as its target reference. The comments are then shown at the specific part of the document, for example as color highlighting that opens a tooltip view.

Rationale

The advantage of sharing comments is that the original document can remain untouched while users have the opportunity to express their views on its content. Comments can play different roles in the group process, as discussed by Weng and Gennari (2004):

— A communication message that coordinates future steps and changes attitudes in the community
— A source of group awareness that explain how other group members react to an annotation or to the annotated document
— An expression of an expert's opinion
— An explanation of changes in the annotated document

Allowing the user to reference a specific part of the annotated artifact makes it easy for the reader to put the annotation in context. However, this is also the most difficult part of the pattern, as we will discuss in the danger spots section.

Check

When applying this pattern, you should answer these questions:

— How can you model the reference to the artifact? Can you identify the artifacts as direct object references, will you use a PROXY OBJECT (Gamma et al., 1995), or can you describe it using a URI?
— Where can you store the comments? Can you create a common comment repository that is accessible by everyone?
— Can you rely on having applications at client sites that interweave comments and the original content?

Danger Spots

Individual users might not want to share all their comments with the whole group. The system should therefore distinguish between private and shared annotations (Marshall and Brush, 2004). Carter et al. (2004) even go a step further and distinguish between personal, collaborative, and social annotations. Personal annotations are used to support "active reading". While perceiving the artifact, users can make comments on the artifact that helps them to capture the content more quickly the next time. Collaborative annotations are used to communicate about the annotated content within a specific group process. One example is the process of writing a book, in which the authors share comments on the book's content. Social or public annotations, on the other hand, are shared between users who are not formally part of a group.

To distinguish the different levels of privacy of annotations, you can extend the annotations with a target group identification (such as all users that have access to a specific part of the collaboration space) to restrict their visibility to members of the group.

Comments can consume a lot of screen space. Therefore, think about making them expandable on demand (see the DETAILS ON DEMAND pattern (Tidwell, 2006)).

Target objects might be subject to changes that cause annotations to be orphaned or mis-positioned. Using IMMUTABLE VERSIONS$_{\rightarrow 5.3.6}$ can prevent the position of an annotation changing. However, after a new version of the document is created, annotations need to be removed from the document, which can be problematic. Selecting smaller units of immutability can help here. You could for example use a reference scheme that uses immutable version names for each paragraph of the document. Brush et al. (2001) discuss how more information about the annotated artifact can be stored in an annotation, so that it becomes more robust to text changes.

If the user does not have access to an application that is comment-aware, you might need to establish a comment proxy. This is an intermediate server that requests the original document for the user and then enriches it with comments. In this case, the proxy plays the role of the user's client in the SHARED ANNOTATION pattern.

Known Uses

Annotea (Kahan and Koivunen, 2001) (also `http://www.w3.org/2001/Annotea/User/Protocol.html`) is a W3C project with the goal of standardizing shared annotation mechanisms for web documents. The Amaya browser is a reference implementation of the Annotea protocol (`http://www.w3.org/Amaya/`), as shown in Figure 4.48.

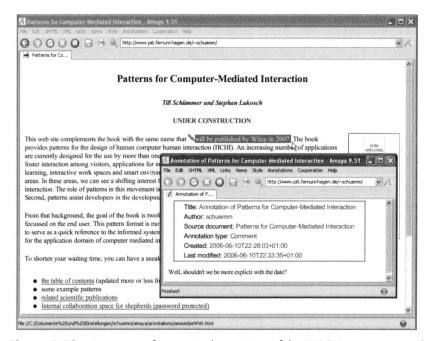

Figure 4.48 Amaya, a reference implementation of the W3C Annotea protocol

The figure shows a web page in which a specific text region is selected. After selecting the text, the user launched the "add comment" command, which opened a new view showing the comment.

Comments are stored as RDF documents. These are XML representations of metadata for a specific object. In the example in Figure 4.48, the comment looks like this:

```
1  <?xml version="1.0" ?>
2  <r:RDF xmlns:r="http://www.w3.org/1999/02/22-rdf-syntax-ns#"
3    xmlns:a="http://www.w3.org/2000/10/annotation-ns#"
```

```
4   xmlns:t="http://www.w3.org/2001/03/thread#"
5   xmlns:http="http://www.w3.org/1999/xx/http#"
6   xmlns:d="http://purl.org/dc/elements/1.1/">
7   <r:Description>
8   <r:type r:resource="http://www.w3.org/2000/10/annotation-ns#Annotation" />
9   <r:type r:resource="http://www.w3.org/2000/10/annotationType#Comment" />
10  <a:annotates r:resource="http://www.pi6.fernuni-hagen.de/~schuemm/" />
11  <a:context>http://www.pi6.fernuni-hagen.de/~schuemm/#xpointer(
12              string-range(/html[1]/p[3]/font[1],"",60,35))</a:context>
13  <d:title>Annotation of Patterns for Computer-Mediated Interaction</d:title>
14  <d:creator>schuemm</d:creator>
15  <a:created>2006-06-10T22:28:03+01:00</a:created>
16  <d:date>2006-06-10T22:33:35+01:00</d:date>
17  <a:body r:resource="http://annotea.pi6.fernuni-hagen.de/annotdzeWWi.html" />
18  </r:Description>
19  </r:RDF>
```

The relevant information starts in line 10 of the example. The a:annotates tag references the resource that should be annotated. The a:context tag details the scope of the comment by providing an explicit location in the document. In this case, it is the first font tag of the third paragraph in the document. In this tag, it is the selection that begins at the sixtieth character and ends thirty-five characters later.

The annotation has a title (line 13) and a reference to the real content (line 17). It includes the name of the user who annotated the document (line 14) and the time when the annotation was entered.

The annotations can be transferred to the annotation server using am HTTP post command. In the example, the annotation is stored on an Annotea server—see line 17.

The Amaya browser queries the annotation server whenever a document is loaded and adds any comments received to the document.

Pink (Takeda and Suthers, 2002), shown in Figure 4.49, is comparable to the Amaya example, but is based on the Zope (http://www.zope.org) document management environment.

It has two main differences from Amaya: first, the annotations target paragraphs rather than user-selected regions of the text. Second, it does not use a standardized RDF format for storing the annotations.

As in Amaya, users can annotate annotations as well. Pink puts special focus on this by representing the annotations as THREADED DISCUSSIONS$_{\to 4.3.3}$.

KOLUMBUS 2 (Kienle, 2006) (Figure 4.50, and see also the known uses section of THREADED DISCUSSIONS$_{\to 4.3.3}$). KOLUMBUS is a collaborative learning

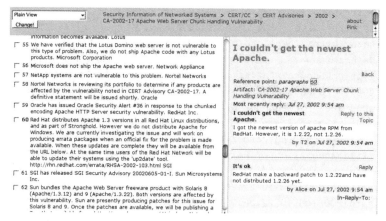

Figure 4.49 The Pink tool for annotating web pages and Wiki documents (from (Takeda and Suthers, 2002))

environment that supports flexible annotations at different levels of granularity. It segments content into a small items that can then be annotated by the users in a very flexible manner. Users can for example decide to annotate a whole chapter, or just a single paragraph.

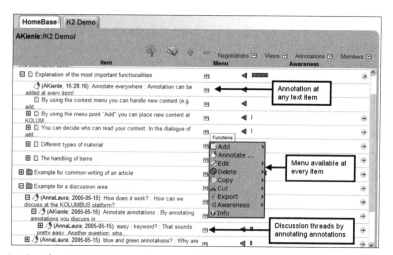

Figure 4.50 The KOLUMBUS environment bases collaborative learning on the concept of shared annotations http://www.imtm-iaw.rub.de/projekte/k2/index.html

Annotations can be inserted at every level of the hierarchy that arises from the segmentation of documents and attached threaded annotations. The higher an annotation is placed in the hierarchy, the more general is its scope. For each annotation the contributor can determine the recipients. In this way they decide whether the annotation is shared or private.

Points of Interest are often placed in an additional layer of electronic maps. While browsing the map, the user can place a flag on interesting places. These places can be stored and exchanged in a community. One concrete example of this is Google Earth, shown in Figure 4.51.

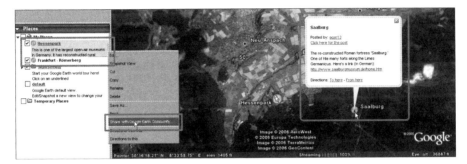

Figure 4.51 Sharing place descriptions places in Google Earth

Users can describe the place and store the description on a community server. The application queries the server for annotation while retrieving the map data.

Related Patterns

LETTER OF RECOMMENDATION$_{\to 3.2.2}$ A positive annotation can serve as a letter of recommendation for the annotated artifact. In the context of computer-mediated interaction, this points to another interesting application of annotations: it is not only possible to annotate artifacts, but also to annotate users.

QUALITY INSPECTION$_{\to 3.2.1}$ can be used to confirm that the annotation is meaningful and of high quality.

FEEDBACK LOOP$_{\to 4.3.6}$ shares with SHARED ANNOTATIONS the idea that a reader should be empowered to discuss the content provided by an author. The difference is that in the case of the FEEDBACK LOOP the reader can only get in contact with the author, not with other readers.

THREADED DISCUSSIONS$_{\to 4.3.3}$ can be used to allow users to comment on other users' comments.

4.3.6 FEEDBACK LOOP *

Alternative name(s): Reply, Ask the Author, Bidirectional Communication

feed·back (fĕd'băk'), NOUN: **1a.** The return of a portion of the output of a process or system to the input, especially when used to maintain performance or to control a system or process. **b.** The portion of the output so returned. **c.** Sound created when a transducer such as a microphone or electric guitar picks up sound from a speaker connected to an amplifier and regenerates it back through the amplifier. **2. The return of information about the result of a process or activity; an evaluative response: asked the students for feedback on the new curriculum. 3.** The process by which a system, often biological or ecological, is modulated, controlled, or changed by the product, output, or response it produces.

Intent

Support readers in clarifying the author's intention and giving feedback to the author.

Context

Authors want to communicate a message to their readers. They create textual content in the community, for example as a web page or a FORUM$_{\rightarrow 4.3.2}$ message. Readers read the content and want to understand the author's message.

Problem

In any communication, the recipient of a message can only refer to the message in order to understand it. However, most messages are ambiguous.

Scenario

Paul has set up a SHARED FILE REPOSITORY$_{\rightarrow 4.1.2}$ *where the project members can place the documentation for the game engine. Marc is doing a good job in documenting the graphics engine. Charley however uses very cryptic language to explain the security model of the game engine. Only Susan has the slightest idea of what Charley is talking about.*

Symptoms

You should consider applying this pattern when . . .

— Authors observe that their message is misinterpreted.
— Readers have problems understanding the author's message.

Solution

Therefore: Provide an easy means for readers to contact the author. Create a user interface element close to the content that opens input fields for the reader's questions and feedback.

Dynamics

The reader sees an author's content. If the reader has a question, they can open a reply view, for example by pressing a "reply-to" button. The reply dialog automatically references the content that is currently viewed. This can mean that the whole content is quoted, or that a pointer to the content is added to the reply message. The reader can pose questions or provide feedback, either by addressing the whole content or annotating just small parts of it. When the reader submits the question, it is transmitted to the author, who can in turn reply to the reader.

Rationale

By asking questions of the author personally, readers can draw attention to those parts of the content out that they find hard to understand. Readers can also qualify their question or feedback by providing more information about their personal context. This helps the author to understand the reader's context better and reshape the message so that it is easier to understand.

Danger Spots

It can make sense to distinguish between questions that are of general relevance and questions that are better discussed bilaterally. In the first case, the question should be sent to the whole group, while in the second case the question should only reach the original author.

This distinction is often not clear, especially in FORUMS$_{\rightarrow 4.3.2}$. In these systems, users are used to replying to a message and reaching the original sender. However, most lists are configured in such a way so that the reply is automatically sent to the address of the list, with the effect that all list members receive the question.

Known Uses

e-Mail Reply. All e-mail clients allow a message recipient to reply to a message. When replying, the system normally quotes the original message, using quotation marks at the beginning of each line. The system also quotes the subject line and precedes it with a special abbreviation such as "Re:".

In many systems, the reader can decide whether or not their reply should reach just the author—often labeled Reply—or all recipients of the original message, labeled as Reply to All.

Contact Buttons on Web Pages. Most web pages provide a link that allows a reader to get in contact with the author of the pages. The easiest way to implement this is to provide a mailto link at the top or bottom of each page. Clicking on the link causes an e-mail window to open in which the required address is already inserted. To fully implement the pattern, the question text should contain a reference to the relevant content. This can also be achieved using the mailto link, by adding additional parameters. For example, the link:

```
<a href=''mailto:stephan.lukosch@fernuni-hagen.de?Subject=
Question%20regarding%20the%20Ask%20the%20Author%20pattern''>
Ask the author</a>
```

opens an e-mail composition view with a completed recipient address and a subject line tailored to the current context. Note that the subject looks quite ugly, because it has to be URL-encoded, which means that spaces have to be replaced by the %20 string. It is even possible to provide content for the body of the message by adding a Body parameter, but this is rarely done.

Writer's workshops (James O. Coplien, 2000) include a non-technical variant of the pattern. Readers discuss a pattern while the authors of the pattern listen to their comments. This helps the authors to understand the readers' perception better. To prevent the authors defending their writing, they have to act like a fly on the wall and not speak. After readers have discussed the content, the authors can ask the readers for clarification of any comments that they were not able to understand.

Related Patterns

FORUM$_{\rightarrow 4.3.2}$ and THREADED DISCUSSIONS$_{\rightarrow 4.3.3}$ are based on the idea that readers of content are allowed to ask the author questions or provide comments. In THREADED DISCUSSIONS$_{\rightarrow 4.3.3}$, the system needs to ensure that a reference to the original content is provided by the reply to show the relationship between questions and answers.

FAQ$_{\rightarrow 4.3.8}$ and QUALITY INSPECTION$_{\rightarrow 3.2.1}$ Authors should consider a rewrite if too many questions address the same problems with the content. In cases where rewriting is not possible, such as when the content is published on paper, the author should apply a QUALITY INSPECTION$_{\rightarrow 3.2.1}$ to create a list of FREQUENTLY ASKED QUESTIONS$_{\rightarrow 4.3.8}$ to shorten the time a reader needs to find an answer to their question.

LETTER OF RECOMMENDATION$_{\rightarrow 3.2.2}$ provides another means of giving feedback.

4.3.7 DIGITAL EMOTIONS **

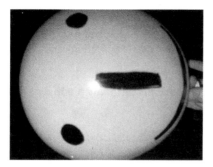

e·mo·tion (ĭ-mō'shən), NOUN: **1. A mental state that arises spontaneously rather than through conscious effort and is often accompanied by physiological changes; a feeling:** *the emotions of joy, sorrow, reverence, hate, and love.* **2.** A state of mental agitation or disturbance: *spoke unsteadily in a voice that betrayed his emotion.* [...] **3.** The part of the consciousness that involves feeling; sensibility: *"The very essence of literature is the war between emotion and intellect"* (Isaac Bashevis Singer).

Intent

Let users express personal feelings.

Context

You are using textual communication without audio or video support.

Problem

In face-to-face communication emotions can be easily communicated by nonverbal clues. In textual communication, it is expensive in time to express emotional connotations in words. Emotions are often not transmitted if the communication focuses on content.

Scenario

John has come across some very cryptic code that was written by Charley. He feels that he should tell Charley that his code is hard to read and that it should be improved. However, Charley quite often misinterprets good advice and feels offended, especially in textual communication.

Symptoms

You should consider applying this pattern when ...

- Users do not recognize ironic remarks and fail to get the joke.
- Users end up in long discussions about a sarcastic message sent by another user.
- Users feel restricted when trying to communicate emotions.

Solution

Therefore: Provide textual means by which users can express their emotions.

Dynamics

There are various means by which users can express their emotions in textual messages:

1. You can rely on *emoticons* by which users express their emotions using ASCII characters, displaying pictograms or whole images composed only of ASCII characters.
2. You can include a toolbar in your communication application that shows graphical images with emotional connotations. Users can select a graphical image to include it in their message.
3. You can include a user interface element that allows users to define their current emotional state on a scale.

Rationale

:-) (Hancock, 2004)

Check

When applying this pattern, you should answer these questions:

— How are going to support users in expressing their emotions: rely on emoticons, support users with a toolbar, or use some sort of emotional scale?
— What kind of emotions are you going to support in the toolbar or scale?
— Where should you place the special user interface element?

Danger Spots

New users have to learn the emoticon conventions for expressing feelings. This can be overcome by applying a FEEDBACK LOOP$_{\rightarrow 4.3.6}$ or FAQ$_{\rightarrow 4.3.8}$.

Automatic expansion of ASCII text can lead to errors when users exchange source code, for example. Therefore, allow users to disable automatic expansion.

Known Uses

E-mail Clients such as Thunderbird automatically expand ASCII emoticons as images, but also allow the user to disable this feature. Well-known examples are:

:-) expresses a smile or happy sentiments

:-(expresses a frown, sadness, or unhappy sentiments

;-) expresses a wink

:p expresses a stuck-out tongue and is used to convey a joke or light-hearted sarcasm

Instant Messaging Systems (IMS) such as ICQ, MSN Messenger, and Yahoo Messenger offer users a list of common emoticons in a toolbar (see Figure 4.52), making it simple for users to express their emotions. Additionally, IMS automatically expands the ASCII characters entered by users as graphical images that reflect the same emotions.

Figure 4.52 Emoticon toolbar in MSN Messenger

Microsoft Chat, formerly known as Comic Chat, displays conversations as an interactive comic strip that unfolds in real time. The text a user types is displayed as comic-style balloons. Gestures generated by conversation semantics and the emotion, selected in the lower-right corner of the screenshot of the user interface shown in Figure 4.53, are reflected in the comic strip.

Active Worlds (http://www.activeworlds.com) is a community system based on a three-dimensional virtual world in which users are represented by avatars. They can navigate through the virtual world and see other users who are in their vicinity.

As in Microsoft Chat, Active Worlds users can exchange textual messages that are visualized as speech balloons. To express emotions, the system provides a tool bar with a predefined set of gestures. In the example in Figure 4.54, Till decided to express joy, which results in the user's avatar performing a pirouette.

Online Role-Playing Games like Dungeons & Dragons Online (Turbine Games, 2006), Everquest 2 (Sony Online Entertainment, 2004), Star Wars

4.3.7 Digital Emotions 305

Figure 4.53 Expressing emotions in Microsoft Chat

Figure 4.54 Expressing emotions in the three-dimensional Active Worlds environment

Galaxies (Sony Online Entertainment, 2003), or World of Warcraft (Blizzard Entertainment, (europäische Server)) make heavy use of DIGITAL EMOTIONS. In all the cases mentioned it is possible to select a target user and execute an emotion. The emotion is acted out by the player's avatar and is also described in the EMBEDDED CHAT$_{\to 4.3.1}$ present in these games.

Related Patterns

EMBEDDED CHAT$_{\to 4.3.1}$ allows textual communication. To express emotions users often use emoticons.

FEEDBACK LOOP$_{\to 4.3.6}$ can be used to find out the meaning of an unknown abbreviation.

FAQ$_{\to 4.3.8}$ can be used to collect emoticons that are common to a community to allow new members to understand the meaning.

4.3.8 FAQ

Alternative name(s): Knowledge Repository, RTFM

FAQ (făk), NOUN: **1. A list of frequently asked questions and their answers about a given subject.**

Intent

Reduce the noise produced by repeated questions.

Context

You are supporting long-term interaction in a large group or community that has experienced members as well as newcomers. You are thinking about how to integrate newcomers.

Problem

Authors have to spend too much effort in answering recurring questions of the recipients. This repetition demotivates the authors from answering at all. Repeated questions disturb most group members.

Scenario

Paul has the idea of better supporting the users of the game engine. He therefore announces a support hotline that the users can use whenever they have problems. Most of the core developers, especially Liam, Ana, and Susan, have volunteered to answer calls to the support hotline. On Monday morning, Adrian calls the hotline and asks how the libraries of the sound support are compiled. Half an hour later, Weigang calls with the same question, and in the afternoon, Molo also poses this question. This is not how the core developers imagined their life as support members.

Symptoms

You should consider applying this pattern when ...

— Community members frequently experience a feeling of *deja vù* when answering questions.
— Users have problems stating the right questions.
— The willingness to answer questions decreases over time.
— You may know questions and answers before establishing a collaboration context.

Solution

Therefore: Maintain a list of frequently asked questions that have been answered already. Treat this list as the knowledge repository of the group. Make this list accessible, especially to newcomers.

Dynamics

A FAQ can be implemented without much technology support. Basically, the author of the FAQ monitors the group interaction and collects recurring questions and answers in a FAQ document. They publish this document in the group space so that other users can refer to the FAQ before asking a question of the group.

A FAQ can also be managed in a more structured way. Figure 4.55 illustrates a possible management process for a FAQ. Users want to find a solution to a specific question. They first look up the FAQ list that includes the most prominent questions—in Figure 4.55, these are all questions with a hit count of thirty or above.

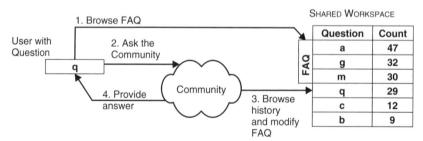

Figure 4.55 Usage of FAQs

If the question is not listed in the FAQ list, the user sends the question to the community. Community members compare the question with previously stated questions. This history of questions can be stored explicitly, for example in a SHARED FILE REPOSITORY$_{\rightarrow 4.1.2}$, or implicitly in the users' memory.

If the question has been asked before, community members refer to the old solution and increase the question's hit count in the question history. If a question passes the threshold for the FAQ, the FAQ list is updated.

Finally, the community member answers the question.

The system ensures that the FAQ list is accessible to all users. In systems that are based on e-mail or Usenet communication, this is done by sending the list to all participants regularly. In systems that provide a SHARED FILE REPOSITORY$_{\rightarrow 4.1.2}$, the list is stored in a prominent place.

Rationale

A FAQ makes important questions and their answers explicit. Users can learn about other users' questions before they finally ask community members. This reduces the number of repeated questions and allows community members to spend their time on challenging new questions.

Check

When applying this pattern, you should answer these questions:

— Where should you store your FAQ list and the list of questions?
— Who will maintain the FAQ list? Is it a responsibility of all community members, or do you have a defined group of moderators?
— How will you distribute the FAQ list?

Danger Spots

Questions that have made their way into the FAQ list will no longer be asked as frequently. However, this can have the effect that other questions seem to be more important, because they have gained a higher number of hits in a specific timeframe. A solution to this can be to count the hits for the FAQ as well. In this case, the questions from the FAQ receive an additional hit whenever a user looks one up in the FAQ.

Another solution to this problem is to use a LETTER OF RECOMMENDATION$_{\rightarrow 3.2.2}$ for each question. Whenever a user finds a solution in the FAQ, they can send feedback about whether the solution was helpful. This increases the question's hit count and ensures that this question will stay important.

Be aware of the fact that users can be reluctant to read a FAQ. Therefore make sure that the FAQ is placed at a prominent place in the community.

Creating a good structure for a FAQ requires a good knowledge of the subject's structure. You should keep this in mind when selecting people who moderate the FAQ and look for the most knowledgeable people in the community.

Known Uses

Newsgroups. Enthusiasts in newsgroups often maintain a list of frequently asked questions that is sent to the group often and in most cases also archived on a website. A typical example of an outline of a FAQ is shown in Figure 4.56.

Related Patterns

HALL OF FAME$_{\to 3.2.5}$ The FAQ can be considered as a HALL OF FAME for famous questions.

FEEDBACK LOOP$_{\to 4.3.6}$ If users do not understand the solution stated in the FAQ, they should be able to ask the user who provided the answer to the question. This may also involve finding an expert on a specific topic. This can be achieved using the EXPERT FINDER$_{\to 3.2.4}$ pattern.

MENTOR$_{\to 3.1.4}$ describes a more personal way of answering questions. This is done by pairing the user with a MENTOR who is an expert in the collaboration context. The expert can be found by applying the EXPERT FINDER$_{\to 3.2.4}$ pattern.

```
========== Questions ==========
*******************************

Part 1: Introduction

    What is this newsgroup for? How shall it be used?
    Where is comp.ai.neural-nets archived?
    What if my question is not answered in the FAQ?
    May I copy this FAQ?
    What is a neural network (NN)?
    Where can I find a simple introduction to NNs?
    Are there any online books about NNs?
    What can you do with an NN and what not?
    Who is concerned with NNs?
    How many kinds of NNs exist?
    How many kinds of Kohonen networks exist? (And what is k-means?)
       VQ: Vector Quantization and k-means
       SOM: Self-Organizing Map
       LVQ: Learning Vector Quantization
       Other Kohonen networks and references
    How are layers counted?
    What are cases and variables?
```

Figure 4.56 The first part of the outline of comp.ai.neural-nets FAQ (Sarle, 1997)

QUALITY INSPECTION$_{\rightarrow 3.2.1}$ It is important that the answers in the FAQ are reliable. The members of the quality inspection team should monitor any changes to the FAQ carefully.

FORUM$_{\rightarrow 4.3.2}$ A forum that keeps the messages persistent can also serve as a repository for finding previously stated questions and their answers. This requires that the FORUM can be searched by the users.

FREQUENTLY ASKED QUESTIONS (Duyne et al., 2002) is a variant of this pattern. In contrast to our description of the FAQ, it stresses the bootstrapping process and advocates creating a FAQ list in the design team at design time. The members of the design team should investigate the topic area and look for competitors' FAQs to find potentially relevant questions. New questions should be gathered from people who are in close contact with the customer. While this approach is valid in the context of mainly unidirectional communication, such as publishing information on a website, we argue that the process of FAQ creation should be more interactive and involve all participants in the interaction setting.

4.3.9 Read me... applied

The community has evolved into a very active group of developers. Paul was happy to see that the pair-programming tools are well accepted and that the code quality has improved significantly. He did not expect a global team to find so many opportunities for synchronous interaction, but this form of working together was new and challenging for the users.

One issue encountered so far was the media gap between the Eclipse environment and communication tools the members used. Three problems were significant. First, the establishment of chat sessions meant an additional overhead for the developers. They had to launch the tools, search their peer's user representation in the chat tool, and then manually establish a chat session before communication could start. The second problem was that the community members used different chat service providers that were not interoperable. Some users were members of the ICQ network, while others favored the Microsoft Messenger network. Finally, there was the problem of persistency of communication. Since most discussions were related to design questions for a specific module of the game engine, it was sad that this information was no longer accessible after a chat session.

Susan therefore suggested using an EMBEDDED CHAT[→4.3.1] that automatically links to the currently focused source code module. This is shown in Figure 4.57. It stores

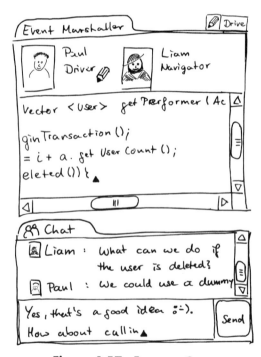

Figure 4.57 EMBEDDED CHAT

4.3 Read me... or how to support textual communication

all contributions, and any user interested in the module can access the chat dialog that took place in the context of the module. Unfortunately, the very persistence of chat sessions was one reason why Paul could not switch all chat communication to the EMBEDDED CHAT. Since other users could read messages after the chat session, there was no longer RECIPROCITY$_{\rightarrow 3.3.1}$ between senders and recipients.

To satisfy the need for asynchronous communication, Paul also added a FORUM$_{\rightarrow 4.3.2}$ that stored the users' contributions as THREADED DISCUSSIONS$_{\rightarrow 4.3.3}$ (see Figure 4.58). The reason for integrating this in the development environment was to focus discussions on a specific package of the project better. Each package has its own forum that can be opened from the package's context menu. Since the system keeps track of the users who are currently working with a package, it can provide them with an additional service: whenever a user creates a message in a forum for a package, the system sends this message directly to the users who are currently working with the package. This allows the forum to serve as a mailing list that automatically adapts to the current work context of the users.

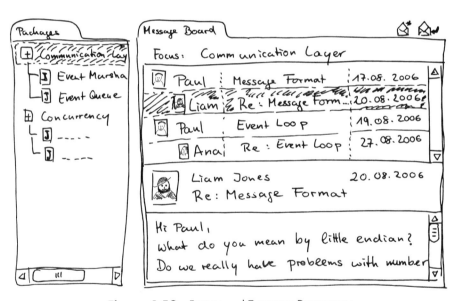

Figure 4.58 FORUM and THREADED DISCUSSION

The third means of communication implemented in the collaboration environment for the game engine is the possibility of creating shared annotations (see Figure 4.59). This is not a new feature—Eclipse already allows users to create annotations. The problem is that no explicit author and date information is stored in these default annotations. Paul's team therefore decided to extend the annotation mechanisms of Eclipse accordingly so that annotations made use of the user information present for the other tools.

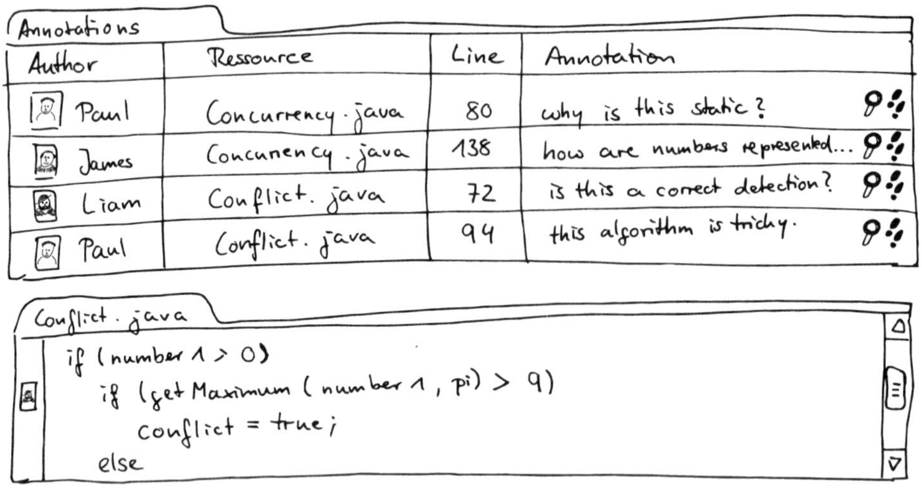

Annotations

Author	Ressource	Line	Annotation
Paul	Concurrency.java	80	why is this static?
James	Concurrency.java	138	how are numbers represented...
Liam	Conflict.java	72	is this a correct detection?
Paul	Conflict.java	94	this algorithm is tricky.

Conflict.java
```
if (number1 > 0)
   if (getMaximum (number1, pi) > 9)
      conflict = true;
   else
```

Figure 4.59 SHARED ANNOTATION

4.4 Feel me... or how to provide synchronous group awareness

Now that the community has found a place for their interaction and is on track, it is ready to work at a very fast pace. Small sub-teams are developing new versions of their components every other day and the quality improves frequently.
This is very satisfying for Paul. When he established the community, he hoped that it would evolve to a very active community of interest, but he did not imagine that it would become so active. Now, he fears that he is losing his overview of activities.

After discussing the basic means for collaboration support, we will now present patterns for supporting awareness of other group members while they are working on shared artifacts. Dourish and Bellotti (1992) provided one of the most widely used definitions of awareness by defining it as "an understanding of the activities of others, which provides a context for your own activity."

You may note that we have already addressed awareness at a coarser scale in previous sections. The patterns in Section 3.1 and Section 3.2 had the purpose of providing awareness at a community level. Users should be supported in socializing with one another and stay aware of relevant activities within the community. As Schlichter et al. (1998b) pointed out, "awareness is needed in both contact facilitation in communities and teams, and for maintaining team work at a high performance level within the team."

We frequently find situations in which users work independently, but at some point in time start tighter collaborations because they share a common need. Figure 4.60 shows this relationship.

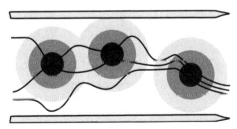

Figure 4.60 The role of awareness for group cohesion

Different levels of awareness are represented in Figure 4.60 by differently shaded circles. If users work at different times or on different artifacts, they share only minimal mutual awareness. The closer they decide to collaborate, the higher becomes their level of awareness. In terms of Figure 4.60, they enter the darker circles.

Related to our scenario, this can lead to the following situation:

Paul and Ana have a hard time keeping track of all the different work group activities that take place in the community.

Coordination by means of detailed group awareness now becomes very important. Paul and Ana have to understand better what the sub-teams are doing, each sub-team needs to understand how their actions interact with other teams' goals and actions, and finally the participants have to understand better the effects of their actions.

Gutwin and Greenberg (1996) have coined the term *workspace awareness* to sum up need for awareness that arises in small teams that work in a shared workspace. They created a reference model by posing the important questions listed in Table 4.1, which typically need to be answered when a group of users interacts in a shared workspace at the same time.

Table 4.1 Elements of workspace awareness proposed by Gutwin and Greenberg (1996).

ELEMENT	RELEVANT QUESTIONS
Presence	Who is participating in the activity?
Location	Where are they working?
Activity Level	How active are they in the workspace?
Actions	What are they doing? What are their current activities and tasks?
Intentions	What will they do next? Where will they be?
Changes	What changes are they making, and where?
Objects	What objects are they using?
Extents	What can they see? How far can they reach?
Abilities	What can they do?
Sphere of Influence	Where can they make changes?
Expectations	What do they need me to do next?

4.4 Feel me... or how to provide synchronous group awareness

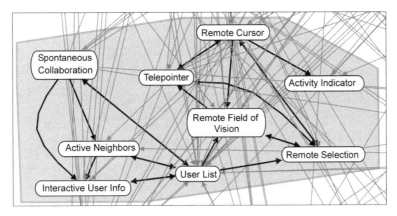

Figure 4.61 Patterns for synchronous awareness

The patterns shown in Figure 4.61 and detailed in this section explain solutions to these questions:

USER LIST$_{\to 4.4.1}$ Show who is currently participating in a session.

SPONTANEOUS COLLABORATION$_{\to 4.4.2}$ Support users in collaboration based on an awareness of other users.

ACTIVE NEIGHBORS$_{\to 4.4.3}$ Display activities not only on the local user's current artifact, but also on related artifacts.

INTERACTIVE USER INFO$_{\to 4.4.4}$ Make the information about other users clickable and connect it with a means of communication and collaboration.

REMOTE FIELD OF VISION$_{\to 4.4.5}$ Provide information to a user in a shared space about the part of the space that is seen by other users.

REMOTE SELECTION$_{\to 4.4.6}$ Let remote users know what the local user has selected.

REMOTE CURSOR$_{\to 4.4.7}$ Allow remote gestures and let remote users know what local users are working on.

TELEPOINTER$_{\to 4.4.8}$ Focus remote users' attention on a specific position in the shared information space.

ACTIVITY INDICATOR$_{\to 4.4.9}$ Provide an indication of other user's activities while not showing the activity's intermediate results.

We can map most of these patterns directly to the questions stated by Gutwin and Greenberg and shown in Figure 4.62. Note that some of these address questions

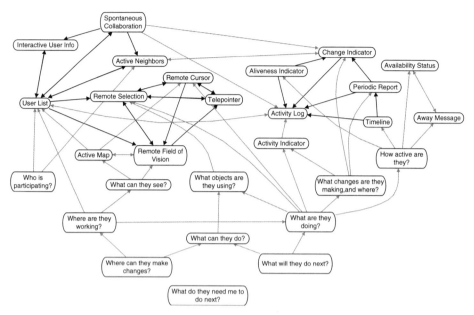

Figure 4.62 Questions addressed by the awareness patterns of our pattern language

that can be considered both in asynchronous and in synchronous contexts. These patterns are shown in Figure 4.62 but are part of Section 4.5. The questions in the lower part point with dotted arrows to patterns or other questions that help to solve the question. The expectation question *What do they need me to do next?* is not explicitly addressed by our pattern language. It would involve patterns for task management that are outside the scope of this book.

4.4.1 User List **

Alternative name(s): This pattern is a refinement of the User List *pattern published in (Schümmer, 2005), with aspects from the* Local Awareness *pattern and the* Presence Indicator *pattern (Schümmer, 2004).*

us·er (yōō'zər), NOUN: **1. One that uses: a user of public transportation. 2.** Law The exercise or enjoyment of a right or property. **3.** One who uses addictive drugs.

Intent

Show who is currently participating in a session.

Context

Many users are working synchronously on a set of shared artifacts.

Problem

Users do not know with whom they are interacting or could interact. Consequently, they do not have a feeling of participating in a group.

Scenario

Charley is working on security-related code. He is thinking about a schema for storing passwords with the user accounts. This requires Charley to modify several files, including the database definition of the user table. At the same time, Ana is working on aspects of making the user representation more personal. She also has to modify the definition of the user table. However, since neither know that the other is working on the user table, they modify the table concurrently, which results in a conflict. They subsequently regret that they could not do the modifications together, which would have prevented the annoying conflict.

Symptoms

You should consider applying this pattern when . . .

— Users consider shared artifacts as private artifacts.

- Users have the impression of being on their own.
- Users don't know whether or not others work with the same artifacts.
- Effective interaction requires that other users can be identified.
- Distributed users cannot see one another.
- Users frequently broadcast requests like "Hi, who else is here?"
- In a COLLABORATIVE SESSION$_{\to 5.1.1}$:
    - Users are inhibited when working with shared artifacts, because they don't know who else will see their changes.
    - Users know that they are interacting with others, but don't know with whom.

Solution

Therefore: Provide awareness in context. **Show who is currently accessing an artifact or participating in a** COLLABORATIVE SESSION$_{\to 5.1.1}$. **Ensure that the information is always valid.**

Dynamics

Users act in an interaction context that may either be a set of shared artifacts or a COLLABORATIVE SESSION$_{\to 5.1.1}$. Whenever users enter an interaction context their names are added to the USER LIST of the interaction context. The user list is a visual representation of all users who are acting in the same interaction context. When a user leaves the interaction context their visual representation is immediately removed from the USER LIST. The USER LIST acts as a subscriber that is informed whenever the underlying model (the set of interacting users) changes (see REMOTE SUBSCRIPTION$_{\to 5.2.2}$).

Rationale

By telling the user explicitly that other users are also working with artifacts (or more generally, work in the same interaction context), these users become aware of each other, which is the basis for group interaction.

By adding a USER LIST, all the participants can see who else is part of the group and get an overview of its current membership. They can be sure that only the users on the USER LIST can see their activities. This is the first condition for establishing group awareness. If the local user is aware of which other users are present, they will act more freely.

Check

When applying this pattern, you should answer these questions:

— What is your interaction context?

- Does it make sense to show a user list for the whole application, or should you distinguish between session-centered user lists?
- Can you identify the artifacts at different levels of scale? If yes, what is the right level of scale for the awareness calculation?

— How many users do you expect in your USER LIST?

— Can you use graphical representations in the USER LIST (VIRTUAL ME$_{\rightarrow 3.1.5}$)?

— Are there situations in which the USER LIST should be turned off?

Danger Spots

Not all representations of the USER LIST scale well for large numbers of users. If you consider for example listing all names in a text field, the number of users is limited by the length of all concatenated user names, which is constrained by the length of the text field. Think about only showing the total number of users, or using icons to represent users to save screen space.

If the system provides access to many artifacts and the group of users is small, the probability of two users working on the same artifact will be small. In this case, you can either reduce the granularity of artifacts or apply ACTIVE NEIGHBORS$_{\rightarrow 4.4.3}$, which gives a feeling of presence by displaying users who are active on other semantically related artifacts.

An important issue for the acceptance of the pattern is trust and privacy. User monitoring only works if it is mutually accepted by all participants. Otherwise, you will soon get the effect that users complain about being monitored or stop using the awareness features. MASQUERADE$_{\rightarrow 3.3.2}$ addresses this problem.

Not all users participate in an interaction context for its entire lifetime. Awareness of who has been participating cannot be achieved by just showing a USER LIST. To overcome this issue, log all activities in an ACTIVITY LOG$_{\rightarrow 4.5.1}$ and display past participation as well. Distinguish between past and present participants by using different display styles.

Known Uses

MSN Messenger shows a user list in each chat window. Each user is shown with their picture (see VIRTUAL ME$_{\rightarrow 3.1.5}$). In contrast to other systems, MSN Messenger only shows remote users in the user list, shown middle-right in Figure 4.63. The local user is shown separately to make it easier to see with which LOGIN$_{\to 3.1.2}$ the user is connected to the system.

Figure 4.63 A user list in MSN Messenger

Textual indication on community websites. Many community web sites show how many users are currently on the site. The size of the interaction context is very large at most sites: users often only have the entire website as context. One example is the home page of phpWebThings, an open source portal system (http://www.phpwebthings.nl/). In its USER LIST the phpWebThings site shows who is currently connected to the site, who of the community members has lately visited the site, and an overview of the connection status according to the membership roles (see Figure 4.64).

Some indicators at websites extend the awareness information to show on which page other users currently are. An example of this is the community page http://www.mvnforum.com (Figure 4.65). This shows the time that users spent on the page and how long they spent on other pages on the same website.

COAST (Schuckmann et al., 2000) generates user lists by showing the set of interested users of a shared application model (see Figure 4.66).

4.4.1 USER LIST

Figure 4.64 Users at the phpWebThings community site

Figure 4.65 USER LIST at the mvnForum community site http://www.mvnforum.com/mvnforum/listonlineusers

Figure 4.66 A COAST user list in the UML editor

UNIX who. The who command in Unix can be used to show the users connected to the same machine.

```
max% who
schuemme    pts/2    Aug  4 10:59    (pd9e9c14c.dip0.t-ipconnect.de)
bourimi     pts/3    Aug  4 11:02    (amsterdam.pi6.fernuni-hagen.de)
max%
```

Although the users do not necessarily collaborate, they share the same resources in their session.

GAMA-Mall (Schümmer, 2002) was a research prototype that used little figures to represent co-present users (Figure 4.67). It extended a virtual bookstore with presence information.

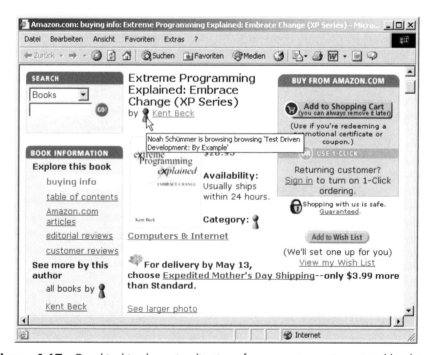

Figure 4.67 Graphical in-place visualization of co-present users in a virtual bookstore

It showed little icons next to bookstore artifacts if users were currently viewing the artifact. Since each icon was an INTERACTIVE USER INFO→4.4.4, they could be used to establish closer interaction with co-present users.

Meeting Mirror (Koch, 2005) is an application that allows participants of (physical) community meetings such as conferences to use interactive large screen displays to explore the attending participants (see Figure 4.68). The meeting mirror implements a USER LIST for synchronous physical events.

Figure 4.68 Participants of the 2004 German conference on human-computer interaction in front of the Meeting Mirror

Related Patterns

ACTIVITY LOG→4.5.1 can be used to log information on other users' activities. By querying the ACTIVITY LOG, one can find out who viewed the artifact and who created it.

BUDDY LIST→3.1.7 limits the set of users shown to known users. This is especially useful if a large number of users share the same session.

COLLABORATIVE SESSION→5.1.1 and ROOM→4.2.1 Sessions or rooms in most cases include a USER LIST.

SPONTANEOUS COLLABORATION→4.4.2 When presence information is shown in the context of artifacts, you should encourage users to enter closer interaction after noticing each other's presence at the same artifact. The GAMA-Mall system described above is one example that shows how a USER LIST supports the establishment of SPONTANEOUS COLLABORATION.

USER GALLERY$_{\rightarrow 3.1.6}$ lists all users who are known by the system, regardless their current collaboration status.

LOGIN$_{\rightarrow 3.1.2}$ allows identification of users and thereby displays their name in the USER LIST.

REMOTE SELECTION$_{\rightarrow 4.4.6}$ and REMOTE FIELD OF VISION$_{\rightarrow 4.4.5}$ both highlight artifacts that are currently accessed by remote users and thereby improve the awareness of collaborating in a group.

VIRTUAL ME$_{\rightarrow 3.1.5}$ supports users in generating an electronic representation of themselves. These representations can be used in the USER LIST to make list entries more personal.

4.4.2 Spontaneous Collaboration *

Alternative name(s): An earlier version of this pattern carried the name From Shared Data to Shared Work.

spon·ta·ne·ous (spŏn-tā'nē-əs), ADJECTIVE: **1.** Happening or arising without apparent external cause; self-generated. **2. Arising from a natural inclination or impulse and not from external incitement or constraint. 3.** Unconstrained and unstudied in manner or behavior. **4.** Growing without cultivation or human labor.

Intent

Support users in establishing collaboration based on an awareness of other users.

Context

Users are working with an application that provides access to shared data. They are working at different locations and consume or manipulate the shared data using their personal clients.

Problem

Although many users work with the same shared data, they may not recognize other users' work. This results in parallel or conflicting work and a lack of collaboration and learning from one another.

Scenario

James is currently refactoring the dialogue interpretation engine. He wants to create a language-independent part as well as a part that performs automatic translation of entered dialogue. Wil is at the same time working on the speech recognition library. At a first glance, everything looks fine and James does not feel the need for collaboration. However, if he knew that Wil was rewriting the way in which recognized texts are stored, James would have restructured his dialogue engine differently.

Symptoms

You should consider applying this pattern when ...

— Managers consider it difficult to predict who should collaborate to reach a specific goal.
— Team members notice that they have worked on the same artifacts after their work is finished.
— Parallel work causes conflicts that could have been resolved if team members had worked together.
— Users are unaware of the potential for collaborative activities that could improve the overall result or minimize conflicting work.

Solution

Therefore: Encourage users to form groups for collaboration spontaneously based on an awareness of other users' presence.

Dynamics

Local users work with an application on shared data. Their work initially takes place in single-user mode. During their work they perform several activities:

— Navigating from one web page to another
— Performing a search query
— Working in the same shared space (and in this case interpreting the content of the shared space as shared data)
— Changing a method of a source file in a programming environment

The application tracks these activities in an ACTIVITY LOG$_{\to 4.5.1}$ to provide awareness to one or more remote users (USER LIST$_{\to 4.4.1}$, CHANGE INDICATOR$_{\to 4.5.4}$, or ACTIVE NEIGHBORS$_{\to 4.4.3}$). Note that the awareness is based on the other users' activities rather than on their existence (VIRTUAL ME$_{\to 3.1.5}$) or their AVAILABILITY STATUS$_{\to 3.3.3}$. After becoming aware of the local user, the remote user can start a collaboration and potentially involve additional remote users.

The newly formed group collaborates using shared tools. The activities in the group are tracked to provide group awareness as well as to give non-group members an awareness of the group's activities.

Rationale

SPONTANEOUS COLLABORATION emphasizes the importance of providing group awareness and reacting to group awareness with tighter collaboration—see Figure 4.69. Users become aware of each other and spontaneously form groups.

Figure 4.69 Interaction between users that leads to SPONTANEOUS COLLABORATION

SPONTANEOUS COLLABORATION starts with a phase of solitary work. While users work independently (a) on shared artifacts (b), the system tracks their activities (1). Based on this information, the system can provide awareness information about the users' solitary activities (2). This information can for example reveal whether other users are currently working on the same artifacts. A user who detects another user working in the same area can establish a contact with this user (3). This mode of group formation is qualitatively different than planned group formation. In planned group formation, a user selects team members based on previous knowledge about the others. In group formation that follows SPONTANEOUS COLLABORATION, interaction partners are selected based on a common current focus, which makes focusing the group and accomplishing collaboration (4) much easier.

Check

When applying this pattern, you should answer these questions:

— Which artifacts are used by more than one user?
— What concurrent activities take place and what effect do these activities have on the artifacts?
— Are there any predefined groups to which activity tracking should be limited? If yes, how will conflicts caused by concurrent groups be resolved?

Danger Spots

Providing mechanisms for dynamic artifact-based collaboration may lead to a practice that disregards formal team management completely. The intent of the pattern is not that formal work flows should be discarded, but rather that they need to be accompanied by dynamic collaboration.

When designing systems you should take into account the fact that users are often reluctant to change their current work environment. Thus it is unlikely that totally new applications will be used solely for the sake of better group awareness (Sohlenkamp et al. (2000)). You should integrate group awareness and collaboration mechanisms as tightly as possible. The ideal case would not require any user action to set up the service, and users would only notice the changed application when collaboration opportunities arose.

Known Uses

TUKAN (Schümmer and Schümmer, 2001; Schümmer, 2001) is a collaborative programming environment that supports dynamic collaboration in eXtreme Programming.

A typical development cycle starts in single-user mode or with two developers working together at one machine. The developer selects an appropriate task and starts solitary coding. At the same time, other developers also start their work. All parties ignore one another until they become aware of each other through browsing or changing semantically related methods.

TUKAN uses colored figures attached to methods to show that other users are working on the same or a related artifact (see Figure 4.70). The developers use built-in communication support to get in contact with each other and to decide whether they should solve any parts of the task that affect both of them together. The system provides means for synchronous collaboration, such as a collaborative code editor.

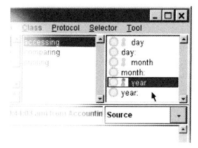

Figure 4.70 Showing the presence of collocated users in TUKAN

I2I (Bradshaw et al., 2002) is a system that provides awareness of other users' activities on the web. Whenever two or more users browse the same or a semantically related artifact, the system visualizes this as an icon that indicates the remote user's presence. Users are provided with the means of communication to establish contacts with others working on related artifacts.

GAMA Mall, also described in the USER LIST$_{\to 4.4.1}$ pattern, extends the web pages of the Amazon.com™ bookstore so that users become aware of others browsing the store. The system informs the user of others browse content that is semantically relevant to the local user. Users can then initiate tighter collaboration, such as chatting or collaborative browsing.

Related Patterns

ACTIVE NEIGHBORS$_{\rightarrow 4.4.3}$ provides a starting point for refining awareness by extending the notion of locality.

CHANGE INDICATOR$_{\rightarrow 4.5.4}$ describes how to keep users aware of changes to shared data.

COLLABORATIVE SESSION$_{\rightarrow 5.1.1}$ describes how collaboration can be planned and organized in synchronous episodes.

MASQUERADE$_{\rightarrow 3.3.2}$ outlines how users can control which data is tracked to provide awareness.

ACTIVITY LOG$_{\rightarrow 4.5.1}$ describes how to track the data required from user activities to provide awareness.

USER LIST$_{\rightarrow 4.4.1}$ outlines the most basic way of providing awareness to users of a system that hosts shared data.

ROOM$_{\rightarrow 4.2.1}$ can be used to offer a virtual place and means of collaboration.

INTERACTIVE USER INFO$_{\rightarrow 4.4.4}$ suggests attaching context menus to a user's VIRTUAL ME$_{\rightarrow 3.1.5}$ so that the start of tighter collaboration becomes easier when the other user is discovered.

ADHOC MEETING (Coldeway, 2003) describes how people should meet dynamically whenever an important issue arises. Although it does not relate to any technical issues or distributed team settings, it shares the same idea.

4.4.3 ACTIVE NEIGHBORS

Alternative name(s): Embodiment Proximity (Gutwin and Greenberg, 2002)

neigh·bor (nā'bər), NOUN: **1.** One who lives near or next to another. **2. A person, place, or thing adjacent to or located near another. 3.** A fellow human. **4.** Used as a form of familiar address.

Intent

Display activities not only on the local user's current artifact, but also on related artifacts.

Context

You are using USER LISTS$_{\rightarrow 4.4.1}$ to inform users about each other's activities. Two or more users are performing work on related artifacts.

The probability of meeting another user on the same artifact is low, since there are many more artifacts than users.

Problem

The USER LIST$_{\rightarrow 4.4.1}$ pattern only shows users with the same focus. If users work on related artifacts, they are not aware of each other, which implies that no collaboration will be established.

Scenario

James has discovered Wil because both worked on the same class in the dialogue interpretation module. They agreed to change some interface code so that both their needs are satisfied. Unfortunately, the interface change affects Charley, who is responsible for securing the dialogue engine and who is currently working on a class that makes heavy use of the dialogue interpretation code.

Symptoms

You should consider applying this pattern when ...

— Users think it could make sense to work with other users who share a common *semantic* focus, but cannot see other users who share exactly the same focus.

- Users rarely work on the same artifact.
- The number of artifacts is much larger than the number of users.
- There are semantic dependencies between the artifacts.
- You are looking for a means to support creative processes and mutual learning.

Solution

Therefore: **Make users aware of other users who are currently performing semantically related activities on the same or related artifacts.**

Dynamics

Model a set of focal artifacts for each user that contains all the artifacts that are the subject of the user's current activities. Extend the set of focal artifacts with related artifacts. Determine the related artifacts, either by similarity metrics such as overlap of terms, or by means of a semantic network.

In the first case, you need to create a function that calculates a semantic distance for two artifacts based on the artifacts' content. Consider using similarity algorithms, such as those proposed by Zobel and Moffat (1998), or external services that identify similar artifacts to a given artifact, such as the Amazon.com web service that calculates related titles for a given book (see http://www.amazon.com/webservices).

In the second case, you should use the associations that are present in your shared data model and interpret it as a semantic network. Weigh the different associations according to their semantic relevance and traverse the object space to find the shortest path between two artifacts. Dijkstra's algorithm that determines the shortest path from one node to any other node can be used, with the modification that you only look for paths that are within a specified distance (Dijkstra, 1959).

Finally, look up presence information for the related artifacts.

Having this information in place, you can determine for each focal artifact who else is present in the artifact's vicinity. Display these users next to the focal artifact and show who is working on which related artifact.

Make this information interactive so that a local user can easily contact remote users or directly move to a remote user's location.

Rationale

To understand why awareness of semantically related activities adds new views for group awareness, it makes sense to look at the history of this model. The awareness model used in this pattern is based on the well-known spatial model, which is used to model interaction in virtual environments (Benford and Fahlén, 1993). Within the spatial model, artifacts are arranged in a three-dimensional space. Users may interact with artifacts by navigating through the space. Other users can always see where their colleagues are positioned within the space. This is called their *presence* position: note that a presence position is already used in the USER LIST$_{\to 4.4.1}$ pattern. In the spatial awareness model, local awareness is extended by relating it to a spatial layout of the artifacts: awareness thus spreads in space.

Rodden (1996) extended the spatial model by introducing the concepts of *focus* and *nimbus*. His focus-nimbus model consists of objects, such as artifacts, and users, who are distributed in space. Each object has a well-defined distance to all other objects. Around objects, there is a focus and a nimbus, which are parts of space. In line with Rodden (1996), we define the *focus* as the set of objects that are of interest to a specific object and the *nimbus* as a set of positions in the object space where the specific object might influence other objects. As an example, the focus of guests at a party consists of anyone they can see, and their nimbus consists of anyone standing next to them. In most cases, interest and influence of an object will fade the further a position in space is away from object.

With focus, nimbus, and presence position as parameters, a suitable awareness function can be defined whose exact formulation is application-dependent. (Additional examples were provided by Rodden (1996)).

While these two models were mainly developed for virtual (three-dimensional) environments, ACTIVE NEIGHBORS generalizes the context to any environment in which it is possible to define a semantic distance between two artifacts.

By making the user aware of others who work on related artifacts, one can ensure that parallel work on semantically related artifacts is detected and coordinated via a social protocol. A conflict, on the other hand, is always bound to parallel work on related artifacts that heads in different directions. Since these parallel activities are minimized with the pattern, conflicts are less likely to occur.

In the same way, users are brought together, which results in collaboration on related artifacts.

Check

When applying this pattern, you should answer these questions:

— How can you calculate the set of artifacts that are semantically related to a user's current set of focal artifacts?

— Up to what semantic distance will you show users with semantically related activities?

— How can you express a user's location? Does every location have a name by which it can be identified?

— Can you provide links that bring a local user to another user's position?

Danger Spots

It is important that you define a good maximum distance threshold for considering other users as semantically related users. Allowing too large a distance will lead to the following problems:

1. The algorithm will find too many users in the set of users who work on artifacts that are not perceived as related artifacts by the local user.
2. It will be hard to calculate the set of users who perform semantically related activities, resulting in long calculation times.

Too small a distance will not consider all relevant artifacts.

Known Uses

I2I (Budzik et al., 2002) shown in Figure 4.71 is a system that tracks users who access web pages. Besides the current page, it recommends other users for collaboration who are currently reading related pages.

Figure 4.71 Recommendations for collaboration in the I2I system (from Budzik et al. (2002))

CoBrow (Wolf and Froitzheim, 1998) displays the presence of other users on web pages by means of presence indicators. The obtrusiveness of these indicators is dependent on the semantic distance between two users in the document space.

TUKAN (Schümmer, 2001) provides awareness of semantically related users, as well as activities that are in conflict with the local user's view of the artifact.

GroupDesk (Fuchs et al., 1995) informs users of activities taking place on semantically related artifacts. It is a generic groupware architecture that was, for example, applied in workflow systems.

Related Patterns

USER LIST$_{\to 4.4.1}$ Semantically related users are shown in the same way as collocated users using a USER LIST that is attached to a specific artifact. Besides the user's

VIRTUAL ME, the list should also show the user's current position and the distance to the position.

INTERACTIVE USER INFO$_{\to 4.4.4}$ You should consider allowing users to move to the location of a semantically related user by following a link in the user's INTERACTIVE USER INFO.

CHANGE INDICATOR$_{\to 4.5.4}$ can be used to visualize information on semantically related activities that have modified an artifact.

4.4.4 Interactive User Info *

in·ter·ac·tive (ĭn'tər-ăk'tĭv), ADJECTIVE: **1.** Acting or capable of acting on each other. **2.** *Computer Science* **Of or relating to a program that responds to user activity. 3.** Of, relating to, or being a form of television entertainment in which the signal activates electronic apparatus in the viewer's home or the viewer uses the apparatus to affect events on the screen, or both.

Intent

Make the information about other users clickable and connect it with a means of communication and collaboration.

Context

You have decided to visualize the presence and actions of other users in the group environment using the user's name and/or a VIRTUAL ME$_{\rightarrow 3.1.5}$. Now you are thinking about how this can lead to real interaction between users.

Problem

Users are aware of other users in the collaboration space and can identify them, but they don't know how to start tighter interaction with a specific user.

Scenario

James sees that Wil is working on the same artifact and decides to drop him a personal message. Unfortunately, this turns out to be quite complicated, since James has to look up Wil's address in his address book, create a new e-mail message, and add Wil to the set of recipients in his e-mail client.

Symptoms

You should consider applying this pattern when . . .

- Contact establishment takes too much time.
- Users have to map the visual representation of the other user to a sequence of actions required to establish a communication or interaction channel with the other user.
- Connection setup requires additional information that is normally not shown in the VIRTUAL ME, such as an IP network address.

Solution

Therefore: Equip the user representation with a context menu that provides commands for finding out more information on a user and for starting tighter collaboration with the user.

Dynamics

For each user, the system defines possible interaction adapters. An interaction adapter defines the interaction channel by which the user can be contacted and provides an address by which the interaction channel can be directed to the user. Whenever a user is shown, all the user's interaction adapters are accessible using a context menu on the user's representation. In cases where context menus are not possible, the user representation may be decorated with links to the user's interaction adapters, or the user representation may link to the user's description (VIRTUAL ME$_{\rightarrow 3.1.5}$). In the latter case, the user's description should include links to use the interaction adapter.

Rationale

Providing an INTERACTIVE USER INFO reduces indirections. In many groupware systems, the users are only shown to other users. There is nothing that a user can "do" with another user. If you consider systems that provide a USER LIST$_{\rightarrow 4.4.1}$ in a shared workspace, for example, this list is often inactive. It serves the purpose of staying aware of who else is working in the workspace, but it does not support establishment of new bilateral interaction channels.

Context menus in general have proved to provide easy access to operations that can be performed with an object. They link an action to the targeted object and thereby ease the complexity of the commands by which a user interacts with the object.

Without interactive user information, users have to identify other users' interaction capabilities manually, for example by looking up the other users' e-mail-addresses in an e-mail directory. With interactive information, this lookup is automated and hidden. In the ideal case, a user does not need to know another user's addresses, but can still contact the other user using interactive user information.

Check

When applying this pattern, you should answer these questions:

— What actions can you add to the context menu?
— How will you reflect the user's state (AVAILABILITY STATUS$_{\rightarrow 3.3.3}$) in the context menu?
— Can you use a context menu, or will you need to provide additional graphical links?

Danger Spots

In some systems not all users share the same interaction capabilities. One user may for example participate in an instant messaging system, while another user can only be reached by e-mail. To reduce the interface's complexity, you should think about showing only those interaction adapters of the remote user that are also available for the local user, or disabling inappropriate actions. This ensures that only interaction channels are shown that can be established by the remote user.

On the other hand, this reduction of interaction adapters has the danger that users never get to know that participation in another interaction service would be beneficial.

Known Uses

Buddy lists in IM systems like the one in MSN Messenger (http://messenger.msn.com/) provide context menus for each user that appears in the BUDDY LIST.

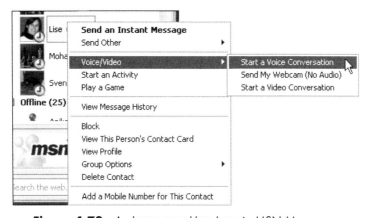

Figure 4.72 An INTERACTIVE USER INFO in MSN Messenger

The example in Figure 4.72 shows the menu actions that are available for contacting the user Lise. The menu dynamically adapts to the capabilities of the local and the remote user. If the remote user is off line, the entries for starting a chat conversation, or the entry for initiating a video connection, would be disabled. The system still allows the local user to send an e-mail to the off-line remote user, however.

vBulletin (http://www.vbulletin.com/) is a web-based discussion forum. Each author is shown in the header of a contribution. Clicking on the author's name shows the different ways in which the author can be contacted (see Figure 4.73).

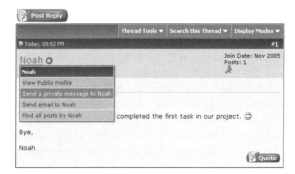

Figure 4.73 An INTERACTIVE USER INFO in the bulletin board system vBulletin

Clicking on one of the context menu items opens the required communication tool to contact the author.

Games. In the genre of massive multiplayer online role-playing games, INTERACTIVE USER INFOS are frequently used to initiate interaction with other players. An example is Everquest 2 (Sony Online Entertainment, 2004) shown in Figure 4.74, in which users can, besides common interactions with other users, trade goods that they carry around with them.

Figure 4.74 Interacting with users in Everquest 2

Other examples of games where a comparable interaction can be observed are Ragnarok Online (Gravity Corp, 2004) and Star Wars Galaxies (Sony Online Entertainment, 2003).

CURE (http://cure.sourceforge.net/) consistently adds context menus to places where users are shown. The options for interaction depend on the capabilities of both the local and the remote user. If both users support synchronous communication, for example, the context menu offers a command for opening a private chat window.

The context menu also reveals where the remote user is currently located in the shared information space. In Figure 4.75, *Svein Johnson* is currently working on the page *Model based Adaptive Product and Process Engineering* in the same room as *Till Schümmer*. By clicking on the name of the page, the local user moves to the remote user's virtual location. This makes it easy to align the focus of distributed users quickly.

Figure 4.75 Interactive User Info in the CURE system

Related Patterns

VIRTUAL ME→3.1.5 The virtual representation of the user serves as context for the INTERACTIVE USER INFO.

BUDDY LIST→3.1.7 All entries in a BUDDY LIST should be equipped with an INTERACTIVE USER INFO. In addition, the INTERACTIVE USER INFO should provide an entry for adding or removing the selected user in a BUDDY LIST.

INVITATION→4.2.5 If possible the INTERACTIVE USER INFO should provide a shortcut for inviting the user to a collaboration context.

LOCALIZED OBJECT ACTIONS (Tidwell, 1999b) argues to "Group object actions together, even more so than for CONVENIENT ENVIRONMENT ACTIONS, and spatially localize them to the object." Transferred to the context of groupware applications, this means that actions that focus on other users should be available in the proximity of the users' representation.

DISABLE IRRELEVANT THINGS (Tidwell, 1999a) argues that actions that cannot be performed on a specific remote user should be disabled but remain visible.

4.4.5 REMOTE FIELD OF VISION   *

Alternative name(s): Remote Scrollbars, Remote Viewport

field of vi·sion (fēld ŏf vĭzh′ən), NOUN: **The space or range within which objects are visible to the immobile eyes at a given time.**

Intent

Provide information to a user in a shared space about the part of the space that is seen by other users.

Context

Many users work simultaneously with a SHARED EDITOR→4.1.6 on shared documents or more generally on artifacts that are laid out in the editor's view. Each user is allowed to scroll through the view area independently.

Problem

Having independent scroll positions in a SHARED EDITOR→4.1.6 opens the opportunity for loosely coupled work. However, it makes the alignment of focus more difficult.

Scenario

James and Wil both edit the diagram that explains dialogue interpretation. James is working in the upper-right corner while Wil has scrolled to the bottom of the diagram. At one point, James has a question about the diagram's title that is shown in the diagram's top right. He asks Wil to look at the top-right part of the screen, but forgets that Wil sees something different there. This results in misunderstandings between Wil and James.

Symptoms

You should consider applying this pattern when ...

— Users express a need to focus on the same area, for example to discuss a part of a document.

— Users interrupt each other to ask about the places on which they are currently working, or they need to notify others every time they change focus.
— Users ask others to look at a specific region of their screen, although others see different parts of the shared editor's view area.

Solution

Therefore: Explicitly indicate the location and scope of each user's view to every other user. In the case of graphical documents this can be achieved by including labeled rectangles that represent—in position and scope—the views seen by remote users. In the case of textual documents, this can be achieved by adding additional, passive scroll bars that represent the scroll position of remote users in the document.

Dynamics

The local *field of vision* is the part of the view area in the shared editor that a local user can see. Depending on the dimensions used in the view area, the field of vision can be described as a geometric form in the view space. In a one-dimensional space as is used to display regions of text, it can also be represented by the index of the first and last visible character.

Whenever the local user scrolls through the shown information, the local field of vision is modified. Its dimensions are stored as a shared object.

This enables all users to access the dimensions of each other's fields of vision. These remote fields of vision are visualized as an additional layer in the shared editor.

Given a two-dimensional space, a remote field of vision is best displayed as a frame. In addition to the shape, you show the name or a VIRTUAL ME$_{\rightarrow 3.1.5}$ of the remote user to whom the remote field of vision refers.

For one-dimensional spaces such as text, it can be enough to show a passive colored scroll bar for each user besides the local scroll bar (see Figure 4.76). Each of these scroll bars shows the current position of a remote user in the text, and each color represents a different user. When two users look at the same part of the text, the scroll bars are positioned at the same position. This implementation is usually called *multiuser scroll bars*.

Rationale

Using a graphical representation of remote fields of vision, the group can easily focus communication on the part of the shared space that is visible to all participants.

Users can be sure that they know where others are. Using this pattern therefore reduces the need of verbal communication to focus discussion or work, and helps the participants to coordinate their activities better.

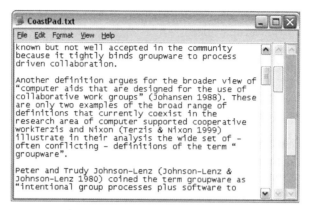

Figure 4.76 Multi user scroll bars

Users can find a part of the document nobody is working on by simply looking at the remote fields of vision of other users. This helps them to divide their work and reduce the potential for conflicting activities.

Check

When applying this pattern, you should answer these questions:

— How can you determine the local user's field of vision? Can you read the scroll position directly from the application?

— How will the field of vision be represented in the shared object space? Will you use a rectangle, an interval, or a polygon?

— How do you help users to understand whose remote field of vision is shown? Can you add user names to the visual representation? Does it make sense to show a picture?

Danger Spots

The representation of the remote field of vision must be clearly distinguishable from other elements in the shared space. Otherwise, it can be mistaken for a diagram object.

As is obvious in Figure 4.76, multiuser scroll bars may use too much screen space. Imagine that a group of ten users works together with the editor shown in Figure 4.76. This would result in half of the user's screen being filled with scroll bars. Other visualizations, such as single lines instead of scroll bars, can help to save screen space. Even so, this solution does not scale for very large groups.

Depending on the implementation, it may be difficult to determine the user's field of vision. A simple implementation takes the view's rectangular bounds and the offset of a scrollable widget as the source of the field of vision. Although this is correct for fully displayed windows, it produces incorrect fields of vision for windows that are obscured by other windows or applications. In this case, the field of vision will be a polygon containing the part of the shared space that is actually visible.

Known Uses

COAST UML-Editor (Schümmer et al., 2001). The open-source collaboration framework COAST ships with a sample application that helps to create UML diagrams collaboratively. It provides awareness by means of remote fields of vision, shown as orange-colored rectangles labeled with the name of the local user. Figure 4.77 shows a remote user called Alejandro Fernández with the short name "casco". In the diagram, his field of vision is shown as a frame on the right of the document.

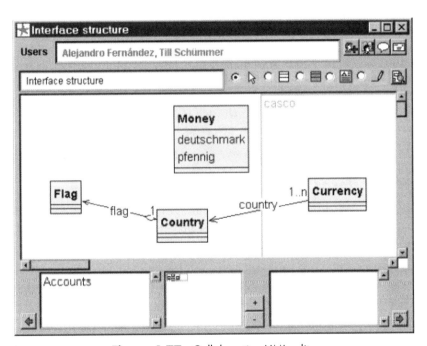

Figure 4.77 Collaborative UML editor

MAUI is a Java toolkit that offers a broad collection of awareness-enhanced user interface components (Hill and Gutwin, 2003, 2004). MAUI supports awareness of remote users' views by adding multiuser scroll bars to the user interface components. These scroll bars show the location of remote users' field of vision. Figure 4.78 shows this for a scroll pane. Additionally, the scroll pane shows each user's viewport as a transparent rectangle inside the pane[4].

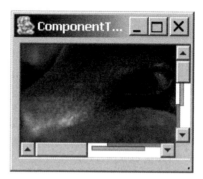

Figure 4.78 REMOTE FIELD OF VISION in MAUI

GroupWEB (Greenberg and Roseman, 1996) includes multiuser scroll bars that show the current position of remote users in a shared HTML document. In (Gutwin and Greenberg, 1998) the authors report on a collaborative construction application in which each user can have an independent field of vision. Remote fields of vision are visualized using semitransparent colored areas in the workspace view.

Related Patterns

TELEPOINTER[→4.4.8] If users still have problems focusing on shared artifacts during communication, they should use telepointers that help to focus on exactly one artifact.

REMOTE SELECTION[→4.4.6] If users still have problems coordinating synchronous work in the shared space, they should think about adding remote selections to identify the artifacts on which other users are working.

ACTIVE MAP[→4.2.2] A local field of vision can be displayed in an ACTIVE MAP to give the user a better idea of location. Remote fields of vision can also be shown in the ACTIVE MAP instead of single points of presence.

VIRTUAL ME[→3.1.5] can be used to obtain and display information on the owner of the REMOTE FIELD OF VISION.

---

[4]This is not visible in Figure 4.78.

SHARED BROWSING$_{\rightarrow 4.1.3}$ describes a case in which the scroll positions of all users are coupled. In this case, all users should have an overlapping REMOTE FIELD OF VISION. For that reason, it makes sense to show a remote field of vision when users are allowed to change their view size (and thereby only see a part of the shared view).

4.4.6 REMOTE SELECTION   *

Alternative name(s): Selection Awareness

se·lec·tion (sĭ-lĕk'shən), NOUN: **1a.** The act or an instance of selecting or the fact of having been selected. **b. One that is selected. 2.** A carefully chosen or representative collection of people or things. **3.** A literary or musical text chosen for reading or performance. **4.** Biology A natural or artificial process that favors or induces survival and perpetuation of one kind of organism over others that die or fail to produce offspring.

Intent

Let remote users know what the local user has selected.

Context

Users collaborate in a shared editor that allows each user to concurrently select and manipulate objects.

Problem

Users select artifacts to start an action on the artifact. Selecting an artifact is considered as taking the artifact under personal control. Whenever two users select the same artifacts, this leads to coordination problems.

Scenario

James and Wil are still collaborating using a shared diagram editor. James selects the abstract class for generic dialogue interpretation, while Wil selects the same class together with all its subclasses. Now James moves the abstract class to another region of the diagram. Will gets quite angry because he thought that he could work on his selected classes independently. He shouts "What have you done with my classes?" at James.

Symptoms

You should consider applying this pattern when . . .

— Users consider selected objects as "their" objects and under their control, but the objects can also be modified by other users.

- Addressing selected elements is often used as a mechanism to focus communication. Phrases like "look at the selected elements" cause confusion, because they don't make any sense to remote users.
- Users are used to selecting an element before they talk about it.

Solution

Therefore: Show remote users' selections to a local user. Make sure that other users who are interested in a specific artifact are aware of all distributed co-workers who have selected the object.

Dynamics

The local user selects objects in the shared space. The selected object is highlighted, for example by using another color or adding a shadow. This makes it easy to distinguish selected objects from objects that are not selected. When shown on remote screens, the locally selected object is also highlighted, but using a different style and revealing the name of the user who selected the object.

Rationale

The fact that each user can have private object selection causes two main problems for usability. First, it produces confusion in actions, since the cognitive absolute of selecting objects and then having control over them no longer holds—other users may have overlapping selections. Second, it hinders communication, because it is not possible to use selection as a focus for communication, as is done in single-user applications.

Remote selection is perceived by users as the desire of the remote user to act on the remotely selected element. Local users will restrain from acting on remotely selected objects in order not to interfere with the work of the remote user. Moreover, in the case of interference, the remote user would have enough clues to realize that the unexpected behavior of the selected object is due to the action of another user.

Remote selection associates a set of visually distinguishable elements with a user. Thus, the sentence "look at the objects that I selected" recovers its value for focusing communication.

Check

When applying this pattern, you should answer these questions:

- What can users select?

— Is it possible to select only part of a specific object?
— How should you display remote selections?

Danger Spots

When implementing remote selections, you need to ensure that they have a different presentation than "local" selections, such as a different color, a flashing outline, shading, and so on.

You should be aware of the problem of multiple overlapping (remote) selections. In the case of diagram elements, you can annotate the selection with multiple user names. If two users have for example selected overlapping sections of text, the selection should be shown in a way that makes it clear that two users selected the text. One option could be to use a pattern as a selection fill that contains colors that correspond to all selecting users. However, this solution does not scale well to large groups of users if all users select the same text.

Known Uses

MAUI (Hill and Gutwin, 2003, 2004) is a user interface toolkit built on top of the JavaBeans framework that eases the creation of multiuser applications. One of its widgets is a collaborative text input field in which each user can have a private selection, but all users share the same text. Selections made by remote users are shown in a different color. In addition, the selection owner's name is shown next to the selection (see Figure 4.79).

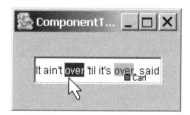

Figure 4.79 REMOTE SELECTION in Maui

Dolphin (Streitz et al., 1994) uses different text colors to represent whether text is selected or not. If it is black, no user has selected it. If it is orange, the local user has selected it. Red indicates that one or more remote users have selected the text.

TUKAN (Schümmer and Haake, 2001) The collaborative method editor in Tukan (Figure 4.80) shows the start and end points of remote text selection as small filled circles under the text. These circles are connected with a line that completes the metaphor of a selection unit. The remote selection indicator is displayed in a color that helps to identify its owner.

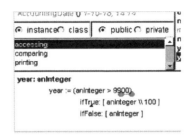

Figure 4.80 Tukan's method editor

COAST UML-Editor (Schümmer et al., 2001). The collaborative COAST UML editor indicates local selection of classes by coloring the class box in soft yellow. Remote selection is indicated by coloring the frame of the class box in soft red and attaching a label with the name of the selector. Figure 4.81 shows that the remote user *till* has selected the Flag class. The local user has selected the Money class. The Country class is not selected.

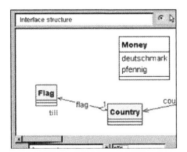

Figure 4.81 User *till* selected the *Flag* class

Related Patterns

TELEPOINTER→4.4.8 REMOTE SELECTION pattern and TELEPOINTER share motivation. Both apply when there is a need to attract another user's attention to a shared artifact. However, REMOTE SELECTION is more suitable than TELEPOINTER when attention needs to be focused on more than one artifact.

REMOTE CURSOR$_{\to 4.4.7}$ If users still have problems coordinating synchronous work in the shared space, they should think about adding remote cursors to identify other users' current work focus better.

REMOTE FIELD OF VISION$_{\to 4.4.5}$ is a less detailed indicator of remote users' foci.

4.4.7 REMOTE CURSOR   **

Alternative name(s): Remote Target Indicator, Telecursor, Remote Mouse Pointer, Remote Caret, Direct Telepointer (ter Hofte et al., 1997)

cur·sor (kûr'sər), NOUN: **Computer Science A bright, usually blinking, movable indicator on a display, marking the position at which a character can be entered, corrected, or deleted.**

Intent

Allow remote gestures and let remote users know what local users are working on.

Context

Users simultaneously manipulate artifacts using diverse input devices such as mouse, keyboard, or other pointing devices.

To act on an artifact, the user first needs to position the pointing device accordingly.

Problem

Users want to be constantly aware of other user's activities. This includes an understanding of other user's interaction with the computer system, such as mouse or cursor movements, which cannot be achieved by merely sharing the document that is currently edited.

Scenario

Juan and Carla met in a distributed session to design the new logo of the game engine collaboratively. They had the idea of using a shared whiteboard on which both of them could draw sketches. Unfortunately, they often draw across each other's sketches. This is something they have never experienced in previous collocated sessions. Probably this was because they could see the hand holding the pen and were polite enough not to push the other person's hand aside.

Symptoms

You should consider applying this pattern when ...

— Other synchronous awareness widgets, such as TELEPOINTER$_{\to 4.4.8}$, REMOTE SELECTION$_{\to 4.4.6}$, or REMOTE FIELD OF VISION$_{\to 4.4.5}$, do not provide sufficient awareness, with the result that users miss the presence and the implicit coordination that would have been experienced in a collocated session.

— Users do not get the impression that other users are active in the shared workspace at the same time.

— Users frequently run into editing conflicts, because they change the same artifact at the same time, and even REMOTE SELECTION does not solve the problem.

— Users frequently want to perform gestures and have the impression that a TELEPOINTER$_{\to 4.4.8}$ is too complicated to use, since it has to be activated before it can be used for gestures.

— Users want to follow how others actually use the shared editor instead of only seeing the results.

Solution

Therefore: Show the mouse cursor or the text cursor of remote users on a local user's view of the shared editor. Ensure that you use different colors and shapes to make remote cursors distinct from the local cursor. Update the cursor position whenever a remote user moves their cursor.

Dynamics

The local user positions the local cursor in a shared artifact or at a position in a shared artifact. The position of the remote cursor is automatically communicated to all other participants of the shared editor, either by storing it as a CENTRALIZED OBJECT$_{\to 5.2.1}$ to which the remote users have a REMOTE SUBSCRIPTION$_{\to 5.2.2}$, or by using DECENTRALIZED UPDATES$_{\to 5.2.6}$. When receiving an updated position, the views of the shared editor are updated so that the remote cursors are shown at the same shared artifact or position in a shared artifact.

The visual presentation of the remote cursor is distinct from that of the local cursor. It should have a different shape or color and be linked to the owner of the cursor. An easy means is to attach the owner's name to the remote cursor's visualization.

Rationale

Remote cursors, especially remote mouse pointers, have been widely studied in the field of CSCW research (see especially (Greenberg et al., 1996; Gutwin and Penner,

2002; Dyck et al., 2004)). Besides other benefits, one core benefit is that remote cursors inform the users of each others activities in a very expressive way. Dyck et al. (2004) stated that remote cursors *"allow people to see when actions begin and end, enable tightly coordinated turn-taking, and allow anticipation of people's actions. This unintentional communication of the fine-grained details of activity is what enables smooth, error-free, and natural real-time interactions in shared workspaces."* [5]

Compared with other awareness patterns, we can state that remote cursors provide the most synchronous and fine-grained level of awareness with respect to a user's current focus and mouse or keyboard interaction. This satisfies the need for constant and detailed awareness.

Check

When applying this pattern, you should answer these questions:

— What shape will you use to display remote cursors?
— Will you capture keyboard cursors, mouse cursors, or both?
— How will a user activate the remote cursor?
— How will you store the state of the cursor positions?

Danger Spots

Tracing remote cursors can be difficult for the local user. One reason for this is that the local user does not steer the remote cursors. Their movements lack the haptic experience that is received when physically moving a mouse or using the keyboard.

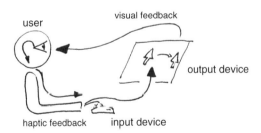

Figure 4.82 Feedback in traditional cursor movements

Figure 4.82 shows the feedback loop involved in traditional cursor control. A user perceives a cursor and relates this to the desired operation that implies a movement

---

[5] Note that (Dyck et al., 2004) did not use the term "remote cursor", but used the term "telepointer" instead.

of the cursor. This movement is performed by hand movements. Since the mouse is placed on a surface, the whole hand using the mouse receives feedback (fingers touch the desk surface). This haptic feedback is related to the feedback received from corresponding movements on the screen. Together this forms a feedback loop that keeps the perception of the cursor position aligned with its real position.

Remote cursors only communicate their position by means of their visual representation on the screen. The remote cursor moves without any intention or physical activity on the part of the local user. This has the effect that the user can loose track of the remote cursor's position. It can also occur that the local user anticipates a movement of the remote cursor that is not correct. Again, users can have problems realigning their idea of the remote cursor's position with its real position.

One widely used solution for keeping track of remote cursors is the use of *trails* (Gutwin and Penner, 2002). These however can make the remote cursors' visualization too prominent, so that it disturbs the local user.

Implementing remote cursors may require small amounts of data to be transferred continuously, consuming a significant part of the communication channel. Compression and interpolation methods can help to reduce the required bandwidth. Examples of this are provided by Dyck et al. (2004).

Be careful when different users have different views on the same artifacts. Consider for example two users who are browsing web pages in differently sized windows. Text paragraphs will wrap differently at each user's machine, so the same information will be displayed in different positions. In this case, deciding on where to display a remote cursor involves some translation, from the positions of the targeted artifacts on the remote user's screen to the position of the same artifacts in the local user's screen—see Greenberg et al. (1996).

Known Uses

SEPIA (Streitz et al., 1992) provides a synchronous collaboration mode in which all authors see a graphical view of the network of nodes in the document. Any modification made to one of the elements in the document is available to all authors automatically. Users usually change the layout of the nodes in the document to make it more readable. To avoid the conflicts that appear when two users try to manipulate the same node simultaneously, the system provides feedback to every user about the position of everyone else's mouse cursors. The mouse cursors of remote users are labeled with the name of their owner (see Figure 4.83). In this way users can anticipate the actions of others and avoid conflicts.

MAUI is a Java toolkit that offers a broad collection of awareness-enhanced user interface components (Hill and Gutwin, 2003, 2004). MAUI shows the remote user's mouse cursors in an additional layer of the graphical user interface.

4.4.7 REMOTE CURSOR

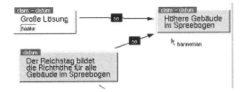

Figure 4.83 Remote cursor in SEPIA

There are several design-time options for REMOTE CURSORS in MAUI, and three different styles, arrow, block, or configurable image. Participant's names can be added to the cursor representation, and cursors can leave fading trails (see Figure 4.84). These fading trails can assist users in interpreting gestural communication.

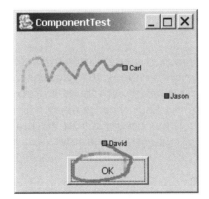

Figure 4.84 REMOTE CURSORS in MAUI

GroupWeb (Greenberg et al., 1996) includes remote cursors, which it refers to as telepointers (see Figure 4.85). GroupWeb's telepointers also convey information about the other user's activity using an icon that represents the activity—for example, a simplified menu if the remote user is currently selecting a command from a menu.

Lotus Sametime (http://www.lotus.com/sametime) is a combination of chat, application sharing, and shared browsing tools that provides "laser" pointers to highlight specific regions on the screen. After activating the laser pointer, the position of the mouse pointer is shown to all remote users, who see the pointer as a large red dot.

Figure 4.85 REMOTE CURSOR in GroupWeb

Related Patterns

TELEPOINTER→4.4.8 A telepointer is used to attract remote users' attention to some artifact in a shared space. In contrast to a telecursor, a telepointer is not bound to an input device. This has the advantage of decoupling gestures from the use of the user interface. Only those gestures that are considered important by the local user (and thus made explicit) are transmitted to remote users. The drawback of the telepointer is that users need to spend time grabbing or activating it.

REMOTE SELECTION→4.4.6 shows the set of artifacts on which a remote user is going to act. REMOTE SELECTION shares with REMOTE CURSOR the intent of indicating the target of future actions. Normally, selections don't change as frequently as cursor positions. Therefore, REMOTE SELECTIONS do not raise bandwidth problems. REMOTE SELECTION applies to a context in which users need first to select in order to act. A REMOTE CURSOR does not impose this overload.

ACTIVITY INDICATOR→4.4.9 REMOTE CURSORS should change their shape according to the remote user's current action. This helps to understand what the remote user is doing better. You could also consider attaching a text to the cursor that explains the remote user's current action. If screen space is scarce, you can follow the advice from the ACTIVITY INDICATOR pattern and provide this text in the application's status bar.

4.4.8 Telepointer *

Alternative name(s): Telecursor[6]

point·er (poin'tər), NOUN: **1.** One that directs, indicates, or points. **2.** A scale indicator on a watch, balance, or other measuring instrument. **3. A long tapered stick for indicating objects, as on a chart or blackboard. 4.** Any of a breed of hunting dogs that points game, typically having a smooth, short-haired coat that is usually white with black or brownish spots.

Intent

Focus remote users' attention on a specific position in the shared information space.

Context

Users interact synchronously in a visual information space.

Problem

When discussing visual artifacts, it is difficult to share a common focus on a specific artifact or a specific part of the artifact.

Scenario

Charley and Paul met in a distributed meeting to discuss the new class layout of the security layer. They opened a class diagram and started to discuss it. Charley pointed with his finger to a specific class and told Paul that the class should be removed. However, since Paul is not collocated, he could not understand what Charley meant by this class.

Symptoms

You should consider applying this pattern when ...

— Users are accustomed to using their fingers to point at artifacts on their screen from experience of collocated settings.

---

[6] Note that the field of HCI research often uses the term "telepointer" to refer to remote cursors. Look at the REMOTE CURSOR[→4.4.7] pattern to understand the difference that we draw in our use of these terms better.

- Remote users have problems relating messages from a local user to the artifacts to which the user is referring.
- Users need a pointing device to interact with the data and not to focus other users' attention.

Solution

Therefore: **Give each user a visual pointer that can be placed in the information space.**

Dynamics

The telepointer owner activates a telepointer, with the effect that the telepointer becomes visible to all other users.

The view has a focal point that identifies a specific artifact or position in the shared information space. It also displays the name of the telepointer owner (VIRTUAL ME$_{\to 3.1.5}$). The telepointer owner can drag the telepointer to gesture within the shared information space. The movements of the telepointer are shared among all group members so that they all see the telepointer at the same position.

When the telepointer owner no longer wants to focus the group's attention, the telepointer can be removed.

Rationale

There are various reasons why a telepointer helps to focus a group's attention better. The main reason is that it is a distinct pointing device. Users know that the telepointer is only used to signal the need for attention. Therefore, they can better interpret it than a REMOTE CURSOR$_{\to 4.4.7}$, for example. The telepointer owner can display the telepointer and continue using the shared application. A REMOTE CURSOR, on the other hand, would also move when the telepointer owner moves the mouse.

Since the telepointer is a distinct widget, it can be used in a more static way: users place their telepointer at a position and then work with the artifacts that are related to that position. This has the effect that there will be less movement on the screen compared to a solution where REMOTE CURSORS are used.

Finally, the availability of a telepointer can make users aware that additional effort is needed to communicate focal positions to other users. Allowing gesturing with the telepointer is an additional means of enriching the non-verbal aspects of communication.

Check

When applying this pattern, you should answer these questions:

- How should you define the space in which telepointers are shown? Is there an intrinsic spatiality in your shared domain model?

— Which icon should you use to display the telepointer?
— Will you show the user's name and/or a picture of the user against the telepointer?
— Will you remove the telepointer when a user leaves the COLLABORATIVE SESSION$_{\rightarrow 5.1.1}$?

Danger Spots

Users can forget to remove their telepointer. This can confuse the group, since it still calls for attention. One solution in this case is to allow a moderator (cf. QUALITY INSPECTION$_{\rightarrow 3.2.1}$) to switch abandoned telepointers off.

Since telepointers normally point to positions in the shared information space, their meaning can be altered if another user moves the artifacts out of the telepointer's focus. A solution could be to link the telepointer to the closest object and move it if the object is moved. However, there are contexts in which behavior would not reflect the user's intention.

As Borghoff and Schlichter (2000) pointed out, you should "note that the telepointer is characterized by the logical position of the information in the shared context rather than by its physical position on its screen display." Therefore, you should consider the same position manipulation as is described in the REMOTE CURSOR$_{\rightarrow 4.4.7}$ pattern.

Known Uses

Netmeeting shared whiteboard (Summers, 1999) (Figure 4.86—see also page 223). The shared whiteboard in NetMeeting allows users to place a pointing hand in the drawing area by pressing a button on the toolbar. User each have their own hand and can use it to point to specific areas of interest. The hands can be distinguished by different colors, but there is no direct mapping to users.

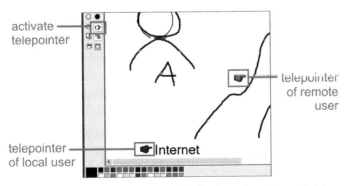

Figure 4.86 Telepointers in the shared whiteboard in Microsoft Netmeeting

Vital allows multiple users to view and manipulate a shared hypertext at the same time. One use case for this system is remote tutoring: a tutor presents material to a class of students and points out relevant parts of the shared material.

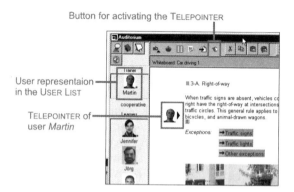

Figure 4.87 Telepointers in the VITAL environment

In Figure 4.87 the tutor *Martin* has activated his Telepointer and is pointing at the text that is the subject of the current audio communication between him and his students.

Related Patterns

Remote Cursor$_{\to 4.4.7}$ A Remote Cursor binds the user's input device to the position that is communicated to remote users, while a Telepointer clearly separates the act of pointing out a position to other users from that of interacting with the shared application.

Remote Selection$_{\to 4.4.6}$ is another way of highlighting specific areas in a shared space. However, like Remote Cursor, it is bound to an input device.

Flag$_{\to 4.3.4}$ A Flag can be considered as a long-term variant of Telepointer. The main difference is that a Flag is used to remember positions in the shared information space. Another difference is that users can set many flags, while they should only have one telepointer.

Embedded Chat$_{\to 4.3.1}$ Telepointers help to relate the communication of an Embedded Chat$_{\to 4.3.1}$ to a specific set of shared artifacts.

Digital Emotions$_{\to 4.3.7}$ describe another means for communicating non-verbally in a computer-mediated setting, apart from gesturing.

Virtual Me$_{\to 3.1.5}$ can be used to provide more information about the telepointer owner.

4.4.9 Activity Indicator *

Alternative name(s): Ticker Tape

ac·tiv·i·ty (ăk-tĭv'ĭ-tē), NOUN: **1. The state of being active. 2.** Energetic action or movement; liveliness. **3a.** A specified pursuit in which a person partakes. **b.** An educational process or procedure intended to stimulate learning through actual experience. **4.** The intensity of a radioactive source. **5.** The ability to take part in a chemical reaction. **6.** A physiological process: *respiratory activity*.

Intent

Provide an indication of other user's activities while not showing the activity's intermediate results.

Context

Users are geographically distributed and interact in a highly synchronous session that involves frequent turn-taking and request-response interaction.

Problem

Users need time to perform a task but only the results are shared among them. In a collocated setting users are accustomed to perceive non-verbal signals such as movement or sounds when another user is active. If the users are distributed, these signals are missing. Users are therefore not aware of other users' activities, which can result in conflicting work or unnecessary delays.

Scenario

Rick and Dimitri both decided to work on graphical aspects of the game engine project. Rick started to work on the rendering of places, while Dimitri looked at the rendering of actors. At one point Dimitri started changing some code that he had currently checked out to his workspace. He planned to check the code in again after he had tested his modifications. However, if Rick also wanted to modify the same section of code, both user's changes would need to be merged after they had finished their tasks.

Symptoms

You should consider applying this pattern when ...

— Users dislike distributed interaction because they do not know what the other users are doing.
— Users perform concurrent actions.
— Users wait a long time for another user's action, even if the other user does not act at all.
— Users act at the same time but do not necessarily share the same focus.
— Users do not want to be distracted from their current task, but still feel the need to stay aware of other users.

Solution

Therefore: **Indicate other user's current activities in the user interface. To reduce interruptions, use a peripheral place or a visually unobtrusive indicator.**

Dynamics

Provide a user interface element in a peripheral location that shows whether remote users are active and what they are currently doing. The current activity of a user can for example be determined using an ACTIVITY LOG$_{\rightarrow 4.5.1}$. Ensure that remote users' activities are shown in the user interface immediately they start to act. Hide the activity if no more activities are detected from the remote users (for example, there is no keyboard input for a specific period of time).

Rationale

The activity indicator is displayed as soon as a remote user starts an activity. This signals to the local user that the remote user is now active and that additional local actions could lead to conflicts.

Check

When applying this pattern, you should answer these questions:

— Where are you going to display the other users' activities? Commonly used places are:
  - The status bar in the collaborative application
  - The status bar on the desktop
  - A pop-up note on the desktop's task bar that disappears automatically after a short period

- A notification pane in your application (comparable to an EMBEDDED CHAT$_{\rightarrow 4.3.1}$)
- A color change in the application's title bar that is also visible when the application is minimized

— What kind of activities are you going to indicate? Is it only important to show modification activities, or should you also indicate other factors such as the navigation activities of users?

Danger Spots

If many users collaborate, displaying their various activities becomes difficult. Therefore, reduce the information provided and cluster the information when several users are performing the same activity, for example.

Known Uses

MSN Messenger shows when another user is typing a message in the status bar of the chat window. This helps the local user to better judge whether a reply can be expected.

Figure 4.88 An ACTIVITY INDICATOR in MSN Messenger

In Figure 4.88 the users *Jutta* and *Till* are involved in a conversation. The status bar tells *Till* that *Jutta* is currently writing a reply.

Palantir (Sarma et al., 2003) is a group awareness component that extends a software configuration management system. Palantir tracks the activities of project team members to provide information about their actions.

Each activity that is of interest to the local user runs through a ticker tape display in the awareness client (see Figure 4.89). This view is intended to stay on the user's desktop and constantly update the user on the most recent activities. Using a scrolling text probably results in a greater level of attention to the information.

A comparable visualization is used in the Elvin system (Parsowith et al., 1998), which tracks and visualizes activities in a shared workspace.

Figure 4.89 The ACTIVITY INDICATOR in Palantír

Mail Clients like Thunderbird (http://www.mozilla.com/thunderbird/) provide a status icon whenever a new message arrives. This prevents the local user from needing to poll a mailbox manually. Compared to more prominent forms of new e-mail alerts, the icon in the status bar will not provide too much distraction: "By having only the new e-mail icon in the system tray, employees' attention would be attracted only when the concentration level is less demanding and the interruption would occur at a more convenient time." (Jackson et al., 2003).

Related Patterns

ATTENTION SCREEN$_{\to 3.3.4}$ can be used to filter the awareness information shown in the ACTIVITY INDICATOR.

ACTIVITY LOG$_{\to 4.5.1}$ describes how to store information on the users' activities and can be used to determine a user's current activity.

4.4.10 Feel me... applied

Since a USER LIST$_{\rightarrow 4.4.1}$ can be considered as the most important pattern for synchronous awareness, it is not surprising that it also makes sense in the context of the game engine community. It terms of the extensions to Eclipse that Paul and Susan created in the previous chapters, there are different levels of scope to which a USER LIST can be attached. Paul decided to provide different USER LISTS for these different scopes.

The global USER LIST is implemented as a filter for the USER GALLERY$_{\rightarrow 3.1.6}$ (see page 116). By enabling the filter, the USER GALLERY only shows users who are currently connected to the system.

The local USER LIST shows all users who collaborate in the same shared editor. This list is always visible when the editor is shown, to promote awareness between the participants of the SHARED EDITOR. You can see an example of this list at the top right of Figure 4.19 on page 231. In addition to the user's identities, this user list shows the users' current roles, and particularly whether or not the user is allowed to manipulate content. This session-specific information only makes sense in the context of the concrete editing session and is one important reason for having an additional user list for the session.

Finally, the third level of scope is the artifact level. Paul and Susan added user lists to the artifacts of the package view in Eclipse. This local USER LIST shows all users who currently have an editor opened on the specific resource (see Figure 4.90). In our definition of work as an interplay between users, artifacts, and tools (see page 187), the three different forms of USER LISTS that Paul decided to implement cover all the different aspects of work. They provide information on the users' state in the global list, they inform users about the use context of the tools in the session-specific USER LIST, and finally they provide awareness of the use of the artifacts in the artifact-centered USER LISTS.

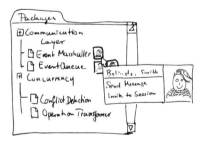

Figure 4.90 Inviting peripheral users to form a spontaneous group

The artifact-centered USER LIST enables SPONTANEOUS COLLABORATION$_{\rightarrow 4.4.2}$. When users see other users, they can INVITE them to a new SHARED EDITING$_{\rightarrow 4.1.6}$

session on this content. The invitation is contextualized with the INTERACTIVE USER INFO$_{\rightarrow 4.4.4}$ shown in Figure 4.90. When a user clicks on another user's VIRTUAL ME in the USER LIST, the system determines potential means for interaction based on each user's status. In Figure 4.90, the local user can invite Belinda to a collaborative session or send her an instant message.

Once in a COLLABORATIVE SESSION$_{\rightarrow 5.1.1}$, the users can use the SHARED EDITOR$_{\rightarrow 4.1.6}$ in which they gain additional awareness of other users' actions. Susan proposed adding a remote selection to the shared code editor. Otherwise, it would be difficult for the driver to communicate about the code with the navigator. Susan could also have decided to implement a TELEPOINTER$_{\rightarrow 4.4.8}$ to solve this problem. The reason for choosing REMOTE SELECTION$_{\rightarrow 4.4.6}$ was that it could be implemented easily using the existing editor classes in Eclipse.

For the diagram editor, the context was different: since users are allowed to work on independent regions of the diagram at the same time, it is crucial to have an overview of other users' working positions. Paul selected the REMOTE FIELD OF VISION$_{\rightarrow 4.4.5}$ pattern to support this (see Figure 4.91).

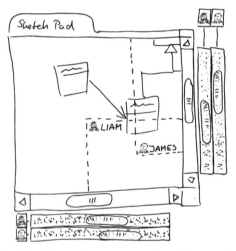

Figure 4.91 Visualizing the group members' REMOTE FIELD OF VISION

The extent of each user's view is shown by frames that are overlaid in the diagram. In addition, multiuser scroll bars help to locate other users when they work outside any overlapping parts of the diagram. Paul decided to decorate each scroll bar with the picture of the scroll bar owner. This information makes it easier to connect working areas with people. However, it made the USER LIST for the diagram editor obsolete, so Paul decided to remove the USER LIST from the diagram editor.

4.5 Remember me... or how to maintain asynchronous group awareness

Tam and Greenberg (2004) extended the questions in Table 4.1 to the context of asynchronous awareness. This has the effect that most questions have not only to be asked for the current point in time, but also for the past.

The reason for doing this is twofold: first, participants should be given a better understanding of the history of individual and group activities. Second, participants are not active in the community all the time.

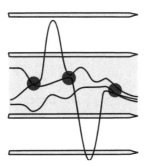

Figure 4.92 The role of awareness in asynchronous collaboration

The latter is shown in Figure 4.92. Participants interact in a shared workspace, but also leave the workspace from time to time. They may even cross the borders of the community, if they are for example on a long vacation or in hospital, from where they have no access to the community's network.

In our scenario, this was the case for Susan:

Susan started to work on a new test framework with George. Unfortunately, she had to interrupt her work and stay in hospital for some weeks because she broke her leg on the way home. After eight weeks she returns, but has problems in understanding what has taken place during her absence.

The patterns in this Section (Figure 4.93) help in comparable contexts. They provide a means for announcing longer absences and present a group history when the user returns—although in Susan's case this might still not work, because she did not plan her absence.

ACTIVITY LOG$_{\to 4.5.1}$ Store information about users' activities in a log to provide a history of their activities and the artifacts' evolution.

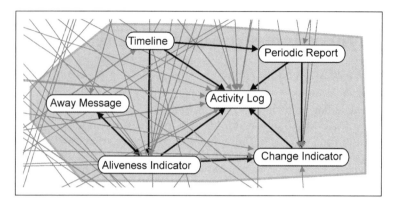

Figure 4.93 Patterns for asynchronous awareness

TIMELINE[→4.5.2] Show who has been active at a specific point in time.

PERIODIC REPORT[→4.5.3] Inform users about changes to relevant artifacts at a predefined frequency.

CHANGE INDICATOR[→4.5.4] Indicate that a shared artifact has been changed.

ALIVENESS INDICATOR[→4.5.5] Include an indicator in a virtual environment that reflects users' activity levels.

AWAY MESSAGE[→4.5.6] Inform active users that a response to their request will be delayed.

4.5.1 Activity Log **

Alternative name(s): Event History, Elephant's Brain

log (lôg), NOUN: **1a.** A usually large section of a trunk or limb of a fallen or felled tree. **b.** A long thick section of trimmed, unhewn timber. **2. Nautical a.** A device trailed from a ship to determine its speed through the water. **b. A record of a ship's speed, its progress, and any shipboard events of navigational importance. c. The book in which this record is kept. 3.** A record of a vehicle's performance, as the flight record of an aircraft. **4.** A record, as of the performance of a machine or the progress of an undertaking: *a computer log; a trip log.*

Intent

Store information about users' activities in a log to provide a history of their activities and the artifacts' evolution.

Context

Users perform parallel activities on shared artifacts without being totally sure about their effects or understanding other users' activities.

Problem

Merging two users' (past or current) activities is a difficult task. It requires the activities to be transferred to the same context and the goals aligned. Many applications do not provide access to the history of an artifact, its use, and its evolution, however. Thus merging is vulnerable to errors and often collaboration does not take place, since the effort of merging exceeds the expected gains from a collaboration.

Scenario

Paul is quite good at keeping an overview of the game engine project. James, on the other hand, only has knowledge of the speech recognition engine. Now James wants to invest some time in the security packages in which Paul has been involved. The only way he can find out more about the evolution of this package is to ask Paul. Paul is tired of telling old stories all over again, however.

Symptoms

You should consider applying this pattern when ...

— Users often notice that an artifact has changed, but can no longer remember how it looked before.
— Users cannot detect who performed incorrect changes, and what these changes were.
— Users cannot find out what user X did to artifact Y yesterday.
— Users don't understand the changes made by other users.

Solution

Therefore: Remember all activities—not only modifications, but also read accesses—that users perform on shared artifacts in a log. Provide access to the log so that it is possible to understand (and merge) the various users' activities.

Dynamics

The log is a container that records activities. Logs should be persistent to allow reference to activities made during previous sessions. Applications interact with the log by adding, consuming, or querying activities.

Activities are performed on shared data. Activities are internally represented as requests from a user interface element (in the broadest sense) to a shared object. An example could be the request to save a file in a text editor. To detect activities, add an additional layer in the communication between the application and the shared data to monitor user's activities. Activities include information about the:

— *Type* of the activity, such as reading, editing, creating, removing, and so on
— *Artifact* that was touched by the activity (often in two versions: the version before the activity and the version after the activity)
— *Time* at which the activity took place (often as a set of two timestamps representing the start and the end of the activity)
— *User* who performed the activity and can be identified by requiring users to LOGIN$_{\rightarrow 3.1.2}$

In several systems, activities also include a user comment, which provides more information on the intent behind an activity. Activities should comprise a single semantic user transaction with the system. Examples could be the selection of a menu command, the insertion of a new paragraph in a text document, or viewing a web page in a web browser. Activities should be updated as soon as a user interacts with the application.

For the display of up-to-date collaboration information, the log can serve as a publisher of new activities according to the PUBLISHER-SUBSCRIBER pattern (Buschmann et al., 1996). Clients who use the log to provide awareness information *subscribe* to activities. They therefore provide an activity pattern that describes relevant activities. The publisher informs the subscriber whenever activities that match the pattern change.

Rationale

Logging all the activities that users perform makes it possible to inspect all activities later. This helps to understand the evolution of a specific artifact, by looking at all activities that took place on the artifact, or a specific user's work, by looking up all the activities initiated by the user.

Since the log is persistent, the information will be remembered after the user has forgotten it.

An ACTIVITY LOG goes beyond version management functionality in two main points:

1. It also remembers accesses that did not change an artifact. These accesses are not mandatory for restoring the system at a specific point of time. However, they help to understand the user's background for a specific activity, and in some cases they can help to reveal conflicting activities.

2. An ACTIVITY LOG provides a means for notifying interested users about activities associated with a specific artifact. Some version management systems also support this, which is the reason why CVS is included in the known uses section, although it does not record non-modifying accesses, as discussed in the previous paragraph.

Check

When applying this pattern, you should answer these questions:

— Do you have a central server on which you can place the log? If not, how do you distribute logs between clients?

— Who will create the activity object, the client or the server? What information is needed to create and initialize the activity object?

— What information will you transmit to the server if you generate activities at the clients?

— How will you support efficient queries of the activity log? How should you handle large numbers of activities? Can you use a database to store the activities?

— Does it make sense in your context to create an activity log for each artifact (to store the activities together with the artifact)?

— Do users agree to their activities being tracked? What happens if a user asks not to be tracked?

Danger Spots

Ensure that many users can add activities to the log at the same time. One way to achieve this is to model the log as a Lovely Bag$_{\to 5.3.5}$ to which users can add activities in any order without producing semantically different activity logs. Since each activity is unique (distinguishable user and time), there will be no conflicts in adding activities to the log.

When referencing artifacts in the activity description, you have to make sure that the right version of the artifact is referenced. In environments where no versioning is available, you should include sufficient information to restore all the different versions of an artifact by inspection of all activities that took place on the artifact.

Prinz (1999) argues that the activity log should be decoupled from the application that generates events. This allows easy extension to support a large variety of events generated by different client applications.

Note that an Activity Log can only store those activities of which it is informed. For off-the-shelf tools such as CAD packages, this might just be the creation of a new document version. You should therefore examine the application carefully to monitor as much information as possible, since this information is crucial for detailed (and intelligent) group support.

Ensure that users knows that activities are logged. Users have to be able to decide on their own whether they want to be monitored (see Masquerade$_{\to 3.3.2}$). They have to feel that being monitored adds value to their activities, for example because of the principle of Reciprocity$_{\to 3.3.1}$. Otherwise, they will in most cases find a way to do their job while bypassing the monitoring mechanisms.

Not all activities should stay in the Activity Log forever. Consider for example a read activity on an artifact. This show that the user involved becomes aware of the artifact's content. However, the user may forget this. Therefore, you should think about the period of validity of activities. Some activities should be cleaned up periodically, others, such as activities that change the state of an artifact, should be permanent.

Known Uses

CVS. The CVS version management system (Price, 2000) maintains a file `history` that stores meta-information on all activities This information includes the user, the touched artifact, and the type of the modification. Version information can be obtained using the `cvs history` command. An example output looks like this:

```
cvs history -c
M 2003-02-27 13:09 schuemm 1.2 README     test == ~test2\test
A 2003-02-27 13:14 schuemm 1.1 short.txt  test == ~test2\test
M 2003-02-27 13:16 schuemm 1.2 short.txt  test == ~test2\test
```

VisualWorks Smalltalk. The VisualWorks Smalltalk environment (Cincom, 2001) writes all changes to a change file. This change file is mainly intended to recover from system crashes, but an important additional use case is the inspection of changes to an artifact. VisualWorks provides a special changes browser for this, which shows all changes to a specific source artifact. Since the programming environment is single-user, it does not provide any multiuser access to the change file.

NESSIE. The NESSIE Awareness Server (Prinz, 1999) is a general-purpose awareness server that stores events. Each event carries information about its originator, the action, the touched artifact, and the time at which the event took place. The events are implementations of activities in the ACTIVITY LOG.

Client applications can add activities to the server using an HTTP-based interface. They can also subscribe to changes by specifying the type of the activity and a desired context (the touched artifact's location).

TUKAN (Schümmer and Schümmer, 2001) is a collaborative programming environment that extends VisualWorks Smalltalk. It logs all activities that users perform in the environment—for example reading source code or modifying a class file—and stores these activities in an activity log.

The ACTIVITY LOG is stored as a shared object, which is replicated to all clients using the COAST framework for synchronous groupware (Schümmer et al., 2001). The replication mechanisms also include a distributed version of PUBLISHER-SUBSCRIBER to trigger view updates or other actions when a log entry changed.

Related Patterns

CENTRALIZED OBJECTS$_{\rightarrow 5.2.1}$ describes how to implement an ACTIVITY LOG that is managed on a central server.

DISTRIBUTED COMMAND$_{\rightarrow 5.2.7}$ When an application uses DISTRIBUTED COMMANDS it is possible to interpret activities according to the COMMAND design pattern (Gamma et al., 1995). The main difference is that commands should be able to execute (and undo) themselves, which exceeds the simple logging purpose of the activities. Commands are therefore more tightly bound to the application.

In contrast to activities, they are potentially active and not just descriptive. If the application uses COMMANDS, it becomes possible to reference commands as activities and store them in the log.

LOGIN$_{\rightarrow 3.1.2}$ allows identification of a user and association of activities with users, as required for the ACTIVITY LOG.

USER LIST$_{\rightarrow 4.4.1}$ Use the USER LIST pattern to inform users of activities that currently take place at the same artifact, to avoid conflicting work.

MODEL-VIEW-CONTROLLER. If the application is implemented following the MODEL-VIEW-CONTROLLER pattern (Krasner and Pope, 1988) and (Buschmann et al., 1996), one way of detecting activities is to hook into the controller's control flow. Whenever the controller receives a startUp message (that is, when it starts its work), an activity is created. The activity is then filled with artifacts that are accessed while the controller is active. When the controller's control flow terminates, it sets the end time of the activity.

CHANGE LOG. A change log (Anderson, 2000) stores different states of an object or an object's attribute together with additional information about the originator of the change. It is comparable to an ACTIVITY LOG because it also stores old states of the artifact, and thus provides the information needed to reconstruct past activities. The focus of the patterns is different: a change log mainly solves the problem of restoring or accessing old states of an object, whereas an ACTIVITY LOG focuses on logging all activities, not necessarily just modifications.

EDITION. The edition pattern (Anderson, 2000) shows how a change to an object's state can be associated with the event that caused the change. It directly binds the activity to the object affected by the activity. For cases in which shared objects can be manipulated, this is an alternative approach to store the activities. The decision whether to store activities on any shared artifact in a repository (ACTIVITY LOG) or directly with the artifact (EDITION) depends on the access patterns for the information. If activities are mainly accessed by time or user they are easier to find in a repository. If they are accessed for a specific artifact, they can also be stored directly with the artifact. For a collaborative setting for an ACTIVITY LOG, you should ensure that all accesses are stored, not just modifying accesses, as it is the case in the original EDITION pattern.

4.5.2 Timeline

time·line (tīm'līn'), NOUN: **1.** A schedule of activities or events; a timetable. **2a.** A chronology. **b. A representation or exhibit of key events within a particular historical period, often consisting of illustrative visual material accompanied by written commentary, arranged chronologically.**

Intent

Show who has been active at a specific point in time.

Context

Your system supports long-term asynchronous and/or synchronous interaction.

Problem

Not all users participate in collaborative sessions continuously. This makes it hard to understand who is working with whom on what topic. Without such an understanding, however, users lack the orientation and coordination required for group interaction.

Scenario

Maurice tries to understand what Paul and his colleagues implemented last week while Maurice was on vacation. He knows that the other developers discussed the strategies for their work frequently and then split work between themselves. He decides to examine the change notifications that were circulated by e-mail, but even after this he still lacks a holistic picture of the development activities.

Symptoms

You should consider applying this pattern when . . .

— Users complain that others do not participate, although they do participate.
— Users stop participating, but this is not detected by the group.

Solution

Therefore: **Display the activities that took place in a workspace as a timeline.**

Dynamics

The timeline is a two-dimensional diagram that relates the time of an activity with either the artifact used in the activity or the performer of the activity.

First group the activities monitored in the ACTIVITY LOG$_{\rightarrow 4.5.1}$ by the days on which each activity took place. Then show, for each day, the activities that took place on that day. Separate the days using bars.

Display each activity as an icon or a dot in the diagram. Use different icons for different users when showing the artifacts accessed by the activities on one of the axis. When showing users on one of the axis, think about different icons for the different artifacts that were accessed.

Use dynamic data visualization techniques such as DATATIPS or LOCAL ZOOMING (Tidwell, 2006) to support the display of long activity logs with many artifacts. This means that additional information is provided on request. Connect the display of activities with the documents that were accessed, so that the timeline can be used for navigating to shared objects.

Rationale

Display of the group's activities supports users in understanding the group's actions. It enhances understanding of the topics with which users were working and to what extent they were collaborating. It also helps to be able to see who has been active in which area of the collaboration space.

Interaction between individuals and subgroups can often be recognized when artifacts are shown on one of axis and these are accessed by different participants. The same is true when users are shown on one of the axis.

Check

When applying this pattern, you should answer these questions:

— Are you more interested in people or in artifacts—are you going to show users or artifacts on one of the axis?

— How will you code the elements in the diagram? How many different targets will your activities have? Would it be helpful to use color codes or different icons?

— Can you provide tool tips that provide details about the activities shown in the diagram?

— Can you link the points in the diagram to the artifacts or the performers of the activity?

— Does it make sense to distinguish between modifying and reading activities, for example by using a different color for the diagram entry?
— Can you support zooming of the timeline or will it be a static image?

Danger Spots

Ensure that you select the data set with the higher cardinality for the Y axis. If your group, for example, has five members who work on fifty documents, the documents should be shown on the Y axis and the members should be shown using different colors or icons. This leads to a diagram with fifty lines and five different icons. Otherwise, one would have a diagram with just five lines but fifty different icons, which would probably be harder to read.

One problem with this pattern can be scalability. As Ganoe et al. (2003) evaluated in a field study, a timeline can become "less effective (and even cluttered) if there are frequent changes to all the documents."

Known Uses

Virtual School is a collaboration space for student interaction. In a user study (Carroll et al., 2003), the authors of the Virtual School environment, found several breakdowns in collaboration that had their causes in a lack of activity awareness. One solution was to integrate a timeline into the students' workspace, as shown in Figure 4.94. The resulting system was then called the BRIDGE awareness center (Ganoe et al., 2004).

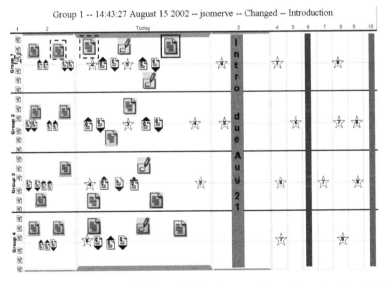

Figure 4.94 TIMELINE in the Virtual School context (from Carroll et al. (2003))

For each project, the timeline showed different documents in the rows. Changes to the documents were represented by the icons on the time axis. To access documents, users were forced to select them in the timeline instead of from a list of documents. Each version could be accessed by clicking on the various icons for each document (using IMMUTABLE VERSIONS$_{\rightarrow 5.3.6}$). This made the timeline an integral part of daily work.

User studies (Ganoe et al., 2003) have shown that the timeline was of great value to people who were observing the group's progress. When there were for example white areas on the timeline, teachers queried the students responsible for those documents about problems in their group process, and provided help.

Babble Timeline (Erickson and Laff, 2001) shown in Figure 4.95 is a visualization widget for better understanding the history of chat conversation. It shows up to one week of the chat log recorded in a Babble chat.

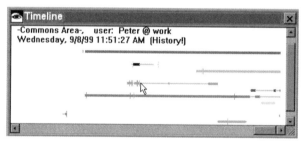

Figure 4.95 TIMELINE in the Babble chat environment (from Erickson and Laff (2001))

Each user is represented by a row. When users send messages to the chat system, they leave a peak on their row of the timeline. Different colors are used to distinguish between contributions to the currently viewed chat and contributions to other chats. Additional information on the time of the contribution and the identity of the user is provided by means of tool tips.

Users make use of the timeline to discover when other users are interacting in the collaboration space. This knowledge helps them to coordinate their work better in future, for example by adjusting their working hours so that synchronous collaboration is possible wherever this is needed.

CVS History Explorer (http://historyflow.sourceforge.net) is a tool that visualizes the history of files stored in CVS, a versioned SHARED FILE REPOSITORY$_{\rightarrow 4.1.2}$. Users can select an artifact and open the timeline for the artifact, which is based on the Flow history visualization first proposed by Viègas et al. (2004).

4.5.2 Timeline

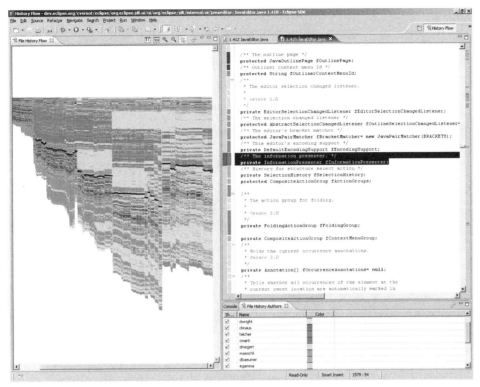

Figure 4.96 Changes to a source file over time visualized as a timeline

Figure 4.96 shows the timeline for a Java source file. Each column maps to one user activity. Note that the view is zoomed out to show the whole history, with the effect that the columns are hard to identify: in the interactive application, one would zoom in to identify the authors. The color of the column header represents a specific user, and the lines in the source file that the user has changed are shown with this color. By comparing the visualizations of the different columns, one can see how different parts of the source code have survived over time. It is also possible to see how the work of a specific user influenced the file over time.

Related Patterns

REPLAY$_{\to 5.1.4}$ also addresses the problem of explaining the activities that took place in the collaboration space to an absent user. The difference is that a TIMELINE visualizes activity information, while the REPLAY pattern shows which artifacts the activities changed.

PERIODIC REPORT→4.5.3 A PERIODIC REPORT provides a more detailed view of changes in a collaboration space. It is well suited to short time spans, but will become very complex when it shows a longer period. A TIMELINE abstracts further from the activities and is therefore capable of providing a longer overview of activities.

ACTIVITY LOG→4.5.1 A TIMELINE displays the activities stored in the ACTIVITY LOG.

ALIVENESS INDICATOR→4.5.5 helps to detect the fact that a user has stopped participating. This can be seen in the TIMELINE when there are no more entries for a specific user—especially when the timeline display shows users on the Y axis.

IMMUTABLE VERSIONS→5.3.6 For each activity, you should be able to link to the version of the document that resulted from the activity. This requires that you keep all versions of the shared artifact, as described in the IMMUTABLE VERSIONS pattern.

TIMELINE in the context of project retrospectives (Kerth, 2001). The technique of project timelines has been widely used in the context of project retrospectives, and captured as patterns by various authors, such as Gottesdiener (2003). The basic idea is that members of a project team place notable project events on a visual timeline. The technical TIMELINE presented in this pattern can support the creation of a project timeline. When using a technically generated TIMELINE in a retrospective, you should allow users to attach SHARED ANNOTATIONS→4.3.5 to the TIMELINE so that they can comment on the events.

DYNAMIC QUERIES and DATA BRUSHING (Tidwell, 2006) discuss how complex diagrams like a TIMELINE can be explored interactively. In the DYNAMIC QUERIES pattern, users can control a set of filters that defines which data elements are included in the diagram. In the context of the TIMELINE a filter could reduce the set of users who are included in the diagram. The DATA BRUSHING pattern suggests simultaneously showing different diagrams and allowing the user to select data in one of the diagrams, with the effect that the other diagram shows more detailed information based on the data selected in the first diagram. Translated to the context of a TIMELINE, you could consider having one global diagram for the collaboration space, with detail diagrams that are shown after the user selects a set of documents in the global diagram.

4.5.3 PERIODIC REPORT **

Alternative name(s): Change Report, Newsletter

pe·ri·od·ic (pîr′ē-ŏd′ĭk), ADJECTIVE: **1.** Having or marked by repeated cycles. **2. Happening or appearing at regular intervals. 3.** Recurring or reappearing from time to time; intermittent. **4.** Characterized by periodic sentences.

Intent

Inform users about changes to relevant artifacts at a predefined frequency.

Context

Users collaborate asynchronously by modifying shared objects.

Problem

Changes in indirect collaboration are only visible by inspecting a changed artifact. Users want to react to actions on artifacts, but they cannot predict when these actions will take place.

Scenario

In January Weigang filed a bug report on a security problem in the login mechanism of the game engine. He then checked the affected components frequently for an update. In January he did this daily, since he really needed the security fix. Nothing happened, however, so Weigang reduced the frequency of his update checks. Now, four months later, he only scans the files every fortnight and has given up hope of a fix. Reflecting on the last few months, Weigang regrets that he spent so much time looking for updates.

Symptoms

You should consider applying this pattern when . . .

— Users rely on each others' activities but cannot predict when they will take place.

- Users frequently scan for changes but rarely find any.
- Collaboration takes longer than it should because users do not scan for changes as frequently as they appear.
- The community performs many modifications a day, so that direct notifications of each change would consume too much attention or would be too expensive.

Solution

Therefore: Inform users periodically about the changes that took place between the time of the current report and the previous one.

Dynamics

Users defines an interest profile manually or automatically based on their access rights in the collaborative system. They also define a notification interval and a communication channel by which they would like to be notified.

After the interest interval has passed (in most cases at night), the system checks whether artifacts matching any interest profiles have been modified within the last time interval. If this is the case, the system puts meta-information on the change into a periodic report. The periodic report, with information on all matching modified objects, is sent to the users using the requested communication channel.

Meta-information can for example contain a short description of the artifact, information about the person who modified it, and the time and type of the modification. It should include a quick reference to the changed artifact to ease access to it.

The check for changed artifacts can take place in two alternative ways:

1. The system can query the timestamps of all objects and search for those that fall within the notification interval. This has the advantage that the artifacts only have to carry a timestamp and no additional data structures are needed to track changes. Information on the performer of the change needs to be stored with the artifact if such information is required in the periodic report.
2. The system tracks all changes in an ACTIVITY LOG$_{\rightarrow 4.5.1}$ and queries the ACTIVITY LOG for activities that took place during the notification interval. Since the activities carry all the required meta-information (performer, time stamp, and the type of activity), this information does not need to be part of the artifact. However, the number of recorded activities may soon grow and slow the system down.

Rationale

Users are informed about changes. This allows them to react to the actions of other users. The fixed interval of change notifications ensures that others can predict when the local user will read the change report. Compared to immediate change notifications, the interval reduces the number of individual interruptions. Since users are able to tailor their reports, the reports will only contain relevant information. For that reason, they will probably be read.

Check

When applying this pattern, you should answer these questions:

— How frequently do changes occur and how long are change authors prepared to wait until their changes are noticed by other group members?

— How can you represent artifacts in the report medium, for example in an e-mail message? Can you provide URLs that let the user access the specific artifact with a single click?

— What is the best time to send your report? Is there a period of low system use in which the report can be sent?

— Should users have to register for the report, or will you send it automatically? If the latter, might it be considered as spam?

— How can users turn the report off?

— How will you support your users in specifying their interests?

— Will reports be able to be personalized to suite different interest profiles, or will everyone share the same report?

Danger Spots

The report can be considered as spam. Make sure that the users know how to tailor the report to their needs.

In most cases it is advisable to avoid empty reports. However, subscribers could think that their report had been lost if they didn't receive one.

Make sure that the report is structured in a way that can be easily grasped. Provide enough information on the artifacts to allow a reader to filter irrelevant changes without looking at the specific artifact in the system.

Known Uses

BSCW is probably one of the best-known collaborative systems to make use of PERIODIC REPORTS. More details can be found in Section 6.1 on page 523.

Forums like Yahoo Groups (http://groups.yahoo.com) often provide options for controlling the frequency of messages sent to subscribers. Subscribers can decide whether they want to receive individual messages or periodic reports, known as *digests*. The digests can contain the entire contents of individual messages, or just the headers with links to the individual messages.

CURE sends a daily report every night. The report lists changes that occurred in rooms to which the recipient has access. These changes include the creation or modification of pages or messages stored in the room, as well as the invitation of new users to the room. Users thus stay aware of documents, communication, and group membership on a regular basis.

e-Commerce websites often allow customers to store their interests and their e-mail address on the server. Whenever a new item is added or an old item is changed, the site sends a notification e-mail informing the potential customer that there might be something new of interest on the site.

Related Patterns

ATTENTION SCREEN$_{\to 3.3.4}$ An attention screen filters notifications and contact requests to ensure users' privacy. It can be combined with a PERIODIC REPORT to ensure that users stay informed about the activities in a collaborative environment. It can also enhance acceptance of the PERIODIC REPORT, since it allows users to define the information that should reach them via the periodic report.

CHANGE INDICATOR$_{\to 4.5.4}$ A change indicator provides information about changed artifacts in the same context as the artifact itself. The notification that an artifact has changed is attached to the artifact. In contrast, a PERIODIC REPORT externalizes this information and transmits it to users' work contexts outside the system, for example via users' mailboxes.

ACTIVITY LOG$_{\to 4.5.1}$ An ACTIVITY LOG keeps track of all activities in a system. A PERIODIC REPORT can be generated from the ACTIVITY LOG by querying it for activities that took place on relevant artifacts since the previous report.

4.5.4 Change Indicator **

change (chānj), NOUN: **1.** The act, process, or result of altering or modifying: *a change in facial expression*. **2.** The replacing of one thing for another; substitution: *a change of atmosphere; a change of ownership*. **3. A transformation or transition from one state, condition, or phase to another:** *the change of seasons*.

Intent

Indicate that a shared artifact has been changed.

Context

Users work on independent copies of shared artifacts.

Problem

While users works on independent local copies of artifacts, their checkout frequency for the artifacts may be low. As a result, they may work on old copies, which leads to potentially conflicting parallel changes. The conflict is worse if two parallel modifications have contradictory intentions.

Scenario

Marc has made some major improvements to the graphics engine. The most important was that he changed the coordinate system from cartesian to polar. Marc documented this change in the manual of the game engine. Martin, who uses the game engine, was not aware of this change. He thinks that he knows how to use the game engine and does not often read the manual. He therefore uses the graphics engine part with cartesian coordinates and is confused when the images look very strange.

Symptoms

You should consider applying this pattern when . . .

— Users apply changes to artifacts based on outdated knowledge of the artifact's state.

— Users report that they would have done things differently if they had been aware of the current state of the artifact.
— Users frequently change artifacts.

Solution

Therefore: Indicate whenever an artifact has been changed by an actor other than the local user. Show this information whenever the artifact or a reference to the artifact is shown on the screen. The information should contain details about the type of change and provide access to the new version of the artifact.

Dynamics

Figure 4.97 shows how the different participants collaborate. Note that we have chosen to demonstrate the pattern on the assumption that shared artifacts are documents kept on a central document server. Without limiting generality, this can be transferred to any shared artifact that is kept at a specific place and that has to be copied to a local system before it can be changed.

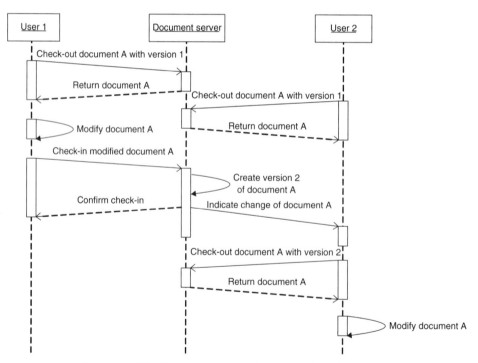

Figure 4.97 Two users are working on a shared document

In Figure 4.97 user 1 downloads a document A from the shared document server. This document has the version 1. Later on, user 2 also checks the document A. Both users now have independent copies of the document A which have the same version. User 1 modifies the local version of the document A and transfer this modified version to the shared document server. The server creates a new version of document A and informs user 2 about the new version. User 2 has not modified the local copy of document A, however, so checks out the new version before performing the planned modifications.

Rationale

There are two main reasons why this pattern works: a technological reason and a cognitive reason.

From a technical point of view, indicating changes alters the point in time at which integration is performed. Whenever an artifact is changed, all older versions will be marked to indicate that the artifact was changed and by whom. In most cases, users wishing to access the artifact will integrate the change immediately to base further work on the most recent version. If this is not possible, they can at least inspect the newer version and adjust their own changes such that integration is easy. This reduces the cost of integration. They can also get in contact with the person who applied the initial change. Both can then discuss and align their changes and—if considered useful—work together in a tightly coupled mode. In all cases the cost of integration is reduced because their conflicting changes are avoided.

The cognitive reasoning is often much more important. Consider a system in which artifacts are not explicitly stored in a local workspace. At a first glance, such systems do not fit into the context of this pattern. If one takes a closer look at typical interactions, however, one can define an implicit local workspace: a local user's knowledge of how the artifacts look. Whenever an artifact is perceived by users, it leaves traces in their memory. All future activities on shared artifacts will be influenced by these memory traces. In many cases, they think they remember the specific artifact and thus do not look at it again.

When the artifact is changed, it is important to inform users that they can no longer be confident about their knowledge of the artifact. The version of the artifact that users remember can lead to other interpretations than those relating to the most recent version. Users therefore need to reprocess the changed artifact and update their semantic representation of the artifact and its context.

Check

When applying this pattern, you should answer these questions:

— How will you display a change warning? Can you add a decorator to the icon representing the changed artifact?

— How important is awareness of the changed artifact? In unimportant cases you can consider simply modifying the artifact's appearance when someone has changed it, while in important cases you should consider a more obtrusive change indicator such as a dialog.

— How soon will you inform other users about a change to an artifact? When the artifact is checked in, or can you have even earlier status updates, for example after modification of the artifact in a local editor?

Danger Spots

Even when indicating changes, people might ignore the indications. To overcome this problem, it is necessary to establish a social protocol that defines how CHANGE INDICATIONS should be handled.

Changes can be complex, and providing details about them can be complex too. In that case, consider providing a comparison view that contrasts a local user's state of a changed artifact with its state as seen by a remote user.

If changes occur too frequently, most artifacts will be shown as changed artifacts, resulting in constant searching for changes and insufficient time to perform constructive actions. One solution could be to highlight unchanged artifacts explicitly, so that users can be confident that such artifacts need no further attention.

Known Uses

TUKAN. The programming environment TUKAN (Schümmer, 2001) uses a weather metaphor to display change warnings. A bold lightning symbol tells programmers that a specific artifact has been changed. The symbols suggest better weather for potential conflicts caused by changes to artifacts that are semantically further away, following the ACTIVE NEIGHBORS$_{\rightarrow 4.4.3}$ pattern. If there is no close conflict, a sun symbol is shown to indicate that everything is up to date and reinforce the user's confidence.

Figure 4.98 shows a browser in TUKAN in which the method day: has been changed by another user, indicated by the thundercloud symbol in front of the method name.

By indication possible configuration conflicts, parallel changes to the same artifact can be avoided. Changes made by other programmers are not instantly reflected in the local programmer's code, but rather in the visualization of the method identifier. Whenever a newer version is signaled, the user can decide to integrate the new version before changing the artifact itself, avoiding parallel versions.

WinEdt. The text editor WinEdt (http://www.winedt.com/) buffers the current file in memory while the user performs edit operations on the file—as do many other editors. If someone or something else has changed the file, WinEdt

4.5.4 CHANGE INDICATOR

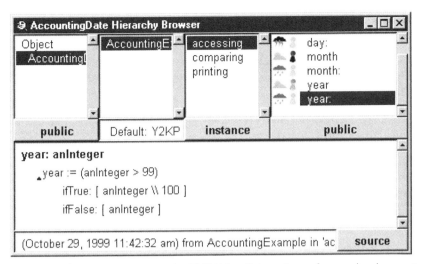

Figure 4.98 Change warnings in the TUKAN collaborative software development environment

displays a warning to indicate that the current file has been modified outside of the application (Figure 4.99).

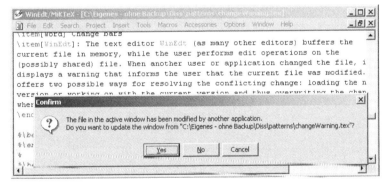

Figure 4.99 Change warnings in a single-user application

WinEdt offers two possible ways for resolving the conflicting change: loading the new version, or continuing to work with the current version and overwriting the external changes when the document is saved.

BSCW. See the explanation in the BSCW case study on page 522.

Related Patterns

ACTIVE NEIGHBORS$_{\rightarrow 4.4.3}$ should be used if artifacts are semantically related. In this case, it is important to highlight not only changes to the current artifact, but also changes that might have an impact on the current artifact at a semantic level.

ACTIVITY LOG$_{\rightarrow 4.5.1}$ Use an ACTIVITY LOG to store the activities that are used to calculate conflicting activities.

USER LIST$_{\rightarrow 4.4.1}$ When attached to artifacts, a USER LIST is comparable to a CHANGE INDICATOR in that it also displays activities on artifacts. The main difference is that a USER LIST only consider activities that are still active. In most cases, CHANGE INDICATORS show activities that are completed.

4.5.5 ALIVENESS INDICATOR

Alternative name(s):   Virtual Tamagotchi, Heartbeat Monitor

a·live (ə-līv'), ADJECTIVE: **1.** Having life; living. See synonyms at living. **2.** In existence or operation; active: *keep your hopes alive.* **3.** Full of living or moving things; abounding: *a pool alive with trout.* **4. Full of activity or animation; lively:** *a face alive with mischief.*
OTHER FORMS: **a·live·ness** — NOUN

Intent

Include an indicator in a virtual environment that reflects users' activity levels.

Context

Users collaborate asynchronously on shared artifacts or in shared virtual or non-virtual collaboration spaces.

Problem

Users who work mainly asynchronously only experience a small subset of activities that take place in the collaboration space. Specifically, they cannot easily see whether other users have been active during their absence. This makes it hard to experience life in the group.

Scenario

Marc just returned from a business trip. He enters his office and wants to continue with the work on the graphics component that he started last week with Carla. However, he does not know whether or not Carla has also done any work in this area while he was out of office.

Symptoms

You should consider applying this pattern when ...

— Users complain that others have stopped participating, although the silent users still follow the interaction.

— Users ask the whole group whether or not they are still participating.
— Users ask each other to visit the collaboration space but are not sure whether or not other users have followed their request.

Solution

Therefore: Show an ALIVENESS INDICATOR **with the user's virtual representation.** For users that have performed activities in the collaboration space recently, use a picture for their indicator that looks very *alive*. Use gradually less *lively* pictures to represent periods of inactivity. Make the picture look like something for which the user can take responsibility.

Dynamics

The system keeps track of users' last activities in the collaboration space. When visualizing the members of the collaboration space (in the context of the collaboration space), the system calculates the time span since the user's last activity. Depending on this interval, the system selects a different indicator to show with each user's representation. For short time spans and hence recent activity, the indicators symbolize a high degree of vivacity, while longer time spans are symbolized by less lively pictures.

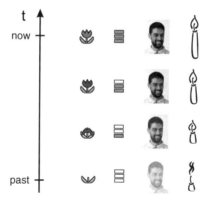

Figure 4.100 Examples of ALIVENESS INDICATORS

Figure 4.100 provides examples of aliveness indicators: a withering flower, a declining bar chart, a fading picture, or a candle burnt down.

Optionally, the indicator can provide additional information, for example by using a tooltip. It could show the time when the user was last active, or provide details about what the user did when active. The indicator can also have different scopes. For a shared workspace system, there can be one indicator for each user in each workspace. In this case, it makes sense to use an indicator that represents an artifact that the user must take care of, such as the flower in Figure 4.100. In systems where the collaboration space is less important, there can be one global scope. This means that the user has the same indicator for the whole system. The fading user image is an example of such a visualization.

The second decision for the scope is whether the indicator should be bound to an individual or to an artifact or region in the collaboration space. An example of the latter could be that the place is symbolized by a virtual flower and that every activity in the place "waters" the flower.

Rationale

The knowledge of other users' last times of participation helps to better understand how closely a group is collaborating. It shows specifically whether there are users who have not been active in the workspace for a long time. Since all group members see this information, the group can think about ways to contact absent users, analyze why they have not participated, and reassign the group's tasks accordingly.

Having indicators with different scopes can help the group to distinguish between the situation in which a user is off line for a while and the situation in which a user is engaged in a different space. Again, this can help to understand the user's context better.

Finally, the indicator can motivate group members to at least enter the collaboration space in order to keep their indicators alive.

When users see other users' wilting, fading or declining indicators, they can contact them using several communication channels and enquire about the reasons for their absence. This helps to keep the group coherent.

Danger Spots

The motivation to keep an activity indicator alive is probably the most important pitfall in this pattern: users can just pretend participation. Whether or not their participation is relevant to the group is not measured by the pattern.

An interesting analogy to this was reported by Dave West at the PLoP writer's workshop: he remembered a UNIX system that scheduled interactive processes with higher priority. The reason for that was that live processes should respond quickly. However, this handicapped non-interactive processes: what happened in his lab was that users started to press the space bar repeatedly just to pretend that their processes were interactive!

In the case of the ALIVENESS INDICATOR, the same phenomenon may emerge if the number of activities is taken as the only measure for participation. You could consider grouping different activities into different classes, so that some activities have a higher impact on the ALIVENESS INDICATOR than others. However, this may only shift the problem somewhere else: users could find new ways to trick the indicator.

In general, this relates to the issue of trust. Aliveness indicators can create a large social pressure to participate, especially if managers observe them. In contexts in which participation is less mandatory, you should think about using MASQUERADE$_{\rightarrow 3.3.2}$ to allow users to turn their indicator off. In any case, this should be coupled with the RECIPROCITY$_{\rightarrow 3.3.1}$ pattern, so that users who turn their indicator off cannot see other users' indicators.

Be aware of different cultural perception for the icons you use for ALIVENESS INDICATORS. In some cultures, an extinguished candle can be interpreted as a sign of death, so people might relate it to a feeling of being dead for the community. Icons thus need to be carefully chosen to suit a community, and should be more abstract than concrete if there is cultural diversity in the community. The same is true for the use of colors: in some cultures, white is for example a color of freshness and birth, while other cultures connect associate it with mourning and death.

Using too many indicators, such as at every place in the collaboration space, can lead to a situation in which users constantly chase their indicators to keep them alive. Consider for example the example of a virtual flower that is bound to a workspace. If users are allowed to enter many workspaces, they will also have many flowers and will need to look for them even if the workspace is deserted for a longer time. A solution to this problem could be either to reduce the number of places that have flowers for specific users, or to slow down the aging of the flowers so that they only fade when both other users are active and the owner of the flower is absent. This however complicates the calculation of the flower's age.

Check

When applying this pattern, you should answer these questions:

— What metaphor will you use to represent the life indicator?
— Will you support different scopes? What are those scopes?
— Should the aliveness indicator be bound to people or to collaboration spaces?
— What is the time scale for your indicator? This is dependent on the level of synchronicity that you want to communicate. In asynchronous systems, this could say be a week, while in more synchronous systems several minutes of inactivity might result in a faded aliveness indicator.
— Will you provide context information?
— What is the scope of the indicator? Is it the whole system, or just one area in the collaboration space?
— Which parts of your collaboration space should be free of indicators?

Known Uses

Flowers in CURE. In the CURE web-based collaboration space (Schümmer, 2005) flowers are used to indicate when a user is active in a group's space (Figure 4.101).

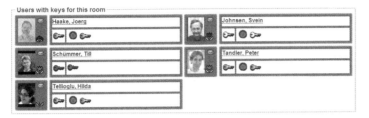

Figure 4.101 Flowers and fading user pictures in CURE

Each space has a property page that lists all the users who are allowed to enter the space. The property page shows the user's picture together with a flower, the user's name, and the user's rights in the collaboration space. Whenever a user performs an activity in the space, such as reading a page or modifying content, the corresponding flower is refreshed so that it blooms. Without activity, the flower ages with time, until after a week of inactivity its bloom falls.

In Figure 4.101, Till Schümmer and Peter Tandler have been active recently. Svein Johnsen has a slightly darker flower, showing that his most recent activity was a short while ago. Joerg Haake's flower had wilted, and Hilda Tellioglu's flower has lost its bloom, indicating that Hilda has been inactive for a long time. The flowers thus provide context information that shows when the corresponding user was last active.

CURE also shows users' global activity by means of fading user pictures. For example, in Figure 4.101, Hilda has been inactive in the current ROOM, but her user picture is still vivid. This implies that she is active in another room.

XING (https://www.xing.com) is a social networking system that shows an *activity meter* (see Figure 4.102) on each user's contact page that represents how active the user has been recently.

Related Patterns

CHANGE INDICATOR→4.5.4 shows a modification on the relevant artifact. The difference between this and an ALIVENESS INDICATOR is that only modification activities are shown, and that time in most cases does not play an important role in the CHANGE INDICATOR pattern.

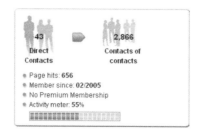

Figure 4.102 An activity meter at XING

ACTIVITY LOG$_{\to 4.5.1}$ allows collection of activity information about users and calculation of how the ALIVENESS INDICATOR should be displayed.

USER LIST$_{\to 4.4.1}$ helps to understand the presence of a user better. An ALIVENESS INDICATOR is also applicable in semi-synchronous or asynchronous settings.

USER GALLERY$_{\to 3.1.6}$ provides a place to display an ALIVENESS INDICATOR.

AWAY MESSAGE$_{\to 4.5.6}$ Users who plan an absence can set up an AWAY MESSAGE$_{\to 4.5.6}$ to explain to the community why their ALIVENESS INDICATOR indicates inactivity.

VIRTUAL ME$_{\to 3.1.5}$ can be combined with an ALIVENESS INDICATOR. Whenever other users browse the page describing the user, they can also see how "alive" the user is.

REWARD$_{\to 3.2.6}$ is another way of honoring participation, but this time by considering the quality of other users' actions. When users perform valuable actions, they receive an award. The difference to an ALIVENESS INDICATOR is that rewards normally do not fade.

4.5.6 Away Message *

Alternative name(s): Auto Reply

a·way (ə-wā'), ADJECTIVE: **1. Absent:** *The neighbors are away.* **2.** Distant, as in space or time: *The city is miles away. The game was still a week away.*

Intent

Inform users that a response to a request will be delayed.

Context

Users interact in a request-response scheme with differing levels of synchronicity.

Problem

Users expect their interaction partners to respond quickly to their actions, but sometimes an interaction partner is unable to respond quickly. The longer initiating users have to wait, the greater their frustration.

Scenario

Martin has encountered problems using the graphics components of the game engine, so he contacts Carla to ask her a question. Normally, Carla responds after several minutes, but by the evening of Martin's working day there is still no response.

Symptoms

You should consider applying this pattern when ...

— Senders ask recipients whether they received a message because the senders did not get a response.

— Senders wait for a recipient's action, but this action does not happen.

— Senders are used to quick replies from their interaction partners based on previous experience. This means that they expect a specific responsiveness from their interaction partner.
— Users are away from the interaction space from time to time.

Solution

Therefore: Let the groupware system respond to a communication with an automatic away message whenever a normal response time cannot be guaranteed. Provide information on when the requesting user can expect a response.

Dynamics

The AWAY MESSAGE pattern suggests following a three-step process when users leave an interaction context temporarily:

Setup. Before users leaves the interaction space, they think about the duration of their absence. They create an away message that explains why they cannot respond and which includes information on the earliest possible reply (their estimated return date).

In most cases, users also provide an explanation that helps senders to handle urgent requests. An example of this is an explanation about who a sender can contact during the recipient's absence.

Design the set-up process so that it is quick and easy. Ideally a user should be able to activate an away message with only one click. It may otherwise be too time-consuming to set up an away message when a user is about to leave.

Execution. When a sender sends a message to an absent recipient, the recipient's system automatically replies with the away message. To avoid duplicate notifications, the recipient's system in addition remembers that the sender was notified. Further e-mails from the sender will not be automatically replied to.

Tear Down. When absent users return and are ready to reply to messages normally, they deactivate their away messages. Optionally, senders who received an away message can be informed that an addressee has returned.

Rationale

The problem of responsiveness to activities has been studied by Tyler and Tang (2003) in the context of e-mail communication. The authors performed a field study in a large technology company and interviewed employees about their e-mail usage habits. Of the twenty-four interviewed subjects, seventeen used away messages frequently to signal their absence. One user reported his expectations of away messages as follows: "You ask someone for information that they know, and you sit around waiting and waiting for them to get back to you, and you find out that they've been out of town." The authors' analysis showed that one third of the subjects turned their away messages on if they were out of office for one day. One subject left it on even after returning from a trip until he had managed to catch up with all the messages sent to him.

The authors finally proposed an *expectation-to-breakdown timeline* that visualizes people's perception of responsiveness. The basic idea is that users have an expectation of the time for which they should wait for a reply. If they do not receive a reply after this threshold has passed, they set it as a breakdown of collaboration. They then start thinking about reshaping the collaboration in order to reach their goal. This can mean that they send a follow-up message or that they try to reach the recipient using another communication medium.

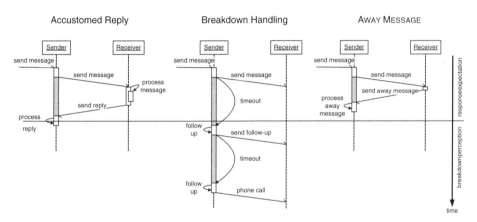

Figure 4.103 Communication patterns in a request-reply interaction

Figure 4.103 illustrates this understanding. The left part shows normal behavior. A user sends a message (or more generally, performs an activity) and the recipient processes the message and generates a reply. The middle part of the figure shows the situation in which the recipient is unable to reply. In this case, the sender will wait for a specific time before trying to remind the recipient that the sender is still expecting a reply. If the recipient still does not reply, the sender will probably try to reach the recipient using another communication channel. Each of these waiting times represent effort on the sender's side.

The AWAY MESSAGE pattern reduces these waiting times, as shown on the right of Figure 4.103. Since the system automatically generates a reply, the sender can enter the breakdown handling immediately. The message provided by the recipient helps the sender to understand the recipient's context better and provides hints on how to handle the problem of not reaching the recipient.

Check

When applying this pattern, you should answer these questions:

— How will you let users configure their away message?

— How can you ensure that an away message contains all the required information, such as the time at which normal communication will resume?

— Will absentees be informed about who has received an away message while they were absent?

Danger Spots

One of the largest problems with away messages is that they often do not distinguish between bilateral and group communication. When communicating via a FORUM$_{\rightarrow 4.3.2}$, for example, which delivers messages to the users' e-mail boxes, the recipient's system may reply with an away message that is received by the whole group instead of the individual sender. The reason for this is that many e-mail dispatching mechanisms modify the message headers so that the sender field is different to the reply-to field. The recipient's system keeps track of message senders, but replies to the reply-to address. This address is again multiplexed to all members of the forum. Forum members may therefore receive multiple away messages, which is annoying.

When discussing this pattern with our copy-editor, he reported a recent case of an employee who had left a company with an active and permanent away message. For many months afterwards every single posting to a mailing list resulted in a reply to each of the several thousand members of the mailing list that stated that "John Doe is no longer at (this company)". Almost no-one on the group had ever even heard of the person or the company involved.

A solution is to keep track of the addresses to which an away message has been sent, instead of the message senders to which the message was a reaction. An alternative solution that is often used is not to auto-reply with an away message if the original message was not personally directed to the absentee. For e-mails, for example, this is the case if the recipient is set to the address of the forum and the member of the forum is only added as a Bcc: (blind) recipient of the message.

A comparable problem is that an absentee cannot know in advance who will receive an away message. Since messages are by default sent to anyone who tries to contact the absentee, the information about their absence can be seen by anybody. This can be valuable information, especially for spam mailers, since it proves that the e-mail address is working and hence valid. A possible solution to this is to define a list of e-mail addresses in advance that may receive an away message.

This leads to a more sophisticated version of the AWAY MESSAGE pattern in which the absentee can define different messages for different groups of senders. If you consider for example the case of a lecturer who leaves university for a month, it makes sense to provide several away messages: one for the students, in which questions on course management might be answered, one for faculty members that discusses issues about project work, and a third for external partners. The problem with such sophisticated messages is it requires more effort to set up the AWAY MESSAGE.

You could think about detecting the absence of a user automatically and providing away messages in this case. However, this may lead to two problems: first, such users will no longer be in control of whether they tell other users about their absence. This violates the users' privacy. Second, such a system will in most cases not know when the absentee returns. This information however needs to be included in effective away messages.

Known Uses

Vacation (Costales, 2002) is probably the most widely used implementation of an away message. In the activation phase, users can specify a message body that is from then on sent to all senders of e-mail to the absent user.

Whenever replying with an away message, the system keeps track of the sender and ensures that no duplicate messages are created. For example:

```
Return-Path: <MAILER-DAEMON@mailstore.fernuni-hagen.de>
Received: from cl-mailhost.FernUni-Hagen.de ([132.176.114.188]
   verified) by mailstore.fernuni-hagen.de (CommuniGate Pro SMTP
   5.0.2) with ESMTP id 15785207 for schuemm@mailstore.FernUni-
   Hagen.de; Sun, 07 May 2006 18:13:32 +0200

... Additional path headers ...

From: "Stephan Lukosch" <Stephan.Lukosch@FernUni-Hagen.de>
Date: Sun, 07 May 2006 18:13:32 +0200
Message-ID: <react-15785210@mailstore.fernuni-hagen.de>
X-Autogenerated: Reply
MIME-Version: 1.0
Content-Type: text/plain; charset="ISO-8859-1"
To: schuemm@mail.pi6.fernuni-hagen.de (Till Schuemmer)
Subject: Re: Committed new files -- please have a look
In-Reply-To: <445E1CAB.mail/3B113JOK@afrika.pi6.fernuni-hagen.de>

I am out of the office until the 15th of May 2006. In urgent cases
please contact Simone Buecker (Simone.Buecker@FernUni-Hagen.de, +49
2331 987 4365). Your e-mail will not be forwarded.

Kind regards

Stephan Lukosch
```

Instant messaging systems like Trillian (http://www.trillian.cc/) allow users to add a message that explains that they are currently away. When another user tries to initiate a chat communication, the system automatically replies with the away message provided. Note that Trillian only keeps track of the sessions to which an away message was sent. Messages are thus not sent twice in the same session, but can be sent repeatedly to the same user in different sessions.

Related Patterns

AVAILABILITY STATUS$_{\to 3.3.3}$ also helps senders to stay aware of the status of a request. However, the availability status normally does not reveal any temporal estimation of response.

ALIVENESS INDICATOR$_{\to 4.5.5}$ An ALIVENESS INDICATOR is an alternative to an away message, since it also signals the requesting users that they may not expect an immediate response. However, it does not explain why the absentee cannot respond, or when the absentee will again be available.

4.5.7 Remember me... applied

Paul has enough experience of distributed software development to know that one of the bigger problems is to maintain a shared understanding of the project and the code artifacts among the developers at different locations.

Since Paul particularly counts on collective code ownership, changes may occur in an unplanned way and traditional management-oriented methods of change propagation may fail. The CHANGE INDICATOR$_{\to 4.5.4}$ pattern looked promising to Paul since it marks artifacts that have been changed since a user last saw them.

Paul decided to add CHANGE INDICATORS at file level. Whenever users save a new version of a file in the SHARED FILE REPOSITORY$_{\to 4.1.2}$, all older versions are shown with a CHANGE INDICATOR. In the example shown in Figure 4.104, Paul has created a new version of the EVENT QUEUE class. Susan, whose user interface is shown in the figure, still has an older version of the file in her local workspace. The triangle icon in front of the artifact informs Susan that a new version of the file is available. By moving her mouse over the file icon she can find out more about the changes. The tooltip shows Susan when Paul created the new version and how he commented his changes. Susan can now decide whether to update the file.

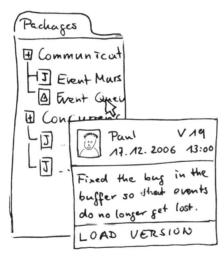

Figure 4.104 Change Indicator

While such indicators help to stay aware of changes when coming across an artifact, Paul and Susan also wanted to maintain a global overview of the changes. They decided to implement the TIMELINE$_{\to 4.5.2}$ pattern to show all changes in the project in one diagram.

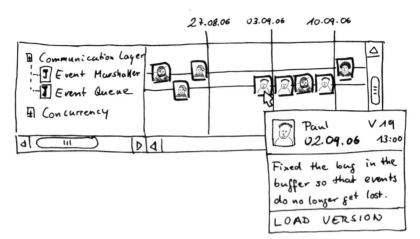

Figure 4.105 Project timeline

Figure 4.105 shows a TIMELINE in the context of the COGE development. The tree view on the left allows users to expand and collapse details in the project's folder structure. The TIMELINE on the right has a row for each item shown in the tree view. Changes are shown by means of the user icons. Details can be obtained by moving the mouse over a user icon.

Figure 4.106 Aliveness Indicator

The third support for asynchronous awareness in the COGE community was the addition of an ALIVENESS INDICATOR$_{\rightarrow 4.5.5}$ for each user (see Figure 4.106). Since all community members are Java programming addicts, they are familiar with the Java icon, which is a hot cup of coffee. This provided the idea for the visual metaphor used for the ALIVENESS INDICATOR. For users who were recently active, the cup was still hot. If users had not participated within the last week, their cup of coffee was shown cold. Users who had not been active in the last month were shown with an empty cup of coffee.

CHAPTER 5

Base Technology

The previous chapters have focused on patterns at a higher level that describe group processes, the use of computer technology to support these processes, and how to design user interfaces for collaborating groups. Compared to these patterns, this chapter focuses on the technical level of groupware applications, and is mainly targeted at developers who have to work out how shared objects should be managed and how information exchange mediated by computer systems.

From a technical perspective, developing groupware applications is a difficult and time-consuming task. Apart from the actual tasks carried out by the application, such as editing texts or spreadsheets:

— Shared data has to be managed
— Parallel input from many users has to be handled
— Collaborating users have to be connected

All the difficulties relate to the management of shared objects—or more generally, shared data. We define a shared object as an object that is used by more than one user. Object usage may be at the same time (synchronous) or at different points in time (asynchronous).

Since users work on different machines, each will be able to use the application and create input at the same time. The input is processed locally by a controller object in the sense of the MODEL-VIEW-CONTROLLER pattern (Buschmann et al., 1996). While in traditional interactive applications, most manipulations are triggered by a local controller object, we have to deal with multiple controller objects at different sites when we consider groupware applications. This means that the control flow within the application becomes much more complicated. Systems based on shared objects must handle multiple requests for changes to a shared object's state at the same time. Maintaining consistency becomes a critical issue in such situations.

To communicate about shared objects and exchange information about the objects' state, different users have to connect their client computers systems using a network connection.

In the context of our scenario, the patterns in this chapter provide the building blocks for creating the synchronous tools. We will look behind the scenes of the development that Paul and Susan carried out to make Eclipse a synchronous pair-programming environment.

Several toolkits and frameworks exist to support developers facing the creation of collaborative applications, such as Rendezvous (Hill et al., 1994), Suite (Dewan and Choudhary, 1992), NSTP (Patterson et al., 1996), GroupKit (Roseman and Greenberg, 1996a), COAST (Schuckmann et al., 1996b), *CBE* (Prakash et al., 1999), *DreamTeam* (Roth, 2000a), Habanero (Chabert et al., 1998), and DyCE (Tietze, 2001). These can help during the development process by providing components that hide most of the *dirty and difficult* work that addresses things like network connection management and process scheduling. They also impose a specific way of shaping the group process, for example by providing the means for starting collaborative sessions.

These frameworks have one big problem, however: they are too prescriptive. They prescribe the context, namely a development language and a specific class structure. This fact makes it difficult (and often impossible) to use a specific framework within a development project that has other constraints, such as a specific database or a specific domain framework (Lukosch and Schümmer, 2004).

Instead, developers need assistance with groupware development that is applicable in the developer's current context. This can be achieved by using the patterns in this chapter. We can group the problems into three clusters: session management has to be considered (Section 5.1) as well as shared data management (Section 5.2) and shared data consistency (Section 5.3).

5.1 Connect me... or how to handle sessions

A key question for development of groupware systems is how distributed users and their systems are set up for collaboration. A common metaphor for setting up collaboration in synchronous groupware systems is handling *groupware as meeting* or COLLABORATIVE SESSIONS$_{\to 5.1.1}$ (Roseman and Greenberg, 1996c).

The session metaphor concentrates on synchronous collaboration and restricts it to *sessions*. Normally, one group member starts a session and other participants join the session later. When their work is done, participants leave the session. Edwards (Edwards, 1994) distinguishes between explicit and implicit session management. Explicit session management requires that users intentionally connect their client to other clients, for example by accepting an INVITATION$_{\to 4.2.5}$ sent by another user, or by joining a session using a INTERACTION DIRECTORY$_{\to 4.2.3}$ that lists available sessions. Implicit session management monitors user activities and automatically connects users when it infers that these users are working on the same document or topic.

> *In the example of the game development community, we have come across sessions frequently in the last chapter. Paul and Susan provided the shared diagram editor, which was built as a collaborative session. Other developers could meet in the session and collaborate on the same data at the same time. Another example of a collaborative session was the pair-programming editor that Paul integrated into Eclipse.*

Both examples emphasize synchronous interaction. From a technical perspective, synchronous collaboration tools are more challenging to implement, mainly because we have to build the tools such that users can modify the same data at the same time. Before users can work on the same data, however, they must be connected in a collaboration context in the technical layer of the application. This means that collaboration episodes are embedded in a COLLABORATIVE SESSION$_{\to 5.1.1}$, which is the main pattern of this section. The other patterns presented in this section (Figure 5.1) all address ways in which sessions may be paused and resumed for all or specific users. This reflects the fact that a user will not always be available for collaboration and that sessions may last too long to be finished in one meeting.

The patterns in this section are shown in Figure 5.1 and provide solutions for establishing sessions and overcoming the difficulties involved in finding a common time for synchronous collaboration. The patterns are:

COLLABORATIVE SESSION$_{\to 5.1.1}$ Allow users to plan and coordinate synchronous collaboration.

PERSISTENT SESSION$_{\to 5.1.2}$ Make results achieved in a collaborative session available for reviewing or resuming collaborative activities.

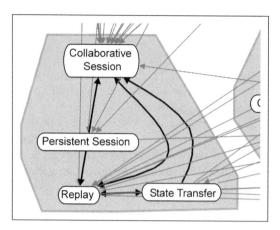

Figure 5.1 Patterns for bootstrapping systems for collaboration

STATE TRANSFER$_{\to 5.1.3}$ Integrate latecomers into running interactions.

REPLAY$_{\to 5.1.4}$ Replay the route by which the current state of a collaboration has evolved.

5.1.1 Collaborative Session **

ses·sion (sĕsh'ən), NOUN: **1a.** A meeting of a legislative or judicial body for the purpose of transacting business. **b.** A series of such meetings. **c.** The term or duration of time that is taken by such a series of meetings. **2.** The part of a year or of a day during which a school holds classes. **3. An assembly of people for a common purpose or because of a common interest: a gossip session. 4.** Law A court of criminal jurisdiction in the United States: *the court of sessions.* **5.** A period of time devoted to a specific activity, as to recording music in a studio.

Intent

Allow users to plan and coordinate synchronous collaboration.

Context

You have a group of users who want to interact synchronously via computer systems. You are concerned about how these users can plan and coordinate their synchronous interaction.

Problem

Users need a shared context for synchronous collaboration. Computer-mediated environments are neither concrete nor visible, however. This makes it difficult to define a shared context and thereby plan synchronous collaboration.

Scenario

Michele and Ana decided that it would make sense to hold a virtual meeting for discussing XML generation for the VRML support in the game engine. They agreed to meet on the 2nd April. However, they forgot to decide on a place for the meeting, so the 2nd April passes without any meeting.

Symptoms

You should consider applying this pattern when ...

— Users are unable to plan and coordinate synchronous collaboration.

— Users need a lot of time to start synchronous interaction, as they first have to start the necessary tools.

Solution

Therefore: Model the context for synchronous collaboration as a shared session object. Visualize the session state and support users in starting, joining, leaving, and terminating the session. When users join a session, automatically start the necessary collaboration tools.

Dynamics

The session object defines the context needed for synchronous collaboration. This may include the goal, the time of interaction, or the state of the session. It links to the participating users and the tools to use.

There are three use cases in which a client interacts with a session object:

Joining a session. When users want to start a new session, the system creates a session object and links it to a configuration of tools. After initializing the session object, the runtime system adds the user object to the session, launches the tools on users' machines, and sets the state of the session to running.

Joining an existing session. When users join an existing session, their runtime system adds the corresponding user object to the set of session users, and launches the tools on the respective machine.

Leaving a session. When users leave a session, their runtime system removes their user object from the shared session object and closes the collaboration tools.

Rationale

The main aspect of this pattern is that the collaboration setting—group members in the form of a set of users and group interaction in the form of a set of tools—is modeled as a shared object. This ensures that meta-information about the group is available to group users and the groupware system, and it is no longer difficult for users to find a shared context for synchronous collaboration. The groupware system monitors this meta-information and launches or shuts down the tools required in specific group situation. Users can thus concentrate on the collaboration task and no longer have to deal with the technical aspects of starting tools and establishing network connections.

Check

When applying this pattern, you should answer these questions:

— How will you bootstrap a session? When is it created? Can you provide a user interface element to create a new session?

- How will users identify sessions? Is it reasonable to name the session? If yes, will users provide a name for the session?
- Where will you keep track of existing sessions? Can you provide a directory service that lists all sessions?
- How will you perform the selection of tools? Will it take place on session creation, or will it take place during the session?

Danger Spots

When you share a session between users, you have to ensure that the information it contains is consistent. Otherwise, some users might for example not start all the applications that are necessary to participate in the session.

When users leave the session abnormally, for example by switching off their computer or losing their network connection, their user objects will stay in the session forever. To detect whether a user is still available, use timeouts for the execution time of a specific function, or use server-side or client-side mechanisms.

Known Uses

COAST models collaborative sessions as shared application models. These objects include references to the shared domain model (the domain data that is intended to be used in the session). Users can express an interest in a shared application model by adding their user objects to the set of interested users of the shared application model. A constraint mechanism ensures that changes to this set are reflected in changes at the users' local visualization. After adding a user object, the constraint mechanism creates a new local application model that is responsible for displaying the application (using an additional view instance) and processing user inputs (with a controller object).

Figure 5.2 shows an example of a collaborative UML editor. Two users Alice and Bob have added their shared user object to the set of interested users of the shared diagram editor instance. The constraint mechanism then created a view and a controller on Alice's and Bob's client.

Note that Alice could also have added Bob's user object to the shared application model of the UML editor. In this case, the windows for the editor would have been automatically opened on Bob's screen without any action from Bob.

DreamTeam is a groupware platform that models a COLLABORATIVE SESSION as a replicated object (Roth, 2000a)—each user owns a copy of a session instance. As long as a session is not running, the session object contains information about the users that are allowed to participate, the time when the session will take place, and which collaborative applications will be used in the

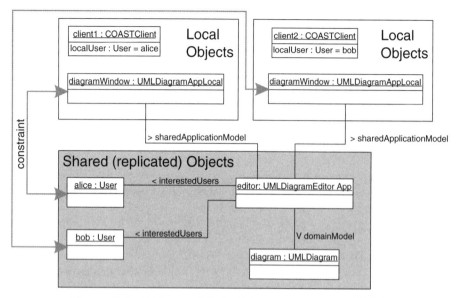

Figure 5.2 Object model of collaborative sessions in COAST

session. When the session is running, the session object includes the user representations of the users participating in the session and references to the collaborative applications used.

GroupKit is a groupware platform that is also based on the session metaphor (Roseman and Greenberg, 1996b). At each site that participates in the session, a specific manager communicates with a central instance to find out which sessions are currently available. Each session consists of a number of conference applications that are used in the session by participating users.

Related Patterns

BELL$_{\rightarrow 4.2.4}$ allows users to ask collaborators if they can join an existing COLLABORATIVE SESSION.

INTERACTION DIRECTORY$_{\rightarrow 4.2.3}$ allows users to look up COLLABORATIVE SESSIONS in which they might be interested.

INVITATION$_{\rightarrow 4.2.5}$ can be used to invite other users to participate in a COLLABORATIVE SESSION.

ROOM$_{\rightarrow 4.2.1}$ provides a place where users can meet to start collaboration. A ROOM can contain collaborative applications or shared documents, and supports asynchronous work by persistently storing the shared documents on a server.

USER LIST$_{\to 4.4.1}$ allows users that are available for collaboration to be identified.

REPLAY$_{\to 5.1.4}$ allows users to join, leave, and rejoin a collaborative session at different times.

SESSION (Sørensen, 2002) focuses on a client/server system in which multiple clients send requests to a server about a specific data set. The server stores the session-specific data as long as the session is active. A COLLABORATIVE SESSION, in contrast, concentrates on managing tools for interacting users.

SESSION (Guerrero and Fuller, 1999) does not focus on how to organize a session. Although it deals with collaborative sessions, the session instance does not include information about the applications that are used in the session.

ABSTRACT SESSION (Pryce, 1997) allows a server object that is accessed by many clients to maintain the status of each client it serves. It is also known as a *Service Access Point* (SAP). In a COLLABORATIVE SESSION, the collaboration instance contains its own status information.

I AM ALIVE (Saridakis, 2003) requests a client to send notifications showing that it is still available. If these notifications fail to appear, the corresponding user is removed from the session.

ARE YOU ALIVE (Saridakis, 2003). When using this pattern, sites regularly check whether another site is available. If not, the corresponding user is removed from the session.

SESSION TIMEOUT (Sørensen, 2002) uses an upper limit for the time during which a session object must to be accessed before the corresponding user is removed from the list of participants.

5.1.2 PERSISTENT SESSION *

per·sis·tent (pər-sĭs'tənt), ADJECTIVE: **1.** Refusing to give up or let go; persevering obstinately. **2.** Insistently repetitive or continuous: *a persistent ringing of the telephone*. **3. Existing or remaining in the same state for an indefinitely long time; enduring: persistent rumors; a persistent infection. 4.** *Botany* Lasting past maturity without falling off, as the calyx on an eggplant or the scales of a pine cone. **5.** *Zoology* Retained permanently, rather than disappearing in an early stage of development: *the persistent gills of fishes.*

Intent

Make results achieved in a collaborative session available for reviewing or resuming collaborative activities.

Context

You have interacted in a COLLABORATIVE SESSION→5.1.1.

Problem

After interacting in a COLLABORATIVE SESSION, users want to resume their collaboration with the results achieved, or want to review them, but the results are not available.

Scenario

Paul hired two marketing specialists, Steven and Andrew, to create a project flyer for the next game developer's fair. During an initial face-to-face meeting they wrote a few pages on the selling points of the game engine and annotated the pages they had written prior to the meeting. They agreed to meet again the next day for further discussion. Paul collected all annotated pages and took these pages home. In the evening, Paul begins to feel ill, and the next morning he is unable to leave home. When Steven and Andrew meet they have to start their work from the beginning, as they cannot access their previous results.

Symptoms

You should consider applying this pattern when . . .

— Users collaborate in a synchronous session and refer to previous results, but they are not available.

— Users in a COLLABORATIVE SESSION are doing the same thing over and over again.
— The groupware system in unable to store results already achieved to be used for reviewing or resuming a collaborative session.

Solution

Therefore: Persistently store the results of a synchronous COLLABORATIVE SESSION on a central server. If shared data is replicated, use the MEDIATED UPDATES pattern to keep a master copy of the shared data and track all changes that are applied to it. Let users access the master copy at the central server for review or session resumption purposes.

Dynamics

By using the MEDIATED UPDATES pattern, you can keep track of all changes applied to shared data. In this pattern, users have to send an update message to the server whenever they change the shared state. The server then distributes the update message to all participating clients. Whenever the server receives an update message, also apply the message to a master copy of the shared data. Offer an interface that allows users to look up and access the results achieved for reviewing or resuming the COLLABORATIVE SESSION.

Rationale

As the central server keeps track of all changes applied to the shared objects used by collaborative tools in a COLLABORATIVE SESSION, users can later access the session's results for reviewing purposes, or continue their collaboration without losing any of the work achieved so far.

Check

When applying this pattern, you should answer these questions:

— Where will you store the results of a session?
— How can a user view the results? Can you provide single-user tools for using the session results alone, or will users use the same tools that were used to create the results?
— Does it make sense to start a new session using the results of a previous session? If yes, how will you start a new session using existing data? Can you extend the user interface for starting a session with commands that allow users to select this existing data?

Danger Spots

If the central server is unavailable, users cannot resume their collaboration or review achieved results. To overcome this, you can either increase availability by using more than one server, or use a decentralized approach in which the runtime system of the last user in the session distributes the session's results to all participants when it completes.

Known Uses

COAST (Schuckmann et al., 2000) is a groupware platform that uses potentially many mediators to ensure consistency of shared data. The mediators keep track of the clients that keep replicas and are connected to the network. Whenever a client changes replicated data (using transactions), a transaction log is sent to the mediators. When the transaction is incorporated into the current state, the master copy at the mediator is updated. Master copies at the mediators are persistent. This ensures that results achieved are always available for reviewing or resuming a COLLABORATIVE SESSION.

CBE (Prakash et al., 1999) provides a computer-based shared workspace that facilitates collaboration over the Internet and World Wide Web. CBE uses the services of the group communication server *Corona* (Shim et al., 1997). Among other services Corona logs all update messages received by the collaborating clients and thereby ensures the persistency of results.

DreamObjects (Lukosch, 2003a) supports transitions between synchronous and asynchronous work by allowing each participant of a session to store, load, and distribute complete session states. To overcome possible problems when using a central server, DreamObjects uses SMTP and NNTP to distribute session results to all relevant participants of a session. Groups therefore do not have to rely on a central server to store and resume states.

Related Patterns

COLLABORATIVE SESSION$_{\to 5.1.1}$ can use a PERSISTENT SESSION to store the results of a session.

MEDIATED UPDATES$_{\to 5.2.5}$ describes how to distribute update messages among collaborating clients using a central server. This functionality of the server can easily be extended to store results persistently.

ROOM$_{\to 4.2.1}$ provides the group with a place where they can meet for collaboration. A room persistently stores documents on a server that are used by participants during collaboration. All users can access all documents in the room. A ROOM thus supports asynchronous interaction.

REPLAY$_{\rightarrow 5.1.4}$ addresses a problem that arises when session state is persisted and a long period of time has passed: not all users may remember the session state of the previous session. Simply restoring the state may not be sufficient, because participants need to understand how the session state evolved.

KEEP SESSION DATA IN THE CLIENT (Sørensen, 2002) focuses on how to keep session-specific data on the client's site when clients are collaborating via a server that is unable to host the data. However, this pattern is not concerned with how to keep the data when a session has ended.

KEEP SESSION DATA IN THE SERVER (Sørensen, 2002) describes the issues involved when keeping session-specific data on a server. Like KEEP SESSION DATA IN THE CLIENT, this pattern is merely concerned with data that is necessary during a session rather than afterwards.

5.1.3 STATE TRANSFER **

Alternative name(s): What's Up?

state (stāt), NOUN: **1. A condition or mode of being, as with regard to circumstances:** *a state of confusion.* **2.** A condition of being in a stage or form, as of structure, growth, or development: *the fetal state.* **3.** A mental or emotional condition: in a manic state. **4.** *Informal* A condition of excitement or distress. **5.** *Physics* **The condition of a physical system with regard to phase, form, composition, or structure:** *Ice is the solid state of water.*

Intent

Integrate latecomers into running interactions.

Context

You allow users to join, leave, and rejoin a COLLABORATIVE SESSION→5.1.1 at different points in time.

Problem

Users are collaborating in a COLLABORATIVE SESSION→5.1.1 but not all of them participate from the beginning. Due to this, some do not know the intermediate results of the COLLABORATIVE SESSION→5.1.1 which makes it difficult for them to collaborate.

Scenario

John and Charley have done some secret, private work on key management for the game engine. Now Paul wants to participate in subsequent steps and asks if he can join their COLLABORATIVE SESSION. However, Paul does not know the current status of the artifacts manipulated by John and Charley.

Symptoms

You should consider applying this pattern when ...

— Users have problems in participating in a COLLABORATIVE SESSION→5.1.1 from the beginning.

— Users cannot participate in a collaboration because they are not familiar with its intermediate results.
— Users need to understand the current interaction focus and context.

Solution

Therefore: Transmit the current state of shared objects to latecomers when they join a COLLABORATIVE SESSION. Since all current participants have the most recent state of the session's shared objects, the system can ask any of the existing clients to perform the state transfer. Ensure the consistency of the state.

Dynamics

Latecomers can join an existing COLLABORATIVE SESSION$_{\rightarrow 5.1.1}$. To participate in the collaboration, they need the current state of the session. For this purpose, a latecomer needs to find someone to provides the current state. This provider has to ensure that the latecomer receives a consistent current state, as otherwise the latecomer will still have problems in participating properly. For this purpose, the state provider must not block the ongoing collaboration.

Two cases have to be distinguished: with and without a central server. In the simplest case, a central server exists, for example when the COLLABORATIVE SESSION$_{\rightarrow 5.1.1}$ uses CENTRALIZED OBJECTS$_{\rightarrow 5.2.1}$ or MEDIATED UPDATES$_{\rightarrow 5.2.5}$ to communicate state changes. In the case of MEDIATED UPDATES$_{\rightarrow 5.2.5}$, the central server has to be enhanced so that it maintains a copy of the current state. We call such an enhanced server a *mediator*.

When a central server is available, a latecomer can contact the server as provider and request the current state of the COLLABORATIVE SESSION$_{\rightarrow 5.1.1}$. After the latecomer has contacted the server (provider), the server includes the latecomer in all subsequent communication about state changes. From now on, whenever the latecomer receives a message concerning a state change, the latecomer buffers this message.

After including the latecomer in communications, the server creates a copy of the shared state and supplies the latecomer with this copy. Additionally, the server informs the latecomer of the most recent change that was applied to the shared state. This can for example be done by using a logical clock (Lamport, 1978) and timestamps for each message that describes a state change. This ensures that the latecomer has an initial copy of the current state.

After receiving the copy of the shared state, the latecomer applies all buffered state changes received after contacting the server. If the state changes are encapsulated as COMMANDS$_{\rightarrow 5.2.7}$, the latecomer has to execute all buffered commands. As soon as the buffer is empty, the latecomer has a consistent state and can participate in the COLLABORATIVE SESSION$_{\rightarrow 5.1.1}$. If state changes are distributed as new versions of the shared objects, the latecomer identifies the latest versions of the affected objects and replaces the received version with the latest version, for example by using IMMUTABLE VERSIONS$_{\rightarrow 5.3.6}$. Figure 5.3 shows these collaborations in the case of a mediator that acts as a provider for the latecomer.

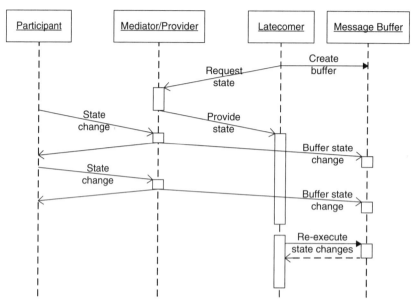

Figure 5.3 A mediator acts as provider for a latecomer

If there is no central server to act as a provider of the current state, state transfer is more complicated. The latecomer has to choose one of the other participants as provider. As the other participants may leave the collaborative session at any time, it is important to select a provider carefully. In the case in which a provider cannot complete the STATE TRANSFER, a new provider should not start from the beginning of the session. For a detailed description of the necessary collaborations, refer to the DreamObjects platform (Lukosch, 2003a) (Lukosch, 2003b).

Rationale

STATE TRANSFER ensures that a latecomer receives a consistent current state of a COLLABORATIVE SESSION$_{\rightarrow 5.1.1}$, so that the latecomer can collaborate with the other participants in the session.

Check

When applying this pattern, you should answer these questions:

— How should the latecomer identify a session state provider? Will the latecomer be prompted for a server name, will the server name be hard-coded, or will you provide a more sophisticated lookup mechanism?

— How can you identify state changes that have not been applied to a session state copy provided to a latecomer? Are you going to use timestamps?

Danger Spots

Using a central server as a state provider for a latecomer is a single point of failure. Additionally, a central server is a bottleneck for network communication. Using DECENTRALIZED UPDATES$_{\rightarrow 5.2.6}$ overcomes this issues.

Known Uses

COAST (Schuckmann et al., 1996b) uses MEDIATED UPDATES$_{\rightarrow 5.2.5}$ and DISTRIBUTED COMMANDS$_{\rightarrow 5.2.7}$ to distribute state changes. Latecomers that join a session contact the mediator, which in turn provides the latecomer with the current state of the session.

Collaboratory Builder's Environment (CBE). CBE (Prakash et al., 1999) uses a communication infrastructure that is based on a central Corona server (Hall et al., 1996) (Shim et al., 1997) (Shim and Prakash, 1998). This server handles group communication, keeps a copy of the shared state, and logs all messages that are sent between participants.

DreamObjects (Lukosch, 2003a) (Lukosch, 2003b) directly transfers the current state of a session to a latecomer without using a central server as a provider. A latecomer can also choose an arbitrary participant of the current session as provider. If this provider disconnects while providing state support, the latecomer chooses another participant to carry on support.

DreamTeam (Roth, 2000b) uses the participant that initiated a COLLABORATIVE SESSION$_{\rightarrow 5.1.1}$ as provider for a latecomer. This is done without blocking other collaborators in their current work. However, if the session originator leaves the current session, it is no longer possible for a latecomer to join the session.

RTP/I (Mauve, 2000b) is an application-level protocol that is derived from Real-Time Transport Protocol (RTP) (Schulzrinne et al., 1996). RTP/I is used by collaborative applications and deals with distributed interactive media that is partitioned into subcomponents. The state of the distributed interactive media is replicated to every participating site and can be changed by events. RTP/I offers some generic services, such as a consistency service (Vogel and Mauve, 2001) and a generic "late-join" service (Vogel et al., 2000). The late-join service defines different late-join policies, such as event-triggered late-join, immediate late-join. These policies can be assigned to the different subcomponents. Based on the policies defined, the subcomponents are transferred to a latecomer. It is the task of the consistency service to ensure that the latecomer gets a consistent state of the subcomponents. The consistency service uses physical timestamps to define the necessary total order of events, and requires that participating sites synchronize their physical clocks, for example with the help of GPS receivers or *Network Time Protocol (NTP)* (Mills, 1992).

Related Patterns

CENTRALIZED OBJECTS$_{\to 5.2.1}$ allows a central server to be chosen as state provider for a latecomer.

COLLABORATIVE SESSION$_{\to 5.1.1}$ allows users to plan and coordinate synchronous collaboration. Latecomers need the current state of the session.

DISTRIBUTED COMMAND$_{\to 5.2.7}$ allows state changes to be encapsulated.

IMMUTABLE VERSIONS$_{\to 5.3.6}$ allows different versions of a shared object to be identified.

MEDIATED UPDATES$_{\to 5.2.5}$ allows the mediator to be chosen as state provider for a latecomer.

DECENTRALIZED UPDATES$_{\to 5.2.6}$ make it difficult to find a provider for a latecomer, as the participants of a COLLABORATIVE SESSION$_{\to 5.1.1}$ communicate in a peer-to-peer network.

REPLAY$_{\to 5.1.4}$ replays the route by which the current state of a COLLABORATIVE SESSION$_{\to 5.1.1}$ has been achieved.

MARSHALLER (Völter et al., 2004) describes how objects can be transferred from one computer to another via the network. The pattern addresses issues like serialization and deserialization.

5.1.4 REPLAY

Alternative name(s): What Has Happened Here?

re·play (rē-plā'), TRANSITIVE VERB: To play over again: replay a tennis match; replay a tape; replay history. NOUN: **1. The act or process of replaying. 2.** Something replayed. **3.** An instant replay.

Intent

Replay the sequence of changes by which the current state of a collaboration has evolved.

Context

You allow users to join, leave, and rejoin a collaboration at different points in time.

Problem

When users join an ongoing collaboration as latecomers or when users rejoin a collaboration after a time of absence, it is hard for them to understand how the current state of the collaboration has been reached, or what has changed since their last participation, by only perceiving the current state of the collaboration.

Scenario

Paul and Susan performed an extremely successful pair-programming session. The next day, Susan wants to continue the session but Paul has contracted flu and cannot participate. Susan therefore asks Liam. Unfortunately, Liam does not know what has been going on in Paul's and Susan's session, which make it hard for him to start collaborating with Susan.

Symptoms

You should consider applying this pattern when ...

— Users have problems participating in a collaboration from its beginning.

— Users have problems understanding how the current state of a collaboration has been reached.

Solution

Therefore: Capture all changes to the shared objects used in the collaboration in an ACTIVITY LOG$_{\to 4.5.1}$. When users join or rejoin a collaboration, replay the captured changes to show them how the current state of the collaboration has been reached.

Dynamics

To replay the sequence of changes by which the current state of a COLLABORATIVE SESSION$_{\to 5.1.1}$ has been reached, it is necessary to capture all changes that are applied to the shared state and to store these changes in a log (see ACTIVITY LOG$_{\to 4.5.1}$).

Two cases have to be distinguished: with or without a central server. In the simplest case, a server can be used as a provider for the latecomer. This is for example the case when using CENTRALIZED OBJECTS$_{\to 5.2.1}$ or MEDIATED UPDATES$_{\to 5.2.5}$ to communicate state changes. In both cases, the server has to be enhanced to keep a log of all state changes already applied to shared state. Depending on how state changes are distributed, this might either be a log of DISTRIBUTED COMMANDS$_{\to 5.2.7}$ or a set of IMMUTABLE VERSIONS$_{\to 5.3.6}$ for all shared objects.

The client system joining the collaboration is called a "latecomer". When a central server is available, a latecomer can contact the server as provider and request the log of state changes. After the latecomer has contacted the provider, the provider includes the latecomer in future communication about state changes. From that point on the latecomer buffers all messages about state changes.

After including the latecomer in communication, the provider supplies the latecomer with a log of state changes. As soon as the latecomer has received the log, it starts to re-execute all state changes and display their execution in the user interface. While executing the state changes, the latecomer displays a control panel that allows the speed used to re-execute the state changes to be set. After replaying the log, the latecomer checks to see whether it has received further state changes. If there are state changes in the buffer, the latecomer executes them. When the buffer is empty, the latecomer has a consistent current state, stops buffering state changes, and participates in the session.

If there is no central server, it is not necessarily the case that any of the clients have been in the session from its beginning and so know of all state changes. To solve this issue, you can model the state changes as shared objects again. All clients synchronize their logs by means of the synchronization mechanisms for REPLICATED OBJECTS$_{\to 5.2.3}$ mentioned in Section 5.3 and keep a full log of all state changes that can then be sent to latecomers. STATE TRANSFER$_{\to 5.1.3}$ can then be used to provide a latecomer with a copy of the log.

Rationale

By keeping a log of all state changes, transmitting this log to latecomers, and re-executing the state changes at a selectable speed, the latecomers can perceive how the current state of the session has been reached.

Check

When applying this pattern, you should answer these questions:

— How can the latecomer identify a provider? Is there a site that is well known to all participants?
— Will users be able to control session state replay? Will they see all changes? Will they be able to adjust the replay speed?
— Which parts of the interaction will latecomers be allowed to see? Are there any areas of privacy in the session history that should be maintained?
— What is the granularity of your change logging? For example, is it on a keystroke level, or on a commit level?

Danger Spots

Transmitting the complete log of state changes might take a lot of time, especially if a latecomer is joining very late in a session. To overcome this issue, make regular copies of the shared state and let latecomers choose the point of time at which replay starts. Then select the copy of the shared state that is closest in time before the time selected by the latecomer. Transmit this copy and only the commands that have been executed afterwards to the latecomer. The latecomer then uses the copy to initialize shared objects and start executing commands from the selected point in time.

It may not be feasible to create a full replay of the interaction. The system can only replay those parts that were performed using the system. However, collaboration normally takes place using many interaction channels. The probability that not all of these channels can be captured and replayed is thus quite high.

A full replay can be too fine-grained, since it shows all operations. The common way to overcome this issue is to abstract from fine-grained changes to high-level changes. You should therefore consider replaying composite changes in one step and augmenting the replay with meta-information. Finding the right level of abstraction is however domain- and case-specific.

Known Uses

Collaboration Bus (Chung et al., 1998) is a groupware development environment that offers a service that allows sessions to be replayed. The service is based on a latecomer accommodation server called the *logger*. At a participant's site, a *loggable* captures all events that change the local user interface and sends these events to the logger. The logger is therefore informed about all the changes that a client applies to the user interface of a shared application. When a latecomer wants to join a session, the logger replays all logged events to the latecomer's loggable. Based on these events, the latecomer's loggable creates the user interface. As the log can become very large, the system uses log compression techniques. These depend on semantic information about the events that a loggable has to provide. Instead of replaying all events, such as mouse movements, the logger can provide the latecomer with just the events that resulted in a state change.

DreamObjects (Lukosch, 2003a,b) is a groupware framework that keeps the log as a replicated object. It therefore does not need a central server to act as a provider of the log. When joining, users can choose what percentage of the current should be replayed and the delay between display of state changes. Figure 5.4 shows a sequence of screenshots taken during replay of a session.

ReplayKit (Manohar and Prakash, 1995a,b) is a groupware environment that encapsulates and records individual users in session objects. Users collaborate asynchronously by annotating, modifying, and exchanging these session objects. The runtime system allows replay of a session object at different speeds.

CatchUp (Henkel and Diwan, 2005) is a plug-in for the Eclipse development environment that allows record and replay of refactorings.

Related Patterns

ACTIVITY LOG$_{\to 4.5.1}$ describes how to log all changes to the shared state.

CENTRALIZED OBJECTS$_{\to 5.2.1}$ allows a central server to be chosen as session state provider for a latecomer.

COLLABORATIVE SESSION$_{\to 5.1.1}$ allows users to plan and coordinate synchronous collaboration. Latecomers need the current state of the session.

DISTRIBUTED COMMAND$_{\to 5.2.7}$ allows state changes to be encapsulated.

IMMUTABLE VERSIONS$_{\to 5.3.6}$ allows different versions of a shared object to be identified.

MEDIATED UPDATES$_{\to 5.2.5}$ allows the mediator to be chosen as state provider for a latecomer.

REPLICATED OBJECTS$_{\to 5.2.3}$ can be used to keep a replicated log of state changes.

DECENTRALIZED UPDATES$_{\to 5.2.6}$ requires that all or a subset of all clients keep the log of state changes, because the participants of a COLLABORATIVE SESSION$_{\to 5.1.1}$ communicate in a peer-to-peer network, so there is no central server that can be chosen as change log providers for latecomers.

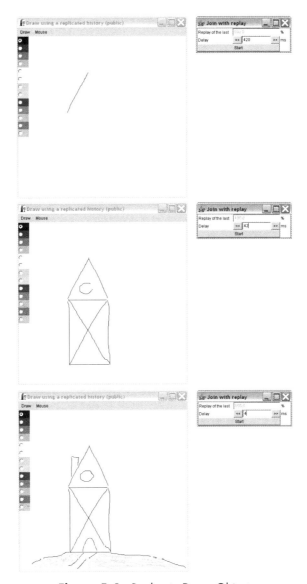

Figure 5.4 Replay in DreamObjects

STATE TRANSFER$_{\to 5.1.3}$ directly transfers the current session state to a latecomer.

TIMELINE$_{\to 4.5.2}$ shows the orchestration of different activities by means of a diagram. A TIMELINE can be compared to a script of activities, while REPLAY executes or animates the script.

5.1.5 Connect me... applied

A COLLABORATIVE SESSION$_{\rightarrow 5.1.1}$ was used to support members of the community in the creation of task-based collaboration contexts. Susan created a new COLLABORATIVE SESSION. Technically, this resulted in a new *XPSession* object that was stored in the INTERACTION DIRECTORY$_{\rightarrow 4.2.3}$ and made accessible to all users of the system. We show in detail how this was done in the next section.

After creating the session, the system automatically added Susan to the session and assigned her the role of driver. Technically, Susan's user object was added to the collection of users in the session object. This list is accessible to all registered users so that session information can be shown in all clients.

Paul—who wants to join Susan in a pair-programming session—can see the new session object in the INTERACTION DIRECTORY. As we mentioned in Section 4.2.7, he can ask to join the session. This causes a pop-up request to appear on Susan's screen. The pop-up request was again implemented as a COLLABORATIVE SESSION: Paul created a *NotifierSession* and added Susan as a user. Since Susan's client will be able to see the new object, it will open the required tools for the session. In this case, it is a simple dialog asking whether or not Paul can join the session.

If Susan agrees that Paul can join her, she takes Paul's user object and adds it to the collection of session users in the XPSession instance. Paul's application will see that the local user—Paul's user object—is now related to the XPSession and it will open an appropriate XPEditor window.

In the XPSession Susan is allowed to alter the current session state. This includes the name of the file that is currently shown in the editor and the position of the text cursor in the editor. This state information is stored in the shared XPSession. To allow Susan to leave the session, perhaps for a lunch break, it is modeled as a PERSISTENT SESSION$_{\rightarrow 5.1.2}$. Susan can therefore decide to leave the session and reenter it when she returns. At this point she gets access to the current state of the session by means of the STATE TRANSFER$_{\rightarrow 5.1.3}$ pattern.

5.2 Share me... or how systems manage common data

Single-user and groupware applications have to manage their data, but groupware applications also have to share their data to allow users to collaborate. Data management is the main difference between developing single-user applications and groupware applications.

> *The Eclipse plug-in for distributed pair programming made use of shared data to enable collaboration. As explained in the previous section, the COLLABORATIVE SESSION$_{\rightarrow 5.1.1}$ was represented by instances of the XPSession class and each user was represented by a shared user object.*

Different approaches exist for sharing data among collaborating users and much discussions has taken place about the best approach for synchronous groupware applications. However, the developers of some groupware platforms, such as Prospero (Dourish, 1996), GEN (O'Grady, 1996), Clock (Graham et al., 1996), or DreamObjects (Lukosch, 2003a) have argued that every strategy for managing shared data has its advantages and drawbacks and that none is well-suited for every groupware application, or even for single data objects in an application. Instead, the appropriate strategy for managing shared data heavily depends on the groupware application that is going to use the shared data.

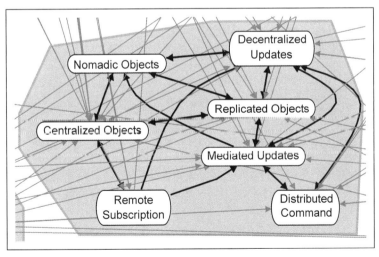

Figure 5.5 Patterns for managing shared data

The patterns in this section, shown in Figure 5.5, describe the different strategies and support developers have in choosing the appropriate strategy for managing shared data. They are:

CENTRALIZED OBJECTS$_{\to 5.2.1}$ Allow users to access shared objects remotely.

REMOTE SUBSCRIPTION$_{\to 5.2.2}$ Let the server notify clients about state changes to shared data.

REPLICATED OBJECTS$_{\to 5.2.3}$ Allow users to access shared objects without network delay.

NOMADIC OBJECTS$_{\to 5.2.4}$ Provide access to shared objects without a network.

MEDIATED UPDATES$_{\to 5.2.5}$ Minimize the administrative load for updates by using a central instance that dispatches the updates.

DECENTRALIZED UPDATES$_{\to 5.2.6}$ Distribute local state changes to the other users to maintain consistency.

DISTRIBUTED COMMAND$_{\to 5.2.7}$ Keep all replicas of a shared object consistent by re-executing commands.

5.2.1 CENTRALIZED OBJECTS **

cen·tral·ize (sĕn'trə-līz'), TRANSITIVE VERB: **1.** To draw into or toward a center; consolidate. **2. To bring under a single, central authority:** *The Constitution centralizes political power in the federal government.*

Intent

Allow users to access shared objects remotely.

Context

You are developing a groupware application. Now you are thinking about how to organize the data so that many users can work with it.

Problem

To enable collaboration, users must be able to share data.

Scenario

Susan wants to structure the whole project a little better. She therefore proposes using shared task lists in which all change requests for the game engine are managed. The open issue, however, is how these task lists should be managed to allow all members of the community to see their tasks and add new ones.

Symptoms

You should consider applying this pattern when ...

— Users have to meet in person to collaborate because they don't know how to exchange data.

— Users with a permanent network connection want to collaborate in an interactive application, but cannot share data.

— Users cannot establish a common ground to get an understanding of shared data.

Solution

Therefore: Manage the data necessary for collaboration on a server that is known to all users. Allow the users to access the data on the server.

Dynamics

The main participant is the server. Users who want to collaborate must know the address of the server. The server stores the data that is shared for collaboration. Users access the server to retrieve shared data and display it locally. When changing the data, they contact the server again, which performs the change. Accessing and changing the data can be implemented for example by using remote procedure calls (RPCs) (Birrell and Nelson, 1984). Figure 5.6 shows these collaborations for two collaborating users who access shared data objects managed by a central server.

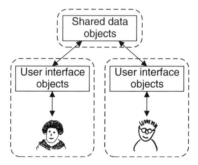

Figure 5.6 Users accessing CENTRALIZED OBJECTS

Rationale

Since all users rely on the same shared data, they can access this data and collaborate. Besides this, the main advantages of this pattern are:

— All users know the address of the server and can therefore find the shared data easily and quickly.

— As the shared data is stored and only changed on the server, it is easy to maintain consistency.

Check

When applying this pattern, you should answer these questions:

— Which protocol are you going to use to let users access the data?

— Are you going to allow changes to the data on the central server? If yes, how are you going to propagate these changes to the users, and how are you going to ensure consistency during concurrent updates?

Danger Spots

The central server is a bottleneck for accessing and changing shared data. When many users access the shared data intensively, the response time of the application may increase. This can make collaboration difficult.

If the central server becomes unavailable, users can no longer access the shared data.

Different clients may change the CENTRALIZED OBJECTS over time, causing the local views at client sites to become outdated. To overcome this problem, use REMOTE SUBSCRIPTION$_{\to 5.2.2}$ to keep the local views up to date.

Known Uses

Suite (Dewan and Choudhary, 1992) uses a DOCUMENT-VIEW variant of the MODEL-VIEW-CONTROLLER pattern (Buschmann et al., 1996) to divide model and presentation. Suite keeps the model objects, called *active variables*, on the server. The views and controllers, called *dialogue managers*, are kept on the clients. Whenever a client's dialogue manager needs to modify the data, it asks the server to change the model.

NSTP (Patterson et al., 1996) provides a service for data sharing in synchronous multiuser applications. The service is offered by an easily accessible notification server. The server provides clients with access to shared state and notifies the clients whenever the shared state changes. The server contains two kinds of objects: *places* and *things*. A place contains the shared state and partitions the resources of the server among several applications. Each application uses at least one place. A client joins a collaborative application by entering the place. Things are the actual objects that maintain the shared state and can be created, changed, locked, unlocked, and deleted.

DreamObjects (Lukosch, 2003a) supports a variety of distribution schemes. Among these is a variant of the centralized distribution scheme. In this variant each participating site can act as server for a central object and thereby easily introduce local data in a collaborative session. Changes to these centralized objects are only performed at the object hosting site. All other sites can transparently access a centralized object via *local substitutes* that handle all necessary mechanisms.

Wikis (Leuf and Cunningham, 2001) are a special kind of web application in which users can modify stored pages using a simple set of editing rules. Typically, a client first requests a page for viewing. The Wiki engine creates an HTML version of the page that is stored (in plain text) on the server. If the user decides to edit the page, the server creates a form version of the page that includes an input field for editing the page's source text. If the client decides to store the edited page, the changed text is sent to the server and stored in the server's pages.

Related Patterns

REMOTE SUBSCRIPTION$_{\rightarrow 5.2.2}$ allows clients to be informed about changes that are applied to CENTRALIZED OBJECTS.

REPLICATED OBJECTS$_{\rightarrow 5.2.3}$ should be used if a collaborative application is highly interactive and many users perform many changes. REPLICATED OBJECTS decrease the response time of the application, but increase the availability of the shared data.

NOMADIC OBJECTS$_{\rightarrow 5.2.4}$ should be used if there is no permanent network connection. NOMADIC OBJECTS make the data accessible for disconnected users.

BLACKBOARD (Buschmann et al., 1996) makes use of structures described in the CENTRALIZED OBJECTS pattern. It is an example of distributed processing with exchange of intermediate results (called *hypotheses*) at a central location. The hypotheses are thus the objects that are shared between processing units. The blackboard that manages hypotheses is an instance of the server in the CENTRALIZED OBJECTS pattern.

AUTHORIZATION (Schumacher et al., 2005) describes how a user's access rights can be linked to a specific centralized object. You can use this pattern if not all users of your system should be allowed to access all shared objects.

NAMING (Völter et al., 2002) describes how shared objects can obtain an identifier that is unique in the space of shared objects. It suggest using a central naming service that manages a book of white pages listing the names and the locations of all shared objects. The naming server is again a CENTRALIZED OBJECT.

COMMON PERSISTENT STORE (Dyson and Longshaw, 2004) also argues for a centralized architecture, but with the purpose of allowing different servers to access common data.

5.2.2 Remote Subscription **

sub·scrip·tion (səb-skrĭp'shən), NOUN: **1a. A purchase made by signed order, as for a periodical for a specified period of time or for a series of performances. b.** An agreement to receive or be given access to electronic texts or services, especially over the Internet. **2.** Acceptance, as of articles of faith, demonstrated by the signing of one's name. **3a.** The raising of money from subscribers. **b.** A sum of money so raised. **4.** The signing of one's name, as to a document. **5.** Something subscribed.

Intent

Let the server notify clients about state changes to shared data.

Context

You provide clients with access to CENTRALIZED OBJECTS$_{\to 5.2.1}$. These objects can change over time. Now you are thinking about avoiding inconsistencies between the state of an object and its visual representation at client sites.

Problem

Clients that show objects maintained from a server assume that the objects are valid. Since the objects may be shown for a long time, however, their displayed state may become outdated. Users consuming the object therefore receive incorrect information.

Scenario

Susan has finally organized all the tasks for resolving change requests as CENTRALIZED OBJECTS. *Each project member can now access open tasks using a web browser and decide to work on a specific task. Charley would like to contribute to security tasks. He opens his browser, reads the list of current tasks, but cannot find open tasks. He therefore decides not to invest any time in the game engine project for the coming month. A day later, Paul adds numerous security tasks. However, Charley has not noticed that Paul has added three new security tasks soon after Charley loaded the task list.*

Symptoms

You should consider applying this pattern when . . .

- Polling for new states is not possible due to resource restrictions such as bandwidth costs or computing resources.
- Clients only visualize information received from a server.
- It is important that users do not use outdated information.

Solution

Therefore: Let clients subscribe to the state of shared data and ensure that the server informs the clients about relevant state changes.

Dynamics

The server keeps track of all the clients that have subscribed to the state of a shared object. Whenever the state of the object is changed, the server informs the clients about the state change. For this purpose, the server can either simply inform the subscribed clients which object has been changed, or the server can include a description of the state change, which allows the clients to update their display of the object. In the first case, it is up to the clients to request the new current state from the server.

Rationale

REMOTE SUBSCRIPTION, in combination with CENTRALIZED OBJECTS$_{\to 5.2.1}$, allows a distributed MODEL-VIEW-CONTROLLER (Buschmann et al., 1996) to be implemented. The server maintains the model, while the views and controllers are kept at the clients. As the clients subscribe to the server, the server knows who has to be informed about changes applied to the model. Thus whenever the model is changed, the server can look up the subscribed clients and inform them about the changes. This allows the clients to keep their views up to date.

Check

When applying this pattern, you should answer these questions:

- Are you going to include the state change in the update information? If yes, how are you going to describe the state change?

Danger Spots

If the server does not include a description of the state change to allow clients to update their view, it may lead to a high communication load when each client requests the new state of the changed object. This worsens the problem of the server being a communication bottleneck.

Clients may crash. To avoid communication problems at the server, the server has to remove a client from the subscription list whenever it detects a crashed client.

In some cases the server does not know how to contact its clients, for example when communicating via HTTP. To overcome this problem you can reverse the roles of client and server by postponing a response to a client's request until new information is available. When the client receives an answer, it contacts the server again immediately and waits for a new update.

Known Uses

CURE. In the web-based computer-supported collaborative learning (CSCL) platform CURE (Haake et al., 2004a), subscriptions are used to update web pages at client sites.

When the web server generates the HTML pages that include the information for the learning environment, it includes several Javascripts that mark sections of pages that may change frequently. Examples are USER LISTS$_{\rightarrow 4.4.1}$ showing users who are currently browsing material from a particular ROOM$_{\rightarrow 4.2.1}$ in the CSCL environment.

Besides marking the location of potentially changing elements in the web page, the script also informs a listener applet that any changes to the model (the shared objects that were used as a model for generating the web pages) that would change an element on the web page should be propagated to the script.

The applet then informs the server that maintains a dictionary, which includes, for each model object, the addresses of the clients that want to be informed of state changes. These clients are the subscribers of the model object.

When a model object changes its state, the server sends a message to the clients registered as subscribers for the model object. The message is received by the applet at the client's site, which dispatches the message to the relevant Javascript.

Finally, the Javascript exchanges the relevant HTML code on the page to ensure that it is again valid.

NSTP. The Notification Service Transfer Protocol (Patterson et al., 1996) provides a service for data sharing in synchronous multiuser applications. The service is offered by a *notification server* that provides clients with access to a shared state, and notifies the clients whenever the shared state changes.

Java Message Service (JMS). The idea behind the JMS infrastructure (http://java.sun.com/products/jms/) is that clients can subscribe to update messages for a given topic that is managed at a JMS server.

Suite (Dewan and Choudhary, 1992) uses a DOCUMENT-VIEW variant of the MODEL-VIEW-CONTROLLER pattern (Buschmann et al., 1996) for dividing model and presentation. Suite keeps the model objects (called *active variables*) on the server. The views and controllers (called *dialogue managers*) are kept on the clients. Whenever a model object changes, the corresponding controllers in the clients are informed and the views are updated.

Related Patterns

CENTRALIZED OBJECTS$_{\rightarrow 5.2.1}$ requires the use of REMOTE SUBSCRIPTIONS to keep clients' views up to date.

DECENTRALIZED UPDATES$_{\rightarrow 5.2.6}$ and MEDIATED UPDATES$_{\rightarrow 5.2.5}$ mainly differ from REMOTE SUBSCRIPTIONS in that the shared objects are kept at the clients. In the case of DECENTRALIZED UPDATES and MEDIATED UPDATES$_{\rightarrow 5.2.5}$, the clients hold replicas of the shared objects while REMOTE SUBSCRIPTION only considers view state. This implies that no state changes to model objects are performed on the client's side, which makes model consistency easier to manage.

MODEL-VIEW-CONTROLLER (Buschmann et al., 1996) can be implemented in a distributed setting using REMOTE SUBSCRIPTIONS.

PUBLISHER-SUBSCRIBER (Buschmann et al., 1996) is the localized version of this pattern.

5.2.3 REPLICATED OBJECTS **

rep·li·ca·tion (rĕp'lĭ-kā'shən), NOUN: **1.** A fold or a folding back. **2.** A reply to an answer; a rejoinder. **3.** Law The plaintiff's response to the defendant's answer or plea. **4.** An echo or reverberation. **5. A copy or reproduction. 6. The act or process of duplicating or reproducing something.**

Photo: Loikkanen, Antti, Finland, www.visipix.com

Alternative name(s): Replicate for Speed

Intent

Allow users to access shared objects without network delay.

Context

You have considered managing shared data using CENTRALIZED OBJECTS$_{\rightarrow 5.2.1}$. Now you are concerned about performance.

Problem

The response time of interactive applications has to be short. Network latency wastes time in distributed systems. Thus interactive applications are inappropriate if their response time depends on client-server communication.

Scenario

Paul and Charley have used CENTRALIZED OBJECTS *as a basis for their shared diagram editor. Each domain model of a class is located at the central server so that both users can see and manipulate all classes. Unfortunately, interactive operations like drag and drop do not work well: the response to each action is too slow. Charley says that this is due to the centralized model because this implies that all operations, such as dragging an element just one pixel, need to be done on the server before the local view gets updated.*

Symptoms

You should consider applying this pattern when . . .

— Users with a permanent network connection collaborate in a highly interactive application.
— Users perform many incremental changes on large objects.
— The response of the application is too slow.

Solution

Therefore: Replicate shared data to client sites. Let a user access and modify the local replicas.

Dynamics

Figure 5.7 shows two collaborating users who access REPLICATED OBJECTS.

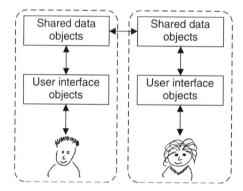

Figure 5.7 Users accessing Replicated Objects

As every user can locally access and modify shared data, the consistency of the data is an issue. To ensure consistency, use DECENTRALIZED UPDATES$_{\to 5.2.6}$ or MEDIATED UPDATES$_{\to 5.2.5}$ to propagate local changes.

When users joins a collaborating group as latecomers, their clients must request all shared data objects from a site that already participates in the collaboration. STATE TRANSFER$_{\to 5.1.3}$ and REPLAY$_{\to 5.1.4}$ are two different approaches to solving this problem.

Rationale

Since users can access data locally, they can perform local changes or display refreshes without network overheads.

Check

When applying this pattern, you should answer these questions:

— How will you identify the shared data that is transferred to the clients?
— How will you distribute local changes to all other clients?
— Is consistency of the replicated objects an issue? If yes, how can you ensure consistency when concurrent updates are performed?

Danger Spots

Replication ensures that the delay in accessing shared objects is low, but it may cause a large initial delay when the common objects are accessed for the first time. Thus you should schedule initial transmission at times when fast response times are not needed.

Replication causes high communication costs (Garcia-Molina, 1986). If this is an issue and you want to reduce the communication costs, use partial replication. For that purpose, let clients only hold a replica of a shared data object which is currently being accessed or will shortly be accessed. Other shared data objects that also belong to the state of the application can be ignored without any adverse effect to the user interface.

As the working style of individual users is not deterministic, this can result in high communication costs. For example, consider a system for editing books. Each section of the book is modeled as a shared object. The unit of replication is a chapter of the book. This means that users interested in one section of the book will request the chapter in which the section is contained and afterwards have replicas of all sections of the book. However, if the users frequently jump between different chapters, the replication does not add performance, and many sections are replicated without being ever used. In the worst case, the system would request a chapter and almost immediately discard it.

For a more sophisticated approach, use heuristics to guess whether a user really needs a shared object or not. Wolfson et al. (Wolfson and Jajodia, 1992a), (Wolfson and Jajodia, 1992b), (Wolfson et al., 1997), introduce several distributed algorithms for adaptive replication. The algorithms use different cost functions to adapt the replication scheme of a shared data object. The cost functions are based on the read write pattern of the shared data object. They also show that their adaptive replication algorithm significantly reduces the network traffic.

Known Uses

GroupKit (Roseman and Greenberg, 1996a) organizes shared objects in *environments* (Roseman, 1995). An environment is a hierarchical data structure in which a node can either hold a value or have other nodes as children. The runtime system transparently replicates an environment. A developer can bind callbacks to an environment and receive a notification when a node is added, changed, or removed.

COAST (Schuckmann et al., 1996b) allows clients to keep replicas of shared objects. To maintain a replica, clients register at a central server, which provides a primary copy of the objects. Clients can directly change their replicas and show the new state of the replica in their user interface. This ensures a high level of interaction in the application. Whenever a client changes the state of a replica, this change is propagated by means of MEDIATED UPDATES$_{\to 5.2.5}$. Changes can be state changes or the creation of new replicated objects.

DreamObjects (Lukosch, 2003a) supports replicated objects for highly interactive applications. All participating sites maintain a replica and can perform read accesses locally. Changes to the replica are handled transparently by a local substitute that wraps the shared object and is automatically created whenever a new shared object is registered in the runtime system.

Additionally, DreamObjects offers two predefined partial replication schemes. These replication schemes dynamically change the distribution of a shared data object according to a user's working style, such as how often a user accesses a shared object, or according to the topology of the connecting network, such as a one replica per subnet policy.

HTTP/1.1 (Fielding et al., 1999) supports caching on both the client and the server. Caching at the client is the most common practice. To ensure consistency of the cached document, HTTP/1.1 uses an expiration mechanism. Instead of requesting a cached document again, the client asks the server if the document is still valid or has expired. In connection with REPLICATED OBJECTS, a cached document can be compared with a replicated shared object.

Related Patterns

CENTRALIZED OBJECTS$_{\to 5.2.1}$ can be used to reduce the communication costs and simplify the management of shared data.

NOMADIC OBJECTS$_{\to 5.2.4}$ support collaboration between users that are not permanently connected to the network.

DECENTRALIZED UPDATES$_{\to 5.2.6}$ can be used to propagate changes to all other sites that maintain replicas of the shared data.

FAIL-STOP PROCESSOR (Saridakis, 2003) discusses replication for another purpose: system failure. As in REPLICATED OBJECTS, different clients keep replicas of shared data. If one client fails, users are redirected to other clients. In the terminology of our pattern language, such behavior would be called REPLICATE FOR RELIABILITY.

SESSION FAILOVER (Dyson and Longshaw, 2004) describes how clients can switch to another server if one server becomes unavailable. In the case of replicated objects, this situation can occur when the provider of the object becomes unavailable.

CACHING (Kircher and Jain, 2004a) and LOCAL CACHE (Dyson and Longshaw, 2004) address the same problem as REPLICATED OBJECTS. In both patterns, the response time becomes critical due to expensive retrieval of shared data. The CACHING pattern focuses more on applications in which users only retrieve data. REPLICATED OBJECTS instead focuses on applications in which users interactively modify shared objects.

DATA REPLICATION (Dyson and Longshaw, 2004) also promotes replication, but in this case at a server level, to ensure high availability of the server.

5.2.4 Nomadic Objects

Alternative name(s): Replicate for Freedom

no·mad (nō'măd'), NOUN: **1.** A member of a group of people who have no fixed home and move according to the seasons from place to place in search of food, water, and grazing land. **2. A person with no fixed residence who roams about; a wanderer.**

Intent

Provide access to shared objects without a network.

Context

You have created an architecture that allows users to access shared objects over a network, for example by using CENTRALIZED OBJECTS$_{\to 5.2.1}$. Now you want to allow them to work when disconnected from the network as well.

Problem

Users may not have a permanent connection to the system where relevant data is kept. Without a permanent connection, or with just a poor connection to the data, users will not be able to finish their work if the data cannot be accessed.

Scenario

Janet implemented some new features for generating context-sensitive menus in the game engine. She started this work last Friday and planned to continue it over the weekend. Unfortunately, she cannot do this because she has no network connection at home to use for accessing the source code repository.

Symptoms

You should consider applying this pattern when ...

— Users work off-line using various devices to work on data that is kept at least on one system.
— Users cannot work wherever they want.

— Users need to work on correct and complete shared objects.

— Users are connected via an unreliable network, such as GSM on trains.

Solution

Therefore: Replicate the data to the user's device and let the user change the local replica even when disconnected from the network. Update the local replicas and distribute local changes whenever two systems that hold copies of the data connect.

Dynamics

Whenever a client connects to the network, it identifies relevant objects provided by a central server or another client. It replicates these objects by asking the publisher of the object for a replica. The client may then disconnect from the network.

When the client connects to the network again, it contacts the publisher of the replicas and ensures that both parties have an updated version of the replicated object. Mechanisms for achieving this are presented in DECENTRALIZED UPDATES$_{\rightarrow 5.2.6}$.

Rationale

Since the required data is always on the user's device, the user is able to access this data when using the device.

Check

When applying this pattern, you should answer these questions:

— How will you identify the relevant objects that are replicated to the client?

— How will you identify those shared objects that have changed since the last connection of the client?

— How will you propagate changes to the client?

— How will you solve conflicts if shared objects have been changed on the client's side as well as on the server side?

Danger Spots

In addition to the danger spots listed for REPLICATED OBJECTS$_{\rightarrow 5.2.3}$, it might be complicated to decide which data is needed in disconnected situations. However, this issue cannot be solved on a technical level, but requires user involvement.

Known Uses

Sync (Munson and Dewan, 1997) is a framework that supports the development of mobile collaborative applications. It is based on replication and offers some basic classes that a developer can use to implement shared data objects. Applications developed with Sync use central asynchronous synchronization—users can connect to the server at any time to synchronize their changes. The basic classes contain mechanisms that solve a set of predefined conflicts that can occur when multiple users change the same data.

IMAP (Crispin, 1996) uses replication of e-mail messages and folders to support users in reading and archiving their e-mail on different clients. Each client can replicate e-mail messages when connected to the IMAP server. In the off-line mode, the client can organize the e-mail, for example by moving messages to other folders or creating new folders. When the client reconnects to the network, it synchronizes its local state with the state on the server and makes the user's changes persistent.

Lotus Notes (http://www.lotus.com/notes) uses replication of shared objects as one of its core principles. Users collaborate on CENTRALIZED OBJECTS that are stored in different Notes databases. To support off-line or remote access to these databases, Notes offers a flexible replication scheme.

Depending on their current location, users can configure which parts of the shared object space should be replicated (and synchronized). Figure 5.8[1] shows the dialogue that is used to configure the replication. The checked resources in Figure 5.8 represent the resources that will be synchronized at the current location.

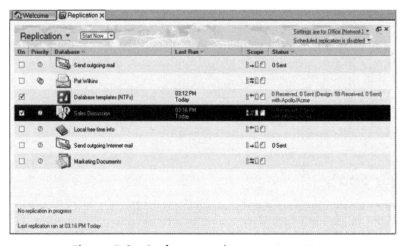

Figure 5.8 Configuring replication in Lotus Notes

---

[1]From http://www.lotus.com/.

offlineCURE (Lukosch et al., 2006) uses NOMADIC OBJECTS to allow users to work with the contents of the web-based collaborative learning platform CURE (Haake et al., 2004b) when disconnected from the Internet. offlineCURE avoids possible conflicts that might arise when users change the same objects while disconnected by using IMMUTABLE VERSIONS$_{\to 5.3.6}$.

CVS. The well-known CVS system is an example of asynchronous collaboration. Users can check out modules from a CVS server. The server transfers the requested module to the user's site. After checkout the user can disconnect from the network and access the module's data locally.

Related Patterns

REPLICATED OBJECTS$_{\to 5.2.3}$ are comparable to NOMADIC OBJECTS in the way they replicate objects to clients. The difference is the way in which changes are handled. Since clients stay connected in REPLICATED OBJECTS, they can ensure consistency directly after a user changes an object.

DECENTRALIZED UPDATES$_{\to 5.2.6}$ can be used to ensure consistency by informing other clients about changes to its replicas.

FAIL-STOP PROCESSOR (Saridakis, 2003) models replication for the purpose of reliability—the discussion in the related patterns section of REPLICATED OBJECTS$_{\to 5.2.3}$.

5.2.5 MEDIATED UPDATES **

Alternative name(s): Update Dispatcher

me·di·at·e (mē'dē-āt-ĭt), ADJECTIVE: **1. Acting through, involving, or dependent on an intervening agency. 2.** Being in a middle position.

Intent

Minimize the administrative load for updates by using a central instance that dispatches the updates.

Context

You have considered using DECENTRALIZED UPDATES$_{\to 5.2.6}$ to inform interested clients about state changes to replicated objects. Now you want to reduce the administrative overhead involved in ensuring consistency and propagating update notifications.

Problem

Clients want to propagate update messages to other clients who keep replicas of the same data. If they contact the other clients directly, they have to maintain information about who those clients are and must establish communication with them. This is complicated and error-prone, particularly if some clients disconnect and reconnect in an unpredictable way—that is, the set of clients changes over time.

Scenario

Michele, Ana, and Maurice have been working for a while on the VRML export features of the game engine. Since one of them had problems accessing the central code repository, the three developers decided to send updates to each other by e-mail. One day Noah joins the group. Michele introduces him to the team and asks all team members to keep also Noah informed about new versions of the code. However, Ana is so used to sending her update notifications only to Michele and Maurice that she forgets to inform Noah of her next update.

5.2.5 MEDIATED UPDATES

Symptoms

You should consider applying this pattern when ...

— The state of the replicated objects often diverges because of missed update notifications.
— Some clients don't know who the other clients are.
— It is hard to manage the set of interested clients, especially when they change frequently.

Solution

Therefore: Let a central site called the *mediator* maintain a list of all clients that are interested in changes to a replicated object. Whenever a client changes a replicated object locally, let the client inform the mediator, which will distribute an update message to all other interested clients.

Dynamics

As shown in Figure 5.9, a user modifies a replica and sends an update message to the mediator. The update message may contain the new object state or the COMMAND$_{\to 5.2.7}$ that led from the old to the new state. Both cases are equivalent regarding update distribution, but different regarding consistency management. The mediator maintains a list of all clients that are interested in the replica and redistributes the update message to these clients. As with DECENTRALIZED UPDATES$_{\to 5.2.6}$, the mediator collects acknowledgments from the other clients and afterwards acknowledges the client that initiated the change. To reduce network communication, the interaction can also work without the acknowledgments of other clients (as shown in Figure 5.9). In this case, the mediator only propagates

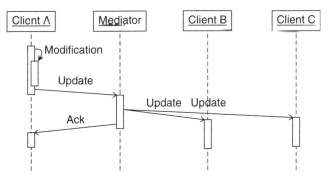

Figure 5.9 Distributing updates via a mediator

update messages if the update can be applied to the mediator's current state. At the same time, the mediator sends an acknowledgment to the initiating client.

Rationale

As the mediator knows who has to receive the update and distributes the update to these clients, clients no longer have to deal with these issues (see DECENTRALIZED UPDATES$_{\to 5.2.6}$). The client list of the mediator is always valid, as the clients have to register themselves at the mediator to be able to maintain a replica.

Since the mediator is informed about all changes, it is also the preferred point for asking for the most recent version of each replicated object. Thus, clients that disconnect, or that enter a collaborative session as latecomers, are provided with a method for retrieving the most current state. In architectures that work without a central mediator, this is impossible (see the discussion in DECENTRALIZED UPDATES$_{\to 5.2.6}$).

Check

When applying this pattern, you should answer these questions:

— Are you going to distribute the action describing the state change, or are you going to distribute the new state of the modified object?
— How will you keep the client lists at the mediator up to date?
— How will you ensure that all clients receive the update message?
— Are you going to use mechanisms to ensure consistency, such as PESSIMISTIC LOCKING$_{\to 5.3.1}$? If yes, how will these mechanisms influence the way you distribute update messages?

Danger Spots

The mediator is a single point of failure and a bottleneck for network communication.

If users change the state at the same time there can be a conflict, which should be resolved by the mediator.

If clients disconnect and then reconnect, the mediator has to ensure that they receive all updates that were distributed during their absence.

Known Uses

COAST (Schuckmann et al., 2000) uses one or more mediators to ensure consistency of shared data. In COAST clients register at a mediator when they want to obtain replicas of shared data. The mediator keeps track of which clients keep replicas and are connected to the network: if they get disconnected, they have to reconnect and obtain a fresh copy of the data.

Whenever the client changes replicated data (using transactions), a transaction log is sent to the mediator. The mediator then decides whether or not the transaction can be incorporated with the current state. If this is possible, the master copy on the mediator is updated and the transaction log is broadcast to all other connected clients that hold replicas of the object.

The mediator is also responsible for storing the shared objects.

DyCE (Tietze, 2001) provides a central object manager that maintains persistent object storage and handles shared objects. Developers have to define transactions to modify a shared data object. The transaction manager at the server acts as a mediator and is responsible for handling and distributing transactions.

Habanero (Chabert et al., 1998) focuses on transforming Java applets into distributed applets called *hablets*. The state of such a hablet is replicated to every participating site. To keep the shared state consistent, Habanero intercepts user interface events and forwards them to a server that acts as mediator. The server serializes all events and forwards them to all clients.

Related Patterns

OPTIMISTIC CONCURRENCY CONTROL$_{\rightarrow 5.3.2}$ provides a way to ensure consistency when different users modify the same parts of shared data at the same time.

DISTRIBUTED COMMAND$_{\rightarrow 5.2.7}$ describes how state changes, instead of the new object state, itself can be re-executed at client sites to ensure consistency of the shared objects.

REPLICATED OBJECTS$_{\rightarrow 5.2.3}$ and NOMADIC OBJECTS$_{\rightarrow 5.2.4}$ can use MEDIATED UPDATES to inform the other participating clients about local changes to a replicated object.

DECENTRALIZED UPDATES$_{\rightarrow 5.2.6}$ at first glance reduce the network load when compared to MEDIATED UPDATES, since communication with the mediator is not necessary. On the other hand, if clients change frequently and therefore the client lists also change frequently, additional network load is produced.

MEDIATOR (Gamma et al., 1995). The MEDIATED UPDATES pattern implements a distributed MEDIATOR. As in MEDIATOR, it decouples single clients and transforms the many-to-many communication between the clients into a one-to-many/many-to-one communication between the mediator and the clients. It also helps to centralize control, which is very helpful when establishing consistency, for example by using CONFLICT DETECTION$_{\rightarrow 5.3.3}$ mechanisms. The main difference between MEDIATOR and MEDIATED UPDATES is that the latter is more focused on the synchronization of replicated objects. It can thus be considered as a more concrete version of MEDIATOR.

OBJECT MANAGER (Buschmann and Henney, 2004) describes how the use of an object can be decoupled from its life-cycle management. The OBJECT MANAGER is responsible for retrieving the object, handing it out to clients, and for keeping it persistent. The mediator in the MEDIATED UPDATES pattern often plays the role of an OBJECT MANAGER.

RECOVERABLE DISTRIBUTOR (Islam and Devarakonda, 1996) describes how local views of global state can be kept consistent at different clients. It describes a comparable interaction between the participants, as was described in this pattern. In this respect it provides a combination of MEDIATED UPDATES and CONFLICT DETECTION$_{\rightarrow 5.3.3}$. Such a combination makes the design of collaborative applications less flexible. Specifically, the focus on only one distribution scheme narrows its applicability.

ACKNOWLEDGEMENT and ROLL FORWARD (Saridakis, 2003) relate to MEDIATED UPDATES as discussed in the DECENTRALIZED UPDATES$_{\rightarrow 5.2.6}$ pattern.

5.2.6 DECENTRALIZED UPDATES *

Alternative name(s): Update Your Friends

de·cen·tral·ize (dē-sĕn'trə-līz), TRANSITIVE VERB: **1. To distribute the administrative functions or powers of (a central authority) among several local authorities. 2a.** To bring about the redistribution of (an urban population and industry) to suburban areas. **b.** To cause to withdraw or disperse from a center of concentration: *decentralize a university complex; decentralize a museum.*

Intent

Distribute local state changes to the other users to maintain consistency.

Context

You have developed support that lets users access REPLICATED OBJECTS$_{\to 5.2.3}$. Now you are thinking about the effects of changes to those objects.

Problem

Users change their local copies of replicated artifacts and want to propagate these changes to other users who keep replicas of the same data, but setting up a central mediator (see MEDIATED UPDATES$_{\to 5.2.5}$) is not possible.

Scenario

Rodrigo and James both manipulate a shared interaction diagram that outlines the dynamics of the dialogue interpretation engine. At the beginning of their interaction, the editor replicates all model objects in order to provide fast feedback. Since both Rodrigo and James change diagram elements at the same time, however, the state of their model objects diverges over time. After saving the diagram locally, they try to integrate their work, but wonder why this is not possible without a lot of errors that have to be resolved manually.

Symptoms

You should consider applying this pattern when . . .

— Users collaborate by sharing and changing replicated artifacts.
— The state of the replicated object diverges as users change their replicas locally.

Solution

Therefore: After changing a replicated object locally, send an update message for the object to all clients that also maintain a replica, take care that all clients receive this update message, and let the clients change their replica according to the information in the update message.

Dynamics

Figure 5.10 shows how the network communication works. A client modifies its replica and distributes an update message to all clients who also hold a replica. This update message may contain the new object state or the COMMAND (Gamma et al., 1995) that led from the old to the new state. Both cases are equivalent as regards update distribution, but different in terms of consistency management. After distributing the update message, the sender collects acknowledgments from the message recipients to ensure that each one received the update message.

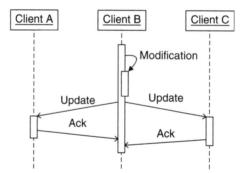

Figure 5.10 A client distributes update messages to all other clients

To know who has to receive the update, each client has to maintain a list of these clients. The time at which the update message is sent depends on the connectivity of the clients.

Rationale

Because all clients eventually receive an update message, they can change the state of their replica to the new state.

Check

When applying this pattern, you should answer these questions:

— Are you going to distribute the action describing the state change, or are you going to distribute the new state of the modified object?
— How will you keep the client lists at the clients' sites up to date?
— How will you ensure that all clients receive an update message?
— Are you going to use mechanisms to ensure consistency, such as PESSIMISTIC LOCKING$_{\to 5.3.1}$? If yes, how will these mechanisms influence the way you distribute update messages?

Danger Spots

You might not know all the client sites that carry a copy of a replicated object. In this case (Datta et al., 2003) suggests using a flooding technique in which informed friends inform their friends. The latter is for example done in the Gnutella peer-to-peer file sharing network (http://www.the-gdf.org/).

Update messages might get lost, so that not all your friends are informed about the update. One possible way to overcome this problem is to use sequence numbers in the update messages. Each client tracks the received sequence numbers and detects a missing update message by a gap in the number sequence. If this occurs, the client has to ask for the lost update message or request a new replica object.

If users change a replicated object's state at the same time, there can be a conflict.

If network bandwidth is an issue, reduce network load by using DISTRIBUTED COMMANDS$_{\to 5.2.7}$ describing the state change instead of the new object state. Be careful, as this might work in every case, such as that of commands that need arguments that are larger than the whole object state.

If the execution of a state-changing action is more time-consuming than transmitting the whole object state to the other clients, distribute the new object state as the update message.

Known Uses

GroupKit (Roseman and Greenberg, 1996a) transparently replicates a programming abstraction called an *environment*. Whenever users change the value of a node in the shared environment, the runtime system automatically distributes the new content of the node to the other participating sites. Additionally, GroupKit supports multicast remote procedure calls (RPCs), as described in (Cooper, 1985). By using multicast RPCs, developers can distribute local changes to all other participating sites.

DreamObjects (Lukosch, 2003a) supports more sophisticated multicast RPC to achieve consistency, as described in (Cooper, 1985). In DreamObjects each site maintains, for each shared object, a list of sites that hold a replica of the shared object. Based on these lists, the DreamObjects runtime system distributes the necessary update messages. These update messages describe the change and allow each receiving site to re-execute the change.

USENET uses a flooding mechanism to exchange messages between the different machines (Horton and Adams, 1987). A message is posted on one machine to a list of newsgroups. This machine accepts it locally, as if applying a local change, and then forwards it to all its neighbors. The neighbors check whether they are really interested in the new message and then apply the change. Furthermore, the neighbors forward the new message to all *their* neighbors. Using this technique a site can apply a change without knowing all the other sites that are interested in the change: it is only necessary to know some sites. However, there are two danger spots with this. First, to reduce network load, loops must be avoided. Second, it is necessary for all sites to be reachable by some means.

Related Patterns

OPTIMISTIC CONCURRENCY CONTROL$_{\rightarrow 5.3.2}$ provides a way to ensure consistency when different users modify the same parts of shared data at the same time.

DISTRIBUTED COMMAND$_{\rightarrow 5.2.7}$ describes how state changes, instead of the new object state, itself can be re-executed at client sites to ensure consistency of the shared objects.

MEDIATED UPDATES$_{\rightarrow 5.2.5}$ can be used to distribute all the changes made by one site. Compared to MEDIATED UPDATES, DECENTRALIZED UPDATES do not have a single point of failure, do not constitute a bottleneck, and have lower communication costs, which reduces the response time of the application.

REPLICATED OBJECTS$_{\rightarrow 5.2.3}$ and NOMADIC OBJECTS$_{\rightarrow 5.2.4}$ can use MEDIATED UPDATES to inform the other participating clients about local changes to a replicated object.

ACKNOWLEDGMENT (Saridakis, 2003). This pattern can be used to model the acknowledgement interaction between the update receivers and the originator.

ROLL FORWARD (Saridakis, 2003) discusses how to replay changes to replicated data. It uses replication at two sites. One site performs a change and the other site replays the change after receiving an update message. If the system at the first site crashes during the update, it will create inconsistent data and probably objects written to the hard disk. The system at the second site will still be operational. Since the first site crashed before it could send an update message, the change at the first system will not affect the second site. When recovering, the first site will replay the changes known at the second site. Both systems will then have a consistent state again.

In the context of collaborative applications, this behavior is also desirable. If one client crashes while performing changes, it may cause inconsistent data, but others will not replay those changes because the first client will no longer be able to send update messages to other clients that hold replicas.

5.2.7 DISTRIBUTED COMMAND *

Alternative name(s): Change Description

dis·trib·ute (dĭ-strĭb'yo͞ot), TRANSITIVE VERB: **1.** To divide and dispense in portions. **2a.** To supply (goods) to retailers. **b.** To deliver or pass out: *distributing handbills on the street.* **3a. To spread or diffuse over an area; scatter: *distribute grass seed over the lawn.* b.** To apportion so as to be evenly spread throughout a given area: *180 pounds of muscle that were well distributed over his 6-foot frame.* **4.** To separate into categories; classify. **5.** *Logic* To use (a term) so as to include all individuals or entities of a given class.

Intent

Keep all replicas of a shared object consistent by re-executing commands.

Context

You allow clients to modify REPLICATED OBJECTS$_{\to 5.2.3}$. Changes are distributed either by DECENTRALIZED UPDATES$_{\to 5.2.6}$ or MEDIATED UPDATES$_{\to 5.2.5}$. Now you are thinking about how to reduce network bandwidth.

Problem

Clients can apply changes to replicated objects locally. When you distribute the new versions of locally changed replicated objects, you might distribute more information than is necessary to keep the other replicas consistent, especially if only a small part of the replicated object has changed. This increases the network load and the response time of your application unnecessarily.

Scenario

Charley and Paul want to debug a new encryption module in the game engine. Charley opens the code and launches his development environment's integrated debugger. Unfortunately, Paul does not see the current debugging state because execution of the program under test is not replicated.

Symptoms

You should consider applying this pattern when ...

— It takes too long to propagate the new state of shared objects.
— Shared data is changed often and the description of the change to the shared data is relatively small compared to the size of the shared data itself.
— User are unsatisfied with the response time of a collaborative application.
— Not all parts of the application's state are replicated.

Solution

Therefore: Capture the method calls that a client uses to manipulate their local replicas as COMMANDS (Gamma et al., 1995). Distribute the captured COMMANDS to all other clients that also maintain replicas via the network. Let these clients re-execute the COMMANDS on their replica.

Dynamics

Figure 5.11 shows how the different participants collaborate when using DECENTRALIZED UPDATES$_{\to 5.2.6}$. In the first step, a client that changes shared state captures the state change. This can be done by requiring each state changing COMMAND to be called via a special interface, by encapsulating the shared object in a WRAPPER (Gamma et al., 1995) that captures the commands invoked, or by using aspect-oriented programming techniques.

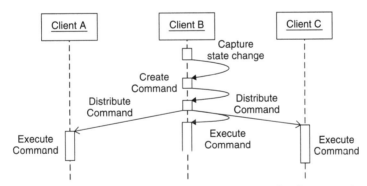

Figure 5.11 A client captures a state change, creates, distributes, and executes a COMMAND

After capturing the state change, this client creates a COMMAND that describes:

— Which object has been changed
— Which method has been called
— Which arguments have been used to execute the command

The client then distributes the COMMAND to other clients that also maintain the replica, while executing the COMMAND locally. Each client that receives the COMMAND uses the information it provides to execute the command on their replica locally.

In the simplest case, using a programming language that allows the dynamic execution of COMMANDS allows them to be re-executed at runtime.

When such a programming language is not available, it is necessary to implement an API that allows the execution of COMMANDS at runtime. To do this, all COMMANDS that need to be replicated have to be identified. These are COMMANDS that manipulate shared data or that execute operations on shared data, or that are relevant for all users in the collaborative session. Setter methods on attributes of shared objects are an example of the first case. An example of the second could be starting the playback of a shared audio resource. Since playback should start at all clients synchronously, the start COMMAND needs to be executed at each site. It is then necessary to implement a mapping between COMMANDS that can be received from other clients and the local execution of these commands. This mapping should include any arguments that might be included in the COMMAND for local execution.

Rationale

As only the COMMAND object is distributed in this pattern, and not the complete object state of the shared object, the amount of network traffic is reduced as long as the command object is smaller than the set of shared objects that is affected by the command. The clients task in producing update messages is eased, as they do not have to determine which parts of any shared data have changed and which have not.

Check

When applying this pattern, you should answer these questions:

— How will you describe the COMMANDS?
— How will you capture COMMANDS?
— How will you re-execute the COMMANDS?

Danger Spots

Clients can execute COMMANDS in parallel. This may lead to inconsistencies in shared data. If you use OPTIMISTIC CONCURRENCY CONTROL$_{\to 5.3.2}$, this is not a problem. Otherwise, mechanisms to ensure consistency, such as PESSIMISTIC LOCKING$_{\to 5.3.1}$, CONFLICT DETECTION$_{\to 5.3.3}$ and OPERATIONAL TRANSFORMATION$_{\to 5.3.4}$ must be applied.

Local re-execution of a command takes time. If you know that distributing the object state is faster than re-executing a COMMAND, distribute the object state.

When distributing COMMANDS you must ensure that each client can execute the COMMAND. This might not always be possible, for example if execution of the COMMAND needs local resources that are unavailable.

COMMANDS may return a result. When re-executing COMMANDS at each client, either skip the result or, if the result has to displayed in the user interface for a consistent view at each client, allow the user interface to subscribe to the COMMAND and its result. Use PUBLISHER-SUBSCRIBER (Buschmann et al., 1996) for this.

COMMANDS may have arguments. These arguments must be transferred either by value or by reference. When transferring arguments by reference, it is necessary that the referenced arguments have the same state at every site when executing the command. Otherwise, the COMMAND execution may lead to inconsistencies in shared data.

COMMANDS may use shared data that is not referenced by their arguments. However, to maintain consistent shared state, all data used must have the same state during COMMAND execution. This can be achieved if the system ensures that commands are always executed in the same order and that they do not rely on local state or user input. How to ensure the same order of command execution is an issue that is discussed in Section 5.3.

COMMANDS may call other commands that also modify the shared data. To maintain consistent state it is necessary to ensure that each client only executes the COMMANDS once. (Mazouni et al., 1995b) call this the *duplicated invocation* problem. They discuss two solutions:

1. *Post-filtering*. A site that receives a message for a COMMAND checks whether it has already received a message for the same distributed action or not. If yes, it simply ignores the additional command. Though this leads to the desired effect, it does not reduce the network traffic.

2. *Pre-filtering*. Only a special coordinating site distributes a message, if one is necessary. This solution avoids a site receiving several messages for the same COMMAND.

Known Uses

Arjuna (Little et al., 1993) (Little and Shrivastava, 1994) is a fault-tolerant distributed system that provides facilities for implementing applications that use replicated objects. Changes to the replicated objects are handled like remote procedure calls. To solve the duplicated invocation problem, Arjuna uses the post-filtering approach.

Amoeba (Tanenbaum et al., 1991) (Wood, 1993) is a distributed operating system that supports method calls to replicated objects. The method calls are handled as DISTRIBUTED COMMANDS. To overcome the duplicated invocation problem, Amoeba uses the pre-filtering approach.

Multicast-RPC, or replicated remote procedure calls, as described in (Cooper, 1985) (Cooper, 1986), allow one-to-many remote procedure calls to keep replicated shared objects consistent.

DreamObjects (Lukosch, 2002) is a platform for the development of synchronous groupware applications. It supports a variety of data distribution strategies. To distribute state changes, DreamObjects uses DISTRIBUTED COMMANDS in combination with the pre-filtering approach, only distributing a command if necessary.

GARF (Mazouni et al., 1995a) is a distributed object system that uses DISTRIBUTED COMMANDS. To overcome the duplicated invocation problem, GARF uses the pre-filtering approach.

Related Patterns

MEDIATED UPDATES$_{\to 5.2.5}$ and DECENTRALIZED UPDATES$_{\to 5.2.6}$ can use DISTRIBUTED COMMANDS to achieve consistency in the shared objects.

PESSIMISTIC LOCKING$_{\to 5.3.1}$, CONFLICT DETECTION$_{\to 5.3.3}$, and OPERATIONAL TRANSFORMATION$_{\to 5.3.4}$ can be used to ensure consistency of the shared objects.

COMMAND (Gamma et al., 1995) describes how a state change can be encapsulated. The DISTRIBUTED COMMAND pattern uses the COMMAND pattern to capture and re-execute the method calls that clients use to manipulate REPLICATED OBJECTS$_{\to 5.2.3}$.

DISTRIBUTED COMMAND (Brown et al., 1999) is an early version of this pattern that focuses mainly on distributed component frameworks like CORBA or EJB. Another version of the DISTRIBUTED COMMAND pattern was provided by Al Zabir (2005). Here, the author emphasized the execution and transportation layers for commands.

PUBLISHER-SUBSCRIBER (Buschmann et al., 1996) allows clients to subscribe to locally executed or re-executed COMMANDS.

WRAPPER (Gamma et al., 1995) allows COMMANDS to be captured by encapsulating a shared object.

SERVER REQUEST HANDLER and INVOKER (Völter et al., 2004) describes how commands from different clients can be translated into the invocation of local methods.

5.2.8 Share me... applied

As promised, we will now describe how Paul implemented the shared objects in the Eclipse plug-in. He thought first about providing only CENTRALIZED OBJECTS$_{\to 5.2.1}$. He implemented a server with various services. One service was to be used for creating new sessions, another for accessing specific users' user objects. Paul likes to use off-the-shelf components, so he designed the server using Web Service technology. This makes it simple to invoke a service on the server: the client simply sends an HTTP request that contains a SOAP message with the name of the desired service.

To create a new session, for example, Susan's application sent the following message to the server:

```
<soap:Envelope xmlns:soap="http://schemas.xmlsoap.org/soap/envelope/">
  <soap:Body>
    <createXPSession xmlns="http://services.coge.co.uk/ws">
      <sessionName>VRML Kernel Performance</sessionName>
    </createXPSession>
  </soap:Body>
</soap:Envelope>
```

In this SOAP message, the service createXPSession is called, which returns a reference to a session object. After successful execution, the server returns a message with meta-information on the newly created session. The server itself stores the session object in a database so that it is persisted across server restarts.

To ensure that all clients maintain the newest state of the CENTRALIZED OBJECTS, Paul added a REMOTE SUBSCRIPTION$_{\to 5.2.2}$ mechanism. Before sending a response to the client, the server adds the client to its list of interested clients. Whenever the state of an object is changed on the server, it informs the clients that their current view is no longer valid.

In our example, Susan created a new session and received meta-information about the session. Before that, she had already queried the server about the interaction directory and received a list with session names and identifiers. Since the server added a new session object to the interaction directory, it now sends all clients who have retrieved a session directory a message that this information is no longer valid. The clients then request the information again and update their local views.

This approach works reasonable well for session management in the Eclipse plug-in. Session information does not change frequently and changes do not require immediate feedback to the user. The situation is different in the case of a shared text cursor. Here, the mechanism described above for interaction between the server and the client is not fast enough. To get around this, the text cursor was implemented as a REPLICATED OBJECT$_{\to 5.2.3}$. Susan can now change the cursor position locally and show it immediately in her local editor. In parallel, her client sends an update message containing the new position of the text cursor to the server. The server changes the value of its master copy of the text cursor object and distributes update notifications to all users who are interested in the text cursor. This is an implementation of the MEDIATED UPDATES$_{\to 5.2.5}$ pattern.

We have only considered cursor position updates so far. These can easily be handled as described above because they are small and an update of the whole object is relatively fast. For edit operations in the pair-programming plug-in's text editor, it can make more sense to DISTRIBUTE COMMANDS$_{\to 5.2.7}$, because edit operations are relatively small, but affect a large text object.

This example shows that data distribution and update mechanisms need to be selected based on the nature of the objects and operations that are used in collaborative applications.

5.3 Control me... or how systems ensure data consistency

Figure 5.12 shows three collaborating users. Imagine these users work with a shared diagram editor that uses REPLICATED OBJECTS$_{\to 5.2.3}$ and DECENTRALIZED UPDATES$_{\to 5.2.6}$. The diagram editor allows the users to modify diagram elements in parallel, for example by moving the elements to a new position. The left-hand and right-hand users modify the same diagram element at the same time and inform the other sites about the modification. Due to network transmission times and network latency, the execution order is not the same at every site. This can lead to inconsistencies.

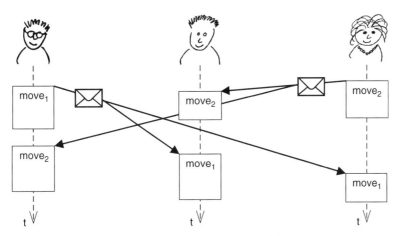

Figure 5.12 Consistency problem

A lot of approaches exist to ensure correct execution order. These approaches are collectively referred to as *concurrency control*. They are based on the idea of coordinating potentially interfering modifications. Some approaches involve the runtime system, while others involve users.

Some platforms rely on a *social protocol* (Greenberg and Marwood, 1994) to ensure the consistency of shared data objects. Social protocols involves users. Normally, when users work together, they mediate their actions such that the actions do not interfere. For example, when they work on a physical whiteboard, they consider it impolite to overwrite another's notes. The same applies for a collaborative whiteboard. To support social protocols, the collaborative application has to make users aware of the actions of others. Even when users follow a social protocol, inconsistencies can arise due to factors such as carelessness. Thus, a social protocol cannot guarantee a consistent state. However, for some applications, such as a sketch editor, this is acceptable, as a sketch editor is often used to develop ideas rather than to produce a final document.

Greenberg and Marwood (1994) compare and classify approaches that are handled by the runtime system and distinguish between *concurrency control through serialization* and *concurrency control through locking*.

Concurrency control through serialization is based on a total ordering of all distributed actions with the help of logical clocks (Lamport, 1978). Normally, a scheduler decides how to execute the actions or how to detect and repair sequencing inconsistencies. Greenberg and Marwood (1994) distinguish *non-optimistic serialization* and *optimistic serialization*. Non-optimistic serialization ensures that all distributed actions are executed in the same order at all participating sites. For this purpose, the scheduler ensures that only one distributed action is executed at a time.

Optimistic serialization is based on two assumptions. First, it assumes that interfering distributed actions are rarely executed out of order. Second, it assumes that it is more efficient to proceed with the execution and then repair any problems produced than to guarantee a correct order. One approach to repairing sequencing problems is to roll back the state of the shared data to its state just before an out-of-order action was executed and then re-execute the actions in order. Another approach is to transform an out-of-order distributed action with a set of rules so that its effect is the same as if it were received in order. Sun and Ellis (1998a) give an overview and evaluation of existing approaches.

Concurrency control through locking requires that a site requests and receives a distributed lock before it executes a distributed action. The lock can have different granularities. The granularity of a lock determines how much of a shared data object, or all shared data, objects can be modified after getting one lock. It is a difficult issue to set the granularity of a lock. Coarse granularity reduces the number of lock requests, but also the concurrency in the application. Fine granularity increases the number of lock requests and the network traffic, but improves concurrency in the application. Similar to the different serialization approaches, Greenberg and Marwood (1994) distinguish between a non-optimistic and an optimistic approach. Non-optimistic locking forces a site to wait until the requested lock is granted before it is allowed to execute a modification. Optimistic locking can be compared with optimistic serialization. A site requests the lock for a modification, but does not wait until the lock is granted to execute the modification locally. If the lock is granted, nothing has to be done. If the lock is not granted, the action has to be rolled back.

From the above approaches to concurrency control, the optimistic approaches especially are highly application-specific, as the application has to support the rollback of an action or the transformation of interfering actions, which is not always possible. All the approaches presented have drawbacks. (Roseman and Greenberg, 1996a) state that concurrency control needs are highly application-specific and that there is no generic method for ensuring the consistency of shared data objects. Different applications, and even single applications, have different requirements over data consistency and how consistency is achieved. The patterns in

5.3 Control me... or how systems ensure data consistency

this section are shown in Figure 5.13 and describe the various strategies for keeping shared data consistent and supporting developers over the choice of an appropriate strategy.

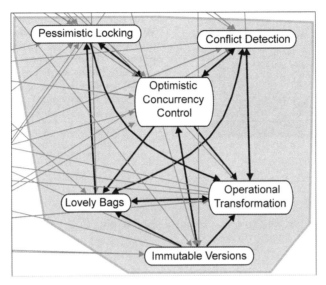

Figure 5.13 Patterns for ensuring data consistency

The patterns are:

PESSIMISTIC LOCKING_{→5.3.1} Allow only one user at a time to change a specific part of the shared state.

OPTIMISTIC CONCURRENCY CONTROL_{→5.3.2} Change data optimistically and roll back conflicting changes.

CONFLICT DETECTION_{→5.3.3} Detect conflicting changes.

OPERATIONAL TRANSFORMATION_{→5.3.4} When executing remote changes, transform these changes such that they take conflicting local changes into account and still lead to a consistent shared state.

LOVELY BAGS_{→5.3.5} Use bags to store shared objects in a container because they provide the best concurrency behavior.

IMMUTABLE VERSIONS_{→5.3.6} Store different versions of a shared object as a version tree.

5.3.1 PESSIMISTIC LOCKING *

Alternative name(s): Don't Trust Your Friends

pes·si·mism (pĕs'ə-mĭz'əm), NOUN: **1. A tendency to stress the negative or unfavorable or to take the gloomiest possible view: "We have seen too much defeatism, too much pessimism, too much of a negative approach" (Margo Jones). 2.** The doctrine or belief that this is the worst of all possible worlds and that all things ultimately tend toward evil. **3.** The doctrine or belief that the evil in the world outweighs the good.

Intent

Allow only one user at a time to change a specific part of the shared state.

Context

Many users work on the same shared data. Now you are thinking about avoiding any inconsistencies.

Problem

You want to ensure that changes performed by the user are definitely applied, even if more than one user wants to modify the same shared object at the same time.

Scenario

Paul planned a small refactoring that will affect most of the classes in the game engine project. He tried to apply the refactoring several times, but each time other developers also modified code while he was refactoring, with the effect that his changes could not easily be merged with those of the other developers. Paul regrets that the team is not collocated. If this were the case, he could simply invite all the developers for a pizza and perform his changes while they were eating.

Symptoms

You should consider applying this pattern when . . .

— Undoing inconsistent changes is hard or impossible—for example, a situation in which changes rely on external events.

5.3.1 PESSIMISTIC LOCKING

— The lack of a social protocol causes synchronous and conflicting changes.
— You have to share critical data and cannot allow inconsistencies in your shared data.

Solution

Therefore: Let a site request and receive a distributed lock before it can change the shared state. The lock can have different grain sizes. The grain size of a lock determines how much of a shared data object, or of all shared data objects, can be modified after getting one lock. After performing the change, let the site release the lock, so that other sites can request and receive it for changing the shared state.

Dynamics

The various sites interact according to Figure 5.14. A site that wants to change the shared state—the content of the replicated objects—first has to request a distributed lock. One strategy for obtaining the lock is by means of a central lock manager. In this case, the lock manager grants the lock to the requesting client. After receiving the distributed lock, the site can perform its change and distribute the change to other participating sites. Finally, the site releases the distributed lock. If a site requests a lock while another site holds the lock, it has to wait until the lock is available again (client B in Figure 5.14).

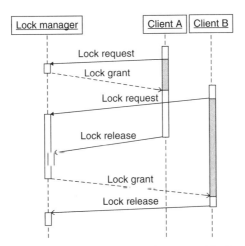

Figure 5.14 Requesting a lock with a central lock manager

There are many strategies for implementing distributed locks (Chang, 1996). The central lock manager described above is only one of these. Selecting a distributed locking algorithm has an impact on the user interface, as users might have to wait before they can interact and thus the response time of the application is increased. When the participating sites are connected via TCP/IP, for example, the use of a token-based algorithm (Singhal, 1989) reduces the number of exchanged messages, thus also decreasing the response time of an application. If the participating sites are connected via a network that supports IP multicasting, an algorithm based on multicasting messages (Ricart and Agrawala, 1981) is the proper choice.

Rationale

By requesting and receiving a distributed lock before performing a change to the shared state, only one site at a time can change the shared state. This prevents inconsistencies in the shared state.

Check

When applying this pattern, you should answer these questions:

— What grain size will the distributed lock have?
— What kind of distributed lock are you going to use?
— How are you going to avoid possible deadlocks that could occur when several distributed locks are necessary to change the shared state?

Danger Spots

Requesting and receiving a distributed lock before changing the shared state can increase the response time of an application. Interactive applications demand a low response time. Therefore, be careful when using distributed locks for concurrency control.

It is a difficult issue to set the grain size of a lock. A coarse grain size, for example for all shared objects, reduces the number of lock requests, but also the concurrency in the application. A fine grain size, for example for each modifying method, increases the number of lock requests and the network traffic, but improves the concurrency in the application. Greenberg and Marwood (1994) discuss these issues and their effect on the user interface.

If a client needs more than one lock to perform its changes, there is the danger of deadlocks. You therefore have to use deadlock avoidance strategies. Havender (1968) for example suggests assigning unique identifiers to the locks, using these identifiers to totally order the locks, and only allowing requests for the locks according to the total order.

Known Uses

DreamObjects (Lukosch, 2003a) supports two different grain sizes for concurrency control. Developers can use one distributed lock per shared object. Whenever a site wants to change a shared object, it first has to request and receive a distributed lock, otherwise the runtime system prevents changes to the object. To achieve more concurrency, developers can specify sets of methods that must be executed mutually exclusively, for example methods that change same parts of a shared object. For each set of methods DreamObjects uses one distributed lock that must be requested and received by a site before executing a method in the set. Requesting and receiving the locks are automatically handled by the runtime system.

DistView (Prakash and Shim, 1994) divides an application into interface and application objects. Both are completely replicated. DistView intercepts all calls to these objects and broadcasts them to the respective replicas to synchronize the states of shared windows. To ensure consistency, DistView associates one distributed lock with each replicated application object. In the application code, developers have to request these locks explicitly before changing an application object.

Related Patterns

OPTIMISTIC CONCURRENCY CONTROL$_{\rightarrow 5.3.2}$ If the response time of the application is a critical issue, this pattern can be used to perform changes in an optimistic way. However, if a conflict occurs, inconsistencies can arise that can be hard to resolve.

OPERATIONAL TRANSFORMATION$_{\rightarrow 5.3.4}$ describes how many users can modify the shared state at the same time without using PESSIMISTIC LOCKING. However, OPERATIONAL TRANSFORMATION also has some drawbacks which can make it difficult to apply—for example, the necessary transformation functions, or the effect of transformed operations on the user.

FLOOR CONTROL$_{\rightarrow 4.1.7}$ describes how mutual exclusion of actions can be achieved either at application level or at the level of a social protocol.

SELECTIVE LOCKING (McKenney, 1996) is a pattern language for locking in parallel programs. It examines constraints such as memory latency or size for this scenario.

PERMIT BASED LOCKING (Schütz, 2001) is a design pattern for requesting and receiving locks that aims to reduce network traffic. For this purpose, it uses a central lock server that passes *permits to lock* to those clients that it guesses next need the lock. If a client has a permit to lock, it need not request the lock and can perform its change immediately. If not, it has to request the permit from the central lock server. If the server has already distributed the requested permit, it revokes the permit. One obvious problem in this pattern is the central lock server, which is a single-point of failure.

COORDINATOR (Jain, 2003) uses a two-phase commit protocol to ensure that all clients perform a change. PESSIMISTIC LOCKING, in contrast, uses a locking approach to ensure that only one client performs a change at a time.

RESOURCE LIFECYCLE MANAGER (Kircher and Jain, 2004c). The lock can be interpreted as a resource in the sense of a RESOURCE LIFECYCLE MANAGER. It is a very simple resource that only controls the right to modify shared objects. A lock therefore does not need a resource environment, as described in the RESOURCE LIFECYCLE MANAGER pattern.

5.3.2 OPTIMISTIC CONCURRENCY CONTROL **

Alternative name(s): Believe in your Group, Optimistic Transactions (Hendrikxs et al., 2001)

op·ti·mism (ŏp'tə-mĭz'əm), NOUN: **1. A tendency to expect the best possible outcome or dwell on the most hopeful aspects of a situation: "There is a touch of optimism in every worry about one's own moral cleanliness" (Victoria Ocampo). 2.** *Philosophy* **a.** The doctrine, asserted by Leibnitz, that this world is the best of all possible worlds. **b.** The belief that the universe is improving and that good will ultimately triumph over evil.

Intent

Change data optimistically and roll back conflicting changes.

Context

Your system allows users to work on replicated objects. You have managed to propagate state changes (DECENTRALIZED UPDATES$_{\to 5.2.6}$ and MEDIATED UPDATES$_{\to 5.2.5}$). Now you are thinking about how to ensure consistency.

Problem

You want to ensure consistency but you want to ensure that changes to the replicated objects are propagated in minimum time.

Scenario

Paul and Charley have found a way to couple their diagram editors such that changes are distributed to all users. They simply distribute commands that include the changes. To prevent conflicting changes, they obtain a lock before they change an element in the diagram (PESSIMISTIC LOCKING). Unfortunately, the application is still slow. Charley assumes that the locks are the problem. Whenever he selects a diagram element, he needs to obtain a lock for it from the server, which takes time.

Symptoms

You should consider applying this pattern when . . .

— The system ensures consistency but is terribly slow.

— Acquiring locks is too time-consuming.
— The application domain is suitable for controlling concurrent interaction by means of a social protocol.

Solution

Therefore: Perform changes to local replicas immediately. If another client has earlier performed a conflicting change, roll back or transform your change.

Dynamics

A client changes a replicated object and informs other clients using DECENTRALIZED UPDATES. The client continues its work and waits either for an acknowledgment or a rejection. If its change conflicts with changes to the same object made at any other client (see CONFLICT DETECTION$_{\to 5.3.3}$) and thus is rejected by the other clients, it has to roll back its change. To be able to roll back a change, the old state has to be recorded before a change is applied. This can be done using the MEMENTO pattern (Gamma et al., 1995). When a conflict is detected, the recorded state has to be restored.

Apart from using MEMENTO, it is also possible to encapsulate all changes as DISTRIBUTED COMMANDS$_{\to 5.2.7}$ and define an inverse COMMAND for each change. Once a conflict over one COMMAND is detected, the corresponding inverse COMMAND has to be executed to roll back the conflicting change.

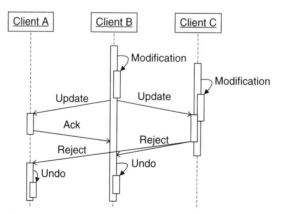

Figure 5.15 Distributing an update message resulting in an undo

Figure 5.15 provides an example of three interacting clients. Client B and Client C perform modifications at almost the same time. After Client B updates the other clients by using DECENTRALIZED UPDATES$_{\to 5.2.6}$, Client C finds that client B's modifications conflict with its own modification. Now assume that Client C is authorized to reject client B's changes. It informs all other clients that client B's modification must be rejected, which causes undo operations at clients A and B. Note that client A also has to undo the change, since it has already integrated B's update with its replicas of the shared data.

Apart from rejecting and rolling back changes, it is also possible to execute local changes immediately and, in case of later conflicting changes, resolve these conflicts by transforming the changes (see OPERATIONAL TRANSFORMATION$_{\to 5.3.4}$).

Rationale

By using this pattern a client avoids waiting in two cases:

1. Before performing a change.
2. After performing a change, updating other client and collecting their acknowledgments.

Check

When applying this pattern, you should answer these questions:

— How are you going to detect a conflict?
— Are you going to keep track of all the different states of an object to allow a rollback on it?
— Will you create inverse COMMANDS to allow rollbacks?

Danger Spots

The optimistic approach can confuse a user by rolling back a modification.

The implementation of a rollback mechanism is very memory intensive when the state of an application has to be stored.

When a lot of changes are performed, recording the state before executing a change can become very memory intensive. In this case, it might be better to encapsulate changes as COMMANDS and define inverse COMMANDS.

Sometimes it can be impossible to define inverse COMMANDS, such as when a COMMAND changes external resources. For example, it is not possible to "unprint" a document.

Rejecting and rolling back conflicting changes also takes time, so too many rollbacks may make the application unusable. You should think about applying OPERATIONAL TRANSFORMATION$_{\to 5.3.4}$ or a redesign of your shared data, for example by using LOVELY BAGS$_{\to 5.3.5}$, in this case.

To reduce the number of rollbacks, you could use the *local lag paradigm* (Mauve, 2000a). The local lag paradigm detects the network delay among participating clients. By using physically synchronized clocks, it further ensures that all COMMANDS are executed at exactly the same time: the local execution of a COMMAND is postponed until the local client can be sure that all participating sites have received and can execute the COMMAND. This reduces the number of rollbacks that are required.

Known Uses

COAST (Schuckmann et al., 1996b) allows clients to perform changes to shared objects directly on their replicas. If a client needs to change a replica, it starts a transaction and modifies the object using COAST's access methods. The transaction manager monitors each access and remembers it in a transaction log. When the transaction is finished it is sent to the mediator, a server that decides whether or not the transaction may survive (comparable to a DISTRIBUTED COMMAND$_{\rightarrow 5.2.7}$). In the meantime, the client that changed its local replica updates all dependent views. If the transaction is accepted by the server, the client has nothing more to do. The client will have been able to continue with the application while the server was deciding whether or not to accept the transaction.

If the transaction is not accepted—that is, if it failed the CONFLICT DETECTION$_{\rightarrow 5.3.3}$ test—the client has to restore the change using the old values that were recorded in the transaction log, and update all dependent views again. This implies that view and controller states are restored.

DyCE (Tietze and Steinmetz, 2000) uses a comparable transaction mechanism to COAST, with optimistic transactions.

DOORS (Preguica et al., 2000) allows independent changes to model objects replicated between clients without requiring a central server. Whenever a client changes a model object, it remembers the change and propagates it to other clients as soon as they are connected. The decision as to whether or not changes are acceptable is made by each client.

GINA (Berlage and Genau, 1993) enables synchronous collaboration on replicated objects. It understands the history of a replicated object as an operation tree and uses the tree for undo/redo mechanisms, optimistic concurrency control, and object merging.

Related Patterns

CONFLICT DETECTION$_{\rightarrow 5.3.3}$ An old Russian saying[2] says "Trust, but control." This implies that even with a high level of trust, a group can produce conflicts. These

---

[2] Lenin is often attributed with this saying, but he was not its author—it was just one of his favorite sayings.

conflicts have to be detected, which is the intent of the CONFLICT DETECTION pattern.

LOVELY BAGS$_{\rightarrow 5.3.5}$ It is crucial to model shared objects in a way that allows many concurrent accesses. Otherwise, OPTIMISTIC CONCURRENCY CONTROL will result in too many changes that need to be undone. The LOVELY BAGS pattern provides one example of how to model shared objects this way.

PESSIMISTIC LOCKING$_{\rightarrow 5.3.1}$ Even when most operations can be performed optimistically, there may be some changes that are hard to undo. For example, changes with large side-effects can be expensive or impossible to undo. In such cases you should perform these changes using locks.

OPERATIONAL TRANSFORMATION$_{\rightarrow 5.3.4}$ describes how conflicting changes can be transformed at each participating site so that the shared state is consistent at all sites.

OPTIMISTIC TRANSACTION (Hendrikxs et al., 2001) explains how to perform concurrent changes optimistically. It proposes performing the changes on a shared resource, then testing whether other clients have performed changes at the same time. To implement this test, this pattern uses a change counter that is compared to the change counter value that is expected for the case in which only the changes of the local client had appeared. The main difference to OPTIMISTIC CONCURRENCY CONTROL is that OPTIMISTIC TRANSACTION does not address the context of replicated objects. This makes the detection of a conflicting change through change counting simpler. If this pattern is applied in a distributed setting, the change counters have to be kept consistent, which on its own results in the management of shared data in a replicated context.

ROLLBACK (Lea and Lea, 1999) discusses how a client can return to a consistent state after a conflicting change has been detected. For this purpose, the old state of the system is recorded before a change is applied. The ROLLBACK pattern has been transferred to the context of replicated systems (Saridakis, 2003).

COMMUNITY OF TRUST (Coplien and Harrison, 2004) discusses the same issue as OPTIMISTIC CONCURRENCY CONTROL, but now on the level of a social process: instead of having strict workflows with heavyweight management, a team should proceed on its own path and at its own pace while staying in control of it actions and processes.

5.3.3 CONFLICT DETECTION **

Alternative name(s): Detect a Conflicting Change

con·flict (kŏn'flĭkt'), NOUN: **1.** A state of open, often prolonged fighting; a battle or war. **2. A state of disharmony between incompatible or antithetical persons, ideas, or interests; a clash. 3.** *Psychology* A psychic struggle, often unconscious, resulting from the opposition or simultaneous functioning of mutually exclusive impulses, desires, or tendencies. **4.** Opposition between characters or forces in a work of drama or fiction, especially opposition that motivates or shapes the action of the plot.

Intent

Detect conflicting changes.

Context

You have managed to distribute state changes and use OPTIMISTIC CONCURRENCY CONTROL$_{\to 5.3.2}$. Now you are worried about conflicting changes.

Problem

If two or more users change the same data at the same time, changes interfere. This can lead to inconsistent data or contradict the users' intentions. If the users are unaware of this conflict, they will no longer have a common base for collaboration.

Scenario

James and Susan both work on the source files of the speech recognition engine. They have copied them from a SHARED FILE REPOSITORY *to their local disk. James changes and uploads the Fourier analysis algorithm and sends his file to the* SHARED FILE REPOSITORY *again. Susan also changes small parts of the algorithm, however. She also copies her version to the* SHARED FILE REPOSITORY, *with the effect that James' changes are overridden.*

Symptoms

You should consider applying this pattern when . . .

— Users perform parallel changes that lead to inconsistent data.
— The social protocol does not ensure consistency.

— Each user works on a local and inconsistent view of the shared data. This means that users are conceptually at cross-purposes.

Solution

Therefore: Let each client remember all local changes that have not yet been applied by all other clients. Whenever a change is received from another client, check it against those changes that affect the same shared object and have not yet been applied by the other client. If performing the changes will produce a conflict, then undo or transform one of the changes such that all clients have a consistent state.

Dynamics

Each client that must be able to detect data conflicts has to maintain a history of all the changes it has performed and note, for each change, whether or not the change has been applied by other clients. If the change has been applied by the other clients, it can be removed from the change list, since no future conflict can arise from this change.

Clients perform changes locally first and use DECENTRALIZED UPDATES$_{\to 5.2.6}$ directly after applying the change. The other clients receive the update information and check their local change history to see whether or not other activities, not perceived by the client that sent the update notification, have changed the same data.

Concurrent changes on the same data are potential candidates for conflicts. The easiest way to decide whether or not a conflict has occurred is to treat all changes that modify the same data as conflicting changes. In general, one can consider two changes as conflicting changes if they produce a different application state if performed in different order. This means that the changes are not commutative. The more detailed is the test for commutativity, the greater the number of concurrent changes can be allowed in the application.

A very common test for whether two changes are commutative that allows more concurrency is based on the use of logical clocks (Lamport, 1978) and timestamps. Each client maintains a local logical clock. Whenever the client performs a local change, it assigns a timestamp to the change from the local logical clock and updates the logical clock. If the logical clock is for example implemented as a counter, the client increases this counter by one to update the clock. Using timestamps allows events to be ordered. As the logical clocks of all clients are not synchronized and each local logical clock is only updated by receiving an external change with a higher timestamp, or by distributing a local change, changes that originate from different clients can have the same timestamp. These changes are assumed not to be commutative.

Consider a linked list as an example of a shared object. One could decide to consider all additions to this list (`addFirst`, `addLast`) as conflicting changes. One could also define `addFirst` and `addLast` as pairwise commutative, since an addFirst operation will not affect the position of the element added with the addLast operation. On the other hand, two concurrent addLast operations are never commutative, since they both affect the end of the list.

In the final phase, the client decides to roll back or transform one of the conflicting changes (see OPTIMISTIC CONCURRENCY CONTROL$_{\to 5.3.2}$ or OPERATIONAL TRANSFORMATION$_{\to 5.3.4}$), or inform the user that the data is inconsistent. In some cases, undoing or transforming is an expensive operation and small inconsistencies can be accepted. Which change is undone or transformed depends on the applied algorithm. It is only necessary to ensure that each client does the same thing.

Rationale

The change history allows each client to detect whether or not conflicting changes have been applied to the same artifact.

Check

When applying this pattern, you should answer these questions:

— How are you going to test changes for commutativity? Are you going to use logical clocks (Lamport, 1978)?

— Are you going to undo or transform changes? How are you going to do this?

Danger Spots

The process of undoing or transforming a change is often complex.

Ensure that you remove those changes from the change history that have been applied by all other clients. To determine what these changes are, a client can include information on its applied changes in the change notifications it sends to the other clients. The more up to date is the list of applied changes, the fewer changes will be stored in the change history. This leads to shorter execution times for detecting a conflict and fewer conflicts.

If the number of clients becomes very large, the management of history lists can become a major bottleneck for the whole system.

Ensure that no additional changes have been applied to an object before undoing or transforming a conflicting change, otherwise the operation may lead to an inconsistent state.

Known Uses

COAST detects conflicting changes at both the mediator and the client. The mediator (see MEDIATED UPDATES$_{\to 5.2.5}$) detects a conflicting change when one client has based a change on data that has been changed by other clients in the meantime. In this case, the mediator ignores the change made on stale data, so that the other clients will not be informed about the conflicting change. The client that performed the conflicting change will receive a change message for the same object from the mediator indicating that the change it made was based on an old state. The client must therefore undo all the changes it performed locally on the shared data for which a conflict was detected, back to the last valid state before the conflicting change. Since each client only needs to detect changes from its local execution and valid changes from the mediator, the management of the state only has to consider two parties, which makes it simple and fast.

Related Patterns

LOVELY BAGS$_{\to 5.3.5}$ can be used to reduce the probability of conflicting changes by modeling the data in a way that is suitable for concurrent changes.

OPERATIONAL TRANSFORMATION$_{\to 5.3.4}$ describes how conflicting changes can be transformed at each participating site so that the shared state is consistent at all sites.

OPTIMISTIC CONCURRENCY CONTROL$_{\to 5.3.2}$ describes how conflicting changes can be rolled back.

RECOVERABLE DISTRIBUTOR (Islam and Devarakonda, 1996) combines CONFLICT DETECTION with MEDIATED UPDATES$_{\to 5.2.5}$. A discussion about how RECOVERABLE DISTRIBUTOR relates to CONFLICT DETECTION is provided in the related patterns section of MEDIATED UPDATES$_{\to 5.2.5}$.

CHANGE INDICATOR reduces the risk of conflicting changes by visualizing another user's change as soon as it happens, without necessarily replaying the change.

5.3.4 OPERATIONAL TRANSFORMATION *

Alternative name(s): Transform a Conflicting Change

trans·for·ma·tion (trăns'fər-mā'shən), NOUN: **1a.** The act or an instance of transforming. **b.** The state of being transformed. **2.** A marked change, as in appearance or character, usually for the better. **3.** *Mathematics* **a.** Replacement of the variables in an algebraic expression by their values in terms of another set of variables. **b.** A mapping of one space onto another or onto itself. **4.** *Linguistics* **a. A rule that systematically converts one syntactic form or form of a sentence into another. b.** A construction or sentence derived by such a rule; a transform.

Intent

When executing remote changes, transform these changes such that they take conflicting local changes into account and still lead to a consistent shared state.

Context

Clients perform concurrent changes on REPLICATED OBJECTS→5.2.3.

Problem

The number of conflicting changes becomes too great because many users perform changes on replicas of the same shared object. Rejecting and rolling back conflicting changes takes too much time, irritates users, and makes the application unusable.

Scenario

Paul and Charley meet in a COLLABORATIVE SESSION→5.1.1 *to work together on an encryption algorithm. They use a synchronous text editor that allows them both to modify the code at the same time. This is good, because they can see each other's changes immediately. When Paul and Charley want to work in parallel, however, much of their input is lost because it results in a concurrency conflict.*

Symptoms

You should consider applying this pattern when ...

— Synchronous work leads to frequent conflicts and response time is crucial for the application.

— Users publish their changes infrequently, increasing the probability of conflicts.
— Users do not want to resolve conflicts manually.

Solution

Therefore: Let each site transform conflicting remote changes such that applying the transformed changes leads to a state that is consistent with the state at all remote sites.

Dynamics

The different clients of a groupware system operate on shared objects as described in the DISTRIBUTED COMMAND$_{\rightarrow 5.2.7}$ pattern: clients cache replicas of shared objects (see REPLICATED OBJECTS$_{\rightarrow 5.2.3}$). Whenever a user executes a command, it is immediately applied to the local replica. After this, it is sent to the other clients, using either MEDIATED UPDATES$_{\rightarrow 5.2.5}$ or DECENTRALIZED UPDATES$_{\rightarrow 5.2.6}$. The other clients then execute the change on their copy of the shared object.

This strategy is extended by two additional processes to achieve consistency:

1. Each client keeps track of an *execution history vector* for each shared object that contains all command objects that have been applied to the shared object. The execution history vector is distributed with the newly created command. This allows remote clients to compare the state of their local copy of the shared object with the state of the initiating client's copy.

2. Before a DISTRIBUTED COMMAND is executed at a site, the execution history of the received command is compared to the execution history attached to the local copy of the shared object. Three different cases can occur:

    — If the execution histories match, the DISTRIBUTED COMMAND is executed and added to the execution history.
    — If the DISTRIBUTED COMMAND's execution history contains additional commands from other sites, the command is buffered until the missing commands can be executed.
    — If the local execution history contains additional commands, the DISTRIBUTED COMMAND is transformed before it is applied.

How the transformation is done is highly dependent on the command and the shared model's data structure. A widely used strategy is to create matrices for each model class that map each possible command to a possible concurrent command. Each specific entry in the matrix then contains the transformed command. For example, for the commands c_i, c_j with $i > j$, the matrix defines transformations $T(c_i, c_j) = c'_i$ that are applied to c_i such that c_i behaves as if c_j had been applied before c_i.

These transformations have to be correct so that both:

1. $c_i \circ T(c_j, c_i)$ is the same as $c_j \circ T(c_i, c_j)$, where $c_i \circ c_j$ means that the command c_i is executed after c_j.
2. $T(c_k, c_i \circ T(c_j, c_i))$ is the same as $T(c_k, c_j \circ T(c_i, c_j))$ with $i < j < k$ (cf. (Sun and Ellis, 1998b)).

The first condition describes the fact that a different order of command execution will finally lead to the same result, while the second condition describes the fact that the order of transformations does not affect the final result.

As an example, consider a shared text object. It contains a list of ordered characters (a String). Possible commands on the text are insert and delete. Imine et al. (2003) elaborate on this example and define the following interface for the shared object:

```
String insert(Number position, Number initialPosition, Character c);
String delete(Number position);
```

The first method inserts a character c at the passed *position*. The parameter *initialPosition* is used to remember the initial position of the character after the command is transformed by a transformation function. The delete command removes the character at the passed *position*.

These two commands can now be arranged in a 2 × 2 matrix so that corresponding transformed functions can be found:

∘	insert (p1, ip1, c1)	delete (p1)
insert (p2, ip2, c2)	tInsIns (p1, ip1, c1, p2, ip2, c2)	tDelIns (p1, p2, ip2, c2)
delete (p2)	tInsDel ((p1, ip1, c1, p2)	tDelDel((p1, p2)

The transformation functions then look as follows according to Imine et al. (2003)[3]:

```
String tInsIns(Number p_1,Number ip_1,Character c_1,Number p_2,
            Number ip_2, Character c_2)
{
// insert the character based on the difference in the insertion index
    if (p_1 < p_2)
      return insert(p_1,ip_1,c_1);
    if (p_1 > p_2)
      return insert(p_1+1,ip_1,c_1);

// same position (p_1 == p_2)
// try to detect differences in the initial index
    if (ip_1 < ip_2)
      return insert(p_1,ip_1,c_1);
    if (ip_1 > ip_2)
      return insert(p_1+1,ip_1,c_1);

// also same initial position (ip_1 == ip_2)
// create an order that is consistent between sites
```

---

[3]The code has been adapted to Java syntax to ease readability.

```
    if code(c_1) < code(c_2))
      return insert(p_1,ip_1,c_1);
    if code(c_1) > code(c_2))
      return insert(p_1+1,ip_1,c_1);

//  also same character
    return id();
}

String tInsDel(Number p_1, Number ip_1, Character c_1, Number p_2)
{
  if (p_1 > p_2)
    return insert(p_1-1,ip_1,c_1);
  else
    return insert(p_1,ip_1,c_1);
}

String tDelDel(Number p_1, Number p_2)
{
  if (p_1 < p_2)
    return delete(p_1);
  if (p_1 > p_2)
    return delete(p_1-1);
  else
    return id();
}

String tDelIns(Number p_1, Number p_2, Number ip_2, Character c_2)
{
  if (p_1 < p_2)
    return delete(p_1);
  else
    return delete(p_1+1);
}
```

Rationale

Since all changes can be applied immediately when this pattern is implemented, the groupware application can respond quickly to user input. In cases where conflicts occur, these are automatically resolved so that all users again share a consistent state.

Check

When applying this pattern, you should answer these questions:

— What are your conflicting commands? What are the corresponding transformation functions?

— How will you keep track of locally executed commands? Will you store them for each shared object, or will you consider a global state?

Danger Spots

The most difficult part of this pattern is to develop a correct set of transformation functions. Research has shown that even for simple data types like strings the process of creating and testing transformation functions is very error-prone (Imine et al., 2003). One therefore should not use this pattern for all data types: transformations should only be used when all other means of achieving concurrency fail.

The size of the execution history can become very large. A site can check whether all other sites have executed a specific command c_i. This is the case if the site received command histories for a new command c_j ($j > i$) that also contained c_i. If this is the case, you can assume there will be no future commands that conflict with c_i and c_i can be removed from the command history. In the same way, you can widen the scope of the execution history. Instead of having an execution history for each shared object, you can have one global execution history. In combination with automatic reduction of the execution history's length, this leads to a minimal execution history for groupware applications.

Finally, and probably most importantly, users may be disturbed by transformed commands. One example of this is the use of transformed commands in a shared text editor. The use of OPERATIONAL TRANSFORMATION ensures that users can type at the same word at the same time and that both users reach the same consistent state. However, the semantics of the result will probably not reflect their intentions.

As an example, imagine that Charley and Susan use a code editor that is based on operational transformations. Susan wants to rename a variable that was initially named count to pagecount. At the same time, Charley wants to change the name to documentcount. Susan starts typing pa and Charley types do. The result will be an interleaving of both users' edits, for example dpaocount. Operational transformations ensure that both Susan and Charley will see dpaocount, but the result is however still meaningless and the conflict has to be resolved between Susan and Charley the next time they talk to each other.

Known Uses

LibreSource (Molli et al., 2003) (http://dev.libresource.org/home/doc/so6-user-manual/concepts/ot) models a SHARED FILE REPOSITORY$_{\to 4.1.2}$ and manages different versions of the files it contains. Depending on the type of file, different transformation functions are used to transform concurrent commands and resolve merge conflicts.

The underlying algorithm (called So6) is based on the algorithm explained in the dynamics section of this pattern. Instead of applying it to strings, however, it can be applied to file operations, line insertion and deletion in text files, or tree operations in an XML document. In text files the algorithm checks for insertions and deletions in overlapping blocks of lines. In XML documents, the algorithm synchronizes the insertion and deletion of nodes, while in file systems, the algorithm considers move, update, add, and delete operations.

GROOVE (Ellis and Gibbs, 1989) is the earliest example of the application of OPERATIONAL TRANSFORMATIONS. It was a structured synchronous text editor that made use of a simple transformation function called dOPT (for *distributed Operational Transformation*). Although the transformation function proved to be incorrect (Cormack, 1995a,b), the basic structure for handling remote commands did not change in later implementations. Sun and Ellis (1998b) collected and discussed other examples of text editors that make use of OPERATIONAL TRANSFORMATION.

Related Patterns

LOVELY BAGS$_{\to 5.3.5}$ are another way of increasing concurrency. While OPERATIONAL TRANSFORMATION focuses on modifying the way in which model objects are modified, LOVELY BAGS change the model's internal representation in such a way that the modifying operation will have better concurrency behavior.

CONFLICT DETECTION$_{\to 5.3.3}$ discusses how conflicting activities can be found.

CHANGE LOG. A change log (Anderson, 2000) stores different states of an object or an object's attribute together with additional information on the originator of the change. It is comparable to the execution history that is necessary for OPERATIONAL TRANSFORMATION.

5.3.5 Lovely Bags

bag (băg), NOUN: **1a. A container of flexible material, such as paper, plastic, or leather, that is used for carrying or storing items. b.** A handbag; a purse. **c.** A piece of hand luggage, such as a suitcase or satchel. **d.** An organic sac or pouch, such as the udder of a cow. **2.** An object that resembles a pouch. **3.** *Nautical* The sagging or bulging part of a sail.

Intent

Use bags to store shared objects in a container because they provide the best concurrency behavior.

Context

You are using mechanisms for CONFLICT DETECTION$_{\to 5.3.3}$. Now you are thinking about reducing the number of conflicting changes.

Problem

Access operations to shared container objects change the contents of the container by adding or removing elements. Most of these operations are very poor in terms of concurrency. This makes synchronous collaboration on container objects often seem impossible.

Scenario

Martin and Weigang communicate using a chat system that is implemented using replicated objects. They thought that this would work well, but the chat often rejects messages and signals that there are concurrent changes. So they consult Charley, who is a real expert on concurrency issues. Charley finds out that the problem is that each contribution is reflected in the shared object model by appending the contribution to a long string. After Charley spots this, it's clear to him that this cannot be good in terms of concurrency, because the append operation modifies the same shared object, leading to different strings depending on the order in which the appends are performed.

Symptoms

You should consider applying this pattern when . . .

— Access operations to container objects are often rejected because two concurrent changes cannot be executed in different orders.

Solution

Therefore: Wherever a high degree of concurrency is needed, model your container objects by means of a bag. If the container's entries need to be ordered, equip the data entries with an order criterion that can be uniquely assigned by each client, such as the current time stamp plus a unique client ID, but still store the entries in the bag.

Dynamics

The main participant is the bag. The bag is a shared container object that can hold references to other objects. It allows duplicates and does not care about the order of the contained elements. From a mathematical point of view, bags are often called *multisets*. Clients perform operations on the bag concurrently. These operations are in most cases commutative because of the ignored order and allowed duplicates. In cases in which the bag may only grow, you no longer have to check for consistency, since clients will never perform operations that are not commutative. In cases in which the clients also remove elements from the bag, ensure that the clients have mechanisms for CONFLICT DETECTION$_{\to 5.3.3}$.

When order is needed while iterating over the collection locally, the collection will be ordered before iterating over it. This conversion requires that the contained elements provide one or more attributes that can be used as sorting criteria.

Rationale

The simple explanation of why this pattern works lies in the "lovely" nature of bags: a bag does not care about order and contained elements in the same way that other container classes do.

Compared to an ordered container object where the add operations are related to an insertion position, such as arrays or lists, bags produce the same result if two elements are added in different orders.

Compared to container objects in which add operations depend on the current set of included objects, such as sets or dictionaries, bags produce the same results if an element is already present in the bag and two clients perform an add and a remove of the object concurrently.

This is illustrated in Figure 5.16. On the left two users collaborate on a list. The list has the initial state abc. Then $User_1$ adds d while $User_2$ adds e at the same time. After both clients have performed their operation, they perform DECENTRALIZED

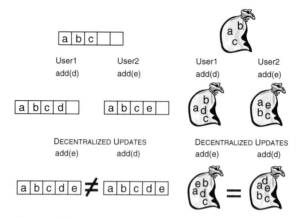

Figure 5.16 Concurrent accesses to lists and bags

UPDATES$_{\rightarrow 5.2.6}$. But since $User_1$'s state differs from $User_2$'s state, they will get different states if they perform the updates. One operation must therefore be undone.

Now consider the right of Figure 5.16: again, the users performed changes and DECENTRALIZED UPDATES$_{\rightarrow 5.2.6}$. But now, the add operations can be performed, since adds do not depend on the object's state or the (non-existent) order of its elements. Both users reach a consistent state after the updates.

In cases in which order is needed, it is often possible to restore this order. Consider for example a sorted collection: this class type ensures that elements stored in instances of sorted collections will be stored according to the sorting order (or iterated according to the sorting order). The main reason for using such a sorted data structure is to speed up the process of iterating over the elements in order.

If a bag needs to be iterated in a sorted way, you can first convert it to a (local) sorted collection, then iterate over the local copy. The ordering, which drastically decreases the possibility of concurrent operations on the data structure, is thus restored locally where needed. This makes access to the ordered collection slower, and requires that each client sorts the elements, but it makes the data structure more robust for concurrent manipulations.

Another reason for storing objects in an ordered collection is the desire to access it via an index. This is often to speed up iteration, for example by using a counter for the index when iterating over an array in Java. As with a sorted access order, the iteration speed is less critical than the lesser degree of concurrency. If the container object needs to be iterated frequently, you can perform the iterations on local copies of the replicated object, which remain valid until the replicated object is changed.

Check

When applying this pattern, you should answer these questions:

- Do the shared objects provide a natural order? If yes, which attributes can be used to order the shared object? If no, can you add an attribute that creates a natural order, such as the combination of client id and creation timestamp?
- What do you need order for? Is it possible to ignore the order?
- Is it feasible to order the objects on the fly, or will you use a local cache in which the bag is ordered and updated whenever the elements change?

Danger Spots

Unfortunately, even a lovely bag is still vulnerable to remove operations. If the same element is removed and added at the same time and the bag did not previously include the element, this will result in different bag states depending on the order of the operations. Prohibiting removes could therefore be an option.

In some cases, arrays can be as attractive as bags, or even more attractive: when the number of elements does not change often and an entry in the array is accessed by its index without relation to the other elements, this change is concurrent to all changes at other array positions. If the array should change its size, however, or have a shared index as a current index, these attributes will reduce the degree of possible concurrent changes on the array.

Sorting large sets may take some time. In cases in which insert operations must be applied to local data, you could consider using a cached sorted replica and inserting new elements using an insertion sort.

Known Uses

Chat in FUB. FUB (Haake and Schümmer, 2003) is a system built on top of COAST for supporting brainstorming in the context of distributed collaborative learning. Its users are provided with two different kinds of chat: a "brainstorming" chat, as well as a "discussion chat" where concepts are discussed. While the brainstorming chat does not require any ordering, allowing it to be directly modeled using a bag, the discussion chat needs to ensure that all chat entries are shown in the same order for all users.

The discussion chat is therefore modeled as a set of chat entries. Each entry has a timestamp that represents the (synchronized) time when the entry was added at the originating client. For displaying the chat log, all entries are sorted with the timestamp as primary key and the message text as a secondary key. This ensures that all entries are shown in the same order at each client.

Arrangement of Messages in Usenet (Horton and Adams, 1987). Usenet newsgroups are represented semantically as trees of messages that model the reply relationships between messages. While these could have been explicitly modeled at the news server, the designers instead decided to hide them within the news entries.

Each entry has a unique id which is determined by the client that generated the entry. The entry can relate to a parent message, while the parent message is not changed at all (it does not know about its child messages). All entries are then stored in an unspecified collection by the server. The important issue here is that the protocol does not demand any order for the entries. When clients request entries, they can ask for a chronologically sorted version, which will then be generated by inspecting the timestamps of the messages.

Related Patterns

PESSIMISTIC LOCKING$_{\rightarrow 5.3.1}$ When the application requires an ordered bag, an additional computation overhead is added to the application, since sorting takes time. This may slow down the responsiveness of the application. If the ordering process takes more time than obtaining a lock, as suggested in PESSIMISTIC LOCKING, you should use a locking mechanism instead.

CONFLICT DETECTION$_{\rightarrow 5.3.3}$ Inconsistencies can occur even when using LOVELY BAGS. CONFLICT DETECTION allows these inconsistencies to be detected.

OPERATIONAL TRANSFORMATION$_{\rightarrow 5.3.4}$ describes another way of increasing the number of possible concurrent changes.

5.3.6 Immutable Versions   *

im·mu·ts·ble (ĭ-myōō'tə-bəl), ADJECTIVE: **Not subject or susceptible to change.**

Intent

Store different versions of a shared object as a version tree.

Context

Users are collaborating with shared objects.

Problem

Performing complex modifications on a shared object usually takes time and requires cognitive effort on the part of the user. If users act on the same shared objects, the probability of conflicting changes increases. However, to discard one of the conflicting changes is inappropriate, since its originator has already expended much effort in performing the change.

Scenario

Charley and Susan both had a free weekend and used this to make the encryption facilities of the game engine more secure. Susan had the bright idea of using elliptic curve cryptography. She changed a set of ten classes and checked in her changes when she came back to the office on Monday. Charley was in favor of using an ElGamal encryption scheme based on discrete logarithms. He changed seven classes and wanted to commit them at midday on Monday. Unfortunately, there is a conflict with three classes, but since Charley simply does not care about elliptic curves, he ignored Susan's changes and committed his classes. The whole build was then broken, since parts of Susan's code were still in the system.

Symptoms

You should consider applying this pattern when . . .

— Users change shared objects concurrently.
— Users modify local replicas of shared objects.
— Users overwrite each others' changes.
— Users are interested in the history of a shared object.

Solution

Therefore: Store all shared objects in a version tree. Make sure that the versions stored in the version tree are immutable, such that they cannot afterwards be changed. Store modifications of a shared object as new versions. Ask users to merge parallel versions in the version tree unless they explicitly branch the version tree.

Dynamics

All versions of a shared object are stored in a version tree. The version tree allows the current version of a shared object, as well as specific versions, to be requested. Whenever a new version is created, a new node is added to the version tree as a child of the preceding version.

The nodes of the version tree can either contain a copy of the shared object in its respective version, the changes that lead to the version when applied to the preceding version, or the differences between the respective version and the preceding version. In all cases, it is important to decide when a new version should be created. This can be done automatically by the system whenever a change is performed or when a user explicitly commits a change.

Figure 5.17 shows a typical evolution of a version tree for a shared object. In Figure 5.17 (a), a user modifies the version V1 of a shared object, which leads to version V2. In Figure 5.17 (b), the version V3 is created and in Figure 5.17 (c) another user creates version V4. The versions V3 and V4 both have the same predecessor V2, which indicates that two users have created a new version starting from version V2. Thus, V3 and V4 are parallel versions. In Figure 5.17 (d) a further parallel version V5 has been created.

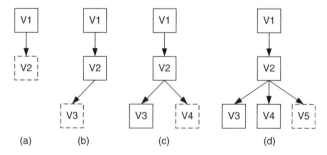

Figure 5.17 Immutable versions tree

In Figure 5.17 (d), V3, V4, and V5 all have the same preceding version V2. These versions exist in parallel. Depending on the collaboration process, there are various ways of handling these parallel versions:

— If it is not necessary to have a single explicit current version, the different branches of the shared object can be kept in parallel.

— If it *is* necessary to have a single explicit current version, the parallel versions must be merged. This can be done either by requesting users to merge the parallel versions manually, or by applying OPERATIONAL TRANSFORMATIONS$_{\to 5.3.4}$.

Rationale

As all versions of a shared object are stored within the version tree, users can modify their local replicas of shared objects concurrently without overwriting each others' changes. Furthermore, the version tree lets them request the newest version of a shared object, as well as specific versions, allowing them to review the history of a shared object.

Check

When applying this pattern, you should answer these questions:

— Are you going to manage the version tree as CENTRALIZED OBJECT$_{\to 5.2.1}$ or REPLICATED OBJECT$_{\to 5.2.3}$?

— Are you going to store the changes that lead to a new version, the differences between two versions, or the versions themselves?

— When are you going to publish a new version? Whenever users change replicas locally, or when they explicitly commit new versions?

— Are you going to offer a user interface for selecting and reviewing the different versions of a shared object?

Danger Spots

Depending on the size of a shared object, storing all the different versions of a shared object can require a lot of memory space. If memory space is limited, you should instead store the changes that lead from one version to another, or the differences between two versions.

Merging different versions can be difficult and time-consuming. If users have to merge versions often, you should offer tools that support merging, for example by highlighting the differences between versions.

Storing different versions of a shared object in a tree increases its access time. If the differences between the versions are stored rather than the versions themselves, access time is increased even further.

If several users are changing a shared object there is a chance of concurrency conflicts when updating the version tree. To overcome this issue, use Lovely Bags$_{\rightarrow 5.3.5}$ for the nodes of the version tree.

Known Uses

Concurrent Versions System (CVS) is a version control system that keeps track of all changes in a set of files. It is typically used in the implementation of a software project and allows several developers to collaborate. The files are stored on a central server that allows users to commit a new version of a file, retrieve the current or a specific version of a file, or create a different version branch for a file. To support this, the server stores all the changes that lead from one version to another.

CURE is web-based collaborative learning platform (Haake et al., 2004c) that allows users to share and edit Wiki pages, as well as documents. CURE and its extension offlineCURE (Lukosch et al., 2006) use Immutable Versions to store the different versions of all artifacts. In case of conflicting versions, CURE requests the user to manually resolve the conflict.

GINA is a framework that supports the development of groupware (Berlage and Genau, 1993) and enables synchronous collaboration by supporting replicated objects. GINA understands the history of a replicated object as an operation tree. This tree stores the operations that lead from one version to another. GINA uses this tree for undo/redo mechanisms, optimistic concurrency control, accessing different object versions, and object merging.

Related Patterns

Lovely Bags$_{\rightarrow 5.3.5}$ allows concurrent modifications of nodes when used for the implementation of the version tree.

Centralized Objects$_{\rightarrow 5.2.1}$ or Replicated Objects$_{\rightarrow 5.2.3}$ can be implemented using Immutable Versions to allow concurrent modifications.

Optimistic Concurrency Control$_{\rightarrow 5.3.2}$ allows shared objects to be changed optimistically and conflicting changes rolled back instead of storing all versions of a shared object.

Private Versioning (Coplien and Harrison, 2004) highlights the fact that individual users may need to keep versions of changed artifacts private until the quality of the artifact has reached a state that complies with the group's quality standards.

EDITION (Anderson, 2000) addresses a comparable problem by arguing that each change to an object should result in a new version of the object, called an *edition*. The edition, in addition, keeps track of the event (or activity) that led to the state change in the object.

5.3.7 Control me... applied

Achieving consistency in the pair-programming plug-in was quite easy. The main reason for this is that the different roles of the users define which artifacts they are allowed to change. According to the FLOOR CONTROL$_{\to 4.1.7}$ pattern, only the driver can change the text of the source code or the position of the cursor.

The situation is different if we consider the case of the shared diagram editor. Here, everyone is allowed to add scribbles and other diagram elements at the same time. They are also allowed to move elements without having to lock them in advance.

This higher level of concurrency was achieved by using an OPTIMISTIC CONCURRENCY CONTROL$_{\to 5.3.2}$ strategy. The diagram canvas and all diagram elements were modeled as REPLICATED OBJECTS$_{\to 5.2.3}$. If Susan for example changes the position of a rectangle with the id r4711, a ChangePosition command is created, sent to the server, and applied to her local replica of the rectangle object. This command contains the following information:

```
ChangePositionCommand c1
    receiver: rectangle r4711
    versionNumber: 0815
    parameters: [17,200]
```

The server performs CONFLICT DETECTION$_{\to 5.3.3}$ by comparing its local version number for the rectangle that has the id r4711 with the version number 0815 contained in the command object. If a conflict is detected, for example if the server also has a version 0815 of the same rectangle, it sends its rectangle the message moveto(17,200) and also distributes the change to all subscribers of the rectangle.

If the server however has a newer version, it sends the originator of the move command a message with the new state of the object. If for example Paul has moved the rectangle to another position before Susan's change is received, the server will send the new state of the rectangle to Susan. The system signals to Susan that a change failed, for example by playing a sound, and displays Paul's state of the same rectangle.

To enhance concurrency, some attributes were implemented as LOVELY BAGS$_{\to 5.3.5}$. One example was the components attribute of the diagram canvas. This allows the server to accept concurrent add operations, so that Susan and Paul could add elements to a diagram at the same time.

CHAPTER 6

Examples of Applying the Pattern Language

In the final chapter we present two examples of collaborative systems and highlight the patterns from our pattern language in these examples. We decided to use the shared workspace system BSCW as an example of asynchronous groupware and the CoWord system as an example of synchronous groupware.

The BSCW system is—besides electronic mail, newsgroups, and instant messaging applications—probably one of the most widely used systems for distributed collaborative work (Bentley et al., 1997a,b; Appelt and Mambrey, 1999; Appelt, 2001; Klöckner, 2002; Orbiteam, 2006). BSCW is an acronym for Basic Support for Collaborative Work. The goal of the system is to provide shared workspaces in which users can collaborate asynchronously. After its first public release in 1995, many thousand installations have been installed and several hundred thousand users have registered with the various BSCW servers. The system is currently offered in a commercial version by OrbiTeam Software, a German software company that collaborates closely with the CSCW (Computer Supported Collaborative Work) research division of Fraunhofer FIT. A free evaluation copy of BSCW and a free license for educational use can be obtained from the OrbiTeam home page at http://www.bscw.de/english/.

CoWord transforms the off-the-shelf single-user application Microsoft Word into a SHARED EDITOR$_{\rightarrow 4.1.6}$ (Sun et al., 2004; Xia et al., 2004; Sun et al., 2006). CoWord supports Microsoft Word 2000, XP, 2003 and even allows users to use different Word versions for SHARED EDITING. When collaborating, users may freely and concurrently edit any object of any type, for example formatted texts, graphic objects, and so on. During this collaboration CoWord ensures the consistency of the edited document. Compared with single-user applications that are reused for collaboration via APPLICATION SHARING$_{\rightarrow 4.1.5}$, CoWord is fully collaboration-aware. A free version of the software can be downloaded from the CoOffice home page at http://cooffice.ntu.edu.sg/coword.

Several aspects influenced our decision to choose these two systems for investigation:

— While BSCW has a special focus on asynchronous collaboration, CoWord has its strengths in synchronous collaboration. This dualism makes it possible to look at the pattern language from two different perspectives.

— Both systems tell a success story: BSCW has attracted a very large number of users and CoWord extends the most widely used word processing system, which makes it relevant to a very large audience.

— We were not personally involved in the development of either system. This gave us an objective view of the implementations and enabled us to show that our patterns represent best practice in the community.

Both the BSCW development team—including members of OrbiTeam and members of Fraunhofer FIT—and the CoWord development team agreed to discuss their implementation decisions with us and support us in the search for patterns in their systems. This last issue is important, because it provides additional evidence of whether or not a specific pattern was intended in the development, and whether or not an extension with additional patterns would fit into the development scope of the teams.

From a methodological perspective, we performed interviews with the developers and made them aware of the patterns. These interviews were conducted in a collocated session in the case of BSCW and by e-mail in the case of CoWord. The developers then confirmed the existence or the absence of each pattern. In both systems, the analysis first focused on patterns that could be detected from examining the user interface. In the second phase we discussed the applications' internal architecture with the teams.

In the third stage we identified possible extensions in the systems. This identification was pattern-driven, which means that we looked at patterns that are related to the patterns that were already in place in the systems. In many cases the development teams agreed to the requirement posed by the pattern and said that they could imagine implementing these patterns in a future version of the software.

The next two sections describe the patterns found in the tools. Each section internally follows the structure of the three main clusters of our pattern language which means that we first look at community support, followed by the support for group work, and finally a discussion of base technology.

6.1 BSCW

Figure 6.1 shows the patterns we found in BSCW. 49% of the patterns in our language can be found in BSCW. These patterns focus mainly on structuring asynchronous interaction, as BSCW is only concerned with asynchronous interaction. In the cluster on group support and the cluster on base technology particularly, we found most of the asynchronous patterns implemented in BSCW. The reason for this is that, unlike in specialized support tools for collaboration, the design goal of BSCW was to cover most of the collaboration settings that occur when teams collaborate at distance.

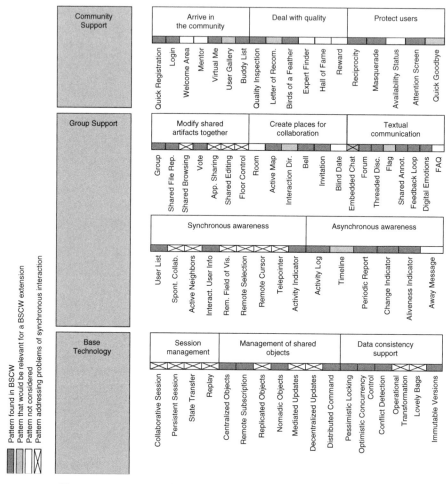

Figure 6.1 Pattern clusters for which known uses exist in BSCW

BSCW is based on the metaphor of a shared workspace, an instance of the SHARED FILE REPOSITORY$_{\rightarrow 4.1.2}$ pattern. Users place documents and other artifacts in folders, for which the users can have different access rights. To modify the documents, users copy them to their local computer and apply the changes in individual work. After finishing their modifications, the users upload the modified file to the shared workspace so that it becomes visible to other group members. This document-centered collaboration is complemented by different means for communication and awareness mechanisms.

Patterns for community support are mainly not implemented in BSCW. This seemed remarkable at first sight, but after talking about it with BSCW's developers it became clear that BSCW's goal was to provide a platform for teams in which the team members already knew one another. The incentives for participating in the community played only a subordinate role. The assumption instead was that the teams had previously agreed on a common goal and that all members had a common incentive for reaching this goal.

6.1.1 Community Support

Arrive in the Community

Before users can access artifacts they have to LOGIN$_{\rightarrow 3.1.2}$ to the system. BSCW uses standard HTTP authentication mechanisms to prompt users for their user name and password. After users successfully log in to the system, they can enter their personal workspace. All other workspaces that they can access are projected into this workspace and the full path of workspaces is always visible on the screen. This ensures that users stay aware of the identity they used to log in.

When users forgot their password, they are taken to an error page that explains how they can select a new password. This is implemented by allowing users to go through the QUICK REGISTRATION$_{\rightarrow 3.1.1}$ process more than once.

QUICK REGISTRATION$_{\rightarrow 3.1.1}$ can be configured by the system administrator to keep it simple. In the simplest case, the system only requests the user's e-mail address, but the administrator can also make additional fields such as name and address mandatory (Figure 6.2–2). After submitting an e-mail address, BCSW creates an account and guides the user through the next steps of the registration process (Figure 6.2–3). They first receive an e-mail with a link pointing to an account activation web page (Figure 6.2–4)—note that the link has a ONE-TIME PASSWORD TOKEN (Schumacher et al., 2005) so that the user can only open the account activation page once. On the account activation page, the user can provide a username and a password (Figure 6.2–5) and finally activate the account.

One problem with the registration process is that users in some cases perform the first steps (provide their e-mail address on the registration page), but forget to click on the verification link. In this case, their account is not yet ready to use but they are already visible in the BSCW system. However, other users can see that the new user

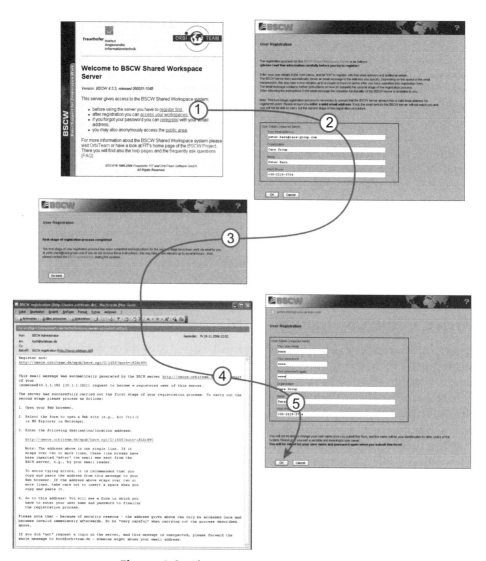

Figure 6.2 The registration process in BSCW

has already been invited to the workspace but has not yet completed the registration process: the system displays the new user's e-mail address rather than user name. Thereby, the current group members are reminded to re-invite new users if they do not finish the registration process.

Another suggestion for improvement that emerged from carefully reading the danger spots of the QUICK REGISTRATION pattern is the selection of a user name. If a user name is already used, the BSCW system simply reports an error message. It could instead make suggestions for unused user names.

Once registered in the system, users can provide more personal information on a personal page (see VIRTUAL ME$_{\rightarrow 3.1.5}$ and Figure 6.3). Whenever users' account names are shown in the system, they link to these personal home pages, on which users can provide a picture, details about their organization, some trivia, and their time zone. The latter is used to personalize the display of any time information in BSCW.

Figure 6.3 VIRTUAL ME by means of a personal profile page

One improvement that could be made based on the VIRTUAL ME pattern would be to show the user's real name whenever users are mentioned, or even the real name and the user's picture. This would make the interaction more authentic than just using the user's account name. However, it can lead to ambiguous names in the system, since real names do not have to be unique.

The users' names can be collected in a personal address book (see BUDDY LIST$_{\rightarrow 3.1.7}$ and Figure 6.4). BCSW's developers preferred this approach instead of using a global USER GALLERY$_{\rightarrow 3.1.6}$ because they assumed that a large number of registered users would make the USER GALLERY too big. The developers also had security concerns. Since BSCW is designed to support different groups and communities on the same server, it was important that the different projects could not see one another. The drawback of the missing USER GALLERY is that it is more difficult to find other users.

Figure 6.4 A picture showing *Koch*'s address book

The only way to find users who do not have access to a shared workspace is to search for them by entering parts of their name. The search result is a list of account names and full names that links to personal profile pages.

If a USER GALLERY were to be added, it would be necessary to ensure that users could control their privacy—this is not ensured by the current solution in which you can search for any user. Users should be able to configure whether or not they appear in the USER GALLERY.

The developers confirmed that there might be interesting applications for a WELCOME AREA even in contexts where community membership is externally defined. One example is the use of BSCW in commercial contexts: new employees could be featured after they had joined the BSCW system. Currently the only notice about new users is a small note in the PERIODIC REPORT.

Find Relevant Users

BSCW distinguishes between public and private workspaces. Each workspace can be made public, with the effect that all users (even unregistered ones) can access the resources in the workspaces. When making a workspace public, the owner of the workspace can define to what extent moderation—following the QUALITY INSPECTION$_{\to 3.2.1}$ pattern—is desired in the workspace. When a contribution is made to a public moderated workspace, it is initially only visible to the managers of the workspace. The system informs the managers, either directly or in the PERIODIC REPORT$_{\to 4.5.3}$, that a new contribution exists. The managers then have to approve or reject contributions.

Managers can also expel users from a workspace. For public workspaces this is more difficult because users cannot be identified. BSCW has a mechanism for granting access rights to users entering the system from specific networks (identified by their IP address), but there is no explicit exclusion for an IP address.

There is no support for QUALITY INSPECTION for the workspaces of closed groups. The current approach of the BSCW design team is to rely on a social process instead of a formal computer-supported moderation mechanism. However, it could be relevant to have moderation in closed groups when the group is larger and less homogeneous.

The second quality-related pattern—LETTER OF RECOMMENDATION$_{\to 3.2.2}$—is not present in BSCW. Users can rate documents but not their interaction with other users. This is a situation that you often find in community systems: one reason for this may be that the rating of documents rather than people is less offensive. A poor assessment of a document only addresses the author's work, while rating the author addresses the author's personality.

Content rating could be used to find users with comparable interests and create BIRDS OF A FEATHER$_{\to 3.2.3}$. However, this is not done in BSCW. What is done to support the BIRDS OF A FEATHER pattern is to display all editors and readers of a specific document. This information can be visualized in a semantic network containing artifacts and users (see Figure 6.5). The figure shows a user *Elke Hinrichs* in the center. She has created a document called *Feedback*. This document has been read by *Oliver Frietsch* and *Thomas Koch*. This means that these three users form BIRDS OF A FEATHER with respect to this specific document. If we consider the whole set of documents that *Elke Hinrichs* created or read, we can see five closely related users, as well as two users who share only knowledge of one or two documents. However, BSCW has no explicit support for forming BIRDS OF A FEATHER.

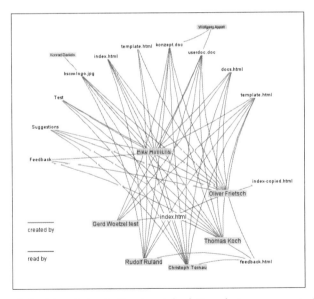

Figure 6.5 Visualizing indirect social relations between users in BSCW

The other patterns in the cluster for dealing with quality address the question of how to find experts in a specific topic and how to keep up a high motivation level for these experts. BSCW does not offer explicit support for this. The only way to find an expert on a specific artifact is to look at the change history of the artifact. If it has been changed mainly by a specific author, one can consider this author as the expert for the artifact. Since there is no further technology support, however, it is still difficult for a user to find the expert on a specific topic.

The lack of a HALL OF FAME$_{\rightarrow 3.2.5}$ is a logical consequence of the lack of an EXPERT FINDER and patternNameLetters of Recommendation. Without these in place, it is not possible to show users in a HALL OF FAME.

Finally, since the designers assumed that the group members have a source of motivation that lies outside the BSCW context, there is no support for acknowledging users following the REWARD$_{\rightarrow 3.2.6}$ pattern.

Protect Users

Privacy issues played an important role in the design of BSCW. Most of this however relates to access right management, which is not covered by the pattern language presented in this book. We were able to identify several patterns from the Security Pattern language (Schumacher et al., 2005) in BSCW, but an in-depth discussion of these patterns is beyond the context of this book.

Several aspects are, however, characteristic of collaborative applications. The most important in connection with security is that of group awareness. BSCW tracks all users' activities and makes them visible to all other users who have at least read access to the corresponding workspaces. The tracking is based on RECIPROCITY$_{\rightarrow 3.3.1}$: users can see which activities were tracked for their VIRTUAL ME$\!$S as well as those for all other users.

The RECIPROCITY found in BSCW does not allow users to control their level of involvement. Users will always share the same amount of data as others unless they connect to the system using anonymous access, following the MASQUERADE$_{\rightarrow 3.3.2}$ pattern. Anonymous access is activated by making a workspace public. Such workspaces can be accessed without authentication so that all users can access the documents and hide their personal identity. This opens up the workspace for any user. There is no way to have anonymous interaction in the group, such as in a brainstorming session where contributions can be made anonymously.

BSCW uses e-mail to keep users informed about changes in their workspaces. This can create an information overload on the recipient. It is important to tailor the notification mechanisms by means of an ATTENTION SCREEN$_{\rightarrow 3.3.4}$. To achieve this, BSCW defines different classes of actions and allows users to define the channel by which they want to be informed about these actions (see Figure 6.6).

The system distinguishes between read, create, move, and change events. These can trigger different awareness channels: event icons as described in CHANGE INDICATOR$_{\rightarrow 4.5.4}$, daily workspace activity reports as described in PERIODIC REPORT$_{\rightarrow 4.5.3}$,

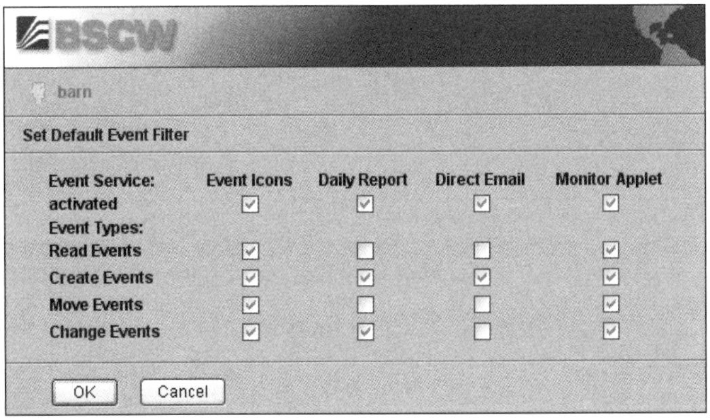

Figure 6.6 Tailoring notification channels in BSCW using an ATTENTION SCREEN

direct e-mails (an e-mail-based ACTIVITY INDICATOR$_{\rightarrow 4.4.9}$), or the monitor applet, which is comparable to a USER LIST$_{\rightarrow 4.4.1}$. The system administrator can define a standard matrix that controls how notifications are sent to users. Each user can also modify the notification profile for each artifact. In this case, the system shows a small exclamation mark next to the artifact to remind the user that this artifact has special notification treatment.

BSCW does not allow users to remove themselves from the system. It is thus difficult to have a QUICK GOODBYE$_{\rightarrow 3.3.5}$. The reason for this is that leaving BSCW completely would in the current implementation require the deletion of user accounts, which is too error prone: users might ask for their accounts to be restored, which would give the system administrators a hard time. When users loose interest in a specific workspace, they can remove themselves from the workspace. This means that they will no longer be able to access workspace resources and that no notifications on events in the workspace will be sent to them. Only administrators can remove accounts completely. On account removal all non-shared (personal) data is removed from the system.

One way to allow users to leave the system entirely would be to tag user accounts as deleted but keep the data. This would ensure that accidentally removed accounts could be restored. Such virtually deleted user accounts would need special treatment in the user interface, which means that this would not be a minor change to BSCW.

6.1.2 Group Support

Modify Shared Artifacts Together

BSCW organizes all shared artifacts in workspaces, implemented as shared folders in a SHARED FILE REPOSITORY$_{\rightarrow 4.1.2}$. Besides documents, users can share tasks, calendars, annotations, and other types of information in the folders.

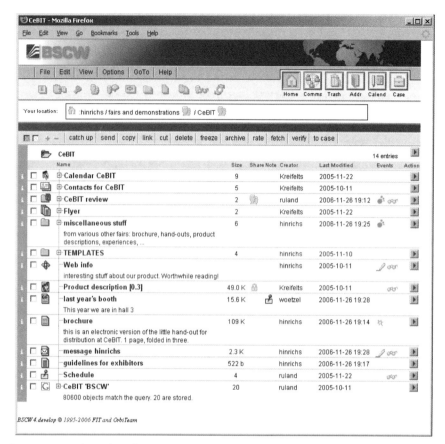

Figure 6.7 Shared workspaces are the BSCW representation of a SHARED FILE SYSTEM

Figure 6.7 is an example of a shared workspace. It shows the documents stored in the workspace, as well as folders, discussions, and stored web queries.

Users can invite other users to any artifact in the shared workspace, including the workspace itself. All users who have access rights to an artifact form a GROUP$_{\to 4.1.1}$. The user interface allows only users to be associated workspaces, although internally this restriction is not mandatory. Conceptually there is a 1:1 relationship between workspaces and groups. Each workspace can be accessed by exactly one group and each group has its home in exactly one workspace. When users are asked to participate in a workspace, the system adds the user to the group that is associated with the workspace.

As proposed by the GROUP pattern, groups can be treated in the same way as individual users, with the effect that groups can be invited to a workspace. If groups are invited to a specific workspace, the workspace will be shown as part of the group's workspace structure (as a sub-workspace of the group's root workspace). If in contrast individual users are invited, they will see the workspace as a new root workspace.

Inviting other groups to a shared workspace requires at least one common workspace with the invited group—to know that the group exists—since groups are invisible to non-group members. This is required because information on group membership should be kept private. However, the system offers query functions by which users can find all groups they have in common with other users.

Creating efficient workspace layouts and memberships is a non-trivial task in BSCW. The designers suggest that you initially create shared workspaces that reflect your company's organization. Each division would then have a shared workspace. From there on, you should invite these groups to other workspaces, so that you can for example have a workspace shared by two divisions. Part of this complexity evolves from the 1:1 relationship between the hierarchical workspace structure and potentially arbitrary group membership. However, the coupling of group membership with artifacts also has the advantage that groups are created implicitly.

From a group process perspective, BSCW offers support for the creation and execution of workflows and additional coordination support by means of circulation folders, task lists, and group calendars that can be shared among all members of a workspace. It also provides a tool for creating and executing a VOTE$_{\rightarrow 4.1.4}$.

Voting is organized in two phases: the set-up phase in which the creator of the vote defines the questions, and the execution phase.

To create a new vote, a vote object is added to the shared workspace and one or more question on which feedback is required are added (Figure 6.8).

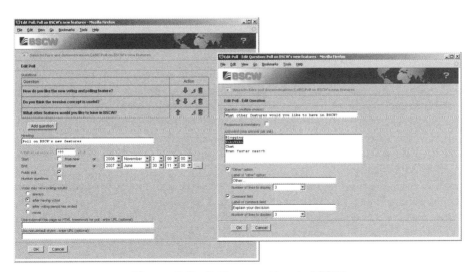

Figure 6.8 Setting up a VOTE in BSCW

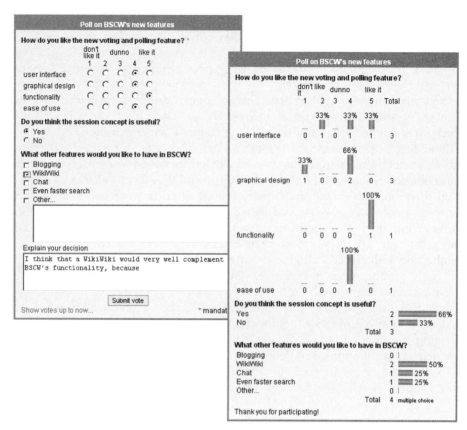

Figure 6.9 Participating in a VOTE

After the vote has been created, users can open it and see the different questions and options (Figure 6.9 left). Each user is only allowed to submit one voting form. Since votes can also be public, BSCW sets cookies to ensure that users can only vote once. However, this can be bypassed by removing the cookies locally and voting again. At the server votes are stored anonymously. After voting users can see the results, as shown on the right of Figure 6.9: the vote creator can define when the results become visible.

BSCW limits its support for SHARED BROWSING$_{\rightarrow 4.1.3}$ to a means for collecting and commenting references to web pages. This can be considered as a minimal version of the concurrent browsing described in the SHARED BROWSING pattern, but it lacks important features. For example, users are not aware of pages that have already been visited by other group members.

Since BSCW was intentionally designed for asynchronous interaction, its developers did not consider more sophisticated support for SHARED BROWSING, SHARED

EDITING, or APPLICATION SHARING$_{\rightarrow 4.1.5}$. The latter may be worth considering when groups want to collaborate more closely on documents stored in the shared workspace. Currently, one user would have to download the shared document, open it locally, start an application sharing system, then tell other users to which computer they should connect.

Create Places for Collaboration

The APPLICATION SHARING scenario mentioned above points to a problem that is solved by the ROOM$_{\rightarrow 4.2.1}$ pattern: for collaboration, users have to share documents, establish communication channels, and launch the collaborative tools that support tighter collaboration on the documents. Due to the asynchronous nature of BSCW, it does not support this shift from asynchronous to synchronous interaction, as it would be supported by the ROOM pattern.

However, if we ignore synchronous collaboration and communication aspects and assume that all the tools that are required to edit shared documents are embedded in the users' web browsers, we could consider the shared workspaces as lightweight ROOMs. This makes sense if we take a closer look at the patterns related to the ROOM pattern and how they are implemented in BSCW. We will first look at means for joining a workspace, then show how workspace structures are represented.

Joining a Workspace. There are basically two ways to become a member of a shared workspace: an INVITATION$_{\rightarrow 4.2.5}$ and a BELL$_{\rightarrow 4.2.4}$. If users want to become members of a shared workspace they have to contact the manager of the workspace directly and ask for an invitation. However, since there is no INTERACTION DIRECTORY$_{\rightarrow 4.2.3}$ that lists *all* workspaces, users will neither be able to find the workspace nor who the manager is. Remember that this is consistent with the assumption that the groups in BSCW should form externally and create their collaboration space after they know who will participate.

The only exceptions to this rule are community spaces. These are workspaces that are visible to the public. These are the only workspaces that are listed in an INTERACTION DIRECTORY$_{\rightarrow 4.2.3}$. Users can request membership of a community space by sending a message to the manager of the community space. Sending this message is explicitly supported from within BSCW by a context menu item for requesting membership (see Figure 6.10). It is therefore a simple implementation of the BELL$_{\rightarrow 4.2.4}$ pattern. If more than one user acts as a manager of the community space, all of them receive a membership request. The request includes a link to accept the request. If the membership request should be rejected, the manager has to use other communication channels to inform the requesting user. Since more than one user may receive the request, it is sufficient that at least one manager accepts it. If more than one manager accepts the request, the requesting user will receive multiple positive responses, but will only have a single membership in the community. In the case of denial of the request, the other managers are not informed, with the result that they might still invite the requesting user.

516 Chapter 6 Examples of Applying the Pattern Language

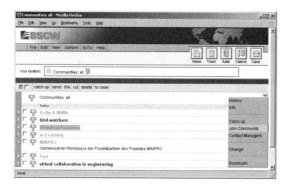

Figure 6.10 Requesting membership in a community space (BELL)

This behavior seems odd at a first glance, but it is related to the philosophy of how members should be added to a workspace: it is sufficient to receive an INVITATION$_{\rightarrow 4.2.5}$ from one user who has the right to invite others. If multiple users have this right, they need to agree on new members at a social protocol level, but the system does not prevent users inviting members against the wishes of the group.

From a user interface perspective, an invitation is expressed by providing either invited users' user names or e-mail addresses (see Figure 6.11). Users already known to the system will be automatically added to the workspace. Users who do not yet have a LOGIN$_{\rightarrow 3.1.2}$ to the system will receive an account creation verification e-mail (see the discussion of the QUICK REGISTRATION pattern). Users cannot reject an invitation, but they can ignore it. They will not receive awareness information about activities in the workspace before they register fully: the only information they receive is the invitation e-mail and information about the existence of the workspace and the member inviting them.

Figure 6.11 Creating an INVITATION in BSCW

An enhancement, especially for large groups, could be to allow users to vote on the acceptance of new members. In the case of a BELL, this would mean that all community managers could vote to accept or reject a membership request and that membership is granted after a specific quorum is reached. In the case of INVITATIONS, a predefined quorum of users would have to agree to the invitation before it is transmitted to the new member.

Visualizing Workspace Structures. Within several scientific projects the developers of BSCW explored the application of maps to display the arrangement of shared workspaces and the activities that take place in the workspaces.

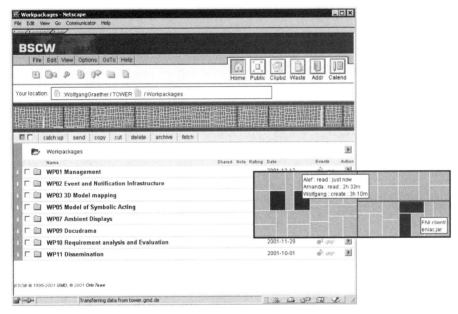

Figure 6.12 SmartMaps in BSCW

SmartMaps (Gräther and Prinz, 2003) shown in Figure 6.12 arrange the folders and artifacts in a shared workspace as treemaps (the TREEMAP pattern, (Tidwell, 2006)). Areas where activities take place are shown in a different color. It is possible to find out more about the activities and the artifacts by exploring the map with the mouse and inspecting the datatip messages (DATATIPS pattern, (Tidwell, 2006)).

SwapIt (Becks and Seeling, 2004) is another visualization and exploration environment that helps to explore the artifacts and activities in a BSCW workspace. It shows clusters of documents on a graphical map (Figure 6.13). Documents are automatically arranged according to their semantic relationships. Users can select

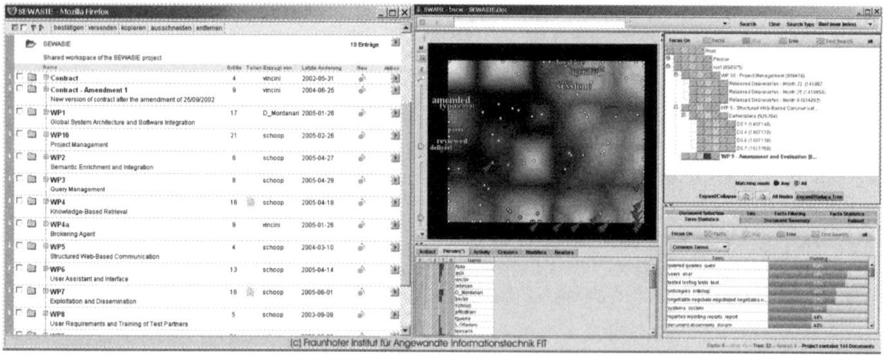

518 Chapter 6 Examples of Applying the Pattern Language

Figure 6.13 SwapIt creates semantic clusters of documents stored in BSCW

regions of this map and receive further details and statistics related to the region. In the context of BSCW, the additional information includes the activities that took place in a BSCW workspace and their performers. Filters can narrow the displayed information, which makes it easier to find activities that are related to a specific area of interest. Colors are used to display connections between information selected in various sub-windows.

Finally, the TOWER project (Pankoke-Babatz et al., 2004) created a three-dimensional map of the shared workspace, called DocuDrama, that is inhabited with avatars representing users (Figure 6.14). When users browse through the shared workspaces, their avatars move on the map as well. When they perform activities on artifacts stored in the shared workspace, their avatars play out symbolic

Figure 6.14 A three-dimensional active map in TOWER

actions that correspond to the respective activities. The developers tested this map as an additional awareness mechanism in distributed teams that have collocated sub-teams. The map was projected in public spaces to raise the awareness of other users' current actions.

Textual Communication

Just as it does for collaboration support, the communication support of BSCW concentrates on asynchronous communication. Users can create Forums$_{\rightarrow 4.3.2}$ that are bound to and stored in a shared workspace. Entries in the Forum are shown as Threaded Discussions$_{\rightarrow 4.3.3}$ (see Figure 6.15). While reading the entries, users can reply to the messages and thereby create a Feedback Loop$_{\rightarrow 4.3.6}$.

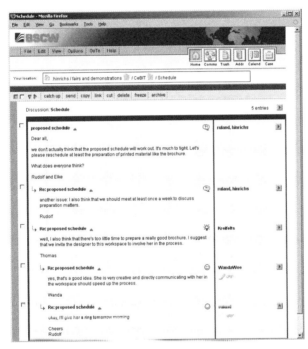

Figure 6.15 A forum in BSCW, including messages of different types

All entries in the forum have to be assigned a specific type. This helps to structure a discussion better. The BSCW administrator can configure the list of available contribution types and give each message type an icon, used when entries of the specific type are shown. In a standard BSCW installation, for example, there are entry types for ideas, notes, pro, contra, expression of anger, and markers for important notes. By selecting an appropriate message type, users can add DIGITAL EMOTIONS$_{\rightarrow 4.3.7}$ to an entire message. However, there is no support for expressing emotions within the messages.

Whether or not entries are sent directly to group members depends on the configuration of their awareness profile (see ATTENTION SCREEN$_{\rightarrow 3.3.4}$). Users who want to be notified directly when a new message is added can enable e-mail notifications on the specific forum.

Messages can be annotated as well as documents. This is implemented by adding a new discussion to the annotated element that serves as a SHARED ANNOTATION$_{\rightarrow 4.3.5}$. Annotating only parts of a specific document or message is not supported by BSCW.

Synchronous Awareness

The patterns for synchronous awareness (see Section 4.4) are in the main not supported, due to the asynchronous nature of BSCW. The only synchronous awareness mechanism is the BSCW monitor applet (see Figure 6.16): this applet enables observation of activities performed by users listed in an address book.

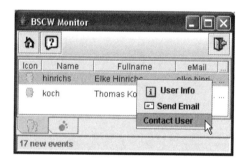

Figure 6.16 The BSCW Monitor applet

The applet provides a synchronous USER LIST$_{\rightarrow 4.4.1}$ but its focus is not bound to a specific workspace. It shows what the users are currently doing (not shown in Figure 6.16). Finally, users can activate a context menu on other users' names to interact with them.

Figure 6.16 shows two collocated users called *hinrichs* and *koch*. By using the context menu, one user could for example write a new e-mail message to the other. The user representation is thus connected to the actions that can be performed with this user, as is suggested in the INTERACTIVE USER INFO$_{\rightarrow 4.4.4}$ pattern.

Actions in general can be directly transmitted to users if they run an external BSCW awareness client. BSCW's TickerTape (Figure 6.17) shows relevant events as they occur, as described in the ACTIVITY INDICATOR$_{\rightarrow 4.4.9}$ pattern.

Figure 6.17 BSCW TickerTape

All the awareness patterns mentioned above can also be found in an asynchronous variant in BSCW. The USER LIST$_{\rightarrow 4.4.1}$, for example, maps to the list of activities stored for each artifact, so that users can see who has read the artifacts.

A TIMELINE$_{\rightarrow 4.5.2}$ is an example of a transformation from a primarily asynchronous setting to a synchronous setting. This is performed in the BSCW TrafficVisualizer applet (Figure 6.18). This applet shows a diagram of users who have performed activities during recent days. The users are represented as small filled circles, except for the local user, who is represented by a square. Depending on the type of their activity, they are placed at a different radius in the diagram. Users who only changed artifacts are placed between 11 and 12 o'clock in the diagram, while users who only read content are positioned between 12 and 1 o'clock. The longer ago the activity was, the more distant from the center is the user's position. The diagram can be read with different goals in mind: users interested in other users who currently share the same focus (USER LIST$_{\rightarrow 4.4.1}$) would look at those positioned in the center, while users interested in who has changed documents would look at those appearing in the 9–12 o'clock region of the diagram. A more traditional TIMELINE (called a *TOA diagram*) was implemented and described for BSCW by Pankoke-Babatz et al. (2004).

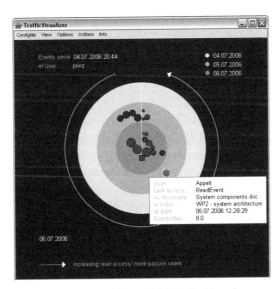

Figure 6.18 The BSCW Traffic Visualizer

Asynchronous Awareness

BSCW offers two different visualizations for understanding past activities: the CHANGE INDICATOR→4.5.4 and a PERIODIC REPORT→4.5.3, which it refers to as a *daily workspace activity report*.

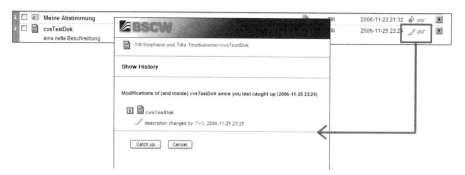

Figure 6.19 Change Indicators in BSCW and the corresponding list of activities

CHANGE INDICATORS show that a document has been changed recently (Figure 6.19). When a change activity on an artifact has taken place, a pen icon is attached to the artifact. In contrast to the collaborations discussed in the CHANGE INDICATOR pattern, users have to reset the indicator explicitly if they are no longer interested in the change.

Change indicators propagate themselves to their enclosing folders. This allows users to stay aware of changes in subfolders more easily. If there is no propagated change indicator, they can be sure that the folder contents have not been changed recently.

Changes, as well as other events, can be communicated to the users in the daily workspace activity report, the BSCW implementation of a PERIODIC REPORT→4.5.3 (Figure 6.20). This lists all the activities that took place during the day and is sent to interested users nightly. As mentioned in the discussion of BSCW's interpretation of the ATTENTION SCREEN→3.3.4, users can configure, for each artifact, whether activities on the artifact will appear in the daily workspace activity report. The reporting period is defined by the system administrator.

All these patterns make heavy use of an ACTIVITY LOG→4.5.1 that stores all the actions that users performed. The ACTIVITY LOG can be queried for activities on a specific document, so that users can better understand the history of the document.

BSCW does not provide an ALIVENESS INDICATOR→4.5.5 for a specific user in a specific workspace. The only information on the user's activity level is the last login time, which is tracked in the user's personal profile page (Figure 6.3). One could argue that users stay aware of all other users' activities, since all of them appear

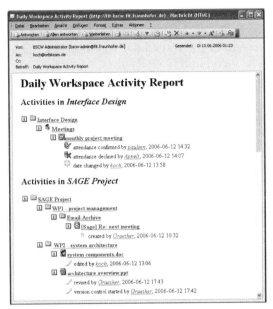

Figure 6.20 BSCW provides asynchronous awareness by means of the daily workspace activity report

in the workspace activity report. However, manual processing is required to find out which of the workspace's members is still participating. It would be useful to have an additional ALIVENESS INDICATOR in the workspace, especially in contexts in which the teams are fully distributed, such as distributed group learning scenarios.

In the same vein, an AWAY MESSAGE$_{\rightarrow 4.5.6}$ could enhance communication in a BSCW workspace FORUM. BSCW relies on external AWAY MESSAGES configured with the user's e-mail system. This informs senders of messages that are directed explicitly to specific members, but would not tell the group that the user is away.

6.1.3 Base Technology

BSCW is built on top of a standard web architecture. It extends the Apache web server with modules written in Python. Web requests are passed on to operation handlers that can be extended to modify or augment the functionality of the core BSCW server.

The web server can be accessed either with a standard web browser or with customized BSCW browsers that communicate with the server using an XML representation of the domain model. These tools can overcome limitations of HTML interfaces and display, for example, tree structures in a TREE TABLE (Tidwell, 2006). The domain data is stored in an object-oriented database that can directly handle

Python objects. A separate server tracks user activities and communicates them to event clients, such as the BSCW Monitor (Figure 6.16).

Using web architecture in the traditional way suggests the use of the following patterns, which can be found in BSCW:

— Shared objects are stored as CENTRALIZED OBJECTS$_{\to 5.2.1}$. BSCW stores all objects except the contents of stored files in the Python database. The files are stored directly in the BSCW server's file system.

— Changes are applied on a first-come-first-serve basis. This means that objects are overwritten in the order in which requests are received by the BSCW web server. We can consider this as very OPTIMISTIC CONCURRENCY CONTROL$_{\to 5.3.2}$.

Applets that react to events, such as the monitor applet, need to extend the restricted client server interaction of the HTTP protocol. As expected, we can find additional patterns here.

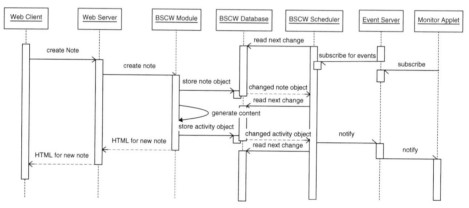

Figure 6.21 Event propagation among BSCW components

The most interesting part is the tracking of activity data. Whenever the user performs an activity using the standard HTTP interface, the BSCW server creates an activity object that is added to the BSCW database as part of an ACTIVITY LOG$_{\to 4.5.1}$.

Another monitoring component, the BSCW scheduler process, observes all changes to the database and propagates the changes to interested components. In the case of events, the relevant component that needs to be informed is the BSCW event server. This component provides access to the CENTRALIZED OBJECTS$_{\to 5.2.1}$ that represent activities. It further allows clients to register a REMOTE SUBSCRIPTION$_{\to 5.2.2}$ for events that will be relevant to them. Whenever new activity events occur, the event monitor informs all subscribed clients, which can then update their awareness information accordingly. These update messages are sent in the form of a DISTRIBUTED COMMAND$_{\to 5.2.7}$.

Besides web-based interaction with documents stored in BSCW, users can replicate entire workspaces to their local machine as NOMADIC OBJECTS$_{\to 5.2.4}$ and work with them connected to the BSCW server. At the user interface level, replication is initiated by placing documents in a virtual briefcase. This briefcase synchronizes resources on the server with locally stored resources (see Figure 6.22). In the case in which both the object on the server and the locally stored copy are modified, the applet asks the user for conflict resolution. The CONFLICT DETECTION$_{\to 5.3.3}$ is based on comparing the timestamps of the different objects.

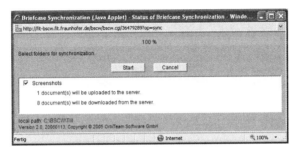

Figure 6.22 Synchronizing objects on the server with local copies

Finally, there is the option of versioning artifacts in BSCW. Although disabled by default, this feature is very valuable for increasing concurrency in distributed work, since it enables users to store documents as IMMUTABLE VERSIONS$_{\to 5.3.6}$.

6.2 CoWord

After discussing how our patterns collaborate in the asynchronous context of BSCW, we can now look for patterns in the synchronous CoWord application. CoWord extends the commercial off-the-shelf word processor Microsoft Word so that it can be used in a synchronous session with other users.

For this purpose, CoWord makes use of a technique called *transparent adaptation* (Sun et al., 2004; Xia et al., 2004; Sun et al., 2006). The key concept behind transparent adaptation is the use of the application programming interface (API) of a single-user application to intercept the user's operations. Intercepted operations are distributed among all clients and the arguments for the operation are adapted at each client to the needs of the Operational Transformation$_{\to 5.3.4}$ pattern. By using the API, no access or change to the application's source code is necessary and the adaptation is transparent to the user.

Figure 6.23 shows the system architecture of CoWord, which consists of three layers:

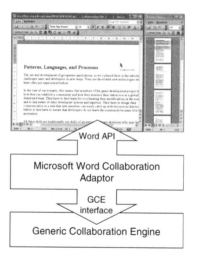

Figure 6.23 CoWord system architecture

1. The Microsoft Word single-user application provides a well-known user interface for creating and editing documents.
2. The *Microsoft Word Collaboration Adaptor* provides collaboration capabilities and adapts the Word data and operation model for the underlying layer.
3. The *Generic Collaboration Engine* provides application-independent collaboration support techniques—the necessary mechanisms for Operational Transformation$_{\to 5.3.4}$.

As shown in Figure 6.24, CoWord implements approximately 34% of the patterns in our pattern language. The main metaphor of CoWord is that of SHARED EDITOR$_{\to 4.1.6}$. To enable collaboration, CoWord also offers a SHARED FILE REPOSITORY$_{\to 4.1.2}$ and an INTERACTION DIRECTORY$_{\to 4.2.3}$. It is therefore obvious that community support as the top-level cluster of our pattern language is not within CoWord's focus. The only pattern that CoWord uses from the top-level cluster is LOGIN$_{\to 3.1.2}$. Users have to identify themselves before they are allowed to access the shared documents in the SHARED FILE REPOSITORY$_{\to 4.1.2}$ (see Figure 6.25). The LOGIN has to be created in advance by the administrator of the SHARED FILE REPOSITORY. In its current version there is no possibility of a QUICK REGISTRATION$_{\to 3.1.1}$ in

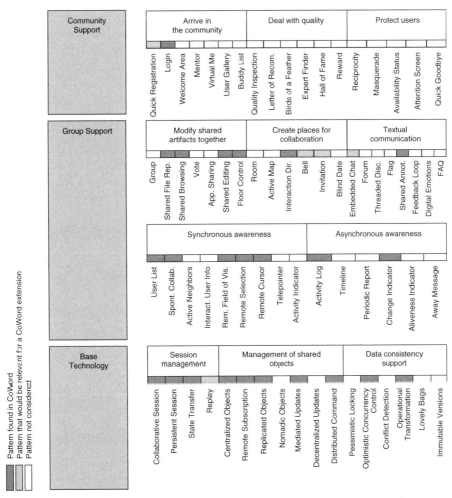

Figure 6.24 Pattern clusters for which known uses exist in CoWord

CoWord. However, the CoWord developers indicated that implementing QUICK REGISTRATION was quite interesting and easily possible.

Figure 6.25 CoWord LOGIN

We now look at the remaining two top-level clusters of the pattern language in more detail.

6.2.1 Group Support

Modify Shared Artifacts Together

CoWord offers a SHARED FILE REPOSITORY$_{\rightarrow 4.1.2}$, called the *collaborative document repository manager* (CDRM), to which users may upload the documents to be shared for collaborative editing. The CDRM allows users to perform basic file operations such as create, remove, rename, and list by using a proprietary browser. Figure 6.26

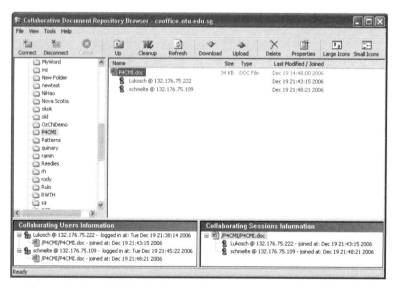

Figure 6.26 CoWord collaborative document repository manager

shows a screenshot of the *collaborative document repository browser* (CDRB) which is the front end for the CDRM. The upper-left part shows the available folders in the repository and the upper-right part shows the contents of the selected folder.

By selecting a document and opening it, a user can start a COLLABORATIVE SESSION$_{\to 5.1.1}$. When the session starts the CoWord SHARED EDITOR$_{\to 4.1.6}$ is opened. Figure 6.27 shows a screenshot of this editor.

CoWord support various kinds of interaction modes, which can be controlled flexibly during the collaborative editing process. These interaction modes are:

— *Multi-actor mode*, which is the default mode and allows multiple users to edit a document concurrently. CoWord automatically preserves the consistency of the shared document by applying OPERATIONAL TRANSFORMATIONS$_{\to 5.3.4}$.

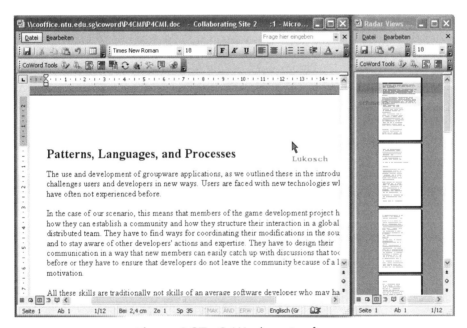

Figure 6.27 CoWord user interface

— *Single-actor mode*, in which only one user can edit a document at a time. CoWord thus supports FLOOR CONTROL$_{\to 4.1.7}$. For this purpose, CoWord uses a distributed protocol that blocks all but one user's input. The floor is passed to the first user who requests it. Other users who want to edit parts of the document have to wait until the current floor holder releases the floor.

— *Multi-view mode*, which is the default mode and allows the interacting users to have an individual view on the shared document. CoWord thus implements relaxed WYSIWIS (what you see is what I see), as discussed in SHARED EDITING$_{\to 4.1.6}$.

— *Single-view mode*, in which all users have the same view of the shared document. This is achieved by a distributed protocol that blocks all but one user's view-changing operations. Again, this protocol is based on a request-and-release protocol, so CoWord also implements strict WYSIWIS.

Users can switch among the different interaction modes via the CoWord toolbar, shown in Figure 6.28. In the mode shown in the figure, single-actor and single-view modes are enabled. When these modes are enabled, all users have the same view of the shared document and only one user can edit its contents. In this configuration CoWord can therefore be used to browse a document collaboratively, as described in SHARED BROWSING$_{\to 4.1.3}$.

Figure 6.28 CoWord toolbar

Create Places for Collaboration

The CoWord CDRB serves as an INTERACTION DIRECTORY$_{\to 4.2.3}$. The interaction context of CoWord is a COLLABORATIVE SESSION$_{\to 5.1.1}$ in which several users can edit a shared document in parallel. When connecting to the CDRM, the CDRB lists all available COLLABORATIVE SESSIONS. Figure 6.29 shows a part of such a list. For each session, the CDRB displays the edited document, the participating users, the users' IP address, and the time at which the users joined. Apart from the special section in the CDRB's user interface, the same information can be discovered when browsing the contents of the file repository. The upper right part of Figure 6.26 shows that this information is also available when viewing the content of a folder in the repository.

Figure 6.29 CoWord INTERACTION DIRECTORY

CoWord thereby allows user to meet and start collaboration. However, each user who has a LOGIN for the CDRM is also allowed to enter a COLLABORATIVE SESSION. As the number of users that have a LOGIN for the CDRM grows, collaborators might be disturbed by uninvited visitors, or fail to notice that someone wants to join. In this case, CoWord could benefit from a BELL$_{\rightarrow 4.2.4}$ that latecomers must use before they are allowed to participate in a session. In our discussions CoWord's developers indicated that they might implement a BELL in the next version of CoWord. A related issue is the possibility of planning a COLLABORATIVE SESSION. By integrating the INVITATION$_{\rightarrow 4.2.5}$ pattern into the CDRB, users could inform each other about planned sessions and invite participation.

Textual Communication

Users who are interacting need to communicate to resolve issues that arise in collaboration. The main patterns in this cluster concentrate on enabling textual communication: EMBEDDED CHAT$_{\rightarrow 4.3.1}$ and FORUM$_{\rightarrow 4.3.2}$. As CoWord is designed to enable synchronous collaborative editing, users would benefit from the possibility of synchronous communication. This could be achieved by integrating an EMBEDDED CHAT$_{\rightarrow 4.3.1}$ into CoWord.

Apart from enabling textual communication, further patterns in this cluster focus on enabling discussion. Of these patterns, CoWord supports SHARED ANNOTATIONS$_{\rightarrow 4.3.5}$ (Figure 6.30). Users can enter comments on specific parts of the shared document: CoWord automatically distributes these comments to all participants, where the comments are displayed against the content.

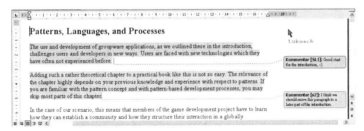

Figure 6.30 SHARED ANNOTATIONS in CoWord

Synchronous Awareness

CoWord contains a lot of features that support group awareness. As we have already seen in the CDRB, CoWord implements the USER LIST$_{\rightarrow 4.4.1}$ pattern, shown at the lower left corner in Figure 6.26. This list contains all the users that are currently connected to the CDRM. It additionally displays the LOGIN time and in which COLLABORATIVE SESSIONS each user is currently participating. Displaying the sessions in which users participate increases awareness of the shared data. CoWord therefore partly implements the SPONTANEOUS COLLABORATION$_{\rightarrow 4.4.2}$ pattern.

In addition to the USER LIST in the CDRB, CoWord offers a *collaborative editing session information panel*. This panel lists the information in the CDRB for a specific user. Figure 6.31 shows a user currently involved in two COLLABORATIVE SESSIONS. The first runs in multiple-actor/view mode, while the second runs in single-actor/view mode. In the second session, *Lukosch* is currently holding the floor for both the view and for interaction. The lower part of Figure 6.31 shows the users participating in the selected first session and thereby provides another USER LIST.

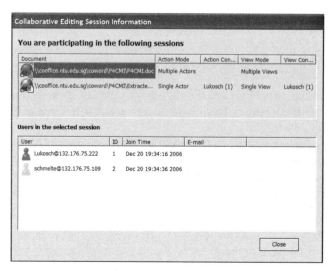

Figure 6.31 Collaborative editing session information panel

Apart from a USER LIST, CoWord supports REMOTE FIELD OF VISION$_{\rightarrow 4.4.5}$ by displaying both local and remote fields of vision. The fields of vision are indicated by transparent layers that are displayed over a miniature view of the shared document. These layers have a different color for each participating user. By clicking on another user's layer it is possible to align your own field of vision with that of the remote user. Figure 6.32 shows the fields of vision for two collaborating users who are currently focusing their work on different parts of the same page of a document. Note that we do not consider this view as an ACTIVE MAP$_{\rightarrow 4.2.2}$, since there is no information reduction in the miniature view other than the reduction of the pixel resolution.

Another pattern from this cluster supported by CoWord is REMOTE CURSOR$_{\rightarrow 4.4.7}$. In CoWord REMOTE CURSORS always trace the actual position of the other users' mice, and associate the users' LOGIN names and a differently colored REMOTE CURSOR for each user. These colors corresponds to the color of users' view ports in the REMOTE FIELD OF VISION. Figure 6.33 shows the *Jutta Schümmer's* REMOTE CURSOR$_{\rightarrow 4.4.7}$.

CoWord allows users to edit the same parts of a shared document concurrently. By displaying REMOTE CURSORS and implementing REMOTE FIELD OF VISION, users

Figure 6.32 REMOTE FIELD OF VISION in CoWord

Figure 6.33 REMOTE CURSOR in CoWord

are aware of the other users' focus. When editing text, especially, users often select text to start an action on it. In CoWord selecting text is considered to be taking the text under personal control. To make users aware of this, CoWord implements the REMOTE SELECTION$_{\rightarrow 4.4.6}$ pattern when the interaction mode is set to single-actor mode. In multi-actor mode REMOTE SELECTION is disabled.

Asynchronous Awareness

The patterns in this cluster are mainly used for providing asynchronous awareness. Although CoWord is designed for synchronous interaction, it uses two patterns from this cluster. The rationale behind this is that users are allowed to have independent work positions in the same document. Although they collaborate on the same document, it can thus happen that users simply do not see what other users are doing. From an abstract point of view, the users perform single-user work on individual parts of the document, and other users need to be informed about changes when they return to a part of the document that has been changed in the meantime by a group member.

CoWord uses an ACTIVITY LOG$_{\rightarrow 4.5.1}$ to remember all the activities that were performed by collaborating users. The information collected is then used to support *collaborative text input highlighting*: text inserted by collaborating users is highlighted using different colors. This highlighting can be saved and made persistent across different sessions, or removed by disabling the feature via the CoWord toolbar. CoWord therefore implements the CHANGE INDICATOR$_{\rightarrow 4.5.4}$ pattern. Figure 6.34

shows this highlighting for two users. Additionally, CoWord uses small images that flash to indicate the type of a remote operation. These images vary when inserting, deleting or updating text. The upper-right corner of Figure 6.34 shows a small pencil, which indicates that the user is inserting text.

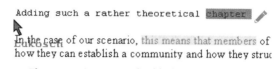

Figure 6.34 Input highlighting in CoWord

CoWord even supports a more sophisticated CHANGE INDICATOR than this by offering *real-time collaborative change tracking*. This feature is a multiuser version of the single-user tracking feature. It tracks all kinds of operations—insert, delete, and update—and maintains all users' identities and change timestamps. Figure 6.35 shows this feature. The tool-tip explains that *Lukosch* has added the beginning of the paragraph and at what time this happened. The text in a different color signals that another has added this text.

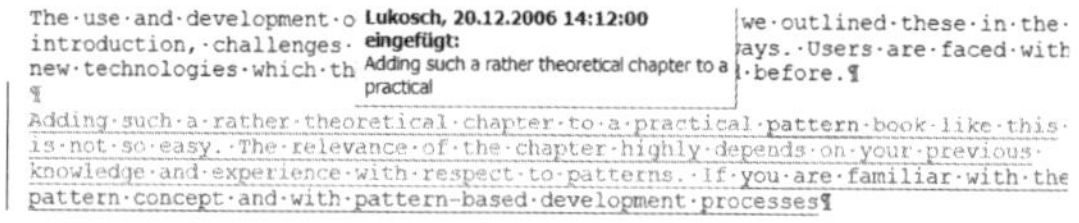

Figure 6.35 Change tracking in CoWord

6.2.2 Base Technology

Bootstrap Collaboration

CoWord relies on COLLABORATIVE SESSION$_{\rightarrow 5.1.1}$ to bootstrap collaboration. Users can start a session by opening a shared document via the collaborative document repository browser (CDRB). The CDRB lists the sessions in an INTERACTION DIRECTORY$_{\rightarrow 4.2.3}$ in the lower-right corner of the user interface (Figure 6.26). When a user starts a session or joins a session via the CDRB, the CDRB automatically opens the shared editor. Users can participate in more than one session. The sessions a user is participating in are listed in the collaborative editing session information panel (Figure 6.31).

When a user wants to leave a session in which a shared document has been changed, CoWord automatically reminds the user to save the results (Figure 6.36). As CoWord is designed for document-centric collaboration, this ensures that session results are stored persistently in the CDRM, thus implementing the PERSISTENT

SESSION$_{\rightarrow 5.1.2}$ pattern. By default the document is saved to the original copy in the CDRM. Additionally, CoWord allows saving the document to the local file system under any name using the *Save as ...* command.

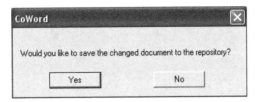

Figure 6.36 Request for PERSISTENT SESSIONS in CoWord

When latecomers join a session, CoWord takes care that they receive the current state of the session by using the STATE TRANSFER$_{\rightarrow 5.1.3}$ pattern. CoWord does not use a central server for the STATE TRANSFER. Instead, a latecomer can be initialized by any collaborating site. CoWord uses a distributed protocol for the initialization that forces the COLLABORATIVE SESSION into a *quiescent state*—a state in which all sites have executed the same set of operations and no operations are in transition. When a *quiescent state* is reached, a latecomer can easily be initialized by any cooperating site by simply transferring the copy of the shared document to the latecomer. When transferring the copy, the CDRM acts as a message relay for communication between the initializing site and the latecomer. When editing large documents, the CoWord approach can block collaborating users. The STATE TRANSFER pattern describes how CoWord could be extended to allow ongoing collaboration while accommodating latecomers.

In some cases users rejoin a COLLABORATIVE SESSION after a time of absence. It can then be hard for them to understand how the current state of a collaboration has been reached by only perceiving the current state of the session. To understand how a specific state has been reached, CoWord could make use of its multiuser real-time change tracking (Figure 6.35) and REPLAY$_{\rightarrow 5.1.4}$ a session to latecomers to show how its current state was reached.

Manage Common Data

Figure 6.37 shows the architecture of CoWord and the interactions among the sites of collaborating users. The collaborative document repository manager(CDRM) allows users to share documents. The CDRM can be located on a central server or at any user's site. The latter approach allows users to share their local documents easily. In both cases, the documents are managed as CENTRALIZED OBJECTS$_{\rightarrow 5.2.1}$ as long as they are not used in a COLLABORATIVE SESSION$_{\rightarrow 5.1.1}$. Information about ongoing sessions and uses that are logged in is also managed as CENTRALIZED OBJECTS.

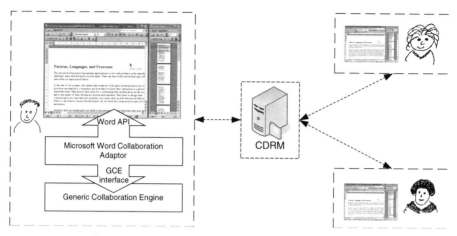

Figure 6.37 CoWord distributed system architecture

When users log into the CDRM, they subscribe to the state of the whole repository. If any user joins, starts, or leaves a session, existing users are notified of the changes. The server *pushes* the notification: the CDRM uses the REMOTE SUBSCRIPTION$_{\rightarrow 5.2.2}$ pattern for this.

As soon as a COLLABORATIVE SESSION$_{\rightarrow 5.1.1}$ has started, the CDRM replicates the document used for the collaboration to the collaborating sites. For the first user the document is copied from the CDRM, while for each latecomer the document is copied from any participating site via the CDRM, using a STATE TRANSFER$_{\rightarrow 5.1.3}$. The users are completely unaware of this mechanisms, as CoWord handles this completely transparently.

When a user changes a local copy of the replicated document, the change is performed immediately, captured in a DISTRIBUTED COMMAND$_{\rightarrow 5.2.7}$, then propagated to the remote sites for re-execution using MEDIATED UPDATES$_{\rightarrow 5.2.5}$. Again, the CDRM acts as message relay to propagate the changes to the other participants of the session.

Ensure Data Consistency

CoWord immediately performs a local user's changes without consulting any other participating site. CoWord therefore relies on OPTIMISTIC CONCURRENCY CONTROL$_{\rightarrow 5.3.2}$. Possible conflicts are resolved and data consistency is achieved by using OPERATIONAL TRANSFORMATION$_{\rightarrow 5.3.4}$, which is the cornerstone technique in CoWord. CoWord follows a strategy of keeping the number of necessary transformation functions low. For that purpose, CoWord's collaboration adaptor (Figure 6.23 on page 526) translates application-specific operations into three generic primitive operations, *insert*, *delete*, and *update*, which are used during OPERATIONAL TRANSFORMATION.

Epilogue

The patterns in this book present an initial step towards a better understanding of computer-mediated interaction in a networked environment. We hope that we have managed to capture many of the basic infrastructure elements that are required to create collaborative applications. At the least, the case studies described in Chapter 6 make us confident that the most important patterns are captured in this collection. Experience gained from development and research projects in which we are currently involved tell the same story.

However, we are not blind to the large potential for mining additional patterns to complement this pattern language. We would like to encourage you to contribute additional experience in the form of patterns or known uses that helps us as a community to cover additional fields. From our experience, we see several promising areas for action, and we would like to close the book by presenting a short overview of these areas.

Workflow management. Workflow management is one of the larger topics that needs to be connected with our pattern language. While the definition of workflows is rather simple on a technical level, it becomes a challenging task as soon as we start to shape team and project structures. However, good work processes are required to create the collaborative companies of the future. We can foresee future companies putting an emphasis on collaboration networks that cross traditional organizational contexts. Helping different cultures to find common ground and helping participants to learn from each others' diverse backgrounds is a challenging but promising task—especially in a global economy in which people with multiple cultural backgrounds join a network.

Computer-mediated collaborative learning. Successful research and development in the area of computer-mediated interaction has often been an interdisciplinary approach. Psychologists, sociologists, or ethnographers often collaborated with system designers to create solutions that fit the end-users' needs. We consider our pattern language to be an important vehicle for communication between members of different disciplines who are often not used to speaking the same special language. However, there is considerable potential for complementary pattern languages from experts in other domains. The field of educational research in the context of computer-supported collaborative learning (CSCL) is relatively advanced in terms of cooperation with system developers. However, we still miss a collection of best practices that focuses on new pedagogical models for CSCL. Since most of these practices should evolve from real-world experience, we can see a large potential for pattern scouts who observe how practitioners extend the practices of our pattern language to enhance distributed learning experiences. The TELL pattern collection (TELL Project Consortium, 2005) is an initial step in this direction, but one that is however still too technology-oriented. For that reason we encourage teachers to take up the challenge of inventing, testing, and documenting good practices for CSCL.

Gaming and entertainment. Another interdisciplinary field that has been ignored by serious CSCW (Computer Supported Collaborative Work) researchers and developers for a long time is that of game design. Some initial scientific studies in the context of cooperation in computer games has however shown that designers of serious collaborative applications can learn a lot from experience in game development and use. We have shown known uses in the gaming area for some of our patterns. However, there are more patterns in computer games. An initial set of rather domain-oriented pattern candidates has been collected in (Björk and Holopainen, 2005). Since these patterns are very focused on shaping game-play, we need additional patterns to bridge the gap between serious and entertainment applications. Identifying these patterns and making them accessible for the development of serious collaboration support is another challenge that we plan to address.

Media use in collaboration. The use of diverse communication media will become more important as soon as basic infrastructural problems are solved. The advent of IP telephony within recent years, such as the Skype network (http://www.skype.com/), or the exchange of video material on platforms like youTube (http://www.youtube.com/) will change the way in which we interact with each other. Capturing patterns for efficient media creation, exchange, and use is probably a valuable endeavor. The process of capturing good practices as patterns should start in such early phases when we can observe the advent of a new trend. This could speed up knowledge transfer within the field and prevent the wheel being invented over and over again, as was the case with the basic support technology for CSCW.

Mobile and other new devices. The more powerful mobile devices become, the better will they be suited to be an integral part of computer-mediated interaction. One example that we recently studied was the case of a German online game manufacturer. The Northworks Software company (http://www.goalunited.org/) offers *Goal United*, a soccer management simulation game with more than 30,000 registered and 20,000 active players in Germany, Austria, and Switzerland. The game follows the idea of being responsible for a soccer team. Users can trade players, create training schedules, or assign players for the next match. All this is done in the context of the game community with communication and interaction support.

The initial version of this game was browser-based, but the company is currently investigating possibilities for staying in touch with the players even when they are not logged in. We were able to observe their development of a client suitable for "smart" phones—mobile phones that have reasonable computing power. The result was a tailored client that allows users to stay in contact using the mobile connection offered by the phone. Players could continue their trading and—most importantly—maintain the contacts that they established in the player community. Wiczniewski (2006) gives a report of these activities.

To what extent the patterns in this book can be embedded in a mobile context is an interesting question for future investigations.

Web 2.0. In the last months of writing this book, the term "Web 2.0" became one of the most important buzzwords for us. We asked ourselves: What is our role in the future of Web 2.0? Musser et al. (2006) define the term as *"a set of economic, social, and technology trends that collectively form the basis for the next generation of the Internet—a more mature, distinctive medium characterized by user participation, openness, and network effects."* Patterns for computer-mediated interaction contribute to this trend by paying special attention to the interaction between users and the technical support that is required to make this interaction happen over distance. We showed that many of the technologies have their known uses in web contexts. New technologies like Ajax (Garrett, 2005) that argue that web browsers should be used not only for viewing content will help to implement the user experience promoted by our patterns in a web context. However, we are optimistic that the current hype around the Web 2.0 will give collaboration support a new arena. Initial examples like Google Docs (http://docs.google.com/) already point to this direction.

Integration, integration, and integration… Looking back at the patterns in this book and the large number of known uses, you may get the impression that there is not much space for creating new applications for collaboration support. It is true that basic support for collaborative work could be handled with BSCW—that is at least the reason for calling it BSCW. We currently see a promising trend to integrate collaboration into domain-specific applications, however. For the same reason that an office suite is not sufficient for all tasks that can be solved with the help of computers, generic systems like BSCW will not be perfect if you have a very domain-specific task to solve in a group. The challenge from our perspective is to create a good balance between collaboration and domain support. Our example scenario, the game development community that used an extended Eclipse system to support collaboration, is just one illustration of this line of action.

We came across another comparable scenario during the research for our book: *intelligent views* (http://www.i-views.de) is a software company that specializes in supporting the creation and use of knowledge networks. This company has created the authoring environment for worldwide operating steel companies, for major German newspaper publishers, and the DUDEN, the German reference dictionary. All these companies use knowledge networks to better understand and compile information that is present in each organization's context. They asked *intelligent views* to support them in this task, but they did not explicitly ask for collaboration support. One potential reason for this is that existing collaboration structures are often based on division of labor rather than on dynamic collaboration of flexible teams. This may also be a reason why some of our reviewers suggested that we remove SPONTANEOUS COLLABORATION$_{\rightarrow 4.4.2}$ and ACTIVE NEIGHBORS$_{\rightarrow 4.4.3}$ from our pattern language.

Intelligent views therefore created support for manipulating knowledge networks, but they used the COAST framework for implementing the application. COAST was invented as a groupware framework, but it has many features that are also needed when creating object-oriented databases with many constraints between the managed objects. By using COAST, the applications had collaboration support almost for free. Users did not mind the fact that the support was integrated, since they could continue their usual way of working. When the system was used, users also got to grips with additional collaborative aspects. Since it was possible to invite other users to an editing session on a knowledge network, the users started to adapt their way of working—initially because they needed support from technicians who were able to demonstrate a specific way of using the knowledge network editor to them.

To trigger more collaboration between the users, the company added a collaborative Sudoku game (http://en.wikipedia.org/wiki/Sudoku) as an "Easter egg"—a hidden command. This had an interesting effect. While users were reluctant to use collaboration in their business tasks, they started to play Sudoku against other company divisions. In this way they experienced collaboration opportunities offered by the system, and so might become accustomed to taking collaborative aspects in domain-specific applications for granted. The future will show whether or not this is sufficient to change their expectations.

Experimental Aspects. While writing this book we have often had discussions about whether a pattern is mature enough to be called a pattern. Most patterns in this collection have—after long discussion—at least a level of maturity that was acknowledged by all the book's reviewers. However, we removed approximately fifty patterns from the collection that were not yet mature enough. For system developers and research departments, these patterns are valuable resources for starting discussions.

Finally, it is you who creates the future… As you can see from the list of interesting areas for extending the work of this book, it is a task list that cannot be addressed by a small group of people. We therefore invite you to participate in the computer-mediated interaction patterns community.

Visit the companion website for this book at `http://www.computer-mediated-interaction-patterns.org` and contribute your experience. Use this site to get in contact with other practitioners of the field. Attach your known uses to patterns from the book, or suggest modifications to the patterns. Browse experimental patterns contributed by us or by other experts in the field. Finally, become your own pattern author by submitting a pattern either to the community website or to one of the PLoP-series conferences such as EuroPLoP (`http://hillside.net/europlop`). We count on you.

Bibliography

Al Zabir, O. (2005). Distributed command pattern-an extension of command pattern for connected systems.
http://www.codeproject.com/cs/design/distributedcommandpattern.asp

Alexander, C. (1964). *Notes on the Synthesis of Form*. Cambridge, Massachusetts: Harvard University Press, 7 (2002) edition.

Alexander, C. (1979). *The timeless way of building*. New York: Oxford University Press.

Alexander, C. (2003a). *The phenomenom of life*, volume 1 of *The nature of order*. Berkeley, California, USA: Center for Environmental Structure.

Alexander, C. (2003b). *The process of creating life*, volume 2 of *The nature of order*. Berkeley, California, USA: Center for Environmental Structure.

Alexander, C., Ishikawa, S., and Silverstein, M. (1968). *A pattern language which generates multi-service centers*. University of California, Berkeley: Center for environmental structure.

Alexander, C., Ishikawa, S., Silverstein, M., Jacobson, M., Fiksdahl-King, I., and Angel, S. (1977). *A pattern language*. New York: Oxford University Press.

Alexander, C., Silverstein, M., Angel, S., Ishikawa, S., and Abrams, D. (1980). *The Oregon Experiment*. New York: Oxford University Press.

Anderson, F. (2000). A collection of history patterns. In Harrison, N., Foote, B., and Rohnert, H. (Editors), *Pattern Languages of Program Design 4*, pp. 263–297. Reading, MA, USA: Addison-Wesley.

Appelt, W. (2001). What groupware functionality do users really use? analysis of the usage of the bscw system. In Klöckner, K. (Editor), *Ninth Euromicro Workshop on Parallel and Distributed Processing 2001*, pp. 337–343. Mantova, Italy: IEEE Computer Society.

Appelt, W. and Mambrey, P. (1999). Experiences with the BSCW shared workspace system as the backbone of a virtual learning environment for students. In *Proceedings of ED-MEDIA99*.

ArenaNet (2005). Guild wars. http://de.guildwars.com/.

Asensio, J. I., Dimitriadis, Y. A., Heredia, M., Martinez, A., Alvarez, F. J., Blasco, M. T., and Osuna, C. A. (2004). Collaborative learning patterns: Assisting the development of component-based cscl applications. In *Proceedings of the 12th Euromicro Conference on Parallel, Distributed and Network-Based Processing*, pp. 218–224. IEEE Press. http://citeseer.ist.psu.edu/678945.html

Autonomy (2002). Collaboration & expertise networks–cen. Aut cen 11.02, Autonomy Inc. http://www.autonomy.com/

Barr, P., Briddle, R., and Noble, J. (2004). Interface ontology: Creating a physical world for computer interfaces. In Henney, K. and Schütz, D. (Editors), *Proceedings of the Eighth European Conference on Pattern Languages of Programs (EuroPLoP'03)*, pp. 1–17. Konstanz, Germany: UVK.

Beck, K. (1999). *eXtreme Programming Explained*. Reading, MA, USA: Addison Wesley.

Becks, A. and Seeling, C. (2004). Swapit: a multiple views paradigm for exploring associations of texts and structured data. In *AVI '04: Proceedings of the working conference on Advanced visual interfaces*, pp. 193–196. New York, NY, USA: ACM Press.

Begole, J. B., Struble, C. A., Shaffer, C. A., and Smith, R. B. (1997). Transparent sharing of java applets: A replicated approach. In *Proceedings of the 10th annual ACM symposium on User interface software and technology*, pp. 55–64. ACM Press. http://doi.acm.org/10.1145/263407.263509

Benford, S. and Fahlén, L. (1993). A spatial model of interaction in large virtual environments. In *Proceedings of the Third European Conference on Computer-Supported Cooperative Work (ECSCW '93)*, pp. 109–124. Milan, Italy: Kluwer.

Bentley, R., Appelt, W., Busbach, U., Hinrichs, E., Kerr, D., Sikkel, K., Trevor, J., and Woetzel, G. (1997a). Basic support for cooperative work on the world-wide web. *International Journal of Human-Computer Studies: Special issue on Innovative Applications of the World-Wide Web*.

Bentley, R., Horstmann, T., and Trevor, J. (1997b). The world wide web as enabling technology for cscw: The case of bscw.

Berlage, T. and Genau, A. (1993). A framework for shared applications with a replicated architecture. In *Proceedings of the 6th annual ACM symposium on User interface software and technology*, pp. 249–257. ACM Press.

Berners-Lee, T., Fielding, R., and Frystyk, H. (1996). Hypertext Transfer Protocol–HTTP/1.0. RFC 1945 (Informational). http://www.ietf.org/rfc/rfc1945.txt

Bikson, T. K. and Eveland, J. D. (1996). Groupware implementation: reinvention in the sociotechnical frame. In *CSCW '96: Proceedings of the 1996 ACM conference on Computer supported cooperative work*, pp. 428–437. New York, NY, USA: ACM Press.

Birrell, A. D. and Nelson, B. (1984). Implementing remote procedure calls. *ACM Transactions on Computer Systems*, 2(1): pp. 39–59.

Björk, S. and Holopainen, J. (2005). *Patterns in Game Design*. Charles River Media.

Blizzard Entertainment (2006). World of warcraft.
http://www.wow-europe.com/de/.

Borchers, J. (2001). *A Pattern Approach to Interaction Design*. John Wiley and Sons Ltd.

Borchers, J. O. (2000). Interaction design patterns: Twelve theses. In *Position Paper for the CHI Workshop "Pattern Languages for Interaction Design: Building Momentum"*.
http://www.it.bton.ac.uk/staff/rng/CHI2K_PLworkshop/PositionPapers/Borchers.pdf

Borghoff, U. M. and Schlichter, J. H. (2000). *Computer-Supported Cooperative Work*. Springer-Verlag Berlin Heidelberg New York.

Bos, N., Olson, J., Gergle, D., Olson, G., and Wright, Z. (2002). Effects of four computer-mediated communications channels on trust development. In *CHI '02: Proceedings of the SIGCHI conference on Human factors in computing systems*, pp. 135–140. New York, NY, USA: ACM Press.

Boyle, M., Edwards, C., and Greenberg, S. (2000). The effects of filtered video on awareness and privacy. In *Proceedings of the 2000 ACM conference on Computer supported cooperative work*, pp. 1–10. Philadelphia, Pennsylvania, United States.

Bradshaw, S., Budzik, J., Fu, X., and Hammond, K. J. (2002). Clustering for opportunistic communication. In *Proceedings of WWW 2002*. ACM Press.

Brown, K., Eskelin, P., and Pryce, N. (1999). A small pattern language for distributed component design. In *Pattern Languages of Programs Conference*. Monticello, Illinois, USA.

Brush, A. J. B., Bargeron, D., Gupta, A., and Cadiz, J. J. (2001). Robust annotation positioning in digital documents. In *CHI '01: Proceedings of the SIGCHI conference on Human factors in computing systems*, pp. 285–292. New York, NY, USA: ACM Press.

Budzik, J., Bradshaw, S., Fu, X., and Hammond, K. J. (2002). Supporting online resource discovery in the context of ongoing tasks with proactive software assistants. *International Journal of Human-Computer Studies*, 56(1): pp. 47–74.

Buschmann, F. and Henney, K. (2004). Explicit interface and object manager–two patterns from a pattern language for distributed computing. In Henney, K. and Schütz, D. (Editors), *Proceedings of the Eighth European Conference on Pattern Languages of Programs (EuroPLoP'03)*, pp. 207–220. Konstanz, Germany: UVK.

Buschmann, F., Meunier, R., Rohnert, H., Sommerlad, P., and Stal, M. (1996). *Pattern-Oriented Software Architecture, Volume 1: A System of Patterns*. Chichester, UK: John Wiley and Sons.

Byrne, D. (1971). *The Attraction Paradigm*. New York: Academic Press.

Carotenuto, L., Etienne, W., Fontaine, M., Friedman, J., Muller, M., Newberg, H., Simpson, M., Slusher, J., and Stevenson, K. (1999). Communityspace: Toward flexible support for voluntary knowledge communities. In *online proceedings of "CHANGING PLACES-the workshop on workspace models for collaboration"*, pp. available online at http://www.dcs.qmw.ac.uk/research/distrib/Mushroom/workshop/final-papers/lotus.pdf. London.

Carr, C. L. (2006). Reciprocity: the golden rule of is-user service relationship quality and cooperation. *Commun. ACM*, 49(6): pp. 77–83.

Carroll, J. M., Neale, D. C., Isenhour, P. L., Rosson, M. B., and McCrickard, D. S. (2003). Notification and awareness: synchronizing task-oriented collaborative activity. *Int. J. Hum.-Comput. Stud.*, 58(5): pp. 605–632.

Carter, S., Churchill, E., Denoue, L., Helfman, J., and Nelson, L. (2004). Digital graffiti: public annotation of multimedia content. In *CHI '04: CHI '04 extended abstracts on Human factors in computing systems*, pp. 1207–1210. New York, NY, USA: ACM Press.

Chabert, A., Grossman, E., Jackson, L., Pietrovicz, S., and Seguin, C. (1998). Java object-sharing in Habanero. *Communications of the ACM*, 41(6): pp. 69–76.

Chang, Y.-I. (1996). A simulation study on distributed mutual exclusion. *Journal of Parallel and Distributed Computing*, 33: pp. 107–121.

Chapman, R. (2001). Community continuum-building online communities on the web. http://web.archive.org/web/20010821070219/http://www.informationhighways.net/mag/mprevious/00apr01.html

Cheng, L.-T., Hupfer, S., Ross, S., and Patterson, J. (2003). Jazzing up eclipse with collaborative tools. In *eclipse '03: Proceedings of the 2003 OOPSLA workshop on eclipse technology eXchange*, pp. 45–49. New York, NY, USA: ACM Press.

Chung, G., Dewan, P., and Rajaram, S. (1998). Generic and composable latecomer accommodation service for centralized shared systems. In Chatty, S. and Dewan, P. (Editors), *IFIP Working Conference on Engineering for HCI*, pp. 129–145. Heraklion, Crete, Greece: Kluwer Academic Publisher.

Cincom (2001). *VisualWorks Application Developer's guide*. Cincinnati: Cincom Systems, Inc.

Coldeway, J. (2003). Interaction patterns of agile development. In O'Callaghan, A., Eckstein, J., and Schwanninger, C. (Editors), *Proceedings of the Seventh European Conference on Pattern Languages of Programs (EuroPLoP'02)*, pp. 329–342. Irsee, Germany: UVK.

Cooper, E. C. (1985). Replicated distributed programs. In *Proceedings of the 10th ACM Symposium on Operating Systems Principles*, pp. 63–78. Orcas Island, Washington, USA: ACM.

Cooper, E. C. (1986). Replicated procedure call. *ACM Operating Systems Review*, 20(1): pp. 44–56.

Coplien, J. O. and Harrison, N. B. (2004). *Organizational Patterns of Agile Software Development*. Prentice Hall.
http://easycomp.info.uni-karlsruhe.de/~jcoplien/HarrisonCoplien.pdf

Coplien, J. O. and Woolf, B. (2000). A pattern language for writers' workshops. In Harrison, N., Foote, B. and Rohnert, H. (Editors), *Pattern Languages of Program Design 4*, pp. 557–580. Addison Wesley.

Cormack, G. V. (1995a). A calculus for concurrent update. Technical Report CS-95-06, Department of Computer Science, University of Waterloo, Waterloo, Ontario N2L 3G1, Canada.
ftp://cs-archive.uwaterloo.ca/cs-archive/CS-95-06

Cormack, G. V. (1995b). A counter example to the distributed operational transform and a corrected algorithm for point-to-point communication. Technical Report CS-95-08, Department of Computer Science, University of Waterloo, Waterloo, Ontario N2L 3G1, Canada.
ftp://cs-archive.uwaterloo.ca/cs-archive/CS-95-08

Costales, B. (2002). *sendmail*. O'Reilly, 3 edition.

Crispin, M. (1996). Internet message access protocol–Version 4rev1. Request for Comments 2060, IETF.

Crocker, D. (1982). RFC 822: Standard for the format of ARPA Internet text messages. Request for Comments 822, IETF.

Curtis, P. (1998). *High Wired : On the Design, Use, and Theory of Educational Moos*, chapter Not Just a Game: How LambdaMOO Came to Exist and What It Did to Get Back at Me, pp. 25–44. University of Michigan Press.

Datta, A., Hauswirth, M., and Aberer, K. (2003). Updates in highly unreliable, replicated peer-to-peer systems. In *Proceedings of the 23rd International Conference on Distributed Computing Systems, ICDCS2003*.
http://citeseer.nj.nec.com/datta03updates.html

Dawkins, R. (1989). *The Selfish Gene*. Oxford University Press.

DeMarco, T. and Lister, T. (1999). *Peopleware (2nd ed.): productive projects and teams*. Dorset House Publishing Co., Inc.

Dewan, P. and Choudhary, R. (1992). A high-level and flexible framework for implementing multiuser interfaces. *ACM Transactions on Information Systems*, 10(4): pp. 345–380.

Dijkstra, E. W. (1959). A note on two problems in connexion with graphs. *Numerische Mathematik*, 1: pp. 269–271.

Dommel, H.-P. and Garcia-Luna-Aceves, J. (1997). Floor control for multimedia conferencing and collaboration. *Multimedia Systems*, 5(1): pp. 23–38.

Dorfman, M. (1997). Requirements engineering. In Thayer, R. H. and Dorfman, M. (Editors), *Software Requirements Engineering*, pp. 7–22. Los Alamitos, CA, USA: IEEE Computer Society Press.

Döring, N. (1999). *Sozialpsychologie des Internets*. Göttingen: Hofgrefe.

Dourish, P. (1996). Open implementation and flexibility in cscw toolkits.
http://citeseer.nj.nec.com/dourish96open.html

Dourish, P. and Bellotti, V. (1992). Awareness and coordination in shared workspaces. In *Conference proceedings on Computer-supported cooperative work*, pp. 107–114.

Duyne, D. K. V., Landay, J., and Hong, J. I. (2002). *The Design of Sites: Patterns, Principles, and Processes for Crafting a Customer-Centered Web Experience*. Addison-Wesley Longman Publishing Co., Inc.

Dyck, J., Gutwin, C., Subramanian, S., and Fedak, C. (2004). High-performance telepointers. In *CSCW '04: Proceedings of the 2004 ACM conference on Computer supported cooperative work*, pp. 172–181. New York, NY, USA: ACM Press.

Dyson, P. and Longshaw, A. (2004). *Architecting Enterprise Solutions: Patterns for High-Capability Internet-based Systems*. Chichester, UK: John Wiley & Sons.

Eckstein, J. (1999). Workshop report on the pedagogical patterns project: Successes in teaching object technology. In *Proceedings of OOPSLA'99 Educator's Symposium*. Denver.

Eckstein, J., Bergin, J., and Sharp, H. (2002). Feedback patterns. In O'Callaghan, A., Eckstein, J., and Schwanninger, C. (Editors), *Proceedings of the Seventh European Conference on Pattern Languages of Programs (EuroPLoP'02)*, pp. 343–373. Konstanz, Germany: UVK.

Edwards, W. K. (1994). Session management for collaborative applications. In *Proceedings of the ACM 1994 Conference on Computer Supported Cooperative Work*, pp. 323–330. Chapel Hill, NC, USA: ACM Press.

Ellis, C. A. and Gibbs, S. J. (1989). Concurrency control in groupware systems. In *SIGMOD '89: Proceedings of the 1989 ACM SIGMOD international conference on Management of data*, pp. 399–407. New York, NY, USA: ACM Press.

Erickson, T. and Laff, M. R. (2001). The design of the 'babble' timeline: a social proxy for visualizing group activity over time. pp. 329–330.

Fielding, R., Gettys, J., Mogul, J., Frystyk, H., Masinter, L., Leach, P., and Berners-Lee, T. (1999). Hypertext transfer protocol–http/1.1. Request for Comments 2616, IETF.

Foner, L. N. (1996). A multi-agent referral system for matchmaking. In *The First International Conference on the Practical Applications of Intelligent Agents and Multi-Agent Technology*. London, UK.
http://foner.www.media.mit.edu/people/foner/Reports/PAAM-96/PAAM.pdf

Frick, A., Ludwig, A., and Mehldau, H. (1995). A fast adaptive layout algorithm for undirected graphs. In *GD '94: Proceedings of the DIMACS International Workshop on Graph Drawing*, pp. 388–403. London, UK: Springer-Verlag.

Fricke, A. and Völter, M. (2000). Seminars–a pedagogical pattern language about teaching seminars effectively. In Devos, M. and Rüpping, A. (Editors), *Proceedings of the Fifth European Conference on Pattern Languages of Programs (EuroPLoP'2000)*, pp. 87–128. Konstanz, Germany: UVK.

Fuchs, L., Pankoke-Babatz, U., and Prinz, W. (1995). Supporting cooperative awareness with local event mechanisms: The groupdesk system. In *Proceedings of ECSCW 1995*, pp. 247–262. Stockholm.
http://citeseer.nj.nec.com/fuchs95supporting.html

Gabriel, R. P. (1996). *Patterns of Software–Tales from the Software Community*. New York: Oxford University Press.

Gamma, E. (2002). Design patterns–ten years later. In Broy, M. and Denert, E. (Editors), *Software Pioneers*, pp. 688–700. Spiringer, Heidelberg.

Gamma, E., Helm, R., Johnson, R., and Vlissides, J. (1995). *Design Patterns: Elements of Reusable Object-Oriented Software*. Reading, MA: Addison-Wesley.

Ganoe, C. H., Convertino, G., and Carroll, J. M. (2004). The bridge awareness workspace: tools supporting activity awareness for collaborative project work. In *NordiCHI '04: Proceedings of the third Nordic conference on Human-computer interaction*, pp. 453–454. New York, NY, USA: ACM Press.

Ganoe, C. H., Somervell, J. P., Neale, D. C., Isenhour, P. L., Carroll, J. M., Rosson, M. B., and McCrickard, D. S. (2003). Classroom bridge: using collaborative public and desktop timelines to support activity awareness. In *UIST '03: Proceedings of the 16th annual ACM symposium on User interface software and technology*, pp. 21–30. New York, NY, USA: ACM Press.
http://doi.acm.org/10.1145/964696.964699

Garcia-Molina, H. (1986). The future of data replication. In *Proceedings of the IEEE Symposium on Reliability in Distributed Software and Database Systems*, pp. 13–19. Los Angeles, CA, USA.

Garfinkel, D., Welti, B., and Yip, T. W. (1994). HP SharedX: A tool for real-time collaboration. *Hewlett Packard Journal*, pp. 23–36.

Garrett, J. J. (2005). Ajax: A new approach to web applications.
http://www.adaptivepath.com/publications/essays/archives/000385print.php

Gergen, K. (1991). *The Saturated Self:Dilemmas of Identityin Contemporary Life*. New York: Basic Books.

Gerosa, M., Fuks, H., Raposo, A., and Lucena, C. (2004). Awareness support in the AulaNet learning environment. In *Proceedings of the IASTED International Conference on Web-Based Education-WBE 2004*, pp. 490–495. Innsbruck, Austria: ACTA Press.

Gettys, J., Karlton, P. L., and McGregor, S. (1990). The x window system, version 11. *Software-Practice and Experience (SPE)*, 20(S2): pp. S2/35–S2/67.

Geyer, W., Richter, H., Fuchs, L., Frauenhofer, T., Daijavad, S., and Poltrock, S. (2001). A team collaboration space supporting capture and access of virtual meetings. In *Proceedings of the 2001 International ACM SIGGROUP Conference on Supporting Group Work*, pp. 188–196. Boulder, Colorado, USA: ACM Press, New York, NY, USA.

Gil-White, F. J. (2005). Common misunderstandings of memes (and genes). In Hurley, S. and Chater, N. (Editors), *Perspectives on Imitation: From Mirror Neurons to Memes*. MIT Press.
http://www.psych.upenn.edu/~fjgil/Memes2.pdf

Girgensohn, A. and Lee, A. (2002). Making web sites be places for social interaction. In *Proceedings of the 2002 ACM conference on Computer supported cooperative work*, pp. 136–145. ACM Press.

Goffman, E. (1959). *The Presentation of Self in Everyday Life*. New York: Doubleday Anchor.

Goland, Y., Whitehead, E., Faizi, A., Carter, S., and Jensen, D. (1999). HTTP Extensions for Distributed Authoring–WebDAV. Request for Comments 2518, IETF.

Goldman, R., Gabriel, R., and Kerievsky, J. (2002). Pattern language for textual electronic communications.
http://c2.com/w4/apl4tec/wiki.cgi?PatternLanguageForTextualElectronic Communications

Gottesdiener, E. (2003). Team retrospectives–for better iterative assessment. *The rational edge*, April.
http://download.boulder.ibm.com/ibmdl/pub/software/dw/rationaledge/apr03/TeamRetrospectivesAppendix_TheRationalEdge_Apr2003.pdf

Graham, I. (2002a). *A Pattern Language for Web Usability*. 0201788888. Addison-Wesley.
http://www.wupatterns.com/

Graham, P. (2002b). A plan for spam.
http://www.paulgraham.com/spam.html

Graham, T. C. N. (1997). Groupscape: Integrating synchronous groupware and the world wide web. In Howard, S., Hammond, J., and Lindgaard, G. (Editors), *Human-Computer Interaction, INTERACT '97, IFIP TC13 Interantional Conference on Human-Computer Interaction*, volume 96 of *IFIP Conference Proceedings*, pp. 547–554. Sydney, Australia: Chapman & Hall.

Graham, T. C. N., Urnes, T., and Nejabi, R. (1996). Efficient distributed implementation of semi-replicated synchronous groupware. In *Proceedings of the ACM Symposium on User Interface Software and Technology (UIST'96)*, pp. 1–10.

Gravity Corp (2004). Ragnarok online. http://www.euro-ro.net/.

Greenberg, S., Gutwin, C., and Roseman, M. (1996). Semantic telepointers for groupware. In *Proceedings of the OzCHI '96 Sixth Australian Conference on Computer-Human Interaction*. Hamilton, New Zealand.
http://www.cpsc.ucalgary.ca/grouplab/papers/1996/96-SemanticTelepointers.OZCHI/cameraready.pdf

Greenberg, S. and Marwood, D. (1994). Real time groupware as a distributed system: Concurrency control and its effect on the interface. In *Proceedings of the ACM 1994 Conference on Computer Supported Cooperative Work*, pp. 207–217. Chapel Hill, NC, USA.

Greenberg, S. and Roseman, M. (1996). Groupweb: A www browser as real time groupware. In *ACM SIGCHI'96 Conference on Human Factors in Computing Systems, Companion Proceedings*, pp. 271–272. Vancouver, Canada.

Greenberg, S. and Roseman, M. (2003). Using a room metaphor to ease transitions in groupware. In Ackermann, M., Pipek, V., and Wulf, V. (Editors), *Sharing Expertise: Beyond Knowledge Management*, pp. 203–256. Cambridge, MA, USA: MIT Press.

Gross, S. E. (2000). *The Compensation Handbook–A state-of-the-art guide to compensation strategy and design*, chapter Team-Based Pay, pp. 261–274. McGraw-Hill, 4th edition.

Gräther, W. and Prinz, W. (2003). Visualizing activity in shared information spaces. In *Proceedings of 10th International Conference on Human-Computer Interaction*, volume 2, pp. 1096–1100. Mahwah, New Jersey: Lawrence Erlbaum Associates.

Grudin, J. (1988). Why cscw applications fail: Problems in the design and evaluation of organizational interfaces. In *Proceedings of the ACM Conference on Computer-Supported Cooperative Work (CSCW88)*, pp. 85–93. Portland, Oregon.

Grudin, J. (1994). Groupware and social dynamics: eight challenges for developers. *Communications of the ACM*, 37(1): pp. 92–105.

Gruen, D., Rohall, S. L., Minassian, S., Kerr, B., Moody, P., Stachel, B., Wattenberg, M., and Wilcox, E. (2004). Lessons from the remail prototypes. In *CSCW '04: Proceedings of the 2004 ACM conference on Computer supported cooperative work*, pp. 152–161. New York, NY, USA: ACM Press.

Guernsey, L. (1996). College "moos" foster creativity and collaboration among users. *The Chronicle of Higher Education*, p. A24.
http://www.bvu.edu/ctown/CHE.html

Guerrero, L. and Fuller, D. (1999). Design patterns for collaborative systems. In *Proceedings of the Fifth International Workshop on Groupware (CRIWG)*.

Gutwin, C. and Greenberg, S. (1996). Workspace awareness for groupware. In *Proceedings of the CHI '96 conference companion on Human factors in computing systems: common ground*, pp. 208–209. Vancouver, BC Canada.

Gutwin, C. and Greenberg, S. (1998). Design for individuals, design for groups: trade-offs between power and workspace awareness. In *Proceedings of the ACM 1998 conference on on Computer supported cooperative work*, pp. 207–216. Seattle, Washington.

Gutwin, C. and Greenberg, S. (1999). The effects of workspace awareness support on the usability of real-time distributed groupware. *ACM Transactions on Computer-Human Interaction*, 6(3): pp. 243–281.

Gutwin, C. and Greenberg, S. (2002). A descriptive framework of workspace awareness for real-time groupware. *Comput. Supported Coop. Work*, 11(3): pp. 411–446.

Gutwin, C. and Penner, R. (2002). Improving interpretation of remote gestures with telepointer traces. In *CSCW '02: Proceedings of the 2002 ACM conference on Computer supported cooperative work*, pp. 49–57. New York, NY, USA: ACM Press.

Haake, J., Schümmer, T., Haake, A., Bourimi, M., and Landgraf, B. (2004a). Supporting flexible collaborative distance learning in the cure platform. In *Proceedings of HICSS-37*. IEEE Press.

Haake, J. M., Haake, A., Schümmer, T., Bourimi, M., and Landgraf, B. (2004b). End-user controlled group formation and access rights management in a shared workspace system. In *CSCW'04: Proceedings of the 2004 ACM conference on Computer supported cooperative work*, pp. 554–563. Chicago, Illinois, USA: ACM Press.

Haake, J. M. and Schümmer, T. (2003). Some experiences with collaborative exercises. In *Proceedings of CSCL'03*. Bergen, Norway: Kluwer Academic Publishers.

Haake, J. M., Schümmer, T., and Haake, A. (2003a). Supporting collaborative exercises for distance education. In *Proceedings of the 36th Annual Hawaii International Conference on System Sciences (HICSS'03)-Track1*, p. 31.2. Big Island, Hawaii: IEEE Computer Society.
http://csdl.computer.org/comp/proceedings/hicss/2003/1874/01/187410031b.pdf

Haake, J. M., Schümmer, T., Haake, A., Bourimi, M., and Landgraf, B. (2003b). Two-level tailoring support for cscl. In Favela, J. and Decouchant, D. (Editors), *Groupware: Design, Implementation, and Use. Proceedings of the 9th International Workshop (CRIWG 2003)*, volume 2806 of *Lecture Notes in Computer Science*, pp. 74–82. Heidelberg: Springer.

Haake, J. M., Schümmer, T., Haake, A., Bourimi, M., and Landgraf, B. (2004c). Supporting flexible collaborative distance learning in the CURE platform. In *Proceedings of the Hawaii International Conference On System Sciences (HICSS-37)*. IEEE Press.

Hall, R. W., Mathur, A., Jahanian, F., Prakash, A., and Rassmussen, C. (1996). Corona: A communication service for scalable, reliable group collaboration systems. In *Proceedings of the ACM 1996 Conference on Computer Supported Cooperative Work*, pp. 140–149. Boston, Massachusetts, USA.

Hancock, J. T. (2004). LOL: humor online. *Interactions*, 11(5): pp. 57–58.

Harrison, S. and Dourish, P. (1996). Re-place-ing space: the roles of place and space in collaborative systems. In *CSCW '96: Proceedings of the 1996 ACM conference on Computer supported cooperative work*, pp. 67–76. ACM Press.

Havender, J. (1968). Avoiding deadlock in multitasking systems. *IBM Systems Journal*, 7(2): pp. 74–84.

Heidegger, M. (1927). *Sein und Zeit*. Tübingen: Niemeyer, 17 (1993) edition.

Henderson, Jr., D. A. and Card, S. (1986). Rooms: the use of multiple virtual workspaces to reduce space contention in a window-based graphical user interface. *ACM Trans. Graph.*, 5(3): pp. 211–243.

Hendrikxs, K., Duval, E., and Oliv´e, H. (2001). Managing shared ressources. In Devos, M. and Rüping, A. (Editors), *Proceedings of the Fifth European Conference on Pattern Languages of Programs (EuroPLoP'2000)*, pp. 411–430. Irsee, Germany: UVK.

Henkel, J. and Diwan, A. (2005). Catchup!: capturing and replaying refactorings to support api evolution. In *ICSE '05: Proceedings of the 27th international conference on Software engineering*, pp. 274–283. New York, NY, USA: ACM Press.

Hentrich, C. (2004). Six patterns for process-driven architectures. In Marquardt, K. and Schütz, D. (Editors), *Proceedings of the 9th European Conference on Pattern Languages of Programs*. Kontanz, Germany: UVK.

Hill, J. and Gutwin, C. (2003). Awareness support in a groupware widget toolkit. In *GROUP '03: Proceedings of the 2003 international ACM SIGGROUP conference on Supporting group work*, pp. 258–267. Sanibel Island, Florida, USA: ACM Press.

Hill, J. and Gutwin, C. (2004). The MAUI toolkit: Groupware widgets for group awareness. *Computer Supported Cooperative Work*, 13: pp. 539–571.

Hill, R. D., Brinck, T., Rohall, S. L., Patterson, J. F., and Wilne, W. (1994). The Rendezvous architecture and language for constructing multiuser applications. *ACM Transactions on Computer-Human Interaction*, 1(2): pp. 81–125.

Holmer, T. and Wessner, M. (2005). *Chat-Kommunikation in Beruf, Bildung und Medien*, chapter Gestaltung von Chat-Werkzeugen zur Verringerung der Inkohärenz, pp. 181–199. Stuttgart: ibidem.

Horton, M. R. (1983). Standard for interchange of USENET messages. Request for Comments 821, IETF.

Horton, M. R. and Adams, R. (1987). RFC 1036: Standard for interchange of USENET messages. Obsoletes RFC0850 (Horton, 1983). Status: UNKNOWN. ftp://ftp.internic.net/rfc/rfc1036.txt, ftp://ftp.internic.net/rfc/rfc850.txt, ftp://ftp.math.utah.edu/pub/rfc/rfc1036.txt, ftp://ftp.math.utah.edu/pub/rfc/ rfc850.txt

Imine, A., Molli, P., Oster, G., and Rusinowitch, M. (2003). Proving correctness of transformation functions in real-time groupware. In *Proceedings of the 8th European Conference on Computer-Supported Cooperative Work*. Helsinki, Finland.
http://www.loria.fr/~molli/rech/ecscw03/ecscw03.pdf

Isaacs, E. A. and Tang, J. C. (1994). What video can and cannot do for collaboration: A case study. *Multimedia Systems*, 2(2): pp. 63–73.
http://www.springerlink.com/content/k6u5j47555154187

Islam, N. and Devarakonda, M. (1996). An essential design pattern for fault-tolerant distributed state sharing. *Communications of the ACM*, 39(10): pp. 65–74.

Jackson, T. W., Dawson, R., and Wilson, D. (2003). Understanding email interaction increases organizational productivity. *Commun. ACM*, 46(8): pp. 80–84.

Jacobs, S., Gebhardt, M., Kethers, S., and Rzasa, W. (1996). Filling html forms simultaneously: Coweb–architecture and functionality. In *5th International WWW Conference*, pp. 1385–1395. Elsevier.

Jain, P. (2003). Coordinator. In O'Callaghan, A., Eckstein, J., and Schwanninger, C. (Editors), *Proceedings of the Seventh European Conference on Pattern Languages of Programs (EuroPLoP'02)*, pp. 521–533. Irsee, Germany: UVK.

Johnson-Lenz, P. and Johnson-Lenz, T. (1981). Consider the groupware: Design and group process impacts on communication in the electronic medium. In Hiltz, S. and Kerr, E. (Editors), *Studies of Computer-Mediated Communications Systems: A Synthesis of the Findings*, volume 16. Newark, New Jersey: Computerized Conferencing and Communications Center, New Jersey Institute of Technology.

Johnson-Lenz, P. and Johnson-Lenz, T. (1990). Rhythms, boundaries, and containers: Creative dynamics of asynchronous group life. Awakening Technology Research Report 4, Awakening Technology.
http://www.awakentech.com/at/Awaken1.nsf/d4cbbb795713bdee88256464007
4729d/cfb70c1957a686e98825654000699e1b!OpenDocument

Kahan, J. and Koivunen, M.-R. (2001). Annotea: an open rdf infrastructure for shared web annotations. In *WWW '01: Proceedings of the 10th international conference on World Wide Web*, pp. 623–632. New York, NY, USA: ACM Press.

Kantor, B. and Lapsley, P. (1986). Network news transfer protocol: A proposed standard for the stream-based transmission of news. Request for Comments 977, IETF.

Karsenty, A., Tronche, C., and Beaudouin-Lafon, M. (1993). GroupDesign: Shared editing in a heterogeneous environment. *Computing Systems*, 6(2): pp. 167–195.

Kerth, N. L. (2001). *Project Retrospectives: A Handbook for Team Reviews*. Dorset House Publishing Company, Incorporated.

Kienle, A. (2006). Integration of knowledge management and collaborative learning by technical supported communication processes. *Education and Information Technologies*, 11(2): pp. 161–185.

Kircher, M. and Jain, P. (2004a). Caching. In Henney, K. and Schütz, D. (Editors), *Proceedings of the Eighth European Conference on Pattern Languages of Programs (EuroPLoP'03)*, pp. 257–268. Konstanz, Germany: UVK.

Kircher, M. and Jain, P. (2004b). *Pattern-Oriented Software Architecture: Patterns for Resource Management*. Chichester, UK: John Wiley & Sons.

Kircher, M. and Jain, P. (2004c). Resource lifecycle manager. In Henney, K. and Schütz, D. (Editors), *Proceedings of the Eighth European Conference on Pattern Languages of Programs (EuroPLoP'03)*, pp. 243–255. Konstanz, Germany: UVK.

Kircher, M., Jain, P., Corsaro, A., and Levine, D. (2001). Distributed extreme programming. In *Proceedings of XP2001-eXtreme Programming and Flexible Processes in Software Engineering*, http://www.cs.wustl.edu/mk1/xp2001.pdf. Villasimius, Sardinia, Italy.

Klöckner, K. (2002). Bscw. cooperation support for distributed workgroups. In Vajda, F. (Editor), *10th Euromicro Workshop on Parallel, Distributed and Network-based Processing.*, pp. 277–282. Canary Islands, Spain: IEEE Computer Society.

Koch, M. (2003). Community support in universities–the Drehscheibe project. In M. Huysman, V. W., E. Wenger (Editor), *Proceedings International Conference on Communities & Technologies (C&T2003)*, pp. 445–464. Kluwer Publishers, Amsterdam, The Netherlands.

Koch, M. (2005). Supporting community awareness with public shared displays. In *Proceedings Bled International Conference on E-Commerce*.

Krasner, G. E. and Pope, S. T. (1988). A cookbook for using the model-view-controller user interface paradigm in Smalltalk-80. *Journal of Object-Oriented Programming*, 1(3): pp. 26–49.

Kuzuoka, H., Oyama, S., Yamazaki, K., Suzuki, K., and Mitsuishi, M. (2000). Gestureman: a mobile robot that embodies a remote instructor's actions. In *CSCW '00: Proceedings of the 2000 ACM conference on Computer supported cooperative work*, pp. 155–162. New York, NY, USA: ACM Press.

Lampe, C. and Resnick, P. (2004). Slash(dot) and burn: distributed moderation in a large online conversation space. pp. 543–550.

Lamport, L. (1978). Time, clocks, and the ordering of events in a distributed system. *Communications of the ACM*, 21(7).

Lauwers, J. C. and Lantz, K. A. (1990). Collaboration awareness in support of collaboration transparency: requirements for the next generation of shared window systems. In *CHI '90 Conference on Human Factors in Computing Systems, Special Issue of the SIGCHI Bulletin*, pp. 303–311. Seattle, Washington, USA.

Lea, D. and Lea, D. (1999). *Concurrent Programming in Java. Second Edition: Design Principles and Patterns*. Addison-Wesley Longman Publishing Co., Inc.

Lee, A., Girgensohn, A., and Schlueter, K. (1997). Nynex portholes: initial user reactions and redesign implications. In *Proceedings of the international ACM SIGGROUP conference on Supporting group work : the integration challenge*, pp. 385–394. ACM Press.

Leuf, B. (2002). *Peer to Peer: Collaboration and Sharing over the Internet*. Addison-Wesley Longman Publishing Co., Inc.

Leuf, B. and Cunningham, W. (2001). *The Wiki Way*. Addison Wesley.

Lewis, D. D. and Knowles, K. A. (1997). Threading electronic mail: A preliminary study. *Information Processing and Management*, 33(2): pp. 209–217.

Little, M., McCue, D., and Shrivastava, S. (1993). Maintaining information about persistent replicated objects in a distributed system. In *Proceedings of the 13th International Conference on Distributed Computing Systems*, pp. 491–498. Pittsburgh, PA, USA.

Little, M. and Shrivastava, S. (1994). Object replication in arjuna. BROADCAST Project Technical Report 50, University of Newcastle.

Lukosch, S. (2002). Adaptive and transparent data distribution support for synchronous groupware. In Haake, J. M. and Pino, J. A. (Editors), *Groupware: Design, Implementation, and Use, 8th International Workshop, CRIWG 2002, LNCS 2440*, pp. 255–274. La Serena, Chile: Springer-Verlag Berlin Heidelberg.
http://kalu.fernuni-hagen.de/Publications/criwg02.pdf

Lukosch, S. (2003a). *Transparent and Flexible Data Sharing for Synchronous Groupware*. Schriften zu Kooperations- und Mediensystemen-Band 2. JOSEF EUL VERLAG GmbH, Lohmar-Köln.

Lukosch, S. (2003b). Transparent latecomer support for synchronous groupware. In Favela, J. and Decouchant, D. (Editors), *Groupware: Design, Implementation, and Use, 8th International Workshop, CRIWG 2003, LNCS 2806*, pp. 26–41. Grenoble (Autrans), France: Springer-Verlag Berlin Heidelberg.
http://kalu.fernuni-hagen.de/Publications/criwg03.pdf

Lukosch, S., Hellweg, M., and Rasel, M. (2006). CSCL, Anywhere and Anytime. In Dimitriadis, Y. A., Zigurs, I., and Gómez-Sánchez, E. (Editors), *Groupware: Design, Implementation, and Use, 12th International Workshop, CRIWG 2006, LNCS 4154*, pp. 326–340. Springer-Verlag Berlin Heidelberg.

Lukosch, S. and Schümmer, T. (2004). Communicating design knowledge with groupware technology patterns–the case of shared object management. In de Vreede, G.-J., Guerrero, L. A., and Raventós, G. M. (Editors), *Groupware: Design, Implementation, and Use, 10th International Workshop, CRIWG 2004, LNCS 3198*, pp. 223–237. San Carlos, Costa Rica: Springer-Verlag Berlin Heidelberg.

Lukosch, S. and Schümmer, T. (2006). Making exam preparation an enjoyable experience. *International Journal of Interactive Technology and Smart Education, Special Issue on 'Computer Game-based Learning'*, 3(4): pp. 259–274.

Manhart, P. (1999). A system architecture for the extension of structured information spaces by coordinated cscw services. In *GROUP '99: Proceedings of the international ACM SIGGROUP conference on Supporting group work*, pp. 346–355. New York, NY, USA: ACM Press.

Mannix, E. and Neale, M. A. (2005). What differences make a difference? the promise and reality of diverse teams in organizations. *Psychological Science in the Public Interest*, 6(2): pp. 31–55.
http://www.psychologicalscience.org/journals/index.cfm?journal=pspi&content=pspi/6_2

Manns, M. L. and Rising, L. (2005). *Fearless Change: Patterns for Introducing New Ideas*. Addison-Wesley.

Manohar, N. R. and Prakash, A. (1995a). Dealing with synchronization and timing variability in the playback of session recordings. In *Proceedings of the Third ACM Multimedia Conference*, pp. 45–56. San Francisco, CA, USA.
http://www.eecs.umich.edu/~aprakash/papers/acm-mm95.pdf

Manohar, N. R. and Prakash, A. (1995b). The session capture and replay paradigm for asynchronous collaboration. In *Proceedings of the Fourth European Conference on Computer Supported Cooperative Work*, pp. 149–164. Stockholm, Sweden.
http://www.eecs.umich.edu/~aprakash/papers/ecscw95.pdf

Marathe, J. (1999). Creating community online. Technical report, Durlacher Research Ltd.

Marshall, C. C. and Brush, A. J. B. (2004). Exploring the relationship between personal and public annotations. In *JCDL '04: Proceedings of the 4th ACM/IEEE-CS joint conference on Digital libraries*, pp. 349–357. New York, NY, USA: ACM Press.
http://www.csdl.tamu.edu/~marshall/p112-marshall.pdf

Mauve, M. (2000a). Consistency in replicated continuous interactive media. In *Proceedings of the ACM 2000 Conference on Computer Supported Cooperative Work*, pp. 181–190. Philadelphia, PA, USA: ACM.

Mauve, M. (2000b). *Distributed Interactive Media*. Ph.D. thesis, Universität Mannheim.

May, D. (2001). Building the cultural artifacts of the organization. In Rüping, A., Eckstein, J., and Schwanninger, C. (Editors), *Proceedings of the Sixth European Conference on Pattern Languages of Programs (EuroPLoP'01)*, pp. 459–476. Irsee, Germany.

Mazouni, K. R., Garbinato, B., and Guerraoui, R. (1995a). Building reliable client-server software using actively replicated objects. In *Proceedings of the International Conference on Technology of Object Oriented Languages and Systems (TOOLS)*, pp. 37–53. Versailles, France.

Mazouni, K. R., Garbinato, B., and Guerraoui, R. (1995b). Filtering duplicated invocations using symmetric proxies. In *Proceedings of the IEEE International Workshop on Object Orientation in Operating Systems (IWOOS)*. Lund, Sweden.

McDonald, D. W. and Ackerman, M. S. (1998). Just talk to me: A field study of expertise location. In *Proceedings of Computer Supported Cooperative Work*, pp. 315–324.

McDonald, D. W. and Ackerman, M. S. (2000). Expertise recommender: A flexible recommendation system and architecture. In *Proceeding of the ACM 2000 Conference on Computer Supported Cooperative Work*, pp. 231–240. Philadelphia, PA.

McKenney, P. E. (1996). Selecting locking primitives for parallel programming. *Communications of the ACM*, 39(10): pp. 75–82.

Mills, D. L. (1992). Network time protocol (version 3) specification, implementation and analysis. Request for Comments 1350, IETF.

Mockus, A. and Herbsleb, J. D. (2002). Expertise browser: A quantitative approach to identifying expertise. In *Proceedings of the 2002 International Conference on Software Engineering*, pp. ALR–2002–001.
http://www.research.avayalabs.com/techreport/ALR-2002-002-paper.pdf

Molli, P., Oster, G., Skaf-Molli, H., and Imine, A. (2003). Using the transformational approach to build a safe and generic data synchronizer. In *GROUP '03: Proceedings of the 2003 international ACM SIGGROUP conference on Supporting group work*, pp. 212–220. New York, NY, USA: ACM Press.

Mørch, A. I. (1997). Three levels of end-user tailoring: Customization, integration, and extension. In Kyng, M. and Mathiassen, L. (Editors), *Computers and design in context*, pp. 51–76. MIT Press, Cambridge, MA, USA.

Munson, J. P. and Dewan, P. (1997). Sync: A java framework for mobile collaborative applications. *IEEE Computer*, 30(6): pp. 59–66.

Musser, J., O'Reilly, T., and the O'Reilly Radar Team (2006). *Web 2.0 Principles and Best Practices*. ISBN 0-596-52769-1. O'Rielly Radar.

Nunamaker, J. F., Dennis, A. R., Valacich, J. S., Vogel, D., and George, J. F. (1991). Electronic meeting systems. *Commun. ACM*, 34(7): pp. 40–61.

O'Grady, T. (1996). *Flexible Data Sharing in a Groupware Toolkit*. Master's thesis, University of Calgary, Department of Computer Science, Calgary, Alberta, Kanada.

Orbiteam (2006). *BSCW 4.3 Manual*. OrbiTeam Software GmbH & Co. KG.
http://www.bscw.de/files/Download/Help/bscw_help_43_en_print.pdf

Pankoke-Babatz, U., Prinz, W., and Schäfer, L. (2004). Stories about asynchronous awareness. In Darses, F., Dieng, R., Simone, C., and Zacklad, M. (Editors), *Cooperative Systems Design–Scenario-Based Design of Collaborative Systems.*, pp. 23–38. IOS Press.

Parsowith, S., Fitzpatrick, G., Kaplan, S., Segall, B., and Boot, J. (1998). Tickertape: Notification and communication in a single line. volume 00, p. 139. Los Alamitos, CA, USA: IEEE Computer Society.
http://citeseer.ist.psu.edu/parsowith98tickertape.html

Patterson, J. F., Day, M., and Kucan, J. (1996). Notification servers for synchronous groupware. In *Proceedings of the ACM 1996 Conference on Computer Supported Cooperative Work*, pp. 122–129. Boston, Massachusetts, USA.

Pfister, H.-R., Schuckmann, C., Beck-Wilson, J., and Wessner, M. (1998). The metaphor of virtual rooms in the cooperative learning environment clear. In Streitz, N., Konomi, S., and Burkhardt, H. (Editors), *Cooperative Buildings-Integrating Information, Organization and Architecture. Proceedings of CoBuild'98*, volume 1370 of *LNCS*, pp. 107–113. Heidelberg: Springer.

Pikrakis, A., Bitsikas, T., Sfakianakis, S., Roure, D. D., Hall, W., Reich, S., and Hill, G. (1998). MEMOIR: Software agents for finding similar users by trails. In Nwana, H. S. and Ndumu, D. T. (Editors), *Proceedings of the 3rd International Conference on the Practical Applications of Agents and Multi-Agent Systems (PAAM-98)*, pp. 453–466. London, UK. http://www.mmrg.ecs.soton.ac.uk/publications/archive/pikrakis1998/html/

Pimentel, M., Fuks, H., and Lucena, C. (2003). Co-text loss in textual chattools. In *4th International and Interdisciplinary Conference on Modeling and Using Context-CONTEXT 2003*, number 2680 in LNAI, pp. 483–490. Stanford, CA, USA.

Pipek, V., Hinrichs, J., and Wulf, V. (2003). Sharing expertise: Challenges for technical support. In Ackermann, M. S., Pipek, V., and Wulf, V. (Editors), *Sharing Expertise: Beyond Knowledge Management*, pp. 111–136. Cambridge, MA, USA: MIT Press.

Postel, J. and Reynolds, J. (1985). File Transfer Protocol (FTP). Request for Comments 0959, IETF.

Prakash, A. and Shim, H. S. (1994). Distview: Support for building efficient collaborative applications using replicated objects. In *Proceedings of the ACM 1994 Conference on Computer Supported Cooperative Work*, pp. 153–164. Chapel Hill, NC, USA.

Prakash, A., Shim, H. S., and Lee, J. H. (1999). Data management issues and trade-offs in cscw systems. *IEEE Transactions on Knowledge and Data Engineering*, 11(1): pp. 213–227.

Preece, J. (2000). *Online Communities*. Chichester, UK: Wiley.

Preguica, N., Martins, J. L., Domingos, H., and Duarte, S. (2000). Data management support for asynchronous groupware. In *Proceedings of the 2000 ACM conference on Computer supported cooperative work*, pp. 69–78. ACM Press.

Price, D. (2000). Cvs-concurrent versions system v1.11. http://www.nongnu.org/cvs/

Prinz, W. (1999). Nessie: An awareness environment for cooperative settings. In Bodker, S., Kyng, M., and Schmidt, K. (Editors), *Proceedings of the Sixth European Conference on Computer Supported Cooperative Work*, pp. 391–410. Copenhagen, Denmark: Kluwer.

Pryce, N. (1997). Abstract session–an object structural pattern. In *Proceedings of the Second European Conference on Pattern Languages of Programs (EuroPLoP'97)*. Konstanz, Germany.

Raha, S. (2004). Sangam project home.
http://sangam.sourceforge.net

Reeves, M. and Zhu, J. (2004). Moomba–a collaborative environment for supporting distributed extreme programming in global software development. In *Lecture Notes in Computer Science : Extreme Programming and Agile Processes in Software Engineering*, pp. 38–50. Springer.
http://www.springerlink.com/content/hlpxh3fn8e639e4a

Ricart, G. and Agrawala, A. K. (1981). An optimal algorithm for mutual exclusion in computer networks. *Communication of the ACM*, 24(1): pp. 9–17.

Richardson, T., Stafford-Fraser, Q., Wood, K. R., and Hopper, A. (1998). Virtual network computing. *IEEE Internet Computing*, 2(1): pp. 33–38. VNC.

Rising, L. (2000). Customer interaction patterns. In Harrison, N., Foote, B., and Rohnert, H. (Editors), *Pattern Languages of Program Design 4*, pp. 585–609. Reading, MA, USA: Addison-Wesley.

Rittel, H. W. J. and Webber, M. M. (1973). Dilemmas in a general theory of planning. *Policy Sciences*, 4: pp. 155–169.

Rittenbruch, M., McEwan, G., Ward, N., Mansfield, T., and Bartenstein., D. (2002). Extreme participation-moving extreme programming towards participatory design. In Binder, T., Gregory, J., and Wagner, I. (Editors), *Participation and Design: Inquiring Into the Poltics, Contexts and Practices of Collaborative Design Work–PDC 2002 Proceedings of the Participatory Design Conference*. Malmo, Sweden.

Rodden, T. (1996). Populating the application: A model of awareness for cooperative applications. In *Proceedings of the ACM 1996 conference on on Computer supported cooperative work*, pp. 87–96.

Roseman, M. (1995). When is an object not an object? In *Proceedings of the Third Annual Tcl/Tk Workshop*, pp. 197–204. Toronto, Canada: Usenix Press.

Roseman, M. and Greenberg, S. (1996a). Building real-time groupware with groupkit, a groupware toolkit. *ACM Transactions on Computer-Human Interaction*, 3(1): pp. 66–106.

Roseman, M. and Greenberg, S. (1996b). Building real time groupware with groupkit, a groupware toolkit. *ACM Transactions on Computer-Human Interaction*, 3(1): pp. 66–106.

Roseman, M. and Greenberg, S. (1996c). TeamRooms: Network places for collaboration. In *Proceedings of the ACM 1996 Conference on Computer Supported Cooperative Work*, pp. 325–333. Boston.

Rossi, G., Garrido, A., and Carvalho, S. (1995). Design patterns for object-oriented hypermedia applications. In Vlissides, J. M., Coplien, J. O., and Kerth, N. L. (Editors), *Pattern Languages of Program Design 2*, pp. 177–191. Reading, MA, USA: Addison-Wesley.

Roth, J. (2000a). 'DreamTeam': A platform for synchronous collaborative applications. *AI & Society*, 14(1): pp. 98–119.

Roth, J. (2000b). *Entwicklungs- und Laufzeitunterstützung für synchrone Groupware*. Ph.D. thesis, FernUniversität–Gesamthochschule–in Hagen.

Roth, J. and Unger, C. (1999). Group rendezvous in a synchronous, collaborative environment. In *11. ITG/VDE Fachtagung, Kommunikation in Verteilten Systemen (KiVS'99)*.

Saridakis, T. (2003). A system of patterns for fault tolerance. In O'Callaghan, A., Eckstein, J., and Schwanninger, C. (Editors), *Proceedings of the Seventh European Conference on Pattern Languages of Programs (EuroPLoP'02)*, pp. 535–582. Irsee, Germany: UVK.

Sarle, W. (1997). Neural network faq, part 1 of 7: Introduction, periodic posting to the usenet newsgroup comp.ai.neural-nets.
ftp://ftp.sas.com/pub/neural/FAQ.html

Sarma, A., Noroozi, Z., and van der Hoek, A. (2003). Palantír: raising awareness among configuration management workspaces. In *ICSE '03: Proceedings of the 25th International Conference on Software Engineering*, pp. 444–454. Washington, DC, USA: IEEE Computer Society.

Schlichter, J., Koch, M., and Xu, C. (1998a). Awareness-the common link between groupware and community support systems. In Ishida, T. (Editor), *Community Computing and Support Systems: Social Interaction in Networked Communities*, LNCS 1519, p. 77. Springer.

Schlichter, J., Koch, M., and Xu, C. (1998b). Awareness-the common link between groupware and communityware. In Ishida, T. (Editor), *Community Computing and Support Systems*, pp. 77–93. Springer Verlag.

Schmidt, D. C., Stal, M., Rohnert, H., and Buschmann, F. (2001). *Pattern-Oriented Software Architecture 2-Patterns for Concurrent and Networked Objects.*. Chichester, UK: John Wiley & Sons.

Schuckmann, C., Kirchner, L., Schümmer, J., and Haake, J. M. (1996a). Designing object-oriented synchronous groupware with COAST. In *Proceedings of ACM CSCW'96 Conference on Supported Cooperative Work*. Boston, Mass.

Schuckmann, C., Kirchner, L., Schümmer, J., and Haake, J. M. (1996b). Designing object-oriented synchronous groupware with COAST. In *Proceedings of the ACM 1996 Conference on Computer Supported Cooperative Work*, pp. 30–38. Boston, Massachusetts, USA.

Schuckmann, C., Schümmer, J., and Schümmer, T. (2000). COAST–ein anwendungsframework für synchrone groupware. In *Proceedings of the net.objectDays*. Erfurt.
http://net.objectdays.org/pdf/00/papers/ooss/schuemmer.pdf

Schulzrinne, H., Casner, S., Frederick, R., and Jacobsen, V. (1996). RTP: A transport protocol for real-time applications. Request for Comments 1889, IETF.

Schumacher, M., Fernandez-Buglioni, E., Hybertson, D., Buschmann, F., and Sommerlad, P. (2005). *Security Patterns*. Chichester, UK: Wiley.

Schümmer, T. (2001). Lost and found in software space. In *Proceedings of the 34th Hawaii International Conference on System Sciences (HICSS-34), Collaboration Systems and Technology*. Maui, HI: IEEE-Press.

Schümmer, T. (2002). Enabling technologies for communities at web shops. In Plaice, J., Kropf, P. G., Schulthess, P., and Slonim, J. (Editors), *Proceedings of the 4th International Workshop on Distributed Communities on the Web (DCW2002)*, number 2468 in Lecture Notes in Computer Science, pp. 253–265. Sydney, Australia: Springer.

Schümmer, T. (2004). GAMA–a pattern language for computer supported dynamic collaboration. In Henney, K. and Schütz, D. (Editors), *Proceedings of the Eighth European Conference on Pattern Languages of Programs (EuroPLoP'03)*. Konstanz, Germany: UVK.

Schümmer, T. (2005). *A Pattern Approach for End-User Centered Groupware Development*. Schriften zu Kooperations- und Mediensystemen-Band 3. JOSEF EUL VERLAG GmbH, Lohmar-Köln.

Schümmer, T. and Haake, J. M. (2001). Supporting distributed software development by modes of collaboration. In *Proceedings of ECSCW 2001*. Bonn.

Schümmer, T. and Lukosch, S. (2006). Structure-preserving transformations in pattern-driven groupware development. *International Journal of Computer Applications in Technology, Special Issue on 'Patterns for Collaborative Systems'*, 25(2/3): pp. 155–166.

Schümmer, T., Lukosch, S., and Slagter, R. (2005). Empowering end-users: A pattern-centered groupware design process. In *Groupware: Design, Implementation, and Use, 11th International Workshop, CRIWG 2005*, LNCS 3706. Porto de Galinhas, Pernambuco, Brazil: Springer-Verlag Berlin Heidelberg.

Schümmer, T., Lukosch, S., and Slagter, R. (2006). Using patterns to empower end-users–the oregon software development process for groupware. *International Journal of Cooperative Information Systems, Special Issue on '11th International Workshop on Groupware (CRIWG'05)'*, 15(2): pp. 259–288.

Schümmer, T. and Schümmer, J. (2001). Support for distributed teams in extreme programming. In Succi, G. and Marchesi, M. (Editors), *eXtreme Programming Examined*. Addison Wesley.

Schümmer, T., Schümmer, J., and Schuckmann, C. (2001). COAST-an open source framework to build synchronous groupware with smalltalk. Technical report, OpenCoast Development Group.
http://www.opencoast.org/documentation/CoastSTBook.pdf

Schümmer, T. and Slagter, R. (2004). The oregon software development process. In *Proceedings of XP2004*.

Schümmer, T., Strijbos, J.-W., and Berkel, T. (2005). A new direction for log file analysis in cscl: Experiences with a spatio-temporal metric. In *Proceedings of CSCL2005*.

Schütz, D. (2001). Permit based locking. In Rüping, A., Eckstein, J., and Schwanninger, C. (Editors), *Proceedings of the Sixth European Conference on Pattern Languages of Programs (EuroPLoP'01)*, pp. 347–359. Irsee, Germany.

Shim, H. S., Hall, R. W., Prakash, A., and Jahanian, F. (1997). Providing flexible services for managing shared state in collaborative systems. In *Proceedings of the Fifth European Conference on Computer Supported Cooperative Work*, pp. 237–252. Lancaster, United Kingdom.

Shim, H. S. and Prakash, A. (1998). Tolerating client and communication failures in distributed groupware systems. In *Proceedings of the 17th IEEE Symposium on Reliable Distributed Systems*, pp. 221–227. West Lafayette, Indiana, USA.

Singhal, M. (1989). A heuristically-aided algorithm for mutual exclusion in distributed systems. *IEEE Transactions on Computers*, 38(5): pp. 651–662.

Smith, M., Cadiz, J. J., and Burkhalter, B. (2000). Conversation trees and threaded chats. In *Proceedings of the 2000 ACM conference on Computer supported cooperative work*, pp. 97–105. Philadelphia, Pennsylvania, USA: ACM Press.

Sohlenkamp, M. and Chwelos, G. (1994). Integrating communication, cooperation, and awareness: the diva virtual office environment. In *CSCW '94: Proceedings of the 1994 ACM conference on Computer supported cooperative work*, pp. 331–343. ACM Press.

Sohlenkamp, M., Prinz, W., and Fuchs, L. (2000). Poliawac–design and evaluation of an awareness enhanced groupware client. *AI and Society–Special Issue on CSCW*, 14: pp. 31–47.

Sony Online Entertainment (2003). Star wars galaxies. http://starwarsgalaxies.station.sony.com/.

Sony Online Entertainment (2004). Everquest 2. http://everquest2.station.sony.com/.

Sørensen, K. E. (2002). Session patterns. In O'Callaghan, A., Eckstein, J., and Schwanninger, C. (Editors), *Proceedings of the Seventh European Conference on Pattern Languages of Programs (EuroPLoP'02)*, pp. 301–321. Konstanz, Germany: UVK.

Stahl, G. (1993). *Interpretation in Design: The Problem of Tacit and Explicit Understanding in Computer Support of Cooperative Design*. Ph.D. thesis, University of Colorado. http://www.cis.drexel.edu/faculty/gerry/publications/dissertations/computer/dissertation.pdf

Stefik, M., Bobrow, D. G., Foster, G., Lanning, S., and Tatar, D. (1987). Wysiwis revised: early experiences with multi-user interfaces. *ACM Transactions on Office Information Systems*, 5(2): pp. 147–167.

Stenmark, D. (2001). The mindpool hybrid: A new angle on ebs and suggestion systems. In *Proceedings of the 34th Annual Hawaii International Conference on System Sciences (HICSS-34)-Volume 1*, p. 1037. IEEE Computer Society.

Stenmark, D. (2002). Group cohesiveness and extrinsic motivation in virtual groups: Lessons from an action case study of electronic brainstorming. In *Proceedings of the 35th Annual Hawaii International Conference on System Sciences (HICSS'02)-Volume 1*, p. 16.1. IEEE Computer Society.
http://csdl.computer.org/comp/proceedings/hicss/2002/1435/01/14350016b.pdf

Stiemerling, O. and Wulf, V. (2000). Beyond 'yes or no'-extending access control in groupware with awareness and negotiation. *Group Decision and Negotiation*, 9: pp. 221–235.
http://www-winfo.uni-siegen.de/wulf/papers/downloads/paper12.pdf

Stotts, D., Prins, J., Nyland, L., and Fan, T. (1998). Cobweb: Tailorable, analyzable rules for collaborative web use. Technical report, Dept. of Computer Science, University of North Carolina, Chapel Hill.

Streitz, N., Geißler, J., Haake, J. M., and Hol, J. (1994). Dolphin: Integrated meeting support across liveboards, local and remote desktop environments. In *Proceedings of the 1994 ACM Conference on Computer-Supported Cooperative Work (CSCW'94)*, pp. 345–358. Chapel Hill, N.C.: ACM Press ACM Press ACM Press ACM Press.

Streitz, N., Geißler, J., Holmer, T., Konomi, S., Müller-Tomfelde, C., Reischl, W., Rexroth, P., Seitz, P., and Steinmetz, R. (1999). i-land: An interactive landscape for creativitiy and innovation. In *ACM Conference on Human Factors in Computing Systems (CHI '99)*, pp. 120–127. New York: ACM Press.

Streitz, N., Haake, J. M., Hannemann, J., Lemke, A., Schuler, W., Schütt, H., and Thüring, M. (1992). Sepia: a cooperative hypermedia authoring environment. In *Proceedings of ACM Hypertext'92 (ECHT92)*, pp. 11–22. Milan, Italy.

Stroebe, w., Hewstone, M., and Stephenson, G. M. (Editors) (1996). *Sozialpsychologie*. Springer.

Summers, R. (1999). *Official Microsoft NetMeeting Book*. Redmond, WA, USA: Microsoft Press International.

Sun, C. and Ellis, C. (1998a). Operational transformation in real-time group editors: Issues, algorithms, and achievements. In *Proceedings of the ACM 1998 Conference on Computer Supported Cooperative Work*, pp. 139–148. Seattle, Washington, USA.

Sun, C. and Ellis, C. (1998b). Operational transformation in real-time group editors: issues, algorithms, and achievements. In *CSCW '98: Proceedings of the 1998 ACM conference on Computer supported cooperative work*, pp. 59–68. ACM Press, New York, NY, USA.

Sun, C., Xia, S., Sun, D., Chen, D., Shen, H., and Cai, W. (2006). Transparent adaptation of single-user applications for multi-user real-time collaboration. *ACM Transactions on Computer-Human Interaction*, 13(4): pp. 1–52.

Sun, D., Xia, S., Sun, C., and Chen, D. (2004). Operational transformation for collaborative word processing. In *CSCW '04: Proceedings of the 2004 ACM conference on Computer supported cooperative work*, pp. 437–446. ACM Press, New York, NY, USA.

Takeda, T. and Suthers, D. (2002). Online workspaces for annotation and discussion of documents. In *ICCE '02: Proceedings of the International Conference on Computers in Education*, p. 1294. Washington, DC, USA: IEEE Computer Society.
http://lilt.ics.hawaii.edu/lilt/papers/2002/Takeda-Suthers-ICCE-2002.pdf

Tam, J. and Greenberg, S. (2004). A framework for asynchronous change awareness in collaboratively-constructed documents. In de Vreede, G.-J., Guerrero, L. A., and Raventós, G. M. (Editors), *Groupware: Design, Implementation, and Use, 10th International Workshop, CRIWG 2004*, LNCS 3198, pp. 223–237. Springer-Verlag Berlin Heidelberg.

Tanenbaum, A., Kaashoek, M., van Renesse, R., and Bal, H. (1991). The amoeba distributed operating system-a status report. *Computer Communications*, 14: pp. 324–335.

TELL Project Consortium (2005). Design patterns for teachers and educational (system) designers. Technical report, TELL EU Project Consortium.
http://cosy.ted.unipi.gr/TELL/media/TELL_pattern_book.pdf

ter Hofte, G. H., Otte, R., and van der Gaast, S. (1997). Supporting telepointing in the mesh groupware platform: Design issues. Technical report, Telematica Instituut, Enschede, NL.
https://doc.telin.nl/dscgi/ds.py/Get/File-19221/t3100101.pdf

Teufel, S., Sauter, C., Mühlherr, T., and Bauknecht, K. (1995). *Computerunterstützung für die Gruppenarbeit*. Addison-Wesley.

Tidwell, J. (1999a). Disabled irrelevant things.
http://www.mit.edu/~jtidwell/language/disabled_irrelevant_things.html

Tidwell, J. (1999b). Localized object actions.
http://www.mit.edu/~jtidwell/language/localized_object_actions.html

Tidwell, J. (2006). *Designing Interfaces*. Sebastopol, CA, USA: O'Reilly.

Tietze, D. A. (2001). *A Framework for Developing Component-based Co-operative Applications*. Ph.D. thesis, Technische Universität Darmstadt.

Tietze, D. A. and Steinmetz, R. (2000). Ein framework zur entwicklung komponentenbasierter groupware. In Reichwald, R. and Schlichter, J. (Editors), *Verteiltes Arbeiten-Arbeit der Zukunft (Proceedings der Fachtagung D-CSCW 2000)*, pp. 49–62. Munich, Germany: B. G. Teubner Stuttgart, Leipzig.

Tönnies, F. (1997). *Gemeinsachft und Gesellschaft*. Darmstadt, Germany: Wissenschaftliche Buchgesellschaft.

Tuckman, B. and Jenson, M. (1977). Stages of small group development revisited. *Group and Organisational Studies*, pp. 419–427.

Turbine Games (2006). Dungeon & dragons online. http://ddo.com.

Twidale, M. M., Nichols, D. M., and Paice, C. D. (1997). Browsing is a collaborative process. *Information Processing and Management*, 33(6): pp. 761–783.

Tyler, J. R. and Tang, J. C. (2003). When can i expect an email response? a study of rhythms in email usage. In Kuutti, K., Karsten, E. H., Fitzpatrick, G., Dourish, P., and Schmidt, K. (Editors), *Proceedings of ECSCW2003*, pp. 239–258. Helsinki, Finland: Kluwer Academic Publishers.

van Welie, M. (2005). Web design patterns.
http://www.welie.com/

Viègas, F. B., Wattenberg, M., and Dave, K. (2004). Studying cooperation and conflict between authors with history flow visualizations. In *CHI'04: Proceedings of the SIGCHI conference on Human factors in computing systems*, pp. 575–582. New York, NY, USA: ACM Press.

Völter, M., Kircher, M., , and Zdun, U. (2004). *Remoting Patterns–Foundations of Enterprise, Internet, and Realtime Distributed Object Middleware.*. Chichester, UK: Wiley.

Völter, M., Schmid, A., and Wolff, E. (2002). *Server Component Patterns: Component Infrastructures Illustrated with EJB*. Chichester, UK: John Wiley & Sons, Inc.

Vogel, J. and Mauve, M. (2001). Consistency control for distributed interactive media. In *Proceedings of the 9th ACM Multimedia, ACM MM 2001*. Ottawa, Canada.

Vogel, J., Mauve, M., Geyer, W., Hilt, V., and Kuhmünch, C. (2000). A generic late join service for distributed interactive media. In *Proceedings of the 8th ACM Multimedia, ACM MM 2000*, pp. 259–268. Los Angeles, CA,USA.

Vogiatzis, D., Tzanavari, A., Retalis, S., Avgeriou, P., and Papasalouros, A. (2005). The learner's mirror. In *Proceedings of the Ninth European Conference on Pattern Languages of Programs (EuroPLoP'04)*. Irsee, Germany: UVK, Konstanz.

Weigert, A. J., Teitge, J. S., and Teitge, D. W. (1986). *Society and Identity: Toward a Sociological Psychology*. Cambridge: CambridgeUniversity Press.

Weng, C. and Gennari, J. H. (2004). Asynchronous collaborative writing through annotations. In *CSCW '04: Proceedings of the 2004 ACM conference on Computer supported cooperative work*, pp. 578–581. New York, NY, USA: ACM Press.

Wessner, M. and Pfister, H.-R. (2001). Group formation in computer-supported collaborative learning. In *Proceedings of the 2001 International ACM SIGGROUP Conference on Supporting Group Work*, pp. 24–31. ACM Press.

Wiczniewski, R. (2006). *Entwicklung eines mobilen Clients für das browserbasierte Massive-Multi-Player-Spiel "goalunited"*. Master's thesis, FernUniversitaet Hagen.
http://kalu.fernuni-hagen.de/downloads/diplomarbeit_wiczniewski.pdf

Wilke, H. and van Knippenberg, A. (1996). Gruppenleistung. In *(Stroebe et al., 1996)*, pp. 455–502. Springer, 3 edition.

Wisneski, C., Ishii, H., Dahley, A., Gorbet, M., Brave, S., Ullmer, B., and Yarin, P. (1998). Ambient displays: Turning architectural space into an interface between people and digital information. In Streitz, N. A., Konomi, S., and Burkhardt, H. J. (Editors), *Cooperative*

Buildings, Integrating Information, Organization, and Architecture, First International Workshop, CoBuild'98, volume 1370 of *LNCS*, pp. 22–32. Darmstadt, Germany: Springer.
http://tangible.media.mit.edu/papers/Ambient_Disp_CoBuild98/Ambient_Disp_CoBuild98.pdf

Wolf, H. and Froitzheim, K. (1998). User space meets document space. In *7th International Conference on the World Wide Web*, pp. 710–712. Brisbane.

Wolfson, O. and Jajodia, S. (1992a). An algorithm for dynamic data distribution. In *Proceedings of the 2nd Workshop on the Management of Replicated Data (WMRD-II)*. Monterey, CA, USA.

Wolfson, O. and Jajodia, S. (1992b). Distributed algorithms for dynamic replication of data. In *Proceedings of the ACM Symposium on Principles of Database Systems (PODS'92)*, pp. 149–163. San Diego, CA, USA.

Wolfson, O., Jajodia, S., and Huang, Y. (1997). An adaptive data replication algorithm. *ACM Transactions on Database Systems*, 22(2): pp. 255–314.

Wood, M. D. (1993). Replicated rpc using amoeba closed group communication. In *Proceedings of the 13th International Conference on Distributed Computing Systems*, pp. 499–507. Pittsburgh, PA, USA.

Xia, S., Sun, D., Sun, C., Chen, D., and Shen, H. (2004). Leveraging single-user applications for multi-user collaboration: the coword approach. In *CSCW '04: Proceedings of the 2004 ACM conference on Computer supported cooperative work*, pp. 162–171. ACM Press, New York, NY, USA.

Yiman, D. (2000). Expert finding systems for organizations: Domain analysis and the demoir approach. In *Beyond Knowledge Management: Sharing Expertise*. Boston, MA: MIT Press.
http://citeseer.nj.nec.com/yimam00expert.html

Zhao, Q. A. and Stasko, J. T. (1998). Evaluating image filtering based techniques in media space applications. In *Proceedings of the 1998 ACM conference on Computer supported cooperative work*, pp. 11–18. 1998, Seattle, Washington, United States.

Ziegler, J., Jerroudi, Z. E., and Böhm, K. (2005). Generating semantic contexts from spoken conversation in meetings. In *IUI '05: Proceedings of the 10th international conference on Intelligent user interfaces*, pp. 290–292. New York, NY, USA: ACM Press.

Zobel, J. and Moffat, A. (1998). Exploring the similarity space. volume 32, pp. 18–34. New York, NY, USA: ACM Press.

Index

Page numbers in *italics* indicate figures and tables

A Pattern Language (C. Alexander), 26, 28, 39
ABSTRACT SESSION, 415
account names, 75
ACKNOWLEDGEMENT, 454, 458
ACTIVE MAP, 46, 234, 235, 242–247
    INTERACTION DIRECTORY and, 251
    REMOTE FIELD OF VISION and, 346
    THREADED DISCUSSION and, 286
ACTIVE NEIGHBORS, 47, 317, 332–336
    BIRDS OF A FEATHER and, 137
    CHANGE INDICATOR and, 392
    SPONTANEOUS COLLABORATION and, 331
Active Worlds, 304, *305*
ACTIVITIES THAT SHAPE, 96
ACTIVITY INDICATOR, 47, 317, 363–366
    EMBEDDED CHAT and, 275
    REMOTE CURSOR and, 358
ACTIVITY LOG, 369, 371–376
    ACTIVITY INDICATOR and, 366
    ALIVENESS INDICATOR and, 398
    BIRDS OF A FEATHER and, 137
    CHANGE INDICATOR and, 392
    CoWord, 533
    EXPERT FINDER and, 139, 142
    GROUP and, 196
    HALL OF FAME and, 147
    MASQUERADE and, 169
    PERIODIC REPORT and, 386
    REPLAY and, 428

    SPONTANEOUS COLLABORATION and, 331
    TIMELINE and, 382
    USER LIST and, 325, 376
Address Book, see BUDDY LIST
ADHOC MEETING, 331
AIM, 111, 178
Alexander, C.,
    A Pattern Language, 26, 28, 39
    The Phenomenon of Life, 35
    The Process of Creating Life, 37
    Timeless Way of Building, 25
Alexandrian patterns, 26–27
ALIVENESS INDICATOR, 48, 370, 393–398
    AVAILABILITY STATUS and, 174
    AWAY MESSAGE and, 404
    QUICK GOODBYE and, 184
    TIMELINE and, 382
Alternating Repetition, 36, 37, 118
Amaya, 294
Amazon.com, 130–131, 145, *147*
Amoeba, 463
anarchistic browsing, 203–204
ANNOTATED SCROLLBAR, 247
Annotea, 294–295
Anonymous Interaction, see MASQUERADE
APPLICATION SHARING, 46, 193, 215–218
    MENTOR and, 94
    SHARED BROWSING and, 206
    SHARED EDITING and, 224

Architecting Enterprise Solutions (Dyson and Longshaw), 53
ARE YOU ALIVE, 415
Area, see ROOM
Arjuna, 463
artifacts, collaborative actions on, 191
ASK FOR HELP, 142
Ask the Author, see FEEDBACK LOOP
asynchronous group awareness, 47–48
    BSCW, 522–523
    CoWord, 533–534
    how to maintain, 369–406
ATTENTION SCREEN, 45, 159, 175–179
    ACTIVITY INDICATOR and, 366
    AVAILABILITY STATUS and, 173
    PERIODIC REPORT and, 386
    QUALITY INSPECTION and, 124
    QUICK GOODBYE and, 184
audio/video conferencing tools, 6
AUGMENTED REALITY, 52
AUTHENTICATOR, 85
AUTHORIZATION, 436
Auto Reply, see AWAY MESSAGE
Autonomy CEN, 136
AVAILABILITY STATUS, 45, 159, 170–174, 185
    ATTENTION SCREEN and, 179
    AWAY MESSAGE and, 404
    BELL and, 254
    MASQUERADE and, 169
AWAY MESSAGE, 370, 399–404
    ALIVENESS INDICATOR and, 398
    AVAILABILITY STATUS and, 174
Avatar, see VIRTUAL ME

Babble Timeline, 380
Ballot, see VOTE
Believe in your Group, see OPTIMISTIC CONCURRENCY CONTROL
BELL, 46, 234, 235, 252–254, 515, 516
    BLIND DATE and, 264
    COLLABORATIVE SESSION and, 254, 414
    INVITATION and, 259
    QUICK REGISTRATION and, 79
    ROOM and, 240
    VOTE and, 214
Bidirectional Communication, see FEEDBACK LOOP

BIG JOLT, 91
BIRDS OF A FEATHER, 45, 91, 119, 134–137, 155, 186
    ATTENTION SCREEN and, 179
    BLIND DATE and, 263
    LETTER OF RECOMMENDATION and, 132
    WELCOME AREA and, 91
Blackboard, 436
BLIND DATE, 46, 234, 235, 260–264
    INVITATION and, 259
BoF-Sessions, 137
bootstrap collaboration, 534–535
Borchers, Jan, *Pattern Approach to Interaction Design*, 52
bots, 75
Boundaries, 35–36, 69
browsing, 203–204, 514–515
    see also SHARED BROWSING
BSCW (Basic Support for Collaborative Work) system, 385, 391, 501, 502, 504–525, 540
    asynchronous group awareness, 522–523
    base technology, 523–525
    browsing, 514–515
    CHANGE INDICATORS, 522
    collaboration, 515
    community support, 505–511
    group support, 515–523
    INVITATION, 516
    joining a workspace, 515–517
    LOGIN, 505
    monitor applet, 520
    pattern clusters, 504
    PERIODIC REPORT, 522, *523*
    protecting users, 510–511
    public and private workspaces, 508–510
    reciprocity, 510
    registration, 505, *506*
    removal from system, 511
    shared artifacts, 511–515
    textual communication, 519–520
    TickerTape, 520, *521*
    TrafficVisualizer, 521
    VIRTUAL ME, 507
    voting, 513–514
    workspace structures, 517–519
BUDDY LIST, 30, 31, 32, 33, 45, 71, 109–114, 117, 163–164

ATTENTION SCREEN and, 179
GROUP and, 197
in IM systems and, 339
INTERACTIVE USER INFO and, 341
RECIPROCITY and, 163–164
USER GALLERY and, 107
USER LIST and, 325
XING and, 33
buddy scouts, 94
bulletin board systems, 164
Bulletin Board, see FORUM

CACHING, 445
CatchUp, 428
CBE, 418, 423
centers, 34
CENTRALIZED OBJECTS, 48, 432, 433–436, 440
   ACTIVITY LOG and, 375
   BUDDY LIST and, 111, 114
   IMMUTABLE VERSIONS and, 498
   REMOTE SUBSCRIPTION and, 440
   REPLAY and, 428
   REPLICATED OBJECTS and, 444
   SHARED EDITING and, 224
   SHARED FILE REPOSITORY and, 201
   STATE TRANSFER and, 424
Change Description, see DISTRIBUTED COMMAND
CHANGE INDICATOR, 48, 370, 387–392
   ACTIVE NEIGHBORS and, 336
   ALIVENESS INDICATOR and, 397
   BSCW, 522
   CONFLICT DETECTION and, 483
   FLAG and, 290
   FORUM and, 280
   PERIODIC REPORT and, 386
   SPONTANEOUS COLLABORATION and, 331
   THREADED DISCUSSIONS and, 286
CHANGE LOG, 376, 489
Change Report, see PERIODIC REPORT
chat systems, 285–286
chat tools, 7
CHIplace, 101, 106
COAST, 52, 322, *324*, 423, 444, 478, 540
   COLLABORATIVE SESSIONS, 413, *414*
   CONFLICT DETECTION, 482–483
   mediators, 452

COAST puzzle, 223–224
COAST UML-Editor, 245, *246*, 345, 351
CoBrow, 335
CobWeb, 205–206
COGE project, 10, 70
   asynchronous group awareness, 405–406
   creating places for collaboration, 265–267
   data consistency, 500
   how to arrive in the community, 115–117
   increasing motivation for participation, 154–156
   managing common data, 465–466
   modifying shared material together, 230–232
   online community, 66
   protecting users, 185–186
   session management, 430
   supporting textual communication, 312–314
   synchronous group awareness, 367–368
   see also Smith, Paul
Collaborative Browsing, SHARED BROWSING
collaboration bus, 427–428
collaborative learning, computer-mediated, 538
COLLABORATIVE SESSION, 47, 48, 230, 409, 411–415
   AVAILABILITY STATUS and, 174
   BELL and, 254, 414
   BLIND DATE and, 264
   GROUP and, 197
   INTERACTION DIRECTORY and, 251
   INVITATION and, 259
   PERSISTENT SESSION and, 418
   REPLAY and, 428
   ROOM and, 240
   SHARED BROWSING and, 207
   SPONTANEOUS COLLABORATION and, 331
   STATE TRANSFER and, 424
   USER LIST and, 325
   VOTE and, 214
collaborative virtual learning environments, 238–239
collaboratory builder's environment (CBE), 418, 423
collective code ownership, 265
CollegeTown, 239, 245
Comic Chat, 304
COMMANDS, 461–464
COMMON PERSISTENT STORE, 436

communities of circumstances, 67
communities of interest, 67
communities, classification of, 67
COMMUNITY OF TRUST, 479
community systems, 7
community websites, 107, 322, *323*
COMPENSATE SUCCESS, 153
Compensation, see REWARD
COMPOSITE, 197
computer-mediated collaborative learning, 538
computer-mediated interaction, 4–9, 30–34
computer-supported collaborative learning, 538
conceptual iterations, 54, *55–58*
concurrency control, 467, 468
CONFLICT DETECTION, 49, 469, 480–483
    DISTRIBUTED COMMAND and, 464
    LOVELY BAGS and, 494
    OPERATIONAL TRANSFORMATION and, 489
    OPTIMISTIC CONCURRENCY CONTROL and, 478–479
    SHARED FILE REPOSITORY and 200–201
contact buttons, 300
Contact List, see BUDDY LIST
Contrast, 36
Control your Privacy, see MASQUERADE
Conversations Threading, see THREADED DISCUSSIONS
cooperation, 5, 6, 8, 9
coordination, 5, 6, 8, 9
COORDINATOR, 474
Corona, 418
CoWord, 501, 502, 526–536
    ACTIVITY LOG, 533
    architecture, 526, *536*
    asynchronous awareness, 533–534
    base technology, 534–536
    change tracking, 534
    collaboration, 530–531
    collaborative document repository manager (CDRM), 528
    collaborative editing session information panel, 531–532
    data consistency, 536
    group support, 528–534
    interaction modes, 29
    managing common data, 535–536
    pattern clusters, 527
    PERSISTENT SESSION, 534–535
    REMOTE CURSOR, 532, *533*
    REMOTE FIELD OF VISION, 532–533
    synchronous awareness, 531–533
    textual communication, 531
CURE, 249–250, 284, *285*, 439
    flowers in, 397
    IMMUTABLE VERSIONS and, 498
    INTERACTIVE USER INFO and, 341
    PERIODIC REPORT and, 386
CVS (Concurrent Versioning System), 200, 374, *375*, 449, 498
CVS History Explorer, 380–381

Daily Report, see PERIODIC REPORT
data, how systems manage common, 431–466
DATA BRUSHING, 382
data consistency, 467–500, 536
data consistency support cluster, 49
DATA REPLICATION, 445
Dawkins, Richard, 38
DECENTRALIZED UPDATES, 49, 432, 455–459
    MEDIATED UPDATES and, 453
    NOMADIC OBJECTS and, 449
    REMOTE SUBSCRIPTION and, 440
    REPLAY and, 428
    REPLICATED OBJECTS and, 444
    STATE TRANSFER and, 424
Deep Interlock and Ambiguity, 35–36
democratic browsing, 204
Design Patterns: Elements of Reusable Object-Oriented Software (E. Gamma), 28
design patterns, Gang of Four, 28, 29, *41*
Designing Interfaces (J. Tidwell), 52
Detect a Conflicting Change, see CONFLICT DETECTION
development iterations, 54
digests, 385
DIGITAL EMOTIONS, 47, 270, 302–306
    EMBEDDED CHAT and, 275
    TELEPOINTER and, 362
digital moderation, 212–214
Direct Telepointer, see REMOTE CURSOR
DISABLE IRRELEVANT THINGS, 341
DISTRIBUTED COMMAND, 49, 432, 460–464
    ACTIVITY LOG and, 375
    DECENTRALIZED UPDATES and, 458

MEDIATED UPDATES and, 453
    REPLAY and, 428
    STATE TRANSFER and, 424
DistView, 473
DIVA, 240
DIVERSE GROUPS, 137
Dolphin, 350
Don't Disturb, see AVAILABILITY STATUS
Don't Trust Your Friends, see PESSIMISTIC LOCKING
Door Knocker, see BELL
DOORS, 478
DreamObjects, 423, 444, 457–458, 464, 472–473
    CENTRALIZED OBJECTS, 435
    REPLAY, 428, 429
DreamTeam, 250, 258, 413–414, 423
Drehscheibe, 101, 106–107, 113, 169
Dungeons & Dragons Online, 304
DyCE, 453, 478
DYNAMIC QUERIES, 382
Dyson, P. and A. Longshaw, *Architecting Enterprise Solutions*, 53

e-COMMERCE websites, periodic reports, 386
E-FORUM, 280
e-mail, 7
    address books, 113–114
    clients, 303–304
    reply, 300
    signatures, 100–101
    threaded discussions, 284
Easy to Unsubscribe, see QUICK GOODBYE
eBay, 83, 129, 132
Echoes, 36, 37
Eclipse, 232, 431
    implementation of shared objects in, 465–466
    ToDo messages in, 289, 290
EDITION, 376, 499
Editorial Board, see QUALITY INSPECTION
efa, 206, 210–212
Election, see VOTE
electronic newspaper, 11
Elephant's Brain, see ACTIVITY LOG
Elvin, 365
EMBEDDED CHAT, 47, 157, 269, 271–276
    DIGITAL EMOTIONS and, 306
    FORUM and, 280
    SHARED BROWSING and, 207
    TELEPOINTER and, 362
    THREADED DISCUSSION and, 286
Embodiment Proximity, see ACTIVE NEIGHBORS
emotions, expressing in text, 302–306
eMule, 151
ENGAGE QUALITY ASSURANCE, 125
entertainment, 538
event history *see* activity log
Event History, see ACTIVITY LOG
Everquest, 304, 340
EXPERT FINDER, 45, 94, 119, 138–142, 154, 155
    BIRDS OF A FEATHER and, 137
    HALL OF FAME and, 146
    MENTOR and, 96
Expert Recommender, see EXPERT FINDER
Expertise Browser, 140–141
Expertise Recommender, 172
Expertise Recommender, see EXPERT FINDER
Expertise selection, see BIRDS OF A FEATHER
Experts-Exchange, 150–151
explicit session management, 409
external merchants, 132

FACE TO FACE BEFORE WORKING REMOTELY, 91
FAIL-STOP PROCESSOR, 444–445, 449
Fair Distribution of Efforts, see RECIPROCITY
FAQ, 47, 270, 307–311
    DIGITAL EMOTIONS and, 306
    FEEDBACK LOOP and, 301
    FORUM and, 279
Fearless Change (Manns and Rising), 49
FEEDBACK LOOP, 47, 269, 298–301
    DIGITAL EMOTIONS and, 306
    FAQ and, 310
    FORUM and, 279
    SHARED ANNOTATION and, 297
FILE AUTHORIZATION, 201
Find the Guru, see EXPERT FINDER
FIREWALLS, 179
FLAG, 47, 269, 287–290
    THREADED DISCUSSIONS and, 286
    TELEPOINTER and, 362
Flagged Messages, see FLAG

FlashMeeting, 228, 229
FLOOR CONTROL, 46, 193, 226–229, 231
   APPLICATION SHARING and, 218
   EMBEDDED CHAT and, 275
   PESSIMISTIC LOCKING and, 473
   SHARED BROWSING and, 207
   SHARED EDITING and, 224
forces, 23–25
FORUM, 47, 269, 277–280, 290
   FAQ and, 311
   FEEDBACK LOOP and, 300
   GROUP and, 197
   INTERACTION DIRECTORY and, 251
   THREADED DISCUSSIONS and, 286
forums, 7, 385
FREQUENTLY ASKED QUESTIONS, 311
freshmeat.net, 145, *146*
Fringe Benefit Remuneration, see REWARD
From Shared Data to Shared Work, see SPONTANEOUS COLLABORATION
FTP (File Transfer Protocol), 200
FUB, 254, 257–258, 493

GAMA-Mall, 324–325, 330–331
game design, 538
games, 7, 90, 172, 179, 304–306, 340
Games at EuroPLoP, 90
Gamma, E., *Design Patterns: Elements of Reusable Object-Oriented Software*, 28
Gang of Four
   design patterns, 28, 29
   patterns and their connection in the, *41*
GARF, 464
GENTLE REMINDER, 290
GestureMan, 95–96
GIA (Group InterAction), 245
GINA, 478, 498
Go Away, see ATTENTION SCREEN
GOOD INTEGRATION WITH OTHER TOOLS, 241
Google, 76–77
Google Docs, 201, 258, *259*
Google Earth, 297
Gradients, 36, 37
GROOVE, 489
GROUP, 45, 192, 194–197
group awareness, 47

   asynchronous, 47–48, 369–406, 522–523, 533–534
   synchronous, 47, 315–326, 531–533
Group Decision Support Systems (GDSS), 7
GROUP IDENTITY, 197
group-based actions, 187, *188*
GroupDesign, 222
GroupDesk, 335
GroupKit, 414, 443–444, 457
groupware, 2, 4–9
   definition, 4
   socio-technical design, 5
GroupWEB, 346, 357, *358*
GUEST ACCOUNT, 79
Guild Wars, 179

Habanero, 453
HALL OF FAME, 45, 119, 143–147
   EXPERT FINDER and, 142
   FAQ and, 310
   LETTER OF RECOMMENDATION and, 132
   QUALITY INSPECTION and, 125
   RECIPROCITY and, 164
   REWARD and, 153
   USER GALLERY and, 107
   WELCOME AREA and, 88, 90
HANDLES, 84
Heartbeat Monitor, see ALIVENESS INDICATOR
Hello Hello, see WELCOME AREA
HONOR QUESTIONS, 153
HP SharedX, 217
HTTP Authentication, 83–84
HTTP/1.1, 444
HyperDialog, 286

I AM ALIVE, 415
I2I, 330, 335
ICQ, 83, 111–112
IMAP, 289, 448
IMMUTABLE VERSIONS, 49, 200, 382, 424, 428, 469, 495–499
implicit session management, 409
impression management, 98
instant messaging systems, 111–112, 178–179, 304, 403–404
integration, 540–541

intelligent views, 540
interaction, in a small group, 188
INTERACTION DIRECTORY, 46, 234, 235, 248–251
 BELL and, 254
 BLIND DATE and, 264
 COLLABORATIVE SESSION and, 414
 FORUM and, 279
 ROOM and, 241
 SHARED FILE REPOSITORY and, 201
INTERACTIVE USER INFO, 47, 317, 337–341
 ACTIVE NEIGHBORS and, 336
 INVITATION and, 259
 SPONTANEOUS COLLABORATION and, 331
 VIRTUAL ME and, 103
Interruption Gradient, see AVAILABILITY STATUS
INTIMACY GRADIENT, 70
INTRODUCTION SESSION, 91
INVITATION, 46, 47, 234, 235, 255–259, 515, 516
 BELL and, 254
 BLIND DATE and, 263
 COLLABORATIVE SESSION and, 414
 INTERACTIVE USER INFO and, 341
involvement hurdles, 69, *118*
iPOCs (intentional points of collaboration), 263
ISDN, 253–254

Jabber, 111, 178
JAMM, 246
Java Message Service (JMS), 439
JIGSAW, 207
JUST SAY THANKS, 133

KEEP SESSION DATA IN THE CLIENT, 419
KEEP SESSION DATA IN THE SERVER, 419
Knowledge Repository, see FAQ
KOLUMBUS, 2 284–285, 295–297

L3, 263
LambdaMOO, 239
Lecture2000, 238
LETTER OF RECOMMENDATION, 45, 119, 126–133, 155
 FEEDBACK LOOP and, 297, 301
 HALL OF FAME and, 146

 MENTOR and, 93, 94, 96
 QUALITY INSPECTION and, 124
 REWARD and, 153
 VOTE and, 214
Levels of Scale, 35, 36
LibreSource, 488
LIMITED ACCESS, 201
Local Awareness, see USER LIST
LOCALIZED OBJECT ACTIONS, 341
locking, 468
LOGIN, 44, 71, 73, 80–85, 505
 ACTIVITY LOG and, 376
 QUICK REGISTRATION and, 79
 SHARED FILE REPOSITORY and, 201
 USER LIST and, 326
Lotus Notes, 448
Lotus Quickplace, 240
Lotus Sametime, 212, 357
LOVELY BAGS, 49, 469, 490–494
 CONFLICT DETECTION and, 483
 IMMUTABLE VERSIONS and, 498
 OPERATIONAL TRANSFORMATION, 489
 OPTIMISTIC CONCURRENCY CONTROL and, 479
 VOTE and, 214

mail clients, 366
mailing lists, 158
Manns, M.L. and L. Rising, *Fearless Change*, 49
MARSHALLER, 424
MASQUERADE, 45, 159, 165–169
 ATTENTION SCREEN and, 179
 SPONTANEOUS COLLABORATION and, 331
 VIRTUAL ME and, 103
 WELCOME AREA and, 90
MASTER AND APPRENTICE, 96
Master and Apprentice, see MENTOR
master-slave browsing, 203
MAUI, 345–346, 350, 356–357
MDA (mobile digital assistant), 15
media, use in collaboration, 538–539
MEDIATED UPDATES, 48, 432, 450–454
 APPLICATION SHARING and, 218
 DECENTRALIZED UPDATES and, 458
 DISTRIBUTED COMMAND and, 464
 PERSISTENT SESSION and, 418

MEDIATED UPDATES (*continued*)
  REMOTE SUBSCRIPTION and, 440
  STATE TRANSFER and, 424
MEDIATOR, 453
mediators, 421, 422, 452
Meeting Area, BLIND DATE
Meeting Mirror, 325
Member Directory, see USER GALLERY
memes, 38–39
MEMOIR, 136, 142
MENTOR, 45, 71, 92–96
  EXPERT FINDER and, 142
  FAQ and, 310
  QUALITY INSPECTION and, 124
  WELCOME AREA and, 90
MESSAGE BOARD, 280
Message Filter, see ATTENTION SCREEN
Microsoft Chat, 304, *305*
Microsoft NetMeeting, 217–218
Mindpool, 153
mobile devices, 539
Mode of Collaboration (MoC), 162–163
MODEL-VIEW-CONTROLLER, 225, 376, 408, 440
moderators, 121
Mojo Nation, 151
MOOs, 239
Mozilla Junk Mail filter, 177–178
MSN Messenger, 83, 94, 172, *173*, 321–322, 365
multi-actor mode, 529
multi-player games, 7
multi-view mode, 529–530
Multicast-RPC, 464
multiuser editors, 8
multiuser scroll bars, 344
mvnForum, 322, *323*

NAMEPLATE, 103
NAMING, 436
NESSIE, 375
NetMeeting, 228, 254
NetMeeting shared whiteboard, 223, 361
newcomers, 87
Newsgroups, 310
Newsletter, see PERIODIC REPORT
NOMADIC OBJECTS, 48, 432, 446–449
  CENTRALIZED OBJECTS and, 436
  DECENTRALIZED UPDATES and, 458
  MEDIATED UPDATES and, 453
  REPLICATED OBJECTS and, 444
non-optimistic serialization, 468
Not-Separateness, 36, 37
NSTP, 435, 439
NYNEX Portholes, 167

OBJECT MANAGER, 454
offlineCURE, 449
ONE GRADE FOR ALL, 153
online communities, definition, 66–67
online games, 172, 179, 304–306, 340
Open Discussion, see FORUM
OPERATIONAL TRANSFORMATION, 49, 469, 484–489
  CONFLICT DETECTION and, 483
  DISTRIBUTED COMMAND and, 464
  LOVELY BAGS and, 494
  OPTIMISTIC CONCURRENCY CONTROL and, 479
  PESSIMISTIC LOCKING and, 473
OPTIMISTIC CONCURRENCY CONTROL, 49, 469, 475–479
  CONFLICT DETECTION and, 483
  DECENTRALIZED UPDATES and, 458
  FLOOR CONTROL and, 229
  IMMUTABLE VERSIONS and, 498
  MEDIATED UPDATES and, 453
  PESSIMISTIC LOCKING and, 473
  SHARED EDITING and, 224
optimistic serialization, 468
OPTIMISTIC TRANSACTION, 479
Optimistic Transactions, see OPTIMISTIC CONCURRENCY CONTROL
OSDP (Oregon Software Development Process), 54–63
  applicability of, 61–63
  conceptual iteration, 55–58
  development iteration, 58–60
  iterations, 54
  tailoring iteration, 61
Overview Diagram, see ACTIVE MAP

Pair Programming, 94
Palantír, 365, *366*

PARTICIPANT'S FEEDBACK FORM, 132
passion, communities of, 67
PASSWORD DESIGN AND USE, 85
password recovery, 82
passwords, 73
pastiche personality, 65–66
Pattern Approach to Interaction Design, Jan Borchers, 52
pattern languages, 2
   for computer-mediated interaction, 43–53
   examples of applying, 501–536
   layers of, 43–44
   related, 49–53
patterns
   Alexandrian form, 26–27
   application of, 34–39
   for designing the infrastructure that is needed by the groupware tools, 44
   for establishing a community, 43
   mathematical description, 25
   morphological law, 25
   and pattern languages, 23–42
   pattern style for computer-mediated interaction, 30–34
   relationship in a pattern language, 39–42
   representations of, 25–29
   for supporting small groups in their interaction, 44
PayPal, 75, 77–79
PERIODIC REPORT, 48, 370, 383–386, 522, 523
   FORUM and, 280
   TIMELINE and, 382
PERMIT BASED LOCKING, 473
PERSISTENT SESSION, 48, 409, 416–419, 534–535
   EMBEDDED CHAT and, 276
   QUICK REGISTRATION and, 73
   ROOM and, 241
PESSIMISTIC LOCKING, 49, 469, 470–474
   DISTRIBUTED COMMAND and, 464
   FLOOR CONTROL and, 229
   LOVELY BAGS and, 494
   OPTIMISTIC CONCURRENCY CONTROL and, 479
   SHARED EDITING and, 224
   SHARED FILE REPOSITORY and, 201
Phenomenon of Life, The (C. Alexander), 35

phpWebThings, 322, *323*
PHYSICAL METAPHORS, 241
Pink, 295, *296*
pixelize filters, 167, *168*
Place, see ROOM
places, creation of, 233–235
Planeshift, 83, *84*
PLAYER-DECIDED DISTRIBUTION OF REWARDS AND PENALTIES, 153
Points of Interest, 297
PoliTeam, 210
Poll, see VOTE
practice, communities of, 67
Presence Indicator, see USER LIST
privacy discrepancy, 158–159
PRIVATE VERSIONING, 498
Process of Creating Life, The (C. Alexander), 38
profiles, user, 99
PUBLISHER-SUBSCRIBER, 440, 464
purpose, communities of, 67

quality, 118–156
QUALITY INSPECTION, 45, 119, 120–125
   EMBEDDED CHAT and, 275
   FAQ and, 311
   FEEDBACK LOOP and, 301
   FORUM and, 279
   LETTER OF RECOMMENDATION and, 132
QUICK GOODBYE, 45, 159, 180–184, 185
   QUICK REGISTRATION and, 79
QUICK REGISTRATION, 44, 71, 72–79, 115
   INVITATION and, 259
   LOGIN and, 84
   MASQUERADE and, 169
   QUICK GOODBYE and, 183
   REWARD and, 156
   SHARED ANNOTATION and, 297
QUICK GOODBYE, 45, 79, 159, 180–184, 185
QUICK REGISTRATION, 44, 71, 72–79, 84, 115, 169, 183, 259

Radar View, see ACTIVE MAP
Ragnarok Online, 340
rate my professor, 123, 130, *131*
Rating, see LETTER OF RECOMMENDATION
RealVNC, 218

RECIPROCITY, 45, 159, 160–164, 510
   BUDDY LIST and, 114
   MASQUERADE and, 166, 167, 169
   REWARD and, 153
RECOMMENDATION COMMUNITY, 132–133
RECOVERABLE DISTRIBUTOR, 453, 483
registration *see* QUICK REGISTRATION
Remote Caret, see REMOTE CURSOR
REMOTE CURSOR, 47, 317, 353–358, 532, 533
   ACTIVE MAP and, 246–247
   REMOTE SELECTION and, 352
   SHARED EDITING and, 225
   TELEPOINTER and, 362
REMOTE FIELD OF VISION, 47, 317, 342–347
   ACTIVE MAP and, 246
   CoWord, 532–533
   REMOTE SELECTION and, 352
   SHARED BROWSING and, 206–207
   SHARED EDITING and, 225
   USER LIST and, 326
Remote Mouse Pointer, see REMOTE CURSOR
REMOTE SELECTION, 47, 317, 348–352
   REMOTE CURSOR and, 358
   REMOTE FIELD OF VISION and, 346
   SHARED EDITING and, 225
   TELEPOINTER and, 362
   USER LIST and, 326
Remote Scrollbars, see REMOTE FIELD OF VISION
REMOTE SUBSCRIPTION, 48, 432, 437–440
   CENTRALIZED OBJECTS and, 436
Remote Target Indicator, see REMOTE CURSOR
Remote Viewport, see REMOTE FIELD OF VISION
REPLAY, 48, 410, 425–430
   COLLABORATIVE SESSION and, 415
   PERSISTENT SESSION and, 419
   SHARED BROWSING and, 207
   STATE TRANSFER and, 424
   TIMELINE and, 381
ReplayKit, 428
Replicate for Freedom, see NOMADIC OBJECTS
Replicate for Speed, see REPLICATED OBJECTS
REPLICATED OBJECTS, 48, 432, 441–445
   APPLICATION SHARING and, 218
   CENTRALIZED OBJECTS and, 436
   DECENTRALIZED UPDATES and, 458
   IMMUTABLE VERSIONS and, 498

   MEDIATED UPDATES and, 453
   NOMADIC OBJECTS and, 449
   REPLAY and, 428
   SHARED EDITING and, 224
Reply, see FEEDBACK LOOP
RESOURCE LIFECYCLE MANAGER, 474
REWARD, 45, 119, 148–153
   ALIVENESS INDICATOR and, 398
   EXPERT FINDER and, 139, 142
   GROUP and, 197
   HALL OF FAME and, 146
   RECIPROCITY and, 164
ROLL FORWARD, 454, 458–459
ROLLBACK, 479
ROOM, 46, 234, 236–241
   ACTIVE MAP and, 247
   COLLABORATIVE SESSION and, 414
   GROUP and, 197
   INTERACTION DIRECTORY and, 251
   PERSISTENT SESSION and, 418
   SHARED EDITING and, 225
   SPONTANEOUS COLLABORATION and, 331
   USER LIST and, 325
Roster, see BUDDY LIST
RTFM, see FAQ
RTP/I, 423–424
rules, for incoming attention requests, 176

Sangam, 94
Schumacher, M., *Security Patterns*, 53
Security Patterns (M. Schumacher), 53
SECURITY SESSION, 84
Selection Awareness, see REMOTE SELECTION
SELECTIVE LOCKING, 473
SEPIA, 356
sequences, 34
SERVER REQUEST HANDLER and INVOKER, 464
service consumers, 149
service directory, 248–251
Service Directory, see INTERACTION DIRECTORY
service providers, 149
SESSION, 415
SESSION FAILOVER, 445
session management, 48, 409–430
SESSION TIMEOUT, 415
SETI@home, 129–130
SHARED ANNOTATION, 47, 269, 291–297

FLAG and, 290
SHARED BROWSING, 46, 193, 202–207, 230
   APPLICATION SHARING and, 218
   REMOTE FIELD OF VISION and, 347
   SHARED EDITING and, 225
   VOTE and, 214
   see also browsing
SHARED EDITING, 46, 193, 219–225, 230, 231
   APPLICATION SHARING and, 218
   SHARED BROWSING and, 206
SHARED FILE REPOSITORY, 46, 192, 198–201, 230
   INTERACTION DIRECTORY and, 251
   ROOM and, 241
   SHARED EDITING and, 225
Shared File System, *see* SHARED FILE REPOSITORY
shared objects, 407
shared whiteboards, 223
shared workspaces, 7, 512
Shared Workspace, *see* SHARED FILE REPOSITORY
SIGN-IN/NEW ACCOUNT, 84
Simplicity and Inner Calm, 36, 37
SINGLE ACCESS POINT, 85
single-actor actions, 187, *188*
single-actor mode, 529
single-view mode, 530
Skype, 83, 196
slashdot.org, 122–123
SmartMaps, 517
Smith, Paul
   a day with, 10–15
   online community, 66
   see also COGE project
social protocol, 467
society, meaning of, 65
socio-technical forces, 23–25
software-engineer.org, 145
SourceForge.net, 152
specialized group tools, 192
SpinChat, 77, *78*, 79
SPONTANEOUS COLLABORATION, 47, 317, 327–331
   USER LIST and, 325
Star Wars Galaxies, 172, *173*, 179, 275
Starcraft, 210, *211*

STATE TRANSFER, 48, 410, 420–424
   REPLAY and, 429
Strong Boundaries, 46
Strong Centers, 35–36, 46
structure preserving transformations, 37
SUBSYSTEM BY SKILL, 137
SubVersion, 200
Suite, 435, 439–440
SwapIt, 517–518
Sync, 447–448
synchronous collaboration, 409

tailoring iterations, 54
Team, *see* GROUP
TEAM PRIDE, 197
TeamSpace, 169
TeamWave Workplace, 239–240
Telecursor, *see* REMOTE CURSOR and TELEPOINTER
TELEPOINTER, 47, 317, 351–352, 359–362
   REMOTE CURSOR and, 358
   REMOTE FIELD OF VISION and, 346
   SHARED EDITING and, 225
ThreadChat, 286
Threaded Chat, 285–286
THREADED DISCUSSIONS, 47, 269, 281–286
   FEEDBACK LOOP and, 300
   FORUM and, 280
   SHARED ANNOTATION and, 297
Thunderbird, 303, 366
Ticker Tape, *see* ACTIVITY INDICATOR
Tidwell, J., *Designing Interfaces*, 52
Timeless Way of Building (C. Alexander), 25
TIMELINE, 48, 370, 377–382
   REPLAY and, 429
ToDo messages, in Eclipse, 289, 290
Tönnies, Ferdinand, 65
topic clusters, 44–49
TOWER project, 3D map of shared workspace, 518
Transform a Conflicting Change, OPERATIONAL TRANSFORMATION
transparent adaptation, 526
travel mates, 12
Travel Together, SHARED BROWSING
TREE TABLE, 286
Trillian, 403–404

TUKAN, 162–163, 167–168, 375
   ACTIVE NEIGHBORS and, 335
   CHANGE INDICATOR and, 390, *391*
   REMOTE SELECTION and, 350, *351*
   SHARED BROWSING and, 205
   SPONTANEOUS COLLABORATION and, 330
TURN TAKING, 229

UNIX, who command, 324
unsubscription, 180–184
Update Dispatcher, see MEDIATED UPDATES
Update Your Friends, see DECENTRALIZED UPDATES
USENET, 279, 283–284, 458, 493–494
User Directory, see USER GALLERY
User Experience Feedback, see LETTER OF RECOMMENDATION
USER GALLERY, 45, 71, 104–108, 116
   ALIVENESS INDICATOR and, 398
   BUDDY LIST and, 110, 114
   GROUP and, 197
   HALL OF FAME and, 147
   QUICK REGISTRATION and, 79
   USER LIST and, 326
   VIRTUAL ME and, 103
   WELCOME AREA and, 91
USER LIST, 47, 157, 230, 317, 319–326
   ACTIVITY LOG and, 325, 376
   ALIVENESS INDICATOR and, 398
   BUDDY LIST and, 114
   CHANGE INDICATOR and, 392
   COLLABORATIVE SESSION and, 415
   EMBEDDED CHAT and, 275
   EXPERT FINDER and, 142
   GROUP and, 197
   INVITATION and, 259
   RECIPROCITY and, 164
   ROOM and, 241
   SHARED FILE REPOSITORY and, 201
   SPONTANEOUS COLLABORATION and, 331
   USER GALLERY and, 108
   VIRTUAL ME and, 103
USER MODEL DEFINITION, 108

Vacation, 403
vBulletin, 339–340
veterans, 87

video systems, 167
VIRTUAL ME, 44, 71, 97–103, 117, 507
   ACTIVE MAP and, 247
   ALIVENESS INDICATOR and, 398
   BUDDY LIST and, 114
   EMBEDDED CHAT and, 276
   GROUP and, 197
   INTERACTIVE USER INFO and, 341
   LOGIN and, 82
   REMOTE FIELD OF VISION and, 346
   TELEPOINTER and, 362
   USER GALLERY and, 108
   USER LIST and, 326
virtual reality conference, 12–13
Virtual School, 379–380
Virtual Tamagotchi, see ALIVENESS INDICATOR
VisualWorks Smalltalk, 375
VITAL (Virtual Teaching and Learning), 238, 239, 362
VITERO, 228
VOTE, 46, 193, 208–214
   LETTER OF RECOMMENDATION and, 132
   QUALITY INSPECTION and, 125
   SHARED BROWSING and, 207

Web 2.0 539
WebDAV, 200
WebWasher, 179
WELCOME AREA, 44, 45, 71, 86–91, 116
   USER GALLERY and, 107
What Has Happened Here?, see REPLAY
What's Up?, see STATE TRANSFER
wholeness, 34, 35
wicked problems, 24
Wiki, 7, 435–436
Wikipedia, 123–124
Win-Win Situation, see RECIPROCITY
WinEdt, 390–391
workflow management, 537–538
workflow management systems (WfMS), 8
workspace awareness, 316
workspace structures, 517–519
workspaces, joining, 515–517
World of Warcraft, 112, 179, 262–263

WRAPPER, 464
writer's workshops, 300
www.communities.com, 88, *89*, 102, 107
www.visualbuilder.com, 88, *89*

XING, 102, 274
   activity meter, 397, *398*
   BUDDY LIST and, 33–34, 112–113

privacy configuration, 168–169
WELCOME AREA and, 88–90

Yahoo groups, 123, 196
   FORUMS and, 196, 279, *280*
   unsubscription, 182, *183*
Yahoo groups directory, 250, *251*
Yahoo Messenger, 83
Yenta, 136–137